AN EXAMINATION

OF THE ALLEGED

DISCREPANCIES OF THE BIBLE.

BY

JOHN W. HALEY, M.A.

WITH

AN INTRODUCTION

BY

ALVAH HOVEY, D.D.,

PROFESSOR IN THE NEWTON THEOLOGICAL INSTITUTION.

B. C. GOODPASTURE

Nashville, Tennessee

1958

FOREWORD

After three quarters of a century Haley's ALLEGED DISCREPANCIES OF THE BIBLE remains the most useful work of its kind. This is the reason for reprinting it at this time. This is not an abridgement of the original. It is an exact reproduction of the work as Mr. Haley left it.

If this edition serves to strengthen faith in the Living Oracles, the present publisher will be gratified.

B. C. Goodpasture   Nashville, Tenn., Oct. 11, 1951

INTRODUCTION.

HAVING read attentively the entire manuscript of the following work, it may be proper for me to express my estimate of its character and value. The topic which it discusses certainly merits examination. First, because of the bearing which it naturally has upon our confidence in the Bible as a revelation from God; and secondly, because of the prominence which has been given to it by those who deny the truthfulness of the Bible. These reasons will be appreciated at once, and therefore need simply to be stated. Any attempt to expand or enforce them would be superfluous.

But hitherto there has been no single treatise in our language which could be said to discuss the subject as thoroughly and minutely as its importance required. Hence the need of a work on the alleged "discrepancies of the Bible," adapted to the wants of men at the present time and taking due account of modern investigation and discovery. Such a work, it seems to me, has been produced by the Rev. Mr. Haley — a work almost equally adapted to meet the wants of scholars and of the people; for on the one hand it is learned and exact, while on the other it is perspicuous and interesting.

The author has made himself familiar with the literature of the subject in various languages, and, with a wise preference of truth to originality, has given the suggestions of others whenever those suggestions appeared to him worthy of special consideration. Thus a great amount of sound learning is comprehended within the limits of a single volume.

Moreover, the statements of the author appear to be unusually exact. This is a result of painstaking care and resolute candor, of a fixed purpose to spare no labor that might tend to the perfection of the work, and of an equally fixed purpose to avoid everything sectarian, as likely to interfere with its usefulness.

The style of the author is uniformly clear and forcible. He comes to the point at once, and either removes the difficulty, or at least shows the reader what it is, and how the writer would dispose of it. This is an admirable quality in such a treatise. If the least circumlocution were allowed the discussion might become tiresome; but, carried forward in the direct and vigorous language of Mr. Haley, it is constantly attractive. The investigation is made interesting by the sense of progress which it awakens. The reader feels that he is moving on, and the danger to which he is exposed is that of advancing too rapidly and eagerly, rather than too slowly and reluctantly. This, however, is a danger which every reader is happy to incur.

The question of discrepancies is a question of interpretation, and it could hardly be expected that any two persons would always agree in their method of reconciling statements which seem to be discordant. I do not in every instance prefer the explanation which Mr. Haley seems to prefer; but the clearness and soberness of his interpretations entitle them to respect in all cases, and to adoption in most. It is, therefore, a pleasure to commend his work to the notice of the public, and especially to the attention of those who for any reason wish to examine the claims of the Bible, as a Divine revelation, to our confidence.

ALVAH HOVEY.

NEWTON CENTRE, June, 1874.

PREFACE.

In making the following contribution to the literature of Christian Apologetics, a brief explanation may be in place.

The author was moved to prepare and publish the present volume by the circulation of a pamphlet, in a certain parish, setting forth in a striking and plausible manner the so-called "self-contradictions of the Bible." This production, cunningly adapted to deceive the ignorant and unwary, was reviewed by me in a course of Sabbath-evening lectures, which form the nucleus of the present work. The pamphlet just mentioned, with many others of a similar character, I afterwards found to be the fruits of an organized and systematic plan to poison the public mind by scattering broadcast, in the cars and upon steamboats, and in other places of public resort, as well as through the mails, a cheap and virulent infidel literature. That these nefarious attempts result, in far too many cases, in subverting the religious faith and the morals of the young, there can be no question. And the means employed by the friends of virtue for exposing and defeating these "devices of Satan" seem, I regret to say, less efficient than is desirable.

During my investigation of the subject I have been impressed with the fact that the so-called "discrepancies" of the Bible have failed to receive due consideration by evangelical authors. The literature of the subject is comparatively meagre and antiquated. True, the discrepancies are discussed to some extent in the various Harmonies, Introductions, and Commentaries, but, for the most part, quite incidentally. Works exclusively devoted to the topic in question are few in number and of comparatively remote date; hence, being scarce and of high price, they are practically inaccessible to most students of the Bible. And were they within reach, they would be found altogether behind the scholarship of the age. *I know of no work, ancient or modern, which covers the whole ground, treating the subject comprehensively yet concisely, and which is, at the same time, adapted to general circulation.* Whoever will examine the appended Bibliography will very probably be convinced that there is a demand for a work of the kind just mentioned. To supply in some degree this want is the aim of the present volume. The measure of the author's success must be determined by the reader.

Some persons may, perchance, question the wisdom of publishing a work in which the difficulties of scripture are brought together and set forth so plainly. They may think it better to suppress, as far as may be, the knowledge of these things. The author does not sympathize with any such timid policy. He counts it the duty of the Christian scholar to look difficulties and objections squarely in the face. Nothing is to be gained by overlooking, evading, or shrinking from them. Truth has no cause to fear scrutiny, however rigid and searching. Besides, the enemies of the Bible will not be silent, even if its friends should hold their peace. It should be remembered that the following " discrepancies " are not now published for the *first* time. They are gathered from books and pamphlets which *are already extensively circulated*. The poison demands an antidote. The remedy should be carried wherever the disease has made its blighting way.

With such views as these I issue this humble volume. Such as it is, making small claim to originality and literary merit, it is committed to the public. If it shall help to vindicate the Bible from the reproaches and misrepresentations of its enemies, and to solve doubts in the minds of honest inquirers, the author's object will have been attained.

Not proposing a discussion of all the difficult questions which arise in studying the Bible, I have restricted my attention to the so-called "discrepancies," that is, to those cases in which the statements or narratives of the Bible are said to conflict with one another. I have kept within the Bible. Cases in which the scriptures seem at variance with secular history or with science have been left to other and abler hands. I have dealt only with those in which the book appears inconsistent with itself. All cases of the latter kind which were of any importance, or which could perplex an honest inquirer of ordinary intelligence, I have aimed to include;[1] and if any such have been omitted, I regret the oversight.

In the preparation of this volume, I first read carefully the works of a large number of English, German, and French rationalists and infidels, with a view to gather up all the "discrepancies" which they adduce from the scriptures. Also, the numerous publications of kindred character — books, pamphlets, and printed sheets — which have been put forth by American sceptics were sedulously collected and collated. This being done, my next care was to classify and solve these discrepancies. In this process I have, as will be seen, laid under contribution a large number of critics and commentators, ancient and modern; in a word, I have gathered from every source whatever seemed pertinent and satisfactory.[2]

One feature of the book, to which the reader's attention is particularly invited, is the copious quotations made with the view to exhibit the *unanimity of scholars* upon certain important points. For this purpose, and generally, an author's exact words could not fail to be more satisfactory to the reader than a mere reference would be. That this copiousness of citation gives to certain portions of the book the aspect of a

---

[1] The whole number of cases treated is nearly nine hundred.

[2] In order to avoid increasing the size and price of the book, it has been found expedient to omit an extended "List of Authorities" which had been prepared. This omission is the less to be regretted since abundant references are given throughout the work.

compilation is a circumstance which I have neither sought to avoid, nor need to excuse. Indeed, my aim throughout has been not *originality*, but *truth ;* not so much to produce *new* ideas, as to present the *best* ideas pertaining to the subject under consideration.

The texts quoted within have been arranged in such a manner that the reader can see at a glance the antithesis or contradiction in each case. As Mr. Andrews[1] has remarked, a great point is gained when we are able to see just what the amount of the discrepancy or contradiction, if it really exists, is. But then, in contrasting isolated texts or phrases, the divergence often seems greater than it actually is, because the modifying power of the context and the general scope of the writer's argument fail to be appreciated by the reader. Hence, in order that a text may be seen in its true bearings and relations, — in its proper framework, — it has sometimes been deemed necessary to extend the citation somewhat beyond the antithetic words. On the other hand, to save space, we have, in cases where the connection of thought would not thereby be destroyed, omitted subordinate clauses, at the same time indicating the omission in the usual manner.

That the adoption of the *alphabetical* order of arrangement has resulted in giving to some chapters a disconnected and fragmentary appearance is obvious. But it was thought that any other method of classification would probably be open to equally great objections of some kind; and that, since the book might be used rather for reference than for consecutive reading, the lack of chronological sequence would not materially detract from its utility.

The work is intended not so much for scholars and critics as for the common people; yet it is hoped that the learned reader will feel that the author has substantiated his positions by the quotations from and references to the highest critical authorities, which occur upon nearly every page.

[1] Life of Our Lord, p. xvi.

Not infrequently several solutions of a difficulty are given, leaving the reader to choose for himself. Of course, not all possible solutions are adduced, but merely those which seem most reasonable.

On the principle that the concessions of its adversaries are weighty arguments in favor of the Bible, these have been made use of, from time to time, as the occasion presented itself.

As to works originally published in foreign languages, whenever approved English translations exist, I have generally followed the latter, instead of giving my own version.

Care has been taken to secure accuracy in the numerous quotations and references; yet it would be vain to claim exemption from what Porson terms "the common lot of authorship." If a reasonable degree of accuracy has been attained, this is the utmost I can expect.

I cannot omit to express here my gratitude to Prof. Edwards A. Park, D.D., for the cordial and unvarying interest which he has manifested in the present work, for timely encouragement, and for practical and valuable advice received by me during its preparation. But for him the work would have been published, if at all, in a less complete and satisfactory form.

My indebtedness to Prof. A. Hovey, D.D., will be sufficiently evinced by the very appreciative Introduction which he has kindly furnished for the volume.

I am also under obligation to Prof. Ezra Abbot, LL.D., of Cambridge, for consenting to revise and complete the bibliography which I had prepared; to Rev. C. F. P. Bancroft, Principal of Phillips Academy, for procuring in Europe for my use rare and important works pertaining to my theme, and for criticisms upon portions of the manuscript; to Rev. Archibald Duff, Jr., of Halle, for explorations on my behalf among the bookstores and libraries of Germany; to Rev. D. P. Lindsley, of Andover, for preparing the full and accurate Index of Texts which is contained in this volume; to Rev.

Selah Merrill, of Andover for the free use of his valuable private library; to Prof. J. H. Thayer, D.D., for various courtesies during my investigations; and to several other literary gentlemen for manifesting a gratifying interest in the progress of the work.

It should, however, be added that no person besides the author is to be held responsible for any opinion or statement expressed in the book, except in those cases where other writers are quoted, or reference is made to them. The plan and the execution of the work are my own. That it has cost me an immense amount of labor and research will be most readily conceded by those most competent to judge.

Moreover, I may be allowed to say that the more thoroughly I have investigated the subject the more clearly have I seen the flimsy and disingenuous character of the objections alleged by infidels. And, whether or not my labors shall result in inducing a similar belief in the minds of my readers, I cannot but avow, as the issue of my investigations, the profound conviction that *every difficulty and discrepancy in the scriptures is, and will yet be seen to be, capable of a fair and reasonable solution.*

Finally, let it be remembered that the Bible is neither dependent upon nor affected by the success or failure of my book. Whatever may become of the latter, whatever may be the verdict passed upon it by an intelligent public, the BIBLE will stand. In the ages yet to be, when its present assailants and defenders are mouldering in the dust, and when their very names are forgotten, the sacred volume will be, as it has been during the centuries past, the guide and solace of unnumbered millions of our race.

J. W. H.

ANDOVER, MASS., June, 1874.

CONTENTS.

	PAGE
INTRODUCTION, by Prof. Hovey,	iii
PREFACE,	v

PART I.
CHAPTER I.

ORIGIN OF THE DISCREPANCIES,	1–29
1. Difference of dates of passages,	3
2. Differences of authorship,	6
3. Differences of stand-point or of object,	7
4. Different methods of arrangement,	9
5. Different methods of computation,	11
6. Peculiarities of Oriental idiom,	14
7. Plurality of names or synonymes,	17
8. Diverse meanings of same word,	18
9. Errors in the manuscripts,	19
10. Imagination of critic,	25

CHAPTER II.

DESIGN OF THE DISCREPANCIES,	30–40
1. To stimulate the intellect,	30
2. Illustrate analogy of Bible and nature,	33
3. Disprove collusion of sacred writers,	36
4. Lead to value the spirit above the letter of the Bible,	37
5. Serve as a test of moral character,	38

CHAPTER III.

RESULTS OF THE DISCREPANCIES,	41–54
1. Text of Bible not unsettled,	41
2. Moral influence of the Bible not impaired,	50

CONTENTS.

PART II.
CHAPTER I.

DOCTRINAL DISCREPANCIES, ... 55–218
   I. Concerning God, ... 55
   II. Concerning Christ, ... 106
   III. Concerning the Holy Spirit, ... 139
   IV. Concerning the Scriptures, ... 143
   V. Concerning Man in relation to the Present, . 158
   VI. Concerning Man in relation to the Future, . 183

CHAPTER II.

ETHICAL DISCREPANCIES, ... 219–311
   I. Duty of Man to God, ... 219
   II. Duty of Man to himself, ... 245
   III. Duty of Man to his fellow-men, . . . 255

CHAPTER III.

HISTORICAL DISCREPANCIES, ... 312–436
   I. Pertaining to Persons, ... 312
   II. Pertaining to Places, ... 363
   III. Pertaining to Numbers, ... 380
   IV. Pertaining to Time, ... 392
   V. Miscellaneous, ... 427

BIBLIOGRAPHICAL APPENDIX, ... 437

INDEX OF SCRIPTURE CITATIONS, ... 445

GENERAL INDEX, ... 462

DISCREPANCIES OF THE BIBLE.
PART I.

CHAPTER I.

ORIGIN OF THE DISCREPANCIES.

"GOD reveals himself in his word, as he does in his works. In both we see a self-revealing, self-concealing God, who makes himself known only to those who earnestly seek him; in both we find stimulants to faith and occasions for unbelief; in both we find contradictions, whose higher harmony is hidden, except from him who gives up his whole mind in reverence; in both, in a word, it is a law of revelation that the heart of man should be tested in receiving it; and that in the spiritual life, as well as in the bodily, man must eat his bread in the sweat of his brow."

In these significant words of the sainted Neander [1] are brought to view the existence and the remedy of certain difficulties encountered by the student of scripture.

It is the object of the present volume to follow out the line of thought indicated by the learned German divine—to survey somewhat in detail the discrepancies of scripture, and to suggest, in the several cases, fair and reasonable solutions.

That no candid and intelligent student of the Bible will deny that it contains numerous "discrepancies," that its statements, taken *prima facie*, not infrequently conflict with or contradict one another, may safely be presumed. This fact

---
[1] Life of Christ, Preface to first edition.

has been more or less recognized by Christian scholars in all ages.

Of the early writers, Origen[1] declares that if any one should carefully examine the Gospels in respect to their historic disagreement, he would grow dizzy-headed, and, attaching himself to one of them, he would desist from the attempt to establish all as true, or else he would regard the four as true, yet not in their external forms.

Chrysostom[2] regards the discrepancies as really valuable as proofs of independence on the part of the sacred writers.

Augustine[3] often recurs, in his writings, to the discrepancies, and handles many cases with great skill and felicity.

Some twenty-five years since, that eminent biblical critic, Moses Stuart,[4] whose candor was commensurate with his erudition, acknowledged that " in our present copies of the scriptures there are some discrepancies between different portions of them, which no learning nor ingenuity can reconcile."[5]

To much the same effect, Archbishop Whately[6] observes: "That the apparent contradictions of scripture *are* numerous — that the instruction conveyed by them, if they be indeed designed for such a purpose, is furnished in abundance — is too notorious to need being much insisted on."

Similarly says Dr. Charles Hodge:[7] "It would require not a volume, but volumes, to discuss all the cases of alleged discrepancies."

Such being the concessions made by Christian scholars, it can occasion no surprise to find sceptical authors expatiating upon the "glaring inconsistencies," "self-contradictions," and

[1] Comm. in Evangelium Joannis, Vol. i. p. 279, Lommatzsch's edition.
[2] Warington on Inspiration, p. 86.
[3] See Rabus in appended Bibliography.
[4] Crit. Hist. and Defence of O. T. Canon, p. 193. Revised ed. p. 179.
[5] When we consider the marked progress of sacred philology and allied sciences during the last quarter of a century, we cannot doubt that the Professor would, were he now living, essentially modify this opinion.
[6] On Difficulties in Writings of St. Paul; Essay 7, Sect. 4.
[7] Theology, Vol. i., p. 169.

"manifest discrepancies" of the Bible, and incessantly urging these as so many proofs of its untrustworthiness and of its merely human origin. The pages of the German rationalists, and of their English and American disciples and copyists, abound with arguments of this character.

Of the importance of our theme, little need be said. Clearly it bears a close and vital relation to the doctrine of inspiration. God, who is wisdom and truth, can neither lie nor contradict himself. Hence, should it be discovered that falsehoods or actual contradictions exist in the Bible, our conclusion must be, that, at any rate, these things do not come from God; that so far the Bible is not divinely inspired. We see, therefore, the need of a patient and impartial examination of alleged falsehoods and contradictions, in order that our theory of inspiration may be made to conform to the facts of the case.

Yet we must guard against the conclusion that, since *we* cannot solve certain difficulties, they are therefore insoluble. This inference — to which minds of a certain temper are peculiarly liable — savors so strongly of egotism and dogmatism as to be utterly repugnant to the spirit of true scholarship.

As in all other departments of sacred criticism, so in the treatment of the discrepancies, there is a demand for reverent, yet unflinching thoroughness and fidelity.

An important preliminary question relates to the ORIGIN of the Discrepancies. To what causes are they to be referred? From what sources do they arise?

1. Many of the so-called discrepancies are obviously attributable to *a difference in the dates* of the discordant passages. Nothing is more common than that a description or statement, true and pertinent at one time, should at a later period, and in a different state of affairs, be found irrelevant or inaccurate. Change of circumstances necessitates a change of phraseology. Numerous illustrations of this principle will be found in the following pages.

A certain infidel, bent upon making the Bible contradict itself, contrasts the two passages: "God saw everything that he had made, and, behold, it was very good"; and "It repented the Lord that he had made man on the earth, and it grieved him at his heart."[1] Taking these texts out of their connection, and, with characteristic fairness, making no mention of the interval of time which divided them, he thus seeks to make it appear that the Bible represents God as, at the same time, satisfied and dissatisfied with his works. Had the unscrupulous pamphleteer told his readers that the fall of man and a period of some fifteen hundred years intervened between the two epochs respectively referred to in these texts, his "discrepancy" would have become too transparent to serve his purpose.

Obviously, after man had fallen, God could no longer be "satisfied" with him, unless a corresponding change had taken place in himself. We thus see that differences of date and circumstances may perfectly explain apparent discrepancies, and remove every vestige of contradiction.

May not these differences also furnish a hint toward the solution of certain moral difficulties in the scriptures? We find some of the patriarchs represented as good men, yet occasionally practising deceit, polygamy, and other sins which are discountenanced in the later books of the Bible. Is not the rule of human conduct, to some extent, a relative one, graduated according to man's knowledge, circumstances, and ability? Did not He who revealed himself "in many portions and in divers manners"[2] make the revelation of human duty in much the same way — not as with the lightning's blinding flash, but like the morning upon the mountains, with a slow and gradual illumination?[3]

In the comparatively unenlightened times in which many of the Old Testament saints lived, many faults and errors of theirs may have been mercifully and wisely passed by. Those "times

---

[1] Gen. i. 31 and vi. 6.   [2] Heb. i. 1, so Alford.
[3] See Bernard, Progress of Doct. in New Test., *passim*.

of ignorance" God "winked at"[1] — "over-looked." Acts committed in that twilight of the world, in the childhood of the race, must be looked at in the light of that period. Nothing could be more unjust or unreasonable than to try the patriarchs by the ethical standard of a later age.

Dr. Thomas Arnold[2] deems that the truest and most faithful representation of the lives of the patriarchs which leads us to think of "a state of society very little advanced in its knowledge of the duties of man to man, and even, in some respects, of the duties of man to God — a state of society in which slavery. polygamy, and private revenge were held to be perfectly lawful, and which was accustomed to make a very wide distinction between false speaking and false swearing." He deprecates the fear that we are "lowering the early scripture history, if we speak of the actors in it as men possessing far less than a Christian's knowledge of right and wrong." Professor Stuart,[3] likewise, repudiates the notion of the absolute perfection of the earlier dispensation, and adds : " It is only a *relative* perfection that the Old Testament can claim ; and this is comprised in the fact that it answered the end for which it was given. It was given to the world, or to the Jewish nation, in its minority." The Professor's conclusion is, that in the early ages, "with the exception of such sins as were highly dishonorable to God and injurious to the welfare of men, the rules of duty were not in all cases strictly drawn."[4]

Now, since our virtue must be judged of in relation to the amount of knowledge we possess, it is easy to see how men are styled "good" who live according to the light they have, even though that light may be comparatively feeble. Therefore, previous to pronouncing upon the moral character of a man or an act, we must take into consideration the date of the act, or

---

[1] "In this word lie treasures of mercy for those who lived in the times of ignorance." — Alford on Acts xvii. 30.
[2] Miscellaneous Works, pp. 149, 150 (N. Y. edition).
[3] History of Old Test. Canon, p. 415. Revised ed. pp. 387, 388.
[4] See further, under Ethical Discrepancies, "Enemies cursed."

the time when the man lived, that we may judge the man or the act by the proper standard. This simple principle will remove many otherwise formidable difficulties.[1]

2. Were it not for the perversity and disingenuousness exhibited by certain writers in dealing with this topic, it would be superfluous to assign *differences of authorship* as a fruitful source of discrepancies. We find recorded in the Bible the words of God and of good men, as well as some of the sayings of Satan and of wicked men. Now, a collision between these two classes of utterances will not seem strange to him who is cognizant of the antagonism of good and evil. For example, we read, "Thou shalt surely die;" and "Ye shall not surely die."[2] When we call to mind that the former are the words of God, the latter those of Satan, we are at no loss to account for the incongruity.

The question of the respective authorship of conflicting texts is an important one: "Whose are these sayings?" "Are they recorded as inspired language, or is one or more of them inserted as a mere matter of history?" "Does the sacred writer endorse, or merely narrate, these statements?" The answer to these simple questions will often be the only solution which the supposed discrepancy needs.

With regard to utterances clearly referable to *inspired* sources, yet which apparently disagree, several things are to be noticed:

(1) The same idea, in substance, may be couched in several different forms of phraseology. Thus we may vary the Mosaic prohibition of murder: "Thou shalt not kill"; "Do not kill"; "Thou shalt do no murder." Any one of these statements is sufficiently exact. No one of them would be regarded by any sensible person as a misstatement of the precept. They all convey substantially the same idea.

(2) Inspiration does not destroy the individuality of the

---

[1] "Distinguite tempora," says Augustine, "et concordabunt scripturae"; "Distinguish as to times, and the scriptures will harmonize."
[2] Gen. ii. 17 and iii. 4.

writers. It deals primarily with *ideas,* rather than with *words.* It suggests ideas to the mind of the writer, allowing him, generally, to clothe them in his own language. In this way his individuality is preserved, and his mental peculiarities and habits of thought make themselves felt in his writings. On this principle we account for the marked difference of style among the sacred writers, as well as for their occasional divergences in setting forth the same idea or in relating the same circumstance.[1]

(3) Inspiration need not always tread in its own track, or follow the same routine of words. A writer may, under the guidance of the Holy Spirit, take the language of a former inspired author, and modify it to suit his own purpose. Thus the New Testament writers often quote those of the Old. They grasp the sense, the ground-thought, of their predecessors, and then mould that thought into such forms as shall best meet the needs of the later age for which they write. This simple principle relieves the apparent discrepancies between the phraseology of the Old Testament and the citations in the New.

3. Other seeming disagreements are occasioned by *differences of stand-point or of object* on the part of the respective authors. Truth is many-sided, flinging back from each of its countless facets a ray of different hue. As Whately says, " Single texts of scripture may be so interpreted, if not compared together, and explained by each other, as to contradict one another, and to be each one of them at variance with the truth. The scriptures, if so studied, will no less mislead you than if they were actually false; for half the truth will very often amount to absolute falsehood."[2]

Often, in looking from different positions, or at different objects, we follow lines of thought, or employ language, which seems inconsistent with something elsewhere propounded by us; yet there may be no real inconsistency in the case. Thus

[1] See several striking cases under " Scriptures, — Quotations."
[2] Future State, Lect. VI., p. 120 (Phila. edition).

we say, in the same breath, "Man is mortal," and "Man is immortal." Both statements are true, each from its own point of view; they do not collide in the least. In respect to his material, visible, tangible organism, he is mortal; but with reference to the deathless, intelligent spirit within, he is immortal. So one may say: "The people of this country are rulers," and, "The American people are ruled." In the sense intended, both assertions may be perfectly correct.

In the "Christian Paradoxes," published in Basil Montagu's edition of Lord Bacon's Works, we find striking contrarieties. Thus, concerning the pious man:

"He is one that fears always, yet is as bold as a lion.

"He loseth his life, and gains by it; and whilst he loseth it, he saveth it.

"He is a peacemaker, yet is a continual fighter, and is an irreconcilable enemy.

"He is often in prison, yet always at liberty; a freeman, though a servant.

"He loves not honor amongst men, yet highly prizeth a good name."

In these cases no uncommon acuteness is requisite to see that there is no contradiction; since the conflicting sayings lie in different planes of thought, or contemplate different ends.

The principle that every truth presents different aspects, and bears different relations, is one of great importance. Sometimes these aspects or relations may seem inconsistent or incompatible with each other; yet, if we trace back the divergent rays to their source, we shall find that they meet in a common centre.

The principle just enunciated serves to reconcile the apparent disagreement between Paul and James respecting "faith" and "works," and to evince, as will be seen elsewhere, the profound, underlying harmony between them. Looking from different points of view, they present different, yet not inconsistent, aspects of the same great truth.

It is scarcely needful to add, that in studying the sacred writings, we should carefully look for and keep in mind the particular point of view and the object of each of the authors. Unless we do this, we risk a total misapprehension of them. We are apt, forgetting the long ages which have intervened, to judge these writers by the standards of our own time. Says Müller: "The great majority of readers transfer without hesitation the ideas which they connect with words as used in the nineteenth century to the mind of Moses or his contemporaries, forgetting altogether the distance which divides their language and their thoughts from the thoughts and language of the wandering tribes of Israel."[1]

This is a timely caution against unconsciously confounding an ancient author's stand-point with our own. We may remark, further, that the historian's stand-point is theoretically a neutral one. So long as he keeps to the mere recital of facts, he does not make himself responsible in any degree for the conduct described by him. When he drops the *role* of the historian, and assumes that of the philosopher and moralist, when he begins to deal out praise or censure, he may be held amenable to the tribunal of ethics for the rectitude and impartiality of his opinions and decisions.

In a word, the Bible writers do not, by simply narrating the misconduct of other persons, make themselves in the slightest degree responsible for that misconduct. Yet many persons, who would not think of holding Macaulay accountable for the crimes recorded in his history, cannot, when they come to read the sacred record, see the difference between a mere historian and a partisan. There is an appreciable distinction between narrating and indorsing an act.

4. Many other apparent discrepancies, of a historical character, are occasioned by the adoption, by the several authors, of *different principles and methods of arrangement.* One writer follows the strict chronological order; another disposes

---

[1] Chips from a German Workshop, i. 133 (Am. edition).

his materials according to the principle of association of ideas. One writes history minutely and consecutively; another omits, condenses, or expands to suit his purpose. From the pen of one writer we receive an orderly, well-constructed biography; another gives us merely a series of anecdotes, grouped so as to illustrate some trait, sentiment, or habit of the person described. Thus, in Xenophon's Memorabilia, we do not find a proper biography of Socrates, but we see various points in his life and character set forth by anecdotes respecting him and by reports of his discussions. These are "thrown together in the manner best suited to illustrate the different topics, without regard to the order of time in which the transactions or conversations actually took place, and without any endeavor to preserve the appearance of continuity of narrative." So our first Gospel, in the words of Professor Stowe,[1] "does not follow any chronological series of events or instructions, but groups together things of the same kind, and shows by a series of living pictures what Christ was in all the various circumstances through which he passed." A similar and intentional disregard of chronological order and sequence is seen, to a greater or less degree, in the three remaining Gospels, and in other historical portions of the Bible.

The methods of the several authors being thus different, it cannot but be that their narratives, when compared, will present appearances of dislocation, deficiency, redundancy, anachronism, or even antagonism — one or all of these. Now, if we put these authors upon a Procrustean bed, and clip or stretch them to suit our notions; if we require them to narrate precisely the same events, in precisely the same order, and with precisely the same fulness or brevity, we do them great violence and injustice. We should let each follow his own method of arrangement, and tell his story in his own way. A different grouping of events does not necessarily bring one author into collision with another, unless it can be shown that both writers intended

[1] Origin and History of Books of Bible, pp. 153, 154.

to follow the order of time. Nor is an author's omission to mention an event equivalent to a denial of that event. It should also be remembered that a writer may employ customary phraseology, involving a historical inaccuracy, yet not be chargeable with falsehood, inasmuch as he does not intend to teach anything in reference to the matter. For example, a historian might incidentally speak of the "battle of Bunker Hill," while he knows perfectly well that the battle was fought on Breed's hill. It is an author's privilege to accommodate himself in this manner, to prevalent opinions and customary forms of speech, provided he does not thereby introduce any material error, which shall vitiate his leading design.

5. Other incongruities arise from the use of *different modes of computation*, particularly of *reckoning time*. Phenomena of this description are not confined to the scriptures, or to the domain of theology. They are found in scientific and other secular literature. Thus, one would think the number of the bones which compose the human skeleton a very simple and easily-settled question; yet the most eminent anatomists disagree on this point. Gray mentions 204 bones; Wilson, 246; Dunglison, 240; others, 208. There is, however, no real discrepancy in the case, since these authors reckon differently.

A historical illustration is also in point. The family record, in an old Bible which belonged to Washington's mother, asserts that he was born "y^e 11th day of February, 173$\frac{1}{2}$." On the other hand, a recent biography [1] of Washington gives the date as "the 22d of February, 1732, New Style." To those who understand the difference between "Old Style" and "New Style," this discrepancy of eleven days will furnish no difficulty. When one historian reckons from one epoch, and another from a different one, there will of necessity be an apparent, if not a real, disagreement.

Many ancient and several modern nations have two kinds of year in use, the civil and the sacred. The Jews employed both

[1] Everett's Life of Washington, pp. 19, 20.

reckonings. "The sacred reckoning was that instituted at the exodus, according to which the first month was Abib; by the civil reckoning the first month was the seventh. The interval between the two commencements was thus exactly half a year."[1]

"The ancient Egyptians, Chaldeans, Persians, Syrians, Phoenicians, and Carthaginians each began the year at the autumnal equinox, about September 22. The Jews also began their civil year at that time; but in their ecclesiastical reckoning the year dated from the vernal equinox, about March 22."

"Among the Latin Christian nations there were seven different dates for the commencement of the year." "In the era of Constantinople, which was in use in the Byzantine empire, and in Russia till the time of Peter the Great, the civil year began with September 1, and the ecclesiastical sometimes with March 21, and sometimes with April 1."[2] Even among us, the academic and the fiscal do not begin and end with the civil year.

It follows, therefore, that when two ancient writers fail to agree as to the month and day of a given event, we must inquire whether or not they employ the same chronological reckoning. If not, their disagreement furnishes no proof that either is wrong. Each, according to his own method of computation, may be perfectly correct. When, in the Fahrenheit thermometer, the mercury stands at 212 degrees, in the Reaumur at 80, and in the Centigrade at 100 degrees, the inference is not valid that any one of the three instruments is inaccurate. The different methods of graduating the scale account for the different indications.

It was one peculiarity of the Jewish reckoning that fractional years were counted for whole ones. Lightfoot[3] says that, according to the rabbins, "the very first day of a year may stand in computation for that year." Aben Ezra, on Lev.

---

[1] R. S. Poole, in Smith's Bib. Dict., Art. "Year."
[2] Appleton's Cyclopaedia; Article "Calendar."
[3] Harmony of New Test., Section 9.

ORIGIN OF THE DISCREPANCIES.

xii. 3, says that, "if an infant were born in the last hour of the day, such hour was counted for one whole day." A similar mode of reckoning prevails in the East at the present time. "Thus, the year ending on a certain day, any part of the foregoing year is reckoned a whole year. A child born in the last week of our December would be reckoned a year old on the first day of January, because born in the old year." Menasseh ben Israel[1] says that, "in respect of the festivals, solemnities, and computations of the reigns of kings, Nisan [March] is the beginning of the year; but in regard to the creation and secular matters, it is Tisri" (September).

That eminent scholar and Egyptologist, Dr. J. P. Thompson,[2] well observes that the study of chronology is "particularly obscure and difficult when we have to do with Oriental modes of computation, which are essentially different from ours. Before the time of Abraham, the narrative given in the book of Genesis may be a condensed epitome of foregoing history — not a consecutive line of historical events, year by year and generation by generation, but a condensed epitome of what had occurred in the world from the creation to that time; for if you will scrutinize it carefully, you will see that in some instances the names of individuals are put for tribes, dynasties, and nations, and that it is no part of the object of the historian to give the consecutive course of affairs in the world at large." He proceeds to express the conviction that there is yet to come to us, from Arabian and other Oriental sources, a mode of interpreting chronology according to these lists of names, which he does not believe we have yet got hold of; hence he is not troubled by any seeming discrepancies. If, then, in dealing with biblical numbers, we encounter methods of computation which differ essentially from our own,[3] this is a fact which no student nor interpreter of scripture can afford to overlook.

[1] Conciliator, i., 126–129. [2] Man in Genesis and in Geology, pp 104–105.
[3] The Hebrew and Arabic allow a peculiar latitude in the expression of numbers. According to Nordheimer(Hebrew Grammar, i. 265), and Wright

It is clear that the Hebrews often employed "round numbers," or, omitting fractions, made use of the nearest whole number. Thus, the ages of the patriarchs, in Gen. v., are given in this manner, unless we adopt the improbable supposition that each of them died upon some anniversary of his birth.

The foregoing considerations evince the folly of hasty decisions in regard to biblical chronology. When the sacred writers disagree as to numbers and dates, unless there is evidence that they intended to reckon from the same point and by the same method, the verdict must be: " Discrepancy not proven."

6. The *peculiarities of the Oriental idiom* are another prolific source of discrepancies. The people of the East are fervid and impassioned in their modes of thought and expression. They think and speak in poetry.[1] Bold metaphors and startling hyperboles abound in their writings and conversation. "The

(Arabic Grammar, p. 211), both these languages permit one to write first the units, then the tens, hundreds and thousands, in their order; or he may reverse the method, writing the highest denomination first, and ending with the lowest.

Rev. Dr. C. S. Robinson, in the Christian Weekly, thus overstates and misapplies the first usage: "This is just the reverse of our habit. We put thousands before hundreds, and hundreds before units. So if a literal rendering of one of those vast numbers be made into English, it will appear positively preposterous.

"In the first book of Samuel, we are told (in our version), that for the impiety of looking into the ark, the Lord smote, in the little town of Bethshemesh, ' of the people fifty thousand and threescore and ten men' (1 Sam. vi. 19). Now, one cannot help thinking that there was no town in all those borders so large as this assumes. Fifty thousand men besides women and children, would populate one of our larger modern cities.

"The difficulty disappears when you recall the idiom I have mentioned. The verse reads, 'seventy, fifties, and a thousand,'—that is, not seventy and fifty thousand, as it is translated, but seventy, two fifties, and one thousand, or one thousand one hundred and seventy men in all."

Dr. R.'s explanation is inapposite. There is quite as much reason for reading "seventies" as "fifties," since *both* the original words are, as they ought to be, in the *plural* number. (See Gesenius, Heb. Gram., Sect. 97, Par. 3). Besides, "fifties" may as well denote *ten* fifties as *two* fifties.

[1] A learned writer observes of Arabian literature: "A poetic spirit pervades all their works. Even treatises in the abstract sciences, geographi-

ORIGIN OF THE DISCREPANCIES. 15

shepherd," says Eichhorn,[1] "only speaks in the soul of the shepherd, and the primitive Oriental only speaks in the soul of another Oriental. Without an intimate acquaintance with the customs of pastoral life, without an accurate knowledge of the East and its manners, without a close intimacy with the manner of thinking and speaking in the uncivilized world, ... you easily become a traitor to the book, when you would be its deliverer and interpreter."

Professor Stuart:[2] "I do not, and would not, summon them [the books of scripture] before the tribunal of Occidental criticism. Asia is one world; Europe and America, another. Let an Asiatic be tried before his own tribunal. To pass just sentence upon him, we must enter into his feelings, views, methods of reasoning and thinking, and place ourselves in the midst of the circumstances which surrounded him."

Lowth,[3] on Metaphors: "The Orientals are attached to this style of composition; and many flights which our ears — too fastidious, perhaps, in these respects — will scarcely bear, must be allowed to the general freedom and boldness of these writers."

Again, he speaks of the difficulties which arise in reading authors "where everything is depicted and illustrated with the greatest variety and abundance of imagery; they must be still more numerous in such of the poets as are foreign and ancient — in the Orientals above all foreigners; they being the farthest removed from our customs and manners, and, of all the Orientals, more especially in the Hebrews."

cal and medical works, have a poetic cast. All their literary productions, from the most impassioned ode to the firman of the Grand Seigneur, belong to the province of poetry."

Michaelis quotes an Arabic poet who expresses the fact, that swords were drawn with which to cut the throats of enemies, thus: "The daughters of the sheath leaped forth from their chambers, thirsting to drink in the jugular vein of their enemies." — See Bib. Repository, Oct. 1836, pp. 439, 442.

[1] See De Wette, Introd. to Old Test., ii. 31-32.
[2] History of Old Test. Canon, p. 187. Revised ed. p. 174.
[3] **Lectures** on Hebrew Poetry, pp. 51, 47 (Stowe's edition).

Dr. Samuel Davidson:[1] "He who does not remember the wide difference between the Oriental and Occidental mind, must necessarily fall into error. The luxuriant imagination and glowing ardor of the former express themselves in hyperbolical and extravagant diction; whereas the subdued character and coolness of the latter are averse to sensuous luxuriance."

Again: "The figures are bold and daring. Passion and feeling predominate. In the Psalms pre-eminently, we see the theology of the feelings, rather than of the intellect. Logic is out of place there. Dogmas cannot be established on such a basis, nor was it ever meant to be so."

Professor Park:[2] "More or less clandestinely, we are wont to interpret an ancient and an Oriental poet, as we would interpret a modern and Occidental essayist. The eastern minstrel employs intense words for saying what the western logician would say in tame language. The fervid Oriental would turn from our modifying phrases in sickness of heart. We shudder at the lofty flights which captivate him. But he and we mean to express the same idea. The Occidental philosopher has a definite thought when he affirms that God exercises benevolence toward good men. Isaiah has essentially the same thought when he cries out: 'As the bridegroom rejoiceth over the bride, so shall thy God rejoice over thee.'"

Such being the genius and idiom of the Orientals, it cannot be deemed strange that their metaphors and hyperboles overlap and collide with one another; that we find David,[3] for example, at one time calling God a rock, and elsewhere speaking of his wings and feathers. Such bold and free imagery, when properly interpreted, develops a felicitous meaning; but when expounded according to literalistic, matter-of-fact methods, it yields discrepancies in abundance. To the interpreter of scripture, no two qualifications are more indispensable than common sense and honesty.

[1] Introduction to Old Test., ii. 409, 310.   [2] Bib. Sacra, xix. 170, 171.
[3] Ps. xlii. 9, and xci. 4.

tained by nothing short of a continuous, unceasing miracle — by making fallible men (nay, many such in every generation) for one purpose absolutely infallible." To the unavoidable errors of copyists is, beyond question, to be attributed a large portion of those minute discrepancies, in both the Old and New Testaments, which we commonly term "various readings." The liability to mistakes in chirography was, moreover, indefinitely augmented by the very close resemblance of certain Hebrew letters to one another. Kalisch[1] gives twelve examples in point.

"Several letters," says Professor Stuart,[2] "bear a great resemblance to each other." As illustrations, he mentions: Beth ב and Kaph כ; Daleth ד and Resh ר; Daleth ד and final Kaph ך; Vav ו and Yod י; Vav ו and Nun final ן; Heth ח and He ה; Heth ח and Tav ת. He might have added, Pe פ and Kaph כ. The reader will observe that, if the left hand perpendicular line of He be accidentally omitted or blurred, we have Daleth left, thus, ה, ד; so Tav and Resh, thus, ת,ר; also Pe and Kaph, פ, כ. "At one time," says Herbert Marsh,[3] "the whole difference consists in the acuteness or obtuseness of an angle; at other times, either on the length or the straightness of a line; distinctions so minute that even when the letters are perfect, mistakes will sometimes happen, and still more frequently when they are inaccurately formed, or are partially effaced. In fact, this is one of the most fruitful sources of error in the Hebrew manuscripts."

Certain Greek letters, also, look very much alike; for example, Nu ν and Upsilon υ, with others.

Every one is aware how easily the English letters b and d are confounded, also p and q; how often we see N placed thus, ᴎ. In print we see the figures 3 and 8, 6 and 9, mistaken for each other. How frequently we find "recieve" for "receive," "cheif" for "chief," "thier" for "their," and the like. Now, if such errors occur, in the most carefully corrected print, what are

---

[1] Hebrew Grammar, i. 3.   [2] Hebrew Grammar, Sec. 17 (ed. of 1821).
[3] Lectures on Criticism and Interpretation, p. 186.

ORIGIN OF THE DISCREPANCIES. 17

7. Other dissonances in scripture are obviously attributable to the Eastern custom of applying a *plurality of names* to the same person or object. In matters of every-day life, this custom is widely prevalent. Thus, in the Arabic,[1] there are 1000 different words or names for "sword," 500 for "lion," 200 for "serpent," 400 for "misfortune," 80 for "honey."

The Hebrew language has as many as fifty words denoting a body of water of some kind.[2] There are at least eighteen Hebrew words used to express different kinds of prickly shrubs or weeds which occur in the Hebrew scriptures.[3] Gesenius gives some eight different Hebrew terms for "counsel," twelve for "darkness," thirty-two for "destruction," ten for "law," and twenty-three for "wealth."[4]

The usage in respect to proper names is quite similar. Thus we find Jacob and Israel, Edom and Esau, Gideon and Jerubbaal, Hoshea or Oshea and Jehoshua or Joshua. One of the apostles bore the following appellations: Simon, Simeon, Peter, Cephas, Simon Peter, Simon Bar-jona, and Simon son of Jonas. So we find Joseph, Barsabas, and Justus designating the same individual.

Not infrequently the names of persons and places were changed on account of some important event. The custom prevails to some extent in modern times. The Persian king, Shah Solyman, began to reign in 1667, under the name Suffee. During the first years of his reign, misfortune attended him. He came to the conclusion that his name was an unlucky one, and must be laid aside, in order to avert further calamities. "He accordingly assumed, with great solemnity, the name of Solyman. He was crowned anew under that name, and all the seals and coins which bore the name of Suffee were broken, as if one king had died, and another succeeded."[5] Chardin, an

---

[1] Bleek, Introd. to Old Test., i. 43. Also, Biblical Repository for October, 1836, pp. 433, 434.
[2] Taylor's Spirit of Hebrew Poetry, p. 91 (Gowans' edition).
[3] Tristram's Natural History of the Bible, p. 423 (London edition).
[4] Potter's English-Hebrew Lexicon, *sub vocibus*.
[5] Bush, Notes on Genesis xvii. 5.

eye-witness, gives an account of the coronation. The custom of changing the name of the pope at the time of his election is not unlike, — Aeneas Sylvius becoming Pius II.

Often, in the Bible, the name of the head of a tribe or nation is put for his posterity. Thus, in a multitude of cases, "Israel" means the Israelitish nation; "Ephraim" and "Moab" signify the descendants of those men respectively. Keeping in mind the great latitude allowed by the Orientals in the use of names, we see the ready solution of many difficulties in the biblical record.

8. Not a few verbal contradictions arise from the use of the same word with *different, sometimes opposite, significations*. As Fuerst says, "Analogy in the Semitic dialects admits of directly opposite meanings in a word as possible." According to this lexicographer and Gesenius, the Hebrew word "bärak" is used in the opposite senses of *to bless* and *to curse*. So "yärash" means both *to possess* and *to dispossess*; "näkar," *to know* and *not to know*; "säqal," *to pelt with stones* and *to free from stones*; "shäbar," *to buy grain* and *to sell grain*. So the Latin word "sacer" means both *holy* and *accursed*.

This infelicity of human speech is not, indeed, peculiar to the East. In our version of the scriptures,[1] and in the early English literature,[2] the word "let" is employed with the contradictory meanings, to *permit* and to *hinder*. In common parlance, a boy "stones" a fruit-tree, and the cook "stones" certain kinds of fruit. "Cleave" affords another example of opposite significations combined in the same word.[3]

When, therefore, we read in the Bible that certain persons "feared the Lord," yet "feared not the Lord"; that God "repents," yet does not repent; that he "tempted" Abraham, yet tempts no man, we find a ready solution of these apparent contradictions.

---

[1] Isa. xliii. 13; Rom. i. 13; 2 Thess. ii. 7.
[2] Two Gent. of Verona, iii. 1; Hamlet, i. 4; Romeo and Juliet, ii. 2.
[3] See Roget's Thesaurus of English Words, Introd. p. 23.

ORIGIN OF THE DISCREPANCIES.

Frequently discrepancies appear in our version, when none exist in the original. This is due to the fact that the same English word has been employed by the translators to represent several original terms. Thus, in Luke xiii. 24 and 2 Tim. ii. 24, two distinct Greek words are in our version rendered "strive." The resulting incongruity disappears when we consider that the term in Luke should have been rendered "agonize." Of course, all such discrepancies are to be attributed to the translators, and not to the book itself.

It is well to remember, also, that in King James's version words are frequently employed in an unusual or obsolete sense. Thus we find "prevent"[1] signifying to *anticipate* or *precede*; "thought"[2] implying *anxiety*. Often a knowledge of the ambiguity of their pivotal words enables us to reconcile two conflicting texts with the greatest ease.

9. A very large number of discrepancies take their rise from *errors in the manuscripts*; these errors being occasioned by the similarity of the alphabetical characters to one another, and by the consequent blunders of transcribers. The reader need not be reminded that previous to the invention of printing, in the fifteenth century, books were produced and multiplied by the slow, laborious method of copying with the pen. In a process so mechanical, mistakes would inevitably occur. The most carefully printed book is not entirely free from typographical errors; the most carefully written manuscript will exhibit defects of some kind. "God *might*," says an eminent critic,[3] "have so guided the hand or fixed the devout attention of copyists, during the long space of fourteen hundred years before the invention of printing, and of compositors and printers of the Bible for the last four centuries, that no jot or tittle should have been changed of all that was written therein. Such a course of providential arrangement we must confess to be quite possible; but it could have been brought about and main-

---

[1] Ps. cxix. 147, 148; 1 Thess. iv. 15.   [2] Matt. vi. 25.
[3] Scrivener, Criticism of New Test., p. 3.

tained by nothing short of a continuous, unceasing miracle — by making fallible men (nay, many such in every generation) for one purpose absolutely infallible." To the unavoidable errors of copyists is, beyond question, to be attributed a large portion of those minute discrepancies, in both the Old and New Testaments, which we commonly term "various readings." The liability to mistakes in chirography was, moreover, indefinitely augmented by the very close resemblance of certain Hebrew letters to one another. Kalisch[1] gives twelve examples in point.

"Several letters," says Professor Stuart,[2] "bear a great resemblance to each other." As illustrations, he mentions: Beth ב and Kaph כ; Daleth ד and Resh ר; Daleth ד and final Kaph ך; Vav ו and Yod י; Vav ו and Nun final ן; Heth ח and He ה; Heth ח and Tav ת. He might have added, Pe פ and Kaph כ. The reader will observe that, if the left hand perpendicular line of He be accidentally omitted or blurred, we have Daleth left, thus, ה, ד; so Tav and Resh, thus, ת,ר; also Pe and Kaph, פ, כ. "At one time," says Herbert Marsh,[3] "the whole difference consists in the acuteness or obtuseness of an angle; at other times, either on the length or the straightness of a line; distinctions so minute that even when the letters are perfect, mistakes will sometimes happen, and still more frequently when they are inaccurately formed, or are partially effaced. In fact, this is one of the most fruitful sources of error in the Hebrew manuscripts."

Certain Greek letters, also, look very much alike; for example, Nu ν and Upsilon υ, with others.

Every one is aware how easily the English letters b and d are confounded, also p and q; how often we see N placed thus, ᴎ. In print we see the figures 3 and 8, 6 and 9, mistaken for each other. How frequently we find "recieve" for "receive," "cheif" for "chief," "thier" for "their," and the like. Now, if such errors occur, in the most carefully corrected print, what are

---

[1] Hebrew Grammar, i. 3.   [2] Hebrew Grammar, Sec. 17 (ed. of 1821).
[3] Lectures on Criticism and Interpretation, p. 186.

the original mode of writing them appears in all countries of which we have any knowledge to have been by signs, not very different from one another; the absence of any context determining in favor of one number rather than another, where the copy is blotted or faded, increases the chance of error, and thus it happens that in almost all ancient works the numbers are found to be deserving of very little reliance."

Mr. Warington:[1] "There is little doubt but that numbers were originally represented in Hebrew, not as now by the names of the numbers in full, but simply by the letters of the alphabet taken in order, at the following numerical value: 1, 2, 3, 4, 5, 6, 7, 8, 9, 10, 20, 30, 40, 50, 60, 70, 80, 90, 100, 200, 300, 400; the five terminal letters supplying the numbers from 500 to 900, and the thousands being obtained by appending certain marks or points to the units."

Mr. Phillott:[2] "Like most Oriental nations, it is probable that the Hebrews in their written calculations made use of the letters of the alphabet. That they did so in post-Babylonian times we have conclusive evidence in the Maccabaean coins; and it is highly probable that this was the case also in earlier times."

Keil:[3] "An interchange of similar letters, on the assumption that letters were used as numerals, also explains many differences in numbers, and many statements of excessive and incredible numbers." Elsewhere, he calls attention to certain "corruptions which have arisen from the blunders of copyists in transcription, and by the resolution of the numerical statements, the numbers having been denoted by letters of the alphabet."

De Wette,[4] speaking of the mistakes of copyists: "They confounded similar letters. Hence, on the supposition that numeral characters were used, we are to explain the difference in numbers." He adduces several pertinent instances. "In this manner," continues his translator, Theodore Parker, "many other mistakes in numbers seem to have arisen."

[1] On Inspiration, pp. 204, 205.   [2] Smith's Bib. Dict., "Number."
[3] Introd. to Old Test., ii. 297 and 85.   [4] Introd. to Old Test., i. 310.

ORIGIN OF THE DISCREPANCIES.

Dr. Kennicott:[1] " That the Jewish transcribers did frequently express the Bible numbers in the original by single letters is well known to the learned."

This author also cites the learned Scaliger, and an ancient Hebrew Grammar, printed with the Complutensian Bible in 1515, to the same effect.

Dr. Samuel Davidson:[2] " Wherever numerous proper names occur, there is greater liability to err. So with regard to numbers; for letters alike in shape being used as numerals, were easily interchanged."

Again, " Letters having been used as numerals in ancient times, one letter was often mistaken for another by transcribers, and hence many corruptions got into the text."

Winer:[3] " In expressing numbers, the Jews, in the post-exile period, as is evident from the incriptions of the so-called Samaritan coins, employed the letters of the alphabet; and it is not improbable that the old Hebrews did the same, just as the Greeks, who derived their alphabet from the Phoenicians, expressed, from the earliest ages, numbers by letters."

" From the confounding of similarly-shaped letters when used for numerals, and from the subsequent writing out of the same in words can be explained satisfactorily in part the enormous sums in the Old Testament books, and the contradictions in their statements of numbers; yet caution is herein necessary."

Gesenius[4] expresses himself in very similar language, adduces examples illustrative of the above hypothesis, and pronounces it " certainly probable " (allerdings wahrscheinlich).

Glassius[5] also decides in favor of the hypothesis, and discusses the subject with no little skill and ability.

[1] On Printed Hebrew Text, i. 96.
[2] Introd. to Old Test., ii. 108, 112.
[3] Real-Wörterbuch, Art. "Zahlen."
[4] Geschichte der Heb. Sprache und Schrift, pp. 173, 174.
[5] Philologia Sacra, Tom. ii. pp. 188–195 (Dathe and Bauer's edition). See, also, J. M. Faber's " Literas olim pro vocibus in numerando a scriptoribus V.T. esse adhibitas." — Onoldi, 1775.

Isaac Taylor:[1] "The frequent use of contractions in writing was a very common source of errors; for many of these abbreviations were extremely complicated, obscure, and ambiguous, so that an unskilful copyist was very likely to mistake one word for another. No parts of ancient books have suffered so much from errors of inadvertency as those which relate to *numbers;* for as one numeral letter was easily mistaken for another, and as neither the sense of the passage, nor the rules of orthography nor of syntax, suggested the genuine reading, when once an error had arisen, it would most often be perpetuated, without remedy. It is, therefore, almost always unsafe to rest the stress of an argument upon any statement of numbers in ancient writers, unless some correlative computation confirms the reading of the text. Hence nothing can be more frivolous or unfair than to raise an objection against the veracity or accuracy of an historian, upon some apparent incompatability in his statement of numbers. Difficulties of this sort it is much better to attribute, at once, to a corruption of the text, than to discuss them with ill-spent assiduity."

On the authority of these scholars and critics, of creeds widely diverse, yet agreeing in this particular, we may, therefore, easily explain many of the contradictory and extravagant numbers [2] which we find in the historical books of the Old Testament. Also certain discrepancies in the New Testament are explicable by the fact that, as is the case in the Codex Bezae, Greek letters bearing a close resemblance were used as *numerals*,[3] and hence were mistaken for one another. In our common Greek text, the number "six hundred three score and six" is indicated simply by three or sometimes four characters.[4]

[1] Transmission of Ancient Books, pp. 24, 25.
[2] Glassius observes, " Modo enim numeros invenimus,qui omnem modum excedunt, modo si eadem res in duobus libris narratur, in altero numerus adfertur, cui alter contradicit." — Phil. Sacra, De Caussis Corrupt. § 23.
[3] In the Sinaitic MS., "numerals are represented by letters, with a straight line placed over them." — Scrivener's Criticism of New Test., p. 73.
[4] Either, as Tischendorf also writes, $\chi\xi\varsigma'$, or else $\chi\xi\sigma\tau'$. Alford writes, in full, ἑξακόσιοι ἑξήκοντα ἕξ. — See Rev. xiii. 18.

ORIGIN OF THE DISCREPANCIES.

We thus see how mistakes in respect to *numbers* have originated.

It hardly need be added that errors as to *names* have arisen in the same way, — from the similarity of certain letters. Thus we find Hadadezer and Hadarezer,[1] a Daleth ד being mistaken for a Resh ר — and many like cases.

The key thus furnished, will unlock many difficulties during the progress of our work.

10. Multitudes of alleged discrepancies are the product of the *imagination of the critic*, influenced to a greater or less degree by *dogmatic prejudice*.

Two classes of writers illustrate this remark. Of one class no names will be mentioned. The character, spirit, and motives of these writers render further notice of them inconsistent with the purpose of our work.

The second class — not to be spoken of in the same connection with the former — comprises men possessing, in not a few cases, valid claims to scholarship, to critical acumen and to great respectability of character. Foremost in this class may be placed De Wette, as he appears in his earlier writings, and Dr. Samuel Davidson, as he is seen in some of his later works. It is painful to add that it seems impossible to acquit even these authors of great occasional unfairness in their handling of the scriptures.[2]

Next — but by a long interval — may stand the names of Strauss, Colenso, and Theodore Parker. One can scarcely read the productions of these three, and some others of their school,

---

[1] 2 Sam. viii. 3; 1 Chron. xviii. 3.

[2] See, under "Ethical Discrepancies, — Enemies treated," an instance from Baur, relative to Rom. xii. 20; also, one from De Wette, under "Historical Discrepancies, — Anak's Sons' Fate."

It may be added that De Wette, as is generally admitted, during his latter years approximated to orthodoxy. On the contrary, Dr. Davidson's tendencies may be gathered from a comparison of the discussion of the Discrepancies, in his "Sacred Hermeneutics," pp. 516—611, with his treatment of the same, in Horne's Introduction (tenth edition), Vol. ii. pp. 503–553. See, also, Dr. Davidson's Introduction to the Old Test., throughout.

without the conviction that the *animus* of these writers is often felicitously expressed by the old Latin motto, slightly modified: "I will either find a discrepancy, or I will make one"—*Aut inveniam discrepantiam, aut faciam.*

Certain rationalistic authors have a convenient method for disposing of answers to the objections adduced by them. They begin at once to talk loftily of the "higher criticism," and to deride the answers and solutions as "gratuitous assumptions."

"Pertness and ignorance," says Bishop Horne,[1] "may ask a question in three lines which it will cost learning and ingenuity thirty pages to answer; and when this is done, the same question shall be triumphantly asked again the next year, as if nothing had ever been written on the subject." Often, when fairly answered and refuted, these authors remind us of the homely old maxim:

"A man convinced against his will,
Is of the same opinion still."

A favorite exegetical principle adopted by some of these critics appears to be, that *similar events are necessarily identical.* Hence, when they read that Abraham twice equivocated concerning his wife;[2] that Isaac imitated his example;[3] that David was twice in peril in a certain wilderness,[4] and twice spared Saul's life in a cave,[5] they instantly assume that in each case these double narratives are irreconcilable accounts of one and the same event. The absurdity of such a canon of criticism is obvious from the fact that *history is full of events which more or less closely resemble one another.* Take, as a well-known example, the case of the two Presidents Edwards, father and son. Both were named Jonathan Edwards, and were the grandsons of clergymen. "Both were pious in their youth, were distinguished scholars, and were tutors for equal periods in the colleges where they were respectively educated. Both were

---

[1] Works, i. 392 (London edition, 4 vols. 1831).
[2] Gen. xii. 19: xx. 2.   [3] Gen. xxvi. 7.   [4] 1 Sam. xxiii. 19; xxvi. 1.
[5] 1 Sam. xxiv. 6; xxvi. 9.

settled in the ministry as successors to their maternal grandfathers, were dismissed on account of their religious opinions, and were again settled in retired country towns, over congregations singularly attached to them, where they had leisure to pursue their favorite studies, and to prepare and publish their valuable works. Both were removed from these stations to become presidents of colleges, and both died shortly after their respective inaugurations; the one in the fifty-sixth, and the other in the fifty-seventh year of his age; each having preached, on the first Sabbath of the year of his death, on the text: 'This year thou shalt die.' "[1]

Now, let these circumstances be submitted for the consideration of rationalistic critics, and, the probable decision will be that there was but *one* Jonathan Edwards.

We thus see that, if critics dared to tamper with the facts of secular, as they do with those of sacred, history, they would justly incur the ridicule of all well-informed persons. Men clamor for the treatment of the Bible like any other book, yet treat it as they *dare* not treat another book. Herein lies the inconsistency of much of the current criticism; particularly of that "higher criticism" of which we hear so much.

The following case illustrates a spirit and practice not seldom exhibited by certain authors: " A Swedish traveller, in looking through Voltaire's library, found Calmet's Commentary, with slips of paper inserted, on which the difficulties noticed by Calmet were set down, without a word about the solutions which were given by him. 'This,' adds the Swede, who was otherwise a great admirer of Voltaire, ' was not honorable.' " " Our modern critics," continues Hengstenberg,[2] " have adopted exactly the same line of conduct."

---

[1] See Memoir prefixed to Works of Edwards the younger, p. xxxiv. Observe that no one of the above cases bears, in respect to *points of coincidence*, worthy comparison with this unquestioned instance in modern times.

[2] Genuineness of Pent. i. 47.

We cannot but concur in the judgment couched in this and the following quotations.

Prof. Henry Rogers,[1] criticising Strauss's Life of Jesus, says it ought to be entitled, " A *collection* of all the difficulties and discrepancies which honest criticism has discovered, and perverted ingenuity has imagined, in the four evangelists."

Again, alluding to Strauss's objections, " The paraded discrepancies are frequently assumed; sometimes even manufactured." This criticism is supported by several illustrations from the German author, and is as applicable to his " New Life of Jesus," as to his earlier work.

The learned translator of Bleek [2] severely, yet fitly, designates the course pursued by certain authors as that " exaggeration of difficulties, that ostentatious parading of grounds of suspicion, which so painfully characterize much of the later biblical criticism, and not unwarrantably give rise to the question whether there be not some secret ground of malevolence, some unacknowledged, but most influential desire to find reasons for an already existing unbelief, to account for the bitter and determined hostility with which the books are treated."

It is a lamentable fact that there is abroad in the world, and bearing the name of Christianity, a spirit which, as Canon Wordsworth [3] well says, " speaks fair words of Christ, and yet it loves to invent discrepancies, and to imagine contradictions in the narratives which his apostles and evangelists delivered of his birth, his temptation, his miracles, his agony, his sufferings, his resurrection, and ascension." We refrain from characterizing that Christianity which seeks to disparage its own sacred books, and to undermine its own foundation.

Such are the spirit and methods of much of the sceptical criticism — even of the so-called "higher criticism"— of our day.

[1] Reason and Faith, pp. 424, 427 (Boston edition).
[2] Preface to Introduction to Old Test.
[3] Preface to Greek Four Gospels, p. viii.

ORIGIN OF THE DISCREPANCIES.

A careful and protracted examination of the works of numerous authors, who from various positions and under various pretences assail the Bible, warrants, as neither unjust nor uncharitable, the remark that a large portion of their alleged "discrepancies" are purely *subjective* — originating, primarily, not in the sacred books, but in the misguided prejudices and disordered imagination of the critic.

We might also have adduced *the very great compression of the narrative* as a fruitful source of apparent incongruities. Such was the condensation which the writers were constrained to employ, that, in any given case, only a few of the more salient circumstances could be introduced. Had the sacred historians undertaken to relate *every* circumstance, the Bible, instead of being comprised in a single volume, would have filled many volumes, and would consequently have proved unwieldy, and well nigh useless to mankind.

If "the world itself could not contain the books" which should minutely detail all our Saviour's acts,[1] how much less could it "contain" those which should narrate circumstantially the history of all the important personages mentioned in the scriptures.

We thus see that, with reference to any given event, a host of minute particulars have dropped from the knowledge of mankind, and are lost beyond recovery. Hence, in many instances, the thread of the narrative is not simply not obvious, but can only be recovered, if at all, by prolonged and searching scrutiny. That circumstances, combined in so fragmentary and disconnected a manner, should sometimes appear incompatible, is a fact too familiar to need illustration.

[1] John xxi. 25.

CHAPTER II.

DESIGN OF THE DISCREPANCIES.

WHY were the discrepancies permitted to exist? What good end do they contemplate?

1. They were doubtless intended as *a stimulus to the human intellect*, as provocative of mental effort. They serve to awaken curiosity and to appeal to the love of novelty.

The Bible is a wonderful book. No other has been studied so much, or called forth a tithe of the criticism which this has elicited. " No book, not nature itself, has ever waked up intellectual activity like the Bible. On the battle-field of truth, it has ever been round this that the conflict has raged. What book besides ever caused the writing of so many other books? Take from the libraries of Christendom all those which have sprung, I will not say indirectly, but directly from it, — those written to oppose, or defend, or elucidate it, — and how would they be diminished! The very multitude of infidel books is a witness to the power with which the Bible stimulates the intellect. Why do we not see the same amount of active intellect coming up, and dashing and roaring around the Koran?"[1]

The discrepancies of the sacred volume have played no insignificant part in this incitement of mental action. Though but a subordinate characteristic, they have prompted men to "search the scriptures," and to ask: How are these difficulties to be resolved? Things which are "hard to be understood," present special attractions to the inquiring mind. Professor Park[2] observes, in an admirable essay on the choice of Texts, "Sometimes a deeper interest is awakened by examining two or more

[1] President Hopkins, Evidences of Christianity, p. 144.
[2] Bib. Sacra, Oct. 1873. pp. 717, 718.

passages which appear to contradict each other than by examining two or more which resemble each other. Men are eager to learn the meaning and force of a text, one part of which is John xv. 15 : 'All things that I have heard of my Father I have made known unto you,' and the other part is John xvi. 12 : 'I have yet many things to say unto you ; but ye cannot bear them now.' Why did our Lord utter the second part of this text *after* the first part, yet in the same hour with it? The Bible rouses the mind from its torpid state by declaring that man dieth and is not, and yet lives forever; that man is a worm of the dust, and yet is made little lower than the angels ; that he must love, and yet hate his father, mother, brother, sister ; that every man must bear his own burden, and yet each one bear the burdens of his brethren ; that man's body will be raised from the grave, and yet not the same body ; that Christ was ignorant of some things, and yet knew all things ; that he could not bear his own cross, and yet upholdeth all things by the word of his power. When two classes of passages stand in apparently hostile array against each other at the opening of a sermon, the somnolent hearer is kept awake in order to see how the conflict will end. He may be raised by the discourse from his natural love of learning the truth to a gracious love of the truth which is learned."

Whately[1] says : " The seeming contradictions in scripture are too numerous not to be the result of design ; and doubtless *were* designed, not as mere difficulties to try our faith and patience, but as furnishing the most suitable mode of instruction that could have been devised, by mutually explaining and modifying or limiting or extending one another's meaning."

Elsewhere, urging the same thought, he observes : " Instructions thus conveyed are evidently more striking and more likely to arouse the attention ; and also, from the very circumstance that they call for careful reflection, more likely to make a lasting impression."

[1] On Difficulties in Writings of St. Paul, Essay vii. Sec. 4.

Again, illustrating, as beautifully as suggestively, by the case of the mariner who steers midway between certain landmarks, he adds: "Even thus, it will often happen that two apparently opposite passages of scripture may together enable us to direct our faith or our practice aright; one shall be calculated to guard us against certain errors on one side, and the other, on the other side; neither, taken alone, shall convey the exact and entire truth; but both taken in conjunction may enable us sufficiently to ascertain it." He also ingeniously compares the colliding texts to several mechanical forces or impulses, acting upon a body to be set in motion; their *resultant* impelling it in the direction required, though no one of the impulses, taken singly, is acting precisely in that direction.

The rabbies have a saying that "the book of Chronicles was given for argument," that is, to incite men to investigation and discussion.[1] The history of sacred criticism demonstrates that the book has answered this purpose remarkably well; its discrepancies being salient points which attract attention.

Not only do these "hard" things induce men to investigate the sacred volume; but meanwhile resolving themselves before the steady and patient eye of the student, they unfold deep and rich meanings which amply reward his toil. This process is exemplified in the case of the scholar quoted above. He observes: "I well remember when it seemed to me that there was a direct contradiction between Paul and James on the subject of faith and works. I can now see that they not only do not contradict each other, but harmonize perfectly."[2]

Says Professor Stuart:[3] "In the early part of my biblical studies, some thirty to thirty-five years ago, when I first began the critical investigation of the scriptures, doubts and difficulties started up on every side, like the armed men whom Cadmus is

---

[1] Rashi, referring to 1 Chron. viii. 38, "And Azel had six sons," quaintly and pithily observes: "What the wise men have said about these 'six sons,' would load thirteen thousand camels."

[2] Evidences of Christianity, p. 354.

[3] History of Old Test. Canon, p. 18. Revised ed. p. 16.

fabled to have raised up. Time, patience, continued study, a better acquaintance with the original scriptural languages and the countries where the sacred books were written, have scattered to the winds nearly all these doubts."

In this manner, the difficulties of scripture often keenly stimulate and richly reward intellectual effort.

2. They were meant to be *illustrative of the analogy between the Bible and nature,* and so to evince their common origin. The "self-contradictions" of the Bible are produced on a grander scale in nature. Wherever we turn our eyes, the material universe affords unmistakable traces of infinite wisdom, power, and benevolence. The starry heavens, the earth robed in vernal green, the bright, glad sunshine, the balmy breezes, the refreshing dews and showers, the sweet song birds, the flowers of brilliant hues and delicious odors, the wonderful and countless forms of vegetation, the infinite varieties of insect and animal life, the nice adaptations and benevolent contrivances for their welfare everywhere visible in nature — all these proclaim the attributes and speak forth the praise of the Creator.

But, looking into the same arena from another point of view, we see a very different spectacle. Want and wo, sorrow and suffering, appear dominant in the world. Frost and fire, famine and pestilence, earthquake, volcano, and hurricane, war and intemperance, a thousand diseases and ten thousand accidents, are doing their deadly work upon our fellow-creatures. All this fearful devastation is going on in a world created and governed by infinite wisdom, power, and love. Milton's terrible picture [1] too often finds its counterpart. Nowhere in the Bible

---

[1]
"Immediately a place
Before his eyes appeared, sad, noisome, **dark**,
A lazar-house it seemed, wherein were laid
Numbers of all diseased, all maladies
Of ghastly spasm or racking torture, **qualms**
Of heart-sick agony, all feverous kinds,
Convulsions, epilepsies, fierce catarrhs,
Intestine stone and ulcer, colic pangs,
Demoniac frenzy, moping melancholy,

do we behold such a gigantic inconsistency, such an irrepressible conflict, as in the scene before us. Let a man solve the grand problem of the ages; let him tell us why an infinitely wise, powerful, and benevolent Creator allowed evil to enter at all his universe — let him explain this contradiction, and we may safely engage to explain those which occur in the Bible. For none of them — not all together — are so dark, unfathomable, and appalling as this one grand, ultimate Discrepancy. Says Origen: " He who believes the scripture to have proceeded from him who is the Author of nature, may well expect to find the same sort of difficulties in it as are found in the constitution of nature." Bishop Butler[1] pertinently adds, that "he who denies the scripture to have been from God, on account of these difficulties, may, for the very same reason, deny the world to have been formed by him."

In nature, then, we perceive mighty discords, tremendous antagonisms, which in appearance seriously involve and militate against the character and attributes of God. Nevertheless, nature is confessedly his work. Now, we find the Bible claiming the same supernatural origin, and exhibiting, among other features of resemblance, similar, though far less important, discrepancies; hence these latter afford a valid presumption in favor of its claim.

Nearly in the same line of thought, says Dr. Charles Hodge:[2] "The universe teems with evidences of design, so manifold, so

> And moon-struck madness, pining atrophy,
> Marasmus, and wide-wasting pestilence,
> Dropsies and asthmas, and joint-racking rheums.
>   Dire was the tossing, deep the groans; Despair
> Tended the sick, busiest, from couch to couch;
> And over them triumphant Death his dart
> Shook, but delayed to strike, though oft invoked
> With vows, as their chief good and final hope.
>   Sight so deform, what heart of rock could long
> Dry-eyed behold?" — Par. Lost, B. xi, line 477–495.

[1] Introduction to Analogy, p. 70 (Malcom's edition).
[2] Theology, i. 170.

DESIGN OF THE DISCREPANCIES.

diverse, so wonderful as to overwhelm the mind with the conviction that it has had an intelligent author. Yet here and there isolated cases of monstrosity appear. It is irrational, because we cannot account for such cases, to deny that the universe is the product of intelligence. So the Christian need not renounce his faith in the plenary inspiration of the Bible, although there may be some things about it, in its present state, which he cannot account for."

If we may credit the philosophers, even the higher walks of science are not free from "stumbling-blocks." Kant, Hamilton, and Mansel teach that our reason, that the necessary laws of thought which govern our mental operations, lead to absolute contradictions.[1] Mansel[2] observes, "The conception of the Absolute and Infinite, from whatever side we view it, appears encompassed with contradictions. There is a contradiction in supposing such an object to exist, whether alone or in conjunction with others; and there is a contradiction in supposing it not to exist. There is a contradiction in conceiving it as one; and there is a contradiction in conceiving it as many. There is a contradiction in conceiving it as personal; and there is a contradiction in conceiving it as impersonal. It cannot without contradiction be represented as active; nor without equal contradiction be represented as inactive. It cannot be conceived as the sum of all existence; nor yet can it be conceived as a part only of that sum."

Again he says, "It is our duty, then, to think of God as personal; and it is our duty to believe that he is infinite. It is true that we cannot reconcile these two representations with each other; as our conception of personality involves attributes apparently contradictory to the notion of infinity."

It would seem that our prospect of escaping contradictions by casting the Bible aside and betaking ourselves to philosophy, is quite unpromising. Notwithstanding the "discrepancies,"

---

[1] Dr. Hodge, Theology, i. 362.
[2] Limits of Religious Thought, pp. 84, 85, and 106 (American edition).

the wisest course may be to retain the Bible for the present, and await further developments.

3. The disagreements of scripture were beyond question designed as a strong incidental proof that *there was no collusion* among the sacred writers. Their differences, go far to establish in this way, the credibility of these authors.

The inspired narratives exhibit " substantial agreement with circumstantial variation." This is precisely what a court of justice requires in respect of the testimony of witnesses. Should their evidence agree precisely in every word and syllable, this fact would be held by the court proof of conspiracy. The well-known " Howland will case,"[1] in New Bedford, some years since, affords an illustration of the principle. In this famous case some one or two millions of dollars was at stake, and over one hundred and fifty thousand dollars were expended for costs and counsel fees in two years. Upon the case were brought to bear the resources of many of the ablest counsel in New England, and the skill of the most ingenious scientific experts of the United States. The main issue of fact raised was whether the signature to the second page was written by Miss Howland, or whether it was a forgery. The minute and exact resemblance of the first and second signatures, in all points, was the grand stumbling-block in the case. In a word, the signatures agreed too well.

Now, had the biblical writers agreed in all particulars, even the minutest, had there been no discrepancies in their testimony, the cry of " Collusion, Collusion ! " would have passed along the whole infidel line, from Celsus and Porphyry down to Colenso and Renan. We maintain, therefore, that the very discrepancies, lying as they do upon the surface, without reaching the subject-matter, the kernel of scripture, — and being, moreover, capable of adjustment,— are so many proofs of its authenticity and credibility.

As to the " various readings,"[2] in the manuscripts of the New

[1] See American Law Review, July, 1870, pp. 625–663.
[2] This term denotes differences in the spelling, choice, and arrangement of words in the Greek text.

Testament, Wordsworth[1] says, "*These discrepancies being such as they are found to be, are of inestimable value.* They show that there has been no collusion among our witnesses, and that our manuscript copies of the Gospels, about five hundred in number, and brought to us from all parts of the world, have not been mutilated or interpolated with any sinister design; that they have not been tampered with by any religious sect, for the sake of propagating any private opinion as the word of God. These discrepancies are, in fact, evidences of the purity and integrity of the sacred text. They show that the scriptures which we now hold in our hands in the nineteenth century, are identical with those which were received by the church in the first century as written by the Holy Ghost." That the "various readings" are thus proofs of the substantial identity of our New Testament with the inspired original is clear. The Greek Testament has come down to us, to all intents and purposes, *unimpaired.* Each of the five hundred manuscripts, with its slight variations in the orthography, selection, and collocation of words, is an independent witness to this fact.

The disagreements of the sacred writers effectually bar the charge of "conspiracy" on their part.

4. Another object of the discrepancies was, it may be presumed, to lead us to *value the spirit beyond the letter* of the scriptures, to prize the essentials of Christianity rather than its form and accidents. Many things point in the same direction. For example, we have no portrait of Jesus, no authentic description of his person. No wood of the "true cross" remains to our day. It is not difficult to divine the reason why no relics of this kind are left to us. Suppose the original text of the holy volume had been miraculously transmitted, in the very hand-writing of the authors, and perfect in every letter and figure. The world would have gone mad over it. Idolatry the most stupendous would have accumulated around it. Crusades more bloody and disastrous than those for the recovery of the holy sepulchre, would have

---

[1] Preface to Greek Four Gospels, p. xxii.

been conducted for its possession. It would have ensanguined and darkened the whole history of the Christian religion. Men would have worshipped the letter in flagrant opposition to the spirit of the sacred book. Doubtless, with a view to counteract this tendency to idolatry and formalism, the scriptures are given to us in their present condition. Our attention is thereby diverted from the external and formal features to the internal and essential elements of scripture.

The numerous manuscripts with their trivial differences, the so-called "imperfections" of our present text, together with the "self-contradictions" of the sacred books — all afford a fresh application and illustration of the inspired saying, "The letter killeth, but the spirit giveth life."

5. The biblical discrepancies were plainly appointed as *a test of moral character;* and, probably, to serve an *important judicial purpose.* They may be regarded as constituting no insignificant element of the means and conditions of man's probation.

There is a peculiar and striking analogy and harmony between the external form and the interior doctrines of the Bible. Both alike present difficulties — sometimes formidable — to the inquirer. Both alike put his sincerity and firmness to full proof. Hence, as Grotius[1] has fitly said, the Gospel becomes a touchstone to test the honesty of men's dispositions.

Our Saviour's teachings were often clothed in forms which to the indifferent or prejudiced hearer must have seemed obscure, if not offensive. To the caviling and sceptical Jews he spoke many things in parables, that seeing they might see and not perceive, and hearing they might hear and not understand.[2] When he said, "Except ye eat the flesh of the Son of Man, and drink his blood, ye have no life in you,"[3] he intentionally used such phraseology as would be repugnant to insincere and squeamish hearers. He thus tested and disclosed

[1] **De** Veritate Religionis Christianae, lib. ii, § 19. [2] **Mark iv. 12.**
[3] **John vi. 53**

men's characters and motives, and sifted out the chaff among his hearers. " From that time, many of his disciples went back, and walked no more with him."[1] The seeming harshness and obscurity of his sayings served to rid him of those followers who were not of teachable spirit, and thoroughly in earnest, and who would not look beneath the surface. The indolent and superficial, the proud and fastidious, were discouraged and repelled by the rough husk in which the doctrinal kernel was encased.

In an analogous manner, the apparent contradictions of the Bible afford "opportunity to an unfair mind for explaining away and deceitfully hiding from itself that evidence which it might see."[2] Our treatment of the external no less than that of the internal difficulties of scripture bears an intimate relation to our moral character.

Those who are disposed to cavil do, in the wise arrangement of God, find opportunities for caviling. *The disposition does not miss the occasion.*

In the words of Isaac Taylor:[3] "The very conditions of a Revelation that has been consigned to various records in the course of thirty centuries involve a liability to the renewal of exceptive argumentation, which easily finds points of lodgment upon so large a surface. .... The very same extent of surface from which a better reason, and a more healthful moral feeling gather an irresistible conviction of the nearness of God throughout it, furnishes to an astute and frigid critical faculty, a thousand and one instances over which to proclaim a petty triumph." Or, as Pascal[4] has beautifully expressed it, God " willing to be revealed to those who seek him with their whole heart, and hidden from those who as cordially fly from him, has so regulated the means of knowing him, as to give indications of himself, which are plain to those who seek him, and obscure to those who seek

---

[1] John vi. 66.   [2] Butler's Analogy, Part ii. chap. vi.
[3] Spirit of Hebrew Poetry, preface.
[4] Thoughts, chap. xiii. Sec. 1 and 2 (Andover edition).

him not. There is light enough for those whose main wish is to see; and darkness enough for those of an opposite disposition."

That the difficulties of the Bible were intended, moreover, to serve a *penal* end seems by no means improbable. Those persons who cherish a cavilling spirit, who are bent upon misapprehending the truth, and urging captious and frivolous objections, find in the inspired volume, difficulties and disagreements which would seem to have been designed as stumbling-stones for those which "stumble at the word, being disobedient: whereunto also they were appointed."[1] Upon the wilful votaries of error God sends "strong delusion, that they should believe a lie,"[2] that they might work out their own condemnation and ruin.

"If we disparage scripture, and treat it 'as any other book,' then Almighty God, who is the author of scripture, will punish us by our own devices. He will 'choose our delusions'; he will 'chastise us by our wickedness,' and 'reprove us by our backslidings,' and 'give us the reward of our own hands.' Our presumption and our irreverence will be the instruments of our punishment."[3] In the divine government of this world, sin not infrequently carries its reward in its own bosom.

When the difficulties of scripture are approached with a docile and reverent mind, they may tend to our establishment in the faith; but, when they are dealt with in a querulous and disingenuous manner, they may become judicial agencies in linking to caviling scepticism its appropriate penalty — even to the loss of the soul.

---

[1] 1 Pet. ii. 8.   [2] 2 Thess. ii. 11.
[3] Replies to Essays and Reviews, p. 485 (English edition).

CHAPTER III.

RESULTS OF THE DISCREPANCIES.

WHAT is the effect of the discrepancies, in relation to the integrity of the text, and to the moral influence of the Bible?

1. They neither *unsettle the text*, nor essentially impair its integrity. They fail to vitiate it, in any appreciable degree. The conclusion reached by eminent scholars and critics, after protracted and thorough investigation, is, that the sacred text has been transmitted to us virtually unaltered.

Says Isaac Taylor,[1] "The evidence of the genuineness and authenticity of the Jewish and Christian scriptures has, for no other reason than a thought of the consequences that are involved in an admission of their truth, been treated with an unwarrantable disregard of logical equity, and even of the dictates of common sense. The poems of Anacreon, the tragedies of Sophocles, the plays of Terence, the epistles of Pliny, are adjudged to be safe from the imputation of spuriousness, or of material corruption; and yet evidence ten times greater as to its quantity, variety, and force, supports the genuineness of the poems of Isaiah, and the epistles of Paul."

Bishop Butler:[2] "There may be mistakes of transcribers; there may be other real or seeming mistakes, not easy to be particularly accounted for; but there are certainly no more things of this kind in the scripture, than what were to have been expected in books of such antiquity; and nothing in any wise sufficient to discredit the general narrative."

That the text of the Old Testament has been transmitted to

---

[1] History of Transmission of Ancient Books, pp. 169-170.
[2] Analogy, p. 288 (Malcom's edition).

us substantially intact, is a conceded point. In all but a few unimportant cases, the genuine reading is *settled* beyond dispute. The candid and scholarly Bleek[1] asserts that "the Hebrew manuscripts have been preserved unaltered *generally;* and this in a measure of which we find no second example in other works which have been multiplied and circulated by numerous manuscripts."

Keil:[2] "The Old Testament, like all the other books of antiquity, has been propagated by transcription. And thus it has happened, even in spite of the great care with which the Jews, who were filled with unbounded reverence for the holy scriptures, watched over their preservation and transmission without injury, that they could not escape the common lot of all ancient books. In the course of repeated copying many small errors crept into the text, and various readings came into existence, which lie before us in the text as it is attested in the records belonging to the various centuries. ... The copyists have committed these errors by seeing or hearing wrongly, by faithlessness of memory, and by other misunderstandings; yet not arbitrarily or intentionally. And by none of them have the essential contents of scripture been endangered."

Even De Wette,[3] comparing the Egyptians, Chaldeans, and Phoenicians with the Hebrews, observes, "From the former, either all the monuments of their literature have perished to the last fragment, or only single melancholy ruins survive, which in nothing diminish the loss of the rest; while, on the contrary, from the latter there is still extant a whole library of authors, so valuable and ancient that the writings of the Greeks are in comparison extremely young." This is a very significant concession from one of the leaders of modern rationalism.

Gesenius[4] says, "To state here in few words my creed, as to the condition of the Hebrew text in a critical respect. It can-

---

[1] Introd. to Old Test., ii. 365. [2] Introd. to Old Test., ii. 294, 295.
[3] Introd. to Old Test., i. 23 (Parker's edition).
[4] Biblical Repository, iii. 41.

RESULTS OF THE DISCREPANCIES.

not be denied, that through the anxious care of the Jewish critics, the text has been in general very well preserved.

"In the Hebrew manuscripts," says Prof. Stuart,[1] "that have been examined, some eight hundred thousand various readings actually occur, as to the Hebrew consonants. How many as to the vowel-points and accents, no man knows. And the like to this is true of the New Testament. But, at the same time, it is equally true, that all these taken together do not change or materially affect any important point of doctrine, precept, or even history. A great proportion, indeed the mass, of variations in Hebrew manuscripts, when minutely scanned, amount to nothing more than the difference in spelling a multitude of English words. What matters it as to the meaning, whether one writes *honour* or *honor*, whether he writes *centre* or *center*?" Such scholars as Buxtorf, Bleek, Hävernick, Keil, and others, affirm that the Jews took such extraordinary care in copying their sacred books, "that it was a practice to count not only the number of verses, but also that of the words, and even of the letters of the various books, in order to ascertain the middle verse, the middle word, and the middle letter of each book."[2]

Keil[3] remarks that the Masora, a rabbinic critical work upon the Old Testament, contains an "enumeration of the verses, words, and letters of each book; information as to the middle word and middle letter of each book; enumeration of verses which contain the whole consonants of the alphabet, or only so many of them; and also of words which occur so many times in the Bible with this or that meaning, and of words written 'plene,' or 'defective.'"

Parker,[4] in De Wette, gives, from Bishop Walton, a list of the number of times which each Hebrew letter occurs in the Old Testament. The same list may be found in Menasseh ben Israel's Conciliator.[5]

[1] History of Old Test. Canon, p. 192. Revised ed. p. 178.
[2] Bleek's Introduction to Old Test., ii. 451, 452.
[3] Introd. to Old Test., ii. 316.
[4] Introduction to Old Test., i. 357.   [5] Vol. i. p. 250.

Bishop Herbert Marsh[1] has the following very just inference: "When we consider the rules which were observed by the Jews in transcribing the sacred writings, rules which were carried to an accuracy that bordered on superstition, there is reason to believe, that no work of antiquity has descended to the present age so free from alteration, as the Hebrew Bible."

The erudite translator[2] of Outram says, "There are not wanting proofs of the most scrupulous care of the Hebrew text on the part of the Jews." "No evidence has been adduced of their wilful alteration of any part of the Hebrew text." It was by such scrupulous and minute care as this, that the Jews preserved their sacred books from any important variation or corruption.

Moreover, notwithstanding its minute discrepancies and "various readings," the text of the New Testament is better established than that of any other ancient book. No one of the so-called "classics," not Homer nor Herodotus, compares favorably, in this respect, with the New Testament. Says Prof. Stowe,[3] "Of the manuscript copies of the Greek Testament, from seven hundred to one thousand of all kinds have been examined already by critics, and of these at least fifty are more than one thousand years old, and some are known to be at least fifteen hundred years old; while the oldest of the Greek classics scarcely reach the antiquity of nine hundred years, and of these the number is very small indeed, compared with those of the Greek Testament."

Among the Greek classical writers, Herodotus and Plato are of the first importance. The earliest manuscripts of Herodotus extant are, one in the Imperial library at Paris, "executed in the twelfth century"; one in the Florentine library, which Montfaucon assigns to the tenth century, and one in the library of Emmanuel College, Cambridge, England, which may possibly

---

[1] Lectures on Criticism and Interpretation, p. 57.
[2] John Allen, in Modern Judaism, pp. 6, 7 (Second edition).
[3] Origin and History of Books of Bible, p. 60.

have been written in the ninth century.[1] One of the earliest manuscripts of Plato is in the Bodleian Library at Oxford, and was executed not earlier than the ninth century.

Among the manuscripts of the New Testament, we have the Alexandrian, written about A.D. 350; the Vatican, written about A.D. 325; the Sinaitic, of date equally early; the Ephraim manuscript, "probably somewhat later than the Alexandrian, but of great critical value"; and the Beza manuscript, dating about A.D. 490.[2] Other scholars substantially concur in these dates, though Alford[3] and Scrivener[4] assign the Alexandrian manuscript to the fifth century; that is, A.D. 400–500.

Here, then, we find *five manuscripts of the Greek New Testament, the youngest of which is about fourteen hundred years old; and all of which may have been prepared by persons who had studied the original manuscripts written by the apostles themselves.*

So far, therefore, as an authenticated and settled text is concerned, the classics are very far behind the New Testament.[5] "There is not," says Tregelles,[6] "such a mass of transmissional evidence in favor of any classical work. The existing manuscripts of Herodotus and Thucydides are modern enough when compared with some of those of the New Testament."

[1] Taylor's History of Transmission of Ancient Books, pp. 276-278; compare Stowe, p. 59.

[2] Stowe, pp. 65-77. See, also, Alford, Prolegomena to Greek Four Gospels, pp. 107-116; and Scrivener, Criticism of New Test., pp. 76-103.

[3] Prolegomena to Four Gospels, p. 107.

[4] Criticism of New Test., p. 82.

[5] Dr. Bentley, in his annihilating reply to Collins, speaking of the manuscript copies of Terence, the oldest and best of which, now in the Vatican library, has "hundreds of errors," observes, "I myself have collated several, and do affirm that I have seen twenty thousand various lections in that little author, not near so big as the New Testament; and am morally sure, that if half the number of manuscripts were collated for Terence with that niceness and minuteness which has been used in twice as many for the New Testament, the number of the variations would amount to above fifty thousand." And yet Terence is one of the best preserved of the classic writers. — Remarks upon a late Discourse, etc. Part i. Sec. 32.

[6] New Testament Historic Evidence, p. 74.

In the fitting words of Scrivener,[1] "As the New Testament far surpasses all other remains of antiquity in value and interest, so are the copies of it yet existing in manuscript, and dating from the fourth century of our era downwards, far more numerous than those of the most celebrated writers of Greece or Rome. Such as have been already discovered and set down in catalogues are hardly fewer than two thousand; and many more must still linger unknown in the monastic libraries of the East. On the other hand, manuscripts of the most illustrious classic poets and philosophers are far rarer and comparatively modern. We have no complete copy of Homer himself prior to the thirteenth century, though some considerable fragments have been recently brought to light which may plausibly be assigned to the fifth century; while more than one work of high and deserved repute has been preserved to our times only in a single copy. Now the experience we gain, from a critical examination of the few classical manuscripts that survive, should make us thankful for the quality and abundance of those of the New Testament. These last present us with a vast and almost inexhaustible supply of materials for tracing the history, and upholding (at least within certain limits) the purity of the sacred text; every copy, if used diligently and with judgment, will contribute somewhat to these ends. So far is the copiousness of our stores from causing doubt or perplexity to the genuine student of holy scripture, that it leads him to recognize the more fully its general integrity in the midst of partial variation."

With equal felicity and truthfulness, Isaac Taylor,[2] on the proof of the genuineness of the scriptures, observes: " And as the facts on which this proof depends are precisely of the same kind in profane, as in sacred literature, and as the same principles of evidence are applicable to all questions relating to the genuineness of ancient books, it is highly desirable that the proof

---

[1] Criticism of New Test., pp. 3, 4.
[2] History of Transmission of Ancient Books, p. 5.

of the genuineness of the sacred writings should be viewed, *in its place*, as forming a part only of a general argument, which bears equally upon the entire literary remains of antiquity. For it is only when so viewed, that the comparative strength and completeness of the proof which belongs to this particular case, can be duly estimated. When exhibited in this light, it will be seen that the integrity of the records of the Christian faith is substantiated by *evidence in a tenfold proportion more various, copious, and conclusive*[1] than that which can be adduced in support of any other ancient writings. If, therefore, the question had no other importance belonging to it than what may attach to a purely literary inquiry, or if only the strict justice of the case were regarded, the authenticity of the Jewish and Christian scriptures could never come to be controverted, till the entire body of classical literature had been proved to be spurious."

Nor does the Bible suffer by comparison with books of later date. For the text of Shakespeare, which has been in existence less than two hundred and fifty years, is "far more uncertain and corrupt than that of the New Testament, now over eighteen centuries old, during nearly fifteen of which it existed only in manuscript. The industry of collators and commentators indeed has collected a formidable array of 'various readings' in the Greek text of the scriptures, but the number of those which have any good claim to be received, and which also seriously affect the sense, is so small that they may almost be counted upon the fingers. With perhaps a dozen or twenty exceptions, the text of every verse in the New Testament may be said to be so far settled by the general consent of scholars, that any dispute as to its meaning must relate rather to the interpretation of the words, than to any doubts respecting the words themselves. But in every one of Shakespeare's thirty-seven plays, there are probably a hundred readings still in

---

[1] The italics are our own.

dispute, a large proportion of which materially affect the meaning of the passages in which they occur."[1]

The probability that trivial variations would be found in considerable numbers will be seen when we reflect that, according to Prof. Norton's[2] estimate, there were, at the end of the second century, as many as *sixty thousand manuscript copies of the Gospels* in existence. That these variations are of slight importance we have already seen; so that in spite of the "fifty thousand various readings"[3] of which we are often told, he must be very ignorant or very mendacious who represents the text of the New Testament as in a dubious and unsettled state. Its antiquity and all other circumstances being taken into the account, there is no other book which compares with it in possessing a settled and authenticated text.

The famous Bentley,[4] one of the ablest critics England has ever seen, observes: "The real text of the sacred writers does not now (since the originals have been so long lost) lie in any single manuscript or edition, but is dispersed in them all. 'Tis competently exact indeed, even in the worst manuscript now extant; nor is one article of faith or moral precept either perverted or lost in them, choose as awkwardly as you can, choose the worst by design, out of the whole lump of readings." Again he adds, "Make your thirty thousand (variations) as many more, if numbers of copies can ever reach that sum; all the better to a knowing and serious reader, who is thereby more richly furnished to select what he sees genuine. But even put them into the hands of a knave or a fool, and yet with the most sinistrous and absurd choice, he shall not extinguish the light of any one chapter, nor disguise Christianity but that every feature of it will be the same."

---

[1] North American Review, quoted in Stowe's Origin and History of Books of Bible, p. 82.
[2] Genuineness of the Gospels, i. 50–53.
[3] See as to the probable number, Scrivener's Criticism of New Test., p. 8
[4] Remarks upon a late Discourse of Free Thinking, Part i. Sec. 82.

RESULTS OF THE DISCREPANCIES.

When men seek to impugn the credibility of the Bible, by alleging "discrepancies" and "various readings," we may safely answer, with Prof. Stuart,[1] that they are so easily accounted for, and of so little importance, that "they make nothing of serious import against the claims which the matter, the manner, and the character of the scriptures prefer as the stable ground of our belief and confidence and obedience."

Very pertinently says Dr. Hodge,[2] "These apparent discrepancies, although numerous, are for the most part trivial; relating in most cases to numbers or dates. The great majority of them are only apparent, and yield to careful examination. Many of them may be fairly ascribed to errors of transcribers. The marvel and the miracle is, that there are so few of any real importance. Considering that the different books of the Bible were written not only by different authors, but by men of all degrees of culture, living in the course of fifteen hundred or two thousand years, it is altogether unaccountable that they should agree perfectly, on any other hypothesis than that the writers were under the guidance of the Spirit of God. In this respect, as in all others, the Bible stands alone. .... The errors in matters of fact which sceptics search out bear no proportion to the whole. No sane man would deny that the Parthenon was built of marble, even if here and there a speck of sandstone should be detected in its structure."

"The subject of various readings," observes President Hopkins,[3] "was at one time so presented as to alarm and disquiet those not acquainted with the facts. When a person hears it stated that, in the collation of the manuscripts for Griesbach's edition of the New Testament, as many as one hundred and fifty thousand various readings were discovered, he is ready to suppose that everything must be in a state of uncertainty. A statement of the facts relieves every difficulty. The truth is,

---
[1] History of Old Test. Canon, p. 104. Revised edition, p. 180.
[2] Theology, i. 169, 170.
[3] Evidences of Christianity, p. 289.

that not one in a thousand makes any perceptible, or at least important, variation in the meaning; that they consist almost entirely of the small and obvious mistakes of transcribers, such as the omission or transposition of letters, errors in grammar, in the use of one word for another of a similar meaning, and in changing the position of words in a sentence. But by all the omissions, and all the additions, contained in all the manuscripts, no fact, no doctrine, no duty prescribed, in our authorized version, is rendered either obscure or doubtful."

2. Moreover, as the *text* of scripture is not vitiated, so its *moral influence* and *efficacy* is not essentially impaired by all the "contradictions" which lynx-eyed infidelity has discovered, or affected to discover, in it. In respect to them, Prof. Bush[1] strikingly and felicitously remarks, "Their apparent contrariety shows at least with what confidence the book of God appeals to our reason on the ground of the general evidence of its origin, exhibiting, as it does, such examples of *literal* self-conflict in particular passages. A work of imposture could not *afford* to be thus seemingly indifferent to appearances."

We thus see how the mighty moral prestige of the Bible resolves these apparent objections into strong presumptions in its favor. The truth of our proposition becomes obvious when we carefully consider the influence of the Bible, both upon individuals and upon society in general, — its effect upon mankind.

We cannot specify here, what every community furnishes, instances of men once dishonest, turbulent, profane, sensual, or drunken, who, under the influence of the Bible, have thoroughly reformed their conduct and life, and become as remarkable for meekness, benevolence, purity, and self-control as they had previously been notorious for the opposite traits.

Among those who have recognized the influence of the Bible, and bowed reverently to its authority, we find many of the "foremost men" of the race — the acutest and most powerful intellects, the most distinguished poets, statesmen, and scholars

[1] Notes on Exodus, Vol. i. p. 295.

whom the world has ever seen. It would be superfluous to name Milton and Dante; Bacon, Newton, and Leibnitz; Boyle, Locke, and Butler; Hale and Grotius; Pascal and Faraday; Washington and Wilberforce.

Had the Bible been, as some assert, full of irreconcilable discrepancies and insoluble difficulties, it could scarcely have commanded the homage of such minds and hearts as these. For, it is not extravagant to say that these men were as acute in detecting imposture, and as competent to discriminate between truth and falsehood as are, in our own time, the Bishop of Natal and the Duke of Somerset.

In proof of the power of the Bible to leaven and renovate society, we need only point to the Sandwich Islands, and to the mission fields and schools of India and Turkey; we need but allude to the marked difference between nations which have received the Bible and those which have rejected it,— between Prussia and France, between England and Spain. On a candid survey of the field, we see the correctness of Chancellor Kent's saying: " The general diffusion of the Bible is the most effectual way to civilize and humanize mankind; to purify and exalt the general system of public morals; to give efficacy to the just precepts of international and municipal law; to enforce the observance of prudence, temperance, justice, and fortitude; and to improve all the relations of social and domestic life."

It was well affirmed by John Locke, " That the holy scriptures are one of the greatest blessings which God bestows upon the sons of men, is generally acknowledged by all who know anything of the value and worth of them."

We, therefore, deem the position an impregnable one, that all the discrepancies and objections which the teeming brain and malignant heart of infidelity have been able to conjure up and rake together, do not in any essential degree detract from the value of the inspired volume, nor diminish its wonderful and beneficent moral power.

—Nor does infidelity furnish any substitute for the Bible. It points us all in vain to Confucius, Zoroaster, and the Vedas, to the cold and arrogant teachings of positivism, to the barren negations and ever-discordant utterances of rationalism. Never book spake like the Bible. No other comes home to the heart and conscience, with light and power and healing as does this. It teaches man how to live and how to die.

A celebrated infidel is said to have exclaimed in his last moments, "*I am about to take a leap in the dark.*" Cast the Bible aside, and every man at death takes a "leap in the dark."

In the language of an eminent writer,[1] "Weary human nature lays its head on this bosom, or it has nowhere to lay its head. Tremblers on the verge of the dark and terrible valley which parts the land of the living from the untried hereafter, take this hand of human tenderness, yet godlike strength, or they totter into the gloom without prop or stay. They who look their last on the beloved dead listen to this voice of soothing and peace, else death is no uplifting of everlasting doors, and no enfolding in everlasting arms, but an enemy as appalling to the reason as to the senses, the usher to a charnel-house where highest faculties and noblest feelings lie crushed with the animal wreck; an infinite tragedy, maddening, soul-sickening — a 'blackness of darkness forever.'"

"Thy word is a lamp unto my feet, and a light unto my path."[2]

We cannot but agree with Lord Chief Justice Hale, that "there is no book like the Bible for excellent learning, wisdom, and use"; we must, with Sir Isaac Newton, "account the scriptures of God to be the most sublime philosophy," and to exhibit "more sure marks of authenticity than any profane history whatsoever."

In considering the solutions hereafter proposed, the legitimate force of a hypothesis should be kept in mind. If a

---

[1] Dr. Rorison, in Replies to Essays and Reviews, pp. 340, 341 (2d edition.).
[2] Ps. cxix. 105.

certain hypothesis meets the exigencies of a given case, then, unless it can be proven false or absurd, its logical value is to set aside any and all objections, and to secure a strong presumption in its own favor.[1] For instance, it is said: " Here is a case in which the Bible contradicts itself." We reply: " Here is a hypothesis which serves to explain and reconcile the disagreement." Now, unless our hypothesis can be proven untrue or irrational, it stands, and the objection is effectually met. In such cases, the burden of proof devolves upon the objector.

The solutions proposed in the following pages are hypothetical; though, in the majority of cases, the probability amounts to almost absolute certainty. In offering these solutions, we neither assert nor undertake to prove that they are the only, or even the actual solutions; we merely affirm that they are reasonable explanations of each case respectively, and, for aught that can be shown to the contrary, they may be the real ones. Therefore, according to the principles of logic and common sense, they countervail and neutralize the discrepancies which are adduced, and leave the unity and integrity and divine authority of the sacred volume unimpaired.

The Discrepancies of Scripture may, perhaps, be most suitably arranged under three heads:[2] the Doctrinal, including

[1] Prof. Henry Rogers well says, " The objector is always apt to take it for granted that the discrepancy is real; though it may be easy to suppose a case (and a *possible* case is quite sufficient for the purpose) which would neutralize the objection. Of this perverseness (we can call it by no other name) the examples are perpetual. ..... It may be objected, perhaps, that the gratuitous supposition of some unmentioned fact — which, if mentioned, would harmonize the apparently counter-statements of two historians — cannot be admitted, and is, in fact, a surrender of the argument. But to say so, is only to betray an utter ignorance of what the argument is. If an objection be founded on the alleged *absolute* contradiction of two statements, it is quite sufficient to show any (not the real, but only a hypothetical and possible) medium of reconciling them; and the objection is in all fairness dissolved; and this would be felt by the honest logician, even if we did not know of any such instances in point of fact. We do know, however, of many." — Reason and Faith, pp. 401-403 (Boston edition).

[2] For other methods of classification, see Davidson's Sacred Hermeneutics, p. 520.

questions of theology; the Ethical, pertaining to human duties and morals; the Historical, relating to persons, places, numbers, and time; with some miscellaneous cases.

Of such a vast and incongruous mass of materials as has accumulated during the investigation, it has seemed well nigh impossible to make a rigorously exact and clearly-defined classification. Obviously, many of the following cases might, from their complex or feebly marked character, fall equally well in some other, or in more than one, of the divisions. In such cases, that arrangement has been adopted which seemed most natural and obvious. The most prominent or important element in a difficult passage has determined the class to which that passage should be referred.

If anything has been lost in scientific precision and nicety, it is believed that much has been gained in simplicity, convenience, and practical utility, by abandoning the attempt at a complex, logical classification, and grouping the discrepancies under a few characteristic heads.

PART II.

CHAPTER I.

DOCTRINAL DISCREPANCIES.

I. GOD.—Omnipotence.

God can do all things.

Behold, I *am* the LORD, the God of all flesh: is there anything too hard for me? Jer. xxxii. 27.
But Jesus beheld *them*, and said unto them, With men this is impossible, but with God all things are possible. Matt. xix. 26.

Can not do some things.

And the LORD was with Judah; and he drave out *the inhabitants of* the mountain; but could not drive out the inhabitants of the valley, because they had chariots of iron. Judg. i. 19.
It was imposssible for God to lie. Heb. vi. 18.

Omnipotence does not imply the power to do every conceivable thing, but the ability to do everything which is the proper object of power. For example, an omnipotent being could not cause a thing to be existent and non-existent at the same instant. The very idea is self-contradictory and absurd. When it is said that God can do "all things," the phrase applies to those things only which involve no inconsistency or absurdity.

According to Voltaire, the quotation from Judges asserts that the Lord "could not drive out the inhabitants of the valley." The fact, however, is that the pronoun "he" refers to the nearest antecedent "Judah." Doubtless, the reason why Judah was not helped, at that time, to drive out the dwellers in the valley, was that too great success might have proved, as it often does, detrimental. God gave to Judah that degree of prosperity which, on the whole, was best for him.

The fourth text refers not to physical but to moral impossibility, — such as is intended when we say, "it was impossible for Washington to betray his country." Our meaning of course is that it was incompatible with Washington's character and principles, to be a traitor. In an analogous yet higher sense, it is "impossible" for God to utter falsehood.

God is tired and rests.	*Is never weary.*
In six days the LORD made heaven and earth, and on the seventh day he rested, and was refreshed. Ex. xxxi. 17.	The everlasting God, the LORD, the Creator of the ends of the earth, fainteth not, neither is weary. Isa. xl. 28.

"Rested and was refreshed" is merely a vivid Oriental way of saying that he ceased from the work of creation, and took delight in surveying that work.

Dr. J. P. Thompson:[1] "To 'rest' here does not mean to seek repose from fatigue, but to suspend activity in a particular mode of operation, to cease from doing thus and so." Maimonides says that the word used in the parallel text, Ex. xx. 11, properly means "ceased." With this explanation the Septuagint agrees.

Murphy:[2] "'Refreshed' includes, at all events, the pure delight arising from the consciousness of a design accomplished, and from the contemplation of the intrinsic excellence of the work."

Omniscience.

God knows all things.	*Tries to find out some things.*
Thou knowest my downsitting and mine uprising, thou understandest my thought afar off. Thou compassest my path and my lying down, and art acquainted *with* all my ways. For *there is* not a word in my tongue, *but*, lo, O LORD, thou knowest it altogether. Ps. cxxxix. 2-4.	Now I know that thou fearest God, seeing thou hast not withheld thy son, thine only *son* from me. Gen. xxii. 12.
I the LORD search the heart, *I* try the reins. Jer. xvii. 10.	The LORD thy God led thee these forty years in the wilderness, to humble thee, *and* to prove thee, to know what *was* in thy heart, whether thou wouldest keep his commandments, or no. Deut. viii. 2.
Thou Lord, which knowest the hearts of all *men*. Acts i. 24.	Thou shalt not hearken unto the words of that prophet, or that dreamer of dreams; for the LORD your God proveth you, to know whether ye love the LORD your God with all your heart, and with all your soul. Deut. xiii. 3.
All things *are* naked and opened unto the eyes of him with whom we have to do. Heb. iv. 13.	

In the texts at the right, the language is accommodated to the human understanding, uttered, as it were, from man's point of view. By the testing process applied to Abraham and the

---

[1] Man in Genesis and in Geology, p. 114.

[2] In the subsequent pages, when an important quotation from an author is given without specific references, the citation is generally from that author's commentary upon the text under consideration.

DOCTRINAL DISCREPANCIES. 57

Israelites, the knowledge which had lain hidden in the divine mind was revealed and verified.

The words addressed to Abraham, " Now I know that," etc., are equivalent to saying, Now I have established by actual experiment that which I previously knew. I have demonstrated, made manifest by evident proof, my knowledge of thy character.

Murphy : " The original *I have known* denotes an eventual knowing, a discovering by actual experiment; and this observable probation of Abraham was necessary for the judicial eye of God, who is to govern the world, and for the conscience of man, who is to be instructed by practice as well as principle."

The language in Genesis may be illustrated as follows : A chemical professor, lecturing to his class, says: " Now I will apply an acid to this substance, and see what the result will be." He speaks in this way, although *he* knows perfectly well beforehand. Having performed the experiment, he says, " I now know that such and such results will follow." In saying this, he puts himself in the place of the class, and speaks from their stand-point.

The texts from Deut. mean simply, The Lord hath dealt with thee *as if* he were ignorant, and wished to ascertain thy sentiments toward him; he hath put thee to as severe a test as would be requisite for discovering the secrets of thine heart. Such is the interpretation which men would give to his treatment of thee.

Forgets not his saints.	*Temporarily forgot Noah.*
Yea, they may forget, yet will I not forget thee. Isa. xlix. 15.	And God remembered Noah. Gen. viii. 1.

The latter text is shaped " after the manner of men." God left Noah in the ark, for many long months, *as if* he had forgotten him. He then " put forth a token of his remembrance."

Does not sleep.	*Sometimes sleeps.*
Behold he that keepeth Israel shall neither slumber nor sleep. Ps. cxxi. 4.	Awake, why sleepest thou, O Lord? arise, cast *us* not off for ever. Ps. xliv 23.

Sometimes God, in wisdom, defers the punishment of the

wicked, and the deliverance of his people, so that he seems oblivious of both. He gives no sign of activity with reference to either, so that a superficial observer might say, "he sleeps." The silence, the long-suffering of God is attributed to indifference or lack of knowledge on his part.[1]

Omnipresence.

God everywhere present.

Whither shall I go from thy Spirit? or whither shall I flee from thy presence? If I ascend up into heaven, thou *art* there: if I make my bed in hell, behold, thou *art there*. *If* I take the wings of the morning, *and* dwell in the uttermost parts of the sea; even there shall thy hand lead me, and thy right hand shall hold me. Ps. cxxxix. 7–10.

Thus saith the LORD, The heaven *is* my throne, and the earth *is* my footstool. Isa. lxvi. 1.

Am I a God at hand saith the LORD, and not a God afar off? Can any hide himself in secret places that I shall not see him? saith the LORD. Do not I fill heaven and earth? saith the LORD. Jer. xxiii. 23, 24.

Though they dig into hell, thence shall my hand take them; though they climb up to heaven, thence will I bring them down: And though they hide themselves in the top of Carmel, I will search and take them out thence; and though they be hid from my sight in the bottom of the sea, thence will I command the serpent, and he shall bite them. Amos ix. 2, 3.

Not in some places.

Adam and his wife hid themselves from the presence of the LORD God amongst the trees of the garden. Gen. iii. 8.

And Cain went out from the presence of the LORD. Gen. iv. 16.

And the LORD came down to see the city and the tower, which the children of men builded. Gen. xi. 5.

And the LORD said, Because the cry of Sodom and Gomorrah is great, and because their sin is very grievous; I will go down now, and see whether they have done altogether according to the cry of it, which has come unto me; and if not I will know. Gen. xviii. 20, 21.

The LORD passed by, and a great and strong wind rent the mountains, and brake in pieces the rocks before the LORD; *but* the LORD *was* not in the wind: and after the wind an earthquake; *but* the LORD *was* not in the earthquake: and after the earthquake a fire; *but* the LORD *was* not in the fire: and after the fire a still small voice. 1 Kings xix. 11, 12.

Jonah rose up to flee unto Tarshish from the presence of the LORD. Jonah i. 3.

The "presence of the Lord," from which Adam hid himself, and Cain and Jonah fled, was the visible and special manifestation of God to them at the time; or else it denotes the place where that manifestation was made.

According to Henderson,[2] either may be meant.

The builders of Babel and the inhabitants of Sodom had pursued their wicked course, as far as divine mercy could permit. God had been far away from these corrupt men; he was "not in all their thoughts." He took the sword of justice and "came down" into the sphere of their consciousness, in a signal and terrible manner.

---

[1] See Ps. l. 21 and lxxiii. 11.
[2] On Minor Prophets, p. 202 (Andover edition).

DOCTRINAL DISCREPANCIES.

Rabbi Schelomo strikingly observes that these texts represent God as " coming down from his throne of mercies to his throne of judgment," — as if mercy were a more serene, exalted, and glorious attribute than justice. Such expressions as " God came down," the Jewish writers term " the tongue, or language, of the event," — that is, the proper interpretation of the event, the lesson it was designed to teach. In such cases, God's *acts* are translated into *words*. The " language of the event" is, God comes down, interposes, to frustrate certain mad schemes of ambition.[1]

Maimonides [2] acutely suggests that, since the word " ascend " is properly applied to the mind when it contemplates noble and elevated objects, and " descend " when it turns toward things of a low and unworthy character, it follows that when the Most High turns his thoughts toward *man* for any purpose, it may be said that God " descends " or " comes down."

Prof. Murphy thinks that, as the Lord, after watching over Noah during the deluge, had withdrawn his visible and gracious presence from the earth, when he again directly interposes in human affairs, there is propriety in saying, " The Lord came down."

God was not in the wind, the earthquake, or the fire; that is, he did not, upon that occasion, choose any one of these as the symbol of his presence, as his medium of communication and manifestation. He did not speak *in* or *by* these, but by " the still small voice."

Herder:[3] " The vision would seem designed to teach the prophet, who, in his fiery zeal for reformation, would change everything by stormy violence, the gentle movements of God's providence, and to exhibit the mildness and longsuffering, of which, the voice spoke to Moses.[4] Hence the beautiful change in the phenomena of the vision."

[1] See Note to Lange on Genesis, p. 364 (American edition).
[2] Moreh Nevochim. Munk's French version, Vol. i. pp. 56, 57.
[3] Spirit of Hebrew Poetry, ii. 40 (Marsh's translation).
[4] See Ex. xxxiv. 5–7.

Eternity.

God from everlasting.
Before the mountains were brought forth, or ever thou hadst formed the earth and the world, even from everlasting to everlasting thou *art* God. Ps. xc. 2.

His origin in time.
God came from Teman, and the Holy One from mount Paran. Hab. iii. 3.

The second text has, singularly enough, been adduced as teaching that God originated in time.

The passage simply refers to the wonderful displays of divine power and glory which the Israelites witnessed in connection with the giving of the law;[1] Teman and Paran being "the regions to the south of Palestine generally, as the theatre of the divine manifestations to Israel." This is clear from the parallel text, "The Lord came from Sinai, and rose up from Seir unto them; he shined forth from mount Paran, and he came with ten thousands of saints; from his right hand *went* a fiery law for them."[2]

Unity.

God is One.
Hear O Israel: The LORD our God *is* one LORD. Deut. vi. 4.
See now that I *even* I *am* he, and *there is* no god with me. Deut. xxxii. 39.
I *am* the LORD, and *there is* none else, *there is* no God besides me. Isa. xlv. 5.
And this is life eternal, that they might know thee, the only true God. John xvii. 3.
But to us *there is but* one God, the Father, of whom *are* all things, and we in him. 1 Cor. viii. 6.

Plurality of Divine Beings.
And God said, Let us make man in our image after our likeness. Gen. i. 26.
And the LORD God said, Behold, the man is become as one of us, to know good and evil. Gen. iii. 22.
And the LORD appeared unto him in the plains of Mamre: and he sat in the tent door in the heat of the day: and he lifted up his eyes and looked, and, lo, three men stood by him: and when he saw *them*, he ran to meet them from the tent door, and bowed himself toward the ground, and said, My Lord, if now I have found favor in thy sight. Gen. xviii. 1-3.
Worship him, all ye gods. Psalm xcvii. 7.
The Lord GOD and his Spirit, hath sent me. Isa. xlviii. 16.
[For there are three that bear record in heaven, the Father, the Word and the Holy Ghost: and these three are one. 1 John v. 7].

The first two texts from Genesis have the word for "God" (Elohim) in the *plural* form. Gesenius considers this a "plural of excellence or majesty"; Nordheimer, a "plural of pre-emi-

---

[1] So Abarbanel, Aben Ezra, Eichhorn, Ewald, Henderson, Herder, Lowth, Michaelis, the Targum, etc.
[2] Deut. xxxiii. 2.

nence"; Baumgarten, a "numerical plural, originally denoting God and angels together"; Delitzsch, a "plural of intensity"; Fuerst, as used "because the ancients conceived of the Deity as an aggregate of many infinite forces." Bush thinks the plural implies "greater fulness, emphasis, and intensity of meaning"; Lange [1] takes it as denoting "intense fulness," and Hengstenberg [2] says, "it calls attention to the infinite riches and the inexhaustible fulness contained in the one divine being."

Ewald: [3] "It was an antique usage, more especially in this Semitic tribe, to designate God, as also every other superior, externally by a plural form, by which no more than the sense of a kind of dignity and reverence was simply expressed."

As to the plural pronouns, "us" and "our," which God here employs, Aben Ezra thinks that he addresses the Intelligences; Philo, Delitzsch, and others, that he spoke to the angels; Davidson, with Sedaiah a Gaon, that he spoke like a sovereign, "We the king": Kalisch, Tuch, and Bush in substance deem it the plural "employed in deliberations and self-exhortations"; Maimonides [4] asserts that God is addressing the earth or the nature already created; Keil that he is speaking of and with himself in the plural number, "with reference to the fulness of the divine powers and essences which he possesses." On the other hand, Lange thinks the phraseology may "point to the germinal view of a distinction in the divine personality," and Murphy that it "indicates a plurality of persons or hypostases in the Divine Being."

We thus see that the above expressions are susceptible of several reasonable interpretations consistent with monotheistic principles.

With reference to Abraham and the "three men" — superhuman beings in the form of man, — the patriarch appeared

---

[1] Introduction to Genesis, pp. 111, 112 (English translation).
[2] Genuineness of Pent. i. 273.
[3] History of Israel, ii. 38 (Martineau's edition).
[4] See Lange on Genesis, p. 173, note.

to single out one as pre-eminent among the three, whom he addressed as "My Lord." Keil says, "Jehovah and two angels: all three in human form." Murphy: "It appears that of the three men, one, at all events, was the Lord, who, when the other two went towards Sodom, remained with Abraham while he made his intercession for Sodom, and afterward he also went his way." Lange: "Abraham instantly recognizes among the three the one whom he addresses as the Lord in a religious sense, who afterwards appears as Jehovah, and was clearly distinguished from the two accompanying angels."

As to the quotation from Psalms, Maimonides and David Kimchi say that the word "Elohim," in this case, means "angelic powers." Others that it means "magistrates" or "judges," as in Exodus xxii. 8, 9. 28.[1] Alexander and Hengstenberg explain it as meaning "false gods"; Delitzsch, as "the superhuman powers deified by the heathen." The Syriac Peshito reads, "all ye his angels."[2]

Isa. xlviii. 16 is ambiguous in the original. "It may mean 'Jehovah and his Spirit have sent me,' or 'Jehovah hath sent both me and his Spirit.'" So Delitzsch: "The Spirit is not spoken of here as jóining in the sending. . . . . The meaning is, that it is also sent, i.e. sent in and with the servant of Jehovah, who is speaking here."

1 John v. 7 is a spurious passage. It is found in no Greek manuscript before the fifteenth or sixteenth century, and in no early version. It is rejected by Alford, Abbot, Bleek, Scrivener, Tischendorf, Tregelles, Wordsworth, and most modern critics.[3]

It should be observed that the texts of the first series teach unequivocally and *designedly* the unity of God, while those of the second series, — intended primarily to teach *other* truths — are fairly explicable in harmony with the former class.

---

[1] In the Hebrew, verses 7, 8, and 27.
[2] Oliver's Translation of Syriac Psalter.
[3] See Orme's Mem. of Controv. on 1 John v. 7 (New York, 1866).

DOCTRINAL DISCREPANCIES.

Immateriality.

God, a Spirit.
A spirit hath not flesh and bones. Luke xxiv. 39.
God *is* a Spirit. John iv. 24.

Has a material body and organs.
Tables of stone, written with the finger of God. Ex. xxxi. 18.
He shall cover thee with his feathers, and under his wings shalt thou trust. Ps. xci. 4.
He had horns *coming* out of his hand. Hab. iii. 4.

These texts, which represent God as having hands, fingers, wings, feathers, horns, and the like, are simply the bold figures and startling hyperboles in which the Orientals are wont to indulge. They would never, for a moment, think of being understood literally in using them.

"Finger of God" is his direct agency: his "wings" and "feathers" are his protecting care, set forth by an allusion to the bird hovering over and guarding her tender young.[1]

Henderson, Delitzsch, Noyes, and Cowles agree substantially in rendering Hab. iii. 4, "Rays streamed from his hand";—a decided improvement upon our version.

Immutability.

God, unchangeable.
God *is* not a man, that he should lie; neither the son of man, that he should repent: hath he said, and shall he not do *it?* or hath he spoken, and shall he not make it good? Num. xxiii. 19.
And also the Strength of Israel will not lie nor repent: for he *is* not a man, that he should repent. 1 Sam. xv. 29.
I the LORD have spoken *it:* it shall come to pass, and I will do *it;* I will not go back, neither will I spare, neither will I repent. Ezek. xxiv. 14.
For I *am* the LORD, I change not. Mal. iii. 6.
The Father of lights, with whom is no variableness, neither shadow of turning. Jas. i. 17.

Repents, and changes his plans.
I will not go up in the midst of thee; for thou *art* a stiffnecked people: lest I consume thee in the way. And he said unto him, If thy presence go not *with me,* carry us not up hence. And the LORD said unto Moses, I will do this thing also that thou hast spoken: My presence shall go *with thee,* and I will give thee rest. Ex. xxxiii. 3, 15, 17, 14.
Doubtless ye shall not come into the land, *concerning* which I sware to make you dwell therein. Num. xiv. 30.
The LORD God of Israel saith, I said indeed *that* thy house, and the house of thy father, should walk before me forever: but now the LORD saith, Be it far from me; . . . . . Behold the days come, that I will cut off thine arm, and the arm of thy father's house, that there shall not be an old man in thine house. 1 Sam. ii. 30, 31.
Then came the word of the LORD unto Samuel, saying: It repenteth me that I have set up Saul *to be* king: for he is turned back from following me, and hath not performed my commandments. 1 Sam. xv. 10, 11.
In those days was Hezekiah sick unto

---

[1] See Deut. xxxii 11.

| *God, unchangeable.* | *Repents, and changes his plans.* |

death. And the prophet Isaiah the son of Amoz came to him, and said unto him, Thus saith the LORD, Set thine house in order; for thou shalt die, and not live. Then he turned his face to the wall, and prayed unto the LORD. ..... And it came to pass, afore Isaiah was gone out into the middle court, that the word of the LORD came to him, saying, Turn again, and tell Hezekiah the captain of my people, Thus saith the LORD, the God of David thy father, I have heard thy prayer, I have seen thy tears: behold, I will heal thee: on the third day thou shalt go up unto the house of the LORD. And I will add unto thy days fifteen years. 2 Kings xx. 1, 4, 5, 6.

Thou hast forsaken me, saith the LORD, thou art gone backward: therefore will I stretch out my hand against thee, and destroy thee; I am weary with repenting. Jer. xv. 6.

And God saw their works, that they turned from their evil way; and God repented of the evil that he had said that he would do unto them; and he did *it* not. Jonah iii. 10.

In respect to his essence, his attributes, his moral character, and his inflexible determination to punish sin and reward virtue, God *is* " without variableness or shadow of turning."

Again, some of his declarations are absolute and unconditional; the greater part, however, including promises and threatenings, turn upon conditions either expressed or implied. The following passage is a very explicit statement of a great principle in the divine administration, — of God's *plan* or *rule of conduct* in dealing with men : " *At what* instant I shall speak concerning a nation, and concerning a kingdom, to pluck up, and to pull down, and to destroy *it ;* if that nation, against whom I have pronounced, turn from their evil, I will repent of the evil that I thought to do unto them. And *at what* instant I shall speak concerning a nation, and concerning a kingdom, to build and to plant *it ;* if it do evil in my sight, that it obey not my voice, then I will repent of the good, wherewith I said I would benefit them."[1]   Here is brought clearly to view the *underlying condition*, which, if not expressed, is implied, in God's promises

---

[1] Jeremiah xviii. 7-10.

and threats. Whenever God, in consequence of a change of character in certain persons, does not execute the threats or fulfil the promises he had made to them, the explanation is obvious. In every such case, the change is in man, rather than in God. For example, God has promised blessings to the righteous and threatened the wicked with punishment. Suppose a righteous man should turn and become wicked. He is no longer the man whom God promised to bless. He occupies a different relation toward God. The promise was made to an entirely different character.

On the other hand, a wicked man repents and becomes good. He is not now the individual whom God threatened. He sustains another relation to his Maker. He has passed out of the sphere of the divine displeasure into that of the divine love. Yet all this while, there is no change in God. His attitude toward sin and sinners, on the one hand, and toward goodness and the good on the other, is the same yesterday, to-day, and forever. It is precisely *because God is immutable*, that his relation to men, and his treatment of them vary with the changes in their character and conduct. In a word, *he changes because he is unchangeable*.

A homely illustration may be permitted. Suppose a rock to be located at the centre of a circle one mile in diameter. A man starts to walk around the circle. On starting he is due north from the rock, which consequently bears due south from him. After travelling a while, he comes to be due east from the rock, and that due west from him. Now the rock does not move, yet its direction from the man changes with every step he takes. In a somewhat analogous manner, God's aspect and feelings toward men change as *they* change. That is, in the words of Whately,[1] "A change effected in one of two objects having a certain relation to each other, may have the same practical result as if it had taken place in the other."

Wollaston:[2] "The respect or relation which lies between

[1] Rhetoric, Part i. chap. 3. Sec. 3.   [2] Religion of Nature, pp. 115, 116.

God, considered as an unchangeable being, and one that is humble, and supplicates, and endeavors to qualify himself for mercy, cannot be the same with that which lies between the same unchangeable God, and one that is obstinate, and will not supplicate, or endeavor to qualify himself. ... By an alteration in ourselves, we may alter the relation or respect lying between him and us."[1] To sum up, *if man changes, the very immutability of God's character requires that his feelings should change toward the changed man.*

Murphy:[2] "To go to the root of the matter, every act of the divine will, of creative power, or of interference with the order of nature, seems at variance with inflexibility of purpose. But, in the first place, man has a finite mind, and a limited sphere of observation, and therefore is not able to conceive or express thoughts or acts exactly as they are in God, but only as they are in himself. Secondly, God is a spirit, and therefore has the attributes of personality, freedom, and holiness; and the passage before us is designed to set forth these in all the reality of their action, and thereby to distinguish the freedom of the eternal mind from the fatalism of inert matter. Hence, thirdly, these statements represent real processes of the divine Spirit, analogous at least to those of the human."

Those passages which speak of God as "repenting" are figurative. They are the "language of the event," the divine acts interpreted in words. We see an artist executing a picture. Having completed, he surveys it, then, without a word, takes his brush and effaces it. We say at once, "he repented that he had made it." We thus interpret his action; we assume that such were his feelings. So God performed such outward acts with reference to the antediluvians and others, that, if they had been performed by a man, we should say "he *repented* of

---

[1] This author has also an illustrative formula which will be appreciated by the mathematician; "The ratio of G to $M + q$ is different from that of G to $M - q$; and yet G remains unaltered."

[2] Commentary on Genesis, vi. 6.

what he had previously said or done." Such is the construction we should naturally put upon his conduct. The language is evidently accommodated to our ideas of things.

Dr. Davidson:[1] "When repentance is attributed to God, it implies a change in his mode of dealing with men, such as would indicate on their part a change of purpose."

Andrew Fuller:[2] "God, in order to address himself impressively to us, frequently personates a creature, or speaks to us after the manner of men. It may be doubted whether the displeasure of God against the wickedness of men could have been fully expressed in literal terms, or with anything like the effect produced by metaphorical language."

Prof. Mansel:[3] "The representations of God which scripture presents to us may be shown to be analogous to those which the laws of our mind require us to form; and, therefore such as may naturally be supposed to have emanated from the same Author."

God's threat not to accompany the Israelites was unquestionably conditional. As Scott says, "such declarations rather express what God might justly do, what it would become him to do, and what he would do, were it not for some intervening consideration, than his *irreversible purpose;* and always imply a reserved exception in case the party offending were truly penitent."

As to the quotation from 1 Sam. ii., by Eli's father's house we are evidently to understand the house of Aaron, from whom Eli was descended through Ithamar. It was Aaron, the tribe-father of Eli, who received the promise that his house should walk forever before the Lord in priestly service. This promise, obviously conditional, was henceforth withdrawn with regard to a certain branch of Aaron's family, and on account of the sinfulness of that branch. So far as Eli and his sons were concerned, the Lord would now cut off the arm of Aaron's house.

[1] Sacred Hermeneutics, p. 527.   [2] Works, i. 669.
[3] Limits of Religious Thought, p. 64 (American edition).

By the expression, "be it far from me," God does not, says Keil, revoke his previous promise, but simply denounces a false trust therein as irreconcilable with his holiness. That promise would only be fulfilled so far as the priests themselves honored the Lord in their office.

The covenant made with Phinehas[1] was not abrogated by the temporary transfer of the high-priest's office from the line of Eleazar to that of Ithamar, since, as Keil reminds us, this covenant contemplated an "everlasting *priesthood*," and not specially the high-priesthood; and the descendants of Phinehas meantime retained the ordinary priesthood.

When Abiathar, the last high-priest — Eli being the first — of the line of Ithamar, was deposed by Solomon,[2] the office of high-priest was restored to the line of Phinehas and Eleazar.[3]

In the case of Hezekiah, the divine declaration was clearly a conditional one. Yet, as Vitringa happily suggests, "the condition was not expressed, because God would draw it from him as a voluntary act."

God satisfied with his works.	*Dissatisfied with them.*
God saw every thing that he had made, and, behold it was very good. Gen. i. 31.	And it repented the LORD that he had made man on the earth, and it grieved him at his heart. Gen. vi. 6.

This case has already been explained.[4]

Will destroy.	*Will not destroy.*
And the LORD said, I will destroy man whom I have created from the face of the earth; both man and beast, and the creeping thing, and the fowls of the air. Gen. vi. 7.	Neither will I again smite any more every thing living, as I have done. Gen. viii. 21.

One of these utterances was made before, the other after, the Flood. Both declarations were strictly fulfilled.

Will abhor.	*Will not abhor.*
And my soul shall abhor you. Lev. xxvi. 30.	I will not cast them away, neither will I abhor them. Lev. xxvi. 44.

The condition is stated plainly in the intervening verse, the

---

[1] Num. xxv. 11–13.
[2] 1 Kings ii. 27. See Bähr in Lange, and Rawlinson in Bible Commentary, on this passage.
[3] 1 Chron. xxiv. 3–6.   [4] See p. 4 of present work.

DOCTRINAL DISCREPANCIES. 69

fortieth. If they should confess their iniquity, the Lord's "abhorrence" of them would be changed into mercy toward them. The whole context of these passages is hypothetical.

Permission granted.	*Permission withheld.*
And God came unto Balaam at night, and said unto him if the men come to call thee, rise up, *and* go with them; but yet the word which I shall say unto thee, that shalt thou do. Num. xxii. 20.	And Balaam rose up in the morning, and saddled his ass, and went with the princes of Moab. And God's anger was kindled because he went. Num. xxii. 21, 22.

The permission given to Balaam was conditional; "If the men come to call thee," etc. Balaam, in his eagerness, "loving the wages of unrighteousness," does not appear to have waited for the men to call him; instead of this, he volunteered to go with them. Hengstenberg[1] observes that Balaam "immediately *availed* himself of the permission of God to go with the Moabites, which he could only do with the secret purpose to avoid the condition which had thereby been imposed upon him, 'The word which I shall say unto thee, that shalt thou do.'" Again, "since God's anger was directed against Balaam's going *with a definite intention*, it involves no contradiction, when afterwards his going was permitted."

Keil thinks that God's anger was not kindled till near the close of Balaam's journey, and then by the *feelings* he was cherishing. A "longing for wages and honor" caused him to set out, and "the nearer he came to his destination, under the guidance of the distinguished Moabitish ambassadors, the more was his mind occupied with the honors and riches in prospect; and so completely did they take possession of his heart, that he was in danger of casting to the winds the condition which had been imposed upon him by God." Hence the divine anger was awakened.

Aben Ezra and Bechayai[2] say that the Lord had already manifested his will to Balaam that he should not go to Balak, but as if imagining God to be mutable, he again inquired if he might go, when the Lord, who impedes not the ways of men,

---
[1] History of Balaam and his Prophecies, pp. 345, 372.
[2] Menasseh ben Israel's Conciliator, i. 205.

permitted it, — If, knowing my will, you still choose to go, do so. Hence his actual going displeased the Lord.

Henry: "As God sometimes denies the prayers of his people in love, so sometimes he grants the desires of the wicked in wrath."

Inaccessibility.

God approachable.	*Not accessible.*
God *is* our refuge and strength, a very present help in trouble. Ps. xlvi. 1.	Why standest thou afar off, O LORD? *why* hidest thou *thyself* in times of trouble? Ps x. 1.
It is good for me to draw near to God. Ps. lxxiii. 28.	Verily thou *art* a God that hidest thyself, O God of Israel, the Saviour. Isa. xlv. 15.
The LORD *is* nigh unto all them that call upon him, to all that call upon him in truth. Ps. cxlv. 18.	Thou hast covered thyself with a cloud, that *our* prayer should not pass through. Lam. iii. 44.
Draw nigh to God and he will draw nigh to you. Jas. iv. 8.	Are ye come to inquire of me! *As* I live, saith the LORD God, I will not be inquired of by you. Ezek. xx. 3.
	Who only hath immortality, dwelling in the light which no man can approach unto. 1 Tim. vi. 16.

Obviously, the expression "draw near to God" is not to be taken in the literal sense. In relation to an omnipresent being there can be, strictly speaking, no nearness, no remoteness. God is as near to one as to another. We "draw nigh" to him, in a figurative sense, by prayer and devout meditation, by engaging in spiritual communion with him.

Ps. x. 1 and Lam. iii. 44 express a degree of impatience that God does not instantly appear, that he sees fit to leave his people temporarily in affliction.

Isa. xlv. 15, Delitzsch renders, "Thou art a mysterious God," and says the meaning is, "a God who guides with marvellous strangeness the history of the nations of the earth, and by secret ways, which human eyes can never discern, conducts all to a glorious issue."

Ezek. xx. 3 was addressed to men who, while cherishing hypocrisy and wickedness in their hearts, attempted to inquire of God. Such inquirers he ever sternly repels.

1 Tim. vi. 16, "Dwelling in light unapproachable," is a statement of the unquestionable truth, that no mortal can literally approach God, endure the ineffable splendor of his presence, or fathom the mysteries of his existence.

No one of these texts intimates that men may not draw near to God, in the only possible way — by penitence and prayer; no one of them denies that he is accessible unto all that "call upon him in truth."

All seekers find.	*Some do not find.*
If thou seek him, he will be found of thee; but if thou forsake him, he will cast thee off for ever. 1 Chron. xxviii. 9.	Seek ye the LORD while he may be found, call ye upon him while he is near. Isa. lv. 6.
I said not unto the seed of Jacob. Seek ye me in vain. Isa. xlv. 19.	Strive to enter in at the straight gate; for many, I say unto you, will seek to enter in, and shall not be able. Luke xiii. 24.
I am sought of *them that* asked not *for me;* I am found of *them that* sought me not. Isa. lxv. 1.	
He that seeketh findeth, and to him that knocketh it shall be opened. Matt. vii. 8.	Ye shall seek me, and shall not find me: and where I am, *thither* ye cannot come. John vii. 34.

Andrew Fuller [1] remarks: "Seeking, in Matthew, refers to the application for mercy through Jesus Christ, in the present life; but in Luke, it denotes that anxiety which the workers of iniquity will discover to be admitted into heaven at the last day. .... Every one that seeketh mercy in the name of Jesus, while the door is open succeeds; but he that seeketh it not till the door is shut will not succeed."

The text from John was addressed to the unbelieving Jews who would not seek Christ, at the right time, nor with the right spirit. Hence, their future seeking would be unavailing. Alford: "My bodily presence will be withdrawn from you; I shall be personally in a place inaccessible to you."

These texts contain nothing whatever to debar those who seek the Saviour at the proper time, and in the right way.

Early seekers successful.	*Some fail to find.*
Those that seek me early shall find me. Prov. viii. 17.	They shall seek me early, but they shall not find me. Prov. i. 28.

These two texts, as the connection evinces, point to entirely different classes of persons. The text from Prov. viii. is taken by many commentators as applicable to the young who seek God. Zöckler [2] says the word here rendered "seek early," coming from a noun denoting the morning dawn, "signifies to seek something while it is yet early, in the obscurity of the morning twilight, and so illustrates eager, diligent seeking." In

[1] Works, i. 675.   [2] In Lange on Prov. i. 28.

this opinion, many critics substantially concur.[1] On this hypothesis, the sense is, " Those who seek me in youth shall find me."

The other text, in the first chapter, rendered by Stuart, " They shall earnestly seek me, but they shall not find me," contemplates obstinate and hardened transgressors. They are described [2] as " fools " and " scorners," are said to have hated knowledge, to have not chosen the fear of the Lord, and to have despised all his reproof. The two texts may, therefore, be paraphrased thus : " Those who early and earnestly seek, shall find me; but impenitent rebels who, in the hour and from the fear of retribution, earnestly seek, shall not find me." Properly explained, there is not the slightest collision between the two texts.

Inscrutability.

God's attributes revealed.	They are unsearchable.
The heavens declare the glory of God; and the firmament sheweth his handy work. Ps. xix. 1.	Canst thou by searching find out God? canst thou find out the Almighty unto perfection? Job. xi. 7.
For the invisible things of him from the creation of the world are clearly seen, being understood by the things that are made; *even* his eternal power and Godhead; so that they are without excuse. Rom. i. 20.	His greatness *is* unsearchable. Ps. cxlv. 3.
	Great *is* our Lord, and of great power: his understanding *is* infinite. Ps. cxlvii. 5.
	There is no searching of his understanding. Isa. xl. 28.
	O the depth of the riches both of the wisdom and knowledge of God! how unsearchable *are* his judgments, and his ways past finding out. Rom. xi. 33.

Neither of the affirmative texts intimates that God can be weighed or measured, or the depths of Deity explored by mortals.

Ps. xix. 1 asserts that the heavens above us, the " upper deep," adorned with sun and moon and stars,

> " Forever singing, as they shine,
> 'The hand that made us is divine,' "

are a proof and illustration of the wisdom, power, and benevolence of the Creator. They thus declare his glory.

Rom. i. 20 merely implies that the invisible attributes of

---

[1] So B. Davidson, Noyes, Parkhurst, Umbreit, Opitius, Stockius, Moore, and Frey.
[2] See verses 22, 29, and 30.

God, particularly his eternal power and divinity, are clearly revealed in his works. Aristotle has a strikingly similar observation, " God, who is invisible to every mortal being, is seen by his works."

Stuart: " God's *invisible* attributes, at least some of them, are made as it were *visible*, i.e. are made the object of clear and distinct apprehension, by reason of the natural creation."

His wonders recounted.	*Innumerable.*
That I may publish with the voice of thanksgiving, and tell of all thy wondrous works. Ps. xxvi. 7	Which doeth great things past finding out; yea, and wonders without number. Job. ix. 10.
Hitherto have I declared thy wondrous works. Ps lxxi. 17.	Many, O LORD my God, *are* thy wonderful works *which* thou hast done, and thy thoughts *which are* to us-ward: they cannot be reckoned up in order unto thee: *if* I would declare and speak *of them*, they are more than can be numbered. Ps. xl. 5.
I have put my trust in the Lord GOD, that I may declare all thy works. Ps. lxxiii. 28.	

These affirmative passages are not to be rigidly interpreted. It is idle to explain the language of emotion according to a strict literalism. David neither asserts nor implies his ability to enumerate and set forth all, in the absolute sense, of God's wonderful works. His meaning is: To the extent of my ability I declare thy marvellous deeds. None of the foregoing texts impinge upon the unsearchableness of God, as to his essence and mode of existence.

Invisibility.

God seen many times.	*Not seen by man.*
And Jacob called the name of the place Peniel: for I have seen God face to face, and my life is preserved. Gen. xxxii. 30.	And he said thou canst not see my face: for there shall no man see me, and live. Ex xxxiii. 20.
Then went up Moses and Aaron, Nadab and Abihu, and seventy of the elders of Israel: and they saw the God of Israel. Ex. xxiv. 9, 10.	Take ye therefore good heed unto yourselves; for ye saw no manner of similitude on the day *that* the LORD spake unto you in Horeb, out of the midst of the fire. Deut. iv. 15.
And the LORD spake unto Moses face to face, as a man speaketh unto his friend. . . . And I will take away mine hand, and thou shalt see my back parts: but my face shall not be seen. Ex. xxxiii 11, 23.	No man hath seen God at any time. John i. 18.
	Ye have neither heard his voice at any time, nor seen his shape. John v. 37.
And Manoah said unto his wife, We shall surely die, because we have seen God. Judg. xiii. 22.	The King eternal, immortal, invisible. 1 Tim. i. 17.
In the year that king Uzziah died, I saw also the Lord sitting upon a throne, high and lifted up, and his train filled the temple. Isa. vi. 1.	Whom no man hath seen nor can see. 1 Tim. vi. 16.
I beheld till the thrones were cast down, and the Ancient of days did sit,	

God seen many times. *Not seen by man.*

whose garment *was* white as snow, and the hair of his head like the pure wool: his throne *was like* the fiery flame, *and* his wheels *as* burning fire. Dan. vii. 9.

Some of the cases mentioned in the first series of texts, — those of Isaiah and Daniel, for example, — were *visions*, in which men "saw" the Deity, not with the physical eye, but with that of the soul. In most of the instances, however, something more real and objective seems to be intended. In some cases, it is said merely that "God" was seen; in others, an "angel" appears, who is identified, during the process of the narrative, with Jehovah.

It is beyond question that God — as a spirit — as he is in himself, — is never visible to men. In what sense, then, may he be said to have been "seen"?

1. He might assume temporarily, and for wise purposes, some visible form in which to manifest himself to his creatures. Cases of this kind are termed "theophanies," in which, as Hengstenberg[1] says, God appears "under a light vesture of corporeity, in a transiently-assumed human form." This seems in some instances the best solution.

2. He might be seen, as we may say, by proxy, — in his accredited representative. This explanation is a very ancient one. In the Samaritan Pentateuch in the narratives of divine appearances, it is not God himself — Jehovah — who is mentioned as the Person appearing, even where this is the case in the Jewish text, but always an Angel.[2] So, in the Chaldee Targum, Jacob's language stands, "I have seen the Angel of God face to face."

It is a striking fact that, in many instances, this "representative Angel" claims for himself divine honors and purposes, and accepts divine worship.[3] Respecting the *nature* and *rank* of this celestial messenger, opinion is divided.[4]

[1] Genuineness of Pent. ii. 370. [2] Bleek, Introduction to Old Test., ii. 393.
[3] See Genesis xviii. 10, 14; xxii. 12; xxxi. 11, 13; Acts vii. 30, 32.
[4] Lange on Genesis, pp. 386-391.

DOCTRINAL DISCREPANCIES. 75

Augustine, Jerome, the Romish theologians, the Socinians, Hofmann, Tholuck, Delitzsch, Kurtz, and others, hold that he was a "created angel" who personated Jehovah, acted as his proxy or nuncius. We know that it is not uncommon for a monarch to depute some nobleman to act as his proxy or representative for the time being with all needful powers and privileges.

The early church, the old Protestant theologians, B.:&h, Hengstenberg, Keil, Hävernick, Lange, Wordsworth, with others, hold that this Angel was the Logos, the second Person in the Trinity, who temporarily assumed the human form, and thus "foreshadowed the incarnation." In this manner God was seen in his Son. On any one of these hypotheses, there is no difficulty, for God was seen, and yet not seen.

In his infinite and incomprehensible essence, as we have just said, Jehovah is seen by no mortal; but in a theophany, in his representative Angel, in the Logos who is "the brightness of his glory and the express image of his person," the "King eternal, immortal, invisible" has often been seen.

Little need be said concerning the specific cases above mentioned. The Lord spake with his servant Moses "face to face," that is, familiarly. Two men may speak face to face, in darkness, neither seeing the other.

As to Ex. xxxiii. 23, Keil says: "As the inward nature of man manifests itself in his face, and the sight of his back gives only an imperfect and outward view of him, so Moses saw only the back, and not the face of Jehovah."

Andrew Fuller:[1] "The difference here seems to arise from the phrase 'face of God.' In the one case, it is expressive of *great familiarity*, compared with former visions and manifestations of the divine glory; in the other, of a *fulness of knowledge of this glory*, which is incompatible with our mortal state, if not with our capacity as creatures.

Murphy: "*My face* is my direct, immediate, intrinsic, self.....

[1] Works, i. 674 (edition in 3 vols.)

My back is my averted, mediate, extrinsic self, visible to man in my works, my word, and my personal manifestations to my people."

Bush: "Nothing could be more expressive than the mode adopted to convey the intimation, that while a *lower* degree of disclosure could be made to him, a *higher* could not." An important truth is couched in highly symbolical language.

As to the apparent collision between John v. 37 and those passages which represent the voice of God as heard at times by men,[1] the citation from John may be taken as asserting that no mortal ever saw the form or heard the voice which is *peculiar* to God. Or, as Alford suggests, the language may have been intended to apply to those persons then present, " Ye have not heard his voice, as your fathers did at Sinai; nor have ye seen his visional appearance, as did the prophets."

On either interpretation there is no difficulty.

Similitude of God seen.	*No similitude visible.*
The similitude of the Lord shall he behold. Num. xii. 8.	And the Lord spake unto you out of the midst of the fire: ye heard the voice of the words, but saw no similitude. Deut. iv. 12.

The first text refers to Moses, the second to the people in general. He saw certain manifestations of God which they were not permitted to see.

Keil thinks that the similitude which Moses saw was simply a manifestation of the glory of God answering to Moses's own intuition and perceptive faculty, and not to be regarded as a form of God which was an adequate representation of the divine nature.

Holiness.

God the Author of evil.	*Not the Author of evil.*
I form the light, and create darkness: I make peace, and create evil: I the Lord do all these *things*. Isa. xlv. 7. Thus saith the Lord; Behold, I frame evil against you, and devise a device against you. Jer. xviii. 11. Out of the mouth of the Most High proceedeth not evil and good? Lam. iii. 38.	A God of truth and without iniquity, just and right *is* he. Deut. xxxii. 4. For thou *art* not a God that hath pleasure in wickedness: neither shall evil dwell with thee. Ps. v 4. For I know the thoughts that I think toward you, saith the Lord, thoughts of peace, and not of evil. Jer. xxix. 11.

[1] See Gen. iii. 8; Ex. xix. 19; Deut. v. 26; Job xxxviii. 1.

God the Author of evil.	Not the Author of evil.
Wherefore I gave them also statutes that were not good, and judgments whereby they should not live. Ezek. xx. 25. Shall there be evil in a city, and the LORD hath not done it? Amos iii. 6.	For God is not *the author* of confusion, but of peace. 1 Cor. xiv. 33.

"Evil," mentioned in the first, second, third, and fifth texts, means natural, and not moral evil, or *sin*. Henderson says, "affliction, adversity"; Calvin, "afflictions, wars, and other adverse occurrences."

When Pompeii is buried by the volcano, Jerusalem destroyed in war, London depopulated by the plague, Lisbon overthrown by an earthquake, Chicago devastated by fire; it is God who sends these "evils" or calamities.

In Psalm v. 4, "evil," as the parallelism shows, is iniquity; in Jer. xxix. 11, it means punitive displeasure.

As to Ezek. xx. 25, the "statutes" which were "not good" are variously referred.

Calvin, Vitringa, and Hävernick say, the customs and practices, the idolatrous and corrupting rites, of heathenism, to which God gave over the Jews as a punishment for their ungodly disposition.[1]

Fairbairn: "The polluted customs and observances of heathenism." Wordsworth: "These evil practices are called 'statutes' and 'judgments,' in verse 18, like the 'statutes of Omri' in Micah vi. 16."[2] Umbreit and Kurtz say, "the liturgical laws which Jehovah prescribed, but which the people abused for heathen purposes."

We know that abused blessings may prove the heaviest curses. May not the meaning be that these "statutes," though good in their original design and adaptation, proved "not good" in their result, through the disobedience of those to whom they were addressed? Are not Paul's words, "And the commandment which *was ordained* to life, I found *to be* unto death,"[3] explanatory of the text under consideration?

---

[1] Compare Ps. lxxxi. 12; Rom. i. 24, 25; 2 Thess. ii. 11.
[2] Compare "statutes of the heathen," 2 Kings xvii. 8.
[3] Rom. vii. 10.

Wines[1] takes the meaning to be, laws not absolutely the best, but relatively so. This view of the meaning and force of the text is confirmed by the words of our Saviour. He has told us that Moses tolerated divorce among the Jews, because of the hardness of their hearts. If the Jews of Moses's time had been less hardhearted, several of his statutes would have been different. These statutes were intended to meet special exigencies, but were not designed for universal application.

Solon, being asked whether he had furnished the best laws for the people of Athens, replied, "I have given them the best that they were able to bear."

"When divine wisdom," observes Montesquieu,[2] "said to the Jews, 'I have given you precepts which are not good,' this signifies that they had only a relative goodness; and this is the sponge which wipes out all the difficulties which are to be found in the law of Moses."

Whichever interpretation may be adopted, none of the above texts, nor any others when properly explained, sanction the revolting proposition that God is the author of sin.

God jealous.	*Free from jealousy.*
I the LORD thy God *am* a jealous God. Ex. xx. 5.	The LORD *is* gracious, and full of compassion; slow to anger, and of great mercy The LORD *is* good to all: and his tender mercies *are* over all his works. Ps. cxlv. 8, 9.
The anger of the LORD and his jealousy shall smoke against that man. Deut. xxix. 20.	
For they provoked him to anger with their high places, and moved him to jealousy with their graven images. Ps. lxxviii. 58.	For jealousy *is* the rage of a man: therefore he will not spare in the day of vengeance. Prov. vi. 34.
Therefore thus saith the Lord GOD; Surely in the fire of my jealousy have I spoken against the residue of the heathen. Ezek. xxxvi. 5.	Wrath *is* cruel, and anger *is* outrageous; but who *is* able to stand before jealousy.[3] Prov. xxvii. 4.
God *is* jealous, and the LORD revengeth. Nahum i. 2.	Jealousy *is* cruel as the grave: the coals thereof *are* coals of fire, *which hath* a most vehement flame. Cantic. viii. 6.

The words "jealous" and "jealousy" are each used in a good and a bad sense.[4] Applied to God, they denote that he

---

[1] Commentary on Laws of Ancient Hebrews, p. 119.

[2] Spirit of Laws, B. 19, c. 21.

[3] Zöckler says the original word denotes here, not "envy," but plainly "jealousy."

[4] In the Hebrew, *jealousy, envy, zeal,* and *anger* may be expressed by a single term, קִנְאָה ; Fuerst and Gesenius.

is intensely solicitous for his own character and honor, that he does not tolerate rivalry of any kind. An infinitely wise and holy Monarch cannot be indifferent as to the loyalty of his subjects.

Keil regards the terms as implying that God "will not transfer to another the honor that is due to himself, nor tolerate the worship of any other god"; and Bush, as denoting "a peculiar *sensitiveness* to everything that threatens to trench upon the honor, reverence, and esteem that he knows to be due to himself. The term will appear still more significant if it be borne in mind that *idolatry* in the Scriptures is frequently spoken of as *spiritual adultery*, and as 'jealousy is the rage of man,' so nothing can more fitly express the divine indignation against this sin than the term in question." According to Newman,[1] the phraseology brings to view "the great principle essential to all acceptance with Jehovah their God; namely to put away the worship of *all other* gods. This is constantly denoted by the phrase that 'Jehovah is a *jealous* God;' and out of it arose the perpetual metaphor of the prophet in which the relation of God to his people is compared to a marriage; the daughter of Israel being his bride or wife, and he a jealous husband. Thus also, every false god is a paramour, and the worship of them is adultery or fornication."

Hence, even in the estimation of this sceptical author, these expressions are not derogatory to the holiness of God.

God tempts men.	*Does not tempt them.*
And it came to pass after these things, that God did tempt Abraham. Gen. xxii. 1. And again the anger of the LORD was kindled against Israel, and he moved David against them to say, Go, number Israel and Judah. 2 Sam. xxiv. 1. And lead us not into temptation, but deliver us from evil. Matt. vi. 13.	Let no man say when he is tempted, I am tempted of God: for God cannot be tempted with evil, neither tempteth he any man. James i. 13.

The Hebrew word "nissäh," *tempt*, in the first text, means as Gesenius says, "to try, to prove any one, to put him to the test."

[1] History of Hebrew Monarchy, p. 26.

It is used in reference to David's trying Saul's armor,[1] and the queen of Sheba's testing the wisdom of Solomon.[2] The meaning therefore is, as in the old Genevan version, "God did *prove* Abraham."

Bush: "God may consistently, with all his perfections, by his providence, bring his creatures into circumstances of *special probation*, not for the purpose of giving *him* information, but in order to manifest to themselves and to others the prevailing dispositions of their hearts." God put Abraham to the proof before angels and men, that his faith and obedience might be made manifest for an example to all coming generations.

As to the second text, it is sufficient to say that God ordered or allowed such influences to affect the mind of David as should lead to a specific wrong act resulting in needful chastisement. Yet the ultimate end in view was the welfare of David and his people.

It should be added that, according to Lord Arthur Hervey,[3] the passage should read, "*For one moved David against them.*" This translation would seem to change the whole aspect of the passage, and to make the numbering of the people the *cause*, rather than the *result*, of the divine displeasure.

Keil:[4] "The instigation consists in the fact that God impels sinners to manifest the wickedness of their hearts in deeds, or furnishes the opportunity and the occasion for the unfolding and practical manifestation of the evil desires of the heart, that the sinner may either be brought to the knowledge of his more evil ways and also to repentance, through the evil deed and its consequences; or, if the heart should be hardened still more by the evil deed, that it may become ripe for the judgment of death. The instigation of a sinner to evil is simply one peculiar way in which God, as a general rule, punishes sins through sinners; for God only instigates to evil actions such as have drawn down the wrath of God upon themselves in consequence of their sin."

---

[1] 1 Sam. xvii. 39. [2] 1 Kings x. 1. [3] In Bible Commentary.
[4] Commentary on 1 Sam. xxvi. 19

"Lead us not into temptation," either " Do not *suffer* us to be tempted to sin ; or, if " temptation " here means *trial, affliction,* " Do not afflict or try us." Such, in substance is Mr. Barnes's view. God " tempts," tests, or tries men, but always for wise reasons, and with a good motive; he never places inducements before men merely *in order* to lead them into sin. His ultimate object is always good.

God, a respecter of persons.	*Does not respect them.*
And the LORD had respect unto Abel and to his offering. But unto Cain and to his offering he had not respect. Gen. iv. 4, 5.	A great God, a mighty, and a terrible, which regardeth not persons, nor taketh reward. Deut. x 17.
And God looked upon the children of Israel, and God had respect unto *them.* Ex. ii. 25.	*There is* no iniquity with the LORD our God, nor respect of persons, nor taking of gifts. 2 Chron. xix. 7.
For I will have respect unto you, and make you fruitful, and multiply you, and establish my covenant with you. Lev. xxvi. 9.	Then Peter opened *his* mouth, and said. Of a truth I perceive that God is no respecter of persons. Acts x. 34.
And the LORD was gracious unto them, and had compassion on them, and had respect unto them. 2 Kings xiii. 23.	For there is no respect of persons with God. Rom ii. 11.
Though the LORD *be* high, yet hath he respect unto the lowly : but the proud he knoweth afar off. Ps. cxxxviii. 6.	God accepteth no man's person. Gal. ii. 6.
	Your Master also is in heaven; neither is there respect of persons with him. Eph. vi. 9.
	The Father, who without respect of persons judgeth according to every man's work. 1 Pet. i. 17.

The first series of texts implies a righteous and benevolent " respect," based upon a proper discrimination as to character ; the second series denotes a " respect" which is *partial,* arising out of selfish and unworthy considerations.

The Hebrew expression, " näsä pänim," in Deut. x. 17 and 2 Chron. xix. 7, is to be taken, according to Gesenius, " in a bad sense, *to be partial,* as a judge unjustly partial or corrupted by bribes." Fuerst gives, among other definitions, " *to take the side of one with partiality.*" In both of the above texts, the connection makes it clear that this is the correct interpretation. The corresponding Greek term " prosopolepsia," expressing concretely the same idea,[1] and occurring in some modification in all but one of the New Testament citations, conveys an unfavorable meaning, uniformly implying *partiality.*

There is therefore no collision between the two series of

---

[1] See Hackett on Acts x. 34.

texts, inasmuch as they refer to widely different kinds of "respect."

God, an angry being.	*Not angry.*
God is angry *with the wicked* every day. Ps. vii. 11.	The LORD God, merciful and gracious, longsuffering, and abundant in goodness and truth, keeping mercy for thousands. Ex xxxiv. 6, 7.
Come, my people, enter thou into thy chambers, and shut thy doors about thee: hide thyself as it were for a little moment, until the indignation be overpast. Isa. xxvi. 20.	A God ready to pardon, gracious and merciful, slow to anger, and of great kindness. Neh. ix. 17.
The fierce anger of the LORD is not turned back from us. Jer. iv. 8.	Great *are* thy tender mercies, O LORD. Ps. cxix. 156.
The LORD revengeth, and *is* furious; the LORD will take vengeance on his adversaries, and he reserveth *wrath* for his enemies. Nah. i. 2.	Fury *is* not in me. Isa. xxvii. 4.

The "anger" ascribed to God in the scriptures is, as Rashi says, "the displeasure and disgust" which he experiences in view of human conduct. Let any one seriously reflect as to what must be the feelings of an *infinitely wise and holy Being* in regard to *sin*, and he can scarcely be at a loss to appreciate the meaning of the term, "anger of God." Prof. Tayler Lewis[1] has the following remarks: "Depart in the least from the idea of indifferentism, and we have no limit but infinity. God either cares nothing about what we call good and evil; or as the heaven of heavens is high above the earth, so far do his love for the good and his hatred of evil exceed in their intensity any corresponding human affection." The Being who loves the good with infinite intensity must hate evil with the same intensity. So far from any incompatibility between this love and this hate, they are the counterparts of each other — opposite poles of the same moral emotion.

"A religion over whose portal is inscribed in letters of flame, 'I AM HOLY,' can without risk represent God as angry, jealous, mourning, repenting. Scrupulosity, under such circumstances, is the sign of an evil conscience."[2]

God, susceptible of temptation.	*Cannot be tempted.*
Ye shall not tempt the LORD your God, as ye tempted *him* in Massah. Deut. vi. 16.	God cannot be tempted with evil. Jas. i. 13.
They that tempt God are even delivered. Mal. iii. 15.	

[1] In Lange on Genesis, p. 288.
[2] Hengstenberg, Genuineness of Pent. ii. 327.

God, susceptible of temptation.	*Cannot be tempted.*
Thou shalt not tempt the Lord thy God. Matt. iv. 7. Now therefore why tempt ye God, to put a yoke upon the neck of the disciples. Acts xv. 10.	

Men are said, in the Bible, to "tempt" God, when they distrust his faithfulness; when they brave his displeasure; when, challenging him to work miracles in their behalf, they presumptuously expose themselves to peril; also, "*by putting obstacles in the way of* his evidently determined course." [1]

The quotation from James, as it stands in our version, simply asserts that there is nothing in God which responds to the solicitations and blandishments of evil; it presents no attractions to him. He is not allured by it in the slightest degree.

Alford, DeWette, and Huther, however, render, in substance, "God is unversed in things evil." With either rendering there is no discrepancy.[2]

Justice.

God is just.	*Unjust.*
That be far from thee to do after this manner, to slay the righteous with the wicked: and that the righteous should be as the wicked, that be far from thee: shall not the Judge of all the earth do right? Gen. xviii. 25. All his ways *are* judgment, a God of truth and without iniquity, just and right *is* he. Deut xxxii. 4. The LORD *is* upright: *he is* my rock, and *there is* no unrighteousness in him. Ps. xcii. 15. Hear now, O house of Israel: Is not my way equal? are not your ways unequal? Ezek. xviii. 25.	For whosoever hath, to him shall be given, and he shall have more abundance: but whosoever hath not, from him shall be taken away even that he hath. Matt. xiii. 12. (For *the children* being not yet born, neither having done any good or evil, that the purpose of God according to election might stand, not of works, but of him that calleth:) It was said unto her, The elder shall serve the younger. As it is written, Jacob have I loved, but Esau have I hated. Rom. ix. 11-13.

As to Matt. xiii. 12, Barnes says: "This is a proverbial mode of speaking. It means that a man who improves what light, grace, and opportunities he has shall have them increased. From him that improves them not, it is proper that they should be taken away."

Alford: "He who *hath* — he who not only hears with the ear, but understands with the heart, has more given to him. ... He who *hath not*, in whom there is no spark of spiritual

---

[1] Alford on Acts xv. 10.

[2] On supposed sanction of Human Sacrifices, see under Ethical Discrepancies.

desire nor meetness to receive the engrafted word, has taken from him even that which he hath ('*seemeth to have*,' Luke); even the poor confused notions of heavenly doctrine which a sensual and careless life allow him are further bewildered and darkened by this simple teaching, into the depths of which he cannot penetrate so far as even to ascertain that they exist."

Dryden's Juvenal furnishes a fine parallel to this text:

> "'Tis true poor Codrus nothing had to boast;
> And yet poor Codrus all that nothing lost."

Stuart says that Rom. ix. 11–13 "refers to the bestowment and the withholding of *temporal blessings*."

John Taylor, of Norwich: "Election to the present privileges and external advantages of the kingdom of God in this world; and reprobation or rejection, as it signifies the not being favored with those privileges and advantages."

Barnes: "He had preferred Jacob, and had *withheld* from Esau those privileges and blessings which he had conferred on the posterity of Jacob."

That temporal privileges and blessings are very unequally distributed, no one can deny. The fact is patent to the most casual observer. "What shall we say then? Is there unrighteousness with God?" If this fact constitutes an objection against the justice of this world's Governor, it is an objection which the infidel is as much bound to answer as is the Christian. The truth is, the All-wise Sovereign has an unquestionable right to bestow his favors as he sees fit.

Punishes for others' sins.	*Does not thus punish.*
And Ham, the father of Canaan, saw the nakedness of his father, and told his two brethren without. And Noah awoke from his wine, and knew what his younger son had done unto him. And he said, Cursed be Canaan; a servant of servants shall he be unto his brethren. Gen. ix. 22, 24, 25. Visiting the iniquity of the fathers upon the children unto the third and fourth *generation* of them that hate me. Ex. xx. 5. And Joshua, and all Israel with him, took Achan the son of Zerah, and the silver, and the garment, and the wedge	The fathers shall not be put to death for the children, neither shall the children be put to death for the fathers: every man shall be put to death for his own sin. Deut. xxiv. 16. Behold, all souls are mine; as the soul of the father, so also the soul of the son is mine: the soul that sinneth, it shall die. The son shall not bear the iniquity of the father, neither shall the father bear the iniquity of the son; the righteousness of the righteous shall be upon him, and the wickedness of the wicked shall be upon him. Ezek. xviii. 4, 20.

Punishes for others' sins.	*Does not thus punish.*
of gold, and his sons, and his daughters, and his oxen, and his asses, and his sheep, and his tent, and all that he had: and they brought them unto the valley of Achor. And all Israel stoned him with stones, and burned them with fire, after they had stoned them with stones. And they raised over him a great heap of stones unto this day. So the LORD turned from the fierceness of his anger. Josh. vii. 24-26. What mean ye, that ye use this proverb concerning the land of Israel, saying, The fathers have eaten sour grapes, and the children's teeth are set on edge? Ezek. xviii. 2.	The righteous judgment of God: Who will render to every man according to his deeds. Rom. ii. 5, 6.

As to the case of Canaan, it cannot be proved, though often assumed, that he was cursed for the misconduct of Ham, his father. Bush thinks that Ham's gross disrespect or contemptuous deportment toward his aged parent became, "under the prompting of inspiration, a *suggesting occasion* of the curse now pronounced. . . . Noah therefore uttered the words from an *inspired foresight* of the sins and abominations of the abandoned stock of the Canaanites."

Keil: "Noah, through the spirit and power of that God with whom he walked, discerned in the moral nature of his sons, and the different tendencies which they already displayed, the germinal commencement of the future course of their posterity, and uttered words of blessing and of curse which were prophetic of the history of the tribes that descended from them." The reason why Canaan alone of Ham's sons was specified "must either lie in the fact that Canaan was already walking in the steps of his father's impiety and sin, or else be sought in the name 'Canaan,'[1] in which Noah discerned, through the gift of prophecy, a significant *omen;* a supposition decidedly favored by the analogy of the blessing pronounced upon Japhet,[2] which is also founded upon the name."

Langè thinks that Noah's malediction is "only to be explained on the ground that, in the prophetic spirit, he saw into

---

[1] That is, "the submissive one"; Keil.
[2] "Widely spreading," so Gesenius.

the future, and that the vision had for its point of departure the then present natural state of Canaan."

Aben Ezra,[1] Rashi, the Talmudists, Scaliger, and others, with Tayler Lewis, hold that Canaan too saw Noah in his exposed condition, and that he committed a cruel and wanton outrage, or some unnamed beastly crime, upon the person of the sleeping patriarch; and that this vile indignity drew down the severe denunciation upon him as the actual offender. Prof. Lewis[2] assigns the following reasons for this opinion: The Hebrew rendered 'his younger son,' cannot refer to Ham, who was *older* than Japheth, but means the *least* or *youngest* of the family, and hence is descriptive of Canaan. The words 'had done unto him' mean something more than an omission or neglect. The expression is a very positive one. Something unmistakable, something very shameful had been done to the old man in his unconscious state, and of such a nature that it becomes manifest to him immediately on his recovery. "There seems to be a careful avoidance of particularity. The language has an euphemistic look, as though intimating something too vile and atrocious to be openly expressed. Thus regarded, everything seems to point to some wanton act done by the very one who is immediately named in the severe malediction that follows: 'Cursed be Canaan.' He was the *youngest son* of Ham, as he was also the youngest son of Noah, according to the well-established Shemitic peculiarity by which all the descendants are alike called sons." This explanation is equally plausible and natural.

On either of the above hypotheses, Canaan was punished not for others' misconduct, but for his own; hence the charge of "injustice" in the case is without foundation.

As to Ex. xx. 5, we may say that Jehovah "visits" the iniquity of the fathers upon their children, in that he permits the latter to *suffer* in consequence of the sins of the former.

---

[1] See Conciliator, i. 33.   [2] In Lange on Genesis, p. 338.

He has established such laws of matter and mind that the sins of parents result in the physical and mental disease and suffering of their offspring. The drunkard bequeaths to his children poverty, shame, wretchedness, impaired health, and not infrequently a burning thirst for strong drink. The licentious man often transmits to his helpless offspring his depraved appetites and loathsome diseases. And this transmission or "visitation" of evil takes place in accordance with the inflexible laws of the universe. Obviously, "injustice" is no less chargeable upon the Author of "the laws of nature" than upon the Author of the Bible.

Even if the above text conveys the idea not only of suffering, but also of *punishment*, yet the language, "unto the third and fourth generation *of them that hate me*," indicates children who are sinful like their parents. Hengstenberg:[1] "The threatening is directed against those children who tread in their fathers' footsteps." Plainly children are intended who imitate and adopt the sinful habits and practices of their parents; hence, being morally, as well as physically, the representatives and heirs of their parents, they may be, in a certain sense, *punished* for the sins of those parents. Bush: "The tokens of the divine displeasure were to flow along the line of those who continued the haters of God."

As to the case of Achan's sons and daughters, Canon Browne[2] says: "The sanguinary severity of Oriental nations, from which the Jewish people were by no means free, has in all ages involved the children in the punishment of the father." Many, however, think that Achan's sons and daughters were simply taken into the valley to be spectators of the punishment inflicted upon the father, that it might be a warning to them. Some explain the execution upon the ground of God's sovereignty, and his consequent right to send death at any time and in any form he pleases.

Keil and others hold that Achan's sons and daughters were

[1] On Gen. of Pent. ii. 448.   [2] In Smith's Bib. Dict., Art. "Achan."

accomplices in his crime. "The things themselves had been abstracted from the booty by Achan alone; but he had hidden them in his tent, buried them in the earth, which could hardly have been done so secretly that his sons and daughters knew nothing of it. By so doing he had made his family participators in his theft; they therefore fell under the ban along with him, together with their tent, their cattle, and the rest of their property, which were all involved in the consequences of his crime."

The "proverb," Ezek xviii. 2, implied that the sufferings of the Jews, at that time, were not at all in consequence of their own sins, but exclusively for the sins of their ancestors — a false and dangerous idea, fitly rebuked by the Almighty.

Slays the righteous with the wicked.	*Spares the righteous.*
This *is* one *thing*, therefore I said *it*, He destroyeth the perfect and the wicked. Job ix. 22. And say to the land of Israel, Thus saith the LORD: Behold I *am* against thee, and will draw forth my sword out of his sheath, and will cut off from thee the righteous and the wicked. Seeing then that I will cut off from thee the righteous and the wicked, therefore shall my sword go forth out of his sheath against all flesh from the south to the north. Ezek. xxi. 3, 4.	Hath walked in my statutes, and hath kept my judgments, to deal truly; he *is* just, he shall surely live, saith the Lord God. When the son hath done that which is lawful and right, *and* hath kept all my statutes, and hath done them, he shall surely live. Ezek. xviii. 9, 19. But if the wicked turn from his wickedness, and do that which is lawful and right, he shall live thereby. Ezek. xxxiii. 19. Now the just shall live by faith. Heb. x. 38.

The first texts do not teach that God, regardless of character, cuts down the evil and the good together. The two classes may be alike in the external circumstances of their death; but they are totally unlike in their destiny. The righteous are, at death and by death, "taken away from the evil to come."[1] It may be the greatest possible blessing, the highest mark of the divine favor, to a good man to be summarily and forever removed from the sorrows and impending evils of earth to the ineffable bliss and repose of heaven. The second series of texts refers to spiritual, and not earthly life. Since the two series of passages contemplate things entirely different, there is no collision between them.

[1] Isaiah lvii. 1, 2.

Benevolence.

God witholds his blessings.

And when ye spread forth your hands, I will hide mine eyes from you: yea, when ye make many prayers, I will not hear: your hands are full of blood. Isa. i. 15.

Then shall they cry unto the LORD, but he will not hear them: he will even hide his face from them at that time, as they have behaved themselves ill in their doings. Micah iii. 4.

Ye ask, and receive not, because ye ask amiss, that ye may consume it upon your lusts. James iv. 3.

Bestows them freely.

For every one that asketh receiveth; and he that seeketh findeth; and to him that knocketh it shall be opened. Luke xi. 10.

If any of you lack wisdom, let him ask of God, that giveth to all men liberally, and upbraideth not: and it shall be given him. James i. 5.

The limiting clauses of the first three texts, "hands full of blood," "ill behavior," and "asking amiss," show clearly why God withholds his blessings in these cases. Moreover, the connection in which the last two texts stand evinces that these texts were not intended to be of universal application. They contemplate those persons only who "ask in faith."[1] Every one that asketh *aright*, receiveth. The principle upon which God, in answer to prayer, bestows his blessings, is thus enunciated: "If we ask anything *according to his will*, he heareth us."[2] It should be added that such limiting clauses as the above are, in order to make out a contradiction, dishonestly suppressed by those writers who engage in the manufacture of "discrepancies."

Hardens men's hearts.

And the LORD hardened the heart of Pharaoh, and he hearkened not unto them. Ex. ix. 12.

And the LORD said unto Moses, Go in unto Pharaoh: for I have hardened his heart, and the heart of his servants, that I might shew these my signs before him. Ex. x. 1.

And Moses and Aaron did all these wonders before Pharaoh: and the LORD hardened Pharaoh's heart, so that he would not let the children of Israel go out of his land. Ex. xi. 10.

But Sihon king of Heshbon would not let us pass by him: for the LORD thy God hardened his spirit, and made his heart obstinate, that he might deliver him into thy hand, as *appeareth* this day. Deut. ii. 30.

For it was of the LORD to harden their hearts, that they should come

They harden their own hearts.

But when Pharaoh saw that there was respite, he hardened his heart, and hearkened not unto them.... And Pharaoh hardened his heart at this time also, neither would he let the people go. Ex. viii. 15, 32.

And when Pharaoh saw that the rain and the hail and the thunders were ceased, he sinned yet more, and hardened his heart, he and his servants. Ex. ix. 34.

Wherefore then do ye harden your hearts, as the Egyptians and Pharaoh hardened their hearts? 1 Sam. vi. 6.

And he also rebelled against king Nebuchadnezzar, who had made him swear by God: but he stiffened his neck, and hardened his heart from turning unto the LORD God of Israel. 2 Chron. xxxvi. 13.

Happy is the man that feareth alway:

---

[1] See James i. 6.

[2] 1 John v. 14.

90 DISCREPANCIES OF THE BIBLE.

Hardens men's hearts.	*They harden their own hearts.*
against Israel in battle, that he might destroy them utterly, *and* that they might have no favor, but that he might destroy them, as the LORD commanded Moses. Josh. xi 20. O LORD, why hast thou made us to err from thy ways, *and* hardened our heart from thy fear? Isa. lxiii. 17. He hath blinded their eyes, and hardened their heart; that they should not see with *their* eyes, nor understand with *their* heart, and be converted, and I should heal them. John xii. 40. Therefore hath he mercy on whom he will *have mercy*, and whom he will he hardeneth. Rom. ix. 18.	but he that hardeneth his heart shall fall into mischief. Prov. xxviii. 14. Harden not your hearts, as in the provocation, in the day of temptation in the wilderness. Heb. iii. 8.

We may premise that the rejection of truth and the abuse of blessings tend ever to "harden the heart." God, therefore, by making known his truth and by bestowing his blessings, indirectly "hardens" men's hearts; that is, furnishes occasion for their hardening. Thus, the divine mercy to Pharaoh in the withdrawal of the plagues at his request became the occasion of increasing his hardness. When he saw that there was respite, that the rain and hail and thunder ceased, he hardened his heart.[1] In brief, God hardened Pharaoh's heart by removing calamities, and bestowing blessings; Pharaoh hardened his own heart by perverting these blessings and abusing the grace of God.

Theodoret:[2] "The sun, by the force of its heat, moistens the wax and dries the clay, softening the one and hardening the other; and, as this produces opposite effects by the same power, so, through the long-suffering of God, which reaches to all, some receive good and others evil; some are softened, and others hardened."

Stuart,[3] concerning Pharaoh: "The Lord hardened his heart, because the Lord was the author of commands and messages and miracles which were the occasion of Pharaoh's hardening his own heart."

Dr. Davidson:[4] "This does not mean that he infused positive

---

[1] See Ex. viii. 15 and ix. 34.
[2] Quaest. 12 in Ex.
[3] Com. on Romans, Excursus xi. p. 483.
[4] Sacred Hermen., pp. 545, 546.

wickedness or obstinacy into the mind, or that he influenced it in any way inconsistent with his perfections, but that he withdrew his grace, allowed the heart of Pharaoh to take its natural course, and thus to become harder and harder. *He permitted it to be hardened.*"

Keil, on Ex. iv. 21, observes: "In this twofold manner God produces hardness, not only *permissive*, but *effective*, i.e. not only by giving time and space for the manifestations of human opposition, even to the utmost limits of creaturely freedom, but still more by those continued manifestations of his will which drive the hard heart to such utter obduracy that it is no longer capable of returning, and so giving over the hardened sinner to the judgment of damnation. This is what we find in the case of Pharaoh."

As to Sihon, Deut. ii. 30, God providentially arranged circumstances so that the malignant wickedness of his heart should develop and culminate in "hardness" and "obstinacy," bringing upon him merited destruction.

Bush, on Josh. xi. 20: "God was now pleased to leave them to *judicial hardness of heart*, to give them up to vain confidence, pride, stubbornness, and malignity, that they might bring upon themselves his righteous vengeance, and be utterly destroyed."

As to the ancient Jews, God hardened their hearts, in that by his providence he sustained them in life, upheld the use of all their powers, caused the prophets to warn and reprove them, and placed them in circumstances where they must receive these warnings and reproofs. Under this arrangement of his providence, they became more hardened and wicked.

Delitzsch, on Isa. lxiii. 17, remarks: "When men have scornfully and obstinately rejected the grace of God, he withdraws it from them judicially, gives them up to their wanderings, and makes their heart incapable of faith. ... The history of Israel, from chap. vi. onwards, has been the history of such a gradual judgment of hardening, and such a curse, eating deeper and deeper, and spreading its influence wider and wider round."

Barnes, on John xii. 40 : " God suffers the truth to produce a regular effect on sinful minds, without putting forth any positive supernatural influence to prevent it. The effect of truth on such minds is to irritate, to enrage, and to harden, unless counteracted by the grace of God. And, as God *knew* this, and knowing it still, sent the message, and suffered it to produce the *regular* effect, the evangelist says, ' *He* hath blinded their minds.' "

Alford, on Rom. ix. 18 : " Whatever difficulty there lies in this assertion that God *hardeneth* whom he will, lies also *in the daily course of his providence*, in which we see this hardening process going on in the case of the prosperous ungodly man."

He is warlike.	*Is peaceful.*
The LORD *is* a man of war: the LORD *is* his name. Ex. xv. 3.	Now the God of peace *be* with you all. Rom. xv. 33.
The LORD of hosts *is* his name. Isa. li. 15.	For God is not *the author* of confusion, but of peace, as in all churches of the saints. 1 Cor. xiv. 33.

These two sets of texts present God in a twofold aspect — in his attitude toward sin and incorrigible sinners, on the one hand, and that toward holiness and the good, on the other. He is hostile in respect to the one, and friendly in relation to the other. All his attributes are at war with evil, but at peace with " that which is good." Every good magistrate and ruler sustains a similar twofold relation. His attitude toward law-abiding citizens is a peaceful one, while in respect to evil-doers he " beareth not the sword in vain." [1]

Mercy.

Unmerciful and ferocious.	*Merciful and kind.*
And thou shalt consume all the people which the LORD thy God shall deliver thee: thine eye shall have no pity upon them. Deut. vii. 16.	O give thanks unto the LORD; for *he is* good; for his mercy *endureth* for ever. 1 Chron. xvi. 34.
And he smote the men of Beth-shemesh, because they had looked into the ark of the LORD, even he smote of the people fifty thousand and three score and ten men. 1 Sam. vi. 19.	The LORD *is* good to all; and his tender mercies *are* over all his works. Ps. cxlv. 9.
Thus saith the LORD of hosts, I remember *that* which Amalek did to Israel, how he laid *wait* for him in the way, when he came up from Egypt. Now go and smite Amalek, and utterly	*It is of* the LORD'S mercies that we are not consumed, because his compassions fail not. Lam. iii. 22.
	The Lord is very pitiful and of tender mercy. Jas. v. 11.
	God is love. 1 John iv. 16.

[1] See Rom. xiii. 3, 4.

DOCTRINAL DISCREPANCIES. 93

Unmerciful and ferocious.	*Merciful and kind.*
destroy all that they have, and spare them not: but slay both man and woman, infant and suckling, ox and sheep, camel and ass. 1 Sam. xv. 2, 3. And I will dash them one against another, even the fathers and the sons together, saith the LORD: I will not pity, nor spare, nor have mercy, but destroy them. Jer. xiii. 14.	For our God *is* a consuming fire. Heb. xii. 29.

As to the injunction to slay the Canaanites, in Deut. vii., see the discussion elsewhere.[1]

In respect to the Bethshemites, there is, in all probability, a mistake in the number specified. "Seventy men" is the true reading, with which Josephus[2] agrees. Copyists often made these mistakes, by taking one numeral letter for another which closely resembled it. In our present Hebrew text the words stand "seventy men, fifty thousand men." But in several manuscripts the Hebrew answering to "fifty thousand men" is entirely wanting. From this circumstance, and the fact that the town of Bethshemesh could by no means furnish anything like fifty thousand men, Keil and others hold that the expression "fifty thousand men" has rightfully no place in the text, but has crept in, by some oversight, from the margin.[3] But it may be asserted that the element of *number* does not necessarily come into the account — that the death of one person, under those circumstances, presents as real a difficulty as would that of fifty thousand persons. It is needful to say only that these Bethshemites evinced a profane and sacrilegious curiosity, and disobeyed the most solemn, explicit, and repeated warnings of Jehovah. For example, we read, in respect to some of the Levites even, "The sons of Kohath shall come to bear it; but they shall not touch any holy thing, lest they die"; and "They shall not go in to see when the holy things are covered, lest

---

[1] Ethical Discrepancies; "Enemies, treatment."

[2] Antiq. vi. 1, 4.

[3] Lord Arthur Hervey, in Bible Commentary, expresses the opinion that the error arose from the use of numeral-letters; Ayin (ע) denoting 70 being mistaken for dotted Nun (נ) representing 50000.

they die."[1] The rabbies say that the Bethshemites actually opened and looked into the ark. It was essential to teach the people, at this time, a solemn and effective lesson with reference to the proper mode of dealing with sacred things and of approaching Jehovah.

The reason for the command in 1 Sam. xv. is as follows: When the Hebrews were toiling along on their weary pilgrimage from Egypt to Canaan, the Amalekites hung upon their rear, laid wait for them, and butchered in cold blood all who were unable to keep up with the main body. The following is the artless language of the sacred historian: "Remember what Amalek did unto thee by the way, when ye were come forth out of Egypt; how he met thee by the way, and smote the hindmost of thee, even all that were feeble behind thee, when thou wast faint and weary; and he feared not God."[2]

They did this, says Keil, "not merely for the purpose of plundering, or of disputing the possession of this district and its pasture grounds with the Israelites, but to assail Israel as the nation of God, and, if possible, to destroy it." The Amalekites, as we gather from the narrative, were, in earlier and in later times a horde of ferocious and bloodthirsty guerrillas. It seemed best to the Almighty to extirpate a race so hardened and depraved, so utterly lost to the nobler feelings of mankind. Hence he said to Saul: "Go, and utterly destroy *the sinners*, the Amalekites."[3] In pursuance of this object, he was ordered to "slay both man and woman, infant and suckling."

It is objected that this command proves God to be "cruel." If so, the fact that in numberless cases he slays tender babes, innocent little ones, by painful diseases, famine, pestilence, earthquakes, hurricanes, and the like, militates equally against him. The charge of "cruelty" lies just as heavily against *the order of things in this world*, by whatever name it may be designated, as it does against Jehovah.

[1] Num. iv. 15 and 20.   [2] Deut. xxv. 17, 18.   [3] 1 Sam. xv. 18.

Besides, had the women and children been spared, there would soon have been a fresh crop of adult Amalekites, precisely like their predecessors. Or, suppose merely the children had been saved; if left to care for themselves, they must have miserably perished of starvation; if adopted and reared in Israelite families, they might, from their hereditary dispositions and proclivities to evil, have proved a most undesirable and pernicious element in the nation. It was, doubtless, on the whole, the best thing for the world that the Amalekite race should be exterminated.

The people so severely threatened in Jer. xiii. 14 were abominably corrupt and depraved. In Jer. vii. 9, they are charged with theft, murder, adultery, perjury, burning incense to Baal, and with idolatry in general. Yet, as the connection [1] clearly shows, the severe threatening above mentioned was a conditional one. They might have repented, and escaped. They would not reform, hence the threatening was strictly carried out.

As to Heb. xii. 29, God is a "consuming fire" in respect to evil and evil-doers. According to Alford, the fact that "God's anger continues to burn now, as then, against those who reject his kingdom, is brought in; and in the back-ground lie all those gracious dealings by which the fire of God's presence and purity becomes to his people, while it consumes their vanity and sin and earthly state, the fire of purity and light and love for their enduring citizenship of his kingdom."

His anger fierce and lasting.	*Slow and brief.*
The fierce anger of the LORD may be turned away from Israel. Num. xxv. 4.	For his anger *endureth but* a moment. Ps. xxx. 5.
And the LORD'S anger was kindled against Israel, and he made them wander in the wilderness forty years, until all the generation, that had done evil in the sight of the LORD, was consumed. Num. xxxii. 13.	The LORD *is* merciful and gracious, slow to anger, and plenteous in mercy. He will not always chide: neither will he keep *his anger* for ever. Ps. ciii. 8, 9.
Wilt thou be angry with us for ever? wilt thou draw out thine anger to all generations? Ps. lxxxv. 5.	

The "fierce anger" of the Lord is his *intense* and *infinite*

---

[1] See Jer. xiii. 15–17.

displeasure at everything unholy and evil. He is "slow to anger"; for though he feels an infinite abhorrence of sin, yet he bears long with the sinner, before giving punitive expression to that abhorrence. He dealt very patiently with the Israelites, as their history abundantly shows.

As to Ps. xxx. 5, Delitzsch observes: "'A moment passes in his anger, a (whole) life in his favor,' that is, the former endures only for a moment, the latter, the whole life of a man."

The anger of God ceases upon the repentance of the sinner. In relation to a certain class of persons, that anger is fierce and lasting, but with respect to a different class, it is slow and brief.

Fearful to fall into his hands.	*Not fearful.*
It is a fearful thing to fall into the hands of the living God. Heb. x. 31.	And David said unto Gad, I am in a great strait: let us fall now into the hand of the LORD: for his mercies *are* great: and let me not fall into the hand of man. 2 Sam. xxiv. 14.

The first text refers to the case of apostates and other incorrigible sinners; the second to the case of those who are truly penitent. Alford: "The two sentiments are easily set at one. For the faithful, in their chastisement, it is a blessed thing to fall into God's hands; for the unfaithful, in their doom, a dreadful one."

Laughs at sinner's overthrow.	*Has no pleasure in it.*
I also will laugh at your calamity: I will mock when your fear cometh. Prov. i. 26.	For I have no pleasure in the death of him that dieth, saith the LORD GOD: wherefore turn *yourselves*, and live ye. Ezek. xviii. 32.

The persons addressed in the first text are obdurate despisers and scorners who have persistently rejected God's admonitions. So, when calamities overtake them, he contemptuously rejects their prayers, which have no trace of penitence in them, but are the offspring of base fear. On this passage Stuart comments as follows: "I shall henceforth treat you as enemies who deserve contempt.... The intensity of the tropical language here makes the expression exceedingly strong. *Laughing at* and *mocking* are expressions of the highest and most contemptuous indignation."

The second text refers to persons who, though sinful, were less hardened and in a more hopeful condition than the former class.

A God of Justice.	*Of Mercy.*
He is the Rock, his work is perfect: for all his ways *are* judgment: a God of truth and without iniquity, just and right *is* he. Deut. xxxii. 4.	The LORD your God *is* gracious and merciful, and will not turn away *his* face from you, if ye return unto him. 2 Chron. xxx. 9.

God's justice is not restricted to what is termed "distributive justice," which gives to every man his exact deserts, leaving no room for the exercise of mercy. The divine justice is that "general justice" which carries out completely all the ends of law, sometimes by remitting, and at other times by inflicting, the penalty, according as the offender is penitent or otherwise. Every wise parent and ruler employs general justice, securing the great ends of government by punishing offenders, or by showing mercy, as circumstances may warrant. The following is a striking passage: "Unto thee, O Lord, belongeth mercy; for thou renderest to every man according to his work."[1] From this text it would seem that, in the Psalmist's view, mercy and justice are so far from being incompatible, that the one attribute is dependent upon the other. "Thou art merciful, for thou art just." Hengstenberg: "He must have loving-kindness, inasmuch as it is involved in the very idea of God as the righteous One, that he recompense every one according to his work, and therefore manifest himself as compassionate to the righteous, while he destroys the wicked."

He hates some.	*Is kind to all.*
Was not Esau Jacob's brother? saith the LORD: yet I loved Jacob, and I hated Esau. Mal. i. 2, 3.	The LORD *is* good to all. Ps. cxlv. 9.

The word "hate" is used here, as often in scripture,[2] in the sense of *to love less.* If one person was preferred to another, the former was said to be "loved," the latter "hated." Henderson observes: "As the opposite of love is hatred, when

---

[1] Ps. lxii. 12.

[2] See Gen. xxix. 30, 31; Prov. xiii. 24; also Luke xiv. 26, compared with Matt. x. 37.

there is only an inferior degree of the former exhibited, the object of it is regarded as being hated, rather than loved."

Veracity.

God cannot lie.	Sends forth lying spirits.
The Strength of Israel will not lie. 1 Sam. xv. 29. That by two immutable things, in which it was impossible for God to lie. Heb. vi. 18.	And he said, Hear thou therefore the word of the LORD; I saw the LORD sitting on his throne, and all the host of heaven standing by him on his right hand and on his left. And the LORD said, Who shall persuade Ahab, that he may go up and fall at Ramoth-gilead? And one said on this manner, and another said on that manner. And there came forth a spirit, and stood before the LORD, and said, I will persuade him. And the LORD said unto him, Wherewith? And he said, I will go forth, and I will be a lying spirit in the mouth of all his prophets. And he said, Thou shalt persuade *him*, and prevail also; go forth, and do so. Now therefore, behold, the LORD hath put a lying spirit in the mouth of all these thy prophets, and the LORD hath spoken evil concerning thee. 1 Kings xxii. 19-23.

The whole declaration of Micaiah, in the passage at the right, is a highly figurative and poetical description of a vision he had seen. Putting aside its rhetorical drapery, the gist of the whole passage is that *God for judicial purposes suffered Ahab to be fatally deceived.* Bähr: " Because Ahab, who had abandoned God and hardened his heart, desired to use prophecy for his own purposes, it is determined that he shall be led to ruin by prophecy. As God often used the heathen nations as the rod of his wrath for the chastisement of Israel (Isa. x. 5), so now he uses Ahab's false prophets to bring upon Ahab the judgment which Elijah had foretold against him."

A. Fuller:[1] "That spirit to whom thou hast sold thyself to work wickedness in the sight of the Lord now desires thee as his prey. He that has seduced thee into sin now asks permission of God to deceive thy prophets, that he may plunge thee into destruction; and God has granted him his desire. And that which Satan is doing for his own ends, God will do for his. There is as much of the judicial hand of God in a

[1] Works, Vol. i. p. 620.

lying spirit having misled thy prophets as of readiness in the evil one to entangle and seize thee as his prey."

Keil: "Jehovah sends this spirit, inasmuch as the deception of Ahab has been inflicted upon him as a judgment of God for his unbelief. But there is no statement here to the effect that this lying spirit proceeded from Satan, because the object of the prophet was simply to bring out the working of God in the deception practised upon Ahab by his prophets. ... Jehovah has ordained that Ahab, being led astray by a prediction of his prophets inspired by the spirit of lies, shall enter upon the war, that he may find therein the punishment of his ungodliness."

Denounces deception.	Sanctions it.
Cursed *be* the deceiver, which hath in his flock a male, and voweth and sacrificeth unto the Lord a corrupt thing. Mal. i. 14.	And Samuel said, How can I go? if Saul hear *it*, he will kill me. And the LORD said, Take an heifer with thee, and say, I am come to sacrifice to the LORD. 1 Sam. xvi. 2.
Peter said, Ananias, why hath Satan filled thine heart to lie to the Holy Ghost, and to keep back *part* of the price of the land? Acts v. 3.	O LORD, thou hast deceived me, and I was deceived: thou art stronger than I, and hast prevailed. Jer. xx. 7.
	And if the prophet be deceived when he hath spoken a thing, I the LORD have deceived that prophet, and I will stretch out my hand upon him, and will destroy him from the midst of my people Israel. Ezek. xiv. 9.
	Even him whose coming is after the working of Satan with all power and signs and lying wonders, and with all deceivableness of unrighteousness in them that perish; because they received not the love of the truth, that they might be saved. And for this cause God shall send them strong delusion, that they should believe a lie: that they all might be damned who believed not the truth, but had pleasure in unrighteousness. 2 Thess. ii. 9-12.

On the text from 1 Samuel, Calvin says: "There was no dissimulation or falsehood in this, since God really wished his prophet to find safety under the pretext of the sacrifice. A sacrifice was therefore really offered, and the prophet was protected thereby, so that he was not exposed to any danger until the time of full revelation arrived."

Keil: "There was no untruth in this; for Samuel was really about to conduct a sacrificial festival, and was to invite Jesse's family to it, and then anoint the one whom Jehovah should point out to him as the chosen one. It was simply a concealment of the principal object of his mission from any who might make inquiry about it because they themselves had not been invited."

It is our privilege to withhold the truth from persons who have no right to know it, and who, as we have reason to believe, would make a bad use of it. Lord Arthur Hervey[1] well observes: "Secrecy and concealment are not the same as duplicity and falsehood. Concealment of a good purpose, for a good purpose, is clearly justifiable; for example, in war, in medical treatment, in state policy, and in the ordinary affairs of life. In the providential government of the world, and in God's dealings with individuals, concealment of his purpose, till the proper time for its development, is the rule, rather than the exception, and must be so."

Jer. xx. 7 is rendered by Davidson[2] thus: "O Lord, thou hast constrained me, and I was constrained."

Henderson: "'Thou didst persuade me, O Jehovah, and I was persuaded.' The prophet alludes to his reluctance to accept the prophetical office, which it required powerful inducements from Jehovah to overcome." Naegelsbach, in Lange, gives a similar version.

Ezek. xiv. 9, which refers to idolatrous prophets, exhibits the fact that when men, without divine authority, set up as prophets, God, in order to expose the falsity of their pretensions, "deceives" them; that is, he so orders circumstances that these prophets will utter false and foolish predictions, which by their failure shall disclose the true character of their authors, and overwhelm them with shame and disgrace.

As to the last text of the second series above, observe the description of the persons contemplated by it. The "deceivableness of unrighteousness" is in them; they neither love nor believe the truth, but have "pleasure in unrighteousness." They deliberately choose error. As they prefer falsehood

---

[1] In Bible Commentary.   [2] Introd. to Old Test., Vol. ii. p. 435.

DOCTRINAL DISCREPANCIES. 101

and delusion to truth, God gives them their choice in full measure. With a judicial purpose, he gives them what they love, together with all its fearful consequences.[1]

Alford: "He is the judicial sender and doer; it is he who hardens the heart which has chosen the evil way."

Ellicott: "The words are definite and significant; they point to that 'judicial infatuation' into which, in the development of his just government of the world, God causes evil and error to be unfolded, and which he brings into punitive agency in the case of all obstinate and truth-hating rejection of his offers and calls of mercy."

Habitation of God.

Dwells in light.	Dwells in darkness.
Who only hath immortality, dwelling in the light which no man can approach unto. 1 Tim. vi. 16.	Then spake Solomon. The LORD said that he would dwell in the thick darkness. 1 Kings viii. 12.
	He made darkness his secret place; his pavilion round about him *were* dark waters *and* thick clouds of the skies. Ps. xviii. 11.
	Clouds and darkness *are* round about him. Ps. xcvii. 2.

The meaning may be that that in which God dwells is "light" to him, but "darkness" to us. The morning sun, which is light to the eagle, is darkness and blindness to nocturnal animals.

A better explanation, perhaps, is the following: Imagery of various and widely diverse kinds is employed in the scriptures to set forth the attributes of God and his immeasurable remove from finite conditions and creatures. Where two or more figures are employed to illustrate the same idea, we should look for the common features of resemblance or common point of comparison. In the case before us, both of the figurative expressions — "unapproachable light" and "thick darkness" — set forth vividly and equally well the *unsearchableness* of God in relation to his creatures. This is the point which, in the present instance, the sacred writers intended to illustrate, and beyond this their language should not be pressed.

[1] See South's Sermon on Falsehood and Lying, Works, i. pp. 192-203. Also, Müller, Doctrine of Sin, ii. pp. 413-415 (second edition).

Dwells in chosen Temples.

And the LORD appeared to Solomon by night, and said unto him, I have heard thy prayer, and have chosen this place to myself for an house of sacrifice. For now have I chosen and sanctified this house, that my name may be there for ever; and mine eyes and mine heart shall be there perpetually. 2 Chron. vii. 12, 16.

Does not dwell there.

Thus saith the LORD, The heaven *is* my throne, and the earth *is* my footstool: where *is* the house that ye build unto me? and where *is* the place of my rest? Isa. lxvi. 1.

Howbeit, the Most High dwelleth not in temples made with hands. Acts vii. 48.

Observe, first, that God does not promise to "dwell" in the temple. He says he had chosen it, not as a residence, but as a "house of sacrifice." So Solomon understood it, for he says: "But who is able to build him an house, seeing the heaven and heaven of heavens cannot contain him? who am I then, that I should build him an house, save only to burn sacrifice before him?"[1] The promise that the name, heart, and eyes of Jehovah should be there, meant simply that he would regard the house with peculiar favor, and manifest his power and grace in it. It is to be noted, secondly, that the whole promise was conditional, as is explicitly stated in the following verses: "But if ye turn away, and forsake my statutes and my commandments, which I have set before you, and shall go and serve other gods, and worship them; Then will I pluck them up by the roots out of my land which I have given them; and this house which I have sanctified for my name will I cast out of my sight, and will make it to be a proverb and a byword among all nations."[2] As the conditions were not complied with, the promise was of course not binding. The quotation from Acts merely affirms that the infinite, omnipresent Spirit is not restricted to any one locality, or confined to any single place of worship.

Inhabits eternity.

For thus saith the high and lofty One that inhabiteth eternity, whose name *is* Holy. Isa. lvii. 15.

Dwells with men.

And I will dwell among the children of Israel, and will be their God. Ex. xxix. 45.

I dwell in the high and holy *place*, with him also *that is* of a contrite and humble spirit, to revive the spirit of the humble, and to revive the heart of the contrite ones. Isa. lvii. 15.

---

[1] 2 Chron. ii. 6.

[2] 2 Chron. vii. 19, 20. Kimchi and Rashi give this explanation of the case.

DOCTRINAL DISCREPANCIES. 103

Inhabits eternity.	*Dwells with men.*
	Jesus answered and said unto him, If a man love me, he will keep my words: and my Father will love him, and we will come unto him, and make our abode with him. John xiv. 23.
	God hath said, I will dwell in them, and walk in *them;* and I will be their God, and they shall be my people. 2 Cor. vi. 16.
	And I heard a great voice out of heaven saying, Behold, the tabernacle of God *is* with men, and he will dwell with them, and they shall be his people, and God himself shall be with them, *and be* their God. Rev. xxi. 3.

An omnipresent Being may do both — dwell in eternity, and with men too. The "omnipresence" of God is his power to develop his activity everywhere at once. Hence, in this view, the passages present no difficulty.

Dwells in heaven.	*Dwells in Zion.*
Unto thee lift I up mine eyes, O thou that dwellest in the heavens. Psalm cxxiii. 1.	Sing praises to the LORD, which dwelleth in Zion. Ps. ix. 11.
	In Salem also is his tabernacle, and his dwelling-place in Zion. Ps. lxxvi. 2.

To a mind capable of comprehending the meaning of the term "omnipresence" these texts are seen to be in perfect harmony. Most simply, yet sublimely, is the idea expressed by the inspired prophet: "Do not I fill heaven and earth? saith the Lord."[1]

Position God assumes.

One Position.	*A different one.*
There will I sit to judge all the heathen round about. Joel iii. 12.	The LORD standeth up to plead, and standeth to judge the people. Isa iii. 13.

This is a fair specimen of the trivial, verbal discrepancies which certain infidel writers palm off upon their careless or ignorant readers as cases of real contradiction. Of course, no person of candor and common sense would think of interpreting the language literally. The figure "sit" brings graphically to view the deliberateness and impartiality with which God judges men; the term "standeth" represents him as in the act of executing his judgments.

[1] Jer. xxiii. 24.

Law of God.

A law of liberty.	*Tends to bondage.*
So speak ye, and so do, as they that shall be judged by the law of liberty. Jas. ii. 12.	These are the two covenants; the one from the mount Sinai, which gendereth to bondage. Gal. iv. 24.

The "law" of the first, is not identical with the "covenant" of the second passage. The former refers to the norm or rule of life contained in the gospel. It is Christ's law of love, purity, and liberty, as embodied in the Sermon on the Mount.

Alford: "It is the law of our liberty, not as in contrast with a former law of bondage, but as viewed on the side of its being the law of the new life and birth, with all its spontaneous and free development of obedience."

On the contrary, the "covenant" is the Mosaic law, with its complicated and burdensome ritual. This gendered to bondage. Ellicott comments thus: "'*Bearing children unto bondage*,' i.e. to pass under and to inherit the lot of bondage." Peter terms it a "yoke," which "neither our fathers nor we were able to bear."[1] As, therefore, the two texts refer to entirely different things, there is no collision.

Law is perfect.	*It perfected nothing.*
But whoso looketh into the perfect law of liberty. Jas. i. 25.	For the law made nothing perfect, but the bringing in of a better hope *did*. Heb. vii. 19.

As in the preceding instance, these texts refer to different things — the former to the Christian, the latter to the Mosaic, law. Besides, were the same law intended in both cases, it would by no means follow that a perfect law necessarily secures perfect obedience.

Observance tends to life.	*Tends to death.*
Ye shall therefore keep my statutes and my judgments: which if a man do, he shall live in them: I *am* the Lord. Lev. xviii. 5. For Moses describeth the righteousness which is of the law, That the man which doeth these things shall live by them. Rom. x. 5.	Because they had not executed my judgments, but had despised my statutes, and had polluted my sabbaths, and their eyes were after their fathers' idols. Wherefore I gave them also statutes *that were* not good, and judgments whereby they should not live; and I polluted them in their own gifts, in that they caused to pass through *the fire* all that openeth the womb, that I might make them desolate, to the end that they might know that I *am* the Lord. Ezek. xx. 24–26.

[1] Acts xv. 10.

Lord. Alford, Wordsworth, Mill, and others adopt the former; Griesbach, Lachmann, Meyer, Davidson, Tischendorf, Tregelles, Green, and Hackett apparently, adopt the latter reading. If we read " the church *of the Lord*," the passage will have no direct bearing upon the point under discussion. On the words, " the only true God," Barnes observes : " The only God in opposition to all false gods. What is said here is in opposition to idols, not to Jesus himself, who, in 1 John v. 20, is called ' the true God and eternal life.' "

Alford: " The very juxtaposition of Jesus Christ here with the Father, and the knowledge of *both* being defined to be eternal life, is a proof by implication of the Godhead of the former. The knowledge of *God and a creature* could not be eternal life, and the juxtaposition of the two would be inconceivable."

Christ, the Son of God.	*Son of man.*
Say ye of him, whom the Father hath sanctified, and sent into the world, Thou blasphemest; because I said, I am the Son of God? John x. 36.	When Jesus came into the coasts of Caesarea Philippi, he asked his disciples saying, Whom do men say that I the Son of man am? Matt. xvi. 13.
And Philip said, If thou believest with all thine heart, thou mayest. And he answered and said, I believe that Jesus Christ is the Son of God. Acts viii. 37.[1]	For the Son of man is come to seek and to save that which was lost. Luke xix. 10.

The term " Son of God," is to be regarded as descriptive of Jesus, in his divine nature ; " Son of man," in his human nature. The latter term, says Alford, is " the name by which the Lord ordinarily in one pregnant word, designates himself as the Messiah — the *Son of God manifested in the flesh of man* — the *second Adam.* And to it belong all those conditions of humiliation, suffering, and exaltation, which it behooves the Son of man to go through." From the following passage, " Hereafter shall the Son of man sit on the right hand of the power of God. Then said they all, Art thou then the Son of God?"[2]

---

[1] This verse is retained by Bornemann, Wordsworth, and the Arabic, Armenian, Syriac, and Vulgate versions. It is omitted by Alford, Hackett, Meyer, Tischendorf, and most other modern critics.

[2] Luke xxii. 69, 70.

Alford: " Christ and the Father are ONE — one in *essence*, primarily, but therefore also one in *working* and *power* and in *will* ; ... not *personally* one, but *essentially*."

Equal to the Father.	*Inferior to him.*
Christ Jesus: who, being in the form of God, thought it not robbery to be equal with God. Philip. ii. 5, 6. After Christ. For in him dwelleth all the fulness of the Godhead bodily. Col. ii. 8, 9.	If ye loved me, ye would rejoice, because I said, I go unto the Father: for my Father is greater than I. John xiv. 28.

The words " greater than I " do not assert Christ's inferiority in respect to *essence*. Barnes: " The object of Jesus here is not to compare his own *nature* with that of the Father, but his *condition*. Ye would rejoice that I am to leave this state of suffering and humiliation, and resume that glory which I had with the Father before the world was. You ought to rejoice at my exaltation to bliss and glory with the Father."

Calvin: " Christ does not here compare the divinity of the Father with his own, neither his own human nature with the divine essence of the Father, but rather his present state with that celestial glory to which he must shortly be received."

In this interpretation concur Luther, Cocceius, De Wette, Tholuck, Stuart, and Alford, with other critics and commentators."[1] This exposition is in perfect keeping with the context.

The Son is God.	*The Father the only God.*
The church of God, which he hath purchased with his own blood. Acts xx. 28. Forasmuch as ye know that ye were not redeemed with corruptible things, *as* silver and gold, from your vain conversation *received* by tradition from your fathers; but with the precious blood of Christ. 1 Pet. i. 18, 19.	And this is life eternal, that they might know thee the only true God. John xvii. 3.

In respect to the quotation from Acts, there are different readings. Some critics read " theos," *God ;* others, " kurios,"

---

[1] Says an eminent Unitarian divine, Rev. Dr. E. H. Sears: " For a mortal man, or for an archangel as well, to announce that God is greater than *he* is, were profane egoism. But for Jesus speaking as the Word to say, ' my Father is greater than I,' is to say only that God as absolute, is more than God revealed." — Heart of Christ, Appendix, p. 550.

DOCTRINAL DISCREPANCIES.   109

it would appear that the Jews took the two expressions, "Son of God" and "Son of man," as nearly or quite synonymous, both denoting the long-expected Messiah.

The only Son of God.	*Men also sons of God.*
The only begotten Son, which is in the bosom of the Father, he hath declared *him.* John i. 18.	For as many as are led by the Spirit of God, they are the sons of God. Rom. viii. 14.
In this was manifested the love of God toward us, because that God sent his only begotten Son into the world, that we might live through him. 1 John iv. 9.	Beloved, now are we the sons of God. 1 John iii. 2.

Observe that the first two texts do not assert that Jesus is the "only," but the "only begotten," Son of God; that is, he is the only being who sustains that peculiar relation to the Father, which is implied in the term "begotten."

One class of theologians hold that, while men may become sons of God by *adoption*,[1] Jesus is son by *generation, and consequent participation in the divine essence and attributes.* Such was the view of the Nicene trinitarians.[2] By analogical reasoning, they maintained that, as the human son participates in the nature and attributes of the human father, the same holds true of the Divine Son in relation to the Divine Father. According to this view, held by many theologians at the present day, Christ is distinctively "*the* Son of God," — or, in the language of Dr. Hodge,[3] "the only person in the universe to whom the word can be applied in its full sense, as expressing sameness of essence."

There is another explanation of the term, "Son of God," which is given by Dr. Watts,[4] Prof. Stuart,[5] Prof. Park, and others. They hold that Christ bears this appellation because, in respect to his human nature, he is derived from God; also because of the elevated dignity which was conferred on him

---
[1] Rom. viii. 15, 16.
[2] Shedd, History of Christian Doctrine, i. 331.
[3] Theology, i. 474. Compare Dr. Miller's Letters on Eternal Sonship, pp. 37-40.
[4] See Works, v. 232-258 (edition in 7 vols.).
[5] Letters to Dr. Miller on Eternal Generation, Letter viii.

as the Messiah, — his resurrection from the dead being the commencement of his elevation to supreme dignity, and being, moreover, the beginning of a *new life;* that is, something analogous to birth or generation. The last-named theologian[1] adduces the additional reason that Christ was greatly beloved of the Father.

On either of the above hypotheses, the fact that men are occasionally styled "sons of God," while Jesus is denominated "the only-begotten Son of God," occasions no difficulty, since the two appellations are respectively used with very different significations.

Omnipotence.

Had all power.	*Was not almighty.*
And Jesus came and spake unto them, saying, All power is given unto me in heaven and in earth. Matt. xxviii. 18	To sit on my right hand, and on my left, is not mine to give, but *it shall be given to them* for whom it is prepared of my Father. Matt. xx. 23.
The Father loveth the Son, and hath given all things into his hand. John iii. 35.	And he could there do no mighty work, save that he laid his hand upon a few sick folk, and healed *them*. Mark vi. 5.

Matt. xx. 23 is rendered by Grotius, Chrysostom, Clarke, Barnes, and others thus: "is not mine to give, *except* to those for whom," etc. With this the Syriac Peshito precisely agrees. The italics in the common version of this text pervert the meaning. The real sense is: "It is not fitting that I should bestow it upon others." The question is not one of power at all, but of fitness.

Mark vi. 5 implies not physical but moral impossibility. It was not lack of power which prevented his working miracles at Nazareth; but, as the next verse shows, the "unbelief" of the people was the reason why it was inconsistent for him, or why he "could not" thus work. So one often says of a thing which he deemed improper, or incompatible with his purposes, "I could not do it."

Alford: "The *want of ability* is not *absolute*, but *relative*. The same voice which could still the tempest, could anywhere

---

[1] MS. Lectures.

and under any circumstances have commanded diseases to obey; but in most cases of human infirmity, it was our Lord's practice to require *faith* in the recipient of aid, and that being wanting, the help *could not* be given."

Omniscience.

Knew all things.	*Ignorant of some things.*
But Jesus did not commit himself unto them, because he knew all *men*, and needed not that any should testify of man: for he knew what was in man. John ii. 24, 25.	And seeing a fig tree afar off having leaves, he came, if haply he might find any thing thereon: and when he came to it, he found nothing but leaves: for the time of figs was not *yet*. Mark xi.13.
Now are we sure that thou knowest all things, and needest not that any man should ask thee. John xvi. 30.	But of that day and *that* hour knoweth no man, no, not the angels which are in heaven, neither the Son, but the Father. Mark xiii. 32.
And he said unto him, Lord, thou knowest all things; thou knowest that I love thee. John xxi. 17.	And said, Where have ye laid him? They said unto him, Lord, come and see. John xi. 34.
Christ, in whom are hid all the treasures of wisdom and knowledge. Col. ii. 3.	Wherefore in all things it behooved him to be made like unto *his* brethren. Heb. ii. 17.

Obviously, some passages represent Christ in the aspect of his Godhead, while others speak of him simply in his human nature, — *as a man*. When he is spoken of as "increasing in wisdom and stature,"[1] the humanity is placed in the foreground; when he claims to have existed "before Abraham was,"[2] he speaks in his inherent divinity. As another has remarked: "His infancy and childhood were no *mere pretence*, but the divine personality was in him carried through these states of weakness and inexperience, and gathered round itself the ordinary accessions and experiences of the sons of men." In the person of Christ, the Divinity voluntarily entered into, and took upon itself, the conditions and limitations of humanity.

Ewald[3] observes: "Even the highest divine power, when it veils itself in mortal body, and appears in definite time, finds, in this body and this time, its limits." To nearly the same purport, Colenso[4] says: "It is perfectly consistent with the most entire and sincere belief in our Lord's divinity, to hold, as many do, that when he vouchsafed to become a 'Son of

---

[1] Luke ii. 52. [2] John viii. 58 [3] Life of Christ, p. 340.
[4] On Pentateuch, Part i. p. xxxi.

man,' he took our nature fully, and voluntarily entered into all the conditions of humanity, and among others, into that which makes our growth in all ordinary knowledge *gradual* and *limited*."

The divinity and humanity were, as we believe, so united that they exerted a reciprocal influence, each modifying the action of the other. If it be said that such a union is improbable, we reply that there is an equal, antecedent improbability that a *spirit*, being immaterial, would be united with a *body* composed of matter, so as to form one personality, one ego; yet we know that this actually occurs in the case of man.

In consequence of the union above mentioned, our Saviour could say "I" of either component of his nature — the divine or the human. Sometimes he spoke in one relation, sometimes in the other, according as circumstances or the exigencies of discourse required.[1] In a somewhat analogous way, a man says, "*I* rejoice at it," and, at another time, "*I* weigh so much." In the first instance, the "I" refers exclusively to the *soul;* in the second, to the *body*. The soul rejoices, the body weighs. Yet the pronoun "I" is applied indifferently to either. We cannot but think that the principle underlying this mode of conception and speech, indicates a simple and correct interpretation of the second series of texts quoted above. They bring Christ before our minds in his lower and subordinate relations, in the humiliation, the "emptying" himself of his Godlike majesty and visible glories, which he voluntarily undertook and endured.[2]

As to the case of the fig-tree, Jesus wished to teach his dis-

---

[1] Dr. Payson, on his death-bed, said, in substance, to his friends, "I suffer as much pain, as if every bone were undergoing dislocation;" and, in the same breath, "I am perfectly, perfectly happy and peaceful — more happy than I can possibly express to you." That is, *he was at the same moment intensely happy*, and *suffering intensely*. Yet this involved no contradiction. The language had respect to different relations, or to different departments of being. See Payson's Memoir, by Cummings, p. 476.

[2] Phil. ii. 7, 8; Greek ἑαυτὸν ἐκένωσε, emptied Himself.

ciples an important lesson. This was enforced upon their minds by his suddenly blighting the tree. The foliage of the tree was in such a state that it was antecedently probable that there was fruit also. Jesus acted " according to the appearance of things; being a man as well as divine he acted, of course, as men *do act* in such circumstances."

As to Mark xiii. 32, Augustine says, " He did not know so that he might at that time disclose to the disciples." He adds elsewhere, " Though as God he could not be ignorant of any thing, yet his human understanding did not know it."

Lightfoot, on the passage: " It is not revealed to him from the Father to reveal to the church."

Wordsworth, on the same text : " It is true that the Son, as Son, knoweth not the day of judgment, because the *Father* ' hath put the times and seasons *in his own power,*' and the Father will reveal them when he thinks meet; and therefore it is no part of the *office* of the Son to *know*, that is, to *determine* and *declare* the day of judgment."

Some of the Lutheran commentators say that our Lord knew " in respect to *possession*, but not in respect to *use*." That is, he might *possess* but not *use* this knowledge.

Waterland :[1] " He denies the knowledge of the day of judgment, but in respect of his *human nature;* in which respect also he is said to have increased in wisdom, Luke ii. 52; the divine *Logos* having, with the human nature, assumed the *ignorance* and other *infirmities* proper to it."

Schaff, in Lange, on Matt. xxiv. 36: " Christ could, of course, not lay aside, in the incarnation, the metaphysical attributes of his divine nature, such as eternity; but he could, by an act of his will, limit his attributes of power and his knowledge, and refrain from their use as far as it was necessary for his humiliation."

Alford: " In the course of humiliation undertaken by the Son, in which he increased in wisdom (Luke ii. 52), learned

[1] Works, ii. 163 (Oxford edition, 1856).

obedience (Heb. v. 8), uttered desires in prayer (Luke vi. 12, etc.) — *this matter was hidden from him.*"

Omnipresence.

Everywhere present.

For where two or three are gathered together in my name, there am I in the midst of them. Matt. xviii. 20.
Lo, I am with you alway, *even* unto the end of the world. Matt. xxviii. 20.

Not omnipresent.

For ye have the poor always with you; but me ye have not always. Matt. xxvi. 11.
Jesus himself drew near, and went with them. Luke xxiv. 15.
Jesus had conveyed himself away, a multitude being in *that* place. John v. 13.
And I am glad for your sakes that I was not there, to the intent ye may believe; nevertheless, let us go unto him. John xi. 15.

The first texts refer to his spiritual presence with his people; the second series relates to his visible presence, in the body. Paul, in Col. ii. 5, employs language of a quite similar import.

Holiness.

He is holy.

He had done no violence, neither *was any* deceit in his mouth. Isa. liii. 9.
In all points tempted like as *we are, yet* without sin. Heb. iv. 15.
Holy, harmless, undefiled, separate from sinners. Heb. vii. 26.

Is sin.

For he hath made him *to be* sin for us, who knew no sin; that we might be made the righteousness of God in him. 2 Cor. v. 21.

The word "sin," in the latter text, doubtless means "sin-offering."[1] In this view concur Augustine, Ambrose, Erasmus, Lightfoot, Macknight, Stuart, Whitby, and many other commentators.

Chrysostom says, " Him who knew no sin, who was righteousness itself, he hath made sin; that is, hath suffered to be condemned as a sinner, to die as a person accursed.

De Wette and Alford give the passage a somewhat different

---

[1] Schleusner, Lexicon to the LXX, defines the original Greek term, ἁμαρτία, as "peccatum, etiam poena peccati, et sacrificium piaculare." Biel gives, also, " sacrificium pro peccato." Examples of the secondary signification are Ezek xliii. 22; xliv. 29; xlv. 22. According to Gesenius, the corresponding Hebrew term חֲטָאָה, with two kindred words, means both *sin* and *sin-offering*. Fuerst says חַטָּאת denotes *sin* in 1 Sam. xx. 1; Psalm lix. 4; Job xiii. 23; and *sin-offering* in Ex. xxix. 14; Lev. iv. 3. The Greek word mentioned above has clearly its secondary or Hebraistic sense in 2 Cor. v. 21.

turn, thus : Sin, i.e. Christ on the cross was the *representative of sin* — of the sin of the world.

With a singular obliquity of mind and heart, F. W. Newman[1] says of our Saviour, as represented in the Gospels, " I almost doubt whether, if one wished to draw the character of a vain and vacillating pretender, it would be possible to draw anything more to the purpose than this," and expresses his " conviction," that " in *consistency* of goodness Jesus fell far below vast numbers of his unhonored disciples."

What must be our estimate of a man who can thus coolly ignore the verdict of the ages, and wantonly revolt the moral sense of Christendom, by suffering his pen to trace such atrocious sentiments as these?

Blessed.	A curse.
God hath blessed thee for ever. Ps. xlv. 2.	Christ hath redeemed us from the curse of the law, being made a curse for us: for it is written, Cursed *is* every one that hangeth on a tree. Gal. iii. 13.
All nations shall call him blessed. Ps. lxxii. 17.	
Worthy is the Lamb that was slain to receive power, and riches, and wisdom, and strength, and honor, and glory, and blessing. Rev. v. 12.	

Luther and some other commentators, taking the language in Galatians too literally, have supposed that by some mysterious transference of human guilt to Christ, he actually became a sinner. This interpretation is, however, uncalled for, and repugnant to our feelings.

Conybeare renders : " He became accursed for our sakes."

Ellicott and Meyer think that the abstract word " katara," *curse*, is chosen instead of the concrete, to " express with more force the completeness of the satisfaction which Christ made to the law."

Barnes : " Jesus was subjected to what was regarded as an accursed death. He was treated in his death *as if* he had been a criminal."

As Christ suffered *in the stead* of those upon whom the curse properly devolved, he might be styled " accursed," or, in the sense just explained, a " curse " for us.

[1] Phases of Faith, chap. vii. (third edition).

Mercy.

He is merciful.
For the Son of man is not come to destroy men's lives but to save *them.* Luke ix. 56.
For the Son of man is come to seek and to save that which was lost. Luke xix. 10.

Unmerciful.
Fall on us, and hide us from the face of him that sitteth on the throne, and from the wrath of the Lamb. Rev. vi. 16.
Called Faithful and True, and in righteousness he doth judge and make war. Rev. xix. 11.
And he *was* clothed with a vesture dipped in blood, and his name is called The Word of God. Rev. xix. 13.
And out of his mouth goeth a sharp sword, that with it he should smite the nations: and he shall rule them with a rod of iron; and he treadeth the wine-press of the fierceness and wrath of Almighty God. Rev. xix. 15.

De Wette[1] says that these latter passages "glow with the spirit of Messianic revenge." The apparent difficulty is easily obviated. Just in proportion as any being loves holiness, in that proportion will he hate sin. Christ, being perfectly holy, being also a wise and benevolent sovereign, cannot but be most powerfully impelled to reward virtue, and to punish and exterminate vice. The texts to which exception is taken, are vivid, figurative expressions of the infinitely wise, just, and righteous principles which Christ displays in the administration of his kingdom.

Spares bruised reed.
A bruised reed shall he not break, and the smoking flax shall he not quench. Isa. xlii. 3.

Wields iron sceptre.
Thou shalt break them with a rod of iron: thou shalt dash them in pieces like a potter's vessel. Ps. ii. 9.

These passages present the Messiah in a twofold attitude; toward the penitent and humble, and toward the proud and rebellious. The "rod of iron" indicates the strength and crushing force with which he would chastise the revolters; the first text brings to view the tender compassion which he would exercise toward the dejected and helpless. The same mouth which breathed the tender words, "Come unto me, all ye that labor and are heavy-laden,"[2] could, without any incongruity, thunder at those scoffing hypocrites, the scribes and Pharisees, the terrible denunciation, "Ye serpents, ye generation of vipers, how can ye escape the damnation of hell."[3]

[1] Introd. to New Test., p. 376.   [2] Matt. xi. 28.   [3] Matt. xxiii. 33.

Courage and Fortitude.

Shrunk at death.	*Met it composedly.*
Now is my soul troubled; and what shall I say? Father, save me from this hour: but for this cause came I unto this hour. John xii. 27.	He humbled himself, and became obedient unto death, even the death of the cross. Philip. ii. 8.
Who in the days of his flesh, when he had offered up prayers and supplications with strong crying and tears unto him that was able to save him from death, and was heard in that he feared. Heb. v. 7.	

Theophylact, Grotius, Tholuck, Barnes, and others, take the Saviour's words interrogatively, thus: " Shall I say, Father, save me from this hour?" This interpretation makes good sense, and accords well with the context.

Heb. v. 7 may be rendered: " He was heard on account of his pious resignation," — or, " because of his reverence." So, in substance, Alford, Barnes, Bleek, Conybeare, Delitzsch, Luther, Robinson, Tyndale, and all the Greek commentators.

Prof. Stuart, following in substance the common version, maintains that it was not death which Christ " feared "; he dreaded lest he should sink under the agony of being deserted by his Father. In this respect he was " heard," and received divine aid.[1] Either interpretation dispels the difficulty.

Veracity.

His witness true.	*Not true.*
Though I bear record of myself, yet my record is true: for I know whence I came and whither I go. John viii. 14.	If I bear witness of myself my witness is not true. John v. 31.

Grotius takes the first passage as a mere hypothesis, " even though I should bear witness of myself," etc. Bishop Pearce, Wakefield, and others render the second text thus: " If I bear witness of myself, is not my witness true?" Should the common version be retained, the meaning is, If I *alone* bear witness of myself." The Mosaic law required at least two witnesses.[2] Jesus therefore admits that his own testimony alone would not be " true "; that is, would not be regarded as *legal proof;* hence he proceeds to adduce the corroborative testimony of another.

---

[1] Luke xxii. 43.   [2] Deut. xix. 15.

Andrew Fuller:[1] "The first passage sets forth his testimony as it was *in itself;* the second as it was *in the account of men.* ... Admitting their laws or rules of evidence, his testimony would not have been credible; and therefore in the verses following he appeals to that of John the Baptist, and the works which he had wrought in his Father's name, which amounted to a testimony from the Father."

Alford: The assertion in chapter v. was, that his own *unsupported* witness (*supposing that possible*) would not be trustworthy, but that his testimony *was* supported by, and in fact coincident with, that of the Father. The very same argument is used in chapter viii., but *the other side of it* presented to us. He *does* witness of himself, *because* his testimony is the testimony of the Father who *witnesseth in him.*

Received human testimony.	*Did not receive it.*
And ye also shall bear witness, because ye have been with me from the beginning. John xv. 27.	But I receive not testimony from man: but these things I say that ye might be saved. John v. 34.

"I receive not," etc.; that is, the "testimony" of which I have spoken is not derived from human sources. It is infinitely more authoritative and conclusive than man's witness would be. I need not human testimony for *myself;* I merely adduce it for your sakes, that "ye might be saved."

Mission.

Peace.	War.
The Prince of Peace. Of the increase of *his* government and peace *there shall be* no end. Isa. ix. 6. 7. Peace I leave with you, my peace I give unto you. John xiv. 27.	Think not that I am come to send peace on earth; I came not to send peace, but a sword. For I am come to set a man at variance against his father, and the daughter against her mother, and the daughter-in-law against her mother-in-law. And a man's foes *shall be* they of his own household. Matt. x. 34–36.

That is, the object of his mission was peace, but a result of it would, in many cases, be strife and war. Often, in securing a valuable end, we cannot avoid certain incidental evils. The object of the surgeon in amputating a diseased limb is the preservation of life, yet pain, as an incidental evil, follows the stroke of his scalpel.

[1] **Works, i. 679.**

DOCTRINAL DISCREPANCIES. 119

A religion of inherent, radical purity could not be promulgated in the world without awakening the fierce antagonism of everything impure and evil. Hence would arise strife and division, bitter conflicts, — as incidental evils, the grand, ultimate, unvarying object being, nevertheless, holiness and peace.

Extended to all men.	*To Israelites alone.*
I will also give thee for a light to the Gentiles, that thou mayest be my salvation unto the end of the earth. Isa. xlix. 6.	Go not into the way of the Gentiles,and into *any* city of the Samaritans enter ye not. But go rather to the lost sheep of the house of Israel. Matt. x. 5, 6.
Christ Jesus; who gave himself a ransom for all. 1 Tim. ii. 6.	I am not sent but unto the lost sheep of the house of Israel. Matt. xv. 24.

He made atonement, "tasted death," for every man, and the benefits of his mediation are, to a certain extent, enjoyed by all, but his *personal* mission was chiefly to the "house of Israel." And the first, but not the later, mission of the apostles was similarly restricted.

To the Samaritans.	*To Jews only.*
And sent messengers before his face; and they went and entered into a village of the Samaritans to make ready for him. Luke ix. 52.	He departed from Galilee, and came into the coasts of Judea, beyond Jordan. Matt. xix. 1.
And it came to pass as he went to Jerusalem, that he passed through the midst of Samaria and Galilee. Luke xvii. 11.	(The woman was a Greek, a Syrophenician by nation,) and she besought him that he would cast forth the devil out of her daughter. But Jesus said unto her, Let the children first be filled: for it is not meet to take the children's bread, and to cast *it* unto the dogs. Mark vii. 26, 27.
He left Judea, and departed again into Galilee. And he must needs go through Samaria. John iv. 3, 4.	
So when the Samaritans were come unto him they besought him that he would tarry with them: and he abode there two days. And many more believed because of his own word. John iv. 40, 41.	

"It is impossible," says Zeller,[1] to reconcile these different accounts." Now the truth is, that the infrequent exceptions alluded to in the first series of texts, only prove the general rule, that Christ's personal mission was to the Jews. The mere fact that, in journeying from Judea to Galilee, he passed through Samaria, which lay between the two, or that he wrought a miracle upon one Samaritan, and virtually commended another,[2] or that he actually tarried two whole days in Sychar, does not, in the slightest, militate against the certainty that *his personal ministry* was among the children of Israel.

[1] Strauss and Renan, p. 79. [2] Luke xvii. 16 and x. 83-87.

To fulfil the law.	To redeem from its curse.
Think not that I am come to destroy the law, or the prophets: I am not come to destroy, but to fulfil. Matt. v. 17.	Christ hath redeemed us from the curse of the law. Gal. iii. 13.

He came to carry out the *great end* of the law, to secure the righteousness of man. He "fulfilled," perfectly obeyed, the moral law, while in him, as the great Antitype, the types and figures of the ceremonial law culminated and were fulfilled. At the same time, he came to redeem, by his atonement, penitent sinners from the "curse," the penalty of the law.

To judge the world.	Not to judge.
For the Father judgeth no man; but hath committed all judgment unto the Son: and hath given him authority to execute judgment also. John v. 22, 27. Jesus said, For judgment I am come into this world, that they which see not might see; and that they which see might be made blind. John ix. 39.	For God sent not his Son into the world to condemn the world; but that the world through him might be saved. John iii. 17. Ye judge after the flesh; I judge no man. John viii. 15. And if any man hear my words, and believe not, I judge him not: for I came not to judge the world, but to save the world. John xii. 47.

The Greek word "krino" has the distinct, though associated, meanings, to *judge* merely, and to *condemn*. In some of the above passages it seems to be used in one sense, in others a different one is employed. Jesus came, in a sense, to "judge" the world, that is, to determine, by means of the gospel, the moral status, and consequent final destiny of men; yet his primary object was not to *condemn* men, though, in the process of judgment, the condemnation of some will be a certain, although incidental, result. "I judge no man," i.e. *after your manner*, or else, *during my present mission*. At his second coming he will in the ultimate and highest sense, "judge the world."

Miracles.

Proof of divine mission.	Not a proof.
And Israel saw that great work which the LORD did upon the Egyptians: and the people feared the LORD, and believed the LORD, and his servant Moses. Ex. xiv. 31. Art thou he that should come, or do we look for another? Jesus answered and said unto them, Go and shew John again those things which ye do hear and see: the blind receive their sight, and the lame walk, the	Then Pharaoh also called the wise men, and the sorcerers: now the magicians of Egypt, they also did in like manner with their enchantments: for they cast down every man his rod, and they became serpents. Ex. vii. 11, 12. And the magicians did so with their enchantments, and brought up frogs upon the land of Egypt. Ex. viii. 7. If there arise among you a prophet, or a dreamer of dreams, and giveth

Proof of divine mission.	*Not a proof.*
lepers are cleansed, and the deaf hear, the dead are raised up. Matt. xi. 3-5. Rabbi, we know that thou art a teacher come from God: for no man can do these miracles that thou doest, except God be with him. John iii. 2. The works which the Father hath given me to finish, the same works that I do, bear witness of me, that the Father hath sent me. John v. 36. God also bearing *them* witness, both with signs and wonders, and with divers miracles, and gifts of the Holy Ghost, according to his own will. Heb. ii. 4.	thee a sign or a wonder, and the sign or the wonder come to pass, whereof he spake unto thee, saying, Let us go after other gods which thou hast not known, and let us serve them; thou shalt not hearken unto the words of that prophet, or that dreamer of dreams: for the LORD your God proveth you, to know whether ye love the LORD your God with all your heart and with all your soul. Deut. xi i. 1-3. For there shall arise false Christs, and false prophets, and shall shew great signs and wonders; insomuch that, if *it were* possible, they shall deceive the very elect. Matt. xxiv. 24. And if I by Beelzebub cast out devils, by whom do your sons cast *them* out? therefore shall they be your judges. Luke xi. 19. *Even him,* whose coming is after the working of Satan, with all power and signs and lying wonders. 2 Thess. ii. 9. And he doeth great wonders, so that he maketh fire come down from heaven on the earth in the sight of men, and deceiveth them that dwell on the earth by *the means of* those miracles. Rev. xiii. 13, 14.

On this general subject, we may say that miracles are one, but not the only, proof of the divine mission of a religious teacher. His own character and claims, as well as the nature of his miracle, and of the doctrine he propounds, must be taken into the account. There are two or three preliminary questions which must be considered before we proceed further.

1. *What constitutes a miracle?* We give various answers. Dr. Charles Hodge:[1] "An event, occurring in the external world, which involves the suspension or counteracting of some natural law, and which can be referred to nothing but the immediate power of God." "After all," he says elsewhere, "the suspension or violation of the laws of nature involved in miracles is nothing more than is constantly taking place around us. One force counteracts another; vital force keeps the chemical laws of matter in abeyance; and muscular force can control the action of physical force. When a man raises a weight from the ground, the law of gravity is neither suspended

---

[1] Theology, Vol. ii. p. 75, and Vol. i. p. 621.

nor violated, but counteracted by a stronger force. The same is true as to the walking of Christ on the water, and the swimming of the iron at the command of the prophet."

Prof. Park:[1] "A miracle is a violation of the laws of matter and of finite mind in their established method of operating." Or, more specifically, "a phenomenon which occurs in violation of the laws of nature as they commonly operate, and which is designed to attest the divine authority of the messenger in whose behalf it occurs."

Archbishop Trench:[2] "An extraordinary divine causality belongs to the very essence of the miracle. ... Beside and beyond the ordinary operations of nature, higher powers, (higher, not as coming from a higher source, but as bearing upon higher ends,) intrude and make themselves felt even at the very springs and sources of her power."

Bleek[3] and Schleiermacher: "A miracle is an event only relatively supernatural; not absolutely violating the laws which God has established, but brought about by a hidden co-operation (rarely exercised in this manner) of other and higher laws than those which appear in ordinary phenomena."

2. *What is the legitimate force of a miracle?* John Foster has the remark that a miracle is the ringing of the great bell of the universe calling the multitudes to hear the sermon. Bishop Butler "Revelation itself is miraculous, and miracles are the proof of it. Pascal: "Miracles test doctrine, and doctrine tests miracles." Rothe: "Miracles and prophecies are not adjuncts appended from without to a revelation in itself independent of them, but constitutive elements of the revelation itself." Gerhard:[4] "The doctrine is the title-deed, and is *essential* to the significance of the seal attached to it. The miracle is the seal,

---

[1] MS. Lectures. See, also, Smith's Bib. Dict., Art. "Miracles," appendix by Professor Park.
[2] Notes on Miracles, p. 18.
[3] Introd. to New Test., i. 221.
[4] Smith's Bib. Dict., Vol. iii. pp. 1960—1968.

and is important for the authority of the title-deed. The seal torn away from the parchment cannot fulfil its main design, and the parchment with the seal cut out is lessened in value."

Dr. Hodge:[1] "When a man presents himself as a messenger of God, whether he is to be received as such or not depends, first, on the doctrines which he teaches, and, secondly, upon the works which he performs. If he not only teaches doctrines conformed to the nature of God and consistent with the laws of our own constitution, but also performs works which evince divine power, then we know not only that the doctrines are true, but also that the teacher is sent of God."

Dr. Thomas Arnold:[2] "You complain of those persons who judge of a revelation not by its evidence, but by its substance. It has always seemed to me that its substance is a most essential part of its evidence; and that miracles wrought in favor of what was foolish or wicked would only prove Manicheism. We are so perfectly ignorant of the unseen world, that the character of any supernatural power can only be judged of by the moral character of the statements which it sanctions: thus only can we tell whether it be a revelation from God or from the devil."

Trench:[3] "A miracle does not prove the truth of a doctrine, or the divine mission of him that brings it to pass. That which alone it claims for him, at the outset, is a right to be listened to; it puts him in the alternative of being from heaven, or from hell. The doctrine must first commend itself to the conscience as being *good*, and only then can the miracle seal it as *divine*. But the first appeal is from the doctrine to the conscience, to the moral nature in man."

John Locke:[4] "Though the common experience and the ordinary course of things have justly a mighty influence on the

---

[1] Theology, i. 636.
[2] Life, ii. 202 (Popular edition, Boston, 1871).
[3] On Miracles, p. 27.
[4] On Human Understanding, Book iv., chap. xvi. sect. 13.

minds of men, to make them give or refuse credit to anything proposed to their belief: yet there is one case wherein the strangeness of the fact lessens not the assent to a fair testimony given of it. For where such supernatural events are suitable to ends aimed at by him who has the power to change the course of nature, there, under such circumstances, they may be the fitter to procure belief, by how much the more they are beyond, or contrary to, ordinary observation. This is the proper case of *miracles*, which, well attested, do not only find credit themselves, but give it also to other truths, which need such confirmation."

Dr. Thomas Brown:[1] "A miracle is *not* a violation of any law of nature. It involves, therefore, primarily, no contradiction nor physical absurdity. It has nothing in it which is inconsistent with our belief of the most undeviating uniformity of nature; for it is not the sequence of a different event when the preceding circumstances have been the same; it is an effect that is new to our observation, because it is the result of new and peculiar circumstances. The antecedent has been, by supposition, different; and it is not wonderful, therefore, that the consequent should be different." "It is essential, indeed, for our belief of any miraculous event, that there should be the appearance of some gracious purpose, which the miracle may be supposed to fulfil; since all which we know of the operation of the divine power in the universe indicates some previous purpose of that kind."

We are now prepared to see the distinction between *true miracles* and other events which might be confounded with them. A genuine miracle tends to confirm the associated doctrine, and is in turn sanctioned by it, while both the doctrine and the miracle commend themselves to our reason as worthy of the Author of nature. It obviously follows that not every *strange feat* is to be regarded as a "miracle." The almost incredible performances of certain jugglers, *contemplating no*

---

[1] On Relation of Cause and Effect, pp. 224, 230.

great moral end, are not to be classed with "miracles," but are to be attributed to "sleight-of-hand," or to a knowledge of certain occult laws and forces of nature. The wonders wrought with *fire*,[1] in the Middle Ages, which men then regarded as miracles, we now see to have been mere tricks, utterly unworthy of the intervention of the Divine Being.

Again, it must be remembered that, as Trench[1] has clearly shown, Satan's kingdom has *its own* miracles, as well as the divine kingdom, and these really involve the intervention of spiritual and supernatural agencies coming from the realm of darkness. Not being "miracles," in the very highest sense of the word, they only partake in part of the essential elements of the miracle. They exhibit " not the omnipotence of God wielding his own world to ends of grace and wisdom and love, but evil permitted to intrude into the hidden springs of things, just so far as may suffice for its own deeper confusion in the end, and, in the meanwhile, for the needful trial and perfecting of God's saints and servants."

Alford: "Miracles, *as such*, are *no test of truth*, but have been permitted to, and prophesied of, false religions and teachers." For illustration of this statement, he refers to several of the texts quoted at the head of this article.

As to the feats of the magicians of Egypt, Bush, Dwight, and others think they were merely the tricks of skilful jugglers.[3] Many commentators, however, seem disposed to recognize the supernatural character of the feats ascribed to the magicians.

Keil: " With our very limited acquaintance with the dark domain of heathen conjuring, the possibility of their working 'lying wonders after the working of Satan,' i.e. supernatural things (2 Thess. ii. 9), cannot be absolutely denied." He adds,

---

[1] See Brewster's Letters on Natural Magic, Letter 12.
[2] Notes on Miracles, pp. 25–27.
[3] Compare Davidson's curt remarks on this point; Introd. to Old Test., i. pp. 221, 222.

"In the persons of the conjurers Pharaoh summoned the might of the gods of Egypt to oppose the might of Jehovah, the God of the Hebrews."

Trench: "Rather was this a conflict not merely between Egypt's king and the power of God; but the gods of Egypt, the spiritual powers of wickedness, which underlay, and were the soul of, that dark and evil kingdom, were in conflict with the God of Israel."

Hengstenberg:[1] "The object to which all of these occurrences were directed, according to chap. viii. 20, was to show that Jehovah is Lord in the midst of the land." This critic thinks that the author of the Pentateuch does not speak definitely upon the nature and origin of the results produced by the Egyptian magicians, and that there is nothing existing which can give us any information concerning his opinion.

As to Deut. xiii., we have seen that the miracle *per se, apart from* the message, is not conclusive proof of the divine mission of the thaumaturgist. In this specific case, if the miracle-worker should inculcate "idolatry," — *which had been most strictly and explicitly forbidden by Jehovah,* — this single circumstance was to be taken as absolute evidence that he was a false prophet and a deceiver. Hence, the "miracle" would, in such case, be simply the work of Satan, which God suffered to be wrought for the purpose of testing man's loyalty and fidelity to him.

The "great signs and wonders," in Matt. xxiv., if of a supernatural character, are like those we have just mentioned.

Luke xi. 19 was a home-thrust, an *argumentum ad hominem*. He said, in substance, "I cast out devils, as also your sons claim to do. Now, if, as you assume, the exorcist is in league with Satan, how is it with your own sons?"

As to 2 Thess. ii. 9, Trench says, "They are '*lying* wonders,' not because in themselves frauds and illusions, but because they are wrought to support the kingdom of lies." Or,

---

[1] Egypt and the Books of Moses, pp. 98, 104, 105.

as Alford says, they "have falsehood for their base and essence and aim."

Much the same may be said with reference to the text in Revelation, which Alford interprets as delineating one characteristic of the Papal church, the claim to work "miracles" of various kinds.

This topic may be dismissed with the single remark that, inasmuch as the *miracles* and the *doctrine* of our Saviour are, at the same time, *congruous with each other*, and *worthy of God*, the miracles may fairly be urged in corroboration of the divinity of his mission.

Modes of Representing Him.

Despised.
He is despised and rejected of men; a man of sorrows, and acquainted with grief: and we hid as it were *our* faces from him; he was despised, and we esteemed him not. Isa. liii. 3.

Honorable.
Unto you therefore which believe *he is* precious.[1] 1 Pet. ii. 7.

These two texts contemplate quite different classes of persons; the one those who, being spiritually enlightened, see the real character and glory of the Messiah; the other those who are still in the darkness and blindness of sin.

Uncomely.
As a root out of a dry ground: he hath no form nor comeliness; and when we shall see him *there is* no beauty that we should desire him. Isa. liii. 2.

Lovely.
My beloved *is* white and ruddy, the chiefest among ten thousand.... His mouth *is* most sweet: yea, he *is* altogether lovely. This *is* my beloved, and this *is* my friend. Cantic. v. 10, 16.

There is no proof that these last texts refer to the Messiah. If they do so, it only need be said that he is despised by some persons, and admired by others.

A lion.
Behold, the Lion of the tribe of Judah. Rev. v. 5.

A lamb.
And looking upon Jesus as he walked, he saith, Behold the Lamb of God! John i. 36.

In one aspect, he is termed a "lion" in another a "lamb." The term "lion" brings out the idea of his dominion, as well as that of his descent from the tribe of Judah;[2] the lamb was an emblem of innocence, and was usually offered in sacrifice.

---

[1] The original word properly means an *honor*.   [2] See Gen. xlix. 9.

High Priest.
We have such a high priest, who is set on the right hand of the throne of the Majesty in the heavens. Heb. viii. 1.

A sacrifice.
He appeared to put away sin by the sacrifice of himself. . . . Christ was once offered to bear the sins of many. Heb. ix. 26, 28.

In making the atonement, he voluntarily laid down his own life; he "*gave himself* a ransom for all"; he was the offerer and the offered, both priest and victim. On the term "high priest," Alford says, "the propitiatory, sacerdotal representative of men before God."

A vine.
I am the vine, ye *are* the branches: he that abideth in me, and I in him, the same bringeth forth much fruit: for without me ye can do nothing. John xv. 5.

A stone.
Jesus Christ himself being the chief corner-*stone*. Eph. ii. 20.
And a stone of stumbling, and a rock of offence, *even to them* which stumble at the word, being disobedient. 1 Pet. ii. 8.

The figure of the "vine" and "branches" sets forth the intimate, vital union of Christ and his people, together with their entire dependence upon him for spiritual nutriment and growth. Alford: "The inner unity of himself and his."

The term "stone" metaphorically presents Jesus as the "foundation" upon which his people build; also as the occasion of the "stumbling" and final overthrow of his enemies.

A shepherd.
I am the good shepherd: the good shepherd giveth his life for the sheep. John x. 11.
Our Lord Jesus, that great Shepherd of the sheep. Heb. xiii. 20.
The Shepherd and Bishop of your souls. 1 Pet. ii. 25.

A sheep.
He was led as a sheep to the slaughter; and like a lamb dumb before his shearer, so he opened not his mouth. Acts viii. 32.
Washed their robes, and made them white in the blood of the Lamb. Rev. vii. 14.

The first figure represents his tender, watchful care and oversight of his "little flock"; the second brings to view the meekness and innocence of his personal character, together with the fact that he, like a lamb, was offered as a sacrifice.

A Door.
I am the door: by me if any man enter in, he shall be saved, and shall go in and out and find pasture. John x. 9.

Bread.
I am the living bread which came down from heaven: if any man eat of this bread, he shall live for ever: and the bread that I will give is my flesh, which I will give for the life of the world. John vi. 51.

The first text points out the fact that Christ is the only medium of access to the Father; that in his name, by his aid, and through his atonement, we come to God. The second text implies that as material bread must be eaten, digested, and assimilated by us, for the maintenance of physical life, so Christ's spirit and teachings must be received into our hearts and incorporated in our lives, in order to our spiritual vitality.

The Light of the world.
That was the true Light, which lighteth every man that cometh into the world. John i. 9.
As long as I am in the world, I am the light of the world. John ix. 5

Men are lights.
Ye are the light of the world. Matt. v. 14.
He was a burning and a shining light. John v. 35.
Among whom ye shine as lights in the world. Phil. ii. 15.

In the primary and highest sense, Christ is the Light of the world; in a secondary and subordinate sense, Christians, viewed as receiving and reflecting his light, may be designated as the "light of the world."

The Foundation.
For other foundation can no man lay than that is laid, which is Jesus Christ. 1 Cor. iii. 11.

Men are foundations.
And are built upon the foundation of the apostles and prophets, Jesus Christ himself being the chief corner-*stone.* Eph. ii. 20.
The church of the living God, the pillar and ground of the truth. And without controversy, great is the mystery of godliness. 1 Tim. iii. 15, 16.

It is not clear that the quotation from Ephesians implies that the apostles and prophets were themselves the "foundation"; the meaning probably is, the foundation which pertained to them, — *their* foundation. Similarly, "sword of the Spirit"[1] means the Spirit's sword. Meyer, Ellicott, Stier, and others say, "the foundation which the apostles and prophets have laid." Alford and Bucer: "the apostles' and prophet's foundation — that upon which they as well as yourselves are built."

On the last quoted text, Ellicott says that "pillar" and "ground," designating the church, are "only simple, metaphorical expressions of the *stability* and *permanence* of the support," and adds, "were there no church, there would be no witness, no guardian of archives, no basis, nothing whereon acknowledged truth could rest." Chrysostom, Theodoret, Tholuck, Luther, Calvin, Beza, Grotius, De Wette, Huther, Alford, and Words-

[1] See Eph. vi. 17.

worth concur in this view, deeming the church "the element in which, and medium by which, the truth is conserved and upheld." But if we admit that, in this secondary sense, the church is the " ground " or basis of the truth, it must be remembered that *Christ* is, after all, the deep substructure, the foundation, of the church itself.

It should be added that Oosterzee, with a host of critics, punctuates the passage differently, thus : " The pillar and ground of the truth, and confessedly great, is the mystery of godliness," etc. With this translation the Syriac Peshito closely corresponds.

Sacrifice.

Died for friends.	*For enemies.*
I lay down my life for the sheep. John x. 15. Greater love hath no man than this, that a man lay down his life for his friends. John xv. 13.	While we were yet sinners, Christ died for us. . . . When we were enemies, we were reconciled to God by the death of his Son. Rom. v. 8. 10

He laid down his life for those who, though "enemies" for the time being, were prospectively "friends." This exhibition of his love broke down their enmity, and transformed their hostility into friendship.

The former passages refer to the prospective, the latter to the present, attitude toward him, of those for whom he died. On the first text from John, Alford says, " The Lord lays down his life strictly and properly, and in the depths of the divine counsel, *for those who are his sheep*." On the second text, " Our Lord does not assert of himself that he laid down his life *only* for his friends (as defined in the next verse), but puts forward *this side* of his love as a great and practical example for his followers."

Laid down his own life.	*Jews murdered him.*
I lay down my life, that I might take it again. No man taketh it from me, but I lay it down of myself. I have power to lay it down, and I have power to take it again. John x. 17, 18.	Him, being delivered by the determinate counsel and foreknowledge of God, ye have taken, and by wicked hands have crucified and slain Acts ii. 23. And killed the Prince of life. Acts iii. 15. The Just One; of whom ye have been now the betrayers and murderers. Acts vii. 52.

Both statements are true, and there is not the slightest discrepancy. The simple fact is, that Jesus, knowing perfectly the hatred, power, and purpose of the Jews, voluntarily surrendered himself into their hands; whereupon they "with malice aforethought and prepense," took his life. He laid down his own life, and they killed him.

Intercession.

The only Mediator.
One mediator between God and men, the man Christ Jesus. 1 Tim. ii. 5.

Holy Spirit intercedes.
Likewise the Spirit also helpeth our infirmities: for we know not what we should pray for as we ought: but the Spirit itself maketh intercession for us, with groanings which cannot be uttered. Rom. viii. 26.

The last text when properly translated, does not assert that the Holy Spirit actually intercedes for Christians, but simply intervenes for their aid.

Barnes: "It simply means that the Holy Spirit greatly *aids* or *assists;* not by praying for us, but in our prayers and infirmities." Stuart: Prayer or supplication made by the Spirit is not here intended. The Spirit "maketh intercession" by exciting in Christians such longings for conformity to God, deliverance from evil, and the enjoyment of future blessedness as no language can adequately express.

Alford: "No *intercession in heaven* is here spoken of, but *a pleading in us* by the indwelling Spirit, of a nature above our comprehension and utterance."

Intercedes not for the world.
I pray for them: I pray not for the world, but for them which thou hast given me; for they are thine. John xvii. 9.

Does intercede for it.
If any man sin, we have an advocate with the Father, Jesus Christ the righteous. 1 John ii. 1.

As the connection evinces, the first text is equivalent to, "I am not now, *at this time*, praying for the world." The prayer in the 17th of John was offered specially for the disciples. This fact, however, furnishes no proof that Jesus does not, at present, intercede for all mankind.

Coming.

In humble guise.
Behold thy King cometh unto thee: he *is* just, and having salvation; lowly, and riding upon an ass, and upon a colt the foal of an ass. Zech. ix. 9.

With regal state.
Behold, *one* like the Son of man came with the clouds of heaven, and came to the Ancient of days, and they brought him near before him. And there was given him dominion, and glory, and a kingdom. Dan. vii. 13, 14.

These passages refer to entirely different events. The first was fulfilled when our Saviour rode into Jerusalem upon the ass; the second will be fulfilled when he shall come again, "in the clouds of heaven, with power and great glory."[1]

Succeeds overthrow of Jerusalem.	Times of Gentiles intervene.
For then shall be great tribulation. ... Immediately after the tribulation of those days, shall the sun be darkened. ... And then shall appear the sign of the Son of man in heaven. Matt. xxiv. 21, 29, 30.	Jerusalem shall be trodden down of the Gentiles, until the times of the Gentiles be fulfilled. ... And then shall they see the Son of man coming in a cloud, with power and great glory. Luke xxi. 24, 27.

This is one of Zeller's objections. He claims that the two accounts are incompatible because one seems to represent the coming of Christ as following, without any interval, the "tribulation"; the other, the two events as separated by the "times of the Gentiles."

The difference, however, is easily accounted for upon the hypothesis that Matthew employs here what we may term "prophetic perspective," while Luke is writing somewhat circumstantially and minutely. By this "perspective," which has a beautiful analogy in a familiar, philosophical experiment, a comparatively small event close to the speaker, appears of equal magnitude with a momentous but remote event, so that the latter seems hidden by the former, or continuous with it. As the observer looks down the vista of the ages, the small covers the large event, and the two seem but one.

On this point, Dr. Davidson[2] says, "Intervening periods were mostly concealed from the sight of the seer." Bleek[3] says that in respect to *time*, "the prophecies are usually so framed that they have a *perspective* character, great developments and catastrophes, occurring at considerable intervals of time, appearing to be brought close together, or to be quite intermixed."

Lange:[4] "According to the *perspective* view of the future, the successive critical events that lie behind each other, are brought near, so that the great *epochs* rise into light like the

---

[1] Compare Matt. xxi. 1–11 and xxiv. 30.
[2] Introd. to Old Test., ii. 481
[3] Introd. to Old Test., ii. 32.
[4] Com. on Matt., p. 430.

tops of mountains, while their times of unfolding, the *periods*, are concealed behind them, or are manifest only in less prominent signs."

Wordsworth : Our Lord's prophecy has a double reference, — to the judgment of Jerusalem, and to that of which *this* judgment was a type, viz. his second coming to judge the world."

Alford maintains that the destruction of Jerusalem and the final judgment are both enwrapped in the words; the former being prominent in the first part of the chapter, while, from verse 28, the lesser subject begins to be swallowed up in the greater, and our Lord's second coming to be the predominant theme.

The word "immediately," verse 29, being supposed to imply the closest consecution, is the only term involving any difficulty. Hammond and Schott render the Greek term *suddenly*, i.e. *unexpectedly*. Glass says it is to be taken, not according to our reckoning, but the divine, in which a thousand days are as one day. Lange : " Describes the nature of the final catastrophe, that it will be at once swift, surpassingly sudden, and following upon a development seemingly slow and gradual. Thus, throughout the whole course of history, the swift epochs follow the slow process of the periods." Owen : " May be taken in the general sense, *very soon after*, referring to the comparative brevity of these intervening centuries or ages, when viewed in relation to the ages of eternity, which are to follow the day of judgment, and in reference to which all time is but as a moment's duration." Alford very satisfactorily says : " All the difficulty which this word has been supposed to involve has arisen from confounding the *partial* fulfilment of the prophecy with the *ultimate* one. The important insertion in Luke [1] shows us that the '*tribulation*' includes '*wrath upon this people*,' which is yet being inflicted; and the treading down of Jerusalem by the Gentiles still going on; and immediately after *that tribulation* which shall happen *when the cup of Gentile iniquity*

[1] Chap. xxi. 23, 24.

is full, and *when the Gospel shall have been preached in all the world* for a witness, and *rejected by the Gentiles*, shall the coming of the Lord himself happen."

His coming at hand.	*It was far off.*
We shall not all sleep, but we shall all be changed, in a moment, in the twinkling of an eye, at the last trump. 1 Cor. xv. 51, 52.	That ye be not soon shaken in mind, or be troubled, neither by spirit, nor by word, nor by letter as from us, as that the day of Christ is at hand. Let no man deceive you by any means. 2 Thess. ii. 2, 3.
The Lord *is* at hand. Phil. iv. 5.	
We which are alive *and* remain unto the coming of the Lord shall not prevent them which are asleep. 1 Thess. iv. 15.	
But the end of all things is at hand. 1 Pet. iv. 7.	

Even De Wette[1] says, "It is no contradiction of the first Epistle that Paul after exhorting them to steadfastly await the second coming of Christ (1 Thess. iv. 15), felt himself bound to moderate their too excited expectations; and 2 Thess. ii. 1, etc., is completely in the spirit of primitive Christianity." Similarly, Dr. Davidson,[2] on 1 Cor. xv. 52: "The expression *we* means such Christians as shall then be alive; all believers then living are grouped together."

On 1 Thess. iv. 15, 17, he says, "Hence ' we which are alive and remain,' etc., can only mean ' such Christians as live and remain.' Paul employs himself and the early Christians as the representatives of those succeeding Christians who should be alive at the Redeemer's second advent. Thus in Deut. xxx. 1, the generation addressed is the representative of a succeeding one; and in John vi. 32, a succeeding generation is employed to represent a past one."

Andrew Fuller:[3] "Everything with respect to degrees is what it is by comparison. Taking into consideration the whole of time, the coming of Christ was ' at hand.' There is reason to believe from this, and many other passages of the New Testament, that the sacred writers considered themselves as having passed the meridian of time, and entered into the afternoon of the world, as we may say. Such appears to be the

---

[1] Introd. to New Test., p. 247.   [2] Introd. to New Test., ii. 458, 465–66.
[3] Works, i. 682.

import of the following among other passages, 'God hath *in these last days* spoken,' etc. ... But taking into consideration only a single generation, the day of Christ was not at hand. The Thessalonians, though a very amiable people, were by some means mistaken on this subject, so as to expect that the end of the world would take place in their lifetime, or within a very few years. To correct this error, which might have been productive of very serious evils, was a principal design of the second Epistle to that people."

It is thus clear that this " discrepancy " of which Baur makes so much, really amounts to nothing.

Before missionary journey completed.	*Not till the world evangelized.*
But when they persecute you in this city, flee ye into another: for verily I say unto you, Ye shall not have gone over the cities of Israel, till the Son of man be come. Matt. x. 23.	And this gospel of the kingdom shall be preached in all the world, for a witness unto all nations; and then shall the end come. Matt xxiv 14. And the gospel must first be published among all nations. Mark xiii. 10.

Strauss[1] works hard to make out a contradiction here. He remarks: " On one occasion Jesus says to his disciples that the Son of man will return before they shall have completed their Messianic preaching in all the cities of Israel; another time he says that the second advent will not occur until the Gospel has been preached in the whole world among all peoples." The difficulty is obviated by the following interpretations, any one of which may be adopted.

Barnes, on Matt. x. 23: " That is, in fleeing from persecutors, from one city to another, you shall not have gone to every city in Judea, till the destruction of Jerusalem, and the end of the Jewish economy."

Wordsworth: " In a primary sense, you will not have completed your missionary work in Judea before I come to judge *Jerusalem*. In a secondary and larger sense, — the missionary work of the church for the *spiritual Israel* will not cease till the second coming of Christ. There is a successive series of 'comings of Christ,' all preparatory to, and consummated in, the great coming."

[1] See New Life of Jesus, i. 325.

Alford maintains that our Lord's prophecies respecting his coming have an *immediate, literal* and a *distant, foreshadowed fulfilment.* Hence he regards "the vengeance on Jerusalem, which historically put an end to the old dispensation, and was, in its place with reference to that order of things, the coming of the Son of man, as a type of the final coming of the Lord." He calls attention to the "wide import of scripture prophecy, which speaks very generally, not so much of *events themselves, points of time,* as of *processions* of events, all ranging under one great description," and adds, "It is important to keep in mind the *great, prophetic parallels* which run through our Lord's discourses, and are sometimes separately, sometimes simultaneously, presented to us by him."

On "Till the Son of man be come," Baumgarten-Crusius says, "Until the victory of the cause of Christ"; Michaelis, "To the destruction of Jerusalem"; Calvin, "To the outpouring of the Holy Spirit;" Norton, "That is, before my religion is established and its truth fully confirmed"; Heubner and Lange, "Till the Son of man shall overtake you," adding, "It points forward to the second coming of Christ; including at the same time the idea that their apostolic labors in Judea would be cut short." Lightfoot: "Ye shall not have travelled over the cities of Israel, preaching the gospel, before the Son of man is revealed by his resurrection."

These interpretations, almost any of which may be adopted without an arbitrary exegesis, serve to show how slight is the foundation for the objection urged by Strauss.

Kingdom.

Not of this world.	Within the Pharisees.
When Jesus therefore perceived that they would come and take him by force, to make him a king, he departed again into a mountain himself alone. John vi. 15. Jesus answered, My kingdom is not of this world: if my kingdom were of this world, then would my servants fight. John xviii. 36.	And when he was demanded of the Pharisees, when the kingdom of God should come, he answered them and said, The kingdom of God cometh not with observation. Neither shall they say, Lo here! or, Lo there! for behold, the kingdom of God is within you. Luke xvii. 20, 21.

Ancient interpreters take the expression "within you," as

pointing out the fact that the kingdom is an inward, spiritual one, having its seat in the heart. Modern critics say that the kingdom had already been set up *among* the Pharisees by John the Baptist and the Messiah, the former introducing it, the latter embodying and representing it. Schoettgen: "It does not imply, in your hearts, but in your land and region." Alford: "The kingdom of God was *begun among them*, and continues thus making its way in the world, without observation of men."

It has no end.	*Will terminate.*
And there was given him dominion, and glory, and a kingdom, that all people, nations, and languages should serve him; his dominion *is* an everlasting dominion, which shall not pass away, and his kingdom *that* which shall not be destroyed. Dan. vii. 14.	Then *cometh* the end, when he shall have delivered up the kingdom to God, even the Father; when he shall have put down all rule, and all authority and power. For he must reign till he hath put all enemies under his feet. . . . And when all things shall be subdued unto him, then shall the Son also himself be subject unto him that put all things under him, that God may be all in all. 1 Cor. xv. 24, 25, 28.
And he shall reign over the house of Jacob for ever: and of his kingdom there shall be no end. Luke i. 33.	
But unto the Son *he saith,* Thy throne, O God, *is* for ever and ever. Heb. i. 8.	

Neander: "Inasmuch as the work of Christ, founded upon his redemptive acts, proceeds toward a definite goal, it must needs come to a termination when this goal is reached." Dr. Hodge: "When he has subdued all his enemies, then he will no longer reign over the universe as Mediator, but only as God, while his headship over his people is to continue forever."

Dr. Davidson[1] holds that Christ's kingdom has two departments or branches, — one relating to his saints, the other to his enemies. When the purposes of the latter department are fulfilled, he will deliver it up to the Father; the former he will retain forever.

Andrew Fuller;[2] "The end of which Paul speaks does not mean the end of Christ's kingdom, but of the world, and the things thereof. The 'delivering up of the kingdom to the Father' will not put an end to it, but eternally establish it in a new and more glorious form. Christ shall not cease to reign, though the mode of his administration be different."

Alford; "The kingdom of Christ over this world, in its

---

[1] Sacred Hermeneutics, p. 571.   [2] Works, i. 678.

beginning, its furtherance, and its completion, has one great end, — *the glorification of the Father by the Son.* Therefore, when it shall be fully established, every enemy overcome, everything subjected to him, he will, — not reign over it and abide its king, but deliver it up to the Father."

Even on this interpretation, the kingdom of the Son will continue. For it is clear that the subjects, laws, and policy of that kingdom will remain unchanged; only the dominion of Christ will " be absorbed in the all-pervading majesty of him for whose glory it was from first to last carried onward." Bengel tersely and admirably expresses the truth, " *omnia erunt subordinata Filio, Filius Patri* " ; All things will be subordinate to the Son, the Son to the Father.

Name.

He bears the Divine Name.	A city bears it.
In his days Judah shall be saved, and Israel shall dwell safely: and this *is* his name whereby he shall be called, The LORD our Righteousness. Jer. xxiii. 6.	In those days shall Judah be saved, and Jerusalem shall dwell safely: and this *is the name* wherewith she shall be called, The LORD our Righteousness. Jer. xxxiii. 16.

Naegelsbach, in Lange, maintains that the word " he," in the expression, " this is his name whereby he shall be called," can refer only to Jerusalem. " Jehovah our Righteousness " is not, then, the name of the scion of David, but of the nation, — the idea being that Israel will be a nation, that will have no other righteousness than Jehovah's. If neither text refers to the Messiah, there is, of course, no discrepancy. Even if otherwise, we see nothing improbable in the supposition that the redeemed nation should be called after the name of its Redeemer and King.

NOTE. — The foregoing are — not indeed *all* the cases adduced by infidel writers, — but all which seem worthy of notice, and to come properly under this head. A considerable number of apparent contradictions pertaining to various events in the life of Christ, are referable to the " historical " department, and will be discussed in a subsequent part of this volume.

III. HOLY SPIRIT.—*Personality.*

He is an Intelligence.

Whosoever speaketh against the Holy Ghost, it shall not be forgiven him, neither in this world, neither in the *world* to come. Matt. xii. 32.

But the Comforter, *which is* the Holy Ghost, whom the Father will send in my name, he shall teach you all things, and bring all things to your remembrance, whatsoever I have said unto you. John xiv. 26.

When he the Spirit of truth is come, he will guide you into all truth: for he shall not speak of himself; but whatsoever he shall hear, *that* shall he speak: and he will show you things to come. He shall glorify me: for he shall receive of mine, and shall show *it* unto you. John xvi. 13, 14.

Then the Spirit said unto Philip, Go near and join thyself to this chariot. Acts viii. 29.

The Spirit of the Lord caught away Philip, that the eunuch saw him no more. Acts viii. 39.

The Holy Ghost said, Separate me Barnabas and Saul for the work whereunto I have called them. Acts xiii. 2.

For it seemed good to the Holy Ghost, and to us, to lay upon you no greater burden. Acts xv. 28.

They assayed to go into Bithynia, but the Spirit suffered them not. Acts xvi. 7.

The flock over the which the Holy Ghost hath made you overseers. Acts xx. 28.

Well spake the Holy Ghost by Esaias the prophet unto our fathers. Acts xxviii. 25

And he that searcheth the hearts knoweth what *is* the mind of the Spirit, because he maketh intercession for the saints, according to *the will of* God. Rom. viii. 27.

The Spirit searcheth all things, yea, the deep things of God. For what man knoweth the things of a man, save the spirit of man which is in him? Even so the things of God knoweth no man, but the Spirit of God. 1 Cor. ii. 10, 11.

For to one is given by the Spirit the word of wisdom; to another the word of knowledge by the same Spirit.... But all these worketh that one and the self-same Spirit, dividing, to every man severally as he will. 1 Cor. xii. 8, 11.

And grieve not the holy Spirit of God. Eph. iv. 30.

It is an Influence.

The Spirit of God moved upon the face of the waters. Gen. i. 2.

Mine elect, *in whom* my soul delighteth; I have put my Spirit upon him. Isa. xlii. 1.

I send the promise of my Father upon you; but tarry ye in the city of Jerusalem, until ye be endued with power from on high. Luke xxiv. 49.

God giveth not the Spirit by measure *unto him.* John iii. 34.

Ye shall be baptized with the Holy Ghost not many days hence. Acts i. 5.

Saith God, I will pour out of my Spirit upon all flesh.... And on my servants and on my hand-maidens, I will pour out in those days of my Spirit. Acts ii. 17, 18.

Peter, filled with the Holy Ghost, said unto them. Acts iv. 8.

God anointed Jesus of Nazareth with the Holy Ghost and with power.... The Holy Ghost fell on all them which heard the word. Acts x. 38, 44.

Quench not the Spirit. 1 Thess. v. 19.

It is obvious that one or the other of these two series of texts must be interpreted figuratively. When we take into consideration the numerical preponderance, as well as the evident literalness and verisimilitude, of the former class of texts, we are led to conclude that they are to be taken according to their natural and obvious import, while those of the latter class must be interpreted tropically.

There are two theories respecting the Holy Spirit; one, that he is a distinction in the Trinity, co-equal, co-essential, co-eternal with the Father and Son; the other, that it is "simply the divine influence, sometimes in creation, and in outward events, but in the great majority of instances, on the soul of man."[1] Between these two theories, we discover no tenable middle ground. Unquestionably the first theory affords a better basis for the explanation of both the foregoing classes of texts, than the second can be made to furnish by any exegetical ingenuity. Some orthodox critics, however, think that in certain cases, the term "spirit of God" is a synonyme for the "power of God;" or that the *name* is put by metonymy for the *effect* of the Spirit.

Clearly, several texts of the second series must, upon any theory of interpretation, be regarded as figurative. The expressions "baptized with," "pouring out," etc., merely indicate that the Holy Spirit would be bestowed in great fulness. It should be carefully noted that this figurative "baptism" took place on the day of Pentecost, when the disciples were "filled with the Holy Ghost."[2] And the fact that they were thus "filled" is not in the least repugnant to the idea that the Holy Spirit is an Intelligence; for Satan is unquestionably represented in the scriptures as a personal being, yet we are told that he "entered into" Judas and "filled the heart" of Ananias.[3] Unless we deny all supra-mundane agencies and influences, we must admit that one intelligence may enter into, possess, and fill another.

The metaphorical nature of the words "anointed with the Holy Ghost and with power," is beyond question, even on the hypothesis that the Holy Ghost is a mere influence. For the

---

[1] Professor Peabody, Lectures on Christian Doctrine, p. 116.
[2] Compare Acts i. 5 with ii. 4. [3] See Luke xxii. 3; Acts v. 3.

idea of a literal "anointing" with an influence or with power is an absurdity. What, then, is the meaning of the metaphor? It appears that, among the Jews, a prophet, priest, or king was "anointed" when he was set apart for, or inducted into, his office. This ceremony, "according to the Hebrew symbology, denoted his receiving the spiritual gifts and endowments which he needed for the performance of his duties."

The "anointing" spoken of, means, says Prof. Hackett, that Christ "possessed the gifts of the Spirit without measure, was furnished in a perfect manner for the work which he came into the world to execute."

In the quotation from 1 Thess., the Holy Spirit is, on account of his purifying and illuminating power, figuratively spoken of as fire. The word "quench" simply keeps up the figure. This representation, however, no more disproves the personality of the Holy Spirit, than does the fact that God is termed a "consuming fire," militate against his personality. Both expressions are figures setting forth certain aspects of the truth.

The methods of interpretation adopted by those who do not admit the personality of the Holy Spirit, are exemplified as follows. Prof. Peabody,[1] on Rom. viii. 26, 27, says, "I do not think that the Spirit of God is referred to in this passage. It is the spirit or soul of *man*, of the *Christian*, that is here spoken of ... for the souls of the righteous intercede for them according to the divine will." With what propriety a man's own soul or spirit could be said to "intercede" for him, the reader must judge.

Divinity.

He is God.	He is subordinate.
Peter said, Ananias, why hath Satan filled thine heart to lie to the Holy Ghost, ... thou hast not lied unto men, but unto God. Acts v. 3, 4.	I will pray the Father, and he shall give you another Comforter. John xiv. 16. When the Comforter is come, whom I will send unto you from the Father, *even* the Spirit of truth which proceedeth from the Father. John xv. 26.

The latter texts refer to an official, but not an essential, sub-

---

[1] Lectures on Christian Doctrine, p. 114.

ordination. It may be inferred from them that there is a fitness in the Holy Spirit's undertaking the function indicated, but not that he is not truly and properly divine. Dr. Hodge[1] terms the Spirit "the executive of the Godhead," and says, "he is subordinate to the Father and Son, as to his mode of subsistence and operation, as he is said to be of the Father and of the Son; he is sent by them, and they operate through him."

While, therefore, his subordination as to office is plainly taught, there is no proof of his inferiority in respect to substance or essence.

Fruits.[2]

Love and Gentleness.	*Vengeance and Fury.*
But the fruit of the Spirit is love, joy, peace, long-suffering, gentleness, goodness, faith, meekness, temperance. Gal. v. 22, 23.	The Philistines shouted against him: and the Spirit of the LORD came mightily upon him, and the cords that *were* upon his arms became as flax that was burnt with fire, and his bands loosed from off his hands. And he found a new jaw-bone of an ass, and put forth his hand, and took it, and slew a thousand men therewith. Judges xv. 14, 15. The evil spirit from God came upon Saul. ... And *there was* a javelin in Saul's hand. And Saul cast the javelin; for he said, I will smite David, even to the wall *with it*. 1 Sam. xviii. 10, 11.

The sense of the quotation from Judges is, that Samson, in this hour of extreme peril, received divine aid so that he broke his bonds, and sucessfully defended himself. The words, "the spirit of the Lord came upon him," imply, says Bush, "a supernatural influence raising the bodily or mental powers to an unwonted pitch of energy," and thus "enabling him to perform achievements to which his unassisted powers would be entirely unequal." It cannot be proved that the Holy Spirit is intended in this passage.

In 1 Sam. xviii. 10, the *article* is not found in the Hebrew, so that the proper rendering is "*an* evil spirit from God." It is said to be "from God," says Keil,[3] "because Jehovah had sent it as a punishment."

---

[1] Theology, i. 529.
[2] On Bestowment of Holy Spirit, see Historical Discrepancies, "Time."
[3] On 1 Sam. xvi. 14.

This passage brings to view God's sovereignty and absolute control in the spiritual as well as in the material world. Not even "evil spirits" go forth without his permission, to exert their influence upon the wicked. And he has a punitive purpose in granting this permission. He uses evil to chastise evil.

IV. THE SCRIPTURES.—Inspiration.

All Scripture inspired.	Some not so.
All scripture *is* given by inspiration of God, and *is* profitable. 2 Tim iii. 16.	But I speak this by permission, *and* not of commandment. . . . But to the rest speak I, not the Lord. 1 Cor. vii. 6, 12. That which I speak, I speak *it* not after the Lord, but as it were foolishly, in this confidence of boasting. 2 Cor. xi. 17.

Many commentators, Origen, Theodoret, Erasmus, Luther, Grotius, Tyndale, Cranmer, Hammond, Adam Clarke, Huther, Ellicott, and Alford, agree substantially with the Syriac Peshito in rendering the first text thus: "Every scripture inspired by God is also profitable." The theory involved in this version is sufficiently elastic to allow Paul, while writing under the guidance of inspiration, to occasionally introduce, upon unimportant points, his own uninspired opinion, — that opinion being in harmony with the general scope and design of the book.

If, however, with Chrysostom, Gregory of Nyssa, Calvin, Wolf, Bengel, Owen, De Wette, Olshausen, Barnes, Conybeare, Oosterzee, Wordsworth, Dr. Hodge apparently, and others, we read: "Is given by inspiration of God, and is profitable," the texts at the right still admit of a facile interpretation. The first of these quotations means, according to Alford and Conybeare, "I am not now speaking by way of command, but merely expressing my permission." If we adopt this very natural interpretation, the passage does not touch the question of inspiration.

The meaning of the 12th verse may, perhaps, be thus expressed: "But to the rest speak I," that is, I Paul in my apostolic office, speaking, not now from special revelation, but under the general supervision of the Holy Spirit. "Not the

Lord," that is, not Christ by any direct command spoken by him, since the question was one with which he *did not deal* in his recorded discourses. Hence, in this case, — as in the language of the 25th verse, " I have no commandment of the Lord, yet I give my judgment," — Paul was permitted to express his own judgment as to the case under consideration, giving us, at the same time, suitable notice that he is speaking in his own proper person. Yet there is no reason to doubt that the " judgment" he thus expressed, was in complete harmony with "the mind of the Spirit."

Dr. Arnold,[1] referring to a text of similar import, the 40th verse of the same chapter, deems it a token of God's " especial mercy to us, that our faith in St Paul's general declarations of divine truth might not be shaken, because in one particular point he was permitted to speak as a man, giving express notice at the time that he was doing so."

" I speak it not after the Lord," 2 Cor. xi., probably means " not after the *example* of the Lord.'' That is, I am constrained to an *apparent* departure from that example. In vindication of myself from the unjust aspersions of my enemies, I am compelled to speak with seeming boastfulness, — as it were " foolishly." This " glorying after the flesh " was not, however, *really* contrary to our Lord's example, because it originated, not in love of boasting, but in the necessities of the case.

We thus see that the above texts may be reconciled upon the basis of an intelligent and comprehensive theory of Inspiration.

Moral Purity.

Purity enjoined.   *Impure ideas suggested.*

It must be conceded by all candid persons that the general tenor of the Bible is decidedly in favor of purity. Yet, it is objected that certain passages, particularly in the earlier books and in Canticles, are calculated to excite impure thoughts and feelings.

To this we reply, 1. Many of the expressions which are

---

[1] Miscellaneous Works, p. 287 (Appleton's edition).

deemed objectionable, are found *in the Mosaic Law*. Every intelligent person is aware that law-books must be very specific and explicit in their phraseology. An examination of any compilation of statutes, or of any standard work on medical jurisprudence, will be conclusive on this point. It is not surprising, then, that the Jewish code of laws contains some expressions that seem coarse. Without great minuteness and perspicuity these statutes would have failed to answer the designed end.

2. We must bear in mind the great freedom of Oriental speech and manners. In the impassioned style of thought and expression prevalent in the East, there is a license, a warmth, a voluptuousness even, which would shock the fastidious ears of Occidentals. Ideas and objects of which they of the Orient would speak with the utmost freedom, we should indicate, if at all, by euphemism and circumlocution. The Bible was written by Eastern authors, and bears traces of its origin among a people whose customs and habits of thought were widely different from ours. Upon this radical divergence are founded many of the so-called "indelicate" expressions of scripture — expressions which would strike an Oriental ear as perfectly chaste and proper. Prof. Stuart,[1] speaking of certain expressions in Canticles, observes, "It is clear that no indecency is intended, and equally clear, as it seems to me, that no improper feelings were excited, by the language in question, in the minds of those who were originally addressed." He also calls attention to the fact that women are excluded, in the East, from public association with men, being kept in seclusion. Hence greater freedom of speech was allowable than in our mixed society. Besides, as Prof. Cowles[2] suggests, the *mode of dress* in the East being different from ours, certain parts of the body are there exposed which would not be among us. Rev. W. M. Thomson[3] says: "While the face is veiled, the bosom is exposed in a way not at all in accordance with our ideas of propriety."

---

[1] Hist. of Old Test. Canon, pp. 377, 378 (Revised edition, p. 353).
[2] Introd. to Com. on Canticles.   [3] Land and Book, i. 174.

An Oriental would, as appears, deem it no more indelicate to praise the breasts, than the hair or eyes or hands of a female.

3. Many expressions which are said to offend the taste are due to the baldness and other infelicities of the English version. The Hebrew is far less objectionable on this score. Prof. Stuart[1] observes: "The perusal of the original makes much less impression on me of an exceptionable kind than the perusal of our version. It is far more delicate, at least to my apprehension. It were easy to exhibit particulars which would justify this statement."

Isaac Taylor:[2] "If a half-dozen heedlessly rendered passages of our English version were amended, as easily they might be, then the Canticle would well consist, throughout, with the purest utterances of conjugal fondness."

Prof. W. H. Green[3] says: "There is not the slightest taint of impurity or immodesty to be found in any portion of this elegant lyric." And we think that no one who carefully reads the elegant translations of Zöckler, Withington, Cowles, or Ginsburg, will dissent from this opinion.

Predictions.

Privately interpreted.	*Not privately interpreted.*
And as he sat upon the mount of Olives, the disciples came unto him privately, saying, Tell us, when shall these things be? and what *shall be* the sign of thy coming, and of the end of the world? Matt. xxiv. 3.	Knowing this first, that no prophecy of the scripture is of any private interpretation: for the prophecy came not in old time by the will of man: but holy men of God spake *as they were* moved by the Holy Ghost. 2 Pet. i. 20, 21.

The Greek corresponding to "of any private interpretation" is confessedly obscure. The word "epilusis" occurs in no other passage of the New Testament. Hence the difficulty in determining its precise signification here. That, however, it has any reference to attempts to explain the scriptures in private, is maintained by no scholar.

We subjoin various renderings of this passage. The Syriac Peshito: "No prophecy is an exposition of its own text."

---

[1] Hist. of Old Test. Canon, p. 382 (Revised edition, p. 357).
[2] Spirit of Hebrew Poetry, pp. 184, 185 (London edition).
[3] Translation of Zöckler, in Lange, p. 102, note.

Bishop Horsley: "Not any prophecy of scripture is of self-interpretation, or is its own interpreter; because the scripture prophecies are not detached predictions of separate, independent events, but are united in a regular and entire system, all terminating in one grand object — the promulgation of the gospel and the complete establishment of the Messiah's kingdom."

Dr. John Owen: "Not an issue of men's fancied enthusiasms, not a product of their own minds and conceptions, not an interpretation of the will of God by the understanding of man, that is, of the prophets themselves."

Dr. Adam Clarke: "'Of any private interpretation' — proceeds from the prophet's own *knowledge* or *invention*, or was the offspring of *calculation* or *conjecture*. Far from inventing the subject of their own predictions, the ancient prophets did not even know the meaning of what they themselves wrote."

Archbishop Whately: "Prophecy is *not to be its own interpreter*, that is, is not to have its full sense made out (like that of any other kind of composition) by the study of the very words of each prophecy itself, but it is to be interpreted by the event that fulfils it."

Dr. Edward Robinson: "'No prophecy of scripture cometh of private interpretation,' i.e. is not an interpretation of the will of God by the prophets themselves."

Dr. Samuel Davidson: "No prophecy admits of a solution *proper to its utterer*."

Dr. Charles Hodge: "What a prophet said was not human, but divine. It was not the prophet's own interpretation of the mind and will of God. He spoke as the organ of the Holy Ghost."

Alford, Tholuck, De Wette, and Huther: "'Prophecy springs not out of human interpretation,' i.e. is not a prognostication made by a man knowing what he means when he utters it."

Upon any reasonable interpretation, the passage no more precludes explanations of prophecy given in private than those made in public.

Prophecy sure.	*Not always fulfilled.*
And if thou say in thy heart, How shall we know the word which the LORD hath not spoken? When a prophet speaketh in the name of the LORD, if the the thing follow not, nor come to pass, that *is* the thing which the LORD hath not spoken, *but* the prophet hath spoken it presumptuously: thou shalt not be afraid of him. Deut. xviii. 21, 22. We have also a more sure word of prophecy: whereunto ye do well that ye take heed, as unto a light that shineth in a dark place. 2 Pet. i. 19.	And Jonah began to enter into the city a day's journey, and he cried, and said, Yet forty days, and Nineveh shall be overthrown. So the people of Nineveh believed God, and proclaimed a fast, and put on sackcloth, from the greatest of them even to the least of them.... And God saw their works, that they turned from their evil way; and God repented of the evil that he had said that he would do unto them; and he did *it* not. Jonah iii 4, 5, 10.

A passage previously cited (Jer. xviii. 7–10)[1] has a bearing upon this point. That passage, however, refers to promises and threatenings, which are, of course, conditional. The text from Deuteronomy seems, on the contrary, to refer to absolute predictions, which are in no way contingent upon human conduct.

Peter terms prophecy "more sure" than the mere "voice" which the apostles heard in the mount, as "being of wider and larger reference, and as presenting a broader basis for the Christian's trust, and not only one fact, however important."

As to the threat uttered by Jonah, it turned upon a condition, either expressed or implied. As Henderson observes, "However absolute the right of God to deal with mankind agreeably to his own good pleasure, his conduct is always in strict accordance with the manner in which they behave toward him. Neither his promises nor his threatenings are unconditional."

Divine promise absolute.	*It was conditional.*
In that same day the LORD made a covenant with Abram, saying, Unto thy seed have I given this land, from the river of Egypt unto the great river, the river Euphrates. Gen. xv. 18. And I will establish my covenant between me and thee, and thy seed after thee, in their generations, for an everlasting covenant; to be a God unto thee, and to thy seed after thee. Gen. xvii. 7.	And the LORD said unto Moses, Behold, thou shalt sleep with thy fathers, and this people will rise up, and go a whoring after the gods of the strangers of the land, whither they go *to be* among them and will forsake me, and break my covenant which I have made with them. Then my anger shall be kindled against them in that day, and I will forsake them, and I will hide my face from them, and they shall be devoured. Deut. xxxi. 16, 17. When ye have transgressed the covenant of the LORD your God, which he commanded you, and have gone and served other gods, and bowed yourselves to them; then shall the anger of the LORD be kindled against you, and ye shall perish quickly from off the good land which he hath given unto you. Josh. xxiii. 16.

---

[1] See pp. 64, 65, of present work.

DOCTRINAL DISCREPANCIES. 149

The covenant with Abraham has a twofold fulfilment: a partial one to his literal posterity — partial, on account of their non-fulfilment of the conditions; also, a grand and glorious fulfilment to Abraham's *spiritual seed*, in bestowing upon them the heavenly Canaan.[1] The "covenant," though not fulfilled in the primary, will be so in the secondary and higher sense.

Judah to reign till Messiah.	Israel's first king a Benjamite.
The sceptre shall not depart from Judah, nor a lawgiver from between his feet, until Shiloh come: and unto him *shall* the gathering of the people *be*. Gen. xlix. 10.	And afterward they desired a king: and God gave unto them Saul the son of Cis, a man of the tribe of Benjamin. Acts xiii. 21.

First. It is very far from being certain that the term "Shiloh" has any reference to the Messiah. Many critics interpret it of "the Ephraimite city where the tabernacle was erected, after the Israelites had entered the promised land." Here, during the judges' rule, the sanctuary remained, God revealed himself, the yearly feasts were kept, and the pious assembled as at their religious centre. On this hypothesis, the sense is, "Till *he*, or *one*, come to Shiloh." That is, Judah should be the leader of the tribes during their march through the wilderness, till they arrive at Shiloh, the centre of the promised inheritance. In this view concur Bleek, Bunsen, Davidson, Delitzsch, Eichhorn, Ewald, Fuerst, Hitzig, Kalisch, Lipmann, Luzzatto, Palfrey, Rödiger, Teller, and Tuch, with others.[2]

Another ancient interpretation is: "Judah shall possess the sceptre till *he* comes to whom it belongs." So, in substance, the Septuagint (according to one reading), Aquila, Symmachus, the Peshito, Onkelos, one Arabic, and most of the ancient versions, the Jerusalem Targum, Jahn, Von Bohlen, De Wette, Krummacher, etc.

Others render the word variously, "Rest-bringer," "Tranquilizer," "Rest," "Peace," "Peacemaker," "Prince of Peace." To this class may be referred Bush, Deutsch, Gesenius finally,

[1] Compare Gal. iii. 29; iv. 28; Heb. xi. 16, 39, 40.
[2] See Article "Shiloh," in Smith's Bib. Dict., Vol. iv. pp. 2997—2999.

150   DISCREPANCIES OF THE BIBLE.

Hengstenberg, Hofmann, Keil, Knobel, Kurtz, Lange, Luther, Rosenmüller, Schröder, Vater, and the Grand Rabbin Wogue. These all, with slight differences, agree in the above interpretation of the term " Shiloh."

It is to be added that nearly all the ancient Jewish commentators, with the early Christian writers, and several modern critics, agree in referring the term to the *Messiah*.

Secondly. Admitting the Messianic reference, the passage still furnishes little difficulty. "Judah," says Keil, "was to bear the sceptre with victorious, lion-like courage, until, in the future *Shiloh*, the obedience of the nations came to him, and his rule over the tribes was widened into the peaceful government of the world." In the camp and on the march, Judah took the first place among the tribes.[1] After the death of Joshua, Judah by divine direction opened the war upon the Canaanites;[2] and the first judge, Othniel, came of that tribe.[3] Then, in David and Solomon, the same tribe gained undisputed pre-eminence. In further proof, it may be added that, later, this tribe gave the name "Jews" to the whole people; "Jehûdim" from "Jehûdah," *Judah*.[4] Moreover, our Lord himself — the Shiloh, upon this interpretation — came as a man of the tribe of Judah.[5] So that *unto* Jesus, and *in* him as Shiloh, that tribe maintained an easy pre-eminence.

Any one of the foregoing interpretations obviates the alleged discrepancy.

Quotations.

Original passages.	Quoted incorrectly.
The Spirit of the Lord GOD *is* upon me: because the LORD hath anointed me to preach good tidings unto the meek; he hath sent me to bind up the broken-hearted, to proclaim liberty to the captives, and the opening of the prison to *them that are* bound; to pro-	The Spirit of the Lord *is* upon me, because he hath anointed me to preach the gospel to the poor; he hath sent me to heal the broken-hearted, to preach deliverance to the captives, and recovering of sight to the blind, to set at liberty them that are bruised, to preach

[1] Num. ii. 2, 3; vii. 12; x. 14.
[2] Judges i. 1–19.
[3] Joshua xv. 13; Judges iii. 9.
[4] Compare Turner's Companion to the Book of Genesis, pp. 371–388. Also, Speaker's (or Bible) Commentary, i. 232, 233 (English edition).
[5] Heb. vii. 14.

DOCTRINAL DISCREPANCIES.

Original passages.	*Quoted incorrectly.*
claim the acceptable year of the LORD, and the day of vengeance of our God. Isa. lxi. 1, 2.	the acceptable year of the Lord. Luke iv. 18. 19.
Behold, I will send my messenger, and he shall prepare the way before me. Mal. iii. 1.	Behold, I send my messenger before thy face, which shall prepare thy way before thee. Mark i, 2.

It will be seen that, in both these cases, the original sense is substantially preserved in the citation. We have elsewhere[1] remarked upon the relation which the inspired authors sustain to one another; and especially, with reference to their use of similar phraseology. A thorough investigation of the subject will show conclusively that the sacred writers, in quoting from one another, quote according to the sense, and not according to the letter. They seldom, almost never, quote *verbatim*.

Original passage.	*Condensed.*
Nevertheless the dimness *shall* not *be* such as *was* in her vexation, when at the first he lightly afflicted the land of Zebulun, and the land of Naphtali, and afterward did more grievously afflict *her by* the way of the sea, beyond Jordan, in Galilee of the nations. The people that walked in darkness have seen a great light: they that dwell in the land of the shadow of death, upon them hath the light shined. Isa. ix. 1, 2.	That it might be fulfilled which was spoken by Esaias the prophet, saying, The land of Zabulon, and the land of Nephthalim, *by* the way of the sea, beyond Jordan, Galilee of the Gentiles; the people which sat in darkness saw great light; and to them which sat in the region and shadow of death light is sprung up. Matt. iv. 14-16.

Here is no contradiction, but a condensation. The fifteenth verse of Matthew is not so much a quotation, as an allusion, designed to arrest the attention of the reader, and prepare the way for the quotation proper.

The following is an example of substantial agreement amid slight circumstantial variations.

Forms of statement.	*Expanded.*
And he said, Go into the city to such a man, and say unto him, The Master saith, My time is at hand; I will keep the passover at thy house with my disciples. Matt. xxvi. 18. And he sendeth forth two of his disciples, and saith unto them, Go ye into the city, and there shall meet you a man bearing a pitcher of water: follow him. And wheresoever he shall go in, say ye to the goodman of the house, The Master saith, Where is the guestchamber, where I shall eat the passover with my disciples? Mark xiv. 13, 14.	And he sent Peter and John, saying, Go and prepare us the passover, that we may eat. . . . Behold, when ye are entered into the city, there shall a man meet you, bearing a pitcher of water, follow him into the house where he entereth in. And ye shall say unto the goodman of the house, The Master saith unto thee, Where is the guest-chamber, where I shall eat the passover with my disciples? Luke xxii. 8, 10, 11.

---

[1] See pp. 6, 7, of present work.

A case of this kind can, we think, furnish difficulty to the advocates of *verbal* inspiration only.

Original passage.	Inexact version.
Sacrifice and offering thou didst not desire; mine ears hast thou opened: burnt-offering and sin-offering hast thou not required. Ps. xl. 6.	Wherefore, when he cometh into the world, he saith, Sacrifice and offering thou wouldest not, but a body hast thou prepared me: In burnt-offerings and *sacrifices* for sin thou hast had no pleasure. Heb. x. 5, 6.

The difficulty, in this case, is, that the apostle follows the Septuagint, "A body hast thou prepared me," instead of the Hebrew, "Mine ears hast thou opened."

We may first ask: Why did the Septuagint translators commit such an error in rendering the Hebrew into Greek? Usher, Semler, Ernesti, Michaelis, Bleek, and Lünemann offer the very plausible suggestion that the translators *misread* the Hebrew, and show how this might readily take place in this particular instance.[1] Cappell, Carpzov, Wolf, Ebrard, Tholuck, and Delitzsch think that the translators deliberately chose this phraseology by which to render the Hebrew, *as being more intelligible to the reader.*

The second question is: Why did the apostle employ this loose rendering, instead of a literal one? In reply, it may be shown that the fundamental idea is retained, even in the inexact phraseology. The expression, "Mine ears hast thou opened," is, according to Hengstenberg,[2] another way of saying, "Thou hast made me hearing, obedient"; while the corresponding words, "A body hast thou prepared me," are equivalent to, "Thou hast fitted me for willing service in the execution of thy designs." We thus see that in both cases the fundamental idea, *the obedience of the Messiah*, is preserved. Therefore, in this deeper view, there is no dissonance between these passages. Such being the case, Paul was at liberty to employ the paraphrastic rendering; especially since this seemed more appropriate to his purpose,[3] as setting forth more fitly than did the

---

[1] See Alford, on Heb. x. 5. [2] Com. on Ps. xl. 6.
[3] Warington on Inspiration, p. 95.

original utterance the incarnation of the Lord Jesus, and his obedience unto death.¹

Original.	*Wrongly referred.*
And I said unto them, If ye think good, give *me* my price: and if not, forbear. So they weighed for my price thirty *pieces* of silver. And the LORD said unto me, Cast it unto the potter: a goodly price that I was prized at of them. And I took the thirty *pieces* of silver, and cast them to the potter in the house of the LORD. Zech. xi. 12, 13.	Then was fulfilled that which was spoken by Jeremy the prophet, saying, And they took the thirty pieces of silver, the price of him that was valued, whom they of the children of Israel did value; and gave them for the potter's field, as the Lord appointed me. Matt. xxvii. 9, 10.

Here is obviously a mistake, either made by Matthew or by subsequent transcribers. The prophecy was uttered by Zechariah, not Jeremiah.

Alford thinks that Matthew quoted from memory and unprecisely. Barnes suggests two explanations. According to the Jewish writers, Jeremiah was reckoned the first of the prophets, and was placed first in the book of the prophets; thus, Jeremiah, Ezekiel, Isaiah, etc. Matthew, in quoting this book, may have quoted it under the name which stood *first* in it; that is, instead of saying, " by the Prophets," he may have said, " by Jeremy the prophet," since *he* headed the list.

Or, the difficulty may have arisen from abridgment of the names. In the Greek, Jeremiah, instead of being written in full, might stand thus, " Iriou "; Zechariah thus, " Zriou." By the mere change of Z into I, the mistake would be made. The Syriac Peshito and several MSS. have simply, " by the prophet." In Henderson's² opinion, the Greek text of the above passage has been corrupted.

Forms of report.	*Different.*
This is my beloved Son, in whom I am well pleased. Matt. iii. 17.	Thou art my beloved Son, in whom I am well pleased. Mark i. 11. Thou art my beloved Son; in thee I am well pleased. Luke iii. 22.
Why are ye fearful, O ye of little faith? Matt. viii. 26 Why are ye so fearful? How is it that ye have no faith? Mark iv. 40.	Where is your faith? Luke viii. 25.
Son be of good cheer; thy sins be forgiven thee. Matt. ix. 2.	Son, thy sins be forgiven thee. Mark ii. 5. Man, thy sins are forgiven thee. Luke v. 20.

¹ See Bib. Sacra, Vol. xxx. p. 309.   ² Minor Prophets, pp. 418, 419.

Forms of report.	Different.
This is Jesus the King of the Jews. Matt. xxvii. 37.	This is the King of the Jews. Luke xxiii. 38.
The King of the Jews. Mark xv. 26.	Jesus of Nazareth, the King of the Jews. John xix. 19.

Taking these several cases into consideration, it is beyond question that in each the fundamental idea is preserved under all the various forms. And this, we think, is all, and precisely what, the sacred writers intended. One might, indeed, say of the last instance that John's report includes the other three; so that, if he is correct, the others of course are so. Or, that, since the superscription was written in Hebrew, Greek, and Latin, Matthew gives a translation of the Hebrew; Mark, a condensed one of the Latin; Luke follows Mark, adding, "This is"; while John gives a summary of the whole. But we see no necessity for such explanations. It is altogether improbable that three inscriptions, in three different languages, should correspond word for word.

The following cases furnish a slightly augmented difficulty.

Provide neither gold, nor silver, nor brass in your purses, nor scrip, for *your* journey, neither two coats, neither shoes, nor yet staves: for the workman is worthy of his meat. Matt x. 9, 10. And commanded them that they should take nothing for *their* journey, save a staff only; no scrip, no bread, no money in *their* purse; but *be* shod with sandals; and not put on two coats. Mark vi. 8, 9.	Take nothing for *your* journey, neither staves nor scrip, neither bread, neither money; neither have two coats apiece. Luke ix. 3.

In this case the trivial differences do not affect the substantial agreement. When we observe that Matthew uses the term "provide,"[1] it is clear that his meaning is: "Do not procure any in addition to what you now have. Go, just as you are."

As to the fact that Matthew forbids "shoes" to be procured, while Mark allows "sandals" to be worn, it may be remarked that "shoes," as the original implies, may have been of a kind such as to cover the whole foot, "while the "sandal" was merely a sole of wood or hide, covering the bottom of the foot.

---

[1] Greek κτάομαι, *to get for oneself, to acquire, to procure, by purchase or otherwise.* Robinson, Lexicon to New Test.

and bound on with thongs.[1] Thus the supposed discrepancy utterly falls away.

| Go into the village over against you, and straightway ye shall find an ass tied, and a colt with her: loose *them*, and bring *them* unto me. And if any *man* say aught unto you, ye shall say, The Lord hath need of them; and straightway he will send them. Matt. xxi. 2, 3. | Go your way into the village over against you: and as soon as ye be entered into it, ye shall find a colt tied, whereon never man sat; loose him, and bring *him*. And if any man say unto you, Why do ye this? say ye that the Lord hath need of him; and straightway he will send him hither. Mark xi. 2, 3.
Go ye into the village over against *you;* in the which at your entering ye shall find a colt tied, whereon yet never man sat: loose him and bring *him hither*. And if any man ask you, Why do ye loose *him?* thus shall ye say unto him, Because the Lord hath need of him. Luke xix. 30, 31. |

This is simply an example of three independent veracious witnesses, each telling his story in his own way. And we cannot feel the least respect for that infinitessimal criticism which cavils and demurs at a case of this kind.

| A wicked and adulterous generation seeketh after a sign; and there shall no sign be given unto it, but the sign of the prophet Jonas. Matt. xvi. 4. | Why doth this generation seek after a sign? Verily, I say unto you, There shall no sign be given to this generation. Mark viii. 12. |

May not Mark mean, there shall no future sign be given? The "sign of the prophet Jonas" was taken from the records of the past. At all events, that kind of sign sought for by the Jews was peremptorily refused.

Other interesting examples of variant quotations are the following:

Till they see the Son of man coming in his kingdom. Matt. xvi. 28. Till they have seen the kingdom of God come with power. Mark ix. 1.	Till they see the kingdom of God. Luke ix. 27.
Let no fruit grow on thee henceforward for ever. Matt. xxi. 19.	No man eat fruit of thee hereafter for ever. Mark xi. 14.
For in the resurrection they neither marry, nor are given in marriage, but are as the angels of God in heaven. Matt. xxii. 30. For when they shall rise from the dead, they neither marry, nor are given in marriage, but are as the angels which are in heaven. Mark xii. 25.	But they which shall be accounted worthy to obtain that world, and the resurrection from the dead, neither marry, nor are given in marriage: neither can they die any more: for they are equal unto the angels; and are the children of God, being the children of the resurrection. Luke xx. 35, 36.
But as touching the resurrection of the dead, have ye not read that which was spoken unto you by God, saying, I	Now that the dead are raised, even Moses showed at the bush, when he calleth the Lord the God of Abraham,

---

[1] So Robinson's New Test. Lexicon.

am the God of Abraham, and the God of Isaac, and the God of Jacob? God is not the God of the dead, but of the living. Matt. xxii. 31, 32. And as touching the dead, that they rise: have ye not read in the book of Moses, how in the bush God spake unto him; saying, I *am* the God of Abraham, and the God of Isaac, and the God of Jacob? He is not the God of the dead, but the God of the living. Mark xii. 26, 27.	and the God of Isaac, and the God of Jacob. For he is not a God of the dead, but of the living: for all live unto him. Luke xx. 37, 38.
But Jesus perceived their wickedness, and said, Why tempt ye me, *ye* hypocrites? Shew me the tribute money. Matt. xxii. 18, 19. But he, knowing their hypocrisy, said unto them, Why tempt ye me? bring me a penny, that I may see *it*. Mark xii. 15.	But he perceived their craftiness, and said unto them, Why tempt ye me? Shew me a penny. Luke xx. 23, 24.
Jesus saith unto him, Thou hast said. Matt. xxvi. 64.	And Jesus said, I am. Mark xiv. 62.
When ye therefore shall see the abomination of desolation, spoken of by Daniel the prophet, stand in the holy place (whoso readeth, let him understand), Then let them which be in Judaea flee into the mountains. Matt. xxiv. 15, 16.	But when ye shall see the abomination of desolation, spoken of by Daniel the prophet, standing where it ought not (let him that readeth understand), then let them that be in Judaea flee to the mountains. Mark xiii. 14. And when ye shall see Jerusalem compassed with armies, then know that the desolation thereof is nigh. Then let them which are in Judaea flee to the mountains. Luke xxi. 20, 21.

Another striking case is that relative to the instituting of the Lord's Supper. The passages are too long to be quoted here, but may be found in Matt. xxvi. 21–29, Mark xiv. 18–24, Luke xxii. 14–20, 1 Cor. xi. 23–26. A no less famous instance is that of Peter's denials of Christ, which is discussed elsewhere.[1]

When we take into consideration the fact that inspiration has reference primarily to *ideas* rather than to *words;* and that, in each of the above cases respectively, *the fundamental idea is, notwithstanding the variations of phraseology, carefully and distinctly preserved,* these and similar instances furnish no real difficulty whatever.[2] In view of these and similar cases, certain eminent critics have felt warranted in deducing two inferences:

1. That the sacred writers, in their citations from one another, *provided the fundamental idea were retained,* were suffered to expand, abridge, or paraphrase the original language,

---

[1] See under Historical Discrepancies, — Persons.
[2] Compare Journal of Sacred Literature (April, 1854), pp. 71–110.

DOCTRINAL DISCREPANCIES. 157

and adapt it to the object which they respectively contemplated. As is observed by Prof. Barrows,[1] "It is manifest that the writers of the New Testament are not anxious about the verbal accuracy of the words cited. The spirit and scope of a passage, which constitute its true life and meaning, are what they have in view, not the exact rendering of the words from the Hebrew into the Greek."

2. That these writers while divinely guarded against any error in communicating *religious* truth, and against any *material* error in narrating matters of fact, were yet not preserved from trivial errors, defects of memory, and the like, which occasionally appear in their writings. In other words, they were neither rendered *omniscient*, nor *infallible* in all respects, but were unerringly guided in the communication of religious truth.

Archbishop Whately,[2] speaking of certain cases in the New Testament, says, " We may plainly perceive that, in point of fact, the sacred writers were *not* supernaturally guarded against trifling inaccuracies in the detail of unimportant circumstances." Again, he speaks of those " trifling inaccuracies as to an insignificant circumstance which occur in the gospel history, and which it was not thought needful to guard against by a special inspiration." Nearly the same view is taken by Mr. Warington[3] who, however, concedes much more than is necessary.

Dean Alford[4] says, "There are certain minor points of accuracy or inaccuracy of which human research suffices to inform men, and on which, from want of that research, it is often the practice to speak vaguely and inexactly. Such are sometimes the conventionally received distances from place to place; such are the common accounts of phenomena in natural history, etc. Now, in matters of this kind, the evangelists and apostles were not supernaturally informed, but left, in common with others, to the guidance of their natural faculties. The

---

[1] Bibliotheca Sacra, Vol. xxx. p. 806.
[2] Future State, appendix to Lecture xi.
[3] On Inspiration, pp. 72–75 and 238, 239.
[4] Prolegomena to Gospels, chap. i., sect. vi., par. 14, 15.

same may be said of citations and dates from history. In the last apology of Stephen, which he spoke being full of the Holy Ghost, and with divine influence beaming from his countenance, we have at least two demonstrable historical inaccuracies. And the occurrence of similar ones in the Gospels does not in any way affect the inspiration or the veracity of the evangelists."

The above theory of inspiration seems very well set forth in the following citation from the late Mr. Parry:[1] "Everything which the apostles have written or taught concerning Christianity — everything which teaches a religious sentiment or duty — must be considered as divinely true, as the mind and will of God, recorded under the direction and guidance of his Spirit. But there is no need to ask whether everything contained in their writings was immediately suggested by the Spirit or not; whether Luke was inspired to say that the ship in which he sailed with Paul was wrecked on the island of Melita, or whether Paul was under the guidance of the Spirit in directing Timothy to bring him the cloak which he had left at Troas; for these things were not of a religous nature, and no inspiration was necessary concerning them." We will simply add that the view of inspiration exhibited in the foregoing extracts, while it very well meets certain exigencies of the case, seems, nevertheless, peculiarly liable to be misunderstood and abused. There is ever far greater danger to be apprehended from a lax than from a strict theory of inspiration.

V. MAN, in relation to the Present. — Creation.

Like God by creation.	This likeness acquired.
So God created man in his *own* image, in the image of God created he him. Gen. i. 27. In the day that God created man, in the likeness of God made he him. Gen. v. 1.	For God doth know that in the day ye eat thereof, then your eyes shall be opened, and ye shall be as gods, knowing good and evil. ... And the LORD God said, Behold, the man is become as one of us, to know good and evil. Gen. iii. 5, 22.

A certain sceptical critic, referring to these two classes of texts, remarks: "In the first, man is *made* in the image of God; in the second, likeness to the Deity comes to him by

[1] Quoted in Journal of Sacred Literature (April, 1854), pp. 104, 105.

subsequently knowing good and evil." The first texts, however, refer to man's spiritual constitution; the second, to his acquired knowledge, or his power to discriminate between good and evil. Man's spirit is made "in the image" of God, who is a Spirit; man's knowledge of good and evil, in virtue of which he is, in a sense, "like God," was acquired.

Made in image of God.	*Created male and female.*
In the image of God made he man. Gen. ix. 6.	Male and female created he them. Gen. v. 2.

The first text contemplates the soul, the immaterial part; the second refers to the material, physical organism of human beings. Maimonides says: "Made in the image of God in respect to the soul and understanding; created male and female in respect to corporeal composition."

Made like God.	*None like Him.*
And God said, Let us make man in our image, after our likeness. Gen. i. 26.	To whom then will ye liken me, or shall I be equal? saith the Holy one. Isa. xl. 25.

The first text conveys the idea of resemblance; the second of equality. We may resemble God in certain respects without being equal to him.

Sinfulness.

No man without sin.	*Some are sinless.*
There *is* no man that sinneth not. 1 Kings viii. 46. The LORD looked down from heaven upon the children of men, to see if there were any that did understand, *and* seek God. They are all gone aside, they are *all* together become filthy: *there is* none that doeth good, no, not one. Ps. xiv. 2, 3 Who can say, I have made my heart clean, I am pure from my sin? Prov. xx. 9. For *there is* not a just man upon earth, that doeth good, and sinneth not. Eccl. vii. 20. Why callest thou me good? *there is* none good but one, *that is* God. Mark x. 18. There is none righteous, no, not one. ... For all have sinned, and come short of the glory of God. Rom. iii. 18, 23. If we say that we have no sin, we deceive ourselves, and the truth is not in us. 1 John i. 8.	Noah was a just man *and* perfect in his generations, *and* Noah walked with God. Gen. vi. 9. Job was perfect and upright, and one that feared God, and eschewed evil. Job i. 1. Who shall ascend into the hill of the LORD? or who shall stand in his holy place? He that hath clean hands, and a pure heart; who hath not lifted up his soul unto vanity, nor sworn deceitfully. Ps. xxiv. 3, 4. Preserve my soul; for I *am* holy. Ps. lxxxvi 2. A good man out of the good treasure of his heart, bringeth forth that which is good. Luke vi. 45. These things write I unto you, that ye sin not. 1 John ii. 1. Whosoever abideth in him sinneth not; whosoever sinneth hath not seen him, neither known him. ... Whosoever is born of God doth not commit sin; for his seed remaineth in him; and he cannot sin, because he is born of God. 1 John iii. 6, 9.

The first series of passages contemplates men in their unregenerate state. These texts teach the undeniable truth that no mere human being has ever reached the age of accountability without violating the moral law, without sinning. They are a strong, emphatic statement of the fact that, *as certainly as human beings arrive at years of discretion, so certainly do they become sinners.* Since "all have sinned," therefore, "if we say that we have no sin"—that we have kept ourselves from sin, and hence do not *need* pardon,—" we deceive ourselves."

Mark x. 18 simply asserts that no being is absolutely good — good *per se* — except God. His is absolute, underived goodness; men are "good," not in the sense in which he is good, but relatively and by derivation.

The citations of the second series, except those from 1 John iii., refer to men possessing the relative goodness just mentioned. The texts excepted are interpreted in the following manner: " *Whosoever sinneth.*" Doddridge says, "Who habitually and avowedly sinneth." " *Doth not commit sin.*" According to Mr. Barnes, the interpretation should be: "Is not *wilfully* and *deliberately* a sinner." He may err, and be " overtaken in a fault," but the misdeed is not intentional. " *He cannot sin,*" that is, it is incompatible with his views, feelings, and purposes. We have here a fresh illustration of that moral impossibility which has been already mentioned more than once.

Andrew Fuller:[1] "It appears that the word 'sin,' in these passages, is of different significations. In the former, it is to be taken properly for any transgression of the law of God. If any man say, in this sense, he has no sin, he only proves himself to be deceived, and that he has yet to learn what is true religion. But in the latter, it seems, from the context, that the term is intended to denote the sin of *apostasy.* If we were to substitute the term 'apostasy' for 'sin,' from the sixth to the tenth verse, the meaning would be clear."

Dr. Davidson[2] calls attention to the form of expression in

[1] Works, i. 682.   [2] Sacred Hermeneutics, p. 579.

the original, 1 John iii. 9, and observes: "There is an emphasis in the verb 'poieo.' It denotes the *habitual working* of sin."

Düsterdieck[1] thinks that the last citations from 1 John present the *ideal standard* which continually, so to speak, floats above the actual life of believers as their rule and aim, and that this norm finds in such actual life only a relative fulfilment, yet that, even in the actual life of all that are born of God, there is something which in full verity answers to the ideal words, "They cannot sin." That is, they sin not, and cannot sin, just in proportion as the new, divine life, unconditionally opposed to all sin, and manifesting itself in godlike righteousness, is present and abides in them.

In a word, the texts just mentioned are *descriptions of the ideal Christian.*

Made upright.	*Made sinful.*
God hath made man upright. Eccl. vii. 29.	Behold, I was shapen in iniquity; and in sin did my mother conceive me. Ps. li. 5.

The latter text is simply an Oriental hyperbolical way of saying that he had begun to sin at the earliest practicable period. This language is no more to be pressed literally than is Job's[2] declaration that he had guided the widow "from his mother's womb." That is, as Delitzsch says, "from earliest youth, so far back as he can remember, he was wont to behave like a father to the orphan and like a child to the widow." To take the language, in either case, in a rigidly literal sense, is a gross absurdity.

Born sinful.	*Infants are sinless.*
For vain man would be wise, though man be born *like* a wild ass's colt. Job xi. 12.	Moreover, your little ones, which ye said should be a prey, and your children, which in that day had no knowledge between good and evil, they shall go in thither Deut. i. 39.
Who can bring a clean *thing* out of an unclean? not one. Job xiv. 4.	Butter and honey shall he eat, that he may know to refuse the evil, and choose the good. For before the child shall know to refuse the evil, and choose the good, the land that thou abhorest shall be forsaken of both her kings. Isa. vii. 15, 16.
What *is* man, that he should be clean? and *he which is* born of a woman, that he should be righteous? Job xv.14.	
The wicked are estranged from the womb: they go astray as soon as they be born, speaking lies. Ps. lviii. 3.	
Foolishness *is* bound in the heart of a child, *but* the rod of correction shall drive it far from him. Prov. xxii. 15.	Except ye be converted, and become as little children, ye shall not enter into

---
[1] Quoted by Alford.   [2] Chap. xxxi. 18.

Born sinful.	Infants are sinless.
That which is born of the flesh is flesh; and that which is born of the Spirit is spirit. John iii. 6.	the kingdom of heaven. Whosoever therefore shall humble himself as this little child, the same is greatest in the kingdom of heaven. Matt. xviii. 3, 4. Suffer little children to come unto me, and forbid them not: for of such is the kingdom of God. Verily, I say unto you, Whosoever shall not receive the kingdom of God as a little child, shall in no wise enter therein. Luke xviii. 16, 17. For *the children* being not yet born, neither having done any good or evil. Rom. ix. 11.

As to the three quotations from Job, we observe, first, that they are couched in poetical and figurative language. Second, as we have remarked elsewhere, there is no proof that Job and his friends were *inspired* as religious teachers, as were the prophets and apostles. That the author of the book was "moved by the Holy Spirit" to record its contents, is beyond doubt; but that we are to take the words of Satan, of Job's wife, of the patriarch himself, and of his friends, as "proof-texts" upon which to build stupendous structures of theology, we cannot for a moment admit. Says Prof. Stuart,[1] "Just as if these angry disputants, who contradict each other, and most of whom God himself has declared to be in the wrong (Job xlii. 7–9), were inspired when they disputed."

Ps. lviii. 3, like li. 5 considered above, is a poetical hyperbole. The absurdity of a literal interpretation is obvious from the fact that the wicked are represented as "speaking lies," *as soon as they are born.* Literalistic exegesis would make them rather precocious. The meaning plainly is, that they begin very early, as soon as possible, to speak lies, and to go astray.

The "foolishness" of Prov. xxii. can hardly be sin, for sin cannot be removed by corporal punishment. A higher power than the "rod" is requisite to the expulsion of sin, and the cleansing of the soul.

As to John iii. 6, there are two interpretations. 1. That given by Meyer: The flesh is the material nature of man, determined ethically by the sinful impulses of which it is the seat. What-

---

[1] History of Old Test., Canon, p. 144 (Revised edition, p. 133).

DOCTRINAL DISCREPANCIES. 163

ever is born from this sensuous and sinfully determined human nature is a being of the same sensuous, sinfully constituted nature without the spiritual and ethical life which first arises through the action of the Divine Spirit. 2. The language may have had a special application. Nicodemus had just suggested the impossibility of a second natural birth. Christ may have meant simply, " even were it possible, you would gain nothing by it: you would still be what you now are." That is, the language may have been designed to teach, not that infants are actually born sinful, but that a second physical birth, were it possible, would fail to introduce a man into the " kingdom of God."

At all events, the theory that children are born with certain *perverted tendencies* or *natural proclivities to sin*, which, though not sinful *per se*, do nevertheless certainly lead the individual into sin as soon as he is capable of moral action, will satisfy the demands of a reasonable exegesis.

Matt. xviii. 3 asserts that we must "become *as little children*" — docile, loving, guileless — in order to enter into " the kingdom of heaven."

Luke xviii. 15 takes up the same thought in respect to infants,[1] and declares that "*of such* is the kingdom of heaven"; that is, *it is composed of little children*, and *of those persons who possess the childlike character and spirit*. It would appear, therefore, that these two passages are utterly incompatible with the theory that children are born into the world laden with guilt, permeated with and steeped in the virus of sin.

Rom. ix. 11 brings to view certain children which, though alive,[2] had " done neither good nor evil." Now, since sin is the " transgression of the law," these children, having violated *no* law, could not possibly be sinners. Nor do we discover anything in the accident of birth which could fix the stain of

---
[1] The original word here is different, and, as Alford says, "points out more distinctly the tender age of the children."
[2] See Gen. xxv. 22, 23.

sin upon their souls. A fair inference, then, is that, since they were not sinners before birth, they did not become such at birth, nor until they wilfully violated, to some extent, the law of God. Nor does it appear that the case of these children was, in respect to this exemption, an exceptional one. Hence the theory that infants come into the world actually sinful or guilty would not seem to be supported either by reason or by the testimony of Scripture.

Children of wrath naturally.	*Keep the law by nature.*
And were by nature the children of wrath, even as others. Eph. ii. 3.	For when the Gentiles, which have not the law, do by nature the things contained in the law, these having not the law, are a law unto themselves. Which shew the work of the law written in their hearts. Rom. ii. 14, 15.

Andrew Fuller: The phrase " by nature " in the latter refers to the *rule* of action; but in the former to the *cause* of it.

Dr. Hodge: " ' By nature,' in virtue of their internal constitution, not by external instruction." Rückert: " We were born children of wrath; i.e. such as we were from our birth, we were exposed to the divine wrath, is the true sense of these words."

Suicer[1] renders the word " phusis," in Eph. ii. 3, " *truly, incontestably.*" The Syriac Peshito reads: " And were *altogether* the children of wrath." Dr. Adam Clarke and Bishop Ellicott doubt whether there is in this text any direct assertion of the doctrine of original sin.

We take the sense to be, " And were, *in our unregenerate condition,* the children of wrath." In this interpretation, Mr. Barnes concurs. Or, a different explanation may be given. The term " nature " may here denote our *natural proclivities and tendencies to sin;* the idea being that, in consequence of the development of these, we were the children of wrath.

Upon any reasonable explanation, the words " were by nature the children of wrath " do not imply that we were *born sinning* or *sinful.* Man is " by nature " a talking being, yet he was not

---

[1] Thesaurus, Vol. ii., col. 1475. Similarly Grotius and several early writers. Compare the German " natürlich."

necessarily *born talking*. We are "by nature" offspring-loving beings, yet it by no means follows that we were born in the actual exercise of this "natural affection." So the fact that we are sinners "by nature" does not necessitate that we were sinners before, or even at birth, but merely that we are such *as the result of* our natural proclivities to evil.

All made sinners by Adam.	*Made righteous by Christ*
Wherefore as by one man sin entered into the world, and death by sin; and so death passed upon all men, for that all have sinned. . . . Therefore, as by the offence of one *judgment came* upon all men to condemnation. Rom. v. 12, 18.	Even so by the righteousness of one *the free gift came* upon all men unto justification of life. For as by one man's disobedience many were made sinners, so by the obedience of one shall many be made righteous. Rom. v. 18, 19.

There are two interpretations of the last two texts. (1) That the "free gift" is *adapted to* all men, and has a *tendency* to restore them to the divine favor. Barnes: "' *Came upon all men*,'— was with reference to all men; had a bearing upon all men; was *originally adapted* to the race." John Taylor: "The drift of the apostle's conclusion is to show that the Gift, in its utmost extent, is free to all mankind." Calvin: The apostle makes the grace "common to all, because it is *offered to all*, not because it is in fact applied to all."

(2) That the words "all" and "many," in the eighteenth and nineteenth verses, are each used in two senses, a wider and a narrower. Dr. Hodge thinks that, in the first clause of each verse, "all" means all who are connected with Adam; in the second clause, all who are connected with Christ. Alford says that both classes of men meet in the word "many." A common term of quantity is found for both; the one extending to its largest numerical interpretation; the other restricted to its smallest. In either view, there is no discrepancy.

Repentance.

Man's own act.	*God's gift.*
Repent ye, and believe the gospel. Mark i. 15.	To give repentance to Israel, and forgiveness of sins. Acts v. 31.
Except ye repent, ye shall all likewise perish. Luke xiii. 5.	Then hath God also to the Gentiles granted repentance unto life. Acts xi. 18.
Now commandeth all men every where to repent. Acts xvii. 30.	If God peradventure will give them repentance to the acknowledging of the truth. 2 Tim. ii. 25.

The word "repentance" is used in two senses. In the first series, it denotes the act of repenting; in the second, the opportunity, motives, and helps of that act. Hackett: "*To give repentance,* i.e. the grace or disposition to exercise it." De Wette: "The opportunity to repent, or the provision of mercy which renders repentance available to the sinner."

Regeneration.

Man active.	Passive.
Circumcise therefore the foreskin of your heart, and be no more stiff-necked. Deut. x. 16.	And the LORD thy God will circumcise thy heart, and the heart of thy seed, to love the LORD thy God with all thy heart. Deut. xxx. 6.
Wash you, make you clean: put away the evil of your doings from before mine eyes. Isa. i. 16.	Wash me thoroughly from mine iniquity, and cleanse me from my sin. Ps. li. 2.
O Jerusalem, wash thine heart from wickedness, that thou mayest be saved. How long shall thy vain thoughts lodge within thee? Jer. iv. 14.	Then will I sprinkle clean water upon you, and ye shall be clean: from all your filthiness, and from all your idols, will I cleanse you. A new heart also will I give you, and a new spirit will I put within you. Ezek. xxxvi. 25, 26.
Make you a new heart and a new spirit: for why will ye die, O house of Israel? Ezek. xviii. 31.	
Turn ye unto me Zech. i. 3.	Turn thou us unto thee, O LORD, and we shall be turned. Lam. v. 21.
Awake, thou that sleepest, and arise from the dead. Eph. v. 14.	But God when we were dead in sins, hath quickened us together with Christ; ... And hath raised *us* up together. ... For we are his workmanship, created in Christ Jesus unto good works. Eph. ii. 5, 6, 10.
Ye have put off the old man with his deeds: and have put on the new *man.* Col. iii. 9, 10.	

The simple fact is, that man is both *active* and *passive* in regeneration. The first series of texts brings to view his activity; the second, his passivity. Man is *active* in thinking upon the truth, in exercising his sensibilities in relation to it, and in giving up his heart to God; he is *passive* in that he is acted upon by the truth, and also by the Holy Spirit. He both acts and is acted upon. God does not, so far as we know, regenerate beings in a state of insensibility or indifference. There is, in a certain sense, a co-operation of the divine agency and the human in the regeneration of the soul. As Prof. Phelps[1] has said: "We cannot mistake in recognizing as another law of the Holy Spirit, that his work shall be concurrent with the will of the regenerate soul itself. Sanctification is a co-operative process. It may be suspended by resistance, and

---

[1] The New Birth, pp. 243, 244.

accelerated by obedience to the divine impulses. ... Not by the breadth of a hair will the sovereignty of God invade the enclosure of that soul's freedom. The soul itself, in its own individuality, is the thing he would save. Its own love is the thing he craves. Its own submission is the right he claims. Its own chosen obedience is the service he requires."

This same idea of co-operation is expressed in the words of Paul;[1] "Work out your own salvation, with fear and trembling; for it is God which worketh in you both to will and to do of his good pleasure."

Justification.

By Faith.	By Works.
Therefore by the deeds of the law, there shall no flesh be justified in his sight. ... We conclude, that a man is justified by faith without the deeds of the law. Rom. iii. 20, 28	For not the hearers of the law *are* just before God, but the doers of the law shall be justified. Rom. ii. 13.
For if Abraham were justified by works, he hath *whereof* to glory, but not before God. Rom. iv 2.	What *doth it* profit, my brethren, though a man say he hath faith, and have not works? can faith save him? ... Faith, if it hath not works, is dead, being alone. ... Was not Abraham our father justified by works, when he had offered Isaac his son upon the altar? ... Seest thou how faith wrought with his works, and by works was faith made perfect? ... Ye see then how that by works a man is justified, and not by faith only. ... For as the body without the spirit is dead, so faith without works is dead also. Jas. ii. 14, 17, 21, 22, 24, 26.
Knowing that a man is not justified by the works of the law, but by the faith of Jesus Christ. Gal. ii. 16.	
But that no man is justified by the law in the sight of God, *it is* evident: for, The just shall live by faith. And the law is not of faith: but, The man that doeth them shall live in them. Gal. iii. 11, 12.	

There is no collision between Paul and James. They merely present different aspects or relations of the same great truth. Paul is arguing against self-righteous religionists, who rely for salvation upon *external morality*, upon *mere works;* James addresses those who maintain that, provided a man's *belief* is correct, it matters little what his *conduct* is; that a "bare assentive faith is sufficient for salvation, without its living fruits in a holy life." In a word, Paul is combating Pharisaism; James, Antinomianism. One asserts: "Works are good for nothing except as they spring from faith"; the other responds: "Faith is of no value except as it produces works." Both together affirm the inseparable connection and unalterable rela-

[1] Phil. ii. 12, 13

tion of faith and works as *cause* and *effect*. John Taylor of Norwich: "The apostle James manifestly speaks of works *consequent* to faith, or of such works as are the fruit and product of faith. Whereas, St. Paul speaks of and rejects works considered as *antecedent* to faith. According to St. Paul, Abraham's justification refers to his state *before* he believed, or when he was ungodly; according to St. James, to his state *after* he believed, or when faith wrought with his works."

Whately: "Abraham is cited by Paul as an example of a man 'justified by *faith*,' and by James, of a man 'justified by *works*'; the faith being manifested by the works which sprung out of it."

Andrew Fuller: "Paul treats of the justification of the *ungodly*, or the way in which sinners are accepted of God, and made heirs of eternal life. James speaks of the justification of the *godly*, or in what way it becomes evident that a man is *approved* of God. The former is by the righteousness of Christ; the latter is by works."

Stuart: "Paul is contending with a *legalist*, i.e. one who expected justification on the ground of his own merit. James is disputing with *antinomians*, viz. such persons as held that mere speculative belief or faith, unaccompanied by works, was all which the gospel demands."

Alford and De Wette understand "faith," as used by James, to denote the result of the reception of the word, especially in a moral point of view; as used by Paul, as consisting in trust on the grace of God revealed in the atoning death of Christ.

Sanctification.

Through the truth.	Through the Spirit.
Sanctify them through thy truth. John xvii. 17.	Elect according to the fore-knowledge of God the Father, through sanctification of the Spirit. 1 Pet. i. 2.

They were sanctified *by* the truth *applied by* the Spirit. The two were instruments in the work of sanctification. In the first passage, Alford employs the preposition "in," since the truth is the *element in which* the sanctifying takes place. As to the second text, the word "spirit" may refer either to the believer's own spirit, or to the Holy Spirit. Alford takes the latter signification; Beza says, " Vel Spiritus Sanctus, vel anima quae sanctificatur." The interpretation, " sanctification *by* the Spirit, *in* the truth," meets the requirements of both texts alike.

The fuller expression,[1] " Through sanctification of the Spirit and belief of the truth," conveys the same idea.

Perfection.

Christians are perfect.	*Paul was not perfect.*
Be ye therefore perfect, even as your Father which is in heaven is perfect. Matt. v. 48.	If by any means I might attain unto the resurrection of the dead. Not as though I had already attained, either were already perfect. Phil. iii. 11, 12.
Let us therefore, as many as be perfect, be thus minded. Phil. iii. 15.	

The term "perfect" is used here in different senses. In Matthew it means complete, all-embracing, godlike in love of others. In Phil. iii. 15 it means mature in Christian life. In the texts at the right it probably refers to the completion of Paul's life by martyrdom. Clement of Alexandria applies the term "perfection," "teleiosis," to the martyrdom of believers. He says: "We call martyrdom 'perfection,' 'teleiosis,' not because man receives it as the completion of life, but because it is the consummation of the work of love." Several other early writers use the word, and its derivatives, in a similar sense.[2] Hence Paul's meaning may be : " My Christian career has not yet culminated in martyrdom."

Many critics, however, think that he is alluding to the games or races of the ancients, and says figuratively that he — as a Christian — had not completed his course, and arrived at the goal, so as to receive the prize.

Final Perseverance.

Impossible to fall from grace.	*Some do fall from grace.*
And I give unto them eternal life; and they shall never perish, neither shall any pluck them out of my hand. John x. 28.	But when the righteous turneth away from his righteousness, and committeth iniquity, *and* doeth according to all the abominations that the wicked *man* doeth, shall he live? All his righteousness that he hath done shall not be
For whom he did foreknow, he also did predestinate *to be* conformed to the	

---
[1] 2 Thess. ii. 13.
[2] Comp. Luke xiii. 32; where the Peshito reads "shall be consummated."

Impossible to fall from grace.

image of his Son, that he might be the first-born among many brethren. Moreover, whom he did predestinate, them he also called: and whom he called, them he also justified: and whom he justified, them he also glorified. ... For I am persuaded, that neither death, nor life, nor angels, nor principalities, nor powers, nor things present. nor things to come, nor height, nor depth, nor any other creature, shall be able to separate us from the love of God which is in Christ Jesus our Lord. Rom. viii. 29, 30, 38, 39.

Some do fall from grace.

mentioned: in his trespass that he hath trespassed, and in his sin that he hath sinned, in them shall he die. Ezek. xviii. 24.

Those that thou gavest me I have kept, and none of them is lost, but the son of perdition. John xvii. 12.

For *it is* impossible for those who were once enlightened, and have tasted of the heavenly gift, and were made partakers of the Holy Ghost, and have tasted the good word of God, and the powers of the world to come, if they shall fall away, to renew them again unto repentance; seeing they crucify to themselves the Son of God afresh, and put *him* to an open shame. Heb. vi. 4-6.

For if we sin wilfully after that we have received the knowledge of the truth, there remaineth no more sacrifice for sins, but a certain fearful looking for of judgment and fiery indignation, which shall devour the adversaries. He that despised Moses' law, died without mercy under two or three witnesses: of how much sorer punishment, suppose ye, shall he be thought worthy, who hath trodden under foot the Son of God, and hath counted the blood of the covenant, wherewith he was sanctified, an unholy thing, and hath done despite unto the Spirit of grace? ... But we are not of them who draw back unto perdition. Heb. x. 26-29, 39.

For if after they have escaped the pollutions of the world through the knowledge of the Lord and Saviour Jesus Christ, they are again entangled therein, and overcome, the latter end is worse with them than the beginning. For it had been better for them not to have known the way of righteousness, than, after they have known *it*, to turn from the holy commandment delivered unto them. 2 Pet. ii. 21, 22.

The first series does not teach the *impossibility* of falling from grace, but merely the *certainty* that this will not occur. The auxiliary "shall" is too strong in these passages. The original expresses futurition, thus; "*will* any pluck them out," "*will* be able to separate us," etc.

The second series may be taken as mere *hypotheses* — suppositions introduced for argument's sake. Such figures of speech are very common. Thus, in Gal. i. 8, Paul introduces this hypothesis: " But though we, or an angel from heaven, preach any other gospel unto you than that which we have preached unto you, let him be accursed." He does not, of course, mean to affirm that an " angel from heaven " ever did, or would, preach a false gospel; he merely says: " On the supposition that one *should* do it." In 1 Cor. xiii. 1–3, we have three of these hypotheses, or "suppositions without regard to fact," as they may be termed.

The hypothetical nature of the quotation from Ezekiel is clearly brought out in the parallel passage, Ezek. xxxiii. 13: " When I shall say to the righteous that he shall surely live; if he trust to his own righteousness," etc.

In John xvii. 12, some construe thus: " None of them is lost; but the son of perdition is lost." This interpretation excludes Judas from the number of those who were "given" to Christ. Otherwise, if Judas is included, it may be said that those of whom Christ spoke were given simply for the "ministry and apostleship";[1] and that nothing more is meant here.

The quotations from Hebrews[2] and Peter are so obviously hypothetical that no comment is needed. Alford has the peculiar remark: " Elect and regenerate are not convertible terms. All elect are regenerate; but all regenerate are not elect. The regenerate may fall away; the elect never can."

Barnes, on Heb. vi. 6: " It is not an affirmation that any *had* actually fallen away, or that, in fact, they *would* do it; but the statement is, that *on the supposition that they had fallen away*, it would be impossible to renew them again.

It may be added that Calvinistic authors interpret the latter series of texts as referring to persons who have been considerably enlightened, but not truly converted; who have never really participated in the spiritual life. Arminian authors, and Alford with them, refer these texts to persons who, after being regenerated, have deliberately apostatized from Christ and his religion. The alleged discrepancy is easily removed by either method of interpretation.

[1] Acts i. 25.
[2] Schoettgen gives a peculiar turn to Heb. vi. 6. See Horae Hebraicae. pp. 954–956.

Christians not destroyed.	*May be destroyed.*
And I give unto them eternal life; and they shall never perish. John x. 28.	Destroy not him with thy meat, for whom Christ died. Rom. xiv. 15. And through thy knowledge shall the weak brother perish, for whom Christ died? 1 Cor. viii. 11.

These cautions and admonitions of the apostle are one of the effective means which God uses in *preventing* the destruction of weak believers.

The "called" all saved.	*Some perish.*
Moreover whom he did predestinate, them he also called: and whom he called, them he also justified: and whom he justified, them he also glorified. Rom. viii. 30.	For many be called, but few chosen. Matt. xx. 16.

The word "call," in the first case, signifies the "effectual call," such as secures its own acceptance, and the salvation of the "called." In the second case, the term denotes the general invitation of the gospel, extended to all men.

Righteous, — earthly lot.

No evil befalls the Godly.	*Evil befalls them.*
There shall no evil happen to the just. Prov. xii. 21. And who is he that will harm you, if ye be followers of that which is good? 1 Pet. iii. 13.	So went Satan forth from the presence of the LORD, and smote Job with sore boils from the sole of his foot unto his crown. Job ii. 7. For whom the Lord loveth he chasteneth, and scourgeth every son whom he receiveth. Heb. xii. 6.

The meaning is, that no *permanent* or *ultimate* evil befalls the good. All apparent evils which overtake them are but temporary, and result in high and lasting good. "All things" — the afflictions which came upon Job and the chastisements which God inflicts upon his people — "work together for good to them that love God."[1] Not seldom the grown-up man is profoundly grateful for the disciplinary chastisement received from parents and teachers in his childhood. So the Christian, looking back from heaven, will doubtless thank God for the trials and sufferings of this earthly life, as for blessings in disguise.

Worldly good and prosperity.	*Worldly misery and destitution.*
And the LORD was with Joseph, and he was a prosperous man. Gen. xxxix. 2. So the LORD blessed the latter end of Job more than his beginning. Job xlii. 12.	There be just *men*, unto whom it happeneth according to the work of the wicked. Eccl. viii. 14. And ye shall be hated of all *men* for my name's sake. Luke xxi. 17.

[1] Compare Rom. viii. 28, and Heb. xii. 11.

Worldly good and prosperity.	*Worldly misery and destitution.*
His leaf also shall not wither; and whatsoever he doeth shall prosper. Ps. i. 3	They were stoned, they were sawn asunder, were tempted, were slain with the sword: they wandered about in sheep-skins, and goat-skins; being destitute, afflicted, tormented. Heb. xi. 37.
They that seek the LORD shall not want any good *thing*. Ps. xxxiv. 10.	
Trust in the LORD, and do good; *so* shalt thou dwell in the land, and verily thou shalt be fed. Ps. xxxvii. 3.	These are they which came out of great tribulation. Rev. vii. 14.

The first texts lay down the general principle that righteousness has a tendency to ensure prosperity in worldly matters; yet they do not assert that this result invariably follows. We say, "Honesty is the best policy," yet we know that some rascals grow rich, while some honest men never succeed in business. Righteousness, because it promotes temperance, industry, frugality, and all other worthy qualities, tends normally to worldly prosperity.

As to Joseph and Job, neither of them escaped very sore trials. The first citation from Psalms is a poetical statement of the principle that righteousness is conducive to worldly prosperity; the second asserts that no actual, ultimate good will be wanting to the righteous.

The second series sets forth certain apparent exceptions to the general rule, and illustrates the truth that, owing to the wickedness of the world, the pious encounter hostility and persecution in some form.

The first text of this series asserts that, in some cases, an apparently similar fate attends the evil and the good. But, as Hengstenberg says, this equality of result is only an external and partial one; while the final issue separates the righteous from the wicked.

The two next passages refer to the disciples and the ancient martyrs. The text from Revelation implies that the righteous enter heaven through "great trials" of various kinds. The combined passages teach that, while righteousness tends normally to secure earthly prosperity; yet, in certain cases, this tendency is temporarily interrupted by certain disturbing influences.

Worldly prosperity, a reward.	*A curse.*
If thou return to the Almighty, thou shalt be built up, thou shalt put away iniquity far from thy tabernacles. Then shalt thou lay up gold as dust, and the *gold* of Ophir as the stones of the brooks. Job xxii. 23, 24.	Lay not up for yourselves treasures upon earth.... For where your treasure is, there will your heart be also. Matt. vi. 19, 21.
His seed shall be mighty upon earth; the generation of the upright shall be blessed. Wealth and riches *shall be* in his house. Ps. cxii. 2, 3.	Blessed *be ye* poor; for yours is the kingdom of God.... But wo unto you that are rich! Luke vi 20, 24.
In the house of the righteous *is* much treasure. Prov. xv. 6.	So *is* he that layeth up treasure for himself, and is not rich toward God. Luke xii. 21.
He shall receive a hundred-fold now in this time, houses, and brethren, and sisters, and mothers, and children, and lands, with persecutions; and in the world to come, eternal life. Mark x 30.	Go to now, ye rich men, weep and howl for your miseries that shall come upon *you*. Your riches are corrupted, and your garments are moth-eaten. Your gold and silver is cankered; and the rust of them shall be a witness against you, and shall eat your flesh as it were fire. James v. 1-3.

As to the quotation from Job, the best critics agree substantially in the rendering, " Cast to the dust thy precious treasure, and to the stones of the brooks the gold of Ophir; then shall the Almighty be thy precious treasure," etc. This is nearly Conant's translation. Delitzsch; "' Put far from thee the idol of precious metal with contempt.' When Job thus casts from him temporal things, by the excessive cherishing of which he has hitherto sinned, God himself will be his imperishable treasure."

The texts from Psalms assert that God will not forsake his people, but will supply their needs. All exceptions to this rule are apparent, not real.

On Prov. xv. 6, Zöckler: " The treasure stored up in such a house is the righteousness that prevails in it, a source and pledge of abiding prosperity."

In Mark x. 30 the limiting clause, " with persecutions," shows clearly that unmixed prosperity is not promised to the Christian.

The opposed texts forbid our idolizing, setting our affections upon, worldly things as our " treasure." They also pronounce blessings upon the " poor in spirit," the humble;[1] and reprove those who " trust in riches."[2] Neither the acquisition nor the possession of earthly riches is forbidden, but the making of wealth our god is prohibited.

---

[1] See Matt. v. 3.   [2] Compare Mark x. 24; 1 Tim. vi. 17.

Poverty a blessing.	*Riches a blessing.*	*Neither desirable.*
Children, how hard is it for them that trust in riches to enter into the kingdom of God. It is easier for a camel to go through the eye of a needle, than for a rich man to enter into the kingdom of God. Mark x. 24, 25. Hath not God chosen the poor of this world, rich in faith, and heirs of the kingdom. Jas. ii. 5.	So the LORD blessed the latter end of Job more than his beginning; for he had fourteen thousand sheep, and six thousand camels, and a thousand yoke of oxen, and a thousand she asses. Job xlii. 12. The rich man's wealth *is* his strong city: the destruction of the poor *is* their poverty. Prov. x. 15.	Remove far from me vanity and lies; give me neither poverty nor riches; feed me with food convenient for me: lest I be full and deny *thee*, and say, Who *is* the LORD? or lest I be poor, and steal, and take the name of my God *in vain.* Prov. xxx. 8, 9.

The "rich man" of Mark x. 25 is described, in the preceding verse, as one who "trusts" in riches, making them his god. James teaches that there is in the humbler walks of life, — in their freedom from the temptations, cares, and anxiety incident to wealth, — something which is peculiarly favorable to the origin and growth of true piety.

As to the great wealth which the Lord bestowed upon Job, it is, says Barnes, substantially that of an Arab ruler or chief like those who, at the present day, are called Emirs.[1] The turn in Job's affairs has its lesson. Mr. Cook, in Smith's Biblical Dictionary : "The restoration of his external prosperity, which is an inevitable result of God's personal manifestation, symbolizes the ultimate compensation of the righteous for all sufferings undergone upon earth."

As to Prov. x. 15, Stuart takes the meaning to be that there are times when the wealth of the rich will avert danger and suffering; and at such times the poor may perish for want of money. Zöckler: "Naturally the author is here thinking of wealth well earned by practical wisdom ; and this at the same time a means in the further efforts of wisdom ; and again, of a deserved poverty which while the consequence of foolish con-

---

[1] The size of Job's flocks and herds is not wonderful. Parallel cases can be adduced in our own time. In an address before the "Hampden Agricultural Society," the lecturer mentioned a farmer in California who owns 100,000 sheep, and another with 135,000; also, a certain farm which produced 40,000 bushels of wheat, and another upon which 2,500 cows are kept. (See "Congregationalist," May 4, 1871). Yet infidels adduce the later wealth of Job as a thing incredible.

duct always causes one to sink deeper in folly and moral need." Lord Bacon: " This is excellently expressed, that riches are as a stronghold in imagination, and not always in fact; for certainly great riches have sold more men than they have bought out."

The prayer of Agur (Prov. xxx.), embodies the sentiment that a moderate competence is better than extreme poverty or enormous wealth.

Wisdom, source of happiness.	*Cause of sorrow.*
Happy *is* the man *that* findeth wisdom, and the man *that* getteth understanding... Her ways *are* ways of pleasantness, and all her paths *are* peace. Prov. iii. 13, 17. For wisdom *is* better than rubies; and all the things that may be desired are not to be compared to it. Prov. viii. 11.	For in much wisdom *is* much grief: and he that increaseth knowledge increaseth sorrow. Eccl. i. 18. Then said I in my heart, As it happeneth to the fool, so it happeneth even to me; and why was I then more wise? Then I said in my heart, that this also *is* vanity. Eccl. ii. 15.

In the first texts, "wisdom" denotes spiritual wisdom, which prepares for and lays hold upon the future life. In the second case, the term implies mere worldly knowledge, unsanctified learning, wisdom limited to the sphere of this life. The "grief" and "sorrow" may refer to the depression of mind and bodily indisposition attendant upon intense and long-continued study and efforts to acquire knowledge, and to the frequent disappointment of this pursuit. The Germans have a proverb, "Much wisdom causeth head-ache."

A good name a blessing.	*A curse.*
A good name *is* rather to be chosen than great riches. Prov. xxii. 1. A good name *is* better than precious ointment. Eccl. vii. 1.	Wo unto you, when all men shall speak well of you! for so did their fathers to the false prophets. Luke vi. 26.

A "good name" does not necessarily imply that "all men speak well" of its possessor. Many a man has a good name — a solid and well-earned reputation — who has nevertheless numerous adversaries and calumniators. The denunciation in Luke is levelled at flatterers and time-serving sycophants, who, like modern politicians and office-seekers, are ever ready to sacrifice principle to popularity. Those ministers whose preaching offends no one, of whom "all men speak well," who prophesy "smooth things,"[1] and "daub with untempered mortar,"[2] are in the direct line of the wo denounced by our Lord.

Righteous not found begging.	*Some righteous beg.*
I have been young, and *now* am old; yet have I not seen the righteous forsaken, nor his seed begging bread. Ps. xxxvii. 25.	And there was a certain beggar named Lazarus. . . . And it came to pass, that the beggar died, and was carried by the angels into Abraham's bosom. Luke xvi. 20, 22.

The occasional and temporary exceptions, which had not fallen under David's notice, only prove the rule.

Hengstenberg: "It is not to be doubted, that God, while he withheld from the righteous of the old covenant, any clear insight into a future state of being, on that account unfolded his righteousness the more distinctly in his dealings towards them during this life, so that they might not err concerning it."

They possess the earth.	*Mere sojourners here.*
Blessed *are* the meek: for they shall inherit the earth. Matt. v. 5.	For we *are* strangers before thee, and sojourners, as *were* all our fathers: our days on the earth *are* as a shadow, and *there is* none abiding. 1 Chron. xxix. 15. For here have we no continuing city, but we seek one to come. Heb. xiii. 14.

Mr. Barnes thinks that the first text is a proverbial expression employed by the Jews to denote any great blessing; perhaps as the sum of all blessings. Schoettgen: "They [the meek] with their religion shall have dominion, not only in the land of Judea, but also through the whole earth." Alford: "That kingdom of God which begins in the hearts of the disciples, and is 'not of this world,' shall work onwards, till it shall become *actually a kingdom over this earth*, and its subjects shall *inherit the earth*, first in its millennial, and finally in its renewed and blessed state forever."

The church of Christ will be a *permanent* institution of ever increasing influence and power; although the individuals who at any given time compose that church are but sojourners and wayfarers here below.

---

[1] Isa. xxx. 10; Jer. xxiii. 31.   [2] Ezek. xiii 10–16; xxii. 28.

Pilgrims and strangers.	*Not pilgrims and strangers.*
And confessed that they were strangers and pilgrims on the earth. Heb. xi. 13. Dearly beloved, I beseech *you*, as strangers and pilgrims, abstain from fleshly lusts, which war against the soul. 1 Pet. ii. 11.	Now therefore ye are no more strangers and foreigners, but fellow-citizens with the saints, and of the household of God. Eph. ii. 19.

The first texts refer to Christians *in their relation to the present world*. They have no permanent home on earth; their citizenship is not here; they expect to remain here but a short time; they are passing on to their eternal home on high. The last quotation depicts them *in their relation to the household of faith*. They have been "adopted" into the holy brotherhood, and are entitled to all its privileges and blessings. Hence they are no longer to be regarded as outcasts and aliens, but as members of the celestial family.

They surely live.	*Some of them die.*
But if a man be just, and do that which is lawful and right, .. hath walked in my statutes, and hath kept my judgments, to deal truly; he *is* just, he shall surely live, saith the Lord God. Ezek. xviii. 5, 9. Whosoever liveth and believeth in me shall never die. John xi. 26.	For he seeth *that* wise men die. Ps. xlix. 10. There is a just *man* that perisheth in his righteousness. Eccl. vii. 15.

The first texts refer to spiritual or eternal life; the last to mere physical or temporal death, which all alike, good and bad, undergo.

Menasseh ben Israel[1] has this suggestion: "Divine justice sometimes chastises the righteous in this world for some sin, that he may receive the full reward of his good actions in the next; and the punishment of the wicked is sometimes delayed to pay him for some good he may have done in this, and to punish him fully in the other when the balance is adjusted."

Will be persecuted.	*Not persecuted.*
All that will live godly in Christ Jesus shall suffer persecution. 2 Tim. iii. 12.	When a man's ways please the Lord, he maketh even his enemies to be at peace with him. Prov. xvi. 7.

Andrew Fuller[2]: "The truth seems to be that neither of the above passages is to be taken *universally*. The peace possessed

---

[1] Conciliator, ii. 214.   [2] Works, i. 683.

by those who please God does not extend so far as to exempt them from having enemies; and, though all godly men must in some form or other be persecuted, yet none are persecuted *at all times*. God has always given his people some seasons of rest. The former of these passages may therefore refer to the native enmity which true godliness is certain to excite; and the latter to the divine control over it. Man's wrath shall be let loose in a degree; but farther than what is necessary for the praise of God it shall not go."

Handled roughly.	*Not touched.*
And the Lord said, Simon, Simon, behold, Satan hath desired *to have* you, that he may sift *you* as wheat. Luke xxii. 31.	He that is begotten of God, keepeth himself, and that wicked one toucheth him not. 1 John v. 18.

The first text does not say that Satan actually gained possession of Peter, but merely that he "desired" to do so; the second avers that the "wicked one" does not inflict any *permanent injury* upon the believer.

Christian yoke, easy.	*Burdensome.*
Come unto me, all *ye* that labour, and are heavy laden, and I will give you rest. For my yoke *is* easy, and my burden is light. Matt. xi. 28, 30.	In the world ye shall have tribulation. John xvi. 33. For whom the Lord loveth he chasteneth, and scourgeth every son whom he receiveth. But if ye be without chastisement, whereof all are partakers, then are ye bastards, and not sons. Heb. xii. 6, 8.

In certain important aspects or relations, the yoke of Christ is "easy." Christianity, being a *spiritual* religion, is far less burdensome than are false religions; it imposes much fewer ceremonies and observances than do they. It is also congruous with man's reason, conscience, and all his nobler instincts, and satisfies the needs and aspirations of his higher spiritual nature. The Christian life is *the normal life of man*.

Looking from another point of view, the Christian's yoke may be deemed "burdensome." For Christianity, being a *pure* religion, comes in direct collision with the deep sinfulness of the human heart; it is in intense antagonism with everything corrupt and evil. Hence the Christian must "crucify the flesh" with the passions and lusts, and in so doing must pass through many a sore trial and conflict.

Wicked, — earthly lot.

Longevity ascribed to them.	Denied to them.
Wherefore do the wicked live, become old, yea, are mighty in power? Their seed is established in their sight with them, and their offspring before their eyes. Job xxi. 7, 8.	They die in youth, and their life *is* among the unclean. Job xxxvi. 14.
Though a sinner do evil a hundred times, and his *days* be prolonged. Eccl. viii. 12.	Bloody and deceitful men shall not live out half their days. Ps. lv. 23.
The sinner *being* a hundred years old shall be accursed. Isa. lxv. 20.	The years of the wicked shall be shortened. Prov. x. 27.
	But it shall not be well with the wicked, neither shall he prolong *his* days, *which are* as a shadow. Eccl. viii. 13.

The affirmative texts do not assert that *all* the wicked live to old age. As to the first citation, Zophar had just asserted that the "portion" of a wicked man is, to be cut off in a moment. Job, in reply, denies the universality of this principle, and says that some of the wicked *do* live, become old, and mighty in power. Yet he evidently regards these as *exceptional* cases: for he adds: "How oft is the candle of the wicked put out! and how oft cometh their destruction upon them!"

The two next quotations do not assert the longevity of sinners, but are purely *hypothetical*.

The four opposed texts assert the general principle that *the tendency of vice is to shorten human life*. Of this the statistics of intemperance, licentiousness, and crime in general afford grim and appalling proof. The sense of the combined texts is, that many of the wicked perish early through their sins, but that some, in exceptional cases, live on to old age.

They prosper.	Will not prosper.
The tabernacles of robbers prosper, and they that provoke God are secure. Job xii. 6.	Evil shall slay the wicked and they that hate the righteous shall be desolate. Ps. xxxiv. 21.
Men of the world, *which have* their portion in *this* life, and whose belly thou fillest with thy hid *treasure*. Ps. xvii. 14.	Evil pursueth sinners. Prov. xiii. 21.
Their eyes stand out with fatness: they have more than heart could wish. Behold, these *are* the ungodly, who prosper in the world; they increase *in* riches. Ps. lxxiii. 7, 12.	
Wherefore doth the way of the wicked prosper? *wherefore* are all they happy that deal very treacherously? Jer. xii. 1.	

The first five texts refer to the *temporary* prosperity which the wicked not infrequently enjoy. The transitory nature of this prosperity was not comprehended by the Psalmist, until he went into the sanctuary of God; then he understood the end of the wicked, that they were " set in slippery places."[1]

Menasseh ben Israel: " God sometimes delays the punishment of the wicked, either that they may repent, or to reward them in this life for some good action they may have performed, or for some secret reason known only to his consummate wisdom."

The last two texts do not assert that evil pursueth and shall slay the wicked without a moment's delay, but merely that this will *ultimately* be the case.

See the Divine glory.	*Will not see it.*
And the glory of the LORD shall be revealed, and all flesh shall see *it* together. Isa. xl. 5.	In the land of uprightness will he deal unjustly, and will not behold the majesty of the LORD. Isa. xxvi. 10.

The wicked will not *voluntarily* recognize the "majesty"— the sovereignty and glory — of the Lord; but he will eventually be *compelled* to see and acknowledge it, as displayed in the final reward of virtue and punishment of vice, at the last great day.

Sin with impunity.	*Promptly punished.*
Their houses *are* safe from fear, neither *is* the rod of God upon them.... Therefore they say unto God, Depart from us; for we desire not the knowledge of thy ways. Job xxi. 9, 14.	The worm shall feed sweetly on him; he shall be no more remembered; and wickedness shall be broken as a tree.... They are exalted for a little while, but are gone and brought low; they are taken out of the way as all *other*, and cut off as the tops of the ears of corn. Job xxiv. 20, 24.

Theodore Parker[2] deems it an evidence of the "exquisite art" and "naturalness" with which the book was written, that Job, in his distraction, is represented as affirming and denying a thing almost in the same breath.

A better explanation of passages like the above is, that in relation to our limited wisdom and impatient feelings, — as we often look at matters — the wicked are not punished promptly, but sin with impunity; while upon a comprehensive and impartial view of the case — as infinite wisdom sees it — they are punished promptly, that is, *at exactly the right time.*

[1] See Ps. lxxiii. 16-18.   [2] Translation of DeWette, ii. 557.

Their punishment denied.	*Affirmed.*
Behold, *as* wild asses in the desert, go they forth to their work; rising betimes for a prey: the wilderness *yieldeth* food for them *and* for *their* children. They reap *every one* his corn in the field.... Men groan from out of the city, and the soul of the wounded crieth out: yet God layeth not folly *to them.* Job xxiv. 5, 6, 12.	This *is* the portion of a wicked man with God, and the heritage of oppressors, *which* they shall receive of the Almighty. If his children be multiplied, *it is* for the sword: and his offspring shall not be satisfied with bread. ... For *God* shall cast upon him, and not spare: he would fain flee out of his hand. Job xxvii. 13, 14, 22.

Hirzel:[1] "While Job's opponents wished to prove this proposition against him, that 'the transgressor did not escape punishment in his life,' and charged it upon Job himself that, since every transgressor was miserable, therefore every miserable man was a transgressor; to parry this argument Job had hitherto, though against his better judgment, denied the entire proposition; and, since his opponents had laid it down as a permanent and universal rule, he had confirmed this denial by adducing numerous examples where the contrary was true. But now he goes on to explain the matter to his friends, and admits that they have rightly apprehended the law by which the transgressor's lot is determined." Yet, while making this concession, he points out an error into which they have fallen in applying the principle. This explanation relieves the difficulty by referring the "apparent contradiction" to the different relations in which Job speaks.

Nor, on the hypothesis that Job was not *inspired* as a religious teacher, is it of the slightest consequence whether or not we can establish the concinnity of all his utterances.

Retribution on Earth.

Reward and punishment here.	*Hereafter.*
Behold, the righteous shall be recompensed in the earth: much more the wicked and the sinner. Prov. xi. 31.	For the Son of man shall come in the glory of his Father, with his angels; and then he shall reward every man according to his works. Matt. xvi. 27. And I saw the dead, small and great, stand before God; and the books were opened: and another book was opened, which is *the book* of life: and the dead were judged out of those things which were written in the books, according to their works. Rev. xx. 12.

It is not asserted, in the first text, that either the righteous

[1] Quoted by De Wette, ii. 561.

or wicked receive *full* recompense in this world. The meaning, doubtless, is that the beginnings of retribution are seen here on the earth. Stuart: " The same retributive government which begins to assert its power in this world, will continue its processes in the world to come '

Melancthon, Bishop Hall, Edwards, Lange, and other critics take the word " recompensed" as referring exclusively to the *punishment of wrong-doing.* Hence, the sentiment is, " If the righteous in this world suffer chastisement for their misdeeds, much more surely shall the impenitent be punished for their wilful transgression." That is, the argument is derived from the corrective discipline experienced by good men on earth in favor of the just retribution which shall be meted out hereafter to the incorrigible sinner. In no aspect is it affirmed that full and final retribution is administered in this world.

VI. MAN, in relation to the Future. — Death.

Men must die.	Some will not die.
So death passed upon all men, for that all have sinned. Rom. v. 12.	If a man keep my saying, he shall never see death. John viii. 51.
And as it is appointed unto men once to die. Heb. ix. 27.	And whosoever liveth and believeth in me shall never die. John xi. 26.
	We shall not all sleep, but we shall all be changed 1 Cor. xv. 51.
	We which are alive *and* remain unto the coming of the Lord shall not prevent them which are asleep. . . . The dead in Christ shall rise first. Then we which are alive *and* remain shall be caught up together with them in the clouds, to meet the Lord in the air. 1 Thess iv. 15, 16, 17.
	He that overcometh shall not be hurt of the second death. Rev. ii. 11.

The two texts from John refer not to *physical* but to *spiritual* death. The Pauline quotations contemplate the righteous who shall be living on the earth at the time of Christ's second coming. These will not indeed literally " die," but will be " changed "; that is, undergo a transformation *equivalent to* death, putting off mortality and putting on immortality. All will experience either death, or what is tantamount to it. As Alford says: " The sleep of death cannot be predicated of all of us, but the resurrection-change *can*."

Rev. ii. 11 also denotes not physical death, but the final punishment of the incorrigibly wicked. It is fitly termed 'death," as being an eternal separation from hope and happiness, and an exclusion from all which is worthy of the name "life."

Lazarus not to die.	*He did die.*
Therefore his sisters sent unto him, saying, Lord, behold, he whom thou lovest is sick. When Jesus heard *that*, he said, This sickness is not unto death, but for the glory of God, that the Son of God might be glorified thereby. John xi. 3, 4.	Then said Jesus unto them plainly, Lazarus is dead. And I am glad for your sakes that I was not there, to the intent ye may believe. John xi. 14, 15.

"This sickness is not unto death"; that is, the *ultimate result* will not be "death," but " the glory of God." And so it proved, for many of the Jews who witnessed the raising of Lazarus from the dead, believed on the Son of God.[1] Thus the Father was glorified in the Son.

Man dies like a beast.	*His death different.*
For that which befalleth the sons of men befalleth beasts; even one thing befalleth them: as the one dieth, so dieth the other; yea, they have all one breath; so that a man hath no preeminence above a beast. Eccl. iii. 19.	Then shall the dust return to the earth as it was: and the spirit shall return unto God who gave it. Eccl. xii. 7.

In *one* aspect of the case, there is no distinction between the death of man and that of beasts. Both are uncertain as to the time of it; both are powerless to prevent it; the *physical phenomena*, in each case, are much the same. In these respects there is a very close resemblance, and this may be the relation of which the author is speaking.

Or, with many commentators, we may say that Solomon raises and answers *objections*, as Paul does so often. Thus the passage in question (Eccl. iii. 18–20), beginning "I said in mine heart," etc., may be merely an *objection* which, being suggested to the mind of Solomon, he proceeds to discuss and solve. Dr. Davidson[2] thinks that the author brings before his readers doubts suggested by observation and reflection, or in some cases presented to him by others. Prof. Stuart: When we view the author in the light of proposing the doubts and

---

[1] Compare John xi. 45.   [2] Introd. to Old Test., ii. 385.

difficulties which perplexed his own mind, and sooner or later as *solving* them, then we meet with no serious embarrassment in interpreting the book.

Prof. Tayler Lewis, in Lange, takes the words, "I said in mine heart concerning," etc., as equivalent to, "I deduced this inference from men's lives, I put this interpretation upon their conduct, that, in their own view, *they are beasts*." It is man's judgment upon himself, as pronounced by his own conduct. It is the language of his life.

A terribly severe, but no less just, estimate of man, from a point of view apparently identical with his own.

Death ceases.	*Still exists.*
Jesus Christ, who hath abolished death, and hath brought life and immortality to light through the gospel. 2 Tim. i. 10.	It is appointed unto men once to die. Heb. ix. 27.

"Hath abolished death"; hath taken away its sting and terror, so that it is no longer *death*, a grim and terrible monster, but a kind angel come to conduct the believer home to heaven. Alford: "By the death of Christ, death has lost his sting; and is henceforth of no more account; consequently the act of natural death is evermore treated by the Lord himself and his apostles as of no account; and its actual and total abolition foretold."

Men, immortal.	*God only, immortal.*
Be not afraid of them that kill the body, and after that have no more that they can do. Luke xii. 4.	The King of kings, and Lord of lords. Who only hath immortality. 1 Tim. vi. 15, 16.

The first text is a strong incidental proof that the *soul* is "immortal," since *it does not die with the body*. It is beyond the power of the persecutor. When he has killed the body his fury has expended itself; he can do no more; he cannot reach or harm the soul. The survival of the soul is thus plainly implied and assumed by our Lord.

The second text is interpreted by "mortal-soulists,"[1] as deιv-

---

[1] We use this term, instead of "Thnetopsychites," the name employed by John Damascenus (see Hagenbach's History of Doctrines, i. 221), to

ing immortality to all beings except God. Hence it would follow that the angels, — Gabriel, and Michael the archangel even, — are mortal! And if, as Alford thinks, the above text refers to the Father exclusively, it would also follow that the Lord Jesus himself is mortal!!

By parity of reasoning the language employed in Rom. xvi. 27, " God only wise," warrants the inference that God is the only being who possesses wisdom!

The meaning in both cases obviously is that only God possesses the given attribute, *inherently* and *underivedly*. Justin Martyr: " He has not this through the will of another, as all the other immortals, but through his own essence." Theodoret: " Immortal by essence, not by participation."

Upon no reasonable interpretation does the passage collide with the derived and dependent immortality of man.

Men kill the soul.	*Cannot kill it.*
Joshua took Makkedah, and smote it with the edge of the sword, and the king thereof he utterly destroyed, them, and all the souls that *were* therein. Josh. x. 28. And they smote all the souls that *were* therein with the edge of the sword, utterly destroying *them:* there was not any left to breathe. Josh. xi. 11.	And fear not them which kill the body, but are not able to kill the soul: but rather fear him which is able to destroy both soul and body in hell. Matt. x. 28.

It is scarcely necessary to allude to the fact that our word " soul" is used in two entirely distinct senses. Thus we say, " The soul is immortal," and, alluding to a marine disaster, " Every soul perished." In the latter case, " soul" is synonymous with " person." This secondary meaning of the word may have arisen from the fact that it is the soul of man which gives him personality. Be this as it may, the most orthodox theologians employ the term in these widely different senses.

designate those who deny the natural immortality of the soul or spirit of man. The term may be extended to include also the denial of consciousness to the soul in the interval between death and the resurrection. Apparently the first attempt to introduce Thnetopsychism into the Christian church was made, A.D. 248, by certain errorists from Arabia. Compare Eusebius's Ecclesiastical History, Book vi., chap. xxxvii.; and Guericke's Ancient Church, p. 228.

DOCTRINAL DISCREPANCIES. 187

The corresponding Hebrew and Greek terms are used with similar latitude. Thus, according to Fuerst, the Hebrew word "nephesh" sometimes means the *soul* or *spirit;* in other cases, an *individual,* a *person, man.* Gesenius says, *spirit, soul, mind;* also a *man, person.*

In view of this fact, when one text asserts that Joshua " slew all the souls " in a city, and another affirms that man is " not able to kill the soul," we see that here is no discrepancy. The term "soul," in one case, refers to man in his earthly make-up, as we see him; in the other, to the deathless intelligence which survives the dissolution of its tabernacle, the body.

If, as mortal-soulists assert, the soul actually dies with the body, then he who "kills" the latter, in that very act kills the former also. If the Siamese twins are so connected that the death of one involves that of the other, then the murderer who kills Chang, by that very stroke kills Eng likewise. That is, according to the theory we are criticising, man is as really "able to kill the soul" as God is.

Immortality possessed.	*To be acquired.*
I will forewarn you whom ye shall fear: Fear him, which after he hath killed, hath power to cast into hell; yea, I say unto you, Fear him. Luke xii. 5.	Who by patient continuance in well doing seek for glory and honor and immortality. Rom. ii. 7.

The first passage implies that there is an *intelligence,* a *spirit,* in man, which outlives and is not affected by the dissolution of the body. Hence God, after he has killed the body, may cast the soul into hell. It is the immortal part which survives to be thus disposed of.

As to Rom. ii. 7, a favorite inference of mortal-soulists is this : " Since man is here spoken of as *seeking* ' immortality,' it follows that he does not possess it by nature." To this characteristic sophism, it is sufficient to reply that, as every scholar is aware, the Greek word used here is not " athanasia," *immortality,* but " aphtharsia," *incorruption,*[1] and points to that *exemption from moral corruption* which the saints are "seeking"

[1] See Eph. vi. 24, where the same word is translated "*sincerity.*"

here, and which they will fully attain in heaven. The passage does not touch the question of man's immortality at all.

Intermediate State.

Dead unconscious.	*Conscious.*
His sons come to honor, and he knoweth *it* not; and they are brought low, but he perceiveth *it* not of them. Job xiv. 21.	But his flesh upon him shall have pain, and his soul within him shall mourn. Job xiv. 22.
Whatsoever thy hand findeth to do, do *it* with thy might; for *there is* no work, nor device, nor knowledge, nor wisdom, in the grave, whither thou goest. Eccl. ix. 10.	The rich man also died, and was buried. And in hell he lifted up his eyes, being in torments. Luke xvi. 22, 23.

As preliminary to the discussion, we repeat that there is no proof that Job or any of his friends were *inspired* — divinely commissioned as religious teachers.[1]

Moreover, the ideas of the ancients, particularly in that early age in which Job lived, were very vague and obscure respecting the future state. "Life and immortality" were not "brought to light" till Christ came.

Whately, following Warburton, says: "To the Israelites of old Moses had no commission to hold out the hopes and fears of another world, but only a 'land flowing with milk and honey,' and long life, and victory, and other temporal rewards. But the 'bringing in of a better hope' by the gospel taught the Christian to 'set his affection on things above, not on things on the earth,' and to look for a heavenly Canaan, a land of promise beyond the grave. God's kingdom of old was a kingdom of this world; but Christ's kingdom is 'not of this world.'"[2]

Dr. Davidson[3] thus sets forth the Hebrew view of the con-

---

[1] Professor Stuart, speaking of the irrelevant appeals which are made to the Old Testament, both in and out of the pulpit, and the unsuitable quotations made from it, observes: "Books of such a peculiar nature as Job and Ecclesiastes, for example, are resorted to with as much confidence for *proof-texts*, as if they were all *preceptive*, and not an account of disputes and doubts about religious matters." — History of Old Test. Canon, p. 409 (Revised edition, p. 382).

[2] Future State, p. 150.

[3] Introd. to Old Test., ii. 290.

dition of the dead in "sheol," the place of departed spirits: "Their time is passed in a kind of sleep, whence they are only roused by some uncommon occurrence. Thus they are represented as shut up in a land of forgetfulness — dreamy shades almost destitute of consciousness."

Dr. Jahn, in his Biblical Archaeology,[1] gives, as will be seen subsequently, a more attractive view than the foregoing rationalistic one of Dr. Davidson. However, in the most favorable aspect of the case, it must be admitted that the notions of the ancient Israelites respecting the future life were not seldom quite obscure and indefinite. Nor is this strange; for *revelation is progressive.* There is an onward march of doctrine in the Bible, from its beginning to its close. The great truths of the Divinity of the Messiah, the atonement, justification by faith, and human immortality, were imperfectly revealed and crudely held in patriarchal times. Hengstenberg: "As far as the saints of the Old Testament attained in their knowledge, they were quite right; they were only excluded from farther light. But it is error alone which inspiration excludes, not the defect and imperfection of knowledge."

Those early times were the dim dawn of revelation; our age beholds the full radiance of the gospel sun at his meridian height. This consideration explains the apparent disagreement between the New Testament and the Old in regard to the intermediate state.

Just here the reader will observe that nearly all of the texts adduced by mortal-soulists to prove the unconsciousness of the dead, are taken *from the Old Testament,* and *particularly from its poetical books.* Now, to go back from *noonday* to *twilight* in search of our eschatology, — to ignore the plain and clear teachings of the New Testament, and adopt as a basis of doctrine the poetic utterances of a preliminary, rudimental, far less spiritual dispensation, — does not indicate the highest wisdom on the part of those who pursue this course. Yet this

[1] Section 314.

is the policy adopted by the mortal-soulists in advocating their theory.

But let us examine the foregoing texts.

Job xiv. 21 simply refers to man in his relation to the present life, and asserts that at death he is entirely *dissociated from* the things of earth; he has no more connection with them. But the very next verse shows that consciousness is not denied to the dead.

As to the next citation, Stuart and Hengstenberg take it as the statement of an objection which is afterwards refuted. The latter says: "The manner of the scriptures is to let doubts and murmurings have free and full expression, and then to vanquish them in open conflict with the sword of faith."

Job xiv. 22 is rendered by Delitzsch: "Only on his own account his flesh suffereth pain, and on his own account is his soul conscious of grief." Similarly Eichhorn, Noyes, Barnes, and Conant. Hofmann: "The pain of his own flesh, the sadness of his own soul alone engage him. He has therefore no room for rejoicing, nor does the joyous or sorrowful estate of others, though his nearest ones, affect him."

As to the text from Luke, if it be a parable, we may then say, with Bishop Bull, "It plainly belongs to the very scope and design of this parable to show what becomes of the souls of good and bad men after death." If it is not a parable its tenor cannot be a matter of doubt.

Prof. Bartlett:[1] "The question whether this is a history or a parable it is not necessary to discuss. In either mode the scripture teaches truth, important and often vital truth. The chief difference is that one mode asserts what has occurred; the other, 'what does occur.'"

In any aspect Christ could not have lent his sanction to falsehood or imposture. As Alford fitly remarks, "In conforming himself to the ordinary language current on these

---

[1] Life and Death Eternal, p. 219.

subjects, it is impossible to suppose that he whose essence is truth could have assumed as existing anything which does not exist. It would destroy the truth of our Lord's sayings, if we could conceive him to have used popular language which did *not point at truth*. And, accordingly, where *such* language was current, we find him not adopting, but protesting against it."[1]

Therefore, with Alford, Trench, Wordsworth, and the best commentators, we take the passage relative to the rich man and Lazarus as teaching, at all events, two things: *first*, that the soul of man is conscious after death; and *secondly*, that, according to its moral character, it goes either into a place of happiness and repose or into one of disquiet and misery. These two thoughts not only lie upon the surface of the narrative; but they also constitute its very life and essence.

The dead, asleep.	*Awake.*
And Jeroboam slept with his fathers, *even* with the kings of Israel. 2 Kings xiv. 29.	Hell from beneath is moved for thee to meet *thee* at thy coming: it stirreth up the dead for thee, *even* all the chief ones of the earth. Isa. xiv. 9.
For now should I have lain still and been quiet, I should have slept. Job iii. 13.	Being put to death in the flesh, but quickened by the Spirit. By which also he went and preached unto the spirits in prison. Which sometime were disobedient. 1 Pet. iii. 18-20.
Our friend Lazarus sleepeth; but I go that I may awake him out of sleep. Then said his disciples, Lord, if he sleep, he shall do well. Howbeit Jesus spake of his death: but they thought that he had spoken of taking of rest in sleep. Then said Jesus unto them plainly, Lazarus is dead. John xi. 11-14.	I saw under the altar the souls of them that were slain for the word of God, and for the testimony which they held. And they cried with a loud voice, saying, How long, O Lord, holy and true, dost thou not judge and avenge our blood on them that dwell on the earth? Rev. vi. 9, 10.
And when he had said this, he fell asleep. Acts vii. 60.	

The language which represents death as a "sleep" is figurative, and is founded upon *a certain resemblance of external phenomena*. But this application of the term does not necessitate the unconsciousness of the "sleeper;" for, as even Whately[2] concedes, "The mind, certainly for the most part, and probably always, continues active during sleep, though in a different manner." A high authority, Dunglison's Medical Dictionary, defines "sleep" as "temporary interruption of our relations with external objects." It is this interruption, with

[1] See Matt. xv. 5, 6. [2] Future State, p. 82.

the attendant inaction, the insensibility to external material objects, and the repose, which makes sleep the "image of death." In neither case have we proof that the mind ceases to act, becomes unconscious, or extinct.

The citation from Isaiah represents the dead as awake and conscious. Delitzsch: "All hades is overwhelmed with excitement and wonder, now that the king of Babel, that invincible ruler of the world, who, if not unexpected altogether, was not expected so soon, is actually approaching."

On the next quotation Alford says: "With the great majority of commentators, ancient and modern, I understand these words to say that our Lord, in his disembodied state, did go to the place of detention of departed spirits, and did there announce his work of redemption, preach salvation in fact, to the disembodied spirits of those who refused to obey the voice of God when the judgment of the flood was hanging over them."

Prof. Tayler Lewis:[1] "We are taught that there was *a work of Christ in hades.* He descended into hades; he makes proclamation 'ekeruxen' in hades to those who are there 'in ward.'" This interpretation, which was almost universally adopted by the early Christian church,[2] and which is far more tenable than any other, involves, of course, the consciousness of departed souls.

The text from Revelation is very explicit, representing the souls of those who had suffered martyrdom, not as insensible, but as awake in the place of rest.

---

[1] In Lange on Eccl., p. 130. Compare Bib. Sacra, Vol. iv. 708; xvi. 309; xix. 1.

[2] Professor Huidekoper: "In the second and third centuries, every branch and division of Christians, so far as their records enable us to judge, believed that Christ preached to the departed." — Christ's Mission to the Underworld, pp. 51, 52. Dietelmair, in his elaborate "Historia Dogmatis de Descensu Christi ad Inferos," says emphatically that this doctrine "in omni coetu Christiano creditum." — See chapters iv. and vi., of that work.

DOCTRINAL DISCREPANCIES.

Devoid of knowledge.	*Possess knowledge.*
For in death *there is* no remembrance of thee: in the grave who shall give thee thanks? Ps. vi. 5. The dead know not any thing, neither have they any more a reward: for the memory of them is forgotten. Also their love, and their hatred, and their envy, is now perished; neither have they any more a portion for ever in any *thing* that is done under the sun. Eccl. ix. 5, 6. For the grave cannot praise thee, death cannot celebrate thee: they that go down into the pit cannot hope for thy truth. Isa. xxxviii. 18.	And he said, For I will go down into the grave unto my son mourning. Gen. xxxvii. 35. And Samuel said to Saul, Why hast thou disquieted me, to bring me up? ... And the LORD hath done to him, as he spake by me: for the LORD hath rent the kingdom out of thy hand, and given it to thy neighbour, *even* to David. ... Moreover, the LORD will also deliver Israel with thee into the hand of the Philistines: and to-morrow *shalt* thou and thy sons *be* with me: the LORD also shall deliver the host of Israel into the hand of the Philistines. 1 Sam. xxviii. 15, 17, 19. But now he is dead, wherefore should I fast? can I bring him back again? I shall go to him, but he shall not return to me. 2 Sam. xii. 23. I pray thee therefore, father, that thou wouldest send him to my father's house: For I have five brethren; that he may testify unto them, lest they also come into this place of torment. ... Nay, father Abraham: but if one went unto them from the dead, they will repent. Luke xvi. 27, 28, 30. For for this cause was the gospel preached also to them that are dead, that they might be judged according to men in the flesh, but live according to God in the spirit. 1 Pet. iv. 6.

David's words are highly poetical and figurative, representing the dead as entirely separated from earthly scenes, employments, and society; and especially as giving, so far as visible and material things are concerned, no evidence of sensation or emotion. They speak of death in its earthly aspect.

The quotation from Ecclesiastes, Hengstenberg and Stuart take as the statement of an objection, with a view to refute it. The bald literalism which mortal-soulists apply to this passage is simply suicidal. For, it is asserted of the dead, including the saint as well as the sinner, and without any qualification, "*Neither have they any more a reward.*" Now a literal exegesis of this language absolutely cuts off Abraham, Moses, David, and all the righteous dead from any future reward! We think the above-named theorists would be slow to admit this logical result of their methods of exposition. Yet there is quite as much reason for insisting upon a literal interpretation of the words just cited, as of the clause, "The dead know not any thing."

The true explanation of this and kindred texts is the following: Zöckler: "The author now sees only the conditions of this world"; he speaks of man merely *in his relation to the present life*. This interpretation agrees admirably with the closing words, "Neither have they any more a portion forever in any thing that is done under the sun." That is, so far as *this* world is concerned, the dead have no knowledge, nor reward, nor portion. They are as completely severed from earthly affairs, as if they had passed into extinction.

The quotation from Isaiah, is the language of king Hezekiah of whose "inspiration" there is no proof.

Of the affirmative passages, the first should be rendered, "I will go down into sheol unto my son mourning."

Prof. Tayler Lewis:[1] "Jacob was going to his son; he was still his son; there is yet a tie between him and his father; he is still spoken of as a personality; he is still regarded as having a being somehow and somewhere." ... "It was not to his son in his grave, for Joseph had no grave. His body was supposed to be lying somewhere in the desert, or torn in pieces, or carried off, by the wild beasts."

Herder:[2] "Abraham was gathered to his fathers,[3] though he was not buried with them, and Jacob wished to go down to the realm of shades to his beloved son, although he supposed him to have been torn in pieces by wild beasts." In a word, Jacob expected, as a disembodied spirit, to meet and recognize the spirit of his son in the underworld. The same idea pervades David's words in 2 Sam. xii. concerning his child. As to 1 Sam. xxviii., apparently the soul of the prophet was permitted to return from sheol, and announce to the terrified Saul his im-

---

[1] In Lange on Genesis, p. 585.

[2] Spirit of Hebrew Poetry, i. 179.

[3] Alger, commenting on this expression, after citing the cases of Abraham and Isaac, of whom language similar is used, adds: "These instances might be multiplied. They prove that to be 'gathered unto one's fathers,' means to descend into sheol, and join there the hosts of the departed." — Hist. of Doct. of Fut. Life, p. 152.

DOCTRINAL DISCREPANCIES.   195

pending destruction. The reproof and the prediction are exactly in keeping with the character of Samuel, and show that he knew whereof he affirmed. He had not, therefore, in death parted with his knowledge.

Keil: " The modern orthodox commentators are unanimous in the opinion that the deceased prophet did really appear, and announce the destruction of Saul, not, however, in consequence of the magical arts of the witch, but through a miracle wrought by the omnipotence of God." Lord Arthur Hervey in Bible Commentary, and Archbishop Trench in " Shipwrecks of Faith," concur in this view. This is far the most natural and reasonable explanation. Saul's sin of " necromancy "[1] was thus made the occasion and commencement of his punishment.

We have elsewhere seen that the narrative of Dives in Luke xvi. presupposes the retention of knowledge by departed souls.

Alford interprets 1 Pet. iv. 6, of the souls of the antediluvians, shut up in hades, to whom Christ made the proclamation referred to in chapter iii. 17, 18. This interpretation assumes the possession of knowledge by disembodied spirits.

Exercise no mental powers.	*Do exercise them.*
The dead praise not the LORD, neither any that go down into silence. Ps. cxv. 17.	Dead *things* are formed from under the waters, and the inhabitants thereof. Job xxvi. 5.
His breath goeth forth, he returneth to his earth; in that very day his thoughts perish. Ps. cxlvi. 4.	Hell from beneath is moved for thee to meet *thee* at thy coming: it stirreth up the dead for thee. . . . All they shall speak and say unto thee, Art thou also become weak as we? Art thou become like unto us. Isa. xiv 9. 10.
	And behold, there talked with him two men, which were Moses and Elias. Who appeared in glory, and spake of his decease which he should accomplish at Jerusalem. Luke ix. 30. 31.
	For he is not a God of the dead, but of the living: for all live unto him. Luke xx. 38.

The first passage is a voice from out the twilight of the Old Dispensation. Life and immortality not having been fully revealed as yet, the author spoke according to his degree of knowledge and illumination.

In the second text, the " thoughts that perish " are the wicked

[1] See Law in Deut. xviii. 10–12.

man's plans and purposes which come to naught at his decease. Hengstenberg: "The thoughts which go to the grave with the dying man are his vain projects."[1]

In the case of the rich fool,[2] his "thoughts" of building larger barns, and of many years of ease and prosperity, — all his selfish and worldly schemes, — "perished" in that same night.

Delitzsch renders Job xxvi. 5, thus: "The shades are put to pain, deep under the waters and their inhabitants." With this rendering Barnes, Conant, and Noyes substantially agree.

Isa. xiv. 9 is rendered by Delitzsch, "The kingdom of the dead below is all in uproar on account of thee, to meet thy coming; it stirreth up the shades for thee." Similarly Henderson, Noyes, and other critics. Now the Hebrew term "rephaim," rendered "dead" in our version of the last two texts, means according to the best Hebraists, not simply the *dead*, but "that part of man which *survives* death."[3]

As to the first text from Luke, all that need be said is this; Moses had been dead nearly fifteen centuries. But the disciples now see and recognize him, and hear him speak. It does not, therefore, seem probable that Moses became extinct at death, but that his soul survived and continued to exercise its faculties. Otherwise, it would seem that *his identity must have been lost* at death; and that for *him* — the original self-same Moses — there could be no after life.

---

[1] In Isa. lv. 7, "Let the wicked forsake his way, and the unrighteous man his thoughts," the term "thoughts" is used in a similar bad sense. According to literalistic principles, this passage amounts to an exhortation to *stop thinking!*

[2] See Luke xii. 16–20.

[3] Professor Conant, in Smith's Bib. Dict., Article "Dead," says the term means "disembodied spirits separated from the body at death, and continuing to live in a separate existence." Fuerst: "A shadow, shadowy being." He adds that, in the two passages just referred to, these shades are represented as stirred up out of their rest, and as feeling the administrative agency of God. Gesenius: "The *shades, manes,* dwelling in hades, whom the Hebrews supposed to be destitute of blood and animal life, but yet not wholly without some faculties of mind." See, also, Boettcher, "De Inferis," pp. 94–100.

Luke xx. 38; He is not a God of *extinct* or *non-existent* beings, therefore Abraham, Isaac, and Jacob are still *living*. The soul then survives the body, and a resurrection is possible.[1] As Lavater and Stier well say, the passage is a "weighty testimony against the 'sleep of the soul' in the intermediate state." The preceding passages clearly presuppose the conscious activity of departed souls.

In darkness and silence.	*In glory and blessedness.*
There the prisoners rest together; they hear not the voice of the oppressor. Job iii. 18.	Thou shalt guide me with thy counsel, and afterward receive me *to* glory. Ps. lxxiii. 24.
Before I go *whence* I shall not return, *even* to the land of darkness, and the shadow of death. Job x. 21.	The path of the just *is* as the shining light, that shineth more and more unto the perfect day. Prov. iv. 18.
Shall thy loving-kindness be declared in the grave? *or* thy faithfulness in destruction? Shall thy wonders be known in the dark? and thy righteousness in the land of forgetfulness? Ps. lxxxviii. 11, 12.	Whilst we are at home in the body, we are absent from the Lord. 2 Cor. v. 6.
	For to me to live *is* Christ, and to die *is* gain. Phil. i. 21.

Of Job's authority as a religious teacher we have previously spoken. As to the language cited from the eighty-eighth Psalm, it is Oriental poetry, therefore hyperbolical and intensely figurative. To interpret it literally, is to do it the utmost possible violence. For example, in the fifth verse it is said of the "slain" that God remembers them no more; in the sixth verse, the Psalmist represents himself as "in the lowest pit, in darkness, in the deeps." Upon these latter words Hengstenberg says, "the *grave of deep places*, in verse 6, is sheol deep in the earth, and 'the dark places' are the dark places of sheol." But was the Psalmist already in sheol, the underworld? This would be the absurd conclusion to which a rigid literalism would lead.

On the theory that the dead are unconscious, in darkness and silence, the "path of the just" instead of growing brighter "unto the perfect day," is disrupted at death by a fearful chasm of black non-existence. In place of a continuous shining track of light, we see a yawning abyss of unfathomable gloom. Nor would Paul lying *unconscious in the grave* be "present with

[1] Consult Alford's significant, but concise, comment on this text.

the Lord" more truly than when he was *living* in the love, service, and fellowship of Christ. Nor does it appear that it would be " gain " for Paul to " die,"— to relinquish his loving, tireless, and blessed labor for the Master, and go into unconscious hibernation or blank nonentity, in the cold sepulchre. A glowing heart like Paul's would hardly count a dormant state, like that of " The Seven Sleepers," to be " gain."

In this connection, we give the views of the Hebrews, particularly those of later and more enlightened times.

Lightfoot:[1] " It was universally believed amongst the Jews, that pure and holy souls when they left this body went into happiness, to Abraham."

Dr. Jahn:[2] In sheol " the departed spirits rejoice in that rest so much desired by the Orientals; and there the living hope to see once more their beloved ancestors and children."

Not with Christ.	*The righteous with him.*
Ye shall seek me; and, as I said unto the Jews, Whither I go, ye cannot come, so now I say to you. John xiii. 33.	And Jesus said unto him, Verily, I say unto thee, To-day shalt thou be with me in paradise. Luke xxiii. 43.
For David is not ascended into the heavens. Acts ii. 34.	Stephen, calling upon *God*, and saying, Lord Jesus, receive my spirit. Acts vii. 59.
	We are confident, *I say*, and willing rather to be absent from the body, and to be present with the Lord. 2 Cor. v. 8.
	For I am in a strait betwixt two, having a desire to depart, and to be with Christ; which is far better. Phil. i. 23.

The first text alludes to the time subsequent to Christ's ascension. Then he was no longer visibly and personally with them; whither he had gone they could not *then* go. Their earthly mission must first be accomplished.

David had not been raised from the dead, and his body and soul re-united. He had not yet ascended to heaven, and *entered upon his full reward*, but was in the intermediate state, tranquilly awaiting the resurrection.

The opposed texts show that the righteous are at death, in a certain sense *with* Christ, present with the Lord, in "disem-

---

[1] Hor. Hebraicae, iii. 171 (Gandell's edition).
[2] Bib. Archaeol., Sec. 314.

DOCTRINAL DISCREPANCIES. 199

bodied and imperfect bliss" which is a foretaste of complete felicity to be awarded them at the last day.

Together in one place.
The LORD will also deliver Israel with thee into the hand of the Philistines: and to-morrow *shalt* thou and thy sons *be* with me. 1 Sam. xxviii. 19.
All go unto one place; all are of the dust, and all turn to dust again. Eccl. iii. 20.

In different places.
And in hell he lifted up his eyes, being in torments, and seeth Abraham afar off, and Lazarus in his bosom. . . . And beside all this, between us and you there is a great gulf fixed. Luke xvi. 23, 26.
Judas by transgression fell, that he might go to his own place. Acts i. 25.

The first two passages teach that the good and bad, at their departure from this life, go alike into the intermediate state, but do not assert that their *condition* there is the same.

In Luke xvi. we see the rich man and Lazarus both in the intermediate state, but one in misery, the other in happiness. In a certain sense, both went " to one place "; in another sense, they went to very different places.

Acts i. 25, teaches that Judas went to "his own place," to the punishment appropriate to his conduct. Such is the view of Olshausen, DeWette, Livermore, Barnes, Hackett, Meyer, Alford, and other commentators.

In the dust and the grave.
And many of them that sleep in the dust of the earth shall awake. Dan. xii. 2.
All that are in the graves shall hear his voice. John v. 28.

Saints, with God.
We are confident, *I say*, and willing rather to be absent from the body, and to be present with the Lord. 2 Cor. v. 8.
Them also which sleep in Jesus will God bring with him. 1 Thess. iv. 14.

The quotation from Daniel refers to man in his physical organism and relations. As to his material, bodily form, in which he is cognizable by our senses, he "sleeps in the dust," at death.

The literalistic exposition of the text from John leads to the conclusion that the *unburied* dead are not to be raised. If the phraseology "all that are *in the graves*" is to be rigidly pressed, then it is a legitimate inference that those who sleep beneath the waves of ocean, those who were devoured by wild beasts, those who were burned at the stake, as not being "in the graves," will *not* " hear his voice and come forth."

Doubtless the expression is equivalent simply to "all the

dead." The last two texts imply that the souls of departed saints are with God, not necessarily in the highest rewards of heaven, but " in the bosom of Abraham," in paradise, joyfully awaiting those rewards.

Resurrection.

Dead to be raised.	Not to be raised.
Thy dead *men* shall live, *together with* my dead body shall they arise. Isa. xxvi. 19. Now that the dead are raised, even Moses shewed at the bush. Luke xx 37. For since by man *came* death, by man *came* also the resurrection of the dead. ... The trumpet shall sound, and the dead shall be raised incorruptible. 1 Cor. xv. 21, 52.	He that goeth down to the grave shall come up no *more*. Job vii. 9. Man lieth down, and riseth not: till the heavens *be* no more, they shall not awake, nor be raised out of their sleep. Job xiv. 12. *They are* dead, they shall not live; *they are* deceased, they shall not rise. Isa. xxvi. 14. They that swear by the sin of Samaria, and say, Thy god, O Dan, liveth; and, The manner of Beer-sheba liveth; even they shall fall, and never rise up again. Amos viii. 14.

The quotations from Job express the opinion, or perhaps, the temporary doubts, of a good, but uninspired, man. They cannot counterbalance the express statements of inspiration.

Isaiah asserts that certain foreign powers, the Assyrians, Babylonians, etc., who had oppressed the Israelites, were deceased and should not " rise"; that is, *to resume their former arbitrary sway.* Not the resurrection of individuals, but the restoration of fallen despotisms, is denied.

The text from Amos has no reference to the future world. It predicts simply the irretrievable overthrow of certain idolaters, in this world.

Universal resurrection.	A partial one.
The hour is coming, in the which all that are in the graves shall hear his voice, and shall come forth. John v. 28, 29.	And many of them that sleep in the dust of the earth shall awake. Dan. xii. 2.

According to Fuerst, the word translated " many," means likewise *crowds* or *masses*.

Calvin: "The word *many* seems here clearly put for *all*." Stuart regards it as " equivalent to our word *multitudes*." Barnes: " There would be a vast or general resurrection from the dead ; so much so that the mind would be interested mainly in the contemplation of the *great hosts* who would thus come forth."

Jesus raised first.

That Christ should suffer, *and* that he should be the first that should rise from the dead. Acts xxvi. 23.

Now is Christ risen from the dead, *and* become the first-fruits of them that slept. 1 Cor. xv. 20.

Others raised previously.

And the LORD heard the voice of Elijah; and the soul of the child came into him again, and he revived. 1 Kings xvii. 22.

And they cast the man into the sepulchre of Elisha: and when the man was let down, and touched the bones of Elisha, he revived, and stood up on his feet. 2 Kings xiii. 21.

And he that was dead sat up, and began to speak. And he delivered him to his mother. Luke vii. 15.

Romans vi. 9 furnishes the solution of the difficulty. Jesus was the first who rose from the dead *to die no more.* All others who were raised, passed a second time through the gates of death. Over *him*, death "hath no more dominion." Hence, he is the "first-begotten of the dead," the first who was raised to immortal life.

Final Judgment.

Ascribed to God.

Shall not the Judge of all the earth do right? Gen. xviii. 25.

The heavens shall declare his righteousness: for God *is* judge himself. Ps. l. 6.

To Christ.

For the Father judgeth no man, but hath committed all judgment unto the Son. John v. 22.

We shall all stand before the judgment-seat of Christ. Rom. xiv. 10.

God will judge the world by Jesus Christ.[1]

Attributed to Christ.

When the Son of man shall come in his glory, and all the holy angels with him, then shall he sit upon the throne of his glory: and before him shall be gathered all nations: and he shall separate them one from another, as a shepherd divideth *his* sheep from the goats. Matt. xxv. 31, 32.

And Jesus said, For judgment I am come into this world; that they which see not might see, and that they which see, might be made blind. John ix. 39.

For we must all appear before the judgment-seat of Christ. 2 Cor. v. 10.

Disclaimed by Him.

Ye judge after the flesh; I judge no man. John viii. 15.

And if any man hear my words, and believe not, I judge him not: for I came not to judge the world, but to save the world. John xii. 47.

These two classes of texts refer, the one to the second, the other to the first advent of our Lord. At his first coming, his object was to present himself, not as the Judge, but as the Saviour, of men; not to condemn but to save them. When he comes the second time, it will be "in flaming fire, taking

---

[1] Acts xvii. 31; Rom. ii. 16.

vengeance on them that know not God, and that obey not the gospel."[1]

Yet the "judging of the world," involving the condemnation of the guilty, was not the *ultimate object* of Christ's mission, but rather a *subordinate* and *incidental result* of that mission.

Administered by God.	*By men also.*
God the Judge of all. Heb. xii. 23. And I saw the dead, small and great, stand before God: and the books were opened. Rev. xx. 12.	Ye which have followed me in the regeneration, when the Son of man shall sit in the throne of his glory, ye also shall sit upon twelve thrones, judging the twelve tribes of Israel. Matt. xix. 28. That ye may eat and drink at my table in my kingdom, and sit on thrones judging the twelve tribes of Israel. Luke xxii. 30. But he that is spiritual judgeth all things, yet he himself is judged of no man. 1 Cor. ii 15. Do ye not know that the saints shall judge the world? and if the world shall be judged by you, are ye unworthy to judge the smallest matters? Know ye not that we shall judge angels? 1 Cor. vi. 2, 3.

Barnes takes Matt. xix. 28, as implying not so much an actual exercise of the power of passing judgment, as the honor attached to the office. The apostles should, at the last day, be relatively honored as judges are.

In 1 Cor. ii. 15, the Greek word employed is the same which in the preceding verse is translated "discerned." It has no reference to the final judgment, but denotes spiritual insight and discrimination in the present life.

As to the last citation, it may be taken simply as asserting that the saints, by their example, would "judge," i.e. *condemn*, sinful men and angels. This interpretation is corroborated by Matt. xii. 41, 42, which asserts that the Ninevites and the queen of Sheba should rise up in the judgment with that generation and "condemn" it; that is, by their example.

Chrysostom: "The saints shall judge the world by their exemplary judgment, because by their example the perfidiousness of the world shall be condemned."

Whately:[2] "Not that he meant, or was ever understood to

---

[1] 2 Thess. i. 8.   [2] Future State, pp. 133–138.

mean, that these persons would themselves take a share in the final judgment; but that their conduct would be a condemnation of the unbelieving generation, who rejected one greater than Jonas, and than Solomon." In another paragraph, the same writer strongly supports this explanation, and continues: "Any one who takes the right course, by so doing, condemns, — in the New Testament language, 'judges,' — those who, with equal opportunities, choose the wrong. This was the case with the Corinthian Christians (or saints); who, by embracing the gospel, judged (in this sense) their unbelieving neighbors, to whom it had been proposed, and who rejected it."

This interpretation relieves the saints of actual participation in the work of judging mankind.

Even if, with Alford and many critics, we feel constrained by the tenor of the passage, to admit this actual participation, still, since the power which the saints exercise is all *derived from God*, the work of judgment may properly be attributed wholly to him.

Future Punishment, — Its Nature.

Continued misery.	*End of consciousness.*
So shall it be at the end of the world: the angels shall come forth, and sever the wicked from among the just, and shall cast them into the furnace of fire. Matt. xiii. 49, 50.	For lo, thine enemies O LORD, for lo, thine enemies shall perish. Ps. xcii. 9.
And shall cut him asunder, and appoint *him* his portion with the hypocrites. Matt. xxiv. 51.	And he shall bring upon them their own iniquity, and shall cut them off in their own wickedness. Ps. xciv. 23.
And cast ye the unprofitable servant into outer darkness: there shall be weeping and gnashing of teeth. Matt. xxv. 30.	All the wicked will he destroy Ps. cxlv. 20.
The same shall drink of the wine of the wrath of God, which is poured out without mixture into the cup of his indignation; and he shall be tormented with fire and brimstone in the presence of the holy angels, and in the presence of the Lamb: And the smoke of their torment ascendeth up for ever and ever: and they have no rest day nor night. Rev. xiv. 10, 11.	They that forsake the LORD shall be consumed. Isa i. 28.
	The soul that sinneth, it shall die. Ezek. xviii. 20.
	Who shall be punished with everlasting destruction. 2 Thess. i. 9.
	The day of judgment and perdition of ungodly men. 2 Pet. iii. 7.

According to the received view, the texts, at the right, while implying *ruin, irremediable overthrow*, do not mean *annihilation* or *extinction*. Mortal-soulists, or "annihilationists" as they are commonly designated, interpret these texts, on the contrary, with a bald and rigid literalism, inferring from them the actual annihilation of the wicked. Mr. Hudson,[1] the ablest author of this class, observes: "The literal sense of the terms in question is manifestly the true one in most instances." Blain asserts that "death" is "extinction of being, soul and body."

Dr. Ives[2] says that death is "the cessation of existence," the first death being a temporary, the second a final cessation. These definitions are founded upon a literalistic, though not self-consistent, exegesis of scripture.

To show the irrelevancy and unsoundness of the arguments employed by writers of this class, the following examples of scripture usage are introduced. The reader will see, at a glance, to what absurdities literalistic interpretation, if consistently carried out, would lead its advocates.

The wicked perish.	The righteous perish.
So let all thine enemies perish, O LORD. Judg. v. 31.	There is a just *man* that perisheth in his righteousness. Eccl. vii. 15.
But the wicked shall perish. Ps. xxxvii. 20.	The righteous perisheth, and no man layeth *it* to heart. Isa. lvii. 1.
He that speaketh lies shall perish. Prov. xix. 9.	The good *man* is perished out of the earth. Micah vii. 2.

In all these cases, the same Hebrew term, "äbadh," is used.

Now, if this term, in the first series of texts, necessarily implies that the wicked are to be annihilated, it is clear that, in the second, it implies, for the same reasons and with the same force, the annihilation of the righteous. Such is the logical conclusion to which literalism conducts us.

Sinners annihilated.	Annihilated objects, existing.
Likewise the fool and the brutish person perish. Ps. xlix. 10 (11).[3]	And with all lost things of thy brother's, which he hath lost, and thou hast found, shalt thou do likewise. Deut. xxii. 3.
For, lo, they that are far from thee shall perish. Ps. lxxiii. 27.	
A false witness shall perish. Prov. xxi. 28.	And the asses of Kish, Saul's father were lost.... And as for thine asses that were lost three days ago, set not thy mind on them; for they are found. 1 Sam. ix. 3, 20.

Here the same word "äbadh" rendered "perish" in the first series, is translated "lost" in the second series. If now in the

---

[1] Debt and Grace, p. 182. [2] Bible Doctrine of the Soul, p. 42.
[3] We put in parenthesis the number of the verse as it is in the Hebrew.

one case it implies the extinction of sinners, in the other it implies the extinction of the "lost things" and of Kish's asses. It would seem that the process of annihilation, in the latter cases, could hardly have been fatal to the existence of the objects mentioned, for they are afterwards " found."

Wicked cut off.	*The Messiah cut off.*
For evil doers shall be cut off. . . . When the wicked are cut off, thou shalt see *it*. Ps. xxxvii. 9, 34.	And after threescore and two weeks shall Messiah be cut off, but not for himself. Dan. ix. 26.

In these three cases, "kärath," is rendered "cut off." If the first texts teach the annihilation of the wicked, the last implies equally strongly that *the Messiah was annihilated!*

Wicked destroyed.	*Persons destroyed, yet alive.*
Thou shalt destroy them that speak leasing. Ps. v. 6.	He hath destroyed me on every side. Job xix. 10.
All the wicked will he destroy. Ps. cxlv. 20.	My people are destroyed for lack of knowledge. Hosea iv. 6.
And he shall destroy the sinners thereof out of it. Isa. xiii. 9.	O Israel thou hast destroyed thyself; but in me *is* thine help. Hos. xiii 9.

If the Hebrew words, and their English equivalent "destroy," used in these cases, imply extinction or termination of conscious existence, we have, in the last citation, a people who, although they had been annihilated, were yet in a hopeful condition.

An odd kind of "annihilation" that must be, which is still susceptible of relief! The sense clearly is, "Thou hast brought great calamities upon thyself, but in me is thine help."

Sinners destroyed.	*Inanimate objects destroyed.*
But the transgressors shall be destroyed together. Ps. xxxvii. 38.	And Pharaoh's servants said unto him, . . . Knowest thou not yet that Egypt is destroyed? Ex. x. 7.
If any man defile the temple of God, him shall God destroy. 1 Cor. iii. 17.	Am I now come up without the LORD against this place to destroy it? The LORD said to me, Go up against this land, and destroy it. 2 Kings xviii. 25.
Who shall be punished with everlasting destruction. 2 Thess. i. 9.	Babylon is suddenly fallen and destroyed; . . . take balm for her pain, if so be she may be healed. Jer. li. 8.
	And shouldest destroy them which destroy the earth. Rev. xi. 18.

It need not be said that in these cases, the literalistic interpretation of the terms "destroy" and "destruction" would land us in the grossest exegetical absurdities.[1]

---

[1] An example of similar kind is furnished by the literalistic exposition of Mal. iv. 1–3. The prophet declares that the wicked shall be burned,

Evil doers consumed.
Let the sinners be consumed out of the earth. Ps. civ. 35.
They that forsake the LORD shall be consumed. Isa. i. 28.
And the scorner is consumed. Isa. xxix. 20.

Things without life consumed.
There shall be an overflowing shower in mine anger, and great hailstones in *my* fury to consume *it*. So will I break down the wall. Ezek. xiii 13, 14.
I have heard all thy blasphemies which thou hast spoken against the mountains of Israel, saying, They are laid desolate, they are given us to consume. Ezek. xxxv. 12.

Of course, a wall "consumed" by "hail-stones," and mountains "consumed" by men, would hardly be understood as having ceased to exist.

Wicked "was not."
Yet he passed away, and lo, he *was not*: yea I sought him, but he could not be found. Ps. xxxvii. 36.

Enoch "was not."
And Enoch walked with God: and he *was* not; for God took him. Gen. v. 24.

The Hebrew for "was not," is exactly the same in these two cases. Now if the first passage teaches the extinction of the wicked, the second teaches that Enoch became extinct. Yet so far from this, we know that he was "translated that he should not see death."[1]

Wicked devoured.
And fire came down from God out of heaven, and devoured them. Rev. xx. 9.

Pious devoured.
If a man bring you into bondage, if a man devour *you*. 2 Cor. xi. 20.
But if ye bite and devour one another, take heed that ye be not consumed one of another. Gal. v. 15.

In these three instances, kindred words of equal intensity are employed. The inference is not difficult.

God's adversaries devoured.
Judgment and fiery indignation, which shall devour the adversaries. Heb. x. 27.

Widows' houses devoured.
Beware of the scribes, ... which devour widows' houses. Mark xii. 38, 40.

The reader will observe that the Greek verb of the first text occurs in the second in a strengthened form.[2] So that, if the first text teaches the annihilation of the wicked, the second teaches that "widows' houses" were *doubly annihilated* by the scribes.

and adds that they shall "*be ashes*," (not "*as* ashes") under the feet of the righteous. The folly of taking such language literally need not be pointed out.

[1] See Heb. xi. 5.
[2] "$\dot{\epsilon}\sigma\theta\acute{\iota}\omega$" in Heb. x. 27, "$\kappa\alpha\tau\epsilon\sigma\theta\acute{\iota}\omega$" in Mark xii. 40; 2 Cor. xi. 20.

Sinners devoured.
But if ye refuse and rebel, ye shall be devoured with the sword. Isa. i. 20.
Therefore all they that devour thee shall be devoured. Jer. xxx. 16.

A forest devoured persons.
For the battle was there scattered over the face of all the country: and the wood devoured more people that day than the sword devoured. 2 Sam. xviii. 8.

In all these passages, the same Hebrew verb "äkal" is used. In the latter instance, literalism, it need not be remarked, would make nonsense of the narrative. Yet there is as much reason for a literal explication of the latter text as of the two former texts.

Wicked torn and broken.
Thy right hand. O LORD, hath dashed in pieces the enemy. Ex. xv. 6.
The adversaries of the LORD shall be broken to pieces. 1 Sam. ii. 10.
Thou shalt break them with a rod of iron; thou shalt dash them in pieces like a potter's vessel. Ps ii. 9.
Consider this, ye that forget God, lest I tear you in pieces. Ps. l. 22.

Righteous likewise.
He teareth me in his wrath; ... he hath broken me asunder: he hath also taken me by my neck, and shaken me to pieces; .. he cleaveth my reins asunder, and doth not spare; he poureth out my gall upon the ground. He breaketh me with breach upon breach. Job xvi. 9, 12, 13, 14.
They break in pieces thy people, O LORD. Ps. xciv. 5.

Here language equally strong and intense is applied to the calamities befalling the righteous and the wicked. If in the former case extinction of existence is intended, why not in the latter case?

Wicked broken in pieces.
Associate yourselves, O ye people, and ye shall be broken in pieces. Isa. viii. 9.

Objects broken, yet still existing.
The sacrifices of God are a broken spirit: a broken and a contrite heart. Ps. li. 17.
And shall devour the whole earth, and shall tread it down, and break it in pieces. Dan. vii. 23.

To show the complete absurdity of insisting upon the literal interpretation of these and similar expressions, it need only be mentioned that Ps. li. 17, "A broken and a contrite heart," is, when rendered literally, "a heart *broken in pieces and shivered.*"[1]

Wicked blotted out.
And the LORD said, I will destroy man whom I have created from the face of the earth: both man and beast, and the creeping thing Gen vi. 7.
Whosoever hath sinned against me, him will I blot out of my book. Ex. xxxii. 33.
Let them be blotted out of the book of the living. Ps. lxix. 28 (29).

Things blotted out, yet existing
I will utterly put out the remembrance of Amalek from under heaven. Ex. xvii. 14.
Blot out all mine iniquities. Ps. li. 9 (11).
I have blotted out, as a thick cloud, thy transgressions. Isa. xliv. 22.
Blotting out the hand-writing of ordinances that was against us. Col. ii 14.

---

[1] Professor Bartlett, "Life and Death Eternal," p. 98.

In all the cases cited here from the Old Testament the expressions "destroy," "blot out," "utterly put out," are translations of the Hebrew term "mächäh."

But this word does not imply annihilation; for when "sins" are "blotted out" they are not annihilated. A *fact*, a *deed*, is not susceptible of annihilation. It may be forgiven, perchance forgotten, but not recalled or undone.

When the "ordinances" of the Mosaic law were "blotted out," they did not cease to exist; they merely became inoperative. Nor does the declaration that God would "utterly put out the remembrance of Amalek" imply the *extinction* of that remembrance; for *the declaration itself perpetuates that remembrance.*

Wicked have an end.	*The righteous also.*
Amalek *was* the first of the nations, but his latter end *shall be* that he perish for ever. Num. xxiv. 20.	Let me die the death of the righteous, and let my last end be like his. Num. xxiii. 10.
The end of the wicked shall be cut off. Ps. xxxvii. 38.	So the LORD blessed the latter end of Job more than his beginning. Job xlii. 12
Whose end *is* destruction. Phil. iii. 19.	For the end of *that* man *is* peace. Ps. xxxvii. 37.

Does the word "end" necessarily imply *termination of being*? If so, the fate of the righteous would not be an enviable one.

Wicked die, are dead.	*Righteous die, are dead.*
And you *hath he quickened*, who were dead in trespasses and sins. Eph. ii. 1.	Likewise reckon ye also yourselves to be dead indeed unto sin, but alive unto God. Rom. vi. 11.
But she that liveth in pleasure is dead while she liveth. 1 Tim. v. 6.	I protest by your rejoicing which I have in Christ Jesus our Lord, I die daily. 1 Cor. xv. 31.
I know thy works, that thou hast a name that thou livest, and art dead. Rev. iii. 1.	For ye are dead, and your life is hid with Christ in God. Col. iii. 3.

From these texts it is perfectly clear that persons may "die," and be "dead," yet all the while be physically alive and conscious. It follows that the phrase "living death," though scouted by certain writers, conveys, nevertheless, a perfectly reasonable and scriptural idea.

We have now passed rapidly in review the strongest, and apparently the most conclusive, proof-texts[1] adduced by annihilationists, and we reach the following results:

---

[1] Our present limits allow only a hasty glance at the subject. The author

(1) Those persons who undertake to build a doctrine upon the figures of poetry and of Oriental idiom are expending their labor just as wisely as they would be in endeavoring to make a pyramid stand upon its apex. Their foundation is inadequate, and their efforts nugatory.

(2) As to the Hebrew terms rendered in our version, "consume," "cut off," "die," "destroy," "devour," "perish," and the like, neither in the original terms, nor in their English equivalents, nor in the connection in which they stand, is there inherent force or aught else which necessitates, or even warrants, the interpretation of them as implying annihilation, extinction of consciousness, or cessation of existence.

(3) On the literalistic hypothesis these words prove *too much*, and so prove nothing. For they would prove that the Messiah was annihilated at his crucifixion; that the righteous are annihilated at death; that after the Israelites had annihilated themselves there was still "help" for them; with all manner of similar absurdities.

Instruments.

Shame and disgrace.

Let them be confounded and troubled forever; yea, let them be put to shame. Ps. lxxxiii. 17.

Some to shame *and* everlasting contempt. Dan. xii. 2.

Friend, how camest thou in hither, not having a wedding-garment? And he was speechless. Matt. xxii. 12.

Of him also shall the Son of man be ashamed, when he cometh in the glory of his Father with the holy angels. Mark viii. 38.

A whirlwind.

A whirlwind of the LORD is gone forth in fury, even a grievous whirlwind: it shall fall grievously upon the head of the wicked. Jer. xxiii. 19.

For they have sown the wind, and they shall reap the whirlwind. Hos. viii. 7.

These and the subsequent texts illustrate different aspects or relations of the punishment which will overtake the wicked.

A worm.

Where their worm dieth not, and the fire is not quenched. Mark ix. 44 (also 46, 48).

A tempest.

Upon the wicked he shall rain snares, fire and brimstone, and a horrible tempest. Ps. xi. 6.

So persecute them with thy tempest, and make them afraid with thy storm. Ps. lxxxiii. 15.

contemplates publishing hereafter a work in which the history of Thnetopsychism, and the arguments adduced in its favor, will be more fully investigated.

Darkness.	Fire.
But the children of the kingdom shall be cast out into outer darkness: there shall be weeping and gnashing of teeth. Matt. viii. 12. Bind him hand and foot, and take him away, and cast *him* into outer darkness. Matt. xxii. 13. And cast ye the unprofitable servant into outer darkness. Matt. xxv. 30.	The Son of man shall send forth his angels, and they shall gather out of his kingdom all things that offend, and them which do iniquity; And shall cast them into a furnace of fire. Matt. xiii. 41, 42. Depart from me, ye cursed, into everlasting fire, prepared for the devil and his angels. Matt xxv. 41. And whosoever was not found written in the book of life was cast into the lake of fire. Rev. xx. 15.

"Darkness" is, in *one* respect, and "fire" in *another* respect, a fit emblem of the punishment.

Dr. J. P. Thompson:[1] "The laws of language require us to understand from these very metaphors, that the future state of the ungodly will be one of conscious and irremediable misery — the 'darkness' of banishment from God, the 'unquenchable fires' of memory, the 'undying worm' of remorse — a state of mental anguish prefigured by physical emblems."

It seems impossible to weigh carefully the foregoing words of scripture, without the resulting conviction that the ruin and overthrow which are threatened to the incorrigible, will be *swift, terrible, and remediless.*

Degrees.

Same for all.	Different gradations.
And when they came that *were hired* about the eleventh hour, they received every man a penny. But when the first came, they supposed that they should have received more; and they likewise received every man a penny. And when they had received *it*, they murmured against the good man of the house: saying, These last have wrought *but* one hour, and thou hast made them equal unto us, which have borne the burden and heat of the day. Matt. xx. 9–12. Then shall he say also unto them on the left hand, Depart from me, ye cursed, into everlasting fire, prepared for the devil and his angels. Matt. xxv. 41. And whosoever was not found written in the book of life was cast into the lake of fire. Rev. xx. 15.	It shall be more tolerable for the land of Sodom and Gomorrah, in the day of judgment, than for that city. Matt. x.15. It shall be more tolerable for Tyre and Sidon at the day of judgment, than for you. Matt. xi. 22. And that servant which knew his lord's will, and prepared not *himself*, neither did according to his will, shall be beaten with many *stripes*. But he that knew not, and did commit things worthy of stripes, shall be beaten with few *stripes*. Luke xii. 47, 48. Who will render to every man according to his deeds. Rom. ii. 6 That every one may receive the things done in *his* body, according to that he hath done, whether *it be* good or bad. 2 Cor. v. 10. And death and hell delivered up the dead which were in them; and they were judged every man according to their works. Rev. xx. 13.

The first series of passages sets forth the *general fact* of

[1] Theology of Christ, p. 234.

future awards, without going into details; the second specifies the *degrees* or *differences* of retribution. Some have supposed that the parable in Matt. xx. is designed to teach "the equality of rewards," and, by implication, that of punishments. Trench interprets it better, as intended to "rebuke the spirit of self-exalting comparison of ourselves with others, and to emphasize the fact that the saints' reward is to be of grace, not of works." Alford takes a similar view.

May not, however, the teaching of the parable be simply this: In cases where the *opportunity* to act is wanting, God rewards the *disposition* in the same manner as he would have done the *action itself*.

The absolute equality of rewards or of punishments is not implied in this parable. As Whately [1] observes: "We may be sure there will be no want of mansions, or of suitable variety of mansions, either in the place of reward or of punishment."

Duration.

Unending.	Will terminate.
Whose fan *is* in his hand, and he will throughly purge his floor, and gather his wheat into the garner; but he will burn up the chaff with unquenchable fire. Matt. iii. 12.	I have sworn by myself, the word is gone out of my mouth *in* righteousness, and shall not return, That unto me every knee shall bow, every tongue shall swear. Isa. xlv. 23.
Whosoever speaketh against the Holy Ghost, it shall not be forgiven him, neither in this world, neither in the *world* to come. Matt. xii. 32.	And thou be cast into prison. Verily I say unto thee, Thou shalt by no means come out thence, till thou hast paid the uttermost farthing. Matt. v. 25, 26.
And these shall go away into everlasting punishment: but the righteous into life eternal. Matt. xxv. 46.	That at the name of Jesus every knee should bow, ... and *that* every tongue should confess that Jesus Christ *is* Lord. Phil. ii. 10, 11.
But he that shall blaspheme against the Holy Ghost hath never forgiveness, but is in danger of eternal damnation.[2] Mark iii. 29.	
He that believeth not the Son, shall not see life; but the wrath of God abideth on him. John iii. 36.	
And he shall be tormented with fire	

[1] Future State, p. 171.

[2] Griesbach, Lachmann, Alford, Tregelles, Tischendorf, and Meyer apparently, read "eternal *sin*." This reading, sustained as it is by the best critical authorities, affords a very strong incidental proof of the endless duration of future punishment. Eternal sin *is* eternal punishment. In this view, Mark iii. 29 is one of the most fearfully significant passages in the New Testament. "Eternal sin!" Who can fathom the meaning of these words?

| *Unending.* | *Will terminate.* |

and brimstone in the presence of the holy angels, and in the presence of the Lamb. And the smoke of their torment ascendeth up for ever and ever: and they have no rest day nor night. Rev. xiv. 10, 11.

And the devil that deceived them was cast into the lake of fire and brimstone, where the beast and the false prophet *are*, and shall be tormented day and night for ever and ever. Rev. xx. 10.

That the texts at the left fairly imply the endless duration of future punishment, we have no doubt. The question is: Do those at the right militate against the doctrine? Such expressions as "unquenchable[1] fire," "not forgiven, neither in this world, neither in the world to come," "everlasting punishment,"[2]

[1] The Greek term ἄσβεστος is defined by Liddell and Scott thus: "Unquenched, inextinguishable, endless, ceaseless." Upon this point annihilationist writers assert that the fire will be "unquenchable" *until it has consumed the chaff*, and will then *go out, of itself!* We refrain from comment. The argument derived by annihilationists from Matt. iii. 12, is peculiarly suicidal. From the fact that the wicked are symbolized by "chaff," it is inferred that they will be *literally burned to ashes*, as chaff is. An equally valid inference from the fact that the righteous are represented by "wheat," would be that they are stored up in the garner, to be *disposed of exactly as wheat is!*

[2] In Matt. xxv. 46, the same Greek adjective, αἰώνιος, is applied both to "punishment" and to "life." Hence it seems a reasonable inference that the "punishment," and the life are of *parallel duration*. As to the words αἰών and αἰώνιος, which, in their various modifications and combinations, are, in our version, rendered "eternal," "everlasting," "forever," "forever and ever," a very interesting discussion may be found in Professor Stuart's Essay on Future Punishment, pp. 56, 66 (new edition). He, following Knapp's Greek text, finds αἰών ninety-four times in the New Testament. In fifty-five of these instances, he says the word "certainly means an *unlimited period of duration* either future or past, *ever, always.*" If we include those cases in which the term refers to future punishment, and to the dominion of the Messiah, we have, says Stuart, sixty-four cases out of ninety-four in which the word means "unlimited period, boundless duration." The same author finds αἰώνιος sixty-six times. Of these, fifty-one are used in relation to the happiness of the righteous; two, in relation to God or his glory; six are of a miscellaneous nature, but the meaning in them all is quite clear; and seven relate to the subject of future punishment." [It should be added that Brüder's

"in danger of eternal sin," the "wrath of God abideth on him," "the smoke of their torment ascendeth up forever and ever," strongly imply *unending misery*. Such is their fair, legitimate meaning. It may be added, as the subjoined note evinces, that, if these expressions do not legitimately convey this idea, then it would seem impossible to prove from the scriptures the eternity of anything; impossible, also, to express in the Greek language the notion itself of endless duration.

The quotations from Isaiah and Philippians simply assert that all men shall, sooner or later, acknowledge the sovereignty of God. But while some do this in love, others may do it in wrath and terror. The subjugation of rebels neither invariably removes their inward hostility, nor transforms them into loyal subjects.

The text from Matt. v. is a caution against litigation, an exhortation to settle difficulties previous to legal process, whenever practicable. There is probably in this place no direct reference to future punishment.

Salvation, — Extent.

All Israel saved.	Only a portion saved.
And so all Israel shall be saved: as it is written, There shall come out of Sion the Deliverer, and shall turn away ungodliness from Jacob. Rom. xi. 26.	But the children of the kingdom shall be cast out into outer darkness: there shall be weeping and gnashing of teeth. Matt. viii. 12.

Alford, De Wette, Meyer, Tholuck, and others take the first text as implying a "future national restoration of Israel to God's favor." Or it may be taken as referring to the *spiritual* Israel; for "he is a Jew which is one *inwardly*."[1] All of the

Concordance, latest edition, gives αἰών one hundred and six times, and αἰώνιος seventy-one times. Probably, however, the proportion remains the same]. In view of these facts, we may conclude with Professor Stuart, that, if these expressions do not fairly imply the eternity of future punishment, "then the scriptures do not decide that God is eternal, nor that the happiness of the righteous is without end, nor that his covenant of grace will always remain, a conclusion which would forever blast the hopes of Christians, and shroud in more than midnight darkness all the glories of the gospel."

[1] Rom. ii. 29.

true Israel will be saved, while many of the nominal will perish.

All men saved.	*Some not saved.*
Until the times of restitution of all things, which God hath spoken by the mouth of all his holy prophets. Acts iii. 21.	The wicked shall be turned into hell, *and* all the nations that forget God. Ps. ix 17.
For God hath concluded them all in unbelief, that he might have mercy upon all. Rom xi. 32.	Salvation *is* far from the wicked. Ps. cxix. 155.
For as in Adam all die, even so in Christ shall all be made alive. 1 Cor. xv. 22.	The wicked is driven away in his wickedness. Prov. xiv. 32.
God our Saviour. Who will have all men to be saved, and to come unto the knowledge of the truth. 1 Tim. ii 3, 4.	*There is* no peace, saith my God, to the wicked Isa. lvii. 21.
The living God, who is the Saviour of all men, specially of those that believe. 1 Tim. iv. 10.	All the proud, yea, and all that do wickedly, shall be stubble: and the day that cometh shall burn them up, saith the LORD of hosts. Mal. iv. 1.
For the grace of God that bringeth salvation hath appeared to all men. Titus ii. 11.	The Son of man shall send forth his angels, and they shall gather out of his kingdom all things that offend, and them, which do iniquity. And shall cast them into a furnace of fire. Matt. xiii. 41, 42.
Not willing that any should perish, but that all should come to repentance. 2 Pet. iii. 9.	And as many as were ordained to eternal life, believed. Acts xiii. 48.
	But the fearful, and unbelieving, and the abominable, and murderers, and whoremongers, and sorcerers, and idolaters, and all liars, shall have their part in the lake which burneth with fire and brimstone: which is the second death. Rev. xxi. 8.

Let us examine the texts at the left, and ascertain whether they teach the actual salvation of all mankind. Hackett, with Meyer and De Wette, interpret the first quotation of the restoration of all things to a " state of primeval order, purity, and happiness, such as will exist for those who have part in the kingdom of Christ at his second coming."

Murdock's version of the Syriac gives the passage a different turn, thus: " Until the completion of the times of those things which God hath spoken." The Arabic has, " Until the times which establish the perfection or completion of all the predictions of the prophets."

Adam Clarke, Barnes, Dr. Jonathan Edwards,[1] and others concur in this latter explanation. Obviously, neither this nor the former one implies the salvation of all men.

On Rom. xi. 32 Alford says that it brings to view God's act, and not man's. The ultimate difference between the " all

[1] Works, i. 284.

men" shut up under disobedience and the "all men" upon whom mercy is shown, lies in the fact that by some men this mercy is not accepted, and so they become *self-excluded* from the salvation of God.

The text from 1 Cor. refers simply to physical death and resurrection. "As Adam caused the physical death of all men, so Christ will effect the resurrection of all." This is the view of Alford, Barnes, De Wette, Meyer, and others.

The citations from 1 Tim. ii. and 2 Peter assert the "wish" or "will" of God that all men should be saved. But this by no means proves that all *will be* saved. For some things which would be *pleasing* to God, *agreeable to his will*, do not take place. For example, he "now commandeth all men everywhere to repent."[1] Need it be said that universal obedience to this command, though it would be agreeable to the divine will, does not exist? Hence, the texts in question, while setting forth the benevolent "wish" or "will" of God, do not intimate that all men will comply with that "will."

1 Tim. iv. 10 terms God "the Saviour of all men." He is such, in that he preserves their lives, and grants them the day and means of grace.

Titus ii. 11 asserts, indeed, that the grace of God bringeth, proffereth, salvation to all men, but does not imply that this "salvation" is *forced upon* them.

It is clear that none of the foregoing texts, fairly interpreted, support the doctrine of universal salvation.

Earth, — Destruction.

Indestructible.	*Will be destroyed.*
The earth which he hath established for ever. Ps. lxxviii. 69.	Of old hast thou laid the foundation of the earth: and the heavens *are* the work of thy hands. They shall perish, but thou shalt endure: yea, all of them shall wax old like a garment Ps. cii. 25, 26.
Who laid the foundations of the earth, *that* it should not be removed for ever. Ps. civ. 5.	
The earth abideth for ever. Eccl. i. 4.	
	Heaven and earth shall pass away: but my words shall not pass away. Luke xxi. 33.

[1] Acts xvii. 30.

Indestructible.	*Will be destroyed.*
	The earth also and the works that are therein shall be burned up. 2 Pet. iii. 10.
	The earth and the heaven fled away; and there was found no place for them Rev. xx. 11.

As to the first texts, the Hebrew word "oläm" rendered "forever," does not imply the metaphysical idea of absolute endlessness, but a period of indefinite length, as Rambach says, "a very long time, the end of which is hidden from us." These texts do not necessarily teach the absolute perpetuity of the earth.

Of the opposed texts, that from Ps. cii. is a kind of comparison between the eternity of God and the dependent existence of material objects: "Though they should perish, thou shalt stand." Similarly Luke: "Though heaven and earth should pass away, my words shall not pass away." That is, my words are more enduring than even heaven and earth.

The quotations from Peter and Revelation imply that the present constitution of things will be changed; that "the cloud-capped towers, the gorgeous palaces, the solemn temples, and the great globe itself" will be subjected to the action of fire. This opinion prevailed among the ancient philosophers, especially the Greek stoics.[1]

The passages which speak of the destruction of the earth may therefore be taken as referring to the change or passing away of its *present form;* those which speak of its durability, as implying the permanence of its *constituent elements.*

Heaven, — Occupants.

Christ only.	*Elijah also.*
And no man hath ascended up to heaven, but he that came down from heaven, *even* the Son of man which is in heaven. John iii. 13.	Elijah went up by a whirlwind into heaven. 2 Kings ii. 11.

In the first text Jesus, setting forth his own superior authority, says, substantially, "No human being can speak *from personal knowledge,* as I do, who came down from heaven." "No man

---

[1] See Wetstein, on 2 Pet. iii. 7.

hath ascended up to heaven *to bring back tidings.*" So we, speaking of the secrets of the future world, should very naturally say: "No man has been there to tell us about them." In saying this, we do not deny that any one has actually entered the eternal world, but merely that any one has gone thither, and *returned* to unfold its mysteries.

Alford applies, however, the words "hath ascended" to Christ's "exaltation to be a Prince and a Saviour."

The former explanation seems the most natural.

Flesh and blood excluded.	*Enoch there.*
Flesh and blood cannot inherit the kingdom of God; neither doth corruption inherit incorruption. 1 Cor. xv. 50.	Enoch was translated that he should not see death. Heb. xi. 5.

A late sceptical writer adduces this and the preceding as cases of discrepancy. It need only be said that, beyond question, Enoch and Elijah, before entering the heavenly world, passed through a change *equivalent* to death. Their corruptible put on incorruption, and their mortal put on immortality.

Publicans and harlots enter.	*Impure not there.*
The publicans and the harlots go into the kingdom of God before you. Matt. xxi. 31.	Neither fornicators, nor idolaters, nor adulterers, nor effeminate, nor abusers of themselves with mankind, nor thieves, nor covetous, nor drunkards, nor revilers, nor extortioners, shall inherit the kingdom of God. 1 Cor. vi. 9, 10.

The first text does not say that publicans and harlots *as such*, but merely that some who *had been* such, and had afterwards repented, should enter heaven. Paul, in the verse succeeding the quotation from Corinthians, observes: "And such *were* some of you, but ye are washed, but ye are sanctified, but ye are justified." They had been corrupt and wicked, but were so no longer. Observe, also, that our Saviour's assertion amounts simply to this, "The publicans and harlots are *more likely* to be saved, *stand a better chance* for salvation, than do you, chief priests and elders."

Neither this passage, nor any other, sanctions the idea of impurity tolerated in heaven.

Employments.

Incessant praise.	Rest and quiet.
And they rest not day and night, saying, Holy, holy, holy, Lord God Almighty, which was, and is, and is to come. Rev. iv. 8.	There remaineth therefore a rest to the people of God. Heb. iv. 9. Blessed *are* the dead which die in the Lord from henceforth: Yea, saith the Spirit, that they may rest from their labors. Rev. xiv. 13.

The two cases are quite different; the former is that of the four wonderful "living creatures," the latter that of departed believers. Moreover, the "rest" attributed to departed saints is "rest *from their labors*," — from every thing painful and wearisome, — but not a "rest" of dormant inactivity, precluding enjoyment, praise, and glorified service.

CHAPTER II.

ETHICAL DISCREPANCIES.[1]

DUTY OF MAN. — *Toward God.*

Blessing gained.

By those who see.
Blessed *are* the eyes which see the things that ye see. Luke x. 23.

Those who see not.
Thomas, because thou hast seen me, thou hast believed: blessed *are* they that have not seen, and *yet* have believed. John xx. 29.

The word "blessed," in the first case seems to mean "highly favored," "enjoying peculiar privileges;" in the latter, "worthy of commendation."

Andrew Fuller: "There is a wide difference between *requiring sight as the ground of faith*, which Thomas did, and *obtaining it as the completion of faith*, which those who saw the coming and kingdom of the Messiah did. The one was a species of unbelief, the other was faith terminating in vision."

Blood, — disposal.

Poured upon altar.
The blood of thy sacrifices shall be poured out upon the altar. Deut. xii. 27.

Sprinkled upon it.
The priests shall sprinkle the blood upon the altar round about. Lev. iii. 2.

Maimonides, whose knowledge of Hebrew customs and traditions was unsurpassed, says that a part of the blood was sprinkled upon the altar, and the remainder poured out at the bottom of it.

The Septuagint and Vulgate render the Hebrew word in Le-

---

[1] The reader need not be reminded that no rigid and precise classification has been attempted. That arrangement which seemed most natural and obvious has generally been adopted. The mere classification of discrepancies is a trivial matter in comparison with their solution.

viticus "pour" and "pour out."[1] A part of the blood was disposed of in one way and the rest in another. Smith's Bib. Dict. says that the priest, after he had sprinkled the altar of incense with the blood, "poured out what remained at the foot of the altar of burnt-offering." Outram:[2] "The blood of the paschal lamb, of the male firstlings, and of the tithes, was considered as rightly sprinkled, if it were only poured out at either corner of the altar."

Covered with dust.	*Poured out as water.*
He shall even pour out the blood thereof, and cover it with dust. Lev. xvii. 13.	Thou shalt pour it upon the earth as water. Deut. xii. 24.

Strange that a recent author who deems this a discrepancy, could not see that the blood might be "poured upon the earth," and afterward "covered with dust."

Christ's execution.

Lawful.	*Unlawful.*
We have a law, and by our law he ought to die. John xix. 7.	It is not lawful for us to put any man to death. John xviii. 31.

The first text refers to the Mosaic code, the second to the restrictions imposed by the Roman government. The meaning of the combined passages is, "By our code of laws he ought to die, but it is not lawful for us (not permitted us by the Roman government) to put any man to death."

Alford: "From the time when Archelaus was deposed (A.D. 6 or 7) and Judea became a Roman province, it would follow by the Roman law, that the Jews lost the power of life and death." From Josephus,[3] we learn that it was not permitted the high-priest even to assemble a sanhedrim without the consent of the Roman procurator.

Covenant basis.

Religious laws.	*Civil laws*
And he said, Behold I make a covenant. . . . Write thou these words: for after the tenor of these words I have made a covenant with thee, and with Israel. Ex. xxxiv. 10-27.	Moses came and told the people all the words of the LORD, and all the judgments. . . . The covenant, which the LORD hath made with you concerning all these words. Ex. xxiv. 3-8.

---

[1] Fuerst says the word means, *to moisten, to wet.*
[2] On Sacrifices, chap. xvi.
[3] Antiq. xx. 9, 1.

The discrepancy which a late writer finds here, has no existence, except in his imagination. The first passage clearly makes the decalogue the foundation of the "covenant."[1] The "words" and "judgments" of the second passage begin with the decalogue in the twentieth chapter, so that both passages concur in making that decalogue the "basis" of the "covenant."

Covering of sin.

Approved.	Denounced.
Blessed *is* he *whose* transgression *is* forgiven, *whose* sin *is* covered. Ps. xxxii. 1.	He that covereth his sins shall not prosper. Prov. xxviii. 13.

In the first text, the parallelism shows that the "covering of sin" means its remission or atonement. The second, as the context evinces, refers to its unjustifiable concealment.

The first text alludes to God's gracious act in forgiving sin; the second to man's wicked act in conniving at it, and hiding it.

Crimes specified.

One list.	A different list.
Cursed be the man that maketh *any* graven or molten image, an abomination unto the LORD, the work of the hands of the craftsman, and putteth *it* in *a* secret *place:* and all the people shall answer and say, Amen, etc. Deut. xxvii. 15-26.	And God spake all these words, saying, I *am* the LORD thy God, which have brought thee out of the land of Egypt, out of the house of bondage. Thou shalt have no other gods before me, etc. Ex. xx. 1-xxiii. 33.[2]

Keil, on Deut. xxvii. 26: "From this last curse, which applies to every breach of the law, it evidently follows, that the different sins and transgressions already mentioned were only selected by way of example, and for the most part were such as could be easily concealed from the judicial authorities."

Similarly Le Clerc and Michaelis.

David's conduct.

Strayed from God	Did not stray.
I have gone astray like a lost sheep. Ps. cxix. 176.	Yet I erred not from thy precepts. Ps. cxix. 110.

David does not charge himself with any moral obliquity, but sets forth his desolate and perilous condition. The Hebrew of

---

[1] See Ex. xxxiv. 28, last clause.
[2] Passages abridged here, and in several cases.

"have gone astray" means, according to Gesenius, "to be thrust hither and thither." Surely this was David's experience.

Menasseh ben Israel takes the first text as alluding to the "troubles and misfortunes which David experienced in this world,— constantly persecuted, and fleeing from one place to another to escape from Saul and his own son."

A man of perfect heart.	*Committed sin.*
His heart was not perfect with the LORD his God, as the heart of David his father. Because David did *that which was* right in the eyes of the LORD, and turned not aside from any *thing* that he commanded him all the days of his life, save only in the matter of Uriah the Hittite. 1 Kings xv. 3, 5. I have found David the *son* of Jesse, a man after mine own heart, which shall fulfil all my will. Acts xiii. 22.	David's heart smote him after that he had numbered the people. And David said unto the LORD, I have sinned greatly in that I have done. 2 Sam. xxiv. 10. Thou *hast been* a man of war, and hast shed blood. 1 Chron. xxviii. 3.

The quotation from Acts refers to David *early in life*,[1] before he had fallen into those great sins which cast such a shadow upon his administration.

Again, the praise bestowed upon David contemplates him in relation to his predecessor and successors in the kingly office. In comparison with them, his heart was "perfect with the Lord his God." Hackett:[2] "This commendation is not absolute, but describes the character of David in comparison with that of Saul." Smith's Bib. Dict. says, the commendation has been made too much of. "It merely indicates a man whom God will approve, in distinction from Saul, who was rejected."

Besides, David's repentance was as deep and thorough as his sins were flagrant and aggravated. On this subject Mr. Carlyle[3] fitly and forcibly remarks: "Who is called 'the man after God's own heart'? David, the Hebrew king, had fallen into sins enough — blackest crimes — there was no want of sin. And, therefore, unbelievers sneer, and ask, 'Is this your man according to God's heart'? The sneer, I must say, seems to me but a shallow one. What are faults, what are the outward details of a life, if the inner secret of it, the remorse, temptations,

---

[1] See 1 Sam. xiii. 14.   [2] On Acts xiii. 22.
[3] *Heroes and Hero-worship*, p. 72.

the often-baffled, never-ended struggle of it, be forgotten? .....
David's life and history, as written for us in those Psalms of his, I consider to be the truest emblem ever given us of a man's moral progress and warfare here below. All earnest souls will ever discover in it the faithful struggle of an earnest human soul towards what is good and best. Struggle often baffled — sore baffled — driven as into entire wreck; yet a struggle never ended, ever with tears, repentance, true unconquerable purpose, begun anew."

In this his constant attitude as a moral hero " striving against sin," who when " cast down is not destroyed," but springs up, Antaeus-like, to renew the conflict, David challenges our admiration.

Fast, — observance.

Enjoined.

On the tenth *day* of this seventh month *there shall be* a day of atonement; it shall be a holy convocation unto you.... And ye shall do no work in that same day; ... for whatsoever soul *it be* that shall not be afflicted in that same day, he shall be cut off from among his people. Lev. xxiii. 27-29.

Disregarded.

And at that time Solomon held a feast, and all Israel with him, ... before the LORD our God, seven days and seven days, *even* fourteen days. On the eighth day he sent the people away. 1 Kings viii. 65, 66.
And on the three and twentieth day of the seventh month he sent the people away into their tents. 2 Chron. vii 10.

It cannot be proved that Solomon did not keep the day of atonement according to the law in Leviticus. The feast of tabernacles began on the fifteenth and ended on the twenty-second of the month; closing with a " holy convocation " the " eighth day,"[1] at the end of which Solomon dismissed the people; the dismission taking effect the next morning, the twenty-third. In this manner the accounts in Kings and Chronicles harmonize perfectly.

We may suppose that the first series of seven days was not entirely consecutive, but began with the seventh, and included three days *before* and four days *after* the tenth, or " day of atonement," which was fitly observed. Or it may be that this series began with the eighth day of the month, while the " day

[1] Lev. xxiii. 33-39.

of atonement," being itself a religious solemnity of high importance, and from the brevity of the narrative, is reckoned in as one of the days of festivity, although it was kept according to the law.

The latter seems to be the opinion of eminent Jewish critics.[1]

Bähr: "Old commentators say that the dedication rendered it unusually solemn; others, that, as it was a fast-day, its observance was for the time omitted."

First-born sons.

Dedicated.	Redeemed.
The first-born of thy sons shalt thou give unto me. Ex. xxii. 29.	All the first-born of man among thy children shalt thou redeem. Ex. xiii. 13.

Keil: "The adoption of the first-born on the part of Jehovah was a perpetual guarantee to the whole nation of the right of covenant fellowship." The first-born sons, though specially consecrated to God, were allowed to be redeemed, and Levites substituted in their stead.[2]

Firstling animals.

Redeemable.	Not redeemable.
Then shalt thou turn *it* into money, etc. Deut. xiv. 22-26.	The firstling of a cow, or the firstling of a sheep, or the firstling of a goat, thou shalt not redeem. Num. xviii. 17.

The first passage does not, as some pretend, sanction the *redemption* of firstlings. It merely allows them, for convenience' sake, to be "turned into money"; but the money must be taken to the prescribed place, and there expended for articles of food and drink to be consumed in the same manner as the original firstlings would have been. It was simply an arrangement for the accommodation of the offerer.

Redeemed with money.	With an animal, or slain.
The firstling of unclean beasts shalt thou redeem. . . . According to thine estimation, for the money of five shekels. Num. xviii. 15, 16.	The firstling of an ass thou shalt redeem with a lamb; and if thou redeem *him* not, then shalt thou break his neck. Ex. xxxiv. 20.

Keil thinks that "the earlier law, which commanded that an ass should be redeemed with a sheep, or else be put to death, was modified in favor of the revenues of the sanctuary and its

---

[1] Conciliator, i. 285. [2] Num. iii. 12, 13.

servants." Money would be more serviceable than numerous animals, by way of commutation.

Sanctified.	*Not sanctified.*
All the firstling males that come of thy herd and of thy flock thou shalt sanctify unto the LORD thy God. Deut. xv. 19.	The firstling of the beasts, which should be the LORD'S firstling, no man shall sanctify it. Lev. xxvii. 26.

Keil: "What belonged to the Lord by law could not be dedicated to him by a vow." It would be mockery to give him what was already his.

Idolatry.

God only, worshipped.	*Other beings adored.*
Thou shalt have no other gods before me.... Thou shalt not bow down thyself to them, nor serve them. Ex. xx. 3, 5.	God, before whom my fathers Abraham and Isaac did walk, the God which fed me all my life long unto this day. The Angel which redeemed me from all evil, bless the lads. Gen. xlviii. 15, 16. Behold, there stood a man over against him with his sword drawn in his hand. ... And Joshua fell on his face to the earth, and did worship. Josh. v. 13, 14.

"God before whom my fathers walked," "God who fed me all my life," and the "Angel who redeemed me" are three appellations of one and the same Being. Lange: "A threefold naming of God." Murphy: "Jacob's threefold periphrasis is intended to describe the one God who wills, works, and wards."

On Josh. v. 14 Keil says the Hebrew word employed here "does not always mean divine worship, but very frequently means nothing more than the deep Oriental reverence paid by a dependant to his superior or king."[1] Gesenius: "This honor was paid not only to superiors, as to kings and princes, but also to equals."[2] There is, then, no idolatry in either case.

Capitally punished.	*Punishment undesired.*
If there be found among you, ... man or woman that hath wrought wickedness in the sight of the LORD thy God, in transgressing his covenant. And hath gone and served other gods, and worshipped them.... The hands of the witnesses shall be first upon him to put him to death, and afterward the hands of all the people. Deut. xvii. 2, 3, 7.[3]	For I have no pleasure in the death of him that dieth, saith the Lord GOD Ezek xviii. 32.

[1] 2 Sam. ix. 6; xiv. 33. [2] Gen. xxiii. 7; Ex. xviii. 7; 1 Kings ii. 19
[3] See Deut. xiii. 6–11.

The capital punishment of idolaters was not a thing desirable *per se*, but it was enjoined out of regard to the welfare of the people and the security of the government. Under the theocracy, in which God was the sole Lawgiver and King, idolatry was simply *high treason*, and must be severely punished, or the very existence of the government would be endangered.

Michaelis [1]: " As the only true God was the civil legislator of the people of Israel, and accepted by them as their King, idolatry was a crime against the state, and therefore just as deservedly punished with death as high treason is with us. Whoever worshipped strange gods shook, at the same time, the whole fabric of the laws, and rebelled against him in whose name the government was carried on."

Dr. Jahn [2]: " Whoever in the Hebrew nation, over which Jehovah was King, worshipped another god, or practised any superstitions, by this very act renounced his allegiance to his king, and deserted to another. He committed high treason, and was properly considered a public criminal. Whoever incited others to idolatry incited them to rebellion, and was a mover of sedition. Therefore death was justly awarded as the punishment of idolatry and its kindred arts, magic, necromancy, and soothsaying; and also of inciting to idolatry."

Image making.

Sanctioned.	*Forbidden.*
And thou shalt make two cherubim *of* gold, *of* beaten work shalt thou make them, in the two ends of the mercy-seat.... And the cherubim shall stretch forth *their* wings on high, covering the mercy-seat with their wings.... And in the candlestick *shall be* four bowls made like unto almonds, *with* their knops and their flowers. Ex. xxv. 18, 20, 34.	Thou shalt not make unto thee any graven image, or any likeness *of any thing*. ... Thou shalt not bow down thyself to them, nor serve them. Ex. xx. 4, 5.
And the Lord said unto Moses, Make thee a fiery serpent, and set it upon a pole. Num. xxi. 8.	Take heed unto yourselves, lest ye forget the covenant of the LORD your God, which he made with you, and make you a graven image, *or* the likeness of any *thing* which the LORD thy God hath forbidden thee. Deut iv. 23.
The throne had six steps.... And twelve lions stood there on the one side and on the other upon the six steps: there was not the like made in any kingdom. 1 Kings x. 19, 20.	Cursed *be* the man that maketh *any* graven or molten image, an abomination unto the LORD, the work of the hands of the craftsman, and putteth *it* in *a* secret *place*. Deut. xxvii. 15.

[1] Commentary on Laws of Moses, iv. 11.
[2] History of Hebrew Commonwealth, p. 19 (English edition).

Some interpret the prohibitions as referring to images intended to represent the Divine Being.

Michaelis [1]: It is evident that images of the Deity are alone spoken of in all these passages, and that, if we infer the prohibition of painting and sculpture from these texts, we might with equal reason from the words that follow, "Thou shalt not lift up thine eyes to heaven, to behold the sun, moon, and stars," infer that we are never to raise our eyes to heaven, and contemplate the sun, moon, and stars, but rather to walk upon all fours forever.

Josephus [2] and Menasseh ben Israel [3] apply the prohibition to images made *for purposes of idolatry*. The latter, with rabbi Isaac Arama, also restricts it to the likeness of existing, and not of imaginary things.

Further, the cherubim were not "graven images," but were of "beaten work," as Murphy says, "formed by the hammer, of malleable gold." Nor were they made "in the likeness" of any created thing whatever. Their form was purely ideal.

Hengstenberg:[4] The cherubim is a representative of creation in its highest grade, an ideal creature. The vital powers communicated to the most elevated existences in the visible creation are collected and individualized in it.

In this view Josephus, Bochart, Stuart,[5] and Fairbairn [6] substantially agree. Thus it is clear that neither the making of the cherubim nor the other cases of sculpture or image-making was a violation of the second commandment. The *idolatrous purpose* at which the prohibition is aimed was wanting in all of the foregoing instances.

Israel's transgression.

Ineradicable.	*To be removed.*
For though thou wash thee with nitre, and take thee much soap, yet thine iniquity is marked before me. Jer. ii. 22.	O Jerusalem, wash thine heart from wickedness, that thou mayest be saved. How long shall thy vain thoughts lodge within thee? Jer. iv. 14.

[1] Com. on Laws of Moses, iv. 52.
[2] Antiq. iii. v. 5.
[3] Conciliator, i. 154–157.
[4] Egypt and Books of Moses, 168.
[5] On Rev. iv. 6–8.
[6] Typology, i. 261, 262 (4th edition).

Abarbanel: "Although you wash and cleanse yourself outwardly, your iniquity is marked." That is, by no external rites and ceremonies can you be cleansed; your hearts must be purified by penitence.

Jerusalem, — ethical aspect.

A delight to God.	A provocation.
The LORD loveth the gates of Zion more than all the dwellings of Jacob. Glorious things are spoken of thee, O city of God. Ps. lxxxvii. 2, 3. For the LORD hath chosen Zion; he hath desired it for his habitation. Ps. cxxxii. 13.	For this city has been to me *as a* provocation of mine anger and of my fury from the day that they built it, even unto this day; that I should remove it from before my face. Jer. xxxii. 31.

In the first passages there is, as Tholuck says, "no reference to Jerusalem according to her earthly aspects, with her streets and walls and palaces." It is the *church*, which is figuratively styled "Zion" and "city of God."

Calvin; "Christ has by his advent extended Mount Zion to the ends of the earth." Jeremiah refers to the literal Jerusalem.

Judging of David.

Desired.	Deprecated.
Judge me, O LORD, according to my righteousness, and according to mine integrity *that is* in me. Ps. vii. 8.	Enter not into judgment with thy servant: for in thy sight shall no man living be justified. Ps. cxliii. 2.

The first text has reference to one particular case, the controversy between David and "Cush[1] the Benjamite." David knew himself to be guiltless of the crimes alleged against him by this enemy; hence his appeal: "As to *this* charge, God knows that I am innocent." But, on a retrospect of his whole life, he acknowledges his ill-desert in general, and exclaims: "Enter not into judgment with thy servant." A man may be absolutely innocent, even in God's sight, with reference to a certain accusation, yet not sinless in respect to his whole life.

Just man's life.

By faith.	By deeds.
The just shall live by his faith. Hab. ii. 4.	If a man be just, and do that whic'. is lawful and right, ... he shall surely live, saith the Lord GOD. Ezek xviii. 5, 9.

---

[1] The Jewish expositors understood Saul to be meant; others say Shimei.

The faith is such as produces good works; the deeds are such as spring from living faith. One text speaks of the subject in one relation; the other, in a different, yet not incompatible one.

Monarchy.

Sanctioned by God.	Offensive to Him.
When thou art come unto the land which the LORD thy God giveth thee, and shalt possess it, and shalt dwell therein, and shalt say, I will set a king over me, like as all the nations that *are* about me; thou shalt in any wise set *him* king over thee, whom the LORD thy God shall choose. Deut. xvii. 14, 15.	Make us a king to judge us like all the nations. . . . And the LORD said unto Samuel, Hearken unto the voice of the people in all that they say unto thee: for they have not rejected thee, but they have rejected me, that I should not reign over them. 1 Sam. viii. 5, 7. *Is it* not wheat-harvest to day? I will call unto the LORD, and he shall send thunder and rain; that ye may perceive and see that your wickedness *is* great, which ye have done in the sight of the LORD, in asking you a king. 1 Sam. xii. 17.

The rationalistic objection is, that the monarchy was contemplated and provided for in the law, yet was afterwards declared to be offensive in the sight of God. To this objection Jewish interpreters[1] reply as follows. It is said, in Tosaphoth, that the sin lay "not in demanding a king, but in the mode of so doing, 'like all the nations,'" virtually equivalent to a wish to become like surrounding idolaters. Maimonides and Nachmanides: In making their demand in the shape of a complaint, as if they were tired of Samuel's administration, and wished to be rid of him. The Cabalists: In acting prematurely, or asking impatiently and at an improper time.

Abarbanel: "The divine will was not that they should elect a king, for God was the true King of Israel." That is, Deut. xvii. was not a command, nor even a permission, to choose a king, but a mere prophetic statement of what God foresaw they would do. It is not said, "When you enter the land, *place* a king over you," but, "When thou art come unto the land, and shalt say, *I* will set," etc.

Professor Keil finds the wrong in their overlooking their own misconduct, and in distrusting God and his guidance. "In

---

[1] See Menasseh ben Israel's Conciliator, i. 285–289.

such a state of mind as this, their desire for a king was a contempt and rejection of the kingly government of Jehovah, and was nothing more than forsaking him to serve other gods."

Motherhood.

Blessed.	To be expiated.
Thy wife *shall be* as a fruitful vine by the sides of thy house. Ps. cxxviii. 3.	She shall bring a lamb of the first year for a burnt-offering. and a young pigeon, or a turtle-dove, for a sin-offering, unto the door of the tabernacle of the congregation, unto the priest: who shall offer it before the LORD, and make an atonement for her. Lev. xii. 6, 7.

Michaelis thinks that Moses, by such laws, intended to " represent theological truths in a figurative manner."

Abarbanel[1]: " As no one bears pains and troubles in this world without guilt; and as there is no chastisement without sin; and lastly, as every woman bears children with pain and danger, hence every one is commanded, after childbirth, to offer an expiatory sacrifice."

Leyrer[2] says that this and all the other rites of purification were intended " to foster the constant humiliation of fallen man; to remind him in all the leading processes of natural life — generation, birth, eating, disease, death — how everything, even his own bodily nature, lies under the curse of sin, that so the law might become a schoolmaster to bring unto Christ, and awaken and sustain the longing for a Redeemer from the curse which had fallen upon his body."

Mr. Clark, in Bible Commentary : " The conclusion, then, appears to be reasonable that all the rites of purification were intended to remind the Israelite that he belonged to a fallen race, and that he needed a purification and atonement which he could not effect for himself."

Paul's moral state.

Nothing good in him.	Christ dwelt in him.
For I know that in me (that is, in my flesh,) dwelleth no good thing. Rom. vii. 18.	I live; yet not I, but Christ liveth in me. Gal. ii. 20.

[1] On Lev. xii.; quoted in Outram on Sacrifices, p. 145.   [2] In Keil.

ETHICAL DISCREPANCIES.   231

In these passages Paul speaks in two distinct relations. "In me, that is, in my flesh," — in my lower, carnal self. "Christ liveth in me," — in my higher, spiritual self, in my renewed heart in which Christ is enthroned. This is Alford's view. Hodge takes substantially the same view. Some interpret the first text as describing Paul previous to his conversion; the latter, as applying to him after that event.

Piety evinced.

By profession.	Profession useless.
No man can say that Jesus is the Lord, but by the Holy Ghost. 1 Cor. xii. 3.	Not every one that saith unto me, Lord, Lord, shall enter into the kingdom of heaven. Matt. vii. 21. And why call ye me Lord, Lord, and do not the things which I say? Luke vi. 46.

The word "say," in the first text, does not imply the *mere utterance* of the words, but the hearty and spontaneous confession of belief in the Messiahship of Jesus. In the last texts the calling of him "Lord," "Lord," is mere lip-service.

Prayer.

May be in public.	Should be in private.
And Solomon stood before the altar of the LORD in the presence of all the congregation of Israel, and spread forth his hands toward heaven. And he said, LORD God of Israel, *there is* no God like thee. 1 Kings viii. 22, 23. His windows being open in his chamber toward Jerusalem, he kneeled upon his knees three times a day, and prayed, and gave thanks before his God, as he did aforetime. Then these men assembled, and found Daniel praying. Dan. vi. 10, 11. I will therefore that men pray every where. 1 Tim. ii. 8.	He went in therefore, and shut the door upon them twain, and prayed unto the LORD. 2 Kings iv. 33. When thou prayest, thou shalt not be as the hypocrites *are:* for they love to pray standing in the synagogues and in the corners of the streets, that they may be seen of men. Verily I say unto you, they have their reward. But thou, when thou prayest, enter into thy closet, and when thou hast shut thy door, pray to thy Father which is in secret. Matt. vi 5, 6. He went out into a mountain to pray, and continued all night in prayer to God. Luke vi. 12. Peter went up upon the house-top to pray, about the sixth hour. Acts x 9.

It is not *publicity*, but *ostentation* in prayer, which is prohibited; not praying in public, but praying in conspicuous places to "be seen of men." The motive, not the place, is the thing in question. Chrysostom and Augustine both caution us against a merely literal interpretation of Matt. vi. 6.

Incessant.	*Brief.*
Because of his importunity he will rise and give him as many as he needeth. Luke xi. 8 Men ought always *to* pray, and not to faint; ... Shall not God avenge his own elect, which cry day and night unto him. Luke xviii. 1, 7.	When ye pray, use not vain repetitions *as* the heathen *do;* for they think that they shall be heard for their much speaking. Be not ye therefore like unto them: for your Father knoweth what things ye have need of, before ye ask him. Matt. vi. 7, 8.

There are abundant examples of the "vain repetitions" which Jesus prohibits. Lightfoot adduces a Jewish maxim, "He who multiplies prayer is heard."

The priests of Baal, in their frantic orgies before their idol's sacrifices, cried from morning even until noon saying, "O Baal, hear us; O Baal, hear us."[1] Another instance is that of the mob at Ephesus, who for about two hours cried out, "Great is Diana of the Ephesians."[2]

The Mohammedan monks in India often practise these "vain repetitions" for days together. They have been known to repeat a single syllable of supposed religious efficacy until their strength was exhausted, and they could no longer speak.[3] A missionary writes that in Orissa some heathen worshippers sit for many hours of the day and night pronouncing the name of Krisnu on a string of beads.

Alford, with great fitness, adduces the "Paternosters" and "Ave Marias" of the Romish church as examples in point.

It is such idle, empty "repetitions" as the above which the Greek term "battalogeo" designates, and which Christ condemns, and not fervent, importunate supplication.

Repentance.

Esau unable to repent.	*Ought to have repented.*
He found no place of repentance, though he sought it carefully with tears. Heb. xii. 17.	God ... commandeth all men every where to repent. Acts xvii. 30.

Most modern commentators, as Stuart, Tholuck, Ebrard, Barnes, interpret the first text, "found no place for a change of mind in his father." But Alford, Bleek, Delitzsch, De Wette,

---

[1] 1 Kings xviii. 26–29.
[2] Acts xix. 34.
[3] Hackett on Acts, p. 322. See, also, Morier's Second Journey, p. 176.

Hofmann, and others take it as meaning that he found no way open to reverse what had been done. " He might change; but the penalty could not, from the very nature of the circumstances, be taken off." He might secure the salvation of his soul; but he could not regain the forfeited birthright, nor secure the revocation of the blessing pronounced prophetically upon Jacob.

Righteousness.

Perilous.	Want of it, perilous.
Be not righteous over much; neither make thyself over wise: why shouldest thou destroy thyself? Eccl. vii. 16.	Be not over much wicked, neither be thou foolish: why shouldest thou die before thy time? Eccl. vii. 17.

The first text is a caution against pharisaic self-righteousness, laying claim to superior wisdom and sanctity, and incurring the penalty which God sends upon arrogance and hypocrisy.

The second admonishes us to be on our guard against crossing the border-line which separates the righteous, who is still subject to weakness and error, from the wilful transgressor. Zöckler, referring to these texts, says: " A recommendation to avoid the two extremes of false righteousness and bold wickedness."

The gist of the whole is: Avoid extremes in all things.

Sabbath.

Sanctioned.	Repudiated.
Remember the sabbath-day to keep it holy. Ex. xx. 8. Blessed *is* the man *that* doeth this, and the son of man *that* layeth hold on it; that keepeth the sabbath from polluting it. Isa. lvi. 2.	The new-moons and sabbaths, the calling of assemblies, I cannot away with; *it is* iniquity, even the solemn meeting. Isa. i. 13. One man esteemeth one day above another: another esteemeth every day *alike*. Let every man be fully persuaded in his own mind. Rom. xiv. 5. Let no man therefore judge you in meat, or in drink, or in respect of a holy-day, or of the new-moon, or of the sabbath-*days*. Col. ii. 16.

The reason why the Sabbath keeping and other observances of the Israelites were not acceptable to God, is set forth by Isaiah, in a subsequent verse, thus: " Your hands are full of blood."

As to the text from Romans, Stuart, Barnes, Hodge, and others think that Paul is not here speaking of the " Lord's day" at all, but of certain Jewish festivals, the passover, feast of tabernacles, and the like, which a man might observe or not, as he saw fit.

Col. ii. 16, is interpreted by Gilfillan [1] as referring to the *Jewish* sabbath, or "seventh day," which had been superseded by "the Lord's day"; the latter being, at the time of Paul's writing, acknowledged and observed by the whole Christian church.

Others, from the fact that the term "sabbath" is applied, in the Old Testament, not only to the seventh day, but to all the days of holy rest observed by the Hebrews, and particularly to the beginning and close of their great festivals, understand the last text as not intended to include the *weekly* day of rest.

Instituted for one reason.	*For a different reason.*
For *in* six days the LORD made heaven and earth, the sea and all that in them *is*, and rested the seventh day: wherefore the Lord blessed the sabbath-day, and hallowed it. Ex. xx. 11.	And remember that thou wast a servant in the land of Egypt, and *that* the LORD thy God brought thee out thence through a mighty hand, and by a stretched-out arm: therefore the LORD thy God commanded thee to keep the sabbath-day. Deut. v. 15.

This is an example of two concurrent reasons for the same observance. The primary reason why all mankind should keep the Sabbath is that the Creator rested on that day. An additional and special reason why the *Israelites* should keep it was the fact that they had been delivered from Egyptian bondage by the Author of the Sabbath.

If it were said to the freedmen of this country, "You should observe the first day of January, because it is the beginning of a new year"; and a little after: "You should observe the first day of January, because it is the anniversary of your emancipation by President Lincoln," there would be no discrepancy.

Sabbath desecration.

Prohibited.	*Countenanced.*
Whosoever doeth *any* work in the sabbath-day he shall surely be put to death. Ex. xxxi. 15. They found a man that gathered sticks upon the sabbath-day.... And	At that time Jesus went on the sabbath-day through the corn, and his disciples were a hungered, and began to pluck the ears of corn, and to eat, etc. Matt. xii. 1-5.

[1] "The Sabbath," pp. 303-313. See, also, Justin Edwards's "Sabbath Manual," pp. 117-127.

ETHICAL DISCREPANCIES.

Prohibited.	*Countenanced.*
all the congregation brought him without the camp, and stoned him with stones, and he died: as the LORD commanded Moses. Num. xv. 32, 36.	And therefore did the Jews persecute Jesus, and sought to slay him, because he had done these things on the sabbath-day. John v. 16.

Deeds of *necessity* and *mercy* were not forbidden by Moses. Eating, drinking, caring for the sick, and like needful acts were not interdicted. Our Saviour did not "break" the Sabbath. He did, indeed, disregard the foolish traditions of the scribes and pharisees relative to that day, but neither by precept nor example did he sanction its real desecration.

Sacrifices.

Appointed.	*Disavowed.*
Thou shalt burn the whole ram upon the altar: it *is* a burnt-offering unto the LORD.... And thou shalt offer every day a bullock *for* a sin-offering for atonement. Ex. xxix. 18, 36.	Will I eat the flesh of bulls, or drink the blood of goats? Offer unto God thanksgiving; and pay thy vows unto the Most High. Ps. l. 13, 14. For thou desirest not sacrifice, else would I give *it*: thou delightest not in burnt offering. Ps. li. 16. To what purpose *is* the multitude of your sacrifices unto me? saith the LORD: I am full of the burnt-offerings of rams and the fat of fed beasts; and I delight not in the blood of bullocks, or of lambs, or of he-goats. When ye come to appear before me, who hath required this at your hand, to tread my courts? Bring no more vain oblations: incense is an abomination unto me. Isa. i. 11–13. Your burnt-offerings are not acceptable, nor your sacrifices sweet unto me. Jer. vi. 20. For I spake not unto your fathers, nor commanded them in the day that I brought them out of the land of Egypt concerning burnt-offerings or sacrifices: but this thing commanded I them, saying, Obey my voice, and I will be your God, and ye shall be my people. Jer. vii. 22, 23. For I desired mercy, and not sacrifice; and the knowledge of God more than burnt-offerings. Hos. vi. 6.

The first quotation from Psalms sets forth God's *spirituality*, as a result of which "the outward sacrifices, as such, can yield him no satisfaction."

The second contrasts mere *external sacrifices* with that *obedience* in default of which all sacrifices are worthless. The offerings spoken of by Isaiah and Jeremiah (sixth chapter) were rejected because of the wickedness of the offerers. Their hands were "full of blood," and they had "rejected" God's law. Reason enough for the non-acceptance of their oblations. Jer. vii. 22, 23 is susceptible of two interpretations.[1]

First. It may be taken as a Hebraistic way of saying, "At that time, I laid no stress upon mere sacrifices in comparison with true obedience. This explanation is given by Calvin and Stuart, also by Dr. Priestley and Prof. Norton.[2] This interpretation is in harmony with Hos. vi. 6, also with Samuel's language to Saul: "Hath the Lord as great delight in burnt-offerings and sacrifices as in obeying the voice of the Lord? Behold, to obey is better than sacrifice, and to hearken than the fat of rams."[3]

Secondly. The quotation may mean, "I gave the command relative to obedience *previous to* that concerning sacrifices." This interpretation, propounded by the Jewish critics, agrees with the facts in the case. The command respecting obedience was given at Marah,[4] just after the Hebrews left the Red Sea; those pertaining to sacrifices were mainly given at Mount Sinai,[5] at a later period of the history.

It is clear that none of the foregoing texts disparage sacrifices offered aright. Heartless offerings are ever rejected.

Expiatory.	*Not expiatory.*
And the priest shall make an atonement for him, as concerning his sin, and it shall be forgiven him. Lev. iv. 26.	For *it is* not possible that the blood of bulls and of goats should take away sins.... The same sacrifices which can never take away sins. Heb. x. 4, 11.
The life of the flesh *is* in the blood: and I have given it to you upon the altar, to make an atonement for your souls. Lev. xvii. 11.	
One kid of the goats *for* a sin-offering, to make an atonement for you. Num. xxix. 5.	

Dr. Davidson[6] says that sin and trespass offerings "were

[1] Magee on Atonement, pp. 146, 147 (Bohn's edition).
[2] Evidences of Genuineness of Gospels, ii. Note D. p. cxl.
[3] 1 Sam. xv. 22.
[4] Ex. xv. 25, 26.
[5] Ex. xxix; Lev. i. to viii.
[6] Introd. to Old Test., i. 287

regarded as possessing an atoning, expiatory power—that they were *substituted in place of* the sinner who brought them, bearing the punishment of his transgression, and so procuring its pardon from God. By their means sins were taken away and covered. The Deity was appeased." Of the sprinkling of the blood, he adds, " The act of sprinkling was *symbolical*, implying that the person who offered the sacrifice had forfeited his life, and the life of the animal was forfeited instead." So Kalisch[1]: " It is impossible to doubt that the doctrine of vicarious sacrifice was entertained by the Hebrews. ... The animal dies to symbolize the death deserved by the offerer on account of his sins."

It does not, however, appear that these sacrifices were deemed to have, *per se*, the power to remove sin. They were a condition, but not the cause, of pardon. As Alford and Ebrard say, they were "not the instrument of complete vicarious propitiation, but an exhibition of the postulate of such propitiation."

Outram also regards them merely as a "condition of pardon."

These sacrifices, being a "yearly remembrance" of sin, since they could not make the offerer "perfect as pertaining to the conscience," pointed him to the great Sacrifice, which "taketh away the sin of the world."

Human sacrifices sanctioned.	*Stringently prohibited.*
Take now thy son, thine only *son* Isaac, whom thou lovest, and get thee into the land of Moriah; and offer him there for a burnt-offering. Gen. xxii. 2. Joshua, and all Israel with him, took Achan the son of Zerah, and the silver, and the garment, and the wedge of gold, and his sons, and his daughters, and his oxen, and his asses, and his sheep, and his tent, and all that he had; and they brought them unto the valley of Achor. ... And all Israel stoned him with stones, and burned them with fire, after they had stoned them with stones. Josh. vii. 24, 25. And Jephthah vowed a vow unto the LORD. ... Whatsoever cometh forth of the doors of my house to meet me, when I return in peace from the chil-	And thou shalt not let any of thy seed pass through *the fire* to Molech. Lev. xviii. 21. Whosoever *he be* of the children of Israel, or of the strangers that sojourn in Israel, that giveth *any* of his seed unto Molech, he shall surely be put to death. Lev. xx. 2.

[1] On Leviticus. Part i. pp. 192, 193.

Human sacrifices sanctioned.	*Stringently prohibited.*
dren of Ammon, shall surely be the LORD's, and I will offer it up for a burnt-offering.... Behold his daughter came out to meet him with timbrels and with d: ces: and she *was his* only child.... Her father, who did with her *according* to his vow which he had vowed; and she knew no man. Judg. xi. 30-40. The king took the two sons of Rizpah, ... and the five sons of Michal the daughter of Saul.... And he delivered them into the hands of the Gibeonites, and they hanged them in the hill before the LORD.... And after that God was entreated for the land. 2 Sam. xxi. 8, 9, 14.	

As to the case of Abraham, God's design was not to secure a certain *outward act,* but a certain *state of mind,* a willingness to give up the beloved object to Jehovah. " The *principle* of this great trial," says Dr. Thomas Arnold,[1] " was the same which has been applied to God's servants in every age, — whether they were willing to part with what they loved best on earth when God's service called for it." Hengstenberg[2]: " Verse 12 shows that satisfaction was rendered to the Lord's command when the spiritual *sacrifice* was completed." In this view concur Warburton, Keil, Murphy, Lange,[3] Bush, Wordsworth, and other authorities.

Kurtz[4] says: " It is true that God did not seek the *slaying* of Isaac *in facto,* but only the implicit *surrender* of the lad in *mind and heart.*" The command, in the original, is somewhat ambiguous: " Make him ascend for a burnt-offering." This Abraham interpreted literally, as implying the actual slaying of his son. This his mistake was the means of developing and testing his faith.

The assumed slaughter of Achan's children a recent author terms " a cruel and unjust thing, forbidden in Deut. xxiv. 16, yet afterwards perpetrated with the Divine sanction."

This case has been already discussed under " Justice of God." It is sufficient to say here that the case furnishes no sanction of

[1] Miscel. Works, p. 150 (N.Y. edition). [2] Genuineness of Pent. ii. 114.
[3] Com. on Genesis, pp. 79, 80. [4] Hist. of Old. Cov. i. 263.

ETHICAL DISCREPANCIES. 239

the abominable custom of slaughtering human beings in sacrifice. As has been elsewhere suggested, for anything that we know to the contrary, Achan's sons and daughters may all have been full-grown, and may have encouraged and participated in the sacrilege in which he took the lead. This is Keil's view of the case.

In reference to Jephthah's supposed sacrifice of his daughter, it may be said, *First. It cannot be proved that he did offer her as a burnt-offering.* The Bible does not say that he did this. If, through ignorance and a misguided fanaticism, he actually committed the cruel deed, *it does not appear that God in any manner sanctioned it.* The sacred historian expresses no opinion in regard to it. The apparent commendation of Jephthah, in Heb. xi. 32, applies to the general tenor of his life, and not, necessarily, to every act performed by him in that remote age.

Secondly. There are good reasons for holding, with Auberlen, Bush, Cassel, Delitzsch, Grotius, Hengstenberg, Houbigant, Keil, the Kimchis, Lange, Le Clerc, Lilienthal, Saalschütz, Schudt, Waterland, and other critics, that, instead of being offered as a burnt-sacrifice, she was simply devoted to perpetual celibacy in the service of the tabernacle.[1]

(*a*) The literal sacrifice of human beings was strictly forbidden in the Mosaic law; and Jephthah was doubtless fully aware of this fact.

(*b*) The Hebrew of Jephthah's vow may be correctly translated, " Shall surely be the Lord's,[2] *or* I will offer it up for a burnt-offering." Dr. Davidson [3]: " It cannot be denied that the conjunction ' vav ' may be rendered *or*. The Hebrew language had very few conjunctions, and therefore *one* had to fulfil the office of *several* in other languages." Dr. Randolph, J. Kimchi,

---

[1] See allusion to something similar; Ex. xxxviii. 8 and 1 Sam. ii. 22.
[2] Compare 1 Sam. i. 11. " I will give him unto the Lord all the days of his life."
[3] Introd. to Old Test., i. 476.

and Auberlen render, "Shall surely be the Lord's, *and* I will offer to him a burnt-offering." Dr. Davidson says: "We admit that the construction is grammatically possible; for examples justify it, as Gesenius shows." Either of these translations removes the difficulty.

(*c*) During the "two months" which intervened between Jephthah's return and the supposed sacrifice, it is scarcely credible that the priests would not have interfered to prevent the barbarous deed, or that Jephthah himself would not have "inquired of the Lord" respecting a release from his vow.

(*d*) As she was Jephthah's only child, to devote her to perpetual virginity would preclude him from all hope of posterity, — *in the estimation of a Jew, a most humiliating and calamitous deprivation.*

(*e*) The phraseology of verses 37–40 points clearly to a life of perpetual and enforced celibacy. On any other hypothesis the language seems irrelevant and unmeaning. As Keil expresses it, to bewail one's virginity does not mean to mourn because one has to die a virgin, but because one has to live and remain a virgin. Inasmuch as the history lays special emphasis upon her bewailing her virginity, this must have stood in some peculiar relation to the nature of the vow. Observe, too, that this lamentation takes place "upon the mountains." Cassel observes that if life had been in question her tears might have been shed at home. But lamentations of *this* character could not be uttered in the town and in the presence of men. For such plaints, modesty required the solitude of the mountains. The words of the thirty-ninth verse are very explicit. They assert that her father fulfilled his vow through the fact that "she knew no man." That is, the vow was fulfilled in the dedication of her life to the Lord, as a spiritual burnt-offering, in a life-long chastity.

"Completeness of consecration as a spiritual sacrifice" seems the pervading idea in the case of Jephthah's sacrifice.

In 2 Sam. xxi. 1 the designation, Saul's "*bloody* house," intimates strongly that the men whom a recent writer pathetically deplores as "innocent grandchildren" were really participants in the crime of their departed progenitor. He had gone beyond the reach of earthly justice; hence the penalty fell upon his surviving partners in treachery and blood. David Kimchi[1] tentatively, and Dr. Jahn[2] confidently propose this very reasonable explanation of the case.

On the whole, none of the foregoing cases represents human sacrifices as sanctioned by the Almighty.

Service of God.

With fear.	*With gladness.*
Serve the LORD with fear, and rejoice with trembling. Ps. ii. 11.	Serve the LORD with gladness. Ps. c. 2.

Reverential fear and devout gladness are quite compatible.

Sin forgiven.

All sin pardonable.	*Some unpardonable.*
And by him all that believe are justified from all things from which ye could not be justified by the law of Moses. Acts xiii. 39.	Whosoever speaketh against the Holy Ghost, it shall not be forgiven him, neither in this world, neither in the *world* to come. Matt. xii. 32.
Where sin abounded, grace did much more abound. Rom. v. 20.	He that shall blaspheme against the Holy Ghost hath never forgiveness, but is in danger of eternal damnation. Mark iii. 29.
If any man sin, we have an advocate with the Father, Jesus Christ the righteous. 1 John ii. 1.	There is a sin unto death: I do not say that he shall pray for it. 1 John v. 16.

The texts at the left by no means assert that every sin, wherever and by whomsoever committed, will be forgiven. The general rule is that *sins repented of will be forgiven*. Matthew and Mark speak of sins which will never be repented of, consequently never forgiven; hence they are sins "unto death."

Sin-offering.

One kind.	*A different kind.*
When the sin which they have sinned against it is known, then the congregation shall offer a young bullock for the sin. ... When a ruler hath sinned, ... if his sin wherein he hath sinned, come to his knowledge; he shall bring his offering, a kid of the goats. Lev. iv. 14, 22, 23.	If *aught* be committed by ignorance without the knowledge of the congregation, that all the congregation shall offer one young bullock for a burnt-offering, ... and one kid of the goats for a sin-offering. Num. xv. 24.

[1] Menasseh ben Israel's Conciliator, i. 167.
[2] History of Hebrew Commonwealth, p. 43 (Ward's edition).

We think the difference here is due to condensation on the part of the later writer. In the first case, the offering for the congregation and that for the ruler are specified *separately ;* in the second case, for brevity's sake, the congregation and the rulers are considered as one, and their respective offerings are spoken of as constituting but one offering.

Mr. Espin, in Bible Commentary, says that, in the citation from Leviticus, the reference is to sins of commission; in that from Numbers, to sins of omission. Hence there is a slight difference in the ritual.

Sinners' feeling.

Feared greatly.	*No fear in the case.*
There were they in great fear. Ps. liii. 5.	Where no fear was. Ps. liii. 5.

" The wicked flee when no man pursueth." Prov. xxviii. 1.

Feared the Lord.	*Feared not the Lord.*
So these nations feared the LORD, and served their graven images. 2 Kings xvii. 41.	Unto this day they do after the former manners: they fear not the LORD. 2 Kings xvii. 34.

An instructive example of the use of the same word in different senses.

Staves of ark.

To remain.	*Might be removed.*
The staves shall be in the rings of the ark: they shall not be taken from it. Ex. xxv. 15.	Aaron shall come, and his sons, and they shall take down the covering vail, and cover the ark of testimony with it; ... and shall put in the staves thereof. Num. iv. 5, 6.

Keil renders Num. iv. 6, " Adjust its bearing-poles." Similarly Bush, Nachmanides, Abarbanel, and Rashi. Bible Commentary, " Put the staves thereof in order."

Swearing and oaths.

Countenanced.	*Prohibited.*
And Abraham said, I will swear. Gen xxi. 24. And Jacob sware by the Fear of his father Isaac. Gen. xxxi. 53. Thou shalt fear the LORD thy God, and serve him, and shalt swear by his name. Deut. vi. 13. I adjure thee by the living God, that thou tell us whether thou be the Christ. Matt. xxvi. 63. I say the truth in Christ, I lie not,	By swearing, and lying, and killing, and stealing. Hos. iv. 2. It hath been said by them of old time, Thou shalt not forswear thyself, but shalt perform unto the Lord thine oaths; but I say unto you, Swear not at all; neither by heaven; for it is God's throne: nor by the earth; for it is his footstool: neither by Jerusalem; for it is the city of the great King. Neither shalt thou swear by thy head;

Countenanced.	Prohibited.
my conscience also bearing me witness in the Holy Ghost. Rom. ix. 1. When God made promise to Abraham, because he could swear by no greater, he sware by himself. Heb. vi. 13. The angel which I saw ... lifted up his hand to heaven, and sware by him that liveth for ever and ever. Rev. x. 5, 6.	because thou canst not make one hair white or black. But let your communication be Yea, yea: Nay, nay: for whatsoever is more than these cometh of evil. Matt. v. 33–37. But above all things, my brethren, swear not, neither by heaven, neither by the earth, neither by any other oath: but let your yea be yea, and *your* nay, nay; lest ye fall into condemnation. James v. 12.

The context puts it beyond doubt that Hosea speaks of *false* "swearing." It is equally clear that our Lord, in Matthew, does not refer to *judicial oaths*, but to *profane swearing*, or oaths in common conversation. In proof, observe:

First. The Jews in that age were in the habit of using vain and frivolous oaths in their ordinary talk. They swore by the temple, by the earth, by heaven, by the head, etc. So long as they did not use the name of God in these oaths, they did not deem them particularly binding. This practice is alluded to in Matt. xxiii. 16–22.

Maimonides[1]: "If any one swears by heaven, by the earth, by the sun, and so forth, although it is the intention of him who swears in these words to swear by him who created these things, yet this is not an oath. Or, if one swears by one of the prophets or by one of the books of scripture, although it be the purpose of the swearer to swear by him who sent that prophet or who gave that book, nevertheless this is not an oath." Michaelis[2] says that such oaths were "at that time so common and so frequently and basely abused as to have become perfectly disgraceful to the Jews, even in the eyes of the less treacherous heathen around them, and justly distinguished by the name of *Jewish oaths*." Against this abuse of language the Lord cautioned his disciples: "Let your speech, or conversation 'logos,' be yea, yea; nay, nay." "Do not attempt to bolster up your veracity by frivolous oaths."

Secondly. So far from condemning judicial oaths, Jesus

---

[1] Quoted by Lightfoot, Hor. Heb., p. 280 (Carpzov's edition).
[2] Commentaries on Laws of Moses, iv. 357.

recognized their validity, and allowed himself to be put under oath. When the high-priest said to him, " I *adjure* thee [put thee under oath, cause thee to swear] by the living God that thou tell us," Jesus submitted to be thus sworn, and responded to the solemn obligation. We find, also, that good men, an angel, even God himself, employed the "oath" for confirmation.[1]

James v. 12 evidently refers to the frivolous oaths we have mentioned. Huther: " It is to be noticed that *swearing by the name of God*[2] is not mentioned; for we must not imagine that this is included in the last member of the clause; the apostle intending, evidently, by 'neither any other oath,' to point only at similar formulae, of which several are mentioned in Matthew."

The inference from these facts we leave to the reader.

Times observed.

May be observed.	*Must not be observed.*
He that regardeth the day, regardeth *it* unto the Lord. Rom. xiv. 6.	There shall not be found among you . . . an observer of times. Deut. xviii. 10.
	Ye observe days, and months, and times, and years. Gal. iv. 10.

Michaelis and Aben Ezra take the expression, "observer of times," in Deuteronomy, as implying "divination from the course of the *clouds*." Gesenius regards it as denoting "some kind of divination connected with idolatry"; Fuerst: "It is better to set out with the fundamental signification, *to cover, to wrap up*." Hence the meaning would be, "to practise enchantment *covertly* or *secretly*." Keil,[3] with certain rabbies, derives the Hebrew term from "ayin," an eye; hence, literally, "to ogle, to bewitch with the evil eye." The passage has no reference to the keeping of the Mosaic feasts.

The texts from Romans and Galatians refer to entirely different classes of persons. Andrew Fuller[4] says that the former text refers to *Jewish converts*, who, having from their youth

---

[1] Compare Gen. xxi. 23, 24; 1 Sam. xx. 42; Heb. vi. 17, 18; Rev. x. 5, 6.
[2] Of course, for judicial purposes only.
[3] On Lev. xix. 26.
[4] Works, i. 680, 681.

observed the Mosaic festivals as instituted by Divine authority, were permitted to continue this observance, and treated as "regarding these days unto the Lord." The latter text has respect to *Gentile converts,* who, having previously done service to idols,[1] showed some inclination to cling to their former unauthorized and superstitious observances; and hence were reproved.

Trespass recompensed.

To the Lord.	To the priest.
He shall bring for his trespass unto the LORD a ram. Lev. v. 15.	He shall bring a ram ... for a trespass-offering unto the priest. Lev. v. 18.

Rashi: "To the Lord for the priest." The latter was the Lord's deputy.

A tax paid to the officer appointed by the government may be said to be paid either to the officer or to the government.

II. DUTY OF MAN. — *To himself.*
Anger.

Approved.	Condemned.
Be ye angry, and sin not: let not the sun go down upon your wrath. Eph. iv. 26.	Make no friendship with an angry man: and with a furious man thou shalt not go. Prov. xxii. 24.
	Be not hasty in thy spirit to be angry: for anger resteth in the bosom of fools. Eccl. vii. 9.
	Slow to wrath: for the wrath of man worketh not the righteousness of God. Jas. i. 19, 20.

Paul, says Alford, "speaks of anger which is an infirmity, but by being cherished may become a sin."

Bishop Butler[2]: "The first text is by no means to be understood as an encouragement to indulge ourselves in anger; the sense being certainly this, 'Though ye be angry, sin not'; yet here is evidently a distinction made between anger and sin — between the natural passion and sinful anger."

The last clause hits the point precisely. There is a normal indignation, which is evoked by exhibitions of meanness, treachery, and injustice, and which may, within certain limits, be indulged without sin. This emotion is to be distinguished from those furious and unreasonable ebullitions of wrath which characterize a passionate man.

---

[1] See Gal. iv. 8–11.   [2] Sermon viii.

Animal Food.

Use unrestricted.	Restricted.
Every moving thing that liveth shall be meat for you. Gen. ix. 3. *There is* nothing unclean of itself. Rom. xiv. 14. Whatsoever is sold in the shambles, *that* eat, asking no question for conscience' sake. 1 Cor. x. 25.	Nevertheless these ye shall not eat, of them that chew the cud, or of them that divide the cloven hoof. . . . They *are* unclean unto you. Deut. xiv. 7.

The first three passages refer to men not under the Mosaic law. Deut. xiv. was addressed to the Israelites whom God, for wise reasons, wished to keep a distinct race.

Dr. Davidson[1]: "It is apparent that *the effect* of these enactments respecting different beasts as proper for food or otherwise, must have been to keep the Hebrews apart from other nations; that, as a distinct people, they might be preserved from idolatry. If certain articles of food common among other races were interdicted, the effect would be to break up social intercourse between them; by which means the Jews would not be in so much danger of learning their barbarous customs, and falling into their superstitions. Thus the separation of meats into clean and unclean was most salutary to a monotheistic people, set apart as the chosen depositaries of the knowledge of God, and exposed on every side to polytheistic tribes."[2]

Certain animals forbidden.	Same allowed.
And every creeping thing that flieth *is* unclean unto you: they shall not be eaten. Deut. xiv. 19.	These may ye eat, of every flying creeping thing that goeth upon *all* four, which have legs above their feet, to leap withal upon the earth. But all *other* flying creeping things, which have four feet, *shall be* an abomination unto you. Lev. xi. 21, 23.

Keil: "The edible kinds of locusts are passed over, in Deut.

---

[1] Introd. to Old Test., i. 258.

[2] Difference of national customs furnishes the solution of several alleged "discrepancies." For example, the wearing of long hair by men is allowed in Num. vi. 5, and repudiated in 1 Cor. xi. 14. But, then, the first passage refers to Jews, the second is addressed to Greeks at Corinth. Among the former, the wearing of long hair was counted honorable, even ornamental, rather than otherwise; among the latter, it indicated effeminacy and the indulgence of unnatural vices. See Stuart, Hist. of Canon of Old Test., p. 375 (Revised edition, p. 351).

xiv., because it was not the intention of Moses to repeat every particular of the earlier laws in these addresses." In the rapid outline given in Deuteronomy it was not practicable to notice unimportant exceptions.

Boasting.

Tolerated.	Repudiated.
I labored more abundantly than they all: yet not I, but the grace of God which was with me. 1 Cor. xv. 10. That which I speak, I speak *it* not after the Lord, but as it were foolishly, in this confidence of boasting. Seeing that many glory after the flesh, I will glory also 2 Cor. xi. 17, 18. In nothing am I behind the very chiefest apostles, though I be nothing. 2 Cor. xii. 11.	Let another man praise thee, and not thine own mouth. Prov. xxvii. 2. That no flesh should glory in his presence. 1 Cor. i. 29.

The limiting clauses, "not I, but the grace of God," "though I be nothing," and the like, show that it was not self-conceit which impelled Paul to "boast" or "glory."

Andrew Fuller,[1] comparing the texts from Proverbs and Corinthians, says: "The *motive* in the one case is the desire of applause; in the other, justice to an injured character and to the gospel which suffered in his reproaches." His apparent boasting was in self-vindication.

"No flesh should glory,"—none should find in the gospel occasion for pride and self-exaltation. Paul did not "glory" thus carnally.

Paul unsurpassed.	Humblest of apostles.
For I suppose I was not a whit behind the very chiefest apostles. 2 Cor. xi. 5. For he that wrought effectually in Peter to the apostleship of the circumcision, the same was mighty in me toward the Gentiles. Gal. ii. 8.	For I am the least of the apostles, that am not meet to be called an apostle, because I persecuted the church of God. 1 Cor. xv. 9. Unto me, who am less than the least of all saints, is this grace given, that I should preach among the Gentiles the unsearchable riches of Christ. Eph. iii. 8.

These passages present the apostle in two distinct aspects.

In respect to his talents, his education, and his missionary zeal and labors he was unmistakably *primus inter pares*, first among his equals of the apostolic rank. But he, unlike the other apostles, had been, before his conversion, a fierce and

---

[1] Works, i. 676.

bloody enemy of Christianity, who "beyond measure persecuted the church of God and wasted it."[1] In his deep sorrow, shame, and humiliation at the remembrance of his former deeds of cruelty, he expresses himself in the language of the second series of texts. The two series contemplate the apostle in entirely different relations.

Moses' self-praise.	Self-praise unworthy.
Moreover, the man Moses *was* very great in the land of Egypt, in the sight of Pharaoh's servants, and in the sight of the people. Ex. xi. 3. Now the man Moses *was* very meek, above all the men which *were* upon the face of the earth. Num. xii. 3.	*It is* not good to eat much honey: so *for men* to search their own glory *is not* glory. Prov. xxv. 27.

The quotation from Exodus is the statement of a simple historical fact. It says nothing of Moses' greatness in respect to personal qualifications, but simply asserts — what is beyond the shadow of doubt — that his miracles had produced a great effect, and had made a deep impression upon the Egyptians. And this statement is introduced not to glorify Moses, but to account in part for the ready compliance of the Egyptians in bestowing upon the Israelites the "jewels" and "raiment" which the latter demanded.

The text from Numbers has by some critics been deemed an interpolation. Others give a different translation of the Hebrew term rendered "meek." Luther says, "harassed or annoyed"; Dr. A. Clarke, "depressed"; Palfrey, "miserable"; Dean Stanley, "enduring, afflicted, heedless of self"; Smith's Bible Dictionary, "disinterested."

There is, however, no need of recourse to these definitions. Moses, under the impulse of the Holy Spirit, was writing history "objectively." Hence he speaks of himself as freely as he would of any other person. It is also to be observed that *he records his own faults and sins*[2] with the same fidelity and impartiality. It is remarked by Calmet: "As he praises himself here without pride, so he will blame himself elsewhere

---

[1] Compare Gal. i. 13; Acts ix. 1.
[2] See Ex. iv. 24; Num. xx. 12; Deut. i. 37.

with humility." The objectionable words were inserted to explain why it was that Moses took no steps in the case to vindicate himself, and why, consequently, the Lord so promptly intervened.

Coveting.

Enjoined.
Covet earnestly the best gifts. 1 Cor. xii. 31.
Wherefore, brethren, covet to prophesy. 1 Cor. xiv. 39.

Forbidden.
Thou shalt not covet ... anything that *is* thy neighbor's. Ex. xx. 17.

"Covet," in the first two texts, implies an earnest desire for that which is legitimately within our reach; in the last, it denotes an unlawful craving for that which properly belongs to another.

Human effort.

Encouraged.
So run, that ye may obtain. 1 Cor. ix. 24.

Depreciated.
So then, *it is* not of him that willeth, nor of him that runneth, but of God that sheweth mercy. Rom. ix. 16.

The latter text teaches that the providing of salvation was God's act, and not attributable to man's "willing" nor "running"—the act of sovereign grace, and not of the creature. The former teaches that the securing of this salvation to the individual depends upon his own exertion. God's mercy in furnishing redemption and man's effort in availing himself of that redemption are the cardinal ideas presented in the two texts.

Idol-meats.

Non-essential.
But meat commendeth us not to God: for neither if we eat are we the better; neither if we eat not, are we the worse. 1 Cor. viii. 8.
What say I then? that the idol is any thing, or that which is offered in sacrifice to idols is any thing? 1 Cor. x. 19.

To be avoided.
The things which the Gentiles sacrifice, they sacrifice to devils, and not to God: and I would not that ye should have fellowship with devils. Ye cannot drink the cup of the Lord, and the cup of devils: ye cannot be partakers of the Lord's table, and of the table of devils. 1 Cor. x. 20, 21.

In the first series, Paul concedes that meat is not affected by being offered in sacrifice to idols, and that the eating of it is *in itself*, a matter of indifference. But he argues, in the eighth chapter,[1] that Christians should refrain from this food, because

---

[1] See verses 9–13.

their participation would be misconstrued by other persons; and in the tenth chapter,[1] because the participant shares, to some extent, in the sin of idolatry.

Andrew Fuller[2]: Your course is *inexpedient*, because it leads others into actual idolatry; it is also positively sinful, because it involves a participation in idol-worship, on the general principle that he who voluntarily associates with others in any act is a partaker of that act.

Laughter.

Commended.	*Condemned.*
A merry heart doeth good *like* a medicine. Prov. xvii. 22.	I said of laughter, *It is* mad: and of mirth, What doeth it? Eccl. ii. 2.
A time to every purpose under the heaven. ... A time to laugh. Eccl. iii. 1, 4.	Sorrow *is* better than laughter: for by the sadness of the countenance the heart is made better. The heart of the wise *is* in the house of mourning; but the heart of fools *is* in the house of mirth. Eccl. vii. 3, 4.
I commended mirth, because a man hath no better thing under the sun, than to eat, and to drink, and to be merry. Eccl. viii. 15.	
I will see you again, and your heart shall rejoice, and your joy no man taketh from you. John xvi. 22.	Wo unto you that laugh now! for ye shall mourn and weep. Luke vi. 25.

The first texts speak approvingly of a cheerful spirit or a seasonable and rational merriment; the second condemn senseless and riotous hilarity. Hengstenberg: "Mirth considered as the highest good, as the end of life, and the too great eagerness displayed in its pursuit." Not laughter in the abstract, but laughter *under certain circumstances*, is condemned.

Man's own way.

Must not be followed.	*May be followed.*
Remember all the commandments of the LORD, and do them; and that ye seek not after your own heart and your own eyes. Num. xv. 39.	Rejoice, O young man, in thy youth; and let thy heart cheer thee in the days of thy youth, and walk in the ways of thy heart, and in the sight of thine eyes. Eccl. xi. 9.

Menasseh ben Israel, Aben Ezra, and Rashi take the second text as ironical: "Well, go your own way, but remember," etc. Ginsburg, Hengstenberg, and Zöckler deem it an injunction to enjoy cheerfully the blessings of life, and, at the same time, to bear in mind man's accountability to the Giver of every good and perfect gift.

---

[1] Verses 20, 21. [2] Works, i. 683, 684.

Mourning.

Commended.	Discountenanced.
Blessed *are* they that mourn : for they shall be comforted. Matt. v. 4.	Rejoice in the Lord always: *and* again I say, Rejoice. Phil. iv. 4.

The "mourning" is that attendant upon true penitence; the "rejoicing" results from the assurance of salvation. The sorrow precedes, the joy follows, pardon.

Purity.

In a preceding part of this work [1] we have discussed at some length, and at one view, the alleged discrepancies which would properly come under this head.

Salvation.

God's work.	Man's work.
For God *is* my King of old, working salvation in the midst of the earth. Ps. lxxiv. 12.	Work out your own salvation with fear and trembling. For it is God which worketh in you both to will and to do of *his* good pleasure. Phil. ii. 12, 13.

The last verse at the right represents God as the prime mover in the work of salvation. Alford: "We owe both the will to do good and the power to his indwelling Spirit." As has been previously said, the divine and human agencies co-operate to a certain extent.[2]

Strong drink.

Use recommended.	Discountenanced.
And thou shalt bestow that money for whatsoever thy soul lusteth after, for oxen, or for sheep, or for wine, or for strong drink. Deut. xiv. 26. And the vine said unto them, Should I leave my wine, which cheereth God and man. Judg. ix. 13. Wine *that* maketh glad the heart of man Ps. civ. 15. Give strong drink unto him that is ready to perish, and wine to those that be of heavy hearts. Let him drink, and forget his poverty, and remember his misery no more. Prov. xxxi. 6, 7. Drink no longer water, but use a little wine for thy stomach's sake, and thine often infirmities. 1 Tim. v. 23.	Wine *is* a mocker, strong drink *is* raging: and whosoever is deceived thereby is not wise. Prov. xx. 1. Who hath wo? who hath sorrow? who hath contentions? who hath babbling? who hath wounds without cause? who hath redness of eyes? They that tarry long at the wine; they that go to seek mixed wine. Look not thou upon the wine when it is red, when it giveth his color in the cup, *when* it moveth itself aright. At the last it biteth like a serpent, and stingeth like an adder. Prov. xxiii. 29–32. Whoredom and wine and new wine take away the heart. Hos. iv. 11. Nor drunkards, nor revilers, nor extortioners, shall inherit the kingdom of God 1 Cor. vi. 10.

For an extended discussion of this point the reader is referred to the literature of the subject. It should, however, be said

---

[1] See pp. 144–146.   [2] Compare pp. 166, 167 of present work.

that *the general tenor of the Bible is clearly and decidedly against intemperance.*

Noah's intoxication[1] — a sad blot upon a character otherwise without reproach — is related merely as a matter of history, and without comment.

As to the miracle at Cana,[2] there is nothing in the act of our Saviour, nor in the circumstances of the case, which goes to sanction drunkenness.

Certain authors maintain, with some plausibility, that in all cases where strong drinks are coupled with terms of commendation, the original word properly means either *unfermented wine* or else *fruit;* and that the notices of fermented wine are restricted to passages of a condemnatory character. This position, if tenable, is one of great importance. For the discussion of this point, we have already referred to the literature of the subject.[3]

In the quotation from Deuteronomy the words rendered "wine" and "strong drink" may not imply here fermented or intoxicating liquors. Even if such be their meaning, the passage does not sanction the use of these drinks to the extent of ebriety.

Judges ix. 13 appears in the sacred record, as a mere fable, with which the uninspired speaker embellished his harangue.

The text in Psalms speaks of "wine" which "maketh glad" the heart of man, and of "bread" which "strengtheneth" it. These two terms apparently stand, by metonymy, for *food* and

---

[1] Gen ix. 21.
[2] John ii 1–11.
[3] Compare Smith's Bib. Dict., "Wine"; also, Lees and Burns' "Temperance Bible Commentary" (American edition, New York, 1870). A writer in Fairbairn's Imperial Bible Dict. says, that תִּירוֹשׁ properly means *vintage fruit*, a solid, instead of a liquid; that שֵׁכָר means *syrup* from various fruits not intoxicating when new. Fuerst takes יַיִן with קָרִץ, Jer. xl. 10, as denoting *bunches of grapes*. Cassell's Bible Dict. says that with the exception of יַיִן, שֵׁכָר, and perhaps of סֹבֶא, the other original terms are not used in connection with drunkenness. But see תִּירוֹשׁ in Hos. iv. 11, above.

drink. Hengstenberg: "What appeases hunger and thirst." It is not an intoxicating drink which is contemplated here.

The passage in Proverbs xxxi. points to a *medicinal* use of the articles in question. In verses 4 and 5 of the same chapter the use of "wine" and "strong drink" is forbidden, for a specified reason, to "kings" and "princes." It is then added: "Give strong drink unto him that is ready to perish [Zöckler: 'who is on the point of perishing, who is just expiring'], and wine unto those that be of heavy hearts." The language indicates persons in a state of great depression and exhaustion.

That Paul's direction to Timothy also contemplates a *strictly medical* use of wine is beyond a shadow of doubt. The conclusion is that the sacred writers are not apologists for drunkenness, and neither directly nor indirectly countenance it.

Temptation.

Desirable.	*Undesirable.*
My brethren, count it all joy when ye fall into divers temptations. Jas. i. 2.	Lead us not into temptation. Matt. vi. 13.

The word rendered "temptations," says Alford, means "not only what we properly call *temptations*, but any kind of distresses which happen to us, from without or from within, which in God's purpose serve as *trials* of us." Matthew inculcates "a humble self-distrust and shrinking from such trials in the prospect"; James teaches that when they *do* providentially overtake us, we are to rejoice that even these things shall work together for our good.

Wealth.

Not to be retained.	*May be retained.*
If thou wilt be perfect, go *and* sell that thou hast, and give to the poor, and thou shalt have treasure in heaven. Matt. xix. 21.	Charge them that are rich in this world, that they be not high-minded, nor trust in uncertain riches.... That they do good, that they be rich in good works, ready to distribute, willing to communicate. 1 Tim. vi. 17, 18.
As many as were possessors of lands or houses sold them, and brought the prices of the things that were sold, and laid *them* down at the apostles' feet. Acts iv. 34, 35.	
They that will be rich fall into temptation, and a snare, and *into* many foolish and hurtful lusts, which drown men in destruction and perdition. For the love of money is the root of all evil. 1 Tim. vi. 9, 10.	

The young ruler's was an *exceptional* case. His " great possessions " were his idol ; love of money was his great sin Jesus shaped the injunction to meet this special case; aiming, as always, at the *besetting sin* of the individual. The only legitimate inference is that every sin, even the most cherished, must be given up, if we would be disciples of Christ.

Of the example in Acts, Alford says that it was a voluntary one, was enforced nowhere by any rule, and that it prevailed only at Jerusalem. Hackett: " The community of goods, as it existed in the church at Jerusalem, was purely a voluntary thing, and not required by the apostles."

Not those who " are rich," but those who " *will*[1] be rich," those who make riches the great object of life, are admonished by the apostle in 1 Tim. vi. The excessive love, rather than the mere possession, of wealth, is the object of reprimand. The Bible forbids neither the acquisition nor the possession of wealth, provided we hold it as God's stewards, and use it for his glory.

Wisdom.

Unprofitable.	*Of great value.*
For in much wisdom *is* much grief: and he that increaseth knowledge increaseth sorrow. Eccl. i. 18.	Wisdom excelleth folly, as far as light excelleth darkness. Eccl. ii. 13.
As it happeneth to the fool so it happeneth even to me : and why was I then more wise? Eccl. ii. 15.	Happy is the man *that* findeth wisdom, and the man that getteth understanding. . . . She is more precious than rubies : and all the things thou canst desire are not to be compared unto her. Prov. iii. 13, 15.
For what hath the wise more than the fool? Eccl. vi. 8.	
This wisdom descendeth not from above, but is earthly, sensual, devilish. Jas. iii. 15.	The wisdom that is from above is first pure, then peaceable, . . . full of mercy and good fruits. Jas. iii. 17.

The term " wisdom " is applied, in the scriptures, to at least three things : 1. Worldly craft, cunning, or policy ; 2. Mere human knowledge or learning ; 3. Enlightened piety. The first is always disapproved ; the second, having in itself no moral quality, is not condemned save when it usurps the place of the third kind, or enlightened piety. The latter is invariably commended. In the case before us ethical wisdom is contrasted with carnal wisdom.

[1] Alford brings out the force of the original word, thus : " 'They who wish to be rich."

III. DUTY OF MAN.— To his fellow-men.
Adultery.

Tolerated.	Prohibited.
All the women children ... keep alive for yourselves. Num. xxxi. 18.	Thou shalt not commit adultery. Ex. xx. 14.
The LORD said to Hosea, Go, take unto thee a wife of whoredoms, and children of whoredoms, for the land hath committed great whoredom, *departing* from the LORD. Hosea i. 2.	Whoremongers and adulterers God will judge. Heb. xiii. 4.

Of the case in Numbers Keil says all the females were put to death who might possibly have been engaged in the licentious worship of Peor,[1] so that the Israelites might be preserved from contamination by that abominable idolatry. The young maidens were reserved to be employed as servants, or, in case they became proselytes, to be married.

With reference to Hosea, Delitzsch takes the prophet's marriages simply as "internal events, i.e. as merely carried out in that inward and spiritual intuition in which the word of God was addressed to him." In this view concur Bleek,[2] Davidson,[3] Hengstenberg, Kimchi, and Knobel; the first of whom dwells upon the unsuitableness of the *outward acts* to make the desired moral impression, while the last pronounces these acts peculiarly inconsistent with a character so severely moral as that of Hosea. Moreover, the word "whoredom," in the first part of the verse may mean, as it certainly does in the last part, simply *spiritual* whoredom, or idolatry.[4]

Assassination.

Sanctioned.	Forbidden.
Ehud said, I have a message from God unto thee. And he arose out of *his* seat. And Ehud put forth his left hand, and took the dagger, ... and thrust it into his belly. ... And Ehud escaped. Judg. iii. 20, 21. 26.	Thou shalt not kill. Ex. xx. 13 If a man come presumptuously upon his neighbor to slay him with guile; thou shalt take him from mine altar, that he may die. Ex. xxi. 14.
Then Jael, Heber's wife, took a nail of the tent, and took a hammer in her hand, and went softly unto him, and smote the nail into his temples, and fastened it into the ground: for he was fast asleep, and weary. So he died. Judg. iv 21.	

[1] See Num. xxv. 1–3.
[2] Introd. to Old Test., ii. 124.
[3] Introd. to Old Test., iii. 287.
[4] Compare p. 79, present work.

The cases of Ehud and Jael are recorded without comment, simply as matters of history. It does not appear that God *sanctioned* their acts, although he *overruled* them for the welfare of his people. Keil admonishes us against supposing that Ehud acted under the impulse of the Spirit of God; also that, though he actually delivered Israel, there is no warrant for assuming that the means he selected were either commanded or approved by Jehovah.

The cases of Joab and Shimei[1] are sometimes adduced as examples of the sanction of assassination. The former was a " man of blood," a deliberate murderer. When the reasons of state, on account of which his punishment had been deferred, ceased to exist, that punishment was justly inflicted. Shimei was guilty of aggravated treason and rebellion. Being reprieved upon a certain condition, he wilfully violated that condition, and met the consequences of his temerity.

Assassination is nowhere sanctioned in the Bible.

Avenging of blood.

Provided for.	*Virtually prohibited.*
The revenger of blood himself shall slay the murderer: when he meeteth him, he shall slay him. Num. xxxv. 19.	Thou shalt not kill. Deut. v. 17.

The practice of blood-revenge, being one of long standing, and founded upon " an imaginary sense of honor,"[2] was tolerated by Moses; but he took measures to prevent its abuse.

According to the original custom, as Burckhardt[3] says, " the right of blood-revenge is never lost; it descends, on both sides, to the latest generation." Moses restricted the avenging of blood to *the nearest male relative* of the deceased, and to the *actual offender.* These two, and no more, were concerned in the affair.

Then, strange as it may seem, such competent witnesses as Burckhardt, Mr. Layard,[4] and Prof. Palmer[5] bear unequivocal

---

[1] 1 Kings ii. 5–9.
[2] Michaelis, Com. on Mosaic Laws, i. 15, 16.
[3] Quoted by Macdonald, Introd. to Pent. ii. 323, 324.
[4] Nineveh and Babylon, p. 260 (New York edition).
[5] **Desert of the Exodus**, p. 75 (Harpers' edition).

testimony to the *salutary influence* of the custom upon the tribes among whom it obtains. The latter traveller says: " Thanks to the terrible rigor of the ' vendetta,' or blood-feud, homicide is far rarer in the desert than in civilized lands." The "killing" forbidden in Deuteronomy is the *crime of murder;* the "blood-revenge" of Numbers is the *recognized punishment* of that crime.

Baptism.

Enjoined. — *Neglected.*

Go ye therefore and teach all nations, baptizing them in the name of the Father, and of the Son, and of the Holy Ghost. Matt. xxviii. 19.

I thank God that I baptized none of you, but Crispus and Gaius. ... For Christ sent me not to baptize, but to preach the gospel. 1 Cor. i. 14. 17.

Obviously, " Christ sent me *not so much* to baptize, as to preach the gospel." Paul did not neglect or undervalue baptism, but gave himself to the work of teaching, leaving his associates to administer baptism.

Burdens.

Must bear others' burdens. — *Bear our own burdens.*

Bear ye one another's burdens, and so fulfil the law of Christ. Gal. vi. 2.

For every man shall bear his own burden. Gal. vi. 5.

The original word for "burden" is not the same in the two cases. The different sense is indicated in accurate versions.

The first text means, " Be sympathetic and helpful to each other in the midst of infirmities and sorrows"; the second, " Every man must bear his own responsibility, under the Divine government."

Calling men " Father."

Forbidden. — *Exemplified.*

And call no *man* your father upon the earth: for one is your Father, which is in heaven. Neither be ye called masters; for one is your Master, *even* Christ. Matt. xxiii. 9, 10.

And Elisha saw *it*, and he cried, My father, my father. 2 Kings ii. 12.

Yet *have ye* not many fathers: for in Christ Jesus I have begotten you through the gospel. 1 Cor. iv. 15.

The texts at the left simply forbid us to take any man *as an infallible guide*. We are to pay to no human being the homage and obedience which rightfully belong to Christ.

Alford: "The prohibition is against loving, and, in any religious matter, using such titles, signifying dominion over the faith of others."

Capital punishment.

Murderer executed.	Spared.
Whoso sheddeth man's blood, by man shall his blood be shed. Gen. ix. 6.	A fugitive and a vagabond shalt thou be in the earth. And Cain said unto the LORD, My punishment *is* greater than I can bear. Gen. iv. 12, 13.

By some unaccountable freak of exegesis, a well-known critic makes the first text *the prohibition of capital punishment.* Instead, it is a most explicit command, sanctioning it.

The case of Cain occurred some fifteen hundred years *before* this command was given to Noah.

Captives.

To be spared.	Put to death.
All the people *that is* found therein, shall be tributaries unto thee, and they shall serve thee.... Thus shalt thou do unto all the cities *which are* very far off from thee, which *are* not of the cities of these nations. Deut. xx. 11, 15.	But of the cities of these people, which the LORD thy God doth give thee *for* an inheritance, thou shalt save alive nothing that breatheth:... That they teach you not to do after all their abominations, which they have done unto their gods; so should ye sin against the LORD your God. Deut. xx. 16, 18.

The general rule was to make captives; the exception was in the case of the "seven nations" of Canaan, to whom, on account of their "abominations," no quarter was to be given.[1]

Chastity tested.

By one method.	A different method.
And the LORD spake unto Moses, saying, Speak unto the children of Israel,... If any man's wife go aside, and commit a trespass against him, etc. Num. v. 11-31.	If any man take a wife, and go in unto her, and hate her, and give occasions of speech against her,... and say, I took this woman, and when I came to her, I found her not a maid, etc. Deut. xxii. 13-21.

A late writer says that, in one case, "great latitude is afforded to the suspicious husband, while the woman's protection against him is only a superstitious appeal to Jehovah; in the other, a judicial investigation is instituted, giving the wife a more reasonable chance of justice."

But the two cases are quite different. The first text refers to unchastity of which the woman was supposed to have been guilty *after* marriage; the other, to similar misconduct of hers

---

[1] See further under "Enemies, — treatment."

before that event. Hence different modes of investigation were adopted. In the first case the way prescribed — the *only* way to arrive at the truth in the matter — was, as Keil says, " to let the thing be decided by the verdict of God himself." In the other case, this would not be true.

Christians bearing weapons.

Permitted.	*Forbidden.*
But now, he that hath a purse, let him take *it*, and likewise *his* scrip: and he that hath no sword, let him sell his garment, and buy one. Luke xxii. 36.	Put up again thy sword into his place: for all they that take the sword, shall perish with the sword. Matt. xxvi. 52.

Some critics take the Greek word ' machaira' as denoting, in the first text, not a " sword," but a " knife." Unquestionably, the word occasionally has this meaning in classical Greek and in the Septuagint.[1] This is a possible, but not probable, interpretation.

The first text may be only another way of saying, " You must henceforth use such precautions, and make such provision for your needs, as men generally do." Wordsworth: " A proverbial expression, intimating that they would now be reduced to a condition in which the men of this world resort to such means of defence. Alford: " The saying is both a description to them of their altered situation with reference to the world without, and a declaration that self-defence and self-provision would henceforward be necessary." Similarly Oosterzee, and many others.

The second quotation may have been a warning to Peter against a *seditious* or *rebellious* use of the sword against rulers. Or it may have been a dissuasive against his attempting to avenge the wrongs inflicted upon Jesus, coupled with the assurance that the latter's persecutors should speedily perish — as they did, in the destruction of their city. That is, rebellion

---

[1] Liddell and Scott give, as one definition, a knife for surgical, sacrificial, and other purposes. In Gen. xxii. 6, 10; Judges xix. 29, such a knife is clearly intended. In the last instance, however, Tischendorf adopts a different reading.

against regularly constituted authorities, together with private, extra-judicial revenge, may be all that is contemplated and prohibited here.

Circumcision.

Instituted.	Discarded.
This *is* my covenant, which ye shall keep, between me and you, and thy seed after thee: Every man-child among you shall be circumcised. Gen. xvii. 10. And the LORD said unto Moses and Aaron, This *is* the ordinance of the passover: ... No uncircumcised person shall eat thereof. Ex. xii. 43, 48.	Is any called in uncircumcision? let him not be circumcised. 1 Cor. vii. 18. Behold, I Paul, say unto you, that if ye be circumcised, Christ shall profit you nothing. Gal. v. 2

The rites and ceremonies of the Mosaic law, among which was circumcision, were intended to serve a temporary purpose. When Christ came the Mosaic ritual ceased to have any binding force. It had fulfilled the designed end.

The first passages were addressed to Abraham and his seed. The second series was written after the rite of circumcision had been set aside by Divine authority.

Not to be omitted.	Neglected for forty years.
And the uncircumcised man-child, ... that soul shall be cut off from his people; he hath broken my covenant. Gen. xvii. 14.	All the people *that were* born in the wilderness by the way as they came forth out of Egypt, ... them Joshua circumcised: for they were uncircumcised) because they had not circumcised them by the way. Josh. v. 5, 7.

Mr. Perowne, in Smith's Bible Dictionary, maintains that "the nation, while bearing the punishment of disobedience in its forty years' wandering, was regarded as under a temporary rejection by God, and was therefore prohibited from using the sign of the covenant."

This explanation is adopted by Calvin, Keil, and Hengstenberg,[1] and is probably the true one. On the same principle the parallel omission of the passover is to be explained.

Profitable.	Useless.
A certain disciple was there, named Timotheus. ... Him would Paul have to go forth with him; and took and circumcised him, because of the Jews which were in those quarters. Acts xvi. 1, 3.	Neither Titus, who was with me, being a Greek, was compelled to be circumcised. And that because of false brethren unawares brought in, who came in privily to spy out our liberty which we have in Christ Jesus, that they might bring us into bondage. Gal. ii. 3, 4.

---

[1] On Genuineness of Pentateuch, ii. 13–15.

Conybeare: The two cases were entirely different. In the latter, there was an attempt to enforce circumcision as necessary to salvation; in the former, it was performed as a voluntary act, and simply on prudential grounds.

Similarly Hackett and Alford. The principle involved is that we may sometimes make concessions to expediency which it would be wrong to make to arbitrary authority seeking to tyrannize over the conscience.

Commutation for murder.

Not allowed.	*Permitted.*
Ye shall take no satisfaction for the life of a murderer, which *is* guilty of death: but he shall be surely put to death. Num. xxxv. 31.	If the ox were wont to push with his horn in time past, and it hath been testified to his owner, and he hath not kept him in, but that he hath killed a man or a woman; the ox shall be stoned, and his owner also shall be put to death. If there be laid on him a sum of money, then he shall give for the ransom of his life whatsoever is laid upon him. Ex. xxi. 29, 30.

In the case of wilful murder, as Abarbanel and Aben Ezra say, absolutely no commutation of the death-penalty was allowed. But the second quotation does not refer to a case of "murder," properly so called. The element of malice was wanting. Gross and criminal carelessness, although resulting in the death of a human being, was yet less heinous than deliberate murder. Hence the judges might, if they saw fit, punish the offender by a heavy fine, instead of death.

This is, substantially, Keil's opinion.

Contention and strife.

Enjoined.	*Forbidden.*
Strive to enter in at the strait gate. Luke xiii 24.	A fool's lips enter into contention. Prov. xviii. 6.
Yea, so have I strived to preach the gospel. . . . Now I beseech you, brethren, that ye strive together with me in *your* prayers to God for me. Rom. xv. 20, 30.	Charging *them* before the Lord that they strive not about words to no profit. . . . The servant of the Lord must not strive. 2 Tim. ii. 14, 24.
It was needful for me to write unto you, and exhort *you* that ye should earnestly contend for the faith. Jude 3.	For where envying and strife *is*, there *is* confusion and every evil work. Jas. iii. 16.

These are interesting examples of the use of the same word in widely different senses. In the first series the words in question imply merely *earnest effort;* in the second, *quarrelsome collision.* We have elsewhere seen that the citation from Luke would be properly rendered, "Agonize to enter in at the strait gate."

Conversion of men.

Man converts his fellow.
In doing this thou shalt both save thyself, and them that hear thee. 1 Tim. iv. 16.
If any of you do err from the truth, and one convert him; Let him know, that he which converteth the sinner from the error of his way shall save a soul from death. Jas. v. 19, 20.

Converts himself.
Lest they see with their eyes, and hear with their ears, and understand with their heart, and convert, and be healed. Isa. vi. 10.

The first text brings to view the influence of another in causing a man to turn; the second, the man's own act in turning from the error of his way. Here is no contradiction.

Distrust.

Enjoined.
Take ye heed every one of his neighbor, and trust ye not in any brother: for every brother will utterly supplant. Jer. ix. 4.
Cursed *be* the man that trusteth in man, and maketh flesh his arm, and whose heart departeth from the Lord. Jer. xvii. 5.
Trust ye not in a friend, put ye not confidence in a guide. Micah vii. 5.

Precluded.
Beareth all things, believeth all things, hopeth all things, endureth all things. Charity never faileth. 1 Cor. xiii. 7, 8.

The first and last texts at the left imply a state of the "most wretched perfidiousness, anarchy, and confusion, in which the most intimate could have no confidence in each other, and the closest ties of relationship were violated and contemned." These two texts are not *commands*, but *advice*—equivalent to saying, "Such is the state of public morals that if you trust any man you will be deceived and betrayed."

Jer. xvii. 5 simply denounces that undue "trust in man" which causes one to "depart from the Lord." None of these passages countenance uncharitable suspicion and distrust.

The first three texts graphically depict the workings and results of human depravity; the last citation sets forth the workings of Christian love. The demoralizing effects of sin are contrasted with the loving, trusting purity arising from the gospel

Divorce.

Largely allowed.

And seest among the captives a beautiful woman, and hast a desire unto her, that thou wouldest have her to thy wife. Then thou shalt bring her home to thy house, . . . And after that, thou shalt go in unto her, and be her husband, and she shall be thy wife. And it shall be, if thou have no delight in her, then thou shalt let her go whither she will. Deut. xxi. 11-14.

When, a man hath taken a wife, and married her, and it come to pass that she find no favor in his eyes, because he hath found some uncleanness in her; then let him write her a bill of divorcement, and give *it* in her hand, and send her out of his house. And when she is departed out of his house, she may go and be another man's *wife*. Deut. xxiv. 1, 2.

Restricted.

Let none deal treacherously against the wife of his youth. For the LORD, the God of Israel, saith, that he hateth putting away. Mal. ii. 15, 16.

Whosoever shall put away his wife, saving for the cause of fornication, causeth her to commit adultery; and whosoever shall marry her that is divorced committeth adultery. Matt. v. 32.

Why did Moses then command to give a writing of divorcement, and to put her away? He saith unto them, Moses, because of the hardness of your hearts, suffered you to put away your wives: but from the beginning it was not so. Matt. xix. 7, 8.

Whosoever putteth away his wife, and marrieth another, committeth adultery; and whosoever marrieth her that is put away from *her* husband, committeth adultery. Luke xvi. 18.

Between these two series of announcements a period of some fifteen hundred years intervened.

God, in the early ages of the Jewish nation, and with a view to prevent greater evils, allowed a limited freedom of divorce. Yet this "putting away," being opposed to the original, divine idea of marriage, was suffered solely on account of the hardness of men's hearts, and in comparatively rude and unenlightened times. We see here the wisdom of God in adapting his statutes and requirements to man's knowledge and position in the scale of civilization.

Besides, as Dr. Ginsburg[1] has observed, "the Mosaic law does not *institute* divorce, but, as in other matters, recognizes and most humanely regulates the prevailing patriarchal practice." The law, moreover, is shaped with a view to mitigate the evils of the practice, and ultimately to restrict it within the proper limits. At our Saviour's coming, he, addressing himself to a more enlightened age, set the matter in the normal light, allowing divorce but for *one* cause.[2]

---

[1] Kitto's Cyclopaedia, iii. 82.

[2] See, further, Professor Hovey, "Scriptural Doctrine of Divorce" (Boston, 1866). President Woolsey, "New Englander" (January, April, and July, 1867).

Enemies, — treatment.

Ammonites tortured.

And he brought forth the people that *were* therein, and put *them* under saws and under harrows of iron, and under axes of iron, and made them pass through the brick-kiln: and thus did he unto all the cities of the children of Ammon. 2 Sam. xii. 31.

And he brought out the people that *were* in it, and cut *them* with saws, and with harrows of iron, and with axes. 1 Chron. xx. 3.

Cruelty prohibited.

But love ye your enemies, **and do** good, and lend, hoping for nothing again; and your reward shall be great, and ye shall be the children of the Highest: for he is kind unto the unthankful and *to* the evil. Be ye therefore merciful, as your Father also is merciful. Luke vi. 35, 36.

If our version of the text from Chronicles is correct, David merely punished the Ammonites for the terrible cruelties which at a previous period his fellow-countrymen had suffered at their hands.[1] Henderson, referring to these cruelties, says: "The object of the Ammonites was to effect an utter extermination of the Israelites inhabiting the mountainous regions of Gilead, in order that they might extend their own territory in that direction."

According to a Jewish tradition, David slew the Moabites,[2] because they had treacherously murdered his parents who had been confided to their care.[3] Wahner, however, gives three explanations "according to which none of the vanquished Moabites were put to death."[4]

The probability is that *our version* of both texts of the first series, as well as the *original* of the second of those texts, is incorrect. Dr. Davidson says: "According to the present reading of Samuel, the meaning could not be *he put them to*. Nor could it be *he put them under*, but only *he put them among* or *between*."

Chandler,[5] Dantz, and others, take the meaning to be that David enslaved the Ammonites, putting them to servile labor, in the midst of suitable implements, — saws, harrows, axes, and the like. The word "vayyäsar," "he sawed," in Chronicles, may be a mere copyist's blunder for "vayyäsem," "he put," as

---

[1] Comp. 1 Sam. xi. 2; Amos i. 13. [2] 2 Sam. viii. 2.
[3] 1 Sam. xxii. 3, 4. [4] See Michaelis, Mos. Laws, i. 334, 335.
[5] Life of David, ii. 227-238 (Oxford, 1853).

in Samuel. The latter word is found in seven of the MSS. collated by Dr. Kennicott. The close resemblance of the two words, especially if the final letter, Mem, were imperfectly formed, accounts for the error of the transcriber.

We, therefore, submit that there is no evidence that David put the Ammonites to the torture. The meaning may be that, he put them to menial service, of the lowest and most laborious kind. If he killed any, it may have been, as Keil suggests, simply the "fighting men that were taken prisoners."

Finally, these passages are *mere history*, and the sacred writer makes himself responsible for nothing more in the case than the simple accuracy of the narrative.

Baal's prophets slain.	*Conciliatory measures enjoined.*
And Elijah said unto them, Take the prophets of Baal; let not one of them escape. And they took them; and Elijah brought them down to the brook Kishon, and slew them there. 1 Kings xviii. 40.	In meekness instructing those that oppose themselves. 2 Tim. ii. 25.

These "prophets" were engaged in promoting treason and rebellion against the theocracy. Leniency shown to them, under these circumstances, would be nothing less than cruelty and treachery toward the highest welfare of the nation.

Keil: "To infer from this act of Elijah the right to institute a bloody persecution of heretics, would not only indicate a complete oversight of the difference between heathen idolaters and Christian heretics, but the same reprehensible confounding of the evangelical standpoint of the New Testament with the legal standpoint of the Old, which Christ condemned in his own disciples, in Luke ix. 55, 56."

Rawlinson: "Elijah's act is to be justified by the express command of the law, that idolatrous Israelites were to be put to death; and by the right of a prophet under the theocracy to step in and execute the law when the king failed in his duty."

Canaanites extirpated.	*Killing forbidden.*
But of the cities of these people, which the LORD thy God doth give thee *for* an inheritance, thou shalt save alive nothing that breatheth; but thou shalt utterly destroy them; *namely*, the	Thou shalt not kill. Deut. v. 17.

Canaanites extirpated.	Killing forbidden.
Hittites, and the Amorites, the Canaanites, and the Perizzites, the Hivites, and the Jebusites; as the LORD thy God hath commanded thee: that they teach you not to do after all their abominations, which they have done unto their gods; so should ye sin against the LORD your God. Deut. xx. 16-18.	

The precept in Deut. v. does not prohibit the punishment of crime. It is to be noted that extraordinary severity was enjoined only in the cases above specified. To other nations the Israelites might propose conditions of peace, and enter into leagues with them.

The reasons for this unexampled severity are the following:

1. *The excessive wickedness* of these seven tribes, the horrible "abominations" of which they were guilty. They burned their children in honor of their gods;[1] they practised sodomy, bestiality, and all loathsome vices.[2] Such was their unmitigated depravity, that the land is represented as "vomiting out her inhabitants," and "spewing them forth," as the stomach disgorges a deadly poison.[3] On account of their loathsome vileness God cut them off by the sword of the Israelites.

2. *Their contaminating example.* This is the reason assigned in the text above quoted. For the same reason, "covenants" and "marriages" between the Israelites and these seven tribes were strictly prohibited.[4] The disastrous consequences of the intercourse of the Israelites with Moab evince the wisdom of this prohibition.[5] It was utterly impossible to live near these degraded idolaters without being defiled by the association.

This fact indicates to us the reason why the Israelites were instructed to "*save alive nothing that breatheth.*" Absolute extermination of the idolaters was the only safeguard of the Hebrews. Any of the former who should be spared, would, owing to their *perverse proclivities*, prove a most undesirable and intractable element in the Hebrew theocracy.[6] It was better for all concerned, that these idolatrous tribes should be

---

[1] Lev. xviii. 21. [2] Lev. xviii. 22-24; xx. 23. [3] Lev. xviii. 25, 28.
[4] Deut. vii. 1-4. [5] Num. xxv. 1-3. [6] Judges ii. 1-3; iii. 1-7.

laid under the ban; that is, altogether exterminated, that they might not teach the Israelites their abominations and sins.

As to the reflex influence, upon the Hebrews themselves, of their extermination of the Canaanites, Prof. Norton[1] bluntly observes: " There is no good moral discipline in the butchery of women and infants. It is not thus that men are to be formed to the service of God." To this, we may reply:

1. The positive and explicit command of Jehovah entirely changed the aspect of the case, and invested the Israelites, while executing this command with a solemn official responsibility as *the instruments of divine justice.*

2. The execution of this command may have been, in that comparatively rude and unenlightened age, the *most effectual means of impressing upon the Hebrews the " exceeding sinfulness" of sin,* together with God's abhorrence[2] of the same, especially, in the form of "idolatry." As the Hebrews looked forth upon the devastated habitations, the slain animals, the dead bodies of the Canaanites, they could not but hear the solemn warning, " *These are the consequences of sin. Behold how Jehovah hates iniquity."*

This view of the case is vigorously presented by Dr. Fairbairn,[3] in words like the following: " What could be conceived so thoroughly fitted to implant in their hearts an abiding conviction of the evil of idolatry and its foul abominations — to convert their abhorrence of these into a national, permanent characteristic, as their being obliged to enter on their settled inheritance by a terrible infliction of judgment upon its former occupants for polluting it with such enormities? Thus the very foundations of their national existence raised a solemn warning against defection from the pure worship of God; and the visitation of divine wrath against the ungodliness of men accomplished by their own hands, and interwoven with the records of their history at its most eventful period, stood as a

---

[1] Genuineness of Gospels, ii. p. cxxx.   [2] Lev. xx. 23.
[3] Typology, ii. 465–471.

perpetual witness against them, if they should ever turn aside to folly. Happy had it been for them, if they had been as careful to remember the lesson, as God was to have it suitably impressed upon their minds."

The language in which Mr. Carlyle[1] characterizes the severe and bloody measures employed by Cromwell against the Irish insurgents, may be applied to the Israelites in their executing the divine commission against the Canaanites, — "An armed soldier, solemnly conscious to himself that he is the soldier of God, the Just, — a consciousness which it well beseems all soldiers and all men to have always, — armed soldier, terrible as death, relentless as doom; doing God's judgments on the enemies of God! It is a phenomenon not of joyful nature; no, but of awful; to be looked at with pious terror and awe."

Viewing the Israelites in this aspect, as the consciously commissioned ministers of heaven's vengeance upon an utterly corrupt and imbruted race, their case is lifted completely out of the common range of warfare, and becomes *entirely unique*, — no longer to be judged of by the ordinary ethical standards.

A late author, who could not be charged with fanaticism, — Dr. Thomas Arnold,[2] — has the following emphatic defence of the Israelites, and of their warfare of extermination: " And if we are inclined to think that God dealt hardly with the people of Canaan in commanding them to be so utterly destroyed, let us but think what might have been our fate, and the fate of every other nation under heaven, at this hour, had the sword of the Israelites done its work more sparingly. Even as it was, the small portions of the Canaanites who were left and the nations around them so tempted the Israelites by their idolatrous practices that we read continually of the whole people of God turning away from his service. But had the heathen lived in the land in equal numbers, and still more, had

---

[1] Cromwell's Letters and Speeches, ii. 53 (Second edition).
[2] Sermon iv. "Wars of the Israelites." See, also, Stanley's Jewish Church. Part i. Lect. xi.

they intermarried largely with the Israelites, how was it possible, humanly speaking, that any sparks of the light of God's truth should have survived to the coming of Christ. ... The whole earth would have been sunk in darkness; and if Messiah had come he would not have found one single ear prepared to listen to his doctrine nor one single heart that longed in secret for the kingdom of God.

"But this was not to be, and therefore the nations of Canaan were to be cut off utterly. The Israelites' sword, in its bloodiest executions, wrought a work of mercy for all the countries of the earth to the very end of the world. ... In these contests on the fate of one of these nations of Palestine the happiness of the human race depended. The Israelites fought not for themselves only, but for us. Whatever were the faults of Jephthah or of Samson, never yet were any men engaged in a cause more important to the whole world's welfare. ... Still they did God's work; still they preserved unhurt the seed of eternal life, and were the ministers of blessing to all other nations, even though they themselves failed to enjoy it."

That these words of an eminent scholar and profound thinker are based upon sound philosophical principles no penetrating mind can fail to perceive. Nor is Dr. Arnold alone in his opinion. Others, of a different creed, and looking from a different point of view, have reached substantially the same conclusions.

That great German critic, Ewald,[1] treating upon this topic, has impressively said: "It is an eternal necessity that a nation such as the great majority of the Canaanites then were, sinking deeper and deeper into a slough of discord and moral perversity, must fall before a people roused to a higher life by the newly-wakened energy of unanimous trust in Divine power." And Dr. Davidson[2]: "In a certain sense, the Spirit of God is a spirit of revenge, casting down and destroying everything opposed to

---

[1] Hist. of Israel, ii. 237.　　　[2] Introd. to Old Test., i. 444.

the progress of man's education in the knowledge and fear of the Lord."

Children slain.	Same loved.
And he went up from thence unto Beth-el; and as he was going up by the way, there came forth little children out of the city, and mocked him, and said unto him, Go up, thou bald-head; go up, thou bald-head. And he turned back, and looked on them, and cursed them in the name of the Lord. And there came forth two she-bears out of the wood, and tare forty and two children of them. 2 Kings ii. 23, 24.	And they brought young children to him, that he should touch them; and *his* disciples rebuked those that brought *them*. But when Jesus saw *it*, he was much displeased, and said unto them, Suffer the little children to come unto me, and forbid them not; for of such is the kingdom of God. And he took them up in his arms, put *his* hands upon them, and blessed them. Mark x. 13, 14, 16.

1. In the person of Elisha, God himself, whose servant the prophet was, was most wantonly and wickedly insulted.

2. The word "neärim," rendered "children" in Kings, may, as a late rationalistic commentator admits, denote a "*youth nearly twenty years old.*" Gesenius says precisely the same; adding that it is also applied to "common soldiers," just as we in English style them, the "boys," the "boys in blue," etc.

Fuerst gives, among other definitions, a person who is twenty years of age, a youth, a young prophet; generally a servant of any kind, a shepherd, a young warrior. The same combination of words as above, "naar qäton," is applied to Solomon[1] after he began to reign at some twenty years of age. Krummacher and Cassel translate the expression in the text, "young people." Hence the theory that these young scoffers were really "little children" at their play is untenable. They were old enough, and depraved enough, to merit the terrible fate which overtook them.

3. Elisha did not slay the young reprobates, nor did he *cause* the bears to come forth. God sent them. The same Being who sometimes cuts off wild, wicked youth by disease or accident, in the present instance punished sinful parents by the violent death of their reprobate children. Prof. Rawlinson suggests that a signal example may have been greatly needed

---

[1] 1 Kings iii. 7. See also the word נַעַר applied to Isaac, Gen. xxii. 5; to Joseph, compare Gen. xxix. 4–6 and xli. 12; to Absalom, 2 Sam. xviii. 5, and to the prophet Jeremiah, Jer. i. 5.

at this time to check the growth of irreligion; and that, as above intimated, the wicked parents were punished by deprivation of offspring.

Edomite hated.
He slew of Edom in the valley of Salt ten thousand.... And he did *that which was* right in the sight of the LORD, yet not like David his father. 2 Kings xiv. 7, 8.

Not to be hated.
Thou shalt not abhor an Edomite, for he *is* thy brother. Deut. xxiii. 7.

As to this characteristically "profound" discrepancy, alleged by an infidel pamphleteer, it may be observed: 1. Not every act of Amaziah's life is commended above. He did, *in the main*, that which was right, but less uniformly or zealously than David. 2. It does not follow that because Amaziah chastised and reconquered the rebellious Edomites he necessarily "abhorred" them.

Enemies cursed.
Let their way be dark and slippery: and let the angel of the LORD persecute them.... Let destruction come upon him at unawares; and let his net that he hath hid catch himself: into that very destruction let him fall. Ps. xxxv. 6, 8.
Let death seize upon them, *and* let them go down quick into hell. Ps. lv.15.
Pour out thine indignation upon them, and let thy wrathful anger take hold of them.... Add iniquity unto their iniquity: and let them not come into thy righteousness. Ps. lxix. 24, 27.
Let them be confounded and troubled for ever: yea, let them be put to shame, and perish. Ps. lxxxiii. 17.
Set thou a wicked man over him: and let Satan stand at his right hand. When he shall be judged, let him be condemned: and let his prayer become sin. Let his days be few; *and* let another take his office. Let his children be fatherless, and his wife a widow. Let his children be continually vagabonds, and beg. Ps. cix. 6-10.
Let there be none to extend mercy unto him: neither let there be any to favor his fatherless children. Let his posterity be cut off; *and* in the generation following let their name be blotted out. Ps. cix. 12, 13.
As he clothed himself with cursing like as with his garment, so let it come into his bowels like water, and like oil into his bones. Let it be unto him as the garment *which* covereth him, and for a girdle wherewith he is girded continually. Ps. cix. 18, 19.

Should be loved.
Love your enemies, bless them that curse you, do good to them that hate you, and pray for them which despitefully use you, and persecute you. Matt. v. 44.
Then said Jesus, Father, forgive them: for they know not what they do. Luke xxiii. 34.
And he kneeled down and cried, with a loud voice, Lord, lay not this sin to their charge. Acts vii. 60.

| *Enemies cursed.* | *Should be loved.* |

O daughter of Babylon, who art to be destroyed; happy *shall he be*, that rewardeth thee as thou hast served us. Happy *shall he be* that taketh and dasheth thy little ones against the stones. Ps.-cxxxvii. 8, 9.

If any man love not the Lord Jesus Christ, let him be Anathema, Maranatha. 1 Cor. xvi. 22.

Some critics take these imprecatory texts as mere *predictions:* " Let his days be few " being equivalent to " His days shall be few." These predictions would also imply the speaker's acquiescence in the foreseen will of Jehovah: "It is the Divine will, therefore *let it be so.*

Others take these passages as *historical*, rather than didactic. It is said that, as the Bible relates impartially the bad as well as the good deeds of the patriarchs, so it does not suppress their wrong thoughts and sayings, but " gives a Shakespearian picture of all the moral workings of the heart." It is precisely this *its fidelity to nature*, keeping back nothing, extenuating nothing, which gives the sacred volume its hold upon the confidence of mankind. " Mr. Barnes admits an element of truth in this explanation, and Dr. Tholuck distinctly holds that a personal feeling has occasionally mixed itself with David's denunciations of the wicked."

Still others think that the duty of forgiveness was not taught nor understood clearly in David's time, as it was in the latter dispensation. This hypothesis, as we have seen elsewhere, is supported by the analogous cases of some other important doctrines and duties, which were revealed progressively, by degrees, as the world was prepared to receive them. In a word, the Psalmist may not have understood, in all its length and breadth, the Christian duty of forgiveness. This explanation is adopted by several eminent authors. Richard Baxter[1] speaks very strongly on this point. So does Mr. Cooper,[2] who says of the Israelitish worthies, " these great and good men

---

[1] Quoted by Davidson, Introd. to Old Test., ii. 306.
[2] " Four Hundred Texts of Holy Scriptures," p. 80.

were not yet acquainted with the perfect rule of charity, or love to enemies, to be taught by a suffering Saviour."

Mr. Warington,[1] with reference to the scripture, asserts that Christ himself lays down the principle, in the plainest manner, that it may contain precepts which, regarded in the abstract, are opposed to God's will, but which were rendered necessary by the imperfect spiritual state of those to whom they were given. In which case this temporary adaptation is to be regarded as a sufficient explanation for the precept given.

Dr. Thomas Arnold[2] deems it a most important exegetical principle "that the revelations made to the patriarchs were only *partial,* or *limited to some particular points*, and that their conduct must be judged of not according to our knowledge, but to theirs." Hence, he says, we may "recognize the divinity of the Old Testament, and the holiness of its characters, without lying against our consciences and our more perfect revelation by justifying the actions of those characters as right, essentially and abstractedly, although they were excusable, or in some cases actually virtuous, according to the standard of right and wrong which prevailed under the law."

Chrysostom,[3] long before, referring to the Israelites, had said, "*Now,* a higher philosophy is required of us than of them. ..... For thus they are ordered to hate not only impiety, but the very persons of the impious, lest their friendship should be an occasion of going astray. Therefore he cut off all intercourse and freed them on every side."

Prof. Moses Stuart[4]: "The Old Testament morality, in respect to some points of *relative* duty, is behind that of the Gospel. Why then should we regard the Old Testament as exhibiting an absolute model of perfection, in its precepts and its doctrines? In some respects, most plainly this is not true."

---

[1] On Inspiration, p. 253.
[2] Miscel. Works, pp. 151, 288 (Appleton's edition).
[3] On 1 Cor. xiii, and alluding to Ps. cxxxix. 22.
[4] On History of Old Test. Canon, pp. 416, 409 (Revised edition, 389, 382). Compare his remarks, pp. 404, 405 (Revised edition, 377, 378).

Elsewhere, he says, "The Psalms that breathe forth imprecations are appealed to by some as justifying the spirit of vengeance under the gospel, instead of being regarded as the expression of a peculiar state of mind in the writer, and *of his imperfect knowledge with regard to the full spirit of forgiveness.*" These last are very pregnant words.

It remains to be observed that the imprecatory texts are explicable on the hypothesis of their full inspiration. The following points must be taken into account.

1. Great allowance must be made for the *strong hyperboles* and *intense vehemence* of Oriental poetry. Where we should ask that the Divine honor and justice might be vindicated, the Eastern poet would pray,

> "That thy foot may be dipped in the blood of thine enemies,
> And the tongue of thy dogs in the same."

The petitions quoted above would, if stated in unimpassioned Occidental style, be greatly modified, and seem far less objectionable.

2. The Psalmist merges his own private griefs in the wrongs inflicted upon the people of God, — counts the Lord's enemies as enemies to himself. He cries out, "Do not I hate them, O Lord, which hate thee? I count them mine enemies." He identified his own interests with those of his heavenly King. "He was situated like the English statesman, who in an attack upon himself sees the crown and government to be actually aimed at." From this representative character of the Psalmist arises the terrible intensity of his language.

3. There is a normal indignation against sin. There are times when "forbearance ceases to be a virtue," when the sense of outraged justice must find expression. Not infrequently a righteous indignation against evil-doers unsheathes the patriot's sword, and kindles the poet's lyre. In the recent history of our own country the imprecatory Psalms seemed *none too strong nor stern* to serve as a vehicle for the loyalty of our citizens,

in giving voice to their indignation, horror, and detestation at the crimes perpetrated by traitors and rebels.

Prof. B. B. Edwards [1] says in substance, that resentment against evil-doers is so far from being sinful, that we find it exemplified in the meek and spotless Redeemer himself (Mark iii. 5). If the emotion and its utterance were essentially sinful, how could Paul wish the enemy of Christ to be accursed ("anathema," 1 Cor. xvi. 22) ; or say of his own enemy, Alexander the coppersmith, "The Lord reward him according to his works" (2 Tim. iv. 14); and especially how could the spirits of the just in heaven call on God for vengeance (Rev. vi. 10)?

4. It is right to pray for the overthrow of the wicked, as a *means*, and not as an *end*, when we are satisfied that *less evil will result from that overthrow than would be occasioned by their triumph*. David felt that the destruction of those wicked persons, while not to be desired *per se*, would nevertheless result in the prevention of incalculable injury to the race. Of two evils he chose the infinitely less. Prayer for the overthrow of the wicked was prayer for the triumph of righteousness.[2]

Treated kindly.	*Put to pain.*
Therefore, if thine enemy hunger, feed him; if he thirst, give him drink. Rom. xii. 20.	For in so doing thou shalt heap coals of fire on his head. Rom. xii. 20.

Baur asserts that in the latter clause Paul's former persecuting spirit crops out, that he cannot repress here the desire to inflict pain upon an enemy. We give Baur credit for too much acuteness to suppose that he was not perfectly aware of the utter disingenuousness of this objection.

The figurative language of the apostle means simply, "By showing kindness to thine enemy thou shalt excite in him such *pain of conscience* as shall lead him to repentance and reformation." The expression is a proverbial one. The Arabs

---

[1] See Bib. Sacra (February, 1844).
[2] See Professor Park in Bib. Sacra, Vol. xix. pp. 165–210. Also, Smith's Bible Dict., iii. 2625–2628.

say, conveying similar ideas, "He roasted my heart," or, "He kindled a fire in my heart."[1] The pain was viewed by Paul as a *means*, not as an *end*; the ultimate object being the *conversion* of the "enemy."

Addressed with ridicule and irony.	With mild words.
And it came to pass at noon, that Elijah mocked them, and said, Cry aloud: for he *is* a god: either he is talking, or he is pursuing, or he is in a journey, *or* peradventure he sleepeth, and must be awaked. 1 Kings xviii. 27. And the king said unto him, Micaiah, shall we go against Ramoth-gilead to battle, or shall we forbear? And he answered him, Go, and prosper: for the LORD shall deliver *it* into the hand of the king. 1 Kings xxii. 15. And Elisha said unto them, This *is* not the way, neither *is* this the city: follow me, and I will bring you to the man whom ye seek. But he led them to Samaria. 2 Kings vi. 19.	Love your enemies, bless them that curse you, do good to them that hate you, and pray for them which despitefully use you, and persecute you. Matt. v. 44. Bless them which persecute you; bless, and curse not. Rom xii. 14. Who, when he was reviled, reviled not again; when he suffered, he threatened not. 1 Pet. ii 23. Not rendering evil for evil, or railing for railing: but contrariwise, blessing. 1 Pet. iii. 9.

In the case of Elijah ridicule was a fit weapon for exposing the folly and absurdity of idol-worship. The prophet employed it with terrible effect.

As to the case of Micaiah; Richter, Keil, Bertheau, and A. Fuller[2] suppose that the words were uttered with ironical gestures and a sarcastic tone. He delivers the words, says Rawlinson, "in so mocking and ironical a tone that the king cannot mistake his meaning, or regard his answer as serious." The succeeding verse shows that Ahab instantly detected the irony.

Bähr, however, takes the language as a reproof for the king's hypocritical question, thus: "How camest thou to the idea of consulting me, whom thou dost not trust? Thy prophets have answered thee as thou desirest. Do, then, what they have approved. Try it. March out. Their oracles have far more weight with thee than mine."

Elisha's statement is regarded by Keil and Rawlinson, apparently, simply in the light of a "stratagem of war," by which the enemy are deceived.

---

[1] See Stuart on Rom. xii. 20.   [2] **Works, i. 619.**

ETHICAL DISCREPANCIES. 277

It is to be remembered, also, that Elisha's motive was a *benevolent* one, for he saved the lives of those whom he had taken captive in this wonderful manner; thus putting a stop to the marauding forays of the Syrians. Thenius: "There is no untruth in the words of Elisha; for his home was not in Dothan, where he was only residing temporarily, but in Samaria; and the words 'to the man' may well mean, to his house." As Bähr has observed, Elisha took the blinded Syrians under his protection, repaid evil with good, and by this very means showed them the man whom they were seeking.

Some regard the prophet's language as mere irony.

Epithets of opprobrium.

Forbidden.	*Their use sanctioned.*
Whosoever shall say to his brother, Raca, shall be in danger of the council: but whosoever shall say, Thou fool, shall be in danger of hell fire. Matt. v. 22.	Ye fools and blind: for whether is greater, the gold, or the temple that sanctifieth the gold? Matt. xxiii. 17. Then he said unto them, O fools, and slow of heart to believe all that the prophets have spoken. Luke xxiv. 25. *Thou* fool, that which thou sowest is not quickened except it die. 1 Cor. xv. 36. O foolish Galatians, who hath bewitched you, that ye should not obey the truth. Gal. iii. 1.

The term "moros," in the texts from Matthew is much more severe than the corresponding terms in the other places. He who "knew what was in man," saw that this word was *exactly descriptive of the moral condition* of the scribes and Pharisees.

As in many other cases, the *spirit* rather than the *words* is aimed at in the prohibition. That is, we are not prohibited calling men "fools" considerately and appropriately; we are forbidden to do so in the spirit of *malevolent contempt.* This obvious principle relieves the whole difficulty.

Fear of persecutors.

Forbidden.	*Exemplified.*
And I say unto you, my friends, Be not afraid of them that kill the body, and after that have no more that they can do. Luke xii. 4.	After these things Jesus walked in Galilee: for he would not walk in Jewry, because the Jews sought to kill him. John vii. 1.

Jesus did not shun death, but avoided dying *prematurely.* When his "hour had come," when his earthly mission was accomplished, he met death with fortitude and composure. To die *before the time* would have measurably defeated his great purpose.

Folly, — treatment.

Folly remediable.	*Remediless.*
Foolishness *is* bound in the heart of a child, *but* the rod of correction shall drive it far from him. Prov. xxii. 15.	Though thou shouldest bray a fool in a mortar among wheat with a pestle, *yet* will not his foolishness depart from him. Prov. xxvii. 22.

These passages refer to entirely different persons. "Foolishness," in the first text, is the incipient waywardness which belongs, in a greater or less degree, to children, and may be corrected by suitable discipline. The "fool" in the second text, is the grown-up fool, whose folly is past cure.

Answered in one way.	*In another way.*
Answer not a fool according to his folly, lest thou also be like unto him. Prov. xxvi. 4.	Answer a fool according to his folly, lest he be wise in his own conceit. Prov. xxvi. 5.

May not this be a simple *dilemma*, equivalent to saying, "Choose between the two evils. If you answer the fool in a foolish manner, you like him will be chargeable with folly. On the other hand, should you undertake to argue with him, he, failing to appreciate your reasoning, will think himself unanswerable, and so become more obtrusive and offensive than ever."

Or, the two texts may refer to different cases, thus: In certain circumstances, do not answer the fool at all. Silence is often the most fitting answer to a foolish question or remark. In other cases, answer the fool with sharp reproof, exposing his folly as it deserves.

Menasseh ben Israel[1]; "Correct and mend him, that he may know his folly and madness. Imitate not his passions, errors, and improper words."

Andrew Fuller[2] makes the meaning depend upon the turn given to the words "according to his folly." In the first text, he takes this phraseology as implying, *in a foolish manner;* in the second, as signifying, *in the manner which his folly requires.* "A foolish speech is not a rule for our imitation; nevertheless

[1] Conciliator, ii. 287. [2] Works, i. 672.

our answer must be so framed by it as to meet and repel it." On this hypothesis, the first text is illustrated by the answer of Moses to the rebellious Israelites;[1] the second text by that of Job to his wife.[2]

Moses answered folly *in a foolish manner;* Job answered it, *not in kind,* but *in the manner it deserved.*

Fruit trees disposed of.

Spared.	*Destroyed.*
When thou shalt besiege a city a long time in making war against it to take it, thou shalt not destroy the trees thereof by forcing an axe against them; for thou mayest eat of them: and thou shalt not cut them down (for the tree of the field *is* man's *life*) to employ them in the siege. Deut. xx. 19.	And this is *but* a light thing in the sight of the LORD: he will deliver the Moabites also into your hand. And ye shall smite every fenced city, and every choice city, and shall fell every good tree, and stop all wells of water, and mar every good piece of land with stones. 2 Kings iii. 18, 19.

Hengstenberg[3] and Keil[4] say that the injunction in Deuteronomy was applicable only in the case of *Canaanitish* cities, which the Israelites were afterward to inhabit. Rawlinson thinks that the text from Deuteronomy really prohibits "only the using of the fruit-trees for timber in siege-works;" and applies only to those countries which the Israelites intended to *occupy.*

Good works.

To be seen by men.	*Not to be seen by them.*
Let your light so shine before men, that they may see your good works, and glorify your Father which is in heaven. Matt. v. 16.	Take heed that ye do not your alms before men, to be seen of them: otherwise ye have no reward of your Father which is in heaven. Matt. vi. 1.

The glory of God, and not the praise of men, must be our ultimate object in exhibiting our "good works" before others. A. Fuller: "This is another of those cases in which the difference lies in the *motive.* It is right to do that which men may see and must see, but not *for the sake* of being seen by them."

Heretics dealt with.

With severity.	*With gentleness.*
Simon *son* of Jonas, lovest thou me? He said unto him, Yea, Lord: thou knowest that I love thee. He saith unto him, Feed my sheep. John xxi. 16. And there came a voice to him, Rise, Peter; kill, and eat. Acts x. 13.	In meekness instructing those that oppose themselves; if God peradventure will give them repentance to the acknowledging of the truth. 2 Tim. ii. 25.

[1] Num. xx. 10.
[3] Genuineness of Pent. i. 176.
[2] Job ii. 10.
[4] On 2 Kings iii. 19.

From the first two passages combined, Cardinal Bellarmine[1] infers the "twofold function of the Roman pontiff, as successor of Peter, viz. *to feed the church* and to *put heretics to death*." One cannot but wonder that this famous exegete did not advance a step further, and infer the duty of *cannibalism* from the same text. The language is certainly very explicit: "Rise, Peter, kill, *and eat!*"

Improvidence.

Sanctioned.

Lay not up for yourselves treasures upon earth. . . . Therefore I say unto you, Take no thought for your life, what ye shall eat, or what ye shall drink; nor yet for your body, what ye shall put on. . . . Take therefore no thought for the morrow: for the morrow shall take thought for the things of itself. Matt. vi. 19, 25, 34.

Give to every man that asketh of thee; and of him that taketh away thy goods, ask *them* not again. . . . But love ye your enemies, and do good, and lend, hoping for nothing again. Luke vi. 30, 35.

Sell that ye have, and give alms. Luke xii. 33.

Make not provision for the flesh, to *fulfil* the lusts *thereof.* Rom. xiii. 14.

Discouraged.

A good *man* leaveth an inheritance to his children's children. Prov. xiii. 22.

But if any provide not for his own, and specially for those of his own house, he hath denied the faith, and is worse than an infidel. 1 Tim. v. 8.

If the texts at the left be carefully examined in their connection with the context, it will be seen that none of them discountenance prudence and true economy, nor encourage wastefulness. The first text simply forbids our making earthly possessions our "treasure," our chief good. We must not set our hearts upon them.

The word "thought," in the next two texts, as in our early English literature, means *solicitude, anxious care.* Thus Bacon[2] mentions an alderman of London who "dyed with *thought* and anguish." Hence the precept is: "Be not unduly anxious concerning your life," etc.

The first two texts from Luke inculcate concretely the abstract principle of benevolence, but do not sanction improvidence.

---

[1] See Horne's Introduction, ii. 632 (Seventh edition).
[2] Eastwood and Wright, "Bible Word-Book," p. 483.

ETHICAL DISCREPANCIES. 281

The text from Luke xii. has, according to Meyer, a specific application, being "addressed only to the apostles and then existing disciples." The quotation from Romans, with its important limiting clause, allows us to make provision for the *needs*, but not for the *lusts* of the flesh.

Incest.

Denounced.

See prohibitions of this crime in Lev. xviii. and xx. Also, denunciations in Deut. xxvii.

Divinely sanctioned.

And God said unto Abraham, As for Sarai thy wife, thou shalt not call her name Sarai, but Sarah *shall* her name *be*. And I will bless her, and give thee a son also of her: yea, I will bless her, and she shall be *a mother* of nations; kings of people shall be of her. Gen. xvii. 15, 16.

And yet indeed *she is* my sister; she *is* the daughter of my father, but not the daughter of my mother; and she became my wife. Gen. xx. 12.

The terms "brother," "sister," and the like are used in the scriptures with great latitude of meaning, much like the Latin term "parentes," or the word "cousin," in modern speech. For example, Lot, Abraham's nephew, is styled his "brother";[1] Rebekah's mother and brother say to her, "Thou art our sister"[2]; Jacob speaks of himself as his uncle's "brother"[3]; Dinah is styled by her brothers, "our daughter."[4]

It is thus clear that the term "sister" makes Sarah a *near relative*, but does not determine the *degree* of relationship. Lange suggests that she may have been merely the "adopted sister" of Abraham. Bush and Delitzsch think she may have been a *niece* of Abraham — daughter of his brother, or, as Delitzsch says, "half-brother," Haran. In this view concur Jerome, Josephus,[5] the Talmud, the Targum of Jonathan, and Rashi, with Jewish writers generally.[6] These authors take Sarah, who was but ten years younger than Abraham,[7] to be identical with Iscah.[8]

All we are warranted in saying is, that Sarah was *nearly*

---

[1] Gen. xiv. 12, 16.
[2] Gen. xxiv. 55, 60.
[3] Gen. xxix. 12.
[4] Gen. xxxiv. 14, 17.
[5] Antiq. I. vi. 5.
[6] Macdonald, Introd. to Pent. i. 70.
[7] Gen. xvii. 17.
[8] Gen. xi. 29.

related — a cousin or niece, perhaps — to Abraham upon his *father's* side. She may have been related to Terah by a former wife, and afterwards adopted by him as a daughter.

As to the case of Lot and his unhappy daughters, recorded in Gen. xix., it is to be noted that the narrative is related in the usual colorless style, without comment, by the sacred writer. There is no concealment, no extenuation, of the crime.

It is clear that their residence in Sodom had blinded the minds of these misguided females, and greatly confused their ideas relative to purity and right and wrong. This case[1] forcibly illustrates the demoralizing influence exerted upon the young by corrupt companions.

Israelites' claim to Canaan.

Derived from God.	*Precluded in the law.*
And I will give unto thee, and to thy seed after thee, the land wherein thou art a stranger, all the land of Canaan, for an everlasting possession. Gen. xvii. 8. And I will set thy bounds from the Red sea even unto the sea of the Philistines, and from the desert unto the river: for I will deliver the inhabitants of the land into your hand; and thou shalt drive them out before thee. Ex. xxiii. 31.	Thou shalt not covet thy neighbor's house, thou shalt not covet thy neighbor's wife, nor his manservant, nor his maidservant, nor his ox, nor his ass, nor any thing that *is* thy neighbor's. Ex. xx. 17.

Widely divergent opinions have been maintained upon the question of the "right of the Hebrews to Palestine." We subjoin the more reasonable.

Michaelis[2] and Dr. Jahn hold that Palestine had from time immemorial been a land of Hebrew herdsmen; and the Israelites, who had never abandoned their right to it, claimed it again of the Canaanites as unlawful possessors.

Ewald[3] expresses the opinion that, though the Canaanites had gained possession of Palestine as its original inhabitants, they had not occupied the whole country. The pasture-lands lay open to those who wished to appropriate them, which was

---

[1] See Lange, Com. on Genesis, p. 81 (American edition).
[2] Commentary on Mosaic Laws, i. 153.
[3] Die Composition der Genesis, pp. 276-278. See Davidson's Introd. i. 487.

done by the ancestors of the Israelites. But during the sojourn in Egypt, the Canaanites unjustly occupied these pastures, and when the returning Hebrews asserted their rights the Canaanites would not acknowledge them. Hence the Israelites took possession of the country, partly in virtue of their ancient possession of some of it, and partly by conquest.

A simpler view is that which derives the claim of the Israelites directly from Jehovah himself.

Hengstenberg[1]: "The Israelites had no human right whatever to Canaan. Their right rested entirely on God's gift. By this no injustice was done to the Canaanites. By their great depravity they had rendered themselves unworthy of being any longer possessors of the land, which God, as in the case of all other nations, only gave them conditionally. The Israelites were sent against them as ministers of the Divine justice; so that their destruction differed only in *form* from that of Sodom and Gomorrah. God's giving Canaan to the Israelites was at once an act of grace and of justice."

This is the scriptural view of the matter.[2] It is the prerogative of him who hath "determined the times before appointed, and the bounds of the habitation of the nations," to bestow a land upon whomsoever he chooses. The same Being who took America out of the hands of the red men, and bestowed it upon the Anglo-Saxon race, took Palestine out of the hands of degraded idolators, and gave it to the Hebrews.

Dr. Davidson[3] well says: "When a nation becomes corrupt and weak, it must give place, in the providence of God, to a stronger. Those that have grown old in superstition and idolatry make way for such as have a more spiritual vitality."

Jewess' marriage.

Restricted to her tribe.	Not thus restricted.
And every daughter that possesseth an inheritance in any tribe of the chil-	If the priest's daughter also be *married* unto a stranger, she may not eat

[1] Genuineness of Pent. ii. 387–417.   [2] Ps. xliv. 1–3; lxxviii. 55.
[3] Introd. to Old Test., i. 444. Compare Fairbairn's Typology, loc. cit.

Restricted to her tribe.	Not thus restricted.
dren of Israel, shall be wife unto one of the family of the tribe of her father, that the children of Israel may enjoy every man the inheritance of his fathers. Num. xxxvi. 8.	of an offering of the holy things. Lev. xxii. 12.

It is clear, as Menasseh ben Israel says, that the first passage applies only to *heiresses*. The object of the precept was to prevent confusion by the transference of landed property from one tribe to another. A daughter who inherited no real estate might marry out of her tribe.

Judging of others.

Forbidden.	Allowed.
Judge not, that ye be not judged. For with what judgment ye judge, ye shall be judged: and with what measure ye mete, it shall be measured to you again. Matt. vii. 1, 2. Judge not, and ye shall not be judged: condemn not, and ye shall not be condemned. Luke vi. 37.	Judge not according to the appearance, but judge righteous judgment. John vii. 24. For what have I to do to judge them also that are without? do not ye judge them that are within? 1 Cor. v. 12.

The text from Matthew forbids *harsh, censorious* judgment, but does not preclude the giving of judicial decisions, nor the expression of our opinions in a proper manner.

The parallelism of the text from Luke, "judge not," "condemn not," indicates the kind of judgment prohibited.

Justice administered.

By one judge.	By several.
Moses sat to judge the people; and the people stood by Moses from the morning unto the evening. Ex. xviii. 13.	And thou shalt come unto the priests the Levites, and unto the judge that shall be in those days, and inquire; and they shall shew thee the sentence of judgment. Deut. xvii. 9. Both the men, between whom the controversy *is*, shall stand before the LORD, before the priests and the judges, which shall be in those days. Deut. xix. 17. Then thy elders and thy judges shall come forth. Deut. xxi. 2.

A recent author discovers, as he thinks, some discrepancy here. But in Ex. xviii. 13–26, we find an account of the change from one judge to a plurality, with the reasons therefor.

Moreover, the altered circumstances of the people upon their exchange of a nomadic life for settlement in Canaan, occasioned the other modifications of earlier laws, which are discoverable in Deuteronomy. In the words of Dr. Davidson,[1] "Should any say that the altered circumstances of the Israelites in Palestine called for these changes; that is true."

Michaelis[2] seems to hold that, because the people "dwelt no longer in round numbers together," the former custom was modified, and judges were appointed in every city.

Killing of Men.

Forbidden.	Sanctioned.
Jesus said, Thou shalt do no murder. Matt. xix. 18.	Then Moses stood in the gate of the camp, and said, Who is on the LORD's side? let him come unto me. And all the sons of Levi gathered themselves together unto him. And he said unto them, Thus saith the LORD God of Israel, Put every man his sword by his side, and go in and out from gate to gate throughout the camp, and slay every man his brother, and every man his companion, and every man his neighbor. Ex. xxxii. 26, 27. And Moses said unto the judges of Israel, Slay ye every one his men that were joined unto Baal-peor. . . . When Phinehas, the son of Eleazar, the son of Aaron the priest, saw it, he rose up from among the congregation, and took a javelin in his hand . . . And he went after the man of Israel into the tent, and thrust both of them through, the man of Israel, and the woman. Num. xxv. 5, 7, 8.

In both cases at the right the slaughter was the signal punishment of an atrocious crime.

In the first case, the Israelites had lapsed into gross idolatry, breaking their covenant with God, and committing treason against their Sovereign. Their offence was of the most aggravated character, and merited capital punishment. Calvin, Keil, Bush, and others think that only those were slain by the Levites who were recognized as the originators and ringleaders of the crime, or who stood boldly forth as its promoters and abettors. These, being found in the open spaces, while the rest of the people had fled to their tents, would alone be slain.

Much the same may be said of the second case. The Hebrews had fallen into the licentious idolatry of Baal Peor.

---
[1] Introd. to Old Test., i. 363.   [2] Mosaic Laws, i. 245.

Moses commanded that all the guilty should be slain. In this hour of national humiliation and sorrow, while the people were weeping at the door of the tabernacle, Zimri, a man of rank, brought into his tent, in the sight of the multitude, a Midianitish paramour. This shameless and flagrant outrage was swiftly and fearfully punished by Phinehas, under the impulse of patriotism and loyalty to God. His zeal in this respect was properly commended.

Kindred, how regarded.

Hated.	Loved.
If any *man* come to me, and hate not his father, and mother, and wife, and children, and brethren, and sisters, yea, and his own life also, he cannot be my disciple. Luke xiv. 26.	Husbands, love your wives, even as Christ also loved the church, and gave himself for it. . . . Let every one of you in particular so love his wife even as himself: and the wife *see* that she reverence *her* husband. Eph. v. 25, 33.
	He that loveth not *his* brother, abideth in death. Whosoever hateth his brother, is a murderer. 1 John iii. 14, 15.

The word " hate " is sometimes used in the Bible in the sense of *to love less*. Thus of Jacob it is said that he " loved Rachel more than Leah," and, a little farther on, that Leah was " hated." [1]

Prof. Stuart: " When the Hebrews compared a stronger affection with a weaker one, they call the first *love*, and the other *hatred*."

Alford: " It hardly need be observed that *this hate* is not only consistent with, but *absolutely necessary* to the very highest kind of love. It is that element in love which makes a man a *wise and Christian friend*, not for time only, but for eternity."

In our day a convert from heathenism is sometimes reproached by his idolatrous kindred with "hating" them, because he does not yield to their solicitations, and renounce Christianity. But the truth is, he loves them better than ever before; he loves them not less, but loves Christ more.

The very fact that, in the first text, the man is spoken of as *hating* " his own life," indicates the figurative or relative sense in which the term is there employed.

[1] Gen. xxix. 30, 31.

Parents honored.	*Treated disrespectfully.*
Honor thy father and thy mother; that thy days may be long upon the land which the LORD thy God giveth thee. Ex. xx. 12.	And call no *man* your father upon the earth: for one is your Father which is in heaven. Matt. xxiii. 9.
Children, obey *your* parents in all things: for this is well-pleasing unto the Lord. Col. iii. 20.	And he said unto another, Follow me. But he said, Lord, suffer me first to go and bury my father. Jesus said unto him, Let the dead bury their dead: but go thou and preach the kingdom of God. Luke ix. 59, 60.

We have elsewhere seen that the text from Matthew speaks of spiritual relations. "Take no man as an *authoritative, infallible guide* in matters of religion." It does not prohibit our paying to our parents due honor. It merely forbids our "trusting in man, and making flesh our arm."[1] As to the case cited from Luke, Theophylact supposes that the disciple asked permission to reside with his father till his death. If the father were still living, Jesus may have foreseen that he would live for a considerable time, so that delay was needless.

Alford[2]: Suffer the spiritually dead to bury the literally dead; the reason of our Lord's rebuke being the peremptory and all-superseding nature of the command, Follow me.

Doubtless Jesus knew that there were a sufficient number of relatives at this man's house to attend to the duty of interment when necessary; also, that, if the man once went back home, he would be over-persuaded to remain, and so never engage in the great work of preaching the gospel.

The case was an exceptional one, simply implying that all other things must be made *subordinate to the gospel.*

Children put to death.	*Tenderly treated.*
If a man have a stubborn and rebellious son, which will not obey the voice of his father, or the voice of his mother, and *that,* when they have chastened him, will not hearken unto them. Then shall his father and his mother lay hold on him, and bring him out unto the elders of his city, and unto the gate of his place. And they shall say unto the elders of his city, This our son *is* stubborn and rebellious, he will not obey our voice; *he is* a glutton, and a drunkard. And all the men of his city shall stone him with stones, that he die: so shalt thou put evil away from among you, and all Israel shall hear, and fear. Deut. xxi. 18-21.	And, ye fathers, provoke not your children to wrath: but bring them up in the nurture and admonition of the Lord. Eph. vi. 4. Fathers, provoke not your children *to anger,* lest they be discouraged. Col. iii. 21.

[1] See Jer. xvii. 5.   [2] On Matt. viii. 21, 22.

With regard to the apparently severe law in **Deuteronomy**, observe:

1. That it is a *son*, and not a daughter.
2. That he is "stubborn" and "rebellious," a "glutton" and a "drunkard."
3. The parents are the only allowed plaintiffs, and *both* must concur in the complaint to make it a legal one.
4. He is brought before the elders of the city, and an investigation is had into the merits of the case.
5. That no case is on record in which a person was put to death under this law.
6. That the mere fact of the existence of such a law would tend strongly to confirm the authority of parents, and to deter youth from disobedience and unfilial conduct.

Levites' Portion.

A fixed residence.	They were sojourners.
Command the children of Israel, that they give unto the Levites of the inheritance of their possession cities to dwell in; and ye shall give *also* unto the Levites suburbs for the cities round about them. . . . *So* all the cities which ye shall give to the Levites *shall be* forty and eight cities. Num. xxxv. 2, 7.	Take heed to thyself that thou forsake not the Levite as long as thou livest upon the earth. Deut. xii. 19. And the Levite that *is* within thy gates; thou shalt not forsake him: for he hath no part nor inheritance with thee. Deut. xiv. 27.

Mr. Plumptre[1]: "If they were to have, like other tribes, a distinct territory assigned to them, their influence over the people at large would be diminished, and they themselves would be likely to forget, in labors common to them with others, their own peculiar calling. Jehovah, therefore, was to be their inheritance. They were to have no territorial possessions."

Ewald[2]: "The Levites, not being destined to agriculture, held with each city only the meadows thereto belonging, for the pasturage of some cattle, but not its arable land or homesteads. Thus the ancient city of Hebron became a priestly city; but its land devolved upon Caleb."

The same great critic, speaking of the subsequent neglect of assigned cities, says the entire system fell into confusion, as is

---

[1] Smith's Bib. Dict., ii. 1640.   [2] Hist. of Israel, ii. 309, 310.

clear not only from its never being mentioned in later times as still existing, but still more from the fact that at a later period quite different places appear as Levitical cities, in which the Levites, driven from their first abodes, had taken refuge.

Keil thinks, that as the Canananites were not immediately destroyed or driven out, the Levites did not forthwith come into possession of their cities, but temporarily sojourned elsewhere. Besides, it does not appear that they were *compelled* to reside in the specified cities. Some of them may have chosen to reside elsewhere; but wherever they were, they were dependent, for their support, upon the tithes and offerings of the people. These considerations relieve the alleged difficulty.

Possessed a stated revenue.	*Classed with mendicants.*
I have given the children of Levi all the tenth in Israel for an inheritance, for their service which they serve, *even* the service of the tabernacle of the congregation. ... The tithes of the children of Israel, which they offer *as* a heave-offering unto the LORD, I have given to the Levites to inherit. Num. xviii. 21, 24.	At the end of three years thou shalt bring forth all the tithe of thine increase the same year, and shalt lay *it* up within thy gates. And the Levite, (because he hath no part nor inheritance with thee,) and the stranger, and the fatherless, and the widow, which *are* within thy gates, shall come, and shall eat and be satisfied. Deut. xiv. 28, 29.

Mr. Plumptre [1] says, "As if to provide for the contingency of failing crops or the like, and the consequent inadequacy of the tithes thus assigned to them, the Levite, not less than the widow and the orphan, was commended to the special kindness of the people."

The tithe spoken of in Deut. xiv. was a second, or "vegetable" tithe, and not the one appointed for the support of the priests and Levites. It was to be employed, not in furnishing a maintenance for the priests and Levites, but to promote charity and brotherly feeling, and to gather the religious life and associations of the people around the sanctuary.[2] In a word, the Levite was to be invited, not because of mendicancy on his part, but to give by his presence a kind of religious character to the feast.

---

[1] Smith's Bib. Dict., loc. cit. [2] Bible Com., Introd. to Deut. Sec. v.

Lying.

Countenanced.

And the king of Egypt called for the midwives, and said unto them, Why have ye done this thing, and have saved the men-children alive? And the midwives said unto Pharaoh, Because the Hebrew women *are* not as the Egyptian women; for they *are* lively, and are delivered ere the midwives come in unto them. Therefore God dealt well with the midwives. Ex. i. 18-20.

And the woman took the two men, and hid them, and said thus, There came men unto me, but I wist not whence they *were*. And it came to pass *about the time* of shutting of the gate, when it was dark, that the men went out: whither the men went, I wot not. Josh. ii. 4, 5.

Likewise also was not Rahab the harlot justified by works. Jas. ii. 25.

Prohibited.

Thou shalt not bear false witness against thy neighbor. Ex. xx. 16.

Lying lips *are* abomination to the LORD. Prov. xii 22.

Wherefore putting away lying, speak every man truth with his neighbor: for we are members one of another. Eph. iv. 25.

Lie not one to another, seeing that ye have put off the old man with his deeds. Col. iii. 9.

All liars, shall have their part in the lake which burneth with fire and brimstone: which is the second death. Rev. xxi. 8.

As to the Hebrew midwives; if they did tell a lie, it was done to avoid *committing murder*. Of two evils, they chose the less. But there is no proof that they were guilty of falsehood. The king seems to have accepted their explanation of the case, which rested upon a well-known physiological fact.

Macdonald: [1] "In proportion as the sentence of toil common to the race, is in any instance mitigated in favor of the female, her own peculiar sentence is only thereby aggravated." The testimony of the rationalist, Von Bohlen,[2] is even more emphatic as to the immunity from pain, enjoyed in certain circumstances by females inured to toil. Murphy suggests that the Hebrew mothers, knowing Pharaoh's order, did not admit the midwife, and she did not intrude, if it could be avoided, until after the birth had occurred.

As to Rahab's case, several things are to be considered.

1. Having been reared in the darkness of heathenism, she could not be expected to understand fully the wrong of falsehood.

2. She was influenced by a desire to preserve her own life. She felt that the only way to secure this end, in the impending

---

[1] Introd. to Pent. i. 386. [2] Illustrations of Genesis, ii. 60.

overthrow of the city, would be to place the victors under previous obligation by saving the lives of their spies.

3. James says she was "justified," not by her words, but by her "works." Keil: The course she adopted was a sin of weakness which was forgiven her in mercy because of her faith.

Several other cases of similar nature, are discussed elsewhere.

Marriage.

Approved.	Disparaged.
And the LORD God said, It is not good that the man should be alone: I will make him a help meet for him. Gen. ii. 18. *Whoso* findeth a wife, findeth a good *thing*, and obtaineth favor of the LORD. Prov. xviii. 22. For this cause shall a man leave father and mother, and shall cleave to his wife: and they twain shall be one flesh? Matt. xix. 5. Let every man have his own wife, and let every woman have her own husband. 1 Cor. vii. 2. Marriage *is* honorable in all. Heb. xiii. 4.	*It is* good for a man not to touch a woman. . . . I say therefore to the unmarried and widows, It is good for them if they abide even as I. . . . I suppose therefore that this is good for the present distress, *I say*, that *it is* good for a man so to be. . . . Art thou loosed from a wife? seek not a wife. . . . He that is unmarried, careth for the things that belong to the Lord, how he may please the Lord. But he that is married, careth for the things that are of the world, how he may please *his* wife. . . . He that giveth *her* not in marriage doeth better. 1 Cor. vii 1, 8, 26, 27, 32, 33, 38.

These last passages which seem to discountenance wedlock were intended for a specific application. Paul foresaw the impending calamity and persecution which was threatening the Corinthian church, and knowing that *the formation of new ties of affection would expose men to increased suffering,* he advised against it. The man who had a wife and children could be made to suffer intensely on their account; the unmarried man would escape this augmented pain. "I think, then," says Paul, "that it is best, by reason of the trials which are nigh at hand, for all to be unmarried."[1] Alford[2] says that the language was addressed to the Corinthians "as advising them under circumstances in which persecution and family divisions for the Gospel's sake, might at any time break up the relations of life." Nothing in this advice discourages matrimony abstractly considered.

[1] Conybeare's translation.   [2] Vol. ii. p. 519.

292 DISCREPANCIES OF THE BIBLE.

With a brother's widow, enjoined.	*The same prohibited.*
If brethren dwell together, and one of them die and have no child, the wife of the dead shall not marry without unto a stranger: her husband's brother shall go in unto her, and take her to him to wife. Deut. xxv. 5.	And if a man shall take his brother's wife, it *is* an unclean thing: he hath uncovered his brother's nakedness; they shall be childless. Lev. xx. 21.

May not the text at the right refer to the *divorced* wife of a living brother? It is provided that, after a woman has received "a bill of divorcement" from her husband, she may "go and be another man's wife."[1] Is not the above text intended to preclude her marriage with a brother of her recent husband? This seems quite possible.

Keil,[2] however, maintains that the prohibition in Leviticus only refers to cases in which the deceased brother had left children; for if he had died childless, the brother not only might, but was required to, marry his sister-in-law. That is, if the widow was childless, her brother-in-law must marry her; if she had children, he was forbidden to do so.

Augustine, Aben Ezra, Michaelis, and the Septuagint take the words, "they shall be childless" as denoting that their children shall be reckoned to the departed brother, they shall be without posterity, so far as the public records show. In a civil sense, they would be childless.

Obedience.

Due to rulers.	*Sometimes to be withheld.*
I *counsel thee* to keep the king's commandment, and *that* in regard of the oath of God. Eccl. viii. 2. Let every soul be subject unto the higher powers. For there is no power but of God: the powers that be, are ordained of God. Whosoever therefore resisteth the power, resisteth the ordinance of God: and they that resist shall receive to themselves damnation. . . . Wherefore *ye* must needs be subject, not only for wrath, but also for conscience' sake. Rom. xiii. 1, 2, 5. Submit yourselves to every ordinance of man for the Lord's sake: whether it be to the king, as supreme; or unto governors, as unto them that are sent by him for the punishment of evildoers, and for the praise of them that do well. 1 Pet. ii. 13, 14.	But the midwives feared God, and did not as the king of Egypt commanded them. . . . Therefore God dealt well with the midwives. Ex. i. 17, 20. Shadrach, Meshach, and Abed-nego, answered and said to the king, O Nebuchadnezzar, we *are* not careful to answer thee in this matter. . . . Be it known unto thee, O king, that we will not serve thy gods, nor worship the golden image which thou hast set up. Dan. iii. 16, 18 Daniel, which *is* of the children of the captivity of Judah, regardeth not thee, O king, nor the decree that thou hast signed, but maketh his petition three times a day. Dan. vi. 13. But Peter and John answered and said unto them, Whether it be right in the sight of God to hearken unto you more than unto God, judge ye. Acts iv. 19. We ought to obey God rather than man. Acts v. 29.

[1] Deut. xxiv. 1, 2. [2] On Lev. xviii. 16.

ETHICAL DISCREPANCIES. 293

The first series of texts involves these principles:

1. That civil government is instituted by God for a specific object, *the encouragement of virtue and the suppression of vice;* "for the punishment of evil-doers, and for the praise of them that do well."

2. That so long as civil government keeps in its proper sphere, we are under solemn obligation to yield obedience.

From the second series may be legitimately inferred:

3. That civil government has no right to command or compel us to do anything contrary to the law of God.

4. That when civil government transcends its proper sphere, when it enjoins unrighteous acts, it then becomes our imperative duty to refuse obedience. In a word, the "higher law" takes the precedence of all human laws. In all the five cases at the right, obedience to *unrighteous,* therefore *non-obligatory,* commands, was properly withheld.

Due to masters.	*To God only.*
Servants, obey in all things *your* masters according to the flesh; not with eye-service, as men-pleasers; but in singleness of heart, fearing God. Col. iii. 22.	Thou shalt worship the Lord thy God, and him only shalt thou serve. Matt. iv. 10.
Servants, *be* subject to *your* masters with all fear; not only to the good and gentle, but also to the froward. 1 Pet. ii. 18.	One is your Master, *even* Christ; and all ye are brethren. Matt. xxiii. 8.
	Ye are bought with a price; be not ye the servants of men. 1 Cor. vii. 23.

The first series refers to civil obedience, or obedience in secular matters; the last relates to worship and religious service.

Rendered to the scribes.	*They must be shunned.*
The scribes and the Pharisees sit in Moses' seat. All therefore whatsoever they bid you observe, *that* observe and do: but do not ye after their works: for they say, and do not. Matt. xxiii. 2, 3.	Beware of the scribes, which love to go in long clothing, and *love* salutations in the market-places.... Which devour widows' houses, and for a pretence make long prayers: these shall receive greater damnation. Mark xii. 38, 40.

The idea is, Follow their precepts, but shun their practice. Do as they say, but not as they do.

Offender rebuked.

Privately.	*Publicly.*
Moreover if thy brother shall trespass against thee, go and tell him his fault between thee and him alone: if he shall hear thee, thou hast gained thy brother. Matt. xviii. 15.	Against an elder receive not an accusation, but before two or three witnesses. Them that sin rebuke before all, that others also may fear. 1 Tim. v. 19, 20.

The first text refers to private, personal wrongs, the second, to open, public offences against peace and good order.

Alford, on the first text: "This direction is only in case of *personal offence* against ourselves, and then the *injured person* is to seek *private explanation*, and that by *going to his injurer*, not waiting till *he* comes to apologize."

This commentator, with Huther and most others, applies the second quotation to sinning presbyters or "elders," who are to be openly rebuked, that the whole church may fear on seeing the public disgrace consequent on sin. Ellicott thinks that the present participle employed directs the thought towards the *habitually* sinful character of the offender, and his need of an open rebuke.

Pleasing of Men.

Practiced.	Condemned.
Let every one of us please *his* neighbor for *his* good to edification. Rom. xv. 2.	For do I now persuade men, or God? or do I seek to please men? for if I yet pleased men, I should not be the servant of Christ. Gal. i. 10.
To the weak became I as weak, that I might gain the weak: I am made all things to all *men*, that I might by all means save some. 1 Cor. ix. 22.	Not with eye-service, as men-pleasers; but as the servants of Christ. Eph. vi. 6.
Even as I please all *men* in all *things*, not seeking mine own profit, but the *profit* of many, that they may be saved. 1 Cor. x. 33.	Even so we speak; not as pleasing men, but God, which trieth our hearts. 1 Thess. ii. 4.

In the first texts, we see that Christian gentleness and self-forgetfulness which is ever ready to waive, so far as is proper, its own claims and preferences, in order to win men to the truth.

The latter texts discountenance that time-serving, sycophantic spirit which unhesitatingly sacrifices principle to popularity, and to the furtherance of its own sinister ends.

A. Fuller:[1] "The one is conduct which has the glory of God and the good of mankind for its object; the other originates and terminates in self. The former is that sweet inoffensiveness of spirit which teaches us to lay aside all self-will and self-importance. The latter is that sordid compliance with the corruptions of human nature, of which flatterers and deceivers have

[1] Works, i. 671.

always availed themselves, not for the glory of God, nor the good of men, but for the promotion of their own selfish designs."

Polygamy.

Tolerated.	Virtually prohibited.
But unto the sons of the concubines which Abraham had, Abraham gave gifts. Gen. xxv. 6.	Let thy fountain be blessed; and rejoice with the wife of thy youth. *Let her be as* the loving hind and pleasant roe; let her breasts satisfy thee at all times; and be thou ravished always with her love. Prov. v. 18, 19.
Then Jacob rose up, and set his sons and his wives upon camels. Gen. xxxi. 17.	
If a man have two wives, one beloved, and another hated. Deut. xxi. 15.	Yet *is* she thy companion, and the wife of thy covenant. And did not he make one? Yet had he the residue of the spirit. And wherefore one? That he might seek a godly seed. Therefore take heed to your spirit, and let none deal treacherously against the wife of his youth. Mal. ii. 14, 15.
And unto David were sons born in Hebron: and his first born was Amnon, of Ahinoam the Jezreelitess. ... His second, Chileab, of Abigail. ... The third, Absalom the son of Maacah. ... And the fourth, Adonijah, the son of Haggith; and the fifth, Shephatiah the son of Abital. And the sixth, Ithream, by Eglah, David's wife. 2 Sam. iii. 2-5.	
And David comforted Bath-sheba his wife. 2 Sam. xii. 24.	For this cause shall a man leave his father and mother, and cleave to his wife. And they twain shall be one flesh: so then they are no more twain, but one flesh. What therefore, God hath joined together, let not man put asunder. Mark x. 7-9.
But king Solomon loved many strange women. ... And he had seven hundred wives, princesses, and three hundred concubines. 1 Kings xi. 1-3.	Let every man have his own wife, and let every woman have her own husband. 1 Cor. vii. 2.

Only this need be said,—that God, on account of "the hardness of men's hearts," suffered polygamy among his people for a time, but "from the beginning it was not so."[1] And, as previously intimated, the patriarchs must be judged by the degree of light which they possessed. Too, it must be remembered that their polygamy differed materially from the "free-love" systems of other times. In polygamy, each wife of the "much-married" man was nevertheless *his wife*, and, *together with her offspring, entitled to be cared for and maintained by him*. Moreover, a "concubine," in those days, was not simply a kept mistress, as the word might now imply, but was a *wife of lower rank*, who was wedded with somewhat less than the ordinary formalities. Dr. Jahn[2] says: "Although this connection was, in fact, a *marriage*, and a *legitimate* one, it was not, nevertheless, celebrated and confirmed by the ceremonies above related." So Mr. Newman[3]: "A concubine, in ancient

---

[1] Matt. xix. 8.   [2] Bib. Archaeol. Sec. 155.
[3] Hist. of Heb. Monarchy, pp. 102, 127.

times, was only a wife *of inferior rank*, and the union was just as permanent as with a wife." The latter author suggests that the usages of the modern court of Persia point to the conclusion that Solomon really took these numerous women as virtual *hostages* for the good behavior of their fathers, who were chieftains of the surrounding heathen nations, and tributary to him. This is a reasonable suggestion.

Poor favored.

Might be favored.	*Must not be favored.*
Blessed is he that considereth the poor. Ps. xli. 1. He that hath mercy on the poor, happy is he. Prov. xiv. 21.	Neither shalt thou countenance a poor man in his cause. Ex. xxiii. 3.

The first two texts commend the exercise of benevolence in cases where no question of law or justice is involved; the last teaches that, in suits between man and man, justice must be done. The judges must not be unduly swayed by the poor man's pleading, but must decide the matter impartially.

Priests' dues.

First-born and firstlings.	*Otherwise disposed of.*
All the best of the oil, and all the best of the wine and of the wheat, the first-fruits of them which they shall offer unto the LORD, them have I given thee. *And* whatsoever is first ripe in the land, which they shall bring unto the LORD, shall be thine. . . . Every thing that openeth the matrix in all flesh, which they bring unto the LORD, *whether it be* of men or beasts, shall be thine. . . . All the heave-offerings of the holy things, which the children of Israel offer unto the LORD, have I given thee, and thy sons and thy daughters with thee, by a statute for ever. Num. xviii. 12, 13, 15, 19.	Thou mayest not eat within thy gates the tithe of thy corn, or of thy wine, or of thy oil, or the firstlings of thy herds or of thy flock, nor any of thy vows which thou vowest, nor thy free-will-offerings, or heave-offering of thine hand. But thou must eat them before the LORD thy God in the place which the LORD thy God shall choose, thou, and thy son, and thy daughter, and thy man-servant, and thy maid-servant, and the Levite that *is* within thy gates. Deut. xii. 17, 18. Thou shalt do no work with the firstling of thy bullock, nor shear the firstling of thy sheep. Thou shalt eat *it* before the LORD thy God year by year in the place which the LORD shall choose, thou and thy household. Deut. xv. 19, 20.

Michaelis[1] says there were two kinds of "firstlings"; the first belonging to the priest as his salary, and the "second firstlings," as he styles them, belonging to the altar, and, of course, consumed by the offerer himself and his guests. He

---

[1] Mosaic Laws, iii. 146-149.

defines the second firstling as that which immediately succeeded the proper firstling.

Davidson[1] recognizes a "second sort of firstlings, which were to be employed for feast-offerings, and therefore to be consumed by the offerer himself and his guests. The name denotes the animals *next in age* to those belonging to the sacerdotal salary. Hence the firstlings referred to were *additional* to such as appear in Exodus, Leviticus, and Numbers."

Similarly Dr. Jahn.[2] Keil thinks there was nothing in the earlier law which would preclude the priest's allowing the persons who presented the firstlings to take part in the sacrificial meals, or handing over to them some portion of the flesh which belonged to himself to hold a sacrificial meal.

Produce of seventh year.

For the poor.	*For owner and his family.*
And six years thou shalt sow thy land, and shalt gather in the fruits thereof. But the seventh *year* thou shalt let it rest and lie still; that the poor of thy people may eat: and what they leave the beasts of the field shall eat. In like manner thou shalt deal with thy vineyard, *and* with thy oliveyard. Ex. xxiii. 10, 11.	But in the seventh year shall be a sabbath of rest unto the land, a sabbath for the LORD: thou shalt neither sow thy field, nor prune thy vineyard. That which groweth of its own accord of thy harvest, thou shalt not reap, neither gather the grapes of thy vine undressed: *for* it is a year of rest unto the land. And the sabbath of the land shall be meat for you; for thee, and for thy servant, and for thy maid, and for thy hired servants, and for thy stranger that sojourneth with thee. Lev. xxv. 4-6.

The first quotation, with its context, teaches that the spontaneous yield of the seventh year is to be left for the poor, and for the wild beasts. The owner of the land is neither to cultivate it, nor to meddle with its produce, for that year.[3] From the second quotation we learn that the "sabbath of the land" was to maintain the owner and his family, with the flocks and herds. In Leviticus xxv. 21, 22, is promised a largely increased crop — "fruit for three years" — in the sixth year. It is, we think, this *surplus* — termed, in the seventh verse, "the increase thereof," — and not the mere spontaneous produce of the year of

---

[1] Introd. to Old Test., i. 353.   [2] Bib. Archaeol. Sec. 388, 389.
[3] Such seems the plain import of Lev. xxv. 5 and 20.

rest, which is designated as "the sabbath of the land." In other words, it is this surplus alone which is to serve the owner and his household during the year of rest, while all that grows during that year is to be relinquished to the destitute.

Keil takes the somewhat different view that the produce arising without tilling or sowing was to be a common good for man and beast. According to Exodus, it was to belong to the poor and needy, but the owner was not forbidden to partake of it also, so that here is no discrepancy.

Property in man.

One man owns another.

And if a man smite his servant, or his maid, with a rod, and he die under his hand; he shall be surely punished. Notwithstanding, if he continue a day or two, he shall not be punished: for he *is* his money. Ex. xxi. 20, 21

And ye shall take them as an inheritance for your children after you, to inherit *them for* a possession, they shall be your bondmen for ever. Lev. xxv. 46.

All men are brethren.

And hath made of one blood all nations of men for to dwell on all the face of the earth, and hath determined the times before appointed, and the bounds of their habitation. Acts xvii. 26.

On account of the "hardness of men's hearts," slavery, like polygamy, was suffered for a time; but the Mosaic code was so shaped as to mitigate its evils, and secure its final extinction. It was doubtless better thus to bring about its gradual abolition than to uproot it by a sudden convulsion. Slavery among the Hebrews was of a much milder type than among their contemporaries. In this opinion Dr. Jahn concurs. Michaelis[1] says that Moses "permitted slavery, but under restrictions by which its rigors were remarkably mitigated, and particularly in the case of Israelitish citizens becoming subjected to it."

Resistance.

Exemplified.

Then said he unto them, But now, he that hath a purse, let him take *it*, and likewise *his* scrip: and he that hath no sword, let him sell his garment, and buy one. Luke xxii. 36.

And when he had made a scourge of small cords, he drove them all out of the temple, and the sheep, and the oxen; and poured out the changers' money, and overthrew the tables. John ii. 15.

Interdicted.

But I say unto you, That ye resist not evil: but whosoever shall smite thee on thy right cheek, turn to him the other also. Matt. v. 39.

Then said Jesus unto him, Put up again thy sword into his place: for all they that take the sword shall perish with the sword. Matt. xxvi. 52.

---

[1] Mosaic Laws, ii. 157.

ETHICAL DISCREPANCIES.

We have previously seen that the first text is equivalent to a declaration that, in the changed circumstances of the disciples, "self-defense and self-provision would henceforward be necessary." The passage sanctions self-defense but not aggression.

Alford says the next passage should read, "He drove all out of the temple, both the sheep and the oxen." The "scourge" was applied to the brutes, not to their owners.

Barnes takes the original of Matt. v. 39, as meaning, Do not *set yourselves against* one who has injured you. We are not to cherish feelings of obstinate and implacable resentment.

The last text means, as noted elsewhere, that those who take the sword in opposition to legal authority, as Peter contemplated doing, or against innocence, as the Jews were about to do, should perish by a violent death.

Retaliation.

Allowed.	Discountenanced.
And if *any* mischief follow, then thou shalt give life for life. Eye for eye, tooth for tooth, hand for hand, foot for foot. Burning for burning, wound for wound, stripe for stripe. Ex. xxi. 23–25.	But I say unto you which hear, Love your enemies, do good to them which hate you. Bless them that curse you, and pray for them which despitefully use you. And unto him that smiteth thee on the *one* cheek offer also the other; and him that taketh away thy cloak forbid not *to take thy* coat also. Luke vi 27–29.

Michaelis[1] and Jahn[2] think that the law of Moses addresses the *perpetrator* of the wrong, admonishing him of the satisfaction he must render for the wrongs inflicted by him. Christ, on the other hand, addresses the *injured* party, forbidding him, as an individual to give vent to his vindictive feelings and take the retribution into his own hands, instead of waiting for the due process of law. Alford observes that " our Lord does not *contradict* the Mosaic law, but *expands* and *fulfils* it, declaring to us that the necessity for it would be altogether removed in the complete state of that kingdom which He came to establish." Warington[3] says, "On what principle are cases of this kind to be explained? Surely by regarding such laws as having

---

[1] Mosaic Laws, iii. 473, 474.　　[2] Bib. Archaeol. Sec. 256.
[3] On Inspiration, p. 252.

been, when given, especially adapted to the people and the times, and for these necessary; but as being for later days and other people not necessary and unadapted, and therefore abrogated."

Robbery.

Forbidden.	Countenanced.
Thou shalt not steal. Ex. xx. 15. Thou shalt not defraud thy neighbor, neither rob *him*. Lev. xix. 13. The wicked borroweth, and payeth not again. Ps. xxxvii. 21. That no *man* go beyond and defraud his brother in *any* matter: because that the Lord *is* the avenger of all such. 1 Thess. iv. 6.	And I will give this people favor in the sight of the Egyptians: and it shall come to pass, that, when ye go, ye shall not go empty. But every woman shall borrow of her neighbor, and of her that sojourneth in her house, jewels of silver, and jewels of gold, and raiment: and ye shall put *them* upon your sons, and upon your daughters: and ye shall spoil the Egyptians. Ex. iii. 21, 22. And the children of Israel did according to the word of Moses: and they borrowed of the Egyptians jewels of silver, and jewels of gold, and raiment. And the LORD gave the people favor in the sight of the Egyptians, so that they lent unto them *such things as they required*: and they spoiled the Egyptians. Ex. xii. 35, 36.

The point of the objection is, that the Israelites *defrauded* the Egyptians, by borrowing, but neglecting to repay. A recent writer styles their conduct "immoral," and adds, "It makes no difference whether the verb translated *borrow* means *ask* or *demand*. The representation made to the Egyptians by the Israelites when they *borrowed* or *asked* the jewels was, that they were going a three days' journey into the wilderness to sacrifice to the Lord God. They conveyed the impression that they were about to return." Knobel also asserts that it was their intention to deceive the king. To this objection, Augustine,[1] Hengstenberg,[2] and Keil reply: God knew the hard heart of Pharaoh, and therefore directed that no more should be asked at first than he must either grant or display the hardness of his heart. Had he consented, God would then have made known to him his whole design, and demanded that His people should be allowed to depart altogether. But when Pharaoh scornfully refused the first and smaller request, Moses was instructed to demand the *entire departure* of Israel from the land. The

---

[1] Quaest. 13 in Ex.   [2] Gen. of Pent., ii. 417–432.

modified request was an act of mercy to Pharaoh, and had he granted it, Israel would not have gone beyond it.

We may add that, on the return of the Israelites from their three days' journey, negotiations would doubtless have been entered into for their final departure. It should be observed that Moses' demand increased in the same proportion as Pharaoh's hardening.[1] Towards the close, there seems to have been no expectation, on either side, that the Israelites would return. After the smiting of the first-born, the Egyptians were desirous to get rid of the Israelites at any price. Hence, they are said to have " thrust them out altogether," and to have been " urgent" upon them to depart " in haste."[2] So far at the last from any promise or expectation of their return, the Egyptians were only too glad to be relieved of their presence.

Michaelis[3] has a peculiar explanation of the "borrowing." He thinks the Hebrews borrowed the articles with the honest intention of restoring them; but, in the haste of their midnight departure, driven out by the pressing command of the king, they had no opportunity to do this. Hence, they took the articles with them, with the view to restore them as soon as possible. In a day or two, the Egyptians made war upon the Israelites. This act of hostility, this "breach of the peace," changed the relations between the two parties, and justified the Israelites in detaining the property of their enemies as a kind of "contraband of war."

Hence, he concludes that the act of the Israelites was no robbery of the Egyptians, but simply *a detention of their property after the breach of peace with the Israelites.*

Ewald[4] maintains that since Israel could not return to Egypt after Pharaoh's treachery and the incidents on the Red Sea, and therefore was not bound to return the borrowed goods, the people kept them and despoiled the Egyptians of them. This sagacious critic sees in this turn of affairs a kind of "divine

---

[1] See Ex. viii. 1, 27; x. 25, 26.   [2] Compare Ex. xi. 1; xii. 31–33.
[3] Com. on Mosaic Laws, iii. 45–47.   [4] Hist. of Israel, ii. 66.

recompense," a piece of "high retributive justice, far above human inequalities, that those who had long been oppressed in Egypt should now be forced to borrow the necessary vessels from the Egyptians, and be obliged by Pharaoh's subsequent treachery to retain them, and thus be indemnified for long oppression."

But there is another view of the case. The Hebrew word, shäal, means, according to Fuerst and Gesenius, to *ask* or *demand*, as well as to *borrow*. It is used in the former sense in Ps. ii. 8, "Ask of me," etc. There is no good reason why we should not adopt this rendering in Exodus. We are told that "the Lord gave the people favor in the sight of the Egyptians," also that Moses was "very great" in their sight.[1] The awe which they felt for Moses, as also for the Israelites so signally favored of God, induced the Egyptians to comply with the demands of the Hebrews to that extent, that the latter "spoiled," that is, *impoverished*, the former. Hengstenberg: "They had spoiled Israel; now Israel carries away the spoil of Egypt." This author, with Rosenmüller, Lilienthal, Tholuck, Winer, Lange, Murphy, Keil, Wordsworth, and a host of critics, understands that the Hebrews asked and received these things simply *as gifts*. And Josephus[2] corroborates this view, saying of the Egyptians, "They also honored the Hebrews with gifts; some in order to secure their speedy departure, and others on account of neighborly intimacy with them." This explanation relieves the entire difficulty.

Slavery and oppression.

Ordained.	Forbidden.
And he said, Cursed *be* Canaan; a servant of servants shall he be unto his brethren. Gen. ix. 25.	And he that stealeth a man, and selleth him, or if he be found in his hand, he shall surely be put to death. Ex. xxi. 16.
Both thy bond-men, and thy bond-maids, which thou shalt have, *shall be* of the heathen that are round about you; of them shall ye buy bond-men and bond-maids. Lev. xxv. 44.	Thou shalt neither vex a stranger, nor oppress him: for ye were strangers in the land of Egypt. Ex. xxii. 21.
And I will sell your sons and your daughters into the hand of the children of Judah, and they shall sell them to the Sabeans. Joel iii. 8.	To undo the heavy burdens, and to let the oppressed go free, and that ye break every yoke? Isa. lviii. 6.

[1] Ex. xi. 3. [2] Antiq. ii. 14, 6 (Bekker's Greek edition).

As to Canaan, we have elsewhere seen that he, being, as the Hebrew requires, the "youngest of Noah's family," was probably the very one indicated as guilty of some unnamed indignity to the sleeping patriarch,[1] and hence was deservedly punished for his crime.

Leviticus refers to a mild form of servitude among the Israelites. Joel threatens captivity as a punishment for sin.

Exodus denounces the kidnapping and oppressing of free persons, foreigners or otherwise.[2] Isaiah admonishes against illegal oppression, rather than against that form of servitude recognized in and regulated by the law.

Hebrew slavery permitted.	Prohibited.
If thou buy a Hebrew servant, six years he shall serve: and in the seventh he shall go out free for nothing. Ex. xxi. 2.	And if thy brother *that dwelleth* by thee be waxen poor, and be sold unto thee: thou shalt not compel him to serve as a bond-servant. *But* as a hired servant, *and* as a sojourner he shall be with thee, *and* shall serve thee unto the year of jubilee. . . . Over your brethren the children of Israel, ye shall not rule one over another with rigor. Lev. xxv. 39, 40, 46.

The latter passages do not, as De Wette seems to think, prohibit the purchase of a Hebrew slave; they merely provide that the service of such should be *more lenient* than that of a stranger. Even a foreigner might buy a Hebrew slave, but always with liberty of redemption.[3] A gentile slave could be held for life-long service.

Emancipation in the seventh year.	In the fiftieth year.
And if thy brother, a Hebrew man, or a Hebrew woman, be sold unto thee, and serve thee six years; then in the seventh year thou shalt let him go free from thee. Deut. xv. 12.	And if thy brother *that dwelleth* by thee be waxen poor, and be sold unto thee. . . He shall be with thee, *and* shall serve thee unto the year of jubilee. And *then* shall he depart from thee. Lev. xxv. 39, 40, 41

That is, his servitude would cease at the end of the six years, or at the end of the jubilee-period, *whichever was nearest*. For example, a man sold under ordinary circumstances must serve six full years; but a man sold in the forty-sixth, would go out in the fiftieth, year of the jubilee-period, thus serving less than six years' time.

---

[1] Gen. ix. 24.   [2] Deut. xxiv. 7.   [3] Lev. xxv. 47-54.

Maid-servant emancipated.	*Not emancipated.*
And if thy brother, a Hebrew man, or a Hebrew woman, be sold unto thee, and serve thee six years; then in the seventh year thou shalt let him go free from thee. Deut. xv. 12.	And if a man sell his daughter to be a maid-servant, she shall not go out as the men-servants do. . . . And if he do not these three unto her, then shall she go out free without money. Ex. xxi. 7, 11.

Michaelis[1] and Jahn think that the first text is a modification of the original law, with a view to a further mitigation of the evils of slavery. Hengstenberg[2] thinks the case specified in Exodus, was an exception to the general rule. It would seldom occur that a father would sell his daughter into servitude, and never but with the expectation that she should become a wife, though of the second rank. The whole matter of the sale was arranged with this object in view. Nachmanides[3] says she did not go out *unconditionally* as the man-servant did. He went out at the end of the sixth year, without let or hinderance. She, on the contrary, might be espoused by her master, or betrothed to his son, in which case she did not go out at all, except for ill-treatment or neglect. Similarly Keil and others.

Saalschütz[4] maintains that Deut. xv. refers to an actual maid-servant whom her owner sells to another, and who gains, by this transaction, the privilege of going out free after six years' service with the second master.

In Ex. xxi, the reference is, he thinks, to one who has previously been free, but whom her father sells into servitude with certain stipulations and guarantees as to her future position and rights in the family.

Sons sharing estate.

Equally.	*Unequally.*
Wherefore she said unto Abraham, Cast out this bondwoman and her son: for the son of this bondwoman shall not be heir with my son, *even* with Isaac. Gen. xxi. 10.	But he shall acknowledge the son of the hated *for* the first-born, by giving him a double portion of all that he hath: for he *is* the beginning of his strength; the right of the first-born *is* his. Deut. xxi. 17.

A late writer says: "According to the Deuteronomist the first-born was to receive a double portion; formerly the sons

---

[1] Vol. ii. p. 180.
[2] Gen. of Pent. ii. 361.
[3] Conciliator, i. 178.
[4] See in Bib. Sacra, xix. 32–75.

shared alike." He, however, gives no quotation sustaining the latter part of his statement, and we have not been able to find any which is conclusive. Even Gen. xxi. 10, quoted above, does not seem satisfactory.

Isaac received "all" of his father's property, with the exception of some "gifts" to his half-brothers.[1] Joseph virtually enjoyed the rights of primogeniture; for his two sons were reckoned among his father's heirs, and on precisely the same footing with them.[2]

Stranger, — treatment.

Loved as a brother.	Not thus loved.
But the stranger that dwelleth with you shall be unto you as one born among you, and thou shalt love him as thyself; for ye were strangers in the land of Egypt. Lev. xix. 34.	Of a foreigner thou mayest exact *it again:* but *that* which is thine with thy brother thy hand shall release. Deut. xv. 3. Unto a stranger thou mayest lend upon usury; but unto thy brother thou shalt not lend upon usury. Deut. xxiii. 20.

The first text need not be pressed as prescribing that absolutely *no* distinction shall be made between a foreigner and a native-born Israelite.

Or, perhaps, the first text alludes to a stranger who has become a *proselyte;* the other two to one who is not such.

Under common regulations.	Some license allowed.
One law shall be to him that is homeborn, and unto the stranger that sojourneth among you. Ex. xii. 49. Ye shall therefore keep my statutes and my judgments, and shall not commit *any* of these abominations; *neither* any of your own nation, nor any stranger that sojourneth among you. Lev. xviii. 26.	Ye shall not eat *of* any thing that dieth of itself: thou shalt give it unto the stranger that *is* in thy gates, that he may eat it; or thou mayest sell it unto an alien; for thou *art* an holy people unto the LORD thy God. Deut. xiv. 21.

In respect to matters of fundamental importance, foreign-born and native citizens were under the same law.

In matters of trivial consequence the foreigner was left more at liberty. There was no forcible proselytism under the Mosaic law.

---

[1] Gen. xxv. 5, 6.

[2] Compare Gen. xlviii. 5; Num. i. 10; 1 Chron. v. 1, 2; Ezek. xlvii. 13; xlviii. 4, 5.

Usury exacted.

Of no poor man.	Of no Hebrew.
If thou lend money to *any of* my people *that is* poor by thee, thou shalt not be to him as an usurer, neither shalt thou lay upon him usury. Ex. xxii. 25.	Thou shalt not lend upon usury to thy brother; usury of money, usury of victuals, usury of anything that is lent upon usury. Deut. xxiii. 19.

Michaelis[1] says that, "in process of time, a prohibition became necessary, otherwise no poor person would ever have got any loan." Jahn[2] thinks that a difficulty arose in determining who was to be considered *a poor person*; hence it became necessary to extend the prohibition to all Hebrews, so that henceforth interest could be taken only of foreigners.

Davidson[3] concedes the wisdom of this arrangement, and adds: "It is easy to see that this would limit their commerce with other nations, and by so doing preserve their religious faith from contamination."

Wicked, — treatment.

Hated.	Loved.
Do not I hate them, O LORD, that hate thee? and am not I grieved with those that rise up against thee? I hate them with perfect hatred: I count them mine enemies. Ps. cxxxix. 21, 22.	But love ye your enemies, and do good. Luke vi. 35. Bless them which persecute you: bless, and curse not. Rom. xii. 14.

The first texts are simply an intense Oriental way of expressing David's utter abhorrence of the vile principles and conduct of the wicked. Viewed simply as depraved and corrupt, he "hated" them; viewed as human beings, he loved them, and desired their repentance and reformation.

Calvin: "Because, devoted to the cultivation of piety, he thoroughly abhorred all impiety."

Justified improperly.	Justified properly.
He that justifieth the wicked, and he that condemneth the just, even they both *are* abomination to the LORD. Prov. xvii. 15. He that saith unto the wicked, Thou *art* righteous; him shall the people curse. Prov. xxiv. 24. Woe unto them that call evil good, and good evil. Which justify the wicked for reward. Isa. v. 20, 23.	But to him that worketh not, but believeth on him that justifieth the ungodly, his faith is counted for righteousness. Rom. iv. 5.

---

[1] Vol. ii. p. 338. [2] Bib. Archaeol. Sec. 251.
[3] Introd. to Old Test., i. 345.

In the first instances, the term "justify" denotes the acquittal of the wicked through bribes; helping the criminal to escape his just deserts. In the last case, the term implies the gracious act of God in pardoning the sinner, and cleansing him from guilt.

Witchcraft, — treatment.

Punished.	Contemned.
Thou shalt not suffer a witch to live Ex. xxii. 18.	But refuse profane and old wives' fables, and exercise thyself *rather* unto godliness. 1 Tim. iv. 7.
A man also or a woman that hath a familiar spirit, or that is a wizard, shall surely be put to death. Lev. xx. 27.	Keep that which is committed to thy trust, avoiding profane *and* vain babblings. 1 Tim. vi. 20.

A critic whom we have quoted often, objects to the Pentateuch, that it "sanctioned the belief in witchcraft by enjoining a wizard to be put to death; whereas we know that such belief was superstition." To this it is a sufficient reply, —

1. Admitting that the terms "witchcraft," "wizard," and the like, were used in their modern signification, as implying the "possession of supernatural or magical power by compact with evil spirits," it would follow, upon theocratic principles, that he who so much as pretends to exercise this power, — thereby deceiving the people, and seducing them from their allegiance to God,— would be worthy of death. The law does not decide as to the validity of his claims, or the success of his attempts; but simply says, "The man or woman who *assumes to exercise witchcraft* shall be put to death."

2. But there is reason to believe that the foregoing terms do not bear, in the Scriptures, their modern meaning. As Sir Walter Scott[1] observes: The sorcery or witchcraft of the Old Testament resolves itself into a trafficking with idols, and asking counsel of false deities; or, in other words, into idolatry. This opinion is entertained by many other writers; as, for example, Dr. Graves,[2] Mr. Denham,[3] and Mr. R. S. Poole.[4] The latter

---

[1] "Letters on Demonology and Witchcraft;" **Letter 2.**
[2] Lect. on Pent. i. 190 (Second edition).
[3] Kitto, iii. 1120 (Alexander's edition).
Smith's Bib. Dict., Art. "Magic."

author regards it as a distinctive characteristic of the Bible that from first to last it warrants no trust or dread of charms and incantations as capable of producing evil consequences when used against a man. In the Psalms, the most personal of all the books of Scripture, there is no prayer to be protected against magical influences. The believer prays to be delivered from every kind of evil that could hurt the body or soul, but he says nothing of the machinations of sorcerers.

These facts go to prove that the modern notion of witchcraft, which the above-named critic justly characterizes as " superstition," was entirely unknown to the early Hebrews. Witchcraft with them and throughout the Scriptures, was a species of idolatry.[1] So that the critic's objection above quoted, falls pointless to the ground.

Woman, — condition and rights.

Should be in subjection.	May bear rule.
Thy desire *shall be* to thy husband, and he shall rule over thee. Gen. iii. 16. The head of the woman *is* the man. 1 Cor. xi. 3. *They are commanded* to be under obedience, as also saith the law. 1 Cor. xiv. 34. Wives, submit yourselves unto your own husbands, as unto the Lord. . . . Therefore as the church is subject unto Christ, so *let* the wives *be* to their own husbands in everything. Eph. v, 22, 24. For after this manner in the old time the holy women also, who trusted in God, adorned themselves, being in subjection unto their own husbands. Even as Sarah obeyed Abraham, calling him lord. 1 Pet. iii. 5, 6.	And Deborah, a prophetess, the wife of Lapidoth, she judged Israel at that time. . . . And the children of Israel came up to her for judgment. And Deborah said unto Barak, Up, for this *is* the day in which the LORD hath delivered Sisera into thy hand: is not the LORD gone out before thee?. . . So Barak went down from mount Tabor, and ten thousand men after him. Judges iv. 4, 5, 14. And when the queen of Sheba heard of the fame of Solomon she came to prove Solomon with hard questions at Jerusalem. 2 Chron. ix. 1. Candace queen of the Ethiopians. Acts. viii. 27.

The cases mentioned in Chronicles and Acts are related as mere matters of history. Besides, the queens of Sheba and Ethiopia were Gentile rulers, and did not arise under the Theocracy.

The case of Deborah is clearly an *exceptional* one; tending therefore to confirm the general rule. Cassel remarks: " That she, a woman, became the centre of the people, proves the relaxation of spiritual and manly energy." Professor Bush has

---

[1] See Deut. xviii. 10, 11; 2 Chron. xxxiii. 5, 6; Gal. v. 20; Rev. xxi. 8

the ingenious suggestion that had her office, at the time, been discharged by a *man*, the circumstance might have excited king Jabin's suspicion, and led to increased violence and oppression on his part.

Must keep silence.	*May prophesy and teach.*
Let your women keep silence in the churches: for it is not permitted unto them to speak; but *they are commanded* to be under obedience, as also saith the law. And if they will learn anything, let them ask their husbands at home: for it is a shame for women to speak in the church. 1 Cor. xiv. 34, 35. Let the woman learn in silence with all subjection. But I suffer not a woman to teach, nor to usurp authority over the man, but to be in silence. 1 Tim. ii. 11, 12.	Miriam the prophetess, the sister of Aaron. Ex. xv. 20. And Deborah, a prophetess, the wife of Lapidoth, she judged Israel at that time. Judges iv. 4. Hilkiah the priest, and Ahikam and Achbor and Shaphan and Asahiah, went unto Huldah the prophetess.... And she said unto them, Thus saith the LORD God of Israel. 2 Kings xxii. 14, 15. And there was one Anna a prophetess, ... which departed not from the temple.... And she coming in that instant, gave thanks likewise unto the Lord, and spake of him to all them that looked for redemption in Jerusalem. Luke ii. 36, 37, 38. And on my servants and on my handmaidens I will pour out in those days of my Spirit: and they shall prophesy. Acts ii. 18. Whom, when Aquila and Priscilla had heard, they took him unto *them*, and expounded unto him the way of God more perfectly. Acts xviii. 26. And the same man had four daughters, virgins, which did prophesy. Acts xxi. 9. Salute Tryphena and Tryphosa, who labor in the Lord. Salute the beloved Persis, which labored much in the Lord. Rom. xvi. 12. But every woman that prayeth or prophesieth with *her* head uncovered dishonoreth her head: for that is even all one as if she were shaven. 1 Cor. xi. 5. Help those women which labored with me in the gospel. Phil. iv. 3.

It is difficult to scan carefully the texts at the right which mention, and by implication commend, female prophets and teachers; and at the same time believe that the texts at the left were meant to overbalance these, and to prohibit, everywhere and for all time, woman's speaking upon religious topics, in promiscuous assemblies, or in public. Yet several of the best commentators, Alford, Ellicott, Wordsworth, Neander, Conybeare, Schaff, Meyer,[1] and Huther, apparently take this view

---

[1] This author in his last edition, concedes that the prohibition does not

of the case. Still, with fitting deference, we may ask whether after all the texts from Corinthians and Timothy may not have been intended for a *local* and *specific*, rather than a *general*, application. Was there not something in the situation and surroundings of those to whom Paul was writing which warrants this supposition? Many circumstances seems to favor this view. We find that sensuality prevailed in the city of Corinth to an almost unprecedented extent. Mr. Conybeare[1] speaks of the "peculiar licentiousness of manners" prevalent there, and adds, "So notorious was this, that it had actually passed into the vocabulary of the Greek tongue, and the very word 'to Corinthianize' meant 'to play the wanton'; nay the bad reputation of the city had become proverbial, even in foreign languages, and is immortalized by the Latin poets."

The same author, enumerating the evils which prevailed at that time in the Corinthian church, says that "women had forgotten the modesty of their sex, and came forward unveiled (contrary to the habit of their country) to address the public assembly." It would seem, then, that any Corinthian woman, making herself conspicuous, or attempting to speak in public, would be deemed *unchaste*. Does not this fact furnish the key to the interpretation of the texts above mentioned? Does Paul in these texts, counsel anything more than a prudent regard to the customs and prejudices of the people, for the sake of *avoiding scandal?* And might not similar circumstances in Ephesus where Timothy was, have prompted the like counsel to him?

Neander[2] thinks that, in 1 Cor. xi. Paul merely refers for example to what was going on in the Corinthian church, reserving his denunciation of it, to the proper place in chapter xiv.

apply to the smaller religious assemblies of the church, which, he thinks, might fall under the head of "churches in the house," *Hausgemeinden.* Compare Rom. xvi. 5; 1 Cor. xvi. 19. See his Com. on 1 Cor. xi. 4.

[1] Life and Epistles of St. Paul, Vol. ii. pp. 27, 31 (American edition).

[2] Planting and Training, p. 150. See also Schaff, Hist. of Apostol Church, 508, 509.

ETHICAL DISCREPANCIES.

The ancient Montanists held that the former passage was meant to be an *exception* to the rule, covering those cases in which the immediate operation of the Divine Spirit raised up prophets from the female sex; also, that Paul meant to restrain females from *didactic* addresses, but not from the public expression of their feelings. Dr. Adam Clarke thinks that the apostle merely prohibits a woman's *questioning, disputing*, etc., as men were allowed to do, in the synagogues and public assemblies. They were to speak, if at all, in a modest manner, by way of *suggestion* rather than *dictation*. Other modern writers take a similar view.

It is beyond reasonable question that the history of missionary enterprises, as well as of revivals, decidedly negatives any such rigid and absolute interpretation and application of the texts in the first series as shall tend to cripple the energies of the church of Christ.

CHAPTER III.

HISTORICAL DISCREPANCIES.

I. CONCERNING PERSONS. — *Names, etc.*

We have elsewhere[1] called attention to the close resemblance of a considerable number of the letters of the Hebrew alphabet, and to the consequent liability of confounding them with each other. These simple facts furnish a reasonable explanation of many " discrepancies " with reference to *names*. The following examples will illustrate the point. In 2 Sam. xxiii. 27, we find the name " Mebunnai"; in 1 Chron. xi. 29, the name " Sibbecai "; both referring to the same person. Now compare these names in the Hebrew, מבני and סבכי, and there is not the least doubt that the variation or " discrepancy " arose through a copyist's blunder. So " Hemdan," Gen. xxxvi. 26; and " Amram," 1 Chr. i. 41, stand in the Hebrew thus; חמדן and חמרן. Also " Zabdi," Josh. vii. 1, and " Zimri," 1 Chron. ii. 6, are written thus: זבדי and זמרי. No reasonable man can look at cases like these — which may be multiplied to an indefinite extent, — and wonder that we find variations among the proper names occurring in the Bible.

Comparing the first eight chapters of 1 Chronicles with corresponding passages in Genesis, numerous discrepancies, like the following, appear: Hadad for Hadar, ד confounded with ר; Aliah for Alvah, Ebal for Obal, Hemam for Homam, Pai for Pau, Shephi for Shepho, Zephi for Zepho, in all which cases, either by design or otherwise, is substituted for ו. Elsewhere we find " Caleb" and " Chelubai," the consonants being

---
[1] See pp. 19-25 of present work.

the same in both words; "Bath-sheba" and "Bath-shua," ב being exchanged for ו; "Achar" and, "Achan," ר being interchanged with נ; "Akan" and "Jakan," י prefixed in the latter case; "Bani" and "Binnui," ו inserted in the second form of the name. In like manner, "Huram" and "Hiram," "Araunah" and "Ornan," "Michaiah" and "Maachah," "Absalom" and "Abishalom," "Shealtiel" and "Salathiel," "Abijah" and "Abijam" are mere variations of names. So Gesenius deems "Uzziah" a popular phonetic corruption of "Azariah," *zz* being pronounced for *zr*.

Dr. Davidson[1] gives a list, taken chiefly from the first eleven chapters of Chronicles, comprising some one hundred and fourteen names which differ from the corresponding names in other parts of Scripture. These "variations" he attributes for the most part to the errors of transcribers.

Here let it be observed, that it is not simply *easy* to commit these errors, but, under the circumstances above described, it is *impossible*, except upon the hypothesis of an unintermitted miracle, to *avoid* committing them. No human skill and patience can preclude occasional slips of the copyist's pen and mistakes of his eye. Yet we regard all errors like those illustrated in the above examples as of very trivial consequence. No doctrine, precept, or promise of the Bible is affected by them in the slightest degree.

Another point to be noticed, as exemplifying the free treatment to which proper names were subjected among the Hebrews, is that of the not uncommon *transposition of letters*. Thus we have "Amiel" and "Eliam," "Jehoiachin" and "Jeconiah" "Ahaziah" and "Jehoahaz,"[2] "Harhas" and "Hasrah." In each of these cases the difference arises from exchanging the

---

[1] Introd. to Old Test., ii. 108–112.
[2] Kennicott illustrates this case thus, *ahaz-ihu*
    ihu-ahaz, the upper word representing the name "Ahaziah" in the Hebrew, the lower word representing the name "Jehoahaz," as it stands in the original. — See Kennicott's Dissertations, ii. 489; also, *passim*.

places of the letters or elements which compose the name. Analogous cases are "keseb" and "kebes," a lamb; "almug" and "algum," the name of a tree; "Shamlai" and Shalmai," a man's name, "Timnath-serah" and "Timnath-heres," the name of the city in which Joshua was buried.

We have in another place,[1] alluded to the Oriental custom of applying several names to the same person or object. This custom is exemplified by several of the cases already cited, and by the following instances. "Esh-baal" and "Ish-bosheth," are two names of the same person; the former name, "Baal's-man," being given to him either at a time when Baal-worship was fashionable in Israel, or else when the term "Baal" conveyed as yet no obnoxious meaning; the latter name, "man of shame," being applied when idolatry was at a discount. Nearly the same may be said as to the names "Merib-baal" and "Mephibosheth." In numerous instances, apparent "discrepancies" are produced by the change of a person's name on account of some trait of character which he has developed, or of some change in his condition and prospects.

The fact, also, that certain names bear forms different in the Old Testament from those in the New must be taken into the account. Thus we find Boaz and Booz, Uriah and Urias, Ezekiel and Ezekias, Isaiah and Esaias, Hosea and Osee, Asher and Aser, Sharon and Saron, Elisha and Eliseus, Elijah and Elias, Korah and Core, Beor and Bosor, Noah and Noe, Hagar and Agar, Hezekiah and Ezekias, Jehoshaphat and Josaphat, Rehoboam and Roboam, Joshua and Jesus, with other similar cases.[2] The fact that the Hebrew and Greek forms of the same name diverge in this manner, serves to explain many apparent inconsistencies in sacred history.

A word may be added concerning the discrepancies adduced by certain critics in reference to the *derivation* of names. For example, they assert that, in Gen. xxx. 16, Issachar receives his name on account of Leah's bestowal of the mandrakes; in

---

[1] Comp. pp. 17, 18 *infra*.   [2] See Bissell's Historic Origin of Bible, p. 384.

verse 18, on account of her surrender of her maid to Jacob. But it should be noted that the sacred writer merely *records* Leah's sayings, yet makes himself in no degree responsible for the correctness of her philology.

It is, however, obvious that we have in the case a kind of "play upon words." Murphy says, " She calls him *Issakar*, with a double allusion. She had hired her husband with the mandrakes, and had received this son as her hire for giving her maid to her husband."

Jacob's name, — one meaning.	*Another signification.*
His hand took hold on Esau's heel; and his name was called Jacob. Gen. xxv. 26.	Is not he rightly named Jacob? for he hath supplanted me these two times. Gen. xxvii. 36.

According to the first passage, the name "Jacob" comes from "äqab" *to seize the heel*, and denotes, as Ewald says, "heel-grasper." According to Esau's insinuation in the second text, the name means "supplanter." Now the truth is, that the word "äqab" has the closely connected secondary signification, *to outwit, to supplant;* and it is to this secondary sense that Esau alludes above. It is manifestly unjust to hold the sacred writer responsible for Esau's bitter and biting pun.[1]

Joseph's name, — derivation.	*A different derivation.*
Gen. xxx. 23.[2]	Gen. xxx. 24.[2]

According to the first text, the name would seem to be derived from "äsaph," *to take away;* according to the second, from "yäsaph," *to add.* The apparent incongruity is dissipated by Keil's suggestion that Joseph's birth was a proof that God had *removed* from Rachel the reproach of barrenness; while it also excited the wish that he would *add* another son. The "taking away" of an evil induced the hope that a good would be "added."

" Moses" a Hebrew name.	*An Egyptian name.*
Ex. ii. 10.	Ex. ii. 10.

The name "Moses" [Hebrew, "Mosheh"] appears to be

---

[1] Compare a similar sarcastic pun upon Nabal's name, 1 Sam. xxv. 25.

[2] In this and many following cases, where the language of scripture presents no *peculiarity*, we have for brevity's sake given simple *references* instead of *quotations*.

derived from the Hebrew verb, mäshäh, *to draw out*. It is, however, objected that an Egyptian princess would not have bestowed upon her foster-child a *Hebrew* name; hence "Moses" must, notwithstanding the intimation of the sacred writer, be an Egyptian name.

Hävernick, Kurtz, and Dean Stanley regard the name as a foreign word Hebraized. The Alexandrian Jews, with Josephus and Philo, attributed to the name an Egyptian origin, with a Greek inflection.

But Canon Cook, in his valuable " Essay on Egyptian Words in the Pentateuch,"[1] points out the existence of an Egyptian word which coincides in *sound* and in *sense*, with the Hebrew verb above mentioned. This Egyptian term " corresponds in form to the Hebrew, letter for letter," and primarily denotes "drawing out." One of the most famous Egyptologists, M. Brugsch, is cited to the effect that the derivation of the name " Moses" from the Hebrew "mäshäh" " would preserve the true sense of the Egyptian." Hence, Mr. Cook concludes that the present is a case of the " simple transcription of words," — that the sacred writer chose the Hebrew term because " it came exceedingly near to, or exactly represented, the Egyptian." Thus the difficulty vanishes.

Zebulun denotes a " dwelling."	*A " dowry."*
Gen. xxx. 20.	Gen. xxx. 20.

The name " Zebulun" is derived from zäbal," *to dwell;*[2] with a play upon, or allusion to, the word " zäbad," *to give, to endow.* The historian, in recording the philological conceits of others, does not thereby vouch for them.

Abigail's father, Nahash.	*Jesse.*
2 Sam. xvii. 25.	1 Chron. ii. 13, 16.

The rabbies say that both names belonged to the same person; Ewald and Keil, that Abigail's mother had a former husband, Nahash, previous to her marriage with Jesse.

---

[1] See Bible Commentary, i. 482–484 (American edition).

[2] This is one of the numerous cases in which the old **maxim applies;** **nomen habet omen.**

HISTORICAL DISCREPANCIES. 317

Abijah's mother, daughter of Abishalom.   *Of Uriel.*
   1 Kings xv. 2.   2 Chron. xiii. 2.

Absalom's daughter, Tamar, probably married Uriel, and became the mother of Maachah or Michaiah. This agrees with Josephus' statement.[1] Hence, in the first text, as often elsewhere, "daughter" denotes "granddaughter": and, in the tenth verse, the "mother" of Asa was, strictly speaking, his "grandmother."

As to the supposed discrepancy between Abijah's wicked course of life, 1 Kings xv. 3, and his "pious" remarks, 2 Chron. xiii. 4–12, it may be said simply that he is not the only wicked person on record who has used pious language when it would serve his purpose.

Abraham's difficulty with Pharaoh.   *With Abimelech.*
   Gen. xii. 11–20.   Gen. xx. 2–18.

We have elsewhere[2] seen that distinct events may bear a very close resemblance. A late rationalist concedes that "in those rude times, such a circumstance might have been repeated," and that the "dissimilarities" of the two cases render their identity doubtful. In king Abimelech, says Keil, we meet with a totally different character from that of Pharaoh. We see in the former a heathen imbued with a moral consciousness of right, and open to receive divine revelation, of which there is not the slightest trace in the king of Egypt. The two cases were evidently quite distinct.

In the first instance, *Sarah* was some sixty-five years of age;[3] hence it has been thought strange that she was spoken of as "very fair." But, since she lived one hundred and twenty-seven years, she was now in only middle age. She had escaped the hardships of maternity, and being "a noble nomadic princess," had led a free and healthful life. In contrast to the swarthy, ugly, early-faded Egyptian women, she possessed no doubt great personal attractions. In the second instance, when she was

---

[1] Antiq. viii. 10, 1.   [2] See pp. 26, 27 of present work.
   [3] Compare Gen. xii. 4; xvii. 17.

some ninety years of age, nothing is said as to her *beauty*. Abimelech was influenced, not by Sarah's personal charms, but simply by a desire to "ally himself with Abraham, the rich nomad prince." [1]

The quite similar case of *Isaac*, Gen. xxvi. 6–11, has been supposed to be a varying account of the one original transaction. But the name "Abimelech," common to the two cases, proves nothing; for, as Keil remarks, it was " the standing official name of the kings of Gerar." [2]

Abraham's inheritance secured.   *Not possessed by him.*
Gen. xiii. 15; xv. 18.   Acts vii. 5.

The explanatory phrase, "Unto thy seed have I given this land," shows that the gift was not to Abraham personally, but to him as the founder and representative of the nation. The land was given to him, as we may say, "in trust."

Abraham's need of divine intervention.   *No occasion for a miracle.*

Then Abraham fell upon his face, and laughed, and said in his heart, Shall *a child* be born unto him that is a hundred years old? Gen. xvii. 17. Therefore sprang there even of one, and him as good as dead, *so many* as the stars of the sky in multitude. Heb. xi. 12.

Then again Abraham took a wife, and her name *was* Keturah. And she bare him Zimran, and Jokshan, and Medan, and Midian, and Ishbak, and Shuah. Gen. xxv. 1, 2.

It is perfectly in keeping with Oriental methods of writing history to suppose that the words "then again," in the second passage, resume the narrative after a digression, and carry us back into the life-time of Sarah. It would then follow that Keturah's children were born to Abraham before the disability of old age overtook him. Or, we may say that the miraculous quickening of his virile powers, by which he was enabled to become the father of Isaac, was continued for some years after.

Abraham weak, and in fear.   *Possessed a large force.*
Gen. xx. 11.   Gen. xiv. 14.

Colenso asserts that Abraham, with his "immense band of trained servants, having routed the combined forces of Eastern kings, could not have feared the petty prince of Gerar." But

---

[1] So Delitzsch.   [2] See Ps. xxxiv. title.

(1) three-hundred and eighteen servants are hardly an "immense band." Abimelech's army may have been twenty times larger. (2) Abraham had not *alone* routed the combined forces of the kings. His "confederates," Aner, Eshcol, and Mamre,[1] may have contributed much the larger portion of the victorious army. So that, humanly speaking, he may have had great reason to fear Abimelech.

Ahaz favored divine worship.	*Closed the temple.*
2 Kings xvi. 15.	2 Chron. xxviii. 24.

The text from Chronicles refers to the latter part of his reign, when he had reached the lowest depths of ungodliness. At an earlier period, he had indeed encouraged a *corrupt* form of worship.[2]

Ahaz invincible.	*Compelled to seek aid.*
2 Kings xvi. 5.	2 Kings xvi. 7; 2 Chron. xxviii. 5, 16, 20.

The first passage refers to an early unsuccessful expedition of the allied kings against Ahaz. Later they overcame him. In this strait, the king of Assyria helped Ahaz, yet helped him not.[3] That is, this warlike monarch, at the request of Ahaz, attacked and conquered Rezin, one of the allies, thus affording temporary relief; but by his subsequent exactions and restrictions he really distressed and weakened Ahaz. For the latter was compelled to become tributary to him, to send him all the treasures of the temple and palace, and finally to appear before him in Damascus as a vassal.

Ahaziah's brethren slain.	*Their sons slain.*
2 Kings x. 13, 14.	2 Chron. xxii. 8.

Bähr, Movers, and Ewald say that the word rendered "brethren" may sometimes imply *near relatives* simply. We thus see how Ahaziah, the "youngest son," and born when his father was but eighteen years of age,[4] could have had forty-two

---

[1] See Gen. xiv. 13, 24.
[2] Compare 2 Kings xvi. 10-16.
[3] 2 Kings xvi. 9; 2 Chron. xxviii. 20, 21.
[4] Compare 2 Kings viii. 17, 26; x. 14; 2 Chron. xxii. 1.

"brethren." His nephews and cousins were all reckoned in the number. In the second text, the term may be used in the strict sense, of his own brothers.

Ahaziah's grandfather, Omri.	*Ahab.*
2 Kings viii. 26.	2 Kings viii. 18.

"Daughter," in the first text, means simply "female descendant." In the twenty-seventh verse, Ahaziah is styled "the son-in-law of the house of Ahab."

Ahimelech, high-priest.	*Ahiah.*	*Abiathar.*
1 Sam. xxi. 1.	1 Sam. xiv. 3.	Mark ii. 26.

Probably, Ahimelech, Abimelech,[1] and Ahiah were names of the same person. As to 2 Sam. viii. 17, which makes Ahimelech the son of Abiathar, instead of the reverse, as elsewhere, Bertheau, Oehler, and Keil think the line ran thus; Ahimelech, Abiathar, Ahimelech, so that Abiathar was the son of Ahimelech, while Ahimelech (the second) was the son of Abiathar. The expression in Mark, "in the days of Abiathar the priest," may denote merely that Abiathar was acting as his father's sägan or substitute.[2] Or, since Abiathar was, from his long association with king David, much more famous than his father, his name, although he was not as yet high-priest, may be used here by a kind of historical anticipation.

Amasa's father, Ithra an Israelite.	*Jether an Ishmaelite.*
2 Sam. xvii. 25.	1 Chron. ii. 17.

The rabbies say that Jether or Jithra was an Ishmaelite by birth, who became an Israelite. So Ewald, who adds that "Jether" is a shorter form for "Ithra." An examination of the two passages in the original makes it evident that the variation is due to a copyist's mistake.

Ammonites' allies.	*Another statement.*
The Syrians of Beth-rehob, and the Syrians of Zoba, twenty thousand footmen, and of king Maacah a thousand men, and of Ish-tob twelve thousand men. 2 Sam. x. 6.	Chariots and horsemen out of Mesopotamia, and out of Syria-maachah, and out of Zobah. So they hired thirty and two thousand chariots, and the king of Maachah and his people. 1 Chron. xix. 6, 7.

---

[1] 1 Chron. xviii. 16. Ewald, "simply a transcriber's error."
[2] See Lightfoot, Horae Hebraicae, on Luke iii. 2 (Carpzov's edition).

HISTORICAL DISCREPANCIES. 321

Beth-rehob was one of the little kingdoms of Mesopotamia, as also were Maacah, Zobah, and Tob petty monarchies of Syria. ("Ish-tob," translated is "men of Tob.")

Thus, the names and numbers agree as follows:

Syrians of Beth-rehob and Zoba,	20,000	Syrians of Zobah, etc.	32,000
Syrians of Ish-tob,	12,000	Syrians of Maachah,	
Syrians of Maacah,	1,000	(number not given),	[1,000]
	33,000		33,000

But one passage names "footmen," the other "chariots." Keil speaks of copyist's errors, and Rawlinson thinks that in the seventh verse, at the right, the words " and horsemen " have dropped out after " chariots." Dr. Davidson[1] cites approvingly Brown of Haddington's explanation, that the Hebrew term rendered "chariots," denotes not only a *chariot*, but a *rider*, and should probably be translated, in a collective sense, *cavalry*. It is suggested that these troops were a kind of auxiliaries, commonly employed in fighting on horse-back or in chariots, but sometimes as foot-soldiers.

Anah, a Hittite.	*Horite.*	*Hivite.*
Gen. xxvi. 34.[2]	Gen. xxxvi. 20.	Gen. xxxvi. 2.

Lange thinks that the term " Hittite " defines the race, " Hivite " the tribe, and " Horite " (" cave-dweller ") the habitation of Anah. There were at least two Anahs, the brother and the son, of Zibeon.[3]

Or, since the three names differ in the Hebrew by one letter only, we may with Michaelis and Bertheau ascribe the disagreement to an error of transcription.

Anak's sons were slain.	*They were expelled.*
And Judah went against the Canaanites that dwelt in Hebron: (now the name of Hebron before *was* Kirjath-arba:) and they slew Sheshai, and Ahiman, and Talmai. Judg. i. 10.	And Caleb drove thence the three sons of Anak, Sheshai, and Ahiman, and Talmai. Josh. xv 14. And they gave Hebron unto Caleb, as Moses said: and he expelled thence the three sons of Anak. Judg. i. 20.

De Wette[4] strangely asserts that the children of Judah " slew

[1] Sacred Hermeneutics, p. 552.   [2] Beeri = Anah.
[3] Compare Gen. xxxvi. 20 and 24.   [4] Introd. to Old Test., ii. 174.

the *same three Anakim* — Sheshai, Ahiman, and Talmai — whom Caleb had killed before." To this we reply :

1. If the three passages refer to the same event, that which in the first is attributed to the men of Judah, is, by a common figure, ascribed in the other two to Caleb, as leader of the expedition. Moreover, the verb " yärash " employed, in the texts at the right, means, not only to *drive out, to expel*, but also according to Fuerst and Gesenius, *to destroy*.[1] Thus the discrepancy vanishes. Caleb expelled the three Anakim from Hebron, and from among the living.

2. Or, with König and others, we may refer the contrasted texts to two different events. On this hypothesis, the first chapter of Judges does not follow the strict chronological order (verses 11–15, 20, being cited almost verbatim from Joshua xv. 13–19, and referring, of course, to the same point of time). So that the sequence of events is as follows: Joshua conquers Hebron, and slaughters or puts to flight the Anakim who dwell there.[2] But while he is occupied elsewhere, the remnant of them return from the land of the Philistines, regain possession of Hebron, and inhabit it. Hence, several years later, when this city was assigned to Caleb, he had first to dislodge the Anakim, the three leaders of whom were slain in their flight, or in some subsequent conflict, by Caleb's adherents.

Apostles named.	*Second list.*	*Third list.*	*Fourth list.*
Matt. x. 2–4.	Mark iii. 16–19.	Luke vi. 13–16.	Acts i. 13.

The names, though arranged differently, agree except in two instances. It is maintained by the best critics, Alford,[3] Meyer, Robinson, Ebrard, Gardiner, and others, that Lebbeus, Thaddeus, and Judas the brother of James, were one and the same person. Simon Zelotes and Simon the Canaanite were identical; " Zelotes " being the Greek form of the Hebrew term rendered " Canaanite." As the name " Bartholomew " (son of

---

[1] Num. xiv. 12 is cited as an example.   [2] Josh. xi. 21, 22.
[3] See his Commentary on Matt. x. 2–4.

Talmai) is merely a patronymic, its bearer is generally believed to have been the same with "Nathanael," John i. 45.

Asa's mother, Maachah. *His grandmother.*
2 Chron. xv. 16.   1 Kings xv. 2, 8, 10.

In ancient Persia, the king sometimes for political reasons *adopted* a mother. When Cyrus conquered Astyages, he, in order to conciliate a certain portion of the people, adopted Amytis, or Mandane as his mother. Mr. Newman [1] ingeniously suggests that Asa adopted, in like manner, the mother of the deceased king; hence she became queen-mother of the realm, though afterwards deposed on account of her idolatry.[2]

Asa removed the high-places. *Left them undisturbed.*
2 Chron. xiv. 3, 5.   1 Kings xv. 14.

Bähr, Thenius, Bertheau, and others say that the high places dedicated to idols were destroyed; while those dedicated to Jehovah were allowed to remain, since his true servants, having been long accustomed to them,[3] might have been grieved by their removal. Keil thinks that the second text merely implies that the king did not succeed in carrying out thoroughly his reforms. Rawlinson suggests that the above texts refer to different times; Asa, in the early part of his reign, putting down idolatry with a strong hand, but in his later years, when his character had deteriorated,[4] allowing idol-worship to creep in again.

Bedan, a judge of Israel. *His name not mentioned.*
1 Sam. xii. 11.   Judges vii.-xii.

Cassel and Davidson, with the Chaldee and the rabbies, refer "Bedan" to Samson,— Bedan being equivalent to Ben-Dan, a Danite. Ewald deems the name a corruption of Abdon.

But Keil and Kennicott, with the Septuagint, Syriac, and Arabic, take it as a copyist's blunder, for Barak, ברק for ברן.

Caleb's father, Jephunneh. *Hur.* *Hezron.*
Josh. xiv. 6.   1 Chron. ii. 50.   1 Chron. ii. 18.

---

[1] Hist. of Heb. Monarchy, p. 150, 151.   [2] 1 Kings xv. 13.
[3] 1 Kings iii. 2, 3.   [4] See 2 Chron. xvi. 7-12.

There were, as Ewald, Keil, and others think, two or three men who bore the name of Caleb. Besides, the term "son," in some of the above texts, may mean simply "descendant."

As to the disagreement of 1 Chron. ii. 19 and 50, respecting Caleb's relation to Ephrath and to Hur, Rawlinson and Bertheau place a period after "Caleb" in the fiftieth verse, and read thus: "These (referring to the preceding) were the sons of Caleb. The sons of Hur, the first-born of Ephratah, were Shobal," etc. This relieves the entire difficulty.

Canaanites were destroyed.	*Were merely subsidized.*
Josh. x. 40; xi. 14, 15.	Judg. i. 28, 30, 33, 35.

It is to be noted that the texts at the left are couched in general terms, and refer particularly to the *southern part* of Palestine.

Masius[1] maintains that Joshua swept over this region in too rapid a manner to depopulate it entirely. All that he needed was to strike such terror into the hearts of his enemies that they would no longer make a stand against him. All whom he pursued, he destroyed; but he did not stop to search into every possible hiding place. This was left to be done by each tribe in its own inheritance.

Canaanites spared, to prove Israel.	*To teach Israel war.*
Judg. ii. 22; iii. 4.	Judg. iii. 2.

They were spared for a two-fold reason; one part being brought out in the two former texts, the other in the latter text Israel was put to the proof by the opportunity of learning to wage war rightly against the enemies of God and his kingdom.

Christ bore his own cross.	*It was borne by Simon.*
John xix. 17.	Luke xxiii. 26.

Jesus may have borne the cross himself, until his failing strength caused a transference of the burden to Simon, whom Meyer takes to have been a slave, selected on account of the indignity of the required service. From Luke, Ebrard infers

---

[1] See in Keil on Josh. x. 40.

that Simon did not bear the cross alone, but merely went behind Jesus, and aided him in carrying it.

Christ's last drink of one kind.	*Of a different kind.*
They gave him vinegar to drink, mingled with gall: and when he had tasted *thereof*, he would not drink. Matt. xxvii. 34.	And they gave him to drink, wine mingled with myrrh: but he received *it* not. Mark xv. 23.

From a comparison of Matt. xxvii. 34 and 48, it is clear that drink was *twice* offered to Jesus while on the cross. The first time, the wine *drugged with bitter narcotics*, the effect of which would be to stupefy him, he did not receive. Afterward, some drink free from drugs was given him, which he accepted.[1]

The word rendered "vinegar" means, according to Grotius, Robinson, Davidson,[2] and others, simply *poor* or *cheap wine*, such as was used by the poorer class. The word translated "gall" denotes, secondarily, anything bitter, — wormwood, poppy, myrrh, and the like.[3]

Christ's genealogy, — one form.	*A diverse form.*
And Jacob begat Joseph the husband of Mary, of whom was born Jesus, who is called Christ. Matt. i. 16.	And Jesus himself began to be about thirty years of age, being (as was supposed) the son of Joseph, which was *the son* of Heli. Luke iii. 23.

There are two principal theories respecting these genealogies.

1. That held by Alford, Ellicott, Hervey, Meyer, Mill, Patritius, Wordsworth, and others — that both genealogies are *Joseph's;* Matthew exhibiting him as the legal heir to the throne of David, that is, naming the successive heirs of the kingdom from David to Jesus the reputed son of Joseph; while Luke gives Joseph's private genealogy or actual descent. This theory is very ingeniously and elaborately set forth in Lord Arthur Hervey's work[4] upon the subject, to which the reader is referred.

2. That held by Auberlen, Ebrard, Greswell, Kurtz, Lange,

---

[1] See John xix. 29, 30.

[2] Sacred Hermeneutics, p. 561.

[3] In the Septuagint it stands for wormwood, Prov. v. 4; for poppy, Deut. xxix. (17) 18.

[4] "The Genealogies of our Lord," London, 1853. See on the other side, Mr. Holmes in Kitto, ii. 92–102 (last edition). Also, Ebrard, "The Gospel History," pp. 149–163.

Lightfoot, Michaelis, Neander, Robinson, Surenhusius, Wieseler, and others — that Matthew gives Joseph's, and Luke, Mary's, genealogy. Although the alleged discrepancies may be removed upon either hypothesis, yet we must give the preference to the second, for the following reasons.

(1) The latter theory seems supported by several early Christian writers, — Origen, Irenaeus, Tertullian, Athanasius, and Justin Martyr.[1]

(2) It is indirectly confirmed by Jewish tradition. Lightfoot[2] cites from the Talmudic writers concerning the pains of hell, the statement that Mary *the daughter of Heli* was seen in the infernal regions, suffering horrid tortures.[3] This statement illustrates, not only the bitter animosity of the Jews toward the Christian religion, but also the fact that, *according to received Jewish tradition, Mary was the daughter of Heli;* hence, that it is *her* genealogy which we find in Luke.

(3) This theory shows us in what way Christ was the " Son of David." If Mary was the daughter of Heli, then Jesus was strictly a descendant of David, not only *legally*, through his reputed father, but *actually*, by direct personal descent, through his mother. The latter consideration is one of the very first interest and importance.

(4) This theory affords a very simple explanation of the whole matter. Mary, since she had no brothers, was an heiress; therefore her husband, according to Jewish law, was reckoned among her father's family, as his *son*. So that Joseph was the actual son of Jacob, and the legal son of Heli. In a word, Matthew sets forth Jesus' *right to the theocratic crown;* Luke, his *natural pedigree*. The latter employs Joseph's name, instead of Mary's, in accordance with the Israelite law that " genealogies must be reckoned by fathers, not mothers." For the remaining difficulties of the case, see discussion elsewhere.

---

[1] See Kitto, ii. 92–94, 547.   [2] Horae Hebraicae on Luke iii. 28.
[3] " Suspensam per glandulas mammarum," etc.

HISTORICAL DISCREPANCIES. 327

Christ's last tour, — one account. *A different statement.*
 Matt. xix. 1; xx. 17, 29; xxi. 1. John x. 40; xi. 17, 54; xii. 1.

These two series of texts seem to represent Jesus' journeyings somewhat differently. But, as Ebrard,[1] Robinson,[2] Gardiner,[3] and others have shown, they refer to different points of time. When Jesus took his final departure from Galilee, he went up to Jerusalem, where he attended the feasts of tabernacles and of dedication; then withdrew to Perea beyond Jordan. Thence he went to Bethany, where he raised Lazarus, and to Jerusalem, whence he retired to "Ephraim," where he tarried a little,[4] and taught. Thence he returned toward Jerusalem, by the way of Jericho, where he healed the blind men and visited Zaccheus, and arrived at Bethany six days previous to his final passover. Some of the above texts refer to one portion, others, to another portion, of these journeys.

Christ's miracles were concealed. *Were promulgated.*
 Matt. ix. 30; Mark v. 43. Mark v. 19; Luke vii. 22.

These two series of texts refer to quite different circumstances. Wherever a report of the signs and wonders wrought by Christ was likely to be conveyed without a right conception of his person and doctrine, there he suffered not the report to be carried.[5] It was fitting that the fears of the Gadarenes should be allayed by knowledge of the "great things" which the Lord had done for the poor demoniac. In Galilee and Judea there was, on the other hand, very great danger, says Ebrard, of confirming the people in their carnal expectations of the Messiah, and even of producing disorder.

Christ's resurrection, — certain narratives. *Different account of it.*
 Matt. xxviii. 1-10; Mark xvi. 1-14. Luke xxiv. 1-12; John xx. 1-18.

Owing to the condensed and somewhat fragmentary nature of these several narratives, and their neglect of strict chronological sequence, they present some difficulties and apparent

---

[1] Gospel History, sections 79-85. [2] English Harmony, sections 81-111.
[3] Greek Harmony, sections 76-112. [4] John xi. 54.
[5] See Smith's Bib. Dict., ii. 1353.

discrepancies. There is, however, not the least doubt that, if we knew *all* the circumstances of the case, those which we *now* know would be seen to fit perfectly into their appropriate places in the narrative.[1] Moreover, it is to be remarked that no one of the sacred writers gives, or intended to give, *all* the circumstances. Each selects those particulars which seemed to him most important, passing by intermediate incidents.

The following summary of the case is given by Robinson,[2] "At early dawn on the first day of the week, the women who had attended on Jesus, viz. Mary Magdalene, Mary the mother of James, Joanna, Salome, and others [3] went out with spices to the sepulchre, in order further to embalm the Lord's body. They inquire among themselves, who should remove for them the stone which closed the sepulchre. On their arrival they find the stone already taken away; for there had been an earthquake, and an angel had descended and rolled away the stone, and sat upon it, so that the keepers became as dead men for terror. The Lord had risen. The women knowing nothing of all this, are amazed; they enter the tomb, and find not the body of the

---

[1] Ebrard (Gospel History, pp. 59–60) gives, from personal observation, a case showing how the knowledge of a hitherto unknown circumstance will often reduce several discordant incidents to harmonious consecution. A messenger N. by name, was sent from Zürich to Pfäffikon on the occasion of an outbreak in the latter place. Accordingly Ebrard was informed by one trustworthy person that N. was sent, late in the evening, with a letter to P.; another told him that N. was sent in the evening to P., but, after going a short distance, returned with the report that the alarm-bell had already been rung in P.; a third related that two messengers had been sent on horseback to P ; and a fourth that N. had sent two men on horseback to P. These seeming discrepancies vanished, when Ebrard afterward learned from N. himself that he had indeed been sent, but met on the way two messengers from P., who reported the outbreak of the riot; that he turned back with them to Zürich, where he immediately procured horses for them, and sent them back to quiet the people in P. We thus see, that once in possession of the *thread of the narrative*, it is an easy matter to arrange upon it seemingly refractory and incompatible circumstances.

[2] See Bibliotheca Sacra for Feb. 1845, pp. 187, 188.

[3] There were two distinct parties of women. This fact relieves several difficulties. See under "Numbers" and "Time."

Lord, and are greatly perplexed. At this time, Mary Magdalene impressed with the idea that the body had been stolen away, leaves the sepulchre and the other women, and runs to the city to tell Peter and John.[1] The rest remain in the tomb, and immediately two angels appear, who announce unto them that Jesus was risen from the dead, and give them a charge in his name for the apostles. They go out quickly from the sepulchre, and proceed in haste to the city to make this known to the disciples. On the way, Jesus meets them, permits them to embrace his feet, and renews the same charge to the apostles. The women relate these things to the disciples; but their words seem to them as idle tales; and they believed them not.

Meantime, Peter and John had run to the sepulchre; and entering in had found it empty; but the orderly arrangement of the grave-clothes and of the napkin convinced John that the body had not been removed by violence or by friends; and the germ of a belief arises in his mind that the Lord had risen. The two returned to the city. Mary Magdalene, who had again followed them to the sepulchre, remained standing and weeping before it; and looking in she saw two angels sitting. Turning around, she sees Jesus, who gives to her also a solemn charge for his disciples."

It will be seen that this summary comprises nearly every incident mentioned by the four evangelists. Ebrard[2] concurs substantially in the view here given.

As to the fact that according to Mark the women said nothing to any man, while according to Matthew they ran to carry the tidings to the disciples, Ebrard thinks that the women actually hastened back to the city with the intention of telling the message, but, on their arrival, found the apostles in such a state of depression and gloom that from fear of ridicule they did not at first venture to do their errand. " Disobedient, indeed, they

---

[1] Peter and John appear to have lodged that night in a place separate from the other apostles. Griesbach thinks that the apostles at this time were scattered throughout the city among those who were friendly to their cause. — See Bib. Sacra, p. 172, note.

[2] Gospel History, pp. 447, 448.

had no wish to be; but they put off from one moment to another what they found it so hard to tell, and what harmonized so little with the lamentations that were heard all around."

Or, it may be that Mark refers as above to one party of the women, while Matthew alludes to the other party.

With reference to the fact that Jesus suffered not Mary Magdalene to touch him, but permitted the other women to embrace his feet,[1] it is to be noted that different Greek words are employed in the two cases. Ebrard, in the latter instance, renders, "Hold me not; I have not yet ascended." Euthymius and Theophylact, followed by Archbishop Thomson,[2] interpret thus: "Death has now set a gulf between us. Touch not, as you once might have done, this body which is now glorified by its conquest over death, for with this body I ascend to the Father." Meyer thinks she wished to ascertain whether the Saviour, whom she recognized, was present in his material form, or with a spiritual body. She sought to obtain by the sense of touch, the knowledge which the eye could not give her.

For other points of difficulty, see under "Numbers" and "Time."

Christ's revelation of truth, complete.	*Much kept back by him.*
All things that I have heard of my Father, I have made known unto you. John xv. 15.	I have yet many things to say unto you, but ye cannot bear them now. John xvi. 12.

May not the first text mean, "All things that I have heard from my Father, *which were designed for you at present*, I have made known to you. The message which I received for you I have faithfully communicated." Everything which the Father had, up to that time, wished him to make known, he had made known to them.

Alford thinks that the first passage is proleptically spoken of the state in which he would place them under the Spirit. A future event, viewed as determined and certain, is spoken of as having already taken place. The "many things," of the

---

[1] Compare John xx. 17 and Matt. xxviii. 9.
[2] Smith's Bib. Dict., ii. 1380.

HISTORICAL DISCREPANCIES. 331

second text, are what was taught by the Saviour after his resurrection,[1] and by the Holy Spirit at a subsequent time.

Christ's use of parables unvarying.	Parables sometimes omitted.
Matt. xiii. 34.	Matt. v.–vii.

Ebrard[2] has correctly pointed out that the first passage has reference to a particular occasion. " Christ's words, that day, were parabolical."

Daniel highly exalted.	Entirely unnoticed.
Dan. ii. 48.	Dan. iii. 12.

Bertholdt thinks it very strange that Daniel, who was so high in office, is not mentioned in connection with his three friends. But, as Bertholdt himself admits, Daniel may have been absent, at this time, from the capital upon some business of state. Herzfeld supposes that not all the dignitaries of the empire were invited to the dedication of the image, and that Daniel was not included among those who received invitations.

David detained at Saul's court.	Not thus detained.
And David came to Saul, and stood before him: and he loved him greatly; and he became his armor-bearer. 1 Sam. xvi. 21.	But David went and returned from Saul to feed his father's sheep at Bethlehem. 1 Sam. xvii. 15.

The mere fact that David " stood before " Saul, and became his " armor-bearer " (adjutant) by no means necessitates the supposition that David remained constantly afterward in Saul's service. If, as we know, Joab had *ten* armor-bearers,[3] Saul probably had at least as many, and, among them, some skilled in war. So that, when Saul's melancholy left him, he doubtless allowed David to return to his father's service. The second text, according to Keil, asserts that David " went back and forth from Saul to feed his father's sheep in Bethlehem." In xviii. 2, we see David taken into *permanent* employ by Saul.

David forbidden to build temple, — one reason.	A different reason.
1 Chron. xvii. 4–6, 12.	1 Chron. xxviii. 3.

Here is not, as De Wette[4] imagines, a contradiction, but two concurrent reasons for the same thing, neither of which ex-

---

[1] See Luke xxiv. 27; Acts i. 3.
[2] Gospel History, pp. 245, 246.
[3] See 2 Sam. xviii. 15.
[4] Introd. to Old Test., ii. 297.

cludes the other. Jehovah had not as yet required the building of a temple, neither would David be the proper man to build such an edifice. Neither the appropriate time nor the fit man had come.

David's officers, — one list.	A different list.
2 Sam. viii. 16–18.	2 Sam. xx. 23–26.

In this case there was an interval of more than twenty years. During that time, as might have been anticipated, some changes occurred, either by death or displacement. As to the fact that, in the first passage, Ahimelech the son, and in the second Abiathar the father, is spoken of as priest,[1] see under "Ahimelech's priesthood." "Seraiah," "Shavsha," "Shisha," and "Sheva" were different forms of the same name.

David's relation to Achish unfriendly.	Pleasant.
1 Sam. xxi. 12–15.	1 Sam. xxvii. 3–6; xxix. 6–9.

Several years intervened between the two visits to the Philistine king. During that period David had been fiercely persecuted by Saul; and Achish, aware of this fact, kindly received the Hebrew fugitive, with the hope that he would prove a valuable ally against Saul, their common enemy. Fuerst, Gesenius, and Hengstenberg think that "Achish" was the personal name, and "Abimelech"[2] the hereditary title of the Philistine monarch.

David's sons, — one list.	A second list.	A third list.
2 Sam. v. 14–16.	1 Chron. iii. 5–8.	1 Chron. xiv. 3–7.
Shammuah.	Shimeah.	Shammua.
Elishua.	Elishama.	Elishua.
Eliada.	Eliada.	Beeliada.
Eliphalet.	Eliphelet.	Eliphalet.
	Eliphelet.	Elpalet.
	Nogah.	Nogah.

We give merely the *differences* of the three lists. There is not the least doubt that these variations arose almost entirely from the blunders of copyists. Of the first two names, and the fourth, in each series, no more need be said. "Beeliada"

---

[1] Comp. Bible Commentary on 2 Sam. viii. 17.   [2] See Ps. xxxiv. title.

is a different form of "Eliada"—compounded with *Baal*, instead of *El*. One "Eliphelet," or "Elpalet," together with "Nogah," as Rawlinson and Keil think, died in infancy, hence is omitted in Samuel. Rashi and others say that "Chileab," 2 Sam. iii. 3, is another name for "Daniel," 1 Chron. iii. 1; Houbigant and Rawlinson maintain that we have here a transcriber's mistake.

David's sons priests.	*No priests except house of Aaron.*
2 Sam. viii. 18.	Num. iii. 10; xvi. 40.

The Hebrew word "cohēn," used in the first text, means not only a *priest*, but also a "servant, a minister, a counsellor performing service." So Fuerst, Keil, Movers, and Saalschütz. Gesenius and De Wette take the meaning to be, domestic priests, or spiritual advisers. Ewald[1] thinks that the priestly dignity was by divine direction extended to David; Mr. Plumptre,[2] that David and his sons may have been admitted to "an honorary, titular priesthood."

David tempted by the Lord.[3]	*Tempted by Satan.*
The anger of the LORD was kindled against Israel, and he moved David against them to say, Go, number Israel and Judah. 2 Sam. xxiv. 1.	And Satan stood up against Israel, and provoked David to number Israel. 1 Chron. xxi. 1.

It is consistent with Hebrew modes of thought that whatever occurs in the world, under the overruling providence of God, —whatever he *suffers* to take place,—should be attributed to his agency. In not preventing, as he might have done, its occurrence, he is viewed as in some sense bringing about the event. Hence the act of Satan might be, in this indirect way, referred back to God, as the Governor of the universe.

Another explanation is, that the Hebrew word "sätän"[4] when used, as in the second text, *without* the article, denotes

---

[1] History of Israel, iii. 133, 200.
[2] Smith's Bible Dict., iii. 2576.
[3] See pp. 79-81 *infra*. Also Stanley, History of Jewish Church, p. 52
[4] See this word applied to the *angel* which withstood Balaam, Num. xxii. 22; to David, 1 Sam. xxix. 4; to Hadad, 1 Kings xi. 14.

simply *an adversary*. Hence Boothroyd, Davidson,[1] and Hervey[2] render, "An adversary stood up against Israel." The latter critic also interprets the first text thus: "For one moved David against them"; adding that some unnamed person, who proved himself an enemy to the best interests of David and Israel, urged the king to number the people.

David's warriors, — one list.	*A different list.*
2 Sam. xxiii. 8–39.	1 Chron. xi. 11–47.

With reference to such copyist's variations as Hararite and Harorite, Shammah and Shammoth, Anethothite and Antothite, Barhumite and Baharumite, further remark is superfluous. The first list contains thirty-one names; the second, forty-seven. Of the first thirty-one names of the passage in Chronicles there are four not found in the list in Samuel, and, conversely, five names in the catalogue of Samuel do not appear in the other list. This difference is explicable upon the hypothesis that the two lists refer to somewhat different times. The list in Chronicles refers to the time when David became king over all Israel (see vs. 10); the other probably points to a later epoch. During the interval, some persons died or left the army, and others took their places.[3]

It is conceded by critics generally that the original text of the eighth verse in Samuel has suffered from copyists, but should be translated substantially thus, "Jashobeam the Hachmonite, the chief of the captains, he swung his spear over eight hundred slain at once." So Hervey, Keil, Kennicott,[4] Gesenius,[5] and others, who decide that the correct reading is found in Chronicles. According to the best authorities, the words rendered "Adino the Eznite" should be interpreted, "*he lifted up, swung, or brandished his spear*"; so that the italic words in the English version are unnecessary.

---

[1] Introd. to Old Test., ii. 88.
[2] Bible Commentary on 2 Sam. xxiv. 1.
[3] See Rawlinson in Bible Commentary on 1 Chron. **xi. 26.**
[4] Dissertations, i. 71–128.
[5] **Thesaurus, pp. 994, 995.**

HISTORICAL DISCREPANCIES. 335

Edomites obstructed Israel's passage.　　　*Permitted it.*
　　Num. xx. 18–21; Judg. xi. 17, 18.　　　Deut. ii. 4, 8.

At first, when the Israelites approached the precipitous, well-nigh impregnable western frontier, the Edomites refused them transit; but when the Israelites had " compassed the land of Edom," and came to the open, unprotected eastern border, the Edomites no longer dared to assume a hostile attitude toward them.[1]

Edomites refused supplies.　　　　*Furnished them.*
　　Num. xx. 19, 20.　　　　　　Deut. ii. 28, 29.

As we have seen, the Edomites at first refused hospitalities to the Israelites; but at the later period they made a virtue of necessity, and sought to turn the matter to their own advantage by selling the necessaries of life to the Israelites.

As to the similar fact that the Moabites did not "meet the Israelites with bread and water" (Deut. xxiii. 3, 4); though they "sold" them these articles (Deut. ii. 28, 29), Kurtz[2] sees, in the first circumstance, " a proof of their indifference, if not of their hostile feelings toward the Israelites," and in the last, "simply a manifestation of their selfish and grasping disposition."

Eli corrected his sons.　　　　　*Did not correct them.*
　　1 Sam. ii. 23, 24.　　　　　　　1 Sam. iii. 13.

That is, he reproved them either too leniently, or not till they had become hardened and ungovernable. His attempts at discipline amounted to nothing.

Eliakim succeeded Josiah.　　　*Succeeded Jehoahaz.*
　　2 Kings xxiii. 34.　　　　　　2 Chron. xxxvi. 4.

Bähr and Rawlinson take the words, "in the room of Josiah," as indicating that Nechoh regarded Jehoahaz simply as a usurper — the latter having been raised to the throne without Nechoh's consent.

Elimelech, indigent.　　　　　*Had a competence.*
　　Ruth i. 1.　　　　　　　　　Ruth i. 21.

To Bertholdt's "discrepancy," Davidson replies that the

---
[1] So Hengstenberg, Keil, Leake, Robinson, and others.
[2] History of O. C. iii. 385.

fulness and *emptiness* relate to Naomi's husband and sons who had died, not to property as Bertholdt imagines.

Elizabeth, of tribe of Aaron.	*Of tribe of Judah.*
Luke i. 5.	Luke i. 27, 36.

The mere fact that Elizabeth was "cousin" to one of the tribe of Judah proves nothing as to her own tribal descent. Intermarriages between the tribes were allowed, except in the case of heiresses. Aaron himself married into the tribe of Judah.¹

Elhanan slew Goliath.	*Slew Lahmi.*
2 Sam. xxi. 19.	1 Chron. xx. 5.

The Goliath here mentioned may, for aught we know, have been Goliath *junior!* Most critics, Michaelis, Thenius, Dathe, Movers, Winer, Keil, Deutsch,² Grove,³ Hervey, and others, maintain, however, that the Hebrew expression in Samuel is defective, and that Chronicles gives the true reading. Dr. Kennicott⁴ shows clearly how the copyist's mistake occurred.

Elkanah, an Ephrathite.	*A Levite.*
1 Sam. i. 1.	1 Chron. vi. 16-27.

He is called an Ephrathite (Ephraimite), because he lived within the borders of the tribe of Ephraim. So far as his civil standing was concerned, he, although a Levite, belonged to the tribe of Ephraim.⁵

Esau's wives, — one list.	*A different statement.*
Judith the daughter of Beeri the Hittite, and Bashemath the daughter of Elon the Hittite. Gen. xxvi. 34. Mahalath the daughter of Ishmael, Abraham's son, the sister of Nebajoth. Gen. xxviii. 9.	Adah the daughter of Elon the Hittite, and Aholibamah the daughter of Anah the daughter of Zibeon the Hivite. And Bashemath, Ishmael's daughter, sister of Nebajoth. Gen. xxxvi. 2, 3.

Some critics think Esau had six wives; others, five; others, three. It will be observed that *all* the wives in the second list bear names different from those corresponding in the first.

---

¹ Compare Ex. vi. 23; 1 Chron. ii. 10.

² See Kitto, i. 763.

³ Smith's Bible Dict., i. 697. See, on the other side, Ewald's History of Israel, iii. 70, and note.

⁴ Dissertations, i. 78-82.

⁵ See similar case of the "Levite of Bethlehem-Judah," Judges xvii. 9.

Hengstenberg,[1] Keil, and Lange account for this by the fact that women at their marriage received new names. On this hypothesis, Bashemath, daughter of Ishmael, is the same with Mahalath; Adah, daughter of Elon the Hittite, is the same with Bashemath; and Aholibamah, daughter of Anah and [grand-] daughter of Zibeon the Hivite, is identical with Judith,[2] daughter of Beeri the Hittite. Anah is also called "Beeri" ("man of the springs"), from the fact that he had found certain "warm springs" in the wilderness.[3] As to his nationality, we have spoken previously.

Eutychus was dead.	His life was in him.
Acts xx. 9.	Acts xx. 10.

The latter words were uttered *after* Paul wrought the miracle. As to the somewhat analogous case of the maiden,[4] of whom, though "dead," Christ said, "She is not dead, but sleepeth," the very obvious explanation is, that, *relatively to his power*, she was not dead. In other words, he could awaken her from death as easily as could others from ordinary sleep.

Genealogical lists, — one form.	Another form.
1 Chron. ix. 1–34.	Neh. xi. 3–36.

The first passage refers to the early inhabitants, previous to the exile. This is clear, from the twentieth verse, which represents Phinehas the son of Eleazar as ruler over them in time past. The second passage refers to the post-exile inhabitants, who lived in the time of Nehemiah. As to the similarity of names in the two lists, it may be said that, after the exile, naturally those very families which, or whose ancestors, had dwelt in Jerusalem in earlier times, went back to that city. Then, too, the recurrence of the same names in families is a familiar incident. People liked to name children after their

---

[1] Gen of Pent. ii. 225, 226.

[2] Murphy and others think that Judith died without male issue, hence her name is omitted in chap. xxxvi.

[3] So Gen. xxxvi. 24 should be interpreted, according to Fuerst, Gesenius, Hengstenberg, Murphy, Keil, and Knobel.

[4] Luke viii. 52 53.

grandfathers, or other near relatives.[1] This is Keil's view. On the other hand, Bertheau, Movers, and Rawlinson maintain that the two lists refer to the same period, and were drawn from much fuller documents; the differences between the lists being due to condensation and omission on the part of the authors, as well as to the blunders of copyists.

Davidson[2] says that the variations between the lists should not be pronounced "corruptions," unless it could be shown that they refer to exactly the same time. The catalogue in Nehemiah relates to an earlier period. Yet the interval between them was not great, since several persons named in Nehemiah were still alive according to the account in Chronicles.

Gershom's relatives, — names.	*Different names.*
His father, Moses, Ex. ii. 22.	Manasseh, Judg. xviii. 30.
His son, Libni, 1 Chron. vi. 20.	Laadan, 1 Chron. xxiii. 7.

It is generally admitted that, in Judges, for "Manasseh" we should read "Moses," — the name having been disguised by Jewish copyists, to prevent supposed disgrace to Moses resulting from the *idolatry* of his grandson.[3] Libni and Laadan are, probably, mere variations of the same name.

Gibeonites were Hivites.	*Remnant of Amorites.*
Josh. xi. 19.	2 Sam. xxi. 2.

The term "Amorite" is often used in a comprehensive sense, as equivalent to "Canaanite"; and especially as denoting that part of the Canaanite nation inhabiting the hill-country, that is, the Hivites.[4] As the Canaanites, with the exception of the Gibeonites and a few others, were supposed to be exterminated, the latter may well have been styled the "remnant" of the Amorites or Canaanites.

Several analogous cases may as well be considered here.

---

[1] See intimation in Luke i. 61. Also see numerous striking examples cited in Hervey's "Genealogies of our Lord," pp. 141-159.
[2] Introd. to Old Test., ii. 137.
[3] So Rashi, Kimchi, and the critics.
[4] Compare Gen. xv. 16, and Num. xiii. 29; Deut. i. 20, 21.

Hiram's mother a Naphtalite.	A Danite.
1 Kings vii. 14.	2 Chron. ii. 14.

Bähr, Blunt,[1] and Thenius say that she was of the neighboring city "Dan," in the tribe of Naphtali, bordering upon Tyre, hence she married a man of the latter country.

Joseph's purchasers Midianites.	Ishmaelites.
Gen. xxxvii. 28, 36.	Gen. xxxvii. 25, 28.

Keil thinks the two tribes were often confounded on account of their common descent from Abraham and the similarity of their customs and mode of life. Lange suggests that Ishmaelites may have been the proprietors of the caravan, which was made up mostly of Midianites.

Moses' wife a Midianite woman.	An Ethiopian.
Ex. ii. 16, 21.	Num. xii. 1.

Possibly "Cushite" and "Midianite" may be used interchangeably (see Hab. iii. 7). A better solution is that Zipporah had died, and Moses was married to a woman of Ethiopian origin. Ewald[2] adopts the latter opinion, also maintaining that Keturah was a wife taken by Abraham during the thirty-eight years which he lived after Sarah's death.

Obed-edom a Gittite.	A Levite.
2 Sam. vi. 10.	1 Chron. xv. 17, 18, 21.

He was called "Gathite," or "Gittite," because born in the Levitical city of Gath-rimmon (Keil), or living at Moreshethgath (Ewald).[3]

Woman a Canaanite.	A Syro-phenician.
Matt. xv. 22.	Mark vii. 26.

She lived in that part of Canaan called "Syro-Phoenicia," and was herself a "Greek," that is, a *Gentile*, as opposed to a Jew[4] (see Rom. ii. 9, 10).

We now return from our digression.

Hazael and Jehu anointed by Elijah.	By Elisha.
1 Kings xix. 15, 16.	2 Kings viii. 7-15; ix. 1-10.

The word "anoint," in the first passage, is used figuratively,

---

[1] Coincidences, pp. 117, 118 (Am. ed.). [2] Hist. of Israel, ii. 178, note.
[3] History of Israel, iii. 127. [4] Smith's Bib. Dict., ii. 967, and iv. 3149.

as in Judges ix. 8, to denote " divine consecration to the regal and prophetic offices.' Elijah did not, says Bähr, understand the anointing literally. He was simply required to announce, either in person or by proxy, to the three men named, their divine call to the performance of regal or prophetic functions. And the injunction (correctly rendered, " And thou shalt go and anoint ") left Elijah free to choose his own time for executing these commissions. Doubtless he gave it in charge to Elisha, his successor, to carry out to the full what remained unaccomplished.

Hezekiah reduced to poverty.   *Possessed great treasures.*
   2 Kings xviii. 14–16.   Isa. xxxix. 2, 6.

The second passage refers to the latter part of Hezekiah's reign, when he enjoyed great prosperity, and many brought " gifts " and " presents " to him, and he was " magnified in the sight of all nations."[1] Thus his fortunes were fully retrieved.

Hezekiah's passover unequalled.   *Surpassed by Josiah's.*
   2 Chron. xxx. 26.   2 Chron. xxxv. 18.

Hezekiah's feast surpassed all that preceded it since the days of Solomon, but was itself eclipsed by the later one of king Josiah. The superiority of Josiah's passover consisted in these points, — " All Judah and Israel " participated; it was held on the legal day; and all the people were ceremonially clean.[2] This was not true of Hezekiah's passover.

Israelites' condition in desert comfortable.   *They endured privations.*
   Deut. ii.7; xxxii. 13, 14.   Ex. xvi. 2, 3; Num. xi. 4–6.

It is clear, from the narrative, that the people were, at some particular times, in a state of destitution,[3] but that generally they were well supplied with food, and abundantly so upon certain occasions. As to the alleged impossibility of so vast a multitude,[4] together with their flocks and herds, finding the needful sustenance during their wanderings in the desert, it is

---

[1] 2 Chron. xxxii. 23, 27–29.
[2] Compare 2 Chron. xxx. 2, 3, 17–20, and xxxv. 18.
[3] Deut. viii. 3, 15.
[4] Ewald says, " about two millions," History of Israel, ii. 196.

HISTORICAL DISCREPANCIES.

to be carefully noted that, from the present sterile and desolate condition of the Sinaitic peninsula, we cannot infer that in former times it was equally barren and dreary as now. Eminent travellers and scholars assign, for believing that that territory was far more productive than at present, the following reasons.

Ewald [1]: " Destruction of good land by sand thrown upon it by the winds of the desert"; " change in the temperature of the soil"; and " increasing idleness or barbarism in the inhabitants, which is indisputable in this case."

Stanley,[2] following Ritter : The considerable decrease of the vegetation of the wâdys (valleys) ; the denudation of the soil by the ruthless destruction of acacia-trees in manufacturing charcoal, the chief article of traffic ; and the diminution of the population, consequently of the size and number of cultivated spots.

" When Niebuhr[3] visited that country, at the beginning of the last century, large supplies of vegetable produce were exported regularly to Egypt, showing that the original fertility was not even then exhausted."

Ritter[4] speaks of the " colonies, chapels, churches, hospices, convents, bishoprics, and Christian communities," existing there so late as between the third and seventh centuries of our era; and of the fact that there was " more building, more artificial irrigation, more culture of the palm-tree, and more agricultural prosperity in general " than is seen there in later times.

Stanley[5] mentions the " numerous remains of cells, gardens, houses, chapels, and churches, now deserted and ruined," which go to show that the desert was not always the dreary waste that it is now. And Ewald[6] says that " the most recent travellers have repeatedly remarked that the country shows clear indications

---

[1] Vol. ii. p. 197.
[2] Sinai and Palestine, pp. 25–29 (American edition).
[3] Bible Commentary, i. 246.
[4] Geography of Palestine and Sinaitic Peninsula, i. 10, 11 (Gage's translation.
[5] Page 29.
[6] Page 197.

of having been formerly much more extensively cultivated." The legitimate inference is, that the "wilderness of Sinai" was formerly vastly more productive and populous than at present.

The following may be enumerated as means of support enjoyed by the Israelites during the forty years' sojourn in the desert:

1. *The miracle of the manna, continued throughout.* Ex. xvi. 35.

2. *The milk and flesh of their flocks and herds.* They came out of Egypt with "very much cattle" (Ex. xii. 38). Prof. Palmer,[1] the latest and most scientific explorer of the Sinaitic country, says that the flocks and herds of the Israelites "would afford them ample means of subsistence, as do those of the Arabs of the present day, whom they undoubtedly resembled in their mode of life."

3. *Agriculture to a certain extent.* We are not to imagine that they spent their time in marching and countermarching, in military order, through the desert, "striking camp in the morning and pitching it again at night, daily, for forty years — and that within the compass of a few hundred miles." It is altogether probable that, during the thirty-eight years[2] the incidents of which were not recorded by the sacred writer, the people led, for the most part, a tranquil and comparatively *settled* life; being scattered over a very wide extent of territory, and engaging somewhat in the cultivation of the soil.

Dr. Davidson[3] observes: "As the tracts in which they roamed were very fertile in some places, producing a great variety of vegetables and fruit; as there were numerous villages and posts throughout it; the Israelites were not without the natural and spontaneous productions of the earth. They tilled the oases, and reaped the produce."

4. *Some intercourse and traffic with other nations.* The

---

[1] Desert of the Exodus, p. 426 (American edition).

[2] See Deut. ii. 14.

[3] Introd. to Old Test., i. 326, 327. As to stations of Israelites, see under "Places."

Israelites had, besides their flocks and herds, gold and silver in considerable quantities, and could procure certain necessaries of life from the Ishmaelites, Midianites, and Edomites, among whom they were.

As to their *flocks and herds*, these found sufficient pasturage in the numerous fertile wâdys through which they roamed.

On the whole, we may conclude, with Ewald,[1] that the Israelites subsisted, at times " in a condition of great privation and trial, certainly, — of which, indeed, in all the traditions, there is frequent complaint, — but still so that a frugal and laborious people would not absolutely perish."

Israelites dwelt in tents.	*They dwelt in booths.*
Ex. xvi. 16.	Lev. xxiii. 42, 43.

The word " ohel," *tent*, means also *a dwelling-house*, or *habitation*, hence might, perhaps, include *booths*. Neither passage asserts that *all* the people dwelt in " tents," or *all* in " booths." It is quite probable that, when they first emerged from Egypt, they were poorly provided with actual " tents," and hence sheltered themselves with " booths " and other rude structures.[2] A little later all may have possessed tents.

Israelites imitated the heathen.	*Did not imitate them.*
Ye have not walked in my statutes, neither executed my judgments, but have done after the manners of the heathen that *are* round about you. Ezek. xi. 12.	Neither have done according to the judgments of the nations that *are* round about you. Ezek. v. 7. Yet hast thou not walked after their ways, nor done after their abominations: but as *if that were* a very little *thing*, thou wast corrupted more than they, in all thy ways. Ezek. xvi. 47.

They had imitated the heathen in some respects, but not in others. The first passage at the right may denote that the Israelites had not commended themselves to the judgment of the heathen, but had pursued a course which even the latter would pronounce inconsistent and discreditable.[3] Or both texts of the series may simply assert that, so far from *imitating* the heathen, the Israelites had gone far beyond them in corruption.

---

[1] pp. 196, 197. [2] Green's Pentateuch Vindicated, pp 69, 70.
[3] See Jer. ii. 10, 11

| *Israelites listened to Moses.* | *Did not listen to him.* |
| Ex. iv. 31. | Ex. vi. 9. |

They gave heed to Moses at first; but since *instant* deliverance did not come, in their disappointment and impatience they would no longer hearken to him.

| *Israelites practised idolatry.* | *They served the Lord.* |
| Josh. xxiv. 14, 23. | Josh. xxii. 2, 11–34; Judg. ii. 7. |

The exhortation, "Put away the strange gods which are among you" (or "within you"), may refer to a lurking adherence of heart to idols. Or, possibly, idolatry may have been practised secretly by a few persons, unsuspected by the people generally. Whichever were the case, the sin was at once broken off.

| *Israelites' repulse of Philistines final.* | *It was not final.* |
| 1 Sam. vii. 13. | 1 Sam. ix. 16; x. 5; xiii. 5, 17. |

The statement that the Philistines "came no more" into the land of Israel, is not to be pressed so as to denote an expulsion for all time to come. It is simply a popular, idiomatic way of saying that they came no more *at that time*, or no more came *successfully*, so as to obtain a permanent foothold.

In a similar manner are to be explained the statements concerning Pharaoh-nechoh, 2 Kings xxiv. 7; Jer. xxxvii. 5; and concerning the Syrians, 2 Kings vi. 23, 24.

| *Israelites resistless.* | *Not irresistible.* |
| Deut. xi. 25. | Josh. vii. 4; Judg. i. 34. |

The first passage was, as is expressly set forth in the context, a conditional promise. The conditions not being complied with, the promise was no longer binding.

| *Israelites very numerous.* | *They were very weak.* |
| Num. i. 46. | Deut. vii. 1, 7. |

The texts at the right refer to the time when Jacob and his family went down into Egypt. From so small a beginning there had sprung a nation like "the stars of heaven for multitude."[1]

---

[1] Compare Deut. x. 22.

HISTORICAL DISCREPANCIES. 345

Jacob brought out of Egypt.   *He died in Egypt.*
      Gen. xlvi. 4.   Gen. xlix. 33.

The words, "I will there make of thee a great nation,"[1] show that the promise was to be fulfilled to Jacob's posterity, and not to him in person. Jacob's body was carried up out of Egypt, and buried in Canaan; his descendants were brought out of Egypt, according to the promise.

Jacob's errand, to procure a wife.   *To escape Esau's anger.*
      Gen. xxviii. 2.   Gen. xxvii. 42-45.

Two reasons for the same thing, — neither excluding the other. Upon the same principle are to be explained the several reasons assigned for Moses' exclusion from Canaan, — "unbelief," Num. xx. 12; "rebellion," Num. xxvii. 14; "trespass," Deut. xxxii. 51; "rash words," Ps. cvi. 33. Also, those adduced for numbering the people, — "taxation," Ex. xxxviii. 26; a "military enrolment," Num. i. 2, 3; ii. 32.[2] In like manner, the reasons named for Saul's rejection, — "unlawful sacrifice," 1 Sam. xiii. 12, 13; "disobedience," 1 Sam. xxviii. 18; "consulting the necromancer," 1 Chron. x. 13.

Jacob purchased the birthright.   *Obtained it by deception.*
      Gen. xxv. 31-33.   Gen. xxvii. 1-29

This "discrepancy" confounds two things which are entirely distinct — the "birthright" and the "blessing."[3] Jacob purchased the former, but obtained the latter by fraud and falsehood.

Jacob supported by the bed's head.   *Supported by his staff.*
      Gen. xlvii. 31.   Heb. xi. 21.

From the fact that the latter passage speaks of Jacob as "dying," while the former (compare xlviii. 1) represents him as not yet "sick," it is probable that they refer to different occasions. If, however, one so extremely old and feeble as

---

[1] Gen. xlvi. 3.

[2] In both cases, only males above twenty years of age were reckoned. See Ex. xxx. 12-14. The second reckoning, Num. i., was probably based on the former one. This would account for the agreement in the sum-total.

[3] See Gen. xxvi. 36.

346 DISCREPANCIES OF THE BIBLE.

Jacob was, might, although not actually death-struck, be spoken of as "dying," it may be observed that the same Hebrew word pronounced "mittäh," denotes *a bed*, but pronounced "matteh," *a staff.* Our present Hebrew Bible exhibits one pronunciation; the Septuagint and the Epistle to the Hebrews follow the other.

Jehoiachin, father of Salathiel.   *He was "childless."*
Matt. i. 12.   Jer. xxii. 30.

The term "childless" is explained by the statement that "no man of his seed shall prosper, sitting upon the throne of David, and ruling any more in Judah." With reference to a lineal successor, he was "childless." Salathiel, or Shealtiel, probably married the daughter and heiress of Neri, hence is reckoned as *his* son (Luke iii. 27).

Jehoiakim had no successor.   *Succeeded by his son Jehoiachin.*
Jer. xxxvi. 30.   2 Kings xxiv. 6.

Jehoiachin's reign lasted but a few months, and was, perhaps, subject to his mother's tutelage. He was then carried captive to Babylon, and his uncle made king in his stead. The Hebrew term rendered "sit," in Jeremiah," implies some degree of *permanence;* hence there is no collision between the passages.

Jehoram's sons taken captive.   *They were put to death.*
2 Chron. xxi. 16, 17.   2 Chron. xxii. 1.

As Keil and Rawlinson say, first taken captive, afterwards slain.

Jehoshaphat declines Ahaziah's aid.   *Made league with him.*
1 Kings xxii. 49.   2 Chron. xx. 35, 36.

The two kings at first engaged in ship-building together. Their ships were wrecked at Ezion-geber. Jehoshaphat, being informed by a prophet as to the cause of this calamity, declined a second proposal from Ahaziah.

Jesus approached by the centurion.   *By the elders of the Jews.*
Matt. viii. 5.   Luke vii. 3.

Alford and Ebrard think that Matthew, writing in a condensed style, speaks of the centurion as *himself* doing that

HISTORICAL DISCREPANCIES.   347

which he really accomplished *by proxy*. So Robinson, who quotes the old law-maxim, " Qui facit per alium, facit per se," He who does a thing by another, does it himself. Still, it is possible that the centurion first sent the elders, and then, in the intensity of his anxiety and distress, went in person to the Saviour.

Upon the above principle is to be explained the case of Zebedee's wife. She makes a certain request for her sons, Matt. xx. 20 ; they make it for themselves, Mark x. 35. So with regard to David : He killed Uriah, 2 Sam. xii. 9 ; the Ammonites killed him, 2 Sam. xi. 17. In like manner, the Levites promulgated the " blessings " and " curses," Deut. xxvii. 14, 15; and Joshua did it, Josh. viii. 34, 35. So the priests bought the potter's field, Matt. xxvii. 6, 7 ; and Judas purchased it, that is, *furnished the occasion* for its purchase, Acts i. 18. Nothing is more common than that figure of speech by which we attribute to the man himself any act which he has either directly or indirectly procured to be done.

Job's children, all dead.	*Some surviving.*
Job i. 19; viii. 4.	Job xix. 17.

Davidson takes the term " children," in the second text, as denoting " grandchildren." Conant, Delitzsch, Gesenius, Schlottmann, Stuhlmann, Umbreit, and Winer take the Hebrew " b'ne bitni " as equivalent to " my brethren." [1] Wetzstein,[2] comparing the Arabic idiom, says that the expression denotes, " all my relations by blood." Nothing in the passage warrants the inference that any of Job's own children were alive.

John identical with Elias.	*He was not Elias.*
Matt. xvii. 12, 13; Mark ix. 13.	John i. 21.

In a figurative, but not in the literal, sense John was Elias. He came in the spirit and power of the Tishbite prophet, and *was* the Elias of his day. Our Saviour's words, " If ye will receive it " (if ye can comprehend the meaning of the prophecy),

[1] Compare the obvious meaning of בְּטָנִי in Job iii. 10.
[2] Delitzsch on Job, Vol. ii. p 416.

"this is Elias which was to come,"[1] show that a literal fulfilment was not intended.

Joseph bound in the prison.   *He was not bound.*
    Gen. xxxix. 20; xl. 3.   Gen. xxxix. 21, 22.

Probably he was bound at first; but after a time, as his true character became apparent, his chains were taken off.

As to the "keeper of the prison,"[2] in whose care Joseph was placed, many critics, Delitzsch, Keil, Kurtz, Lange, and others think that he was a subordinate official, to whom Potiphar intrusted the immediate oversight of the prison and its inmates. The "captain of the guard" mentioned Gen. xl. 4, was probably the successor of Potiphar.[3]

The statement that Joseph was "stolen" (that is, carried away secretly and by force) from his native land (Gen. xl. 15) does not conflict with the fact that he was "sold" to the Ishmaelites (xxxvii. 28).

Joshua conquered certain kings.   *Their cities not captured.*
    Josh. xii. 10, 12, 16, 21, 23.   Josh. xv. 63; xvi. 10; xvii. 11, 12;
                                                    Judg. i. 22-25.

There is an appreciable difference between defeating a king in battle, and gaining possession of his capital city. Hannibal several times vanquished the Roman consuls, but never captured the city of Rome.

Josiah extirpated idolatry.   *It had been destroyed by Manasseh.*
   2 Kings xxiii. 5-12; 2 Chron. xxxiv. 3.   2 Chron. xxxiii. 15.

Manasseh did not root out the love of idolatry, and his son Amon countenanced and powerfully encouraged the worship of false gods. Hence, when Josiah, in his twelfth year, began to overthrow idolatry, he needed to do the whole work over again. The statement that Josiah destroyed the altars which "*Manasseh* had made"[4] is explained by the fact that these altars had been *not* "destroyed," but "cast out of the city," by Manasseh,[5] and were restored by his successor Amon; hence

---

[1] Matt. xi. 14.   [2] Gen. xxxix. 21.   [3] Smith's Bib. Dict., ii. 1465.
[4] 2 Kings xxiii. 12.   [5] 2 Chron. xxxiii. 15.

the religious zeal of Josiah was very properly directed against them.

Josiah's sons, — one list.	*A different list.*
The first-born Johanan, the second Jehoiakim, the third Zedekiah, the fourth Shallum. 1 Chron. iii. 15.	Jehoahaz, Eliakim (Jehoiakim), Mattaniah (Zedekiah). 2 Kings xxiii. 30, 34; xxiv. 17.

Jehoahaz is called Shallum in Jer. xxii. 11. Bleek[1] thinks that Shallum assumed the name "Jehoahaz" at his coronation. In Rawlinson's opinion, Johanan died before his father, or with him at Megiddo.

Judas' death, — one manner.	*A diverse statement.*
And he cast down the pieces of silver in the temple, and departed, and went and hanged himself. Matt. xxvii. 5.	And falling headlong, he burst asunder in the midst, and all his bowels gushed out. Acts i. 18.

Neither of these statements excludes the other. Matthew does not deny that Judas, *after* hanging himself, fell and burst asunder; Peter does not assert that Judas did not hang himself *previous* to his fall. Probably the circumstances were much as follows: Judas suspended himself from a tree on the brink of the precipice overhanging the valley of Hinnom, and the limb or the rope giving way, he fell, and was mangled as described in Acts.

Prof. Hackett,[2] who recently visited the supposed scene of this tragic event, deems the above explanation "entirely natural." As he stood in the valley, and looked up to the rocky terraces which hang over it, and which he found by measurement to vary from twenty-five to forty feet almost perpendicular height, he felt "more than ever satisfied" with the solution just given. He speaks of trees as still growing upon the margin of these precipices, and of a rocky pavement at the bottom of the ledges, upon which the traitor would be crushed and mangled, as well as killed, in his fall. The Professor suggests that Judas may have struck upon some pointed rock, which entered his body, and caused his bowels to gush out.

Besides, we do not know *how long* Judas remained suspended, nor how far decomposition was advanced when he fell.

[1] Introd. to Old Test., ii. 67.   [2] Illustrations of Scripture, pp. 275, 276.

Prof. Gaussen,[1] exemplifying different versions of the same affair, mentions a man who, having determined to commit suicide, placed himself upon the sill of a lofty window, and aimed a pistol at his head, then discharged the pistol, and leaped at the same instant. Now, it might be said, with sufficient accuracy, that the man took his life by shooting, or by throwing himself from a height. So, in the case in question, Matthew gives one aspect of the affair, and Peter another, yet there is no contradiction between them.

Judges appointed by Moses.	*Appointed by the people.*
Ex. xviii. 25; Deut. i. 15.	Deut. i. 9–13.

Jethro suggested the appointment to Moses; and the latter, after obtaining the consent of Jehovah,[2] referred the matter to the people; and the men whom the people nominated he admitted to share his authority, as subordinate judges.[3] Thus, since both Moses and the people participated in the choice, it might be ascribed indifferently to either. The omission of mention of Jethro's part in the matter, which De Wette and Köster style a "contradiction," Stähelin says is no contradiction, since it was the intention of the Deuteronomist simply to state *the fact*, and not *the manner* of the appointment. A quite similar case is that of the spies sent by the Lord, Num. xiii. 1, 2; by Moses, Num. xxxii. 8; by the people, Deut. i. 22; the true solution being that the people suggested the matter to Moses, who laid it before the Lord, and received from him an injunction to comply with the people's request. Yet in the condensed statements of the two latter passages there is no mention of the Divine co-operation in the sending.

Upon the shallow and delusive hypothesis that the historian's omission of an event is equivalent to a denial of that event, are founded many of the alleged "contradictions" of the Bible. The following are examples: Levites' participation in the inauguration of Joash, 2 Chron. xxiii. 1–20; omitted, 2 Kings

---

[1] Theopneusty, p. 117 (Kirk's translation).   [2] See Ex. xviii. 23, 24.
[3] Graves on the Pentateuch, i. 87.

xi. 4–19. Manasseh's repentance, 2 Chron. xxxiii. 11–17; omitted, 2 Kings xxi. 17. Moses' family sent back to Midian, Ex. xviii 2–6; the sending back omitted, Ex. iv. 20; Moses' fast at his *first* ascent of Mount Sinai, Deut. ix. 9, 18; omitted, Ex. xxiv. 18; with many analogous cases elsewhere. In such instances, the omission is due to condensation on the part of the writer, or to his selection of those circumstances only which he deemed important.

Kish the son of Abiel.	*The son of Ner.*
1 Sam. ix. 1; xiv. 50, 51.	1 Chron. viii. 33; ix. 39.

There were probably two men named Ner — one the grandfather, the other the brother of Kish. Hence the genealogy would stand thus:

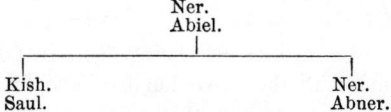

Hervey renders 1 Sam. xiv. 50, 51 thus: "And Kish the father of Saul, and Ner the father of Abner, were the sons of Abiel."[1]

Kohath's son, Izhar.	*Amminadab.*
Ex. vi. 18.	1 Chron. vi. 22.

Two names of the same person. So Rawlinson and other critics.

It may be added here that, upon the hypothesis (1) that the same person bears several names; or (2) that several persons bear the same name; or (3) that copyists have blundered in respect to names; or (4) that the terms "father" and "son," etc., are used in a loose sense for "progenitor," "descendant," and the like, we are able to explain a large number of "apparent contradictions" like the following: Laadan's posterity, 1 Chron. vi. 20; xxiii. 8 and xxvi. 21, 22; Laban's father, Gen. xxviii. 5 and xxix. 5; Machir's wife, 1 Chron. vii. 15 and 16; Mahol's sons, 1 Kings iv. 31 and 1 Chron. ii. 6;

---

[1] Smith's Bible Dict., iv. 2853, makes Abiel the father of Ner.

Salah's father, Gen. xi. 12 and Luke iii. 35, 36; Samuel's first-born, 1 Sam. viii. 2 and 1 Chron. vi. 28; Saul's sons, 1 Sam. xiv. 49 and 1 Sam. xxxi. 2; 1 Chron. viii. 33; Timnah's relationship, Gen. xxxvi. 12 and 1 Chron. i. 36, 51; Zedekiah's relationship, 2 Kings xxiv. 17; 1 Chron. iii. 15 and 1 Chron. iii. 16; 2 Chron. xxxvi. 10; Zechariah's father, Ezra v. 1; vi. 14 and Zech. i. 1; Zerubbabel's father, 1 Chron. iii. 19 and Ezra iii. 2; Neh. xii. 1.

As to the differences,[1] some twenty-seven in number, between the two lists of names, Ezra ii. 2–60 and Neh. vii. 7–62, they are due either to copyists' mistakes, or to variations in our English method of spelling proper names.

Korah swallowed up by the earth.   *He was burned.*
Num. xvi. 31-33; xxvi. 10.   Num. xvi. 35; Ps. cvi. 18.

There are two theories respecting Korah's fate: (1) That he was burned, with the "two hundred and fifty men" who offered incense. Dr. Graves[2] has a very ingenious argument in defence of this hypothesis, which is also supported by Boothroyd, Bush, Geddes, Hervey,[3] Josephus,[4] and the Samaritan version. But Num. xxvi. 10 seems fatal to this theory. (2) That, as the passage just named implies, Korah was engulfed, together with Dathan and Abiram. Ewald,[5] Keil, Kurtz,[6] and Knobel adopt the latter view.

The following would seem to have been the circumstances of the case. Dathan and Abiram, being brothers and Reubenites, probably had tents near together, and with their tribe, on the south side of the encampment.[7] Korah, as a Kohathite, would pitch his tent "on the side of the tabernacle southward."[8] This would bring the three ringleaders into such contiguity that they could conveniently take counsel together.[9]

---

[1] See more than a hundred similar cases collected by Davidson, Introd. to Old Test., ii. 108-112.
[2] On Pentateuch, i. 119, 120.   [3] Smith's Bib. Dict., ii. 1576.
[4] Antiq. iv. 3, 4.   [5] History of Israel, ii. 180.
[6] History of Old Covenant, iii. 296.   [7] Num. ii. 10.
[8] Num. iii. 29.   [9] Blunt, Coincidences. *See* Korah.

HISTORICAL DISCREPANCIES. 353

On the appointed day Korah and his faction assembled at the door of the tabernacle of the congregation. Dathan and Abiram scornfully refused to come (vs. 12–14), and remained in their tents. After the events recorded in vs. 18–24, Moses, leaving the tabernacle, went with the elders of Israel to the tents of Dathan and Abiram. Doubtless Korah, who was the prime mover of the rebellion, left the "two hundred and fifty men" burning incense at the tabernacle, and followed Moses, with the purpose of strengthening Dathan and Abiram in their contumacy. Arrived at their tents, he stood with them and their families in the door to see what Moses would do. At the command of the latter, the people withdrew from about the "tabernacle [tents or dwelling-place] of Korah, Dathan, and Abiram," who were instantly swallowed up by the opening earth. At the same moment, a fire sent of God destroyed the two hundred and fifty men offering incense at the tabernacle. Probably Korah is mentioned, in vs. 24–27, with the other two, because he was so closely linked with them in conduct and fate. It is clear that Korah was not in *his own* tent, which must have been at some little distance, and which seems not to have been destroyed. Some think that "the tabernacle of Korah, Dathan, and Abiram" (vs. 24–27) was one which these men had set up in opposition to the tabernacle proper.

That a portion, at least, of Korah's family did not perish with him is explicitly asserted in Num. xxvi. 11. The prophet Samuel was a descendant of Korah,[1] and some of David's musicians belonged to the same family.[2] So that the expression, "all the men that appertained unto Korah"[3] (literally, "all unto Korah") denotes simply his *adherents* — his servants and retainers, with, possibly, the adult males of his family.

Lazarus came forth from the tomb.   *He was bound hand and foot.*
        John xi. 44.   John xi. 44.

The Jewish sepulchres were caves or rooms excavated in

---

[1] 1 Chron. vi. 22–28.   [2] 1 Chron. vi. 31, 33; Ps. xliv.–xlix, titles.
[3] Num. xvi. 32.

the rock. The dead were not put in coffins, but into niches cut into the sides of these rooms, and radiating outward. The corpse, as Meyer thinks, was not so swathed with bandages as to preclude all motion; and the wrappings would be loosened by the movements of the living man. At Jesus' word, Lazarus raised himself from his recumbent position in the niche, put forth his feet over the edge, then, sliding down, stood upright on the floor.[1] When he thus "came forth," Jesus bade them "loose him, and let him go."

Man's fear and dread upon all beasts.	*Not upon the lion.*
Gen. ix. 2.	Prov. xxx. 30.

The second passage, "A lion which is strongest among beasts, and turneth not away for any," may mean, "for any *beast*," — another way of designating the lion as the "king of beasts." If, however, it implies, "for any *man*," the exceptional cases which this statement covers only prove the general rule that the presence of man intimidates all the lower animals.

Moses somewhat infirm.	*His physical powers well preserved.*
And he said unto them, I *am* a hundred and twenty years old this day; I can no more go out and come in: also the LORD hath said unto me, Thou shalt not go over this Jordan. Deut. xxxi. 2.	And Moses *was* an hundred and twenty years old when he died: his eye was not dim, nor his natural force abated. Deut. xxxiv. 7.

The fact that Moses' eyesight and physical vigor were unimpaired does not preclude his knowing that he had already passed far beyond the ordinary limit of human life, and that his mission — inasmuch as the time for crossing the Jordan had come, and he himself was not to go over — was accomplished. In view of these facts, he admonished the Israelites that he could no longer "go out and come in" *as their leader.*

Moses' father-in-law, Jethro.	*Reuel or Raguel.*	*Hobab.*
Ex. iii. 1; iv. 18; xviii 5.	Ex. ii. 18; Num. x. 29.	Judg. iv. 11.

Observe, (1) That "Reuel" and "Raguel" are exactly the same in the Hebrew. (2) That "Jether," or "Jethro," is not a proper name, but simply a title of honor, denoting "excellency," and about equivalent to the Arabic "Imâm." So

---

[1] So Macknight, Paxton, and others.

Aben Ezra, Ewald, Gesenius, Keil, Kimchi, Knobel, Kurtz, Winer, and others.

The following seems the best explanation of the other difficulties in the case. Hobab was the son of Raguel, and hence the brother-in-law of Moses. He appears to have remained with the Israelites when his father Jethro returned to his own land, and to have settled among them.[1] So Josephus, Bertheau, and Keil. As to Num. x. 29, the original is ambiguous, and may denote either that Raguel or that Hobab was Moses' father-in-law. The English version of Judg. iv. 11 favors the latter theory; but the Hebrew word "chothēn" means properly "a relative by marriage,"[2] or, as Fuerst says, "one who makes an alliance." So that, as Ranke maintains, the term, being ambiguous, proves nothing.

Some think that Hobab was the brother of Jethro — both being sons of Raguel; others, that Hobab and Jethro were different names of the same man, who was actually the father-in-law of Moses, and the son of Raguel. On this hypothesis, the terms "father" and "daughter," Ex. ii. 16–21, are equivalent to "grandfather" and "granddaughter."

Moses peerless among prophets.   *Others wrought equal miracles.*
Deut. xxxiv. 10–12.   1 K. xvii. 22; 2 K. i. 10; ii. 14; iv. 34.

The first passage does not say that no such prophet ever would arise, but merely that, up to the time of writing, no prophet equal to Moses *had* arisen. Moreover, in certain aspects, not simply as a miracle-worker, but as a *lawgiver*, Moses has never been equalled. In this respect he has no human peer.

Moses' veil worn in addressing the people.   *Not worn at such times.*
Ex. xxxiv. 33–35.   2 Cor. iii. 7, 13.

The best commentators agree that the citation from Exodus

---

[1] Compare Ex. xviii. 27; Num. x. 29–32; Judg. i. 16; iv. 11; 1 Sam. xv. 6.

[2] See Gen. xix. 14; 2 Kings viii. 27, where a word differing only in vowel-points is employed.

should be rendered, " And *when* Moses had done speaking with them, he put a veil," etc.

| *Naboth's sons slain with him.* | *Their slaughter not mentioned.* |
| 2 Kings ix. 26. | 1 Kings xxi. 13. |

The omission in the condensed narrative of 1 Kings cannot be construed into a denial. The murder of the sons is not mentioned in this place, because, as Ewald[1] says, it is "here understood as a matter of course." Jezebel, who was not wont to do things by halves, would see to it that Naboth's sons were not left alive to inherit his possessions (which would not then have escheated to the crown), nor to revenge their father's cruel death.

| *Poor not found in Israel.* | *Poor always found.* |
| Deut. xv. 4. | Deut. xv. 11. |

Michaelis, Rosenmüller, Dathe, and others give the sense of the first passage thus, "Thou must release the debt, except when *no poor person is concerned in the matter*, — which may happen, for the Lord shall greatly bless thee," etc.

| *Priests styled sons of Aaron.* | *Classed as Levites.* |
| Lev. i. 5, 8, 11; Num. vi. 23. | Deut. x. 8, 9; xviii. 1, 7. |

Certain critics have affected to see a discrepancy, in that the " sharp distinction " between the priests and Levites in the first passages is not kept up in the second series. To which it is sufficient to reply:

1. The priests were not only "sons of Aaron," but were *also* "Levites."

2. The term "sons of Aaron," applied to the priests, is not found in the last part of Numbers at all, but only in the first fourteen chapters. These relate to the *second*, while Deuteronomy relates to the *fortieth*, year after the exodus. Now, during the intervening thirty-eight years, a change of phraseology may have obtained currency.

3. In Deuteronomy Moses is speaking in general terms. To enter into minute and unimportant details would be quite

---

[1] Hist. of Israel, iv. 75, note 2. So also J. D. Michaelis, and others.

foreign to his purpose, and tend to defeat it. The man who addresses a large and mixed audience will, if he knows his business, take care to shun irrelevant details and distinctions.[1]

Purchaser of sepulchre, Jacob.	It was Abraham.
And the bones of Joseph, which the children of Israel brought up out of Egypt, buried they in Shechem, in a parcel of ground which Jacob bought of the sons of Hamor the father of Shechem for a hundred pieces of silver. Josh. xxiv. 32.	So Jacob went down into Egypt, and died, he, and our fathers. And were carried over into Sychem, and laid in the sepulchre that Abraham bought for a sum of money of the sons of Emmor, *the father* of Sychem. Acts vii. 15, 16.

Alford thinks that the use of the name "Abraham," in the latter passage, is due to "haste or inadvertence" on the part of Stephen. Hackett, following Beza, Kuinoel, Schoettgen, and others, is in favor of omitting the word "Abraham," and rendering, "which was purchased."

The simplest explanation is that suggested by Mr. Garden.[2] It is known that Sychem (Shechem) was the place where God first appeared to Abraham in the land of Canaan, and where the patriarch built an altar.[3] There is reason to believe that a man so scrupulous as was Abraham in respect to property would *purchase* the field where he built his altar. In the one hundred and eighty-five years which intervened, the Shechemites may have reoccupied the location, and Jacob may have renewed the purchase made by his grandfather. Of this consecrated field a portion may have been set apart by Jacob as a burial-place.

According to the usage of New Testament Greek, we should read, "of the sons of Emmor *the son* of Sychem." We are thus carried back to a Shechem and Hamor antecedent to Abraham, and quite different from those of whose sons Jacob made the purchase, Gen. xxxiii. 18–20. The way is thus cleared. Abraham made the original purchase, and Jacob renewed and confirmed the transaction.

Rebellious Israelites all dead.	Spoken of as living.
Num. xxvi. 64, 65.	Deut. i. 6, 9, 14; v. 2, 5; xi. 2, 7.

That the congregation which remained after the death of the

---

[1] See Bible Com., i. 797, 798.   [2] Smith's Bib. Dict., iv. 3114, 3115.
[3] Gen. xii. 6, 7.

rebels might still be considered *identical* with that which came out from Egypt is clear, from the following considerations. Only the males above twenty years of age were "numbered," and placed under the ban.¹ It would follow, beyond question, that a very large number of *women* were present, who remembered the servitude in Egypt and the events in the wilderness. Besides, the *Levites* were exempted from the ban, as well as *all the males under twenty years of age*.² Here, then, were three classes of persons who survived, and who formed the large majority of the congregation to whom Moses discoursed, as recorded in Deuteronomy. He was, therefore (Colenso to the contrary, notwithstanding), perfectly right in saying to the assembled multitudes, "*Your* eyes have seen all the great acts of the Lord which he did."

Rulers knew Christ.	*They knew him not.*
Matt. xxi. 38.	John xvi. 3; Acts iii. 17; 1 Cor. ii. 8.

A. Fuller deems it very probable that there were some of each description; and that the former passages refer to one; the latter, to the other.

Alford suggests that the "ignorance" mentioned admitted of all degrees, from that of the unlearned, who followed their leaders implicitly in rejecting Jesus, to that of the most learned scribes, who rightly understood the Messianic predictions, yet, from moral blindness or perverted expectations, failed to recognize the fulfilment in our Lord.

Samaritans received not Jesus.	*Treated him hospitably.*
Luke ix. 52, 53.	John iv. 39, 40.

Baur finds a "discrepancy" here; but Bleek³ replies that Luke is speaking of a certain Samaritan *village*, while John refers to a *city* in the land of Samaria.

Samuel visited Saul no more.	*Saul prophesied before him.*
1 Sam. xv. 35.	1 Sam. xix. 24.

De Wette⁴: "It is said that Samuel did not see Saul again

---

¹ Compare Num. i. 2, 3, 45, 46.   ² Num. i. 3, 45, 49.
³ Introd. to New Test., ii 220.   ⁴ Introd. to Old Test., ii. 222.

till the day of his death." This statement conveys a wrong impression. "To see" is used in Hebrew for *to visit*, that is, *to go to see*,[1] as in 2 Sam. xiii. 5; 2 Kings viii. 29; 2 Chron. xxii. 6. Samuel went no more to see Saul; but the latter came to see *him*. Our version gives the true sense.

Saul's attendants heard the voice.	They heard it not.
Acts ix. 7.	Acts xxii. 9; xxvi. 14.

The Greek "akouo," like our word "hear," has two distinct meanings, *to perceive sound*, and *to understand*.[2] The men who were with Saul of Tarsus, heard the sound, but did not understand what was said to him. As to the fact that one passage represents them as "standing"; the other, as having "fallen to the earth," the word rendered "stood" also means *to be fixed, to be rooted to the spot*. Hence the sense may be, not that they stood erect, but that they were rendered *motionless*, or *fixed to the spot*, by overpowering fear. Or, perhaps, when the light with such exceeding brilliancy burst upon them, they all "fell to the earth," but afterward rose and "stood" upon their feet.[3]

Saul chosen king by lot.	Chosen by the Lord.	Demanded by people.
1 Sam. x. 20, 21.	1 Sam. ix. 17; x. 24.	1 Sam. viii. 19.

Here is no collision. The people persisted in demanding a king. God granted their request, and guided the lot in the choice of Saul to be king over Israel.[4]

Saul's death, — one manner.	A different manner.
1 Sam. xxxi. 3–5.	2 Sam. i. 6–10.

The latter statement is given as that of an "Amalekite," and is not vouched for by the sacred historian. It was doubtless colored by its author to suit the supposed occasion.

Saul inquired of the Lord.	Did not thus inquire.
1 Sam. xxviii. 6.	1 Chron. x. 14.

[1] See Gesenius, Hebrew Lexicon, p. 951, Rem. g.
[2] On use of ἀκούω with different cases, see Winer's Grammar of N. T. Idiom, pp. 199, 200 (Thayer's edition); also, Buttmann's Grammar, pp. 165, 166.
[3] Compare Hackett, Commentary on Acts ix. 7.
[4] Ewald's History of Israel, iii. 25.

It is sufficient to notice that two different Hebrew words of diverse meaning are employed here. Or, it may be correctly remarked that Saul's attempts at inquiry were of so unworthy a nature that it would be an abuse of language to speak of him as really "inquiring of Jehovah." As to the apparent conflict between 1 Sam. xiv. 18, 37 and 1 Chron. xiii. 3, relative to asking counsel at the ark of God, the latter passage, which denies this custom in the days of Saul, doubtless refers to the later years of that monarch, after he had slain the priests of the Lord, and sunk in the depths of sin and shame.

Saul's family died with him.   *Some of the family survived.*
1 Chron. x. 6.   2 Sam. ii. 8.

The expression "all his house," in the first text, is explained by "all his men," 1 Sam. xxxi. 6. Keil: "All those who were about the king, i.e. the whole of the king's attendants who had followed him to the war." Similarly Rawlinson. Fuerst gives *people, servants* among the significations of the Hebrew word "bayith," *house,* used in the first text.

Saul unacquainted with David.   *Knew him very well.*
1 Sam. xvii. 55-58.   1 Sam. xvi. 21-23.

The point of the difficulty is, How could Saul and Abner too be so ignorant in respect to one who had been armor-bearer and musician to Saul? Various solutions of this difficulty are given.

Some critics, Horsley, Townsend, Gray, and others, think that these passages are not chronologically arranged, and that verses 14-23 of chapter xvi. belong *between* verses 9 and 10 of chapter xviii. In the Vatican MS. of the Septuagint, chapters xvii. 12-31 and 55-xviii. 5 — twenty-nine verses in all — are *omitted.*[1] Houbigant, Kennicott,[2] Michaelis, Eichhorn, Dathe, and Bertheau, on this account, deem these verses "interpolations." But such critics as De Wette, Thenius, Ewald,[3]

---

[1] Davidson on Hebrew Text, pp. 57, 58.   [2] Dissertations, ii. 418-430
[3] History of Israel, iii., 71, note.

Bleek, Stähelin, Keil, and Davidson[1] reject this theory, and explain the passages in another manner.

As to Abner's ignorance of David, it is entirely conceivable that the former, as commander of Saul's army, and constantly busied with military affairs, may have known very little of David (who was probably with Saul only upon infrequent occasions),[2] and nothing whatever as to his family connections.

Saul's ignorance of the young hero may be accounted for upon some one or more of the following considerations:

1. Possible anticipation of events, or transposition of passages. Oriental historians sometimes pursue the leading idea of the narrative to its result, and then return to fill up the omitted details.[3] Hence, contemporaneous events *appear* consecutive.

2. Lapse of time, and consequent change in David's personal aspect. We do not know how much time intervened; and the change in Eastern youths with respect to physical development is very marked and sudden.[4]

3. Bustle of war and court life, with the multiplicity of Saul's servants and attendants. So Kalkar, Saurin, and others.

4. Diseased mental state of Saul. Persons suffering from mania or insanity often forget their nearest friends. So Abarbanel and Bertholdt.

5. Ignorance of Saul, not as to David himself, but as to his family,[5] of which, as we have seen, Abner might well be

---

[1] Introd. to Old Test., i. 530.
[2] See p. 331 infra, "David's detention."
[3] See Bible Commentary on 1 Sam. xvi. 21.
[4] Thomson (Land and Book, ii. 366, American edition), speaking of the sudden change of boys in such cases, says: "They not only spring into full-grown manhood as if by magic, but all their former beauty disappears; their complexion becomes dark; their features hard and angular, and the whole expression of countenance stern and even disagreeable. I have often been accosted by such persons, formerly intimate acquaintances, but who had suddenly grown entirely out of my knowledge, nor could I without difficulty recognize them." Mr. Thomson thinks that David, having returned to shepherd life, had probably undergone a change like that above described, hence was not recognized by Saul.
[5] So Kurtz in Herzog's Real-Encyklopädie, iii. 300.

ignorant. Kimchi thinks that Saul wished to know simply whether David's valor was hereditary, that, if so, his family might be "made free in Israel."[1]

As to the fact that David is represented as "a mighty, valiant man, and a man of war" (xvi. 18), but as a "stripling," a youth unaccustomed to arms (xvii. 39, 42, 56), it may be said that the first epithets may have been applied to David not because he had already fought bravely in war, but on account of the courage and strength displayed by him in killing the lion and the bear (xvii. 34–36), and which pointed him out as a future hero. On the other hand, the Hebrew term rendered "stripling" denotes, says Gesenius, "a youth, young man of marriageable age." Fuerst, "properly, a strong one."

Satan under restraint. *Suffered to roam at liberty.*
2 Pet. ii. 4; Jude vi.   Job i. 6, 7; 1 Pet. v. 8; Rev. xii. 12.

While the leader and some others of the fallen spirits are permitted to roam the earth, and to tempt mankind, the majority of these beings may be confined within the limits of their dark abode. Even those which are let loose have only a *restricted* liberty. Beyond certain environing lines they are not suffered to go; they are under strict surveillance — as we might express it by a borrowed figure, " bound over," or so secured that they cannot escape the judgment of the last day. Davidson[2] thinks that " chains of darkness " signify metaphorically *misery, obdurateness in wickedness,* and *despair.* A being may possess physical liberty, yet wear, at the same time, the heaviest mental and spiritual chains.

Solomon reduced Hebrews to bondage. *Did not enslave them.*
1 Kings v. 13, 15; xii. 4.   1 Kings ix. 22.

None of the Israelites were reduced to *actual slavery.* Nevertheless, Solomon's taxes and levies became very oppressive to the people in general. Enforced service, even though it be paid service, is commonly deemed distasteful and burdensome.

---

[1] See chap. xvii. 25.   [2] Introd. to New Test., iii. 438.

| *Zedekiah carried to Babylon.* | *Did not see Babylon.* |
| Jer. xxxiv. 3. | 2 Kings xxv. 7; Ezek. xii. 13. |

The first passage does not assert that Zedekiah should actually see Babylon, but that he should see its king, and go thither. The facts were these: The king of Babylon ordered the captive Zedekiah to be brought before him at his headquarters at Riblah. There, at the king's command, Zedekiah's eyes were put out, and he was bound with brazen fetters and carried to Babylon. Thus the above predictions were strictly fulfilled. Zedekiah saw the *king* of Babylon, but not the *city itself*, although he was carried thither and died there.

There are many other discrepancies of a transparent or trivial character, like the following cases: Israel's sight, Gen. xlviii. 8 and 10; Egyptians visible, Ex. xiv. 13 and 30; receivers of Moses' book, Deut. xxxi. 9 and 25, 26; reception of promises, Heb. xi. 13, 39, and 33; remover of stone, Gen. xxix. 2 and 4; speaker in a given case, Matt. xxi. 41 and Mark xii. 9; Luke xx. 16; survivors of Sennacherib's army, 2 Kings xix. 35. Now we cannot suppose that cases like these — founded as they are upon free and popular modes of thought and speech, common to all ages and countries — will furnish difficulty to persons possessed of *candor and common sense — two qualities which the Bible invariably demands and presupposes in its readers.*

II. CONCERNING PLACES.

| *Aaron died upon Mount Hor.* | *Died at Mosera.* |
| Num. xx. 27, 28; xxxiii. 38. | Deut. x. 6. |

Mosera or Moseroth was a station near to Mount Hor, and within sight of it. During the encampment of the Israelites at Mosera Aaron ascended the mountain and died. Prof. J. L. Porter [1] thinks Mosera was the general name of the district in which Mount Hor is situated.

---

[1] Kitto, iii. 221.

| *Abraham's destination Canaan.* | *Unknown to him.* |
| Gen. xii. 5. | Heb. xi. 8. |

At first, the *name* of the country was not revealed to him.[1] It is designated simply as a "land that I will show thee" (Gen. xii. 1). Even if the name "Canaan" had been mentioned to Abraham at the outset, it might still be true that he went forth "not knowing whither he went." For, in those days of slow transit, imperfect intercommunication, and meagre geographical knowledge, the mere name of a country several hundred miles distant would convey almost *no* idea of the country itself. In our own time, even, of how many an emigrant on his way to America it might well be said, "He knows not whither he is going."

| *Ahab slain at Jezreel.* | *Slain at Ramoth-gilead.* |
| 1 Kings xxi. 1, 19. | 1 Kings xxii. 37, 38. |

Gerlach, Keil, Rawlinson, and others think that the prediction was fulfilled, *in part* upon Ahab, whose blood was actually licked by the dogs, and *in part* upon his wicked son Jehoram, whose dead body was cast into the very plat of ground which had been Naboth's.[2] Bähr maintains that the word "place," in the passage at the right, is a general term, equivalent to "outside the city"; both Naboth and Ahab meeting their death in a certain "place," that is, *outside the walls of a city.*

| *Ahaz slept with his fathers.* | *Not in the royal sepulchres.* |
| 2 Kings xvi. 20. | 2 Chron. xxviii. 27. |

If Ahaz was buried *in close proximity to*, though not *in*, the royal sepulchres, the conditions of the case would be fully met.

Ahaziah died at Megiddo.	*Apparently elsewhere.*
But when Ahaziah the king of Judah saw *this*, he fled by the way of the garden-house. And Jehu followed after him, and said, Smite him also in the chariot. *And they did so* at the going up to Gur, which *is* by Ibleam. And he fled to Megiddo, and died there. 2 Kings ix. 27.	And he sought Ahaziah: and they caught him (for he was hid in Samaria), and brought him to Jehu: and when they had slain him, they buried him. 2 Chron. xxii. 9.

[1] Gen. xi. 31 merely shows that Abraham's destination was known to Moses writing at a later date. "Went forth to go," points to the *result* in the case.

[2] 2 Kings ix. 25, 26.

HISTORICAL DISCREPANCIES.

It is to be noticed that the second passage is very much condensed, and is supplementary to the other. The closing words, "and when they had slain him, they buried him," indirectly attribute the burial to Jehu's emissaries, inasmuch as they ordered, or at all events allowed, the burial, when they might have prevented it.[1]

Probably Ahaziah really escaped to Samaria, and concealed himself for a time, but was then ferreted out and captured by Jehu's soldiers, who brought him to their master. Attempting again to escape, he received a fatal wound at the pass of Gur near Ibleam, whence he fled to Megiddo, where he breathed his last. So Keil and Hackett.[2]

The passage at the left is elliptical, if not defective. Leaving out the words supplied by our translators, Jehu's injunction was, "Smite him also in the chariot at the going up to Gur, which is by Ibleam."[3] The passage then contains no mention of the fulfilment of the command, which must therefore be supplied from the parallel passage.

Amalekites were in the valley.	*They were on the hill.*
Num. xiv. 25.	Num. xiv. 45

The Hebrew word here rendered "valley" denotes "a broad sweep between hills."[4] In the present instance the valley itself is in one sense styled a "hill," because it lay on the top of the mountain-plateau or table-land where the conflict occurred. The Amalekites and Canaanites "came down" from the heights above to this plateau.

Ammonites' land not forfeited.	*Some of it given to Israelites.*
Deut. ii. 19.	Josh. xiii. 25.

The land which the Ammonites occupied in the days of Moses the Israelites were not permitted to appropriate. But the Amorites had, at some time in the past, overpowered the Ammonites, and wrested from them a large portion of their

---

[1] See 2 Kings ix. 28.
[2] Smith's Bible Dict., i. 48.
[3] Compare Bible Commentary on 2 Kings ix. 27.
[4] Stanley, Sinai and Palestine, under "emek," עֵמֶק, p. 476.

territory. This tract — Sihon being its king and Heshbon its capital — was reconquered, and (apparently with the tacit consent of the Ammonites) taken possession of by the Israelites.[1] It is this territory which is referred to in the passage from Joshua.

Ark placed in the midst of camp.   *In the van of the army.*
Num. ii. 17; x. 21.   Num. x. 33.

Rashi, Kimchi, and the Talmudists maintain that there were two arks — one made by Moses, carried in the van of the army, and afterwards captured by the Philistines; the other made by Bezaleel, which contained the tables of the law, and remained in the midst of the encampment.[2] Abarbanel, Nachmanides, and others hold that the one ark was generally placed in the midst of the encampment, but in exceptional cases, as during the three days' journey, and in the crossing of the Jordan,[3] was borne in advance of the host. Keil and Kurtz say that the ark, as distinguished from the sanctuary, always went foremost. Bishop Patrick thinks that the words "went before them" do not imply local precedence, but leadership; the expression being often applied to a general, who, of course, in leading his forces to battle, does not necessarily go *before them*, in the local sense.

Balaam returned to his place.   *He went instead to Midian.*
Num. xxiv. 25.   Num. xxxi. 8.

He set out upon his journey home, visiting Midian on the way. According to Hengstenberg,[4] Kurtz,[5] and Winer, the Hebrew word rendered "returned" means *to turn away*, or *to turn back;* and the attainment of the object is not included in the word itself. Hence we may read, with Keil, "went and turned towards his place."

---

[1] Ewald, History of Israel, ii. 204, 205, 295.
[2] Conciliator, i. 246, 247; Prideaux, Connections, i. 310, 311 (Charlestown, Mass. 1815).
[3] Josh. iii. 3–6.
[4] History of Balaam and his prophecies, pp. 508, 509.
[5] History of O. C., iii. 458.

HISTORICAL DISCREPANCIES.

Beasts slain at door of tabernacle.   *Slain elsewhere.*
     Lev. xvii. 3, 4.   Deut. xii. 15, 16.

The stringent law of Leviticus, designed to prevent the private and idolatrous rites to which the people were inclined is, now that they are about to enter Canaan, relaxed, so far as animals *intended simply for food* are concerned.

Bethsaida in one locality.   *In a different situation.*
     Mark vi. 32, 45, 53.   Luke ix. 10-17.

Reland and others have shown that there were *two* cities of this name, one on the eastern, the other on the western, shore of the Sea of Galilee.[1]

Benjamin born in Canaan.   *Born in Padan-aram.*
     Gen. xxxv. 16-19.   Gen. xxxv. 24-26.

Aben Ezra says that the latter passage speaks summarily. The author, writing in a condensed manner, took it for granted that his readers, acquainted with what he had written a few verses previously, would make the necessary exception here.

Canaan in a state of famine.   *Fruits not cut off.*
     Gen. xli. 56, 57; xlii. 1-5.   Gen. xliii. 11, 15.

To this discrepancy adduced by Von Bohlen, Kurtz[2] replies, "Only the cereal products of the land had suffered.... Fertility in fruit-trees does not depend on the same circumstances as that of grain crops."

Christ ascended at Bethany.   *At the mount called Olivet.*
     Luke xxiv. 50, 51.   Acts i. 9, 12.

Bethany lay on the eastern slope of Mount Olivet. Persons returning from Bethany to Jerusalem would pass over the top of Olivet, and hence might be said to "return from this mount."

Christ's first re-appearance in Galilee.   *At Jerusalem.*
     Matt. xxviii. 16, 17.   Luke xxiv. 33, 36; John xx. 19.

Matthew does not deny, but simply passes over, earlier appearances of our Lord, and dwells upon that in Galilee as

---

[1] See articles in Smith and Kitto; also, Thomson's Land and Book, ii. 9, 29-32; and Ebrard, Gospel History, p. 335, 336.

[2] History of Old Covenant, i. 376, 377.

being one of great importance. Then, probably, it was that the risen Saviour was "seen of above five hundred brethren at once."[1] This manifestation seems to have been our Lord's last great act in Galilee, his final interview with his disciples in that region.

Christ's first sermon on a mountain.   *In the plain.*
Matt. v. 1, 2.   Luke vi. 17, 20.

Mr. Greswell thinks that these passages refer to entirely different occasions. Stanley[2] says that the words in Luke should be rendered "a level place,"[3] and not "the plain." He describes a hill with flattened top, "suitable for the collection of a multitude," and having also two peaks (now called "the Horns of Hattin"), from one of which Christ "came down," and stood "upon the level place" to address the people.

Cities in the territory of Dan.   *Within that of Ephraim.*
Josh. xxi. 23, 24.   1 Chron. vi. 69.

In the opinion of Keil and Rawlinson, the Hebrew text of 1 Chron. vi. is defective, some words having dropped out between verses 68 and 69, through an oversight of copyists.

Cities pertained to Judah.   *Pertained to Dan.*
Josh. xv. 33; 1 Chron. ii. 53.   Josh. xix. 40, 41; Judg. xviii. 2, 8.

The explanation is, that the inheritance of Dan proving inadequate,[4] Judah gave up some of its northern towns, and Ephraim some of its southern towns, to the Danites, thus furnishing them with a territory proportionate to their number. Zorah and Eshtaol were among the towns relinquished by Judah, hence are spoken of sometimes as belonging to the latter tribe, and sometimes to Dan.[5] The statement in Judges xviii. 1, that "the inheritance of the Danites had not fallen unto them among the tribes of Israel," Cassel regards simply as a causeless complaint by the Danites, who had not sufficient enterprise to conquer the territory which had been assigned to them by lot. Bertheau,

---

[1] 1 Cor. xv. 6.   [2] Sinai and Palestine, p. 360.
[3] Greek ἐπὶ τόπου πεδινοῦ.   [4] Josh. xix. 47.
[5] Compare Keil on Josh. xix. 40–48.

Keil, Kimchi, and Rashi take the words as meaning, "no *adequate* inheritance."

The assignment of the same cities to Judah (Josh. xv. 26–32, 42), and to Simeon (Josh. xix. 2–7), is due to the simple fact that the inheritance of Simeon fell *within* that of Judah.[1] Differences in the names are due to copyists.

Country of the Gergesenes.	*Country of the Gadarenes.*
Matt. viii. 28.	Mark v. 1.

A general geographical designation applying to the territory in which Gadara and Gergesa were situated.[2]

David took Metheg-ammah.	*Captured Gath.*
2 Sam. viii. 1.	1 Chron. xviii. 1.

Fuerst and Gesenius interpret the first passage thus: "David took the bridle of the metropolis," that is, he subdued Gath the metropolis of the Philistines. Hävernick:[3] "David took the rein of dominion out of the hand of the Philistines." Ewald:[4] "Tore from the hand of the Philistines the bridle of the arm; that is, he tore from them the supremacy by which they curbed Israel, as a rider curbs his horse by the bridle, which the strength of his arm controls."

Disciples went into Galilee.	*Tarried in Jerusalem.*
Matt. xxviii. 10, 16.	Luke xxiv. 49.

The command "tarry ye in Jerusalem," etc., means simply, "Make Jerusalem your head-quarters. Do not leave it *to begin your work*, until ye be endued," etc. This injunction would not preclude a brief excursion to Galilee. Besides, the command may not have been given until *after* the visit to Galilee. Alford adopts the latter hypothesis.

Ephraim's land east of Jordan.	*West of Jordan.*
2 Sam. xviii. 6.	Josh. xvii. 15–18.

Blunt, Ewald,[5] Hervey, and Stanley[6] think that "the wood

---

[1] Josh. xix. 1, 9.
[2] See Smith's Bible Dict., Art. "Gadara." Some of the best critics, Tischendorf, Tregelles, etc., give a different reading in the first passage, agreeing with that of the second.
[3] Introd. to Old Test., p. 208. [4] Vol. iii. 148.
[5] Vol. ii. 321, 322; iii. 186, note. [6] Sinai and Palestine, pp. 322, 323.

of Ephraim" (2 Sam. xviii. 6), was not within the territory of that tribe, but was on the eastern side of Jordan. This forest probably derived its name from the slaughter of the Ephraimites long before in that vicinity.[1]

Forces stationed in certain places.	In different places.
2 Kings xi. 5-7.	2 Chron. xxiii. 4, 5.

From the fact that the young king spent six years in the house of the Lord, it is designated as "the king's house."[2] Keil maintains that the forces under the command of the centurions who occupied the various posts in the temple consisted partly of Levitic temple-guards, and partly of royal body-guards. In Kings the latter class, in Chronicles the former class, come prominently into view. The posts or stations of the forces agree well. One division was to be " at the gate of Sur " (Kings), " at the gate of the foundation " (Chronicles) ; a second was to be " keepers of the watch of the king's house " (Kings), " at the king's house " (Chronicles) ; a third was to be " at the gate behind the guard " (Kings), " porters of the doors," better " watchers of the thresholds " (Chronicles). Here is no discrepancy.

Goliath's armor put in David's tent.	Carried to Nob.
1 Sam. xvii. 54.	1 Sam. xxi. 9.

The first passage does not assert that David *kept* it in his tent. During the interval, he or some one carried the sword to Nob.

Goliath's head carried to Jerusalem.	That city held by Jebusites.
1 Sam. xvii. 54.	2 Sam. v. 6, 9.

To the "discrepancy" which De Wette[3] sees here, Ewald[4] answers, that clearly David did not carry the head to Jerusalem till afterwards, when he was king. Then, as we learn from the passage at the right, he captured that city.

Gospel to be preached everywhere.	Not to be preached in Asia.
Matt. xxviii. 19.	Acts xvi. 6.

For wise reasons, and *for a brief time only*, Paul was not

---

[1] See Judg. xii. 1-6.
[2] See 2 Kings xi. 3-5.
[3] Introd. to Old Test., ii. 216.
[4] History of Israel, iii. 72.

allowed to preach in Asia. When the fitting time arrived, the prohibition was removed.

Halting-places of Israelites, — names.   *Stated differently.*
Num. xxxiii. 44–49.   Num. xxi. 10–20.

We have previously seen [1] that the Israelites, during a large portion of the thirty-eight years were comparatively stationary, or as nearly so as tribes of nomadic habits could well be; and that they doubtless were spread over a large extent of territory, in quest of water and pasturage for their flocks and herds. Prof. Porter [2] has more than once passed through a moving tribe of Arabs, spreading over a tract *twenty miles in diameter*. We doubt not that the Israelites covered a vastly larger territory; and that when they moved, it was, as Prof. Palmer [3] says, " in Bedawîn order, subdivided into numerous encampments, and spread over an immense surface of country."

Many critics agree with Kurtz [4] that the stations mentioned in Num. xxxiii. 19–36 are simply the places successively occupied as *the head-quarters of Moses and the tabernacle*. " It was absolutely necessary that the scattered parties of Israelites should be visited by Moses and the sanctuary, to prevent their connection with one another, and more especially their connection with Moses and the sanctuary, being entirely dissolved during so long a period as thirty-seven years. Hence the stations named in Num. xxxiii. 19–36 must be regarded in the light of a circuit, which was made through the desert by Moses and the tabernacle." Prof. J. L. Porter,[5] Dieterici,[6] Davidson,[7] and Messrs. Espin [8] and Cook take a similar view. Dr. Robinson [9] also maintains that " the stations as enumerated refer to the headquarters of Moses and the elders, with a portion of the people who kept near them; while other portions preceded or followed

---

[1] See p. 342 infra.   [2] Kitto's Cyclopedia, iii. 1075.
[3] Desert of Exodus, p. 433.   [4] History of Old Covenant, iii. 301.
[5] Kitto, iii. 1079.   [6] See in Kurtz, iii. 90.
[7] Introd. to Old Test., i. 326, 327.   [8] Bible Commentary, i. 654, 720.
[9] Bib. Researches, i. 106 (1st edition).

them at various distances as the convenience of water and pasturage might dictate." Prof. Porter thinks that the number of "marshalled men" who constantly attended Moses was not more than one tenth of the whole.

The differences between the lists of stations above arose from the fact that the same station had several names, or that two contiguous stations were occupied at the same time;[1] or, as Kurtz[2] thinks, that the object in the thirty-third chapter is a *statistical* one, that is, to set forth not all the halting-places, but merely the places where a regular camp was formed and the sanctuary erected, while in earlier passages the object is a *historical* one, hence more places are enumerated. Hence, Num. xxi. 11—xxii. 1, *seven* places are mentioned between Ije-abarim and the plains of Moab; in Num. xxxiii. 44–48, only *three* places.

In Num. xxxiii. 30–33, we find the names Moseroth, Bene-jaakan, Hor-hagidgad, and Jotbathah; in Deut. x. 6, 7 they stand thus: Beeroth[3] Bene-jaakan, Mosera, Gudgodah, and Jotbath. As to the trivial variations of the names, nothing need be said. The latter passage, which puts Bene-jaakan *before* Mosera, probably refers to a second visit of the Israelites to these places, in the fortieth year of the wandering. The first time, they pursued a circuitous course; the second time, the shortest and most direct route, thus reversing the order of the two places named.[4]

The "wilderness of Paran," Num. x. 12 and xii. 16, is probably mentioned in the first of these texts by anticipation. Ranke says: "Before entering more minutely into the details of the march, which he does from x. 33 onwards, the author mentions at the very outset (x. 12) the ultimate destination, viz. Paran, on the borders of the promised land." So Tuch and Hengstenberg.

---

[1] So Davidson, i. 326, and Keil on Num. xxi. 16–20.
[2] History of Old Covenant, iii. 384.
[3] That is, "wells of Bene-jaakan" = Bene-jaakan in the other passage.
[4] See Hengstenberg, Gen. of Pent. ii. 355–357; Kurtz, Hist. of Old Cov., iii. 254, 255.

Kurtz[1] thinks that x. 12 names the most southerly, and xii. 16 the most northerly, station in the wilderness of Paran.

The fact that different names were applied to the same localities explains such cases as the following: Israelites' station in wilderness of Kedemoth, Deut. ii. 26; on Pisgah, Num. xxi. 20, 21. Moses' outlook, from Abarim, Num. xxvii. 12; from Pisgah, Deut. iii. 27; from Nebo, Deut. xxxiv. 1. Simeon's cities and towns, one list, Josh. xix. 2–6; a varying list, 1 Chron. iv. 28–31. Also, Abel-beth-maachah, 1 Kings xv. 20; Abel-maim, 2 Chron. xvi. 4. Gezer, 1 Chron. xx. 4; Gob, 2 Sam. xxi. 18, with a multitude of similar cases.

Kadesh is said to have been located in the wilderness of Paran, Num. xiii. 26; in the desert or wilderness of Zin, Num. xx. 1; Deut. xxxii. 51. With respect to this point there are several hypotheses.

1. That there were two places named Kadesh, situated, respectively, as above. So Reland, Rabbi Schwarz, and Stanley[2] qualifiedly. The term "Kadesh," which denotes "holy place," may well have been applied to several localities.

2. That the name was applied both to a certain city and to an extensive region in which this city lay. So Prof. Palmer,[3] Mr. Hayman,[4] and others.

3. That the one city Kadesh was situated in such relation to the deserts of Paran and Zin that it might be popularly assigned to either. It may have been located upon the dividing line of the two deserts, or, if they overlapped, in the territory common to them both.[5] It is the opinion of Fries, Hengstenberg, Keil, Kurtz, Raumer, Robinson, and others that the Israelites were *twice* at Kadesh — once in the second year, and again in the fortieth year of their wanderings.[6] Ewald thinks that "Kadesh

---

[1] See authorities cited, History of Old Covenant, iii. 220.
[2] Sinai and Palestine, pp. 93, 94, notes.
[3] Desert of Exodus, p. 420.
[4] Smith's Bible Dict., ii. 1519.
[5] See Smith's Bible Dict., Art. "Paran."
[6] Kurtz iii. 246, 247, 305–309.

was only the resting-place of Moses and the tabernacle, and the meeting-place of the community on appointed days."

As to the location of Meribah, near Rephidim, Ex. xvii. 1-7; near Kadesh, Num. xx. 13, we know that on two distinct occasions the Israelites rebelled for want of water. Hence both localities were appropriately named " Meribah " (strife).[1] On the second occasion Moses and Aaron transgressed, and offended Jehovah.

Israel's boundary the Euphrates.   *A different limit.*
Gen. xv. 18; Deut. xi. 24; 2 Sam.viii. 3.   Num. xxxiv. 10-12; Josh. xiii.9-12.

Keil suggests that these different passages give the limits — the *maxima* and *minima* — of the promise; the actual extent to be determined by, and proportionate to, Israel's loyalty and fidelity to God. It is thought by Ewald,[2] Hervey, and Newman[3] that "his border," in 2 Sam. viii. 3, refers not to David's border, but to that of his opponent.

Israelites returned to Gilgal.   *Returned to Makkedah.*
Josh. x. 15, 43.   Josh. x. 21.

Davidson, Espin, Hengstenberg, Keil, and others take the fifteenth verse as a part of the quotation from the "book of Jasher," — the citation beginning with the twelfth, and ending with the fifteenth verse. The return to the temporary camp at Makkedah preceded that to Gilgal.

Jehoiakim carried to Babylon.   *Died at Jerusalem.*

Against him came up Nebuchadnezzar king of Babylon, and bound him in fetters, to carry him to Babylon. 2 Chron. xxxvi. 6.

So Jehoiakim slept with his fathers. 2 Kings xxiv. 6.
He shall be buried with the burial of an ass, drawn and cast forth beyond the gates of Jerusalem. Jer. xxii. 19.
His dead body shall be cast out in the day to the heat, and in the night to the frost. Jer. xxxvi. 30.

Bertheau, Hasse, and Movers think that the Hebrew of the first passage implies that Jehoiakim was not actually carried to Babylon. Bleek[4] pertinently suggests that he may have gone out against the enemy, and been slain outside the city. Rawlinson supposes that he was bound with the intention of

---

[1] See Kitto, iii. 138.   [2] History of Israel, iii. 150, note.
[3] History of Hebrew Monarchy, p. 80.   [4] Introd. to Old Test., ii. 72, 73.

carrying him to Babylon, but instead was slain, and his corpse ignominiously treated. After the withdrawal of the Babylonians the remains were collected and interred in the royal burial-place, so that, ultimately, the unhappy prince "slept with his fathers." Winer[1] thinks that, at the capture of Jerusalem in the next reign, the enemy, or even his former subjects, may have vented their rage upon the remains of the deceased Jehoiakim in the manner above described. Wordsworth[2] calls attention to the fact that, of all the kings of Judah whose deaths are spoken of in scripture, Jehoiakim is the only one whose *burial* is not mentioned.

Jeroboam's residence Shechem.	*He resided at Tirzah.*
1 Kings xii. 25.	1 Kings xiv. 12–17.

He lived at one place in the early, at the other in the later, part of his reign. Bähr suggests that Tirzah may have been merely a summer residence of this monarch.

Jerusalem in Judah.	*In land of Benjamin*
Josh. xv. 8.	Josh. xviii. 28.

The city was actually within the limits of the territory of Benjamin, yet on the very border line of Judah,[3] so that it might be popularly assigned to either tribe. Stanley,[4] indeed, maintains that the Jebusite fortress stood upon "neutral ground in the very meeting-point of the two tribes"; and Lightfoot[5] mentions a Jewish tradition that the altars and sanctuary were in Benjamin, the courts of the temple in Judah.

Jordan, — *"this side," east of river.*   *Phrase denotes west of river.*
Num. xxxv.14; Deut. i.1; Josh. i.14.   Josh. xii.7; xxii.7; 1Chron. xxvi. 30.

The expression "this side Jordan," like its Hebrew equivalent,[6] is ambiguous, and may denote *either* side of that river, according to the *mental stand-point* which the sacred historian occupies at the time of writing. So Fuerst, Gesenius, and others.

---

[1] Real-Wörterbuch, i. 595.   [2] Replies to Essays and Reviews, p. 434.
[3] Smith's Bible Dict, ii. 1273.   [4] Sinai and Palestine, p 175.
[5] Prospect of Temple, chap. 1.   [6] See different senses, Num. xxxii.19, 32.

Joshua conquered all Canaan.	*Conquered only a part.*
Josh. xi. 16, 17, 23; xii. 7, 8; xxi. 43.	Josh. xiii. 1–6; Judg. ii. 23.

The solution appears to be that Joshua had *virtually* conquered the whole land. He had so thoroughly broken the power of the Canaanites that they could no longer make head against him. The land was now *within the grasp* of the Israelites. All they needed to do was to go forward valiantly, and *occupy* it. But, through indolence and unbelief, they did not avail themselves fully of that dominion which was within their reach.

Josiah died at Megiddo.	*Died at Jerusalem.*
And his servants carried him in a chariot dead from Megiddo, and brought him to Jerusalem, and buried him in his own sepulchre. 2 Kings xxiii. 30.	And they brought him to Jerusalem, and he died, and was buried in *one of* the sepulchres of his fathers. 2 Chron. xxxv. 24.

Davidson,[1] Fuerst, Gesenius, and Rawlinson agree that the word "mēth," in the first text, may mean *dying,* or *in a dying state.*[2] Josiah was carried off the field in a dying condition; he expired on the way to Jerusalem.[3]

Law given at Sinai.	*Given in Horeb.*
Ex. xix. 11, 18.	Deut. iv. 10–15.

1. Sinai may be the older, and Horeb the later name. So Davidson, Stanley [4] apparently, and Ewald.[5]

2. Horeb may be a general name of the district or range of mountains, and Sinai the specific name of some peak. So Hengstenberg,[6] Robinson, Palmer,[7] Rödiger, Ritter, Kurtz, Dr. J. P. Thompson,[8] and others.

3. Sinai may be taken as the original name of the entire group, whilst Horeb is restricted to one particular mountain. Gesenius takes this view; and Lepsius thinks that the two names are applied alike to the mountain of the law. Any one of these hypotheses relieves the difficulty completely.

---

[1] Sacred Hermeneut., p. 551.
[2] See use in Gen. xx. 3.
[3] Compare Zech. xii. 11.
[4] Sinai and Palestine, 31, note.
[5] History of Israel, ii. 43, note.
[6] Gen. of Pent., ii. 327.
[7] Desert of Exodus, p. 103.
[8] Smith's Bible Dict., iv. 3054.

HISTORICAL DISCREPANCIES. 377

Moses commissioned in Midian.   *Received commission in Egypt.*
   Ex. iii. 10; iv. 19.   Ex. vi. 10–13.

His failure to persuade Pharaoh to a dismission of the Israelites, as well as the sudden revulsion, on their part, from buoyant hope to unseemly dejection, rendered it absolutely necessary that Moses' wavering faith should be strengthened by a solemn renewal of his commission.

Nebuchadnezzar encamped at Riblah.   *Came against Jerusalem.*
   2 Kings xxv. 6.   2 Kings xxv. 1.

The expression "came against" does not imply that he came *to* the city in person. He sent his army to besiege the city; but he himself made his head-quarters at Riblah, from which place he could conveniently direct hostile operations against Jerusalem and Tyre, both of which cities he was besieging at the time.

Passover slain at home.   *Slain at sanctuary.*
   Ex. xii. 7.   Deut. xvi. 1–7.

The first precept was addressed to the Israelites in Egypt, when they had "no common altar" nor sanctuary; hence the houses in which they dwelt were, so to speak, consecrated as altars and sanctuaries. The second passage contemplates them as settled in Palestine, where they had a common sanctuary, around which it was desirable that their religious sentiments, services, and associations should be clustered. Kurtz[1] thinks that the words "in the place which the Lord thy God shall choose"[2] include the whole city in which the tabernacle was located; so that the passover might be slain upon any spot within that city.

Peter's residence Capernaum.   *Apparently Bethsaida.*
   Mark i. 21, 29.   John i. 44.

Peter and his brother were "of Bethsaida," in that they were *natives* of that city; yet they afterward *dwelt* in Capernaum.

Sanctuary at Shiloh.   *Located at Shechem.*
   Josh. xviii. 1; 1 Sam. iii. 21; iv. 3.   Josh. xxiv. 1, 26.

Masius, Michaelis, and other critics say that "miqdäsh,"

[1] History of Old Covenant, iii. 213.   [2] In Deut. xvi. 7.

sanctuary, in the last text, denotes simply the holy place which Abraham consecrated,[1] and in which Jacob dwelt a long time, and where he purified his family from idolatry.[2] This place, however, was different from the "sanctuary" proper, where the ark had its seat. Hengstenberg[3] has clearly shown that the phrase "before God" does not invariably imply the presence of the sacred ark or tabernacle.

Solomon's ships went to Ophir.   *They went to Tarshish.*
1 Kings ix. 26–28.   1 Kings x. 22; 2 Chron. ix. 21.

Rawlinson thinks that different fleets are intended; also that the name "Tarshish" was applied to two different places, one of which was situated on the shores of the Indian Ocean or the Persian Gulf, since the Phoenicians had trading establishments in this quarter, and were in the habit of repeating their local names. Hence this name, like our term "Indies," may have been applied to places widely separated. It was to this eastern Tarshish, and not to that in Spain, that Solomon's fleet made the triennial voyage.[4]

Bähr, Bleek,[5] Davidson,[6] DeWette, Ewald, Gesenius, Hävernick, Movers, Winer, and Mr. Twistleton,[7] however, take the expression "ships of Tarshish," not as denoting that these vessels actually went to Tarshish, but that they were of the kind ordinarily employed in commerce with that place. That is, "Tarshish-ships," like our term "East-Indiamen," would loosely indicate the larger class of merchant vessels. On this hypothesis, the chronicler[8] misunderstood the appellation, as if it denoted that these ships actually went to Tarshish.

Tabernacle located without the camp.   *Within the camp.*
Num. xi. 16, 24–26; xii. 4.   Num. ii. 2, 3.

The encampment of the Israelites was arranged in the form of a hollow square, with a large unoccupied space in the middle.

[1] See Gen. xii. 6, 7.
[2] Gen. xxxiii. 19; xxxv. 2, 4
[3] Gen. of Pent. ii. 32–46.
[4] 1 Kings x. 22.
[5] Introd. to Old Test., i. 441.
[6] Introd. to Old Test., ii. 90.
[7] Smith's Bible Dict., iv. 3178–3181. See references, p. 3180.
[8] 2 Chron. ix. 21; xx. 36, 37.

HISTORICAL DISCREPANCIES.

At the centre of this space the tabernacle was located; being thus, as is thought, some two thousand cubits removed, on all sides, from the tents of the people. In consequence of this isolation of the tabernacle, those who visited it were necessitated, as it were, to leave the encampment, and "go out" to the tabernacle. The latter was *within*, yet virtually *outside of* the camp.

A recent writer[1] finds, in 1 Kings xix. 3, 8, a "geographical anomaly," in that, as he thinks, "Elijah is represented as travelling uninterruptedly *forty days and forty nights* from Beersheba to Horeb; whereas the distance is little more than forty geographical miles." To which we reply: (1) That, according to the best maps, such as those of Kiepert, and Smith and Grove, the distance is some *two hundred* statute miles; and (2) that there is no intimation that Elijah was walking the whole time, neither that he pursued a straight course in his wanderings.

The same author[2] finds a similar difficulty in 1 Sam. x. 1–9, where, as he maintains, Saul went first to Rachel's sepulchre, near Bethlehem, and thence to (Mount) Tabor in Zebulon, across the territory of four tribes, making the whole circuit in a single day. But the Hebrew "ēlon täbor," rendered *plain of Tabor* in vs. 3, means, according to Fuerst, Gesenius, and the Septuagint, *oak of Tabor*. Keil and Ewald[3] say, the "terebinth of Tabor"; the latter adding that "Tabor" is certainly only "a dialectic variation" for "Deborah," and, with Thenius, maintaining that the tree in question was that under which Deborah was buried.[4] There is not the least proof that Mount Tabor is here intended.

---

[1] See in Davidson's Introd. to Old Test., ii. 36, 37.
[2] In Davidson, Vol. i. 515.
[3] History of Israel, iii. 21, and note.
[4] Gen. xxxv. 8.

III. CONCERNING NUMBERS.

We have previously, more than once, called attention to the marked resemblance of Hebrew letters to one another;[1] also, to the fact, generally conceded by scholars, that these letters were in ancient time employed to represent numbers.[2] These two facts indicate at once the *cause* and the *solution* of the numerical discrepancies of scripture. For, when ב denotes 2; כ, 20; נ, 50; and פ, 80; when ד stands for 4, ה for 4000, ר for 200, and ת for 400, mistakes in numbers, especially when the numeral letters were blurred or unskilfully written, would be *inevitable*. But, as elsewhere intimated, these mistakes, which we find in considerable numbers, touch no vital point of scripture. No precept, promise, or doctrine is in the least degree impaired by them; nor do they militate against any well-balanced theory of inspiration. That the larger part of the following cases arose through the mistakes of copyists we have not a shadow of doubt; yet, since other solutions have been given in most cases, they will be adduced when it seems worth while.

Abraham's only son Isaac.	*Had several sons.*
Gen. xxii. 2; Heb. xi. 17.	Gen. xxv. 6.

Isaac was Abraham's "only son" by Sarah, as well as the only one in the line of promise — the theocratic line. Or the term may be equivalent to "*beloved* son." Josephus[3] employs the term "monogenes," *only-begotten*, in this latter sense.

Absalom had three sons.	*He had no sons.*
2 Sam. xiv. 27.	2 Sam. xviii. 18.

Previous to the time referred to in the latter text, his three sons had died.

Arah's sons seven hundred seventy-five.	*Six hundred and fifty-two.*
Ezra ii. 5.	Neh. vii. 10.

Most probably the difference is due to copyists' blunders.

---

[1] See pp. 20, 312, 313, infra.   [2] See pp. 21–24, infra.
[3] See Antiq. i. 13, 1, and xx. 2, 1.

HISTORICAL DISCREPANCIES. 381

The other cases, some twenty in number, which appear from a comparison of Ezra ii. 6–65, with Neh. vii. 11–67, are to be explained in the same manner.[1] The "gifts" of the people, as set down by the two writers, vary as follows:

Ezra, ii. 69.	Nehemiah, vii. 70–72.
Gold, 61000 drams (a copyist's mistake).	Gold, from Tirshatha, 1,000 drams " from chief fathers, 20,000 " " people, 20,000 " 41,000
Silver, 5000 lbs. (a round number).	Silver, from Tirshatha, 500 lbs " chief fathers, 2,200 " " people, 2,000 " 4,700 "
Garments, 100 (a round number).	Garments, given by Tirshatha, 30 " people, 67 97

Keil and Bertheau think that, in the seventieth verse from Nehemiah, the Hebrew for *pounds of silver* has dropped out, so that, as assumed in the above reckoning, the passage would stand, "five hundred pounds of silver and thirty priests' garments."

Alting points out the fact that Ezra's sum total is 29818; Nehemiah's, 31089; and that the latter mentions 1765 persons, and the former 494 persons, omitted in the parallel record. It is a curious coincidence that Ezra's sum total added to Nehemiah's surplus is just equal to the latter's sum total added to the former's surplus. That is, $29818 + 1765 = 31089 + 494 = 31583$. If from the whole amount, 42360, given by both authors, we deduct 31583, the remainder will be 10777; "omitted," says Davidson,[2] following Alting, "because they did not belong to Judah and Benjamin, or to the priests, but to the other tribes."

Ambuscade, thirty thousand men.	Five thousand men.
Josh. viii. 3–9.	Josh. viii. 12.

The Jewish interpreters[3] maintain that there were *two* ambuscades. The twelfth and thirteenth verses are not found in the

---

[1] See lists in Keil's Commentary; also, in De Wette, Introd. to Old Test., ii. 331, 332. Compare Bib. Comment. in loc.

[2] Sacred Hermeneutics, p. 554.

[3] Conciliator, ii. 11.

Septuagint;[1] hence, some critics regard them as a marginal note which has crept into the text. The best explanation is, that the copyist wrote, by mistake, in the third verse, ל, 30000, for ה, 5000.

Upon the same hypothesis, that of the confounding of similar numeral letters, may be explained all such cases as the following: Chapter's length, 5 cubits, 1 Kings vii. 16; 3 cubits, 2 Kings xxv. 17. Deaths by plague, 24000, Num. xxv. 9; 23000, 1 Cor. x. 8 (Paul[2] *may* have intended to include only those who fell "in one day"). Edomites slain, 18000, 2 Sam. viii. 13 and 1 Chron. xviii. 12; 12000,[3] Ps. lx. title (the slaughter is attributed to king David, to his general-in-chief, and to a subordinate, according to a common figure of speech). Foreskins, 200, 1 Sam. xviii. 25, 27; 100, 2 Sam. iii. 14. Horsemen, 700, 2 Sam. viii. 4; 7000, 1 Chron. xviii. 4 (Nun final, ן, mistaken for dotted Zayin, ז̇).[4] Horsemen 40000, and chariots 700, 2 Sam. x. 18; footmen 40000, and chariots 7000, 1 Chron. xix. 18 (Keil: It is very evident that there are copyist's errors in both texts). House and porch, — height, 30 cubits, 1 Kings vi. 2; 120 cubits, 2 Chron. iii. 4. Levites, — number, 22000, Num. iii. 39; 23000, Num. xxvi. 62 (the 1000 excess may have been the increase during the interval). Molten sea held 2000 baths, 1 Kings vii. 26; 3000 baths, 2 Chron. iv. 5 (the Hebrew verb rendered "contained" and "held" is different from that translated "received"; and the meaning may be that the sea ordinarily contained 2000, but when filled to its utmost capacity received and held 3000 baths.[5] Or, with Bähr and Keil, we may say that ב, 2000, has been confounded with ג, 3000). Officers, — chief, 550, 1 Kings ix. 23; 250, 2 Chron. viii. 10. Overseers, 3300, 1 Kings v. 16; 3600, 2 Chron. ii.

---

[1] Davidson, on Hebrew Text, p. 44.
[2] Ewald (ii. 181, note), deems it "a slight slip" of Paul's pen.
[3] Ewald says (iii. 157, note), "a clerical error."
[4] Davidson, Sacred Hermeneutics, p. 544.
[5] So Rawlinson; also, Taylor's Calmet.

HISTORICAL DISCREPANCIES.

18 (the *sum* of the officers and overseers is the same, 3850, in each case. In Kings *authority*, in Chronicles *nationality*, seems the principle of division).[1] Pillars' length, 18 cubits, 1 Kings vii. 15; 35 cubits, 2 Chron. iii. 15 (possibly the two were cast in one piece 35 cubits long, which, cut in two, made two pillars, in round numbers 18 cubits long).[2] Pomegranates, 200, 1 Kings vii. 20; 400, 1 Kings vii. 42 and 2 Chron. iv. 13; 100, Jer. lii. 23; 96 on a side, Jer. lii. 23 (if the two pillars had each two rows, with 100 pomegranates in a row, the first three numbers are accounted for. Bähr and Rawlinson think that 96 faced the cardinal points, while the other four were placed at the angles). Persons slain, 800, 2 Sam. xxiii. 8; 300, 1 Chron. xi. 11 (ש, the initial letter of the Hebrew words for *three* and *eight*, being used as an abbreviation, a mistake arose).[3] Persons slain, 5, 2 Kings, xxv. 19; 7, Jer. lii. 25 (ה, 5, confounded with ז, 7). Stalls, 40000, 1 Kings iv. 26; 4000, 2 Chron. ix. 25 (Ewald[4]: Hebrew terms for *four* and *forty* confounded). Talents, 420, 1 Kings ix. 28; 450, 2 Chron. viii. 18 (כ, 20, confounded with נ, 50). Temple's length, 40 cubits, 1 Kings vi. 17; 60 cubits, 1 Kings vi. 2 (the whole temple, exclusive of the porch, was 60 cubits long, vs. 2; the sanctuary 20 cubits, vs. 16; hence the temple *par excellence* was 40 cubits in length). Temple vessels, 2499, Ezra i. 9, 10; 5400, Ezra i. 11 (ancient interpreters maintain that, in the first two verses, only the larger and more valuable articles are specified; while the sum total, in vs. 11, includes the greater and the less together).[5] In all these cases the hypothesis of copyist's errors affords a very facile and reasonable explanation.

[1] See Bib. Com. on 1 Kings v. 16.
[2] Davidson, Sacred Hermeneutics, pp. 548, 549.
[3] Kennicott, Dissertations, i. 95, 96.
[4] History of Israel, iii. 170, note. See another solution, Davidson's Sacred Hermeneutics, p. 548.
[5] Keil, Commentary in loc.

Animals employed, — one.	More than one.
Mark xi. 7.	Matt. xxi. 5, 7.

To this objection of Strauss, Davidson[1] replies that "kai," in the last clause of the fifth verse, is exegetical, and should be rendered *even*. Hence the passage would read, "upon an ass, *even* a colt," etc.

As to the fact that the seventh verse seems to represent Christ as riding upon *both* animals, Winer[2] notes that by a vague idiom the "plural of class" is often put for the singular; as when we say, *He sprang from the horses*, though only one of the team, the saddled horse, is meant. Upon this idiomatic use of the plural instead of the singular may be explained the following cases: Jacob's daughters, Gen. xlvi. 7 and 15. Reviling malefactors, Matt. xxvii. 44 and Luke xxiii. 39–41 (Chrysostom, Jerome, Theophylact, and others say that at first *both* malefactors reviled our Lord, but that later one repented).[3] Tables of shew-bread, 1 Kings vii. 48 and 2 Chron. iv. 19.

Animals sacrificed, thirteen.	Eleven only.
Lev. xxiii. 18, 19.	Num. xxviii. 27, 30.

Jewish interpreters in the Mishna and Gemara,[4] as well as Josephus, Keil, Kurtz, and others,[5] maintain that the offerings mentioned in Numbers are *additional* to those prescribed in Leviticus. The former were to be offered *before* the latter, and subsequent to the daily morning sacrifice. As the passages refer respectively to different points of time, there is no collision. Upon the same theory of reference to different occasions or times, we may readily solve cases like the following: Benjamin's sons, Gen. xlvi. 21, and Num. xxvi. 38, 40; 1 Chron. vii. 6 (the same individual may have borne different names; and, during the interval between the epochs referred to, some of the sons may have died).[6] Captives, 2 Kings xxiv. 14, 16

---

[1] Introd. to New Test., i. 86. [2] Grammar of New Test. Idiom, p. 175.
[3] Davidson's Sacred Hermeneutics, p. 562. [4] Conciliator, i. 233.
[5] See Bible Commentary on Lev. xxiii.
[6] Davidson, Introd. to Old Test., ii. 50, says these accounts must "relate to different periods of time, and different branches of the same line."

HISTORICAL DISCREPANCIES. 385

and Jer. lii. 28-30 (here may be a numerical error, or the 10000 in Kings may have included not only the 4600 of Jeremiah, but also those captured on certain other occasions). Cities of refuge, Num. xxxv. 13; Josh. xx. 7, 8 and Deut. iv. 41 (Moses himself appointed three cities, and Joshua subsequently confirmed this appointment, and added three more cities). Heads of people, Ezra ii. 3-35 and Neh. x. 14-27 (Davidson[1]: "The number had increased in the interval between Zerubbabel and Nehemiah"). Jair's cities, Judg. x. 4 and Josh. xiii. 30; 1 Chron. ii. 22, 23 (these passages refer to different times. Rawlinson suggests that, as the "Havoth" were properly "villages" or "small hamlets," it might be difficult to fix their number exactly. According to Keil and Bertheau,[2] Kenath and her daughter-towns, thirty-seven in number, are included by the chronicler among Jair's cities, thus making the number "sixty"). Jeduthun's sons, 1 Chron. xxv. 3. Jesse's sons, 1 Sam. xvi. 6-11; and 1 Chron. ii. 13-15 (the later writer omits the sons who died early). Michal's sons, 2 Sam. xxi. 8 and vi. 23 ("Had no child unto the day of her death" may mean simply "had no child henceforward." Ewald[3] and De Wette[4] say, with the greatest probability, that *Michal*, in the first passage, is a copyist's mistake for *Merab*). Ransom, Ex. xxx. 13 and Neh. x. 32 (the first was a census tax; the latter, an annual tax). Shemaiah's sons, 1 Chron. iii. 22 (Jewish critics say that one son died in infancy). Simeonites, Num. i. 23 and Num. xxvi. 14 (here may be a numerical error; or, since Zimri, one of the ringleaders, was a Simeonite, the 24000 who died in the matter of Baal-Peor[5] may have belonged chiefly to the tribe of Simeon; hence its remarkable diminution). Solomon's gifts to Hiram, 1 Kings v. 11 and 2 Chron. ii. 10 (Davidson[6]: The first passage specifies

---

[1] Introd. to Old Test., ii. 139. [2] Die Bücher der Chronik, pp. 16, 17.
[3] Vol. iii. 74, note; also p. 136. [4] Introd. to Old Test., ii. 219.
[5] Num. xxv. 6-14. [6] Sacred Hermeneutics, p. 548.

the articles intended for Hiram's household; the second, those for his workmen).

Angels seen, one seated.	Two standing.	Two seated.
Matt. xxviii. 2, 5; Mark xvi. 5.	Luke xxiv. 4.	John xx. 12.

Ebrard,[1] with other critics, has made it clear that these passages relate to different persons and times. This point will be considered hereafter. One angel appeared at a given time; two appeared at another time. The position assumed, also, may have varied at different times. Yet the Greek word in Luke, rendered "stood by," also means *to come near, to appear to*. In Luke ii. 9; Acts xii. 7, it is translated, "came upon"; hence, in the text in question, the sense may be, "suddenly appeared to them."

Appearances of Christ, — one number.	Different numbers.
John xx. and xxi.	Luke xxiv.; 1 Cor. xv. 5-8.

No one of the sacred writers claims to have mentioned all the appearances of our Lord. Certain cases are mentioned by one writer, other cases by another writer, — each laying stress upon those instances which seemed to him most important, yet not denying the existence of other instances.

In a similar manner may be resolved the subjoined cases: Blind men, Matt. xx. 30 and Mark x. 46; Luke xviii. 35, 38 (some think there were *three*[2] blind men healed, — one when Jesus entered the city, the other two when he left it; others suppose that *two* were healed, — one in the approach to Jericho, the other in the departure from it, — and that Matthew, greatly condensing the narrative, speaks of both events as if occurring during the departure from the city.[3] Others give to the Greek verb in Luke the sense *to be nigh* or *near*,[4] and take the passage as meaning simply that Jesus was *still near* the city; Mark and Luke mentioning only the better known of the two

---

[1] Gospel History, pp. 447, 448, 452.
[2] So Davidson, Sacred Hermeneutics, pp. 558, 559.
[3] See Ebrard, pp. 362-366.
[4] See ἐγγίζω in Liddell and Scott; also in Robinson's New Test. Lexicon.

blind men). Convocations and feasts, Lev. xxiii.; Num. xxviii., xxix. and Ex. xxiii. 14–16; xxxiv. 18–23; Deut. xvi. 1–16 (in the latter passages only the three feasts are mentioned in which all the males were required to present themselves at the sanctuary). Demoniacs, Luke viii. 27 and Matt. viii. 28 (only the more prominent one mentioned by Luke). Levites, — classes, Neh. x. 9–13 and Neh. xii. 8, 9 (in the latter case only the more noticeable are specified). Tribes loyal, 1 Kings xi. 32, 36 and xii. 21 (of the two contiguous tribes, Judah and Benjamin, the former was vastly more powerful, and virtually absorbed the latter, hence the two were spoken of as one tribe).

Beasts in ark, two of each kind.   *Seven of a kind.*
Gen. vi. 19, 20.   Gen. vii. 2, 3.

The second injunction may be simply an amplification of the former given some hundred and twenty years previously. At first, it was said that a pair of every kind of beasts should be preserved; afterwards, that, in the case of the few clean beasts, there should be preserved not one pair only, but seven pairs.[1] Abarbanel[2] takes the first passage as simply asserting that the beasts should come *paired*, male and female; the second as specifying the *number* of the pairs — seven of the clean, two of the unclean, animals.

Benjamites slain, 26,100.   *The number, 25,000.*
Judg. xx. 15, 47.   Judg. xx. 46, 47.

The Jewish interpreters say that 25000 were slain on the last day — "that day" (vs. 35, 46); while the other 1100 were slain on the preceding days. Or, if vs. 46 gives in "round numbers" the exact statement of vs. 35 (25000 for 25100), we have still 1000 slain previous to the last day of the contest.

Cities and villages, twenty-nine.   *Thirty-eight in number.*
Josh. xv. 32.   Josh. xv. 21–32.

Rashi, Kimchi, and Menasseh ben Israel[3] call attention to

---

[1] Bible Commentary, in loc.   [2] Conciliator, i. 37.
[3] Conciliator, ii. 22, 23.

the fact that in Josh. xix. 1–6 we find nine of these cities (if Chesil and Bethul are identical, as is probable) set off to Simeon. As nine from thirty-eight leaves twenty-nine, the first passage gives the remainder *after* the cession, the second sets forth the *original* number. Or, with Keil, we may suppose a slight numerical error in the case.

City's dimensions, 1000 *cubits.*   *Two thousand cubits.*
Num. xxxv. 4.   Num. xxxv. 5.

There are various explanations of this case.[1] The Jewish interpreters say that the city and lands thereto belonging were arranged in three concentric circles. Of these the city occupied the inner one; the next larger, with a radius 1000 cubits greater, formed the suburb proper; while the outmost, with a radius still increased by 1000 cubits, was devoted to fields and vineyards.

Davidson, J. D. Michaelis, and Keil suppose the city to be 1000 cubits square. Around this square another is formed, with its corresponding sides parallel to, and 1000 cubits distant from, those of the first. The outer square or suburb will therefore be 3000 cubits on a side. Measuring from any corner of the city along its wall and across the suburb to the side of the external square, we have a line of 2000 cubits, in conformity with the dimensions given above.

Mr. Espin[2] thinks that, whatever the shape of the city, the suburbs were to extend a thousand cubits outward from any point in the city wall; while on the four sides, north, south, east, and west, the frontage was to be not less than 2000 cubits in length.

Generations, forty-two.   *A different number.*
Matt. i. 17.   Matt. i. 2–16.

The first "fourteen" extends from Abraham to David; the second, from David to the *deportation;* the third, from Jechonias to Christ, inclusive in each case. So Alford, Robinson,

---

[1] See some eight solutions in Kitto, ii. 823–825.
[2] Bible Commentary, in loc.

Gardiner, and others. Ebrard[1] makes the first series begin with Abraham and end with David, the second begin with Solomon and end with Jechonias, the third begin with Salathiel and end with Christ, inclusive. He maintains, with Spanheim and Lightfoot, that certain kings are omitted by Matthew because of their great wickedness, and their intermarriage with, or descent from, heathen women.[2] Dr. Mill[3] shows that it was a common practice among the Jews to distribute their genealogies into divisions according to some favorite or mystical number; and that, in order to do this, generations were repeated or left out.

Many critics think that, since Jehoiakim and Jehoiachin differ in Greek *only by a single letter,* " Jechonias " in Matt. i. 11 denotes the *former,* in vs. 12 the *latter,* individual. On this hypothesis, the second "fourteen" ends with "Jechonias" (Jehoiakim), and the third begins with "Jechonias" (Jehoiachin); and there is no deficiency.

Jacob's family, seventy persons.	Seventy-five persons.
Gen. xlvi. 27.	Acts vii. 14.

Jacob's children, grandchildren, and great-grandchildren amounted to sixty-six.[4] Adding Jacob himself, and Joseph with his two sons, we have seventy. If to the sixty-six we add the nine wives of Jacob's sons (Judah's and Simeon's wives were dead; Joseph could not be said to call himself, his own wife, or his two sons into Egypt; and Jacob is specified separately by Stephen), we have seventy-five persons, as in Acts.[5]

People, — number.	A different statement.
2 Sam. xxiv. 9.	1 Chron. xxi. 5.
800,000 men of Israel.	1100,000 men of Israel.
500,000 men of Judah.	470,000 men of Judah.

The difference may arise from the fact that the statements are founded upon oral tradition, and not upon public records.

[1] Gospel History, pp. 149, 150. As the pedigree is "juridical, and not strictly genealogical," he reckons *Mary herself* as one of the third series.
[2] See Deut. vii. 2–4; Ezra ix. 1, 2.
[3] On Mythical Interpretation of Gospels, pp. 150–161.
[4] Gen. xlvi. 8–26. [5] Davidson's Sacred Hermeneutics, pp. 582, 583.

Or there may be copyist's errors in one or both cases. An elaborate explanation based upon the supposition that the difference is due to the inclusion or exclusion of the standing army may be seen in Davidson's Sacred Hermeneutics.[1]

Priests, — classes, four.	Twenty-two classes.
Ezra ii. 36–39.	Neh. xii. 1–7.

The number in Ezra is that which was fixed upon at the outset. It was immediately enlarged, in the attempt to conform to the pre-exile arrangement.

Shekels paid by David.	A different statement.
So David bought the threshing-floor and the oxen for fifty shekels of silver.	So David gave to Ornan for the place six hundred shekels of gold by weight.
2 Sam. xxiv. 24.	1 Chron. xxi. 25.

Of a variety of explanations, three may be adduced: (1) That we have here a copyist's mistake, which could very easily happen. (2) That the first passage gives the price of the *oxen* simply, thus: "So David bought the threshing-floor, and the oxen for fifty shekels of silver." The phraseology of the second passage, "So David gave to Ornan *for the place*," etc., seems to favor this view. (3) That David purchased, first, the threshing-floor — a plat of ground "probably not 100 feet in diameter," with the oxen; then, afterwards, bethought himself to buy the place, "mäqom," — the whole hill of Moriah, — for which latter he paid "600 shekels of gold."

Solomon's wives, one thousand.	One hundred and forty.
1 Kings xi. 3.	Cant. vi. 8.

Perhaps the "virgins without number" — who may have been, as Newman[2] thinks, held merely as hostages, — made up the one thousand. Ginsburg, Kleuker, Magnus, and Rosenmüller take the expression in Canticles as a poetical one, denoting simply *a large number*. Zöckler thinks it refers to an earlier period in the reign of Solomon, before he fell into idolatry and other sins.

Things in ark, three.	The tables of stone only.
Heb. ix. 4.	Ex. xl. 20; Deut. x. 5; 1 Kings viii. 9.

We have previously seen that the "book of the law" was

---

[1] Pp. 546, 547. Also, Bib. Com. on 1 Chron. xxi. 5.   [2] See p. 296 infra.

not put *into*, but by the side of, the ark.[1] The text from Hebrews, which asserts that the "pot of manna" and "Aaron's rod" were *in* the ark, probably refers to the *original* arrangement. Later the two were removed.

Unclean birds, twenty.	*Twenty-one mentioned.*
Lev. xi. 13–19.	Deut. xiv. 12–18.

The Hebrew terms "dääh" and "rääh," translated, in the first and second passages, respectively, *vulture* and *glede*, differ only in their initial letters ד and ר. Critics generally assume a slight error of transcription in the case. On this hypothesis, if we drop the superfluous word "dayyäh" (omitted in the Samaritan version, the Septuagint, and several MSS.[2]) rendered *vulture* in the second passage, the discrepancy vanishes. Or, with Aben Ezra and Keil, we may take the term "rääh," in the second passage, as the name of the *genus* which includes the several species, some of which are subsequently named.[3]

Visitors at the sepulchre.	*Different statements.*
One woman. John xx. 1.	Three women. Mark xvi. 1.
Two women. Matt. xxviii. 1.	Five or more women. Luke xxiv. 10.

Observe (1) that no one of the evangelists denies that more women were present than those he mentions by name. John does not assert that Mary Magdalene *only* was present; in fact, he intimates the contrary, for he represents her as saying, in vs. 2, "*We* know not where they have laid him." Each writer seems, while not denying the presence of other persons, to single out one or more whom, for some reason, he mentions with particularity. This explanation of the case is perfectly reasonable, as the following illustration will evince. In the year 1824 Lafayette visited the United States, and was everywhere welcomed with honors and pageants. Historians will describe these as a noble incident in his life. Other writers will relate the same visit as made, and the same honors as

---

[1] Deut. xxxi. 26.   [2] Davidson, on Hebrew Text, p. 37.

[3] Ben Gershon thinks that רָאָה *keen-sighted*, and הָאָה (דָּיָה another form of the same word) *swift-flying*, both denote the same bird. See Conciliator, i. 225. Also, compare Wood's Bible Animals, p. 360.

enjoyed, by *two* persons, Lafayette and his son.[1] Yet there will be no contradiction between these two classes of writers. No more is there between the evangelists relative to the number of women who visited the sepulchre.

Or (2) we may take the sacred writers as referring to *different points of time*, each specifying the number present at the time to which *he* refers. There were two distinct parties[2] of women — the Marys and their friends, and the Galilean women — who followed our Lord. Probably the women, having lodged among their friends in different parts of the city, and to avoid suspicion on the part of the Jews, would come by different paths to the sepulchre, and would not arrive at the same moment. We may, therefore, suppose that Mary Magdalene arrived first (so John); soon the other Mary arrives (so Matthew); then Salome comes (so Mark); finally, the "other women" make their appearance (so Luke). As we shall see hereafter, a hypothesis of this kind removes the difficulty as to the *time* of the visit to the tomb.[3]

IV. CONCERNING TIME.

It would be superfluous to repeat what has been said relative to discrepancies resulting from the confounding of similar numeral letters. Obviously, in those cases where questions of *time* are involved, the liability to errors of the above kind becomes an element of prime importance. Taking this factor into account, together with others we have pointed out,[4] — the use of different methods of reckoning time, and the grouping of events not chronologically, but upon the principle of association, — and we are enabled to solve with facility such cases of discrepancy as the following relative to time.

Abraham's age at migration 75 *years.*   *Apparently* 135 *years.*
      Gen. xii. 4.   Gen. xi. 26, 32; Acts vii. 4.

In the twenty-sixth verse, Abraham may be mentioned first,

---

[1] See Robinson's English Harmony, p. 181.   [2] See Kitto, ii. 582, 585.
[3] Comp. pp. 327–330 infra.   [4] See pp. 9–14 infra.

simply on account of his theocratic importance; as Moses is usually named before Aaron, who was the elder. So that Abraham may have been the *youngest* son, born when Terah was 130 years old.[1] It would then follow that Abraham left Haran at the age of 75, his father having previously died, at the age of 205 years. This removes the difficulty.

Some Jewish interpreters, however, think that Abraham actually left Haran sixty years *before* his father's death. On this theory, Stephen, in asserting that Abraham left *after* his father's death, simply followed the then commonly received, though inaccurate, chronology. So Ewald,[2] Keil, Kurtz,[3] Lange, Murphy, and others.

Absalom's tarry forty years.   *Could not have been so long.*
        2 Sam. xv. 7.   1 Kings ii. 11.

De Wette[4] observes, "We are not told from what point of time the forty years are reckoned." But Josephus,[5] followed by Ewald,[6] Hervey, and most critics, assumes that there is a copyist's error in the case. In the same manner such cases as the following are to be explained. Famine—duration, 2 Sam. xxiv. 13 and 1 Chron. xxi. 11, 12 (De Wette: ג, 3, mistaken for ז, 7). Jerusalem burned, 2 Kings xxv. 8 and Jer. lii. 12 (Bähr: ז, 7, confounded with י, 10). Jerusalem captured, Jer. xxxvi. 9 and Dan. i. 1 (Pusey[7] thinks that the bare mention that Jehoiakim was captured implies that the *city* was not then captured. Keil renders Dan. i. 1: Nebuchadnezzar *went, set out*, to Jerusalem).

Adam died on the day of his fall.   *Lived 930 years.*
            Gen. ii. 17.   Gen. v. 5.

In that very day he became *spiritually* dead — "dead in trespasses and sins";[8] "alienated from the life of God."[9] Also, in a *physical* point of view, death began then to prey

---

[1] Davidson, Sacred Hermeneutics, p. 528; also, Hackett on Acts.
[2] Vol. i. 325, note.   [3] Vol. i. 204, 205.
[4] Introd. to Old Test., ii. 212.   [5] Ant. vii. 9, 1.
[6] Vol. iii. 170, note.   [7] Lectures on Daniel the Prophet, p. 399.
[8] Eph. ii. 1.   [9] Eph. iv. 18.

upon him; the seeds of mortality were sown in his body. That which might have been but a painless and longed-for translation became a painful and dreaded dissolution.

Agag mentioned at a certain time.   *Did not live till later.*
      Num. xxiv. 7.   1 Sam. xv. 2-8.

Balaam was, for the time, uttering predictions under the influence of the Spirit of God,[1] hence he may have mentioned a man not yet born. Besides, the name "Agag" was probably hereditary to the chieftains of Amalek, as "Pharaoh" was to the Egyptian monarchs. Hence the Agag of the second passage would be a later one bearing the same name.

Other examples of alleged *premature mention* are the following: Amalek; compare Gen. xiv. 7; Num. xxiv. 20 and Gen. xxxvi. 12 (Esau's son may have been named after the original Amalek; or the "country of the Amalekites," Gen. xiv. 7, may have been styled thus by *historical anticipation*, having acquired the name previous to the time when Moses wrote. Amalek may be termed the "first of the nations,"[2] as being the first that *assailed Israel*, or as pre-eminent[3] among the neighboring nations at the time when Balaam uttered the words). Gilgal, Deut. xi. 30 and Josh. iv. 19, 20; v. 9 (two different places are intended; one of which may have been that now known as Jiljilia or Jiljûlieh;[4] the site of the other is not determined). Hebrews, — land, Gen. xl. 15 and Josh. i. 11 (since Abraham, Isaac, and Jacob had "effected something like permanent settlements" at various points in the land of Canaan, it may have been popularly termed the "land of the Hebrews,"[5] although the latter had not as yet taken possession of it. Besides, Joseph doubtless knew very well that, according

---

[1] Num. xxiv. 2, 16.
[2] See Num. xxiv. 20.
[3] See same Hebrew expression in Amos vi. 1.
[4] Robinson, Later Bib. Res., pp. 138, 139
[5] This name seems to mean "*trans-Euphratics*," that is, those who had come across the Euphrates. See Josh. xxiv. 14; also Kurtz, i. 167-169, and Gesenius, Thesaurus, p. 987.

to the divine promise, the land of Canaan *belonged* to the Hebrews). Hebron, Gen. xiii. 18 and Josh. xiv. 15; xv. 13 (the best critics agree that the original name was Hebron; afterwards Kirjath-arba was substituted; then the old name Hebron was revived. Quite similar has been the fate of Jerusalem. After Hadrian's conquest the early name "Jerusalem" was displaced, and, dropping out of contemporaneous history, was forgotten. The new city bore the name of "Ælia Capitolina." Not till the reign of Constantine did the old name come again into use).[1] Joshua, Ex. xvii. 9; xxiv. 13 and Num. xiii. 16 (the author, as Kurtz thinks, writing after the name Joshua had become common, employs it by *anticipation*. Or Joshua may have received the name at the defeat of Amalek,[2] in which case Num. xiii. 16 should be rendered, "And Moses *had called* Oshea,"[3] etc.). Kings in Israel, Gen. xxxvi. 31 and 1 Sam. x. 24, 25 (the idea of monarchy was familiar to the Israelites from the example of the surrounding nations, all of which had kings. Besides, there were express promises[4] to Abraham and Jacob that *kings* should spring from them). Levites' land, Lev. xxv. 32–34; Num. xxxv. 2–8 and Josh. xxi. 2, 3, 41 (in the first two passages the land is mentioned by anticipation). Luz, Josh. xvi. 2 and Judg. i. 26 (Eichhorn and Bertholdt say that different places are meant. The name "Luz" was, according to the second text, transferred to another town).[5] Ophir, Gen. x. 29 and 1 Kings ix. 28 (the Ophir of the first text seems to have been a *man*, or else a *tribe*. Either might give name to the place). Sabbath, Gen. ii. 2, 3; Ex. xvi. 23 and Ex. xx. 8 (the Sabbath may have been observed from early times, although no explicit injunction to that effect

---

[1] See "Jerusalem, the City of Herod and Saladin," by Besant and Palmer, pp. 54, 55; also, **Smith's** Bible Dict., ii. 1309.

[2] Ex. xvii. 9.

[3] So Rosenmüller, Eichhorn, and Kanne; and substantially **Hengstenberg** and Ranke.

[4] Gen. xvii. 6, 16; xxxv. 11.

[5] **See Smith's** Bib. Dict., ii. 1699, 1700.

is recorded previous to the giving of the law at Sinai). Tabernacle, Ex. xxxiii. 7 and Ex. xl. 17 (it is possible that the narrative does not follow the chronological order, and that the tabernacle proper was completed before the time referred to in the first text. Or, since the usual word for tabernacle, "mishkän," is not used in the thirty-third chapter at all, the reference may be to an old sanctuary or sacred tent which had come down from the days of the patriarchs. So Michaelis, Le Clerc, and Rosenmüller. Otherwise, it may have been Moses' own tent, set apart for this temporary purpose. So the Septuagint, Syriac, Aben Ezra, Rashi, Keil, Kurtz, and Wogue). Temple, 1 Sam. i. 9; iii. 3, and 1 Kings vi. 14 (the Hebrew word "hēkäl," in the first two texts, means *a large building or dwelling, an edifice*, and is not restricted to the Temple proper. Gesenius says it is applied to "the sacred tabernacle in use before the building of the Temple"). Temple-mount, Ex. xv. 13–17 and 2 Chron. iii. 1 (there is no proof that the real temple-mount is here specified. That Jehovah would, however, select a "high and stately mountain"[1] in Canaan as the place of his sanctuary was the natural inference of Miriam, who was doubtless familiar with the promises and with the history of the patriarchs).[2] Testimony, Ex. xvi. 34 and Ex. xl. 20 (the first passage was written, probably, near the close of Moses' life, by historic anticipation, in order to finish the story about the manna).

Ahab died in 19th year of Jehoshaphat.	In his 17th year.
1 Kings xv. 10; xvi. 29; xxii. 41.	1 Kings xxii. 51.

Most probably the difference arose from a slight mistake in numeral letters. It is to be remembered, however, that the Hebrews had peculiar methods of reckoning the length of reigns. Regnal years seem to have been counted from the beginning of the year, not from the day of the king's accession. Thus, if a king began to reign in the last month of one year, reigned the whole of the next year, and one month of the third,

---

[1] Kurtz, ii. 856.   [2] See Gen. xxii. 2; Ex. iii. 1, 2.

HISTORICAL DISCREPANCIES. 397

we should, although his reign lasted not over fourteen months, have dates in his first, second, and third years. Any dates in the year of his accession, but previous to that event, or in the year of his death, but subsequent to it, would be assigned to the last year of his predecessor or to the first of his successor.[1] Thus, as Rashi [2] says, since parts of years are reckoned as whole ones, we shall have the same year sometimes twice reckoned, once to the father, and then again to the son. The Talmudists say that the years of the kings are reckoned from the month Nisan to Nisan again, and that with such precision that even a single day before or after Nisan is counted for a year. Hence, if a king reigned from the first day of Nisan, a year and a day, to the second day of the next Nisan, he was reckoned as reigning *two* years. So Keil and Bähr. Taking these facts into account, together with the use of round numbers, and of different and sometimes obscure eras of computation,[3] and it is obvious that Hebrew chronology becomes somewhat complicated and intricate.

Should it be objected that the above methods of computation adopted by the Hebrew historians are *incorrect*, we reply that those were *their methods*, and *the writers are to be judged by their own standards, not by ours*. Unless, then, it can be shown that according to their own Oriental ideas and methods of constructing history and of reckoning time these writers disagree with themselves, the charge of " discrepancy " does not fairly lie against them.

Upon some one of the foregoing principles are to be explained the following cases, pertaining to various monarchs.

---

[1] Smith's Bib. Dict., i. 439; also, compare pp. 11-14 infra, where the subject is discussed more fully.

[2] Conciliator, ii. 86.

[3] Browne, " Ordo Saeclorum," p. 221-248, maintains that some of the reigns are enumerated in years current, others in years complete; and that the kings of Judah reckoned their reigns from an epoch different from that employed by the kings of Israel.

Ahaziah of Judah, — age, twenty-two.   *It was forty-two.*
2 Kings viii. 26.   2 Chron. xxii. 2.

According to the latter text, Ahaziah must have been two years older than his own father! The perfectly simple explanation adopted by Gesenius[1] and most critics is, that the copyist mistook one numeral letter for another — כ, 20, for מ, 40.

Ahaziah's reign begun in the eleventh year of Joram, 2 Kings ix. 29; in the twelfth year, 2 Kings viii. 25 (Rashi says that, on account of Joram's sickness,[2] his son Ahaziah was associated with him in the eleventh year of Joram's reign, but began to reign alone in the twelfth year). Ahaziah of Israel began to reign in the seventeenth year of Jehoshaphat, 1 Kings xxii. 51; apparently later, compare 2 Kings iii. 1; (the difference probably arises from the fact that, instead of fractional, the nearest whole numbers, above or below, are employed). Amaziah's reign began in the fourth year of Joash, 2 Kings xii. 1; xiii. 10; in the second year, 2 Kings xiv. 1 (Rawlinson mentions a double accession of this Joash; one as co-partner with his father; the other two years later, as sole king. Amaziah's reign dated in the fourth year from one accession; in the second from the other). Asa had ten years of peace, 2 Chron. xiv. 1; xv. 19; at war with Baasha all their days, 1 Kings xv. 16, 32 (Asa reigned forty-one years.[3] Baasha, beginning in Asa's third year, reigned twenty-four years.[4] Asa's ten years of peace may have occurred *after* Baasha's death. Or, possibly, there may have been ten years of their contemporaneity, during which, though there was "war" i.e. unre-

---

[1] He says, "Geschichte der Heb. Sprache und Schrift," p. 174, "Nach 2 Kön. viii. 26 ist offenbar zu lesen 22 (בכ für מב)." Lightfoot and Ben Gershon think that, in Chronicles, the whole reign of the house of Omri is reckoned in, to make the forty-two; thus, Omri 6 + Ahab 22 + Ahaziah 2 + Joram 12 = 42. It is a singular fact that this peculiarly rabbinic method of computation will, in a considerable number of cases, remove apparent discrepancies. — See Conciliator, passim.

[2] 2 Chron. xxi. 18, 19.

[3] 1 Kings xv. 10.

[4] 1 Kings xv. 33.

HISTORICAL DISCREPANCIES.   399

mitting hostility, between them, there was no actual resort to arms.[1] Critics agree that, in 2 Chron. xv. 19 and xvi. 1, thirty-fifth and thirty-sixth years are a copyist's mistake for fifteenth and sixteenth, or twenty-fifth and twenty-sixth). Azariah's reign begun in the twenty-seventh year of Jeroboam. 2 Kings xv. 1; in the fifteenth year, 2 Kings xiv. 2, 17, 23 (some say, the twenty-seventh year of Jeroboam's co-partnership with his father, but the sixteenth since he began to reign alone. The best critics maintain that כז, 27, has been confounded with טו, 15).[2] Azariah's reign ended in the first year of Pekah, 2 Kings xv. 2, 27; in the second year of Pekah, 2 Kings xv, 32 (parts of years are reckoned as whole years).

Baasha died in Asa's twenty-seventh year, 1 Kings xv. 33; in his twenty-sixth, 1 Kings xvi. 8 (here, again, the same principle applies).

Ela's reign two years, 1 Kings xvi. 8; one year, 1 Kings xvi. 10 (he actually reigned a part of two years. These parts are called years).

Hezekiah's age, twenty-five, 2 Kings xviii. 2; probably less, 2 Kings xvi. 2 (Ahaz, dying at the age of thirty-six, would hardly leave a son aged twenty-five. Hence, with many critics, we may assume a slight mistake in numeral letters).[3] Hoshea's reign begun in the twentieth year of Jotham, that is, the third or fourth of Ahaz, 2 Kings xv. 27, 30, 32; in the twelfth year of Ahaz, 2 Kings xvii. 1 (the rabbies[4] say that because Hoshea was tributary to the Assyrians in the early part of his reign, the first nine years are not reckoned; his reign properly beginning with his independence. Mr. Browne[5] admits an interregnum, or a period of anarchy, lasting eight years).

[1] See Browne's Ordo Saeclorum, pp. 231-234.
[2] Compare the translator's note in Bähr, p. 151.
[3] Davidson, Vol. ii. p. 22, and Ewald, Vol. iv. 167, with the Septuagint, Syriac, and Arabic of 2 Chron. xxviii. 1, make Ahaz *twenty-five years* old at his accession.
[4] Conciliator, ii. 98, 99.
[5] Ordo Saeclorum, p. 242. He thinks that Isa. ix. 17-21 refers to this period of anarchy.

Ishbosheth's reign two years, 2 Sam. ii. 10; apparently some seven years, 2 Sam. ii. 11; v. 5 (Ewald[1] and Keil maintain that, after Saul's death, five years were spent in warfare against the Philistines, before Ishbosheth was anointed king over Israel).

Jehoahaz's reign begun in the twenty-third year of Joash, 2 Kings xiii. 1; about the nineteenth year, 2 Kings x. 36; xii. 1 (Bähr thinks that בכ, 23, has been substituted, in the first text, for בא, 21).[2] His reign lasted seventeen years, 2 Kings xiii. 1; fourteen, 2 Kings xiii. 10 (we may adopt the above emendation; or, with the old expositors, suppose that his son shared the throne the last two or three years of the reign). Jehoash began to reign in the thirty-seventh year of Joash, 2 Kings xiii. 10; apparently in the fortieth, 2 Kings xiii. 1. Jehoiachin's age, eighteen years, 2 Kings xxiv. 8; eight years, 2 Chron. xxxvi. 9 (Bähr thinks that ר, 10, has dropped out of the latter text). His capture in Nebuchadnezzar's eighth year, 2 Kings xxiv. 12; in the seventh year, Jer. lii. 28 (either a slight mistake in numeral letters, or else a different method of counting regnal years). His deliverance on the twenty-seventh day of the month, 2 Kings xxv. 27; on the twenty-fifth day, Jer. lii. 31 (a mistake as to a single numeral letter). Jehoiakim's fourth year corresponded to Nebuchadnezzar's first, Jer. xxv. 1; xlvi. 2; to his second, Dan. i. 1 (the fourth year of Jehoiakim, being reckoned by a different method, might correspond to the *latter* part of Nebuchadnezzar's *first*, and the *earlier* part of his *second* year. Nebuchadnezzar *set out* upon his expedition against Jerusalem in Jehoiakim's *third* year, Dan. i. 1; and continued it, after the battle of Carchemish, in his *fourth* year). Joram of Israel, — reign begun in the second year of Jehoram of Judah, 2 Kings i. 17; apparently five years before,

---

[1] Vol. iii. 113.

[2] Josephus agrees with this emendation. Obviously, upon the principles of computation already explained, a discrepancy of one or two years arises and is accounted for so easily, as to be of no consequence whatever.

HISTORICAL DISCREPANCIES. 401

2 Kings viii. 16 (Joram of Israel seems to have begun to reign in the second year of the *joint* rule of Jehoram and his father; Jehoram of Judah began to reign *alone* in the fifth year of Joram of Israel.[1] Or, with Mr. Bullock,[2] we may hold that Jehoram of Judah had two or three "accessions": (1) When Jehoshaphat, on going to the battle of Ramoth-gilead, about the seventeenth year of his reign, intrusted the regency to Jehoram; (2) when Jehoshaphat, in the twenty-third year, made him joint king; (3) when, in the twenty-fifth year, Jehoshaphat died. So that the accession of Joram of Israel in Jehoshaphat's eighteenth year would coincide with the second year after the first accession, and the fifth year before the second accession, of Jehoram of Judah). Jeroboam II. contemporary with Uzziah (Azariah) fourteen years, 2 Kings xiv. 23; xv. 1; thirty-eight years, 2 Kings xv. 8 (Bähr, Thenius, and Wolff say that in xiv. 23 we should read *fifty-one*, נא, for *forty-one*, מא; Ewald[3] says *fifty-three*. Browne[4] suggests that "in the twenty-seventh year of Jeroboam," xv. 1, means *the twenty-seventh year before the end* of Jeroboam's reign. Most critics think that כז, 27, is put here by mistake for טו 15. Some[5] suppose an interregnum of eleven or twelve years between the death of Jeroboam and the accession of his son). Josiah's reformation in his twelfth year, 2 Chron. xxxiv. 3–7; in the eighteenth year, 2 Kings xxii. 3; xxiii. 4 (what he did at the earlier period was but the commencement and preparation for what he, under the influence of the newly-discovered book of the law, carried out rigidly and thoroughly in his eighteenth year). Jotham's reign, twenty years, 2 Kings xv. 30; sixteen years, 2 Kings xv. 33 (it has been suggested that, since Uzziah was a leper, his son Jotham reigned in connection with him four years.[6] Some Jewish critics maintain that "the twentieth year of Jotham" means the twentieth *from*

---

[1] See Davidson, Sac. Herm., p. 550.
[2] Smith's Bible Dict., ii. 1178.
[3] Vol. iv. p. 118.
[4] Ordo Saeclorum, p. 239, note
[5] Ordo Saeclorum, loc. cit.
[6] See Sac. Herm., p. 550.

the beginning of his reign, that is, the fourth year of his successor Ahaz. Bähr thinks the thirtieth verse an interpolation). Nebuchadnezzar's nineteenth year, Jer. lii. 12; eighteenth year, Jer. lii. 29 (either a numerical error, or else different events are intended). His dream explained in the second year of his reign, Dan. ii. 1; not till he had reigned three years, Dan. i. 1, 5, 18 (in i. 1 he is styled "king of Babylon" by historical anticipation. He was at the time crown prince and commander-in-chief in behalf of his father; or, as Berosus[1] intimates, he may have been actually co-regent. The "second year," in ii. 1, dates from the beginning of his real reign. Besides, as Rawlinson[2] observes, the "three years" of Daniel's training means, according to the Hebrew usage, "no more than one whole year, and parts, however small, of two other years)." Omri's reign began in the twenty-seventh year of Asa, 1 Kings xvi. 15; in the thirty-first year, 1 Kings xvi. 23 (he began, at the first date to reign over *one half* of Israel, at the second date to reign over the *whole*).[3] Pekah's reign twenty years, 2 Kings xv. 27; about thirty, 2 Kings xv. 32, 33; xvii. 1 (Bähr thinks that ב, 20, has been substituted improperly for ל, 30. Oppert and Lenormant[4] assert, upon the authority of the Assyrian inscriptions, that Pekah's reign was *interrupted* above seven years, he being dethroned about B.C. 742 by a second Menahem, and re-instated by another revolution about B.C. 733. The thirty years date from his first inauguration, while his actual reign was twenty years). As to Saul's reign, 1 Sam. xiii. 1, 2, the

---

[1] He says that the father "conferred upon his son Nebuchadnezzar, now a man, some share of the government." See Hengstenberg's Genuineness of Daniel, p. 50.

[2] Historical Illustrations, pp. 168, 169 (American edition).

[3] 1 Kings xvi. 21, 22.

[4] Manual of Ancient History of the East, i. 172 (Amer. edition). See a summary of regnal discrepancies in Movers' Kritische Untersuchungen über die biblische Chronik, pp. 54, 55, note (*a*). For tabular and synchronistic lists of the kings of Judah and Israel, the reader is referred to the various Commentaries and Bible Dictionaries.

best critics agree that some numeral letter has dropped out in both verses.

Ai destroyed at a certain time.	*Still inhabited.*
Josh. viii. 28.	Neh. vii. 32.

Parker[1]: " It may have been rebuilt in the interval."

Amalekites utterly destroyed.	*Overthrown at a later period.*
1 Sam. xv. 7, 8.	1 Sam. xxx. 1, 17.

The Hebrew expression in the first passage is, literally, " *devoted to destruction,*" and means no more than that he *destroyed all whom he caught.* The words " all the people" are to be interpreted, as Thenius[2] says, " with a restriction," and not to be pressed so as to preclude the idea that *some* escaped, who, twenty years later, gathering a band of their Bedouin neighbors, made a predatory excursion against Ziglag.

Bethel and Gezer conquered.	*Apparently not till later.*
Josh. xii. 12, 16.	Judg. i. 22–25, 29.

Some critics[3] think that all, or nearly all, of Judg. i.–ii. 6 refers to events *previous to* the death of Joshua. Hence the above passages would relate to substantially the same period, and there would be no collision. Otherwise, we may adopt the solution of the difficulty indicated a little further on.

Canaan conquered speedily.	*Conquest delayed.*
Josh. x. 42.	Josh. xi. 18.

The first text refers especially to the southern part of Palestine, which was conquered in a single campaign; the second relates to the northern part, the conquest of which occupied a longer period.

As to the fact that the Canaanites were to be destroyed *quickly* (" mahēr "), Deut. ix. 3; yet not *at once* (" mahēr "), Deut. vii. 22, the Hebrew term is employed in these two cases

---

[1] De Wette's Introd. to Old Test., ii. 177, note.

[2] Die Bücher Samuels, p. 68.

[3] Compare Bib. Com. Introd., to Judges, pp. 123–125. On this hypothesis, we must read in Judg. i. 1, "after the death of *Moses,*" etc. This seems plausible, since the death of *Joshua* is related in ii. 8, 9.

in a *relative* sense. The overthrow by the Israelites of "seven nations greater and mightier" than they, was, in respect to the *magnitude* of the work, done "quickly"; but, with reference to the fact that *the rapidity of their conquest was graduated to the rate of their actual occupation*, so that the depopulated land was not left to become the haunt of wild beasts, it was not done "at once," that is, not too suddenly.

As to those passages which seem to represent the subjugation of Canaan and the extirpation of its inhabitants as already effected and complete, in contrast with others which speak of "very much land" as still in possession of the native inhabitants (compare Josh. xi. 16, 17, 23; xii. 7, 8 and xiii. 1; xvii. 14; xxiii. 5) it has been suggested[1] (1) that in the former passages the writer speaks from the *theocratic* point of view, intimating that everything has been done *on the part of God*, it only remaining for the Israelites to faithfully execute *their* part of the work; (2) that "territory was undoubtedly overrun by Joshua at the first onset which was afterwards recovered by the Canaanites, and only again and finally wrested from them at a subsequent, sometimes a long subsequent, date."

Cities smitten at one time.	Not till a later period.
Josh. xii. 10–23.	Josh. xv. 63; xvii. 12; Judg. i. 22, 29.

Some make a distinction between *smiting the kings* and *capturing their cities* in the present instance. But all such cases as these may be explained by the supposition that, in the irregular warfare which the Israelites waged, the Canaanites which escaped at the conquest of the cities would, as soon as the attention of the victors was turned in another direction, return and re-occupy their former haunts. Soon they would rebuild and fortify these cities, and in process of time must be again dislodged by armed force. Hence it would happen that some of the Canaanite cities would be conquered *several times over* by the Israelites, under Joshua, Caleb, and other leaders.

---

[1] See Bible Com., Introd. to Josh. p. 12; also, p. 376 infra.

Ewald,[1] in his sketch of the "never-ending hostilities and counter-hostilities of those early times," hits the mark precisely. Having pointed out the inferiority of the Hebrews in all the practical arts, including even arms and military tactics, and their superiority to the Canaanites in respect to martial courage, he adds: "With these striking differences, the warlike daring of the Hebrews might easily achieve most extraordinary momentary successes, and yet their first campaigns could not be much more than what the Arabs in all three continents called 'alghars,' or rather (since the Hebrews had no cavalry) 'razzias,' that is, sudden *raids*, overpowering the land for the moment, rather than permanently subduing it; and when the camp of the invaders was remote, the thick ranks of the former inhabitants, regardless of their promised submission, soon closed again behind their invaders." In these characteristically graphic words of the great critic, we have the key to such cases of *repeated* conquest as are subjoined. Debir conquered, Josh. x. 38, 39 and Josh. xv. 15–17; Judg. i. 11–13. Dor and Taanach, Josh. xii. 21, 23 and Judg. i. 27. Hazor, Josh. xi. 1, 10 and Judg. iv. 24. Hebron, — king, Josh. x. 23, 26 and 36, 37 (Bleek[2] suggests that the latter passage may refer to a successor of the king mentioned in the former. König[3] thinks that there were two conquests of Hebron). Hormah, Num. xxi. 3 and Josh. xii. 14; Judg. i. 17 (the name "Hormah," denoting *accursed*, or *devoted to destruction*, may have been applied to more than one place.[4] Or, the vow or ban made by Moses may not have been fully carried out till the time of Joshua. Kurtz[5] suggests that the *city* may not have been conquered at the same time with its king, or that Hormah may have

---

[1] History of Israel, ii. 263.
[2] Introd. to Old Test., i. 349. Several other passages referring to Hebron, Josh. xi. 21; xiv. 12, 13; Judg. i. 9–11, indicate its varying fortunes.
[3] Alttestamentliche Studien, i. 22.
[4] Some have reckoned *three* places with this name. Num. xiv. 45 may mean, unto the place *now* known as Hormah.
[5] Vol. iii. 335.

been recaptured by the Canaanites, and only definitively conquered and placed under the ban at the time indicated in Judg. i. 17). Jebus or Jerusalem, Josh. xii. 10; Judg. i. 8 and Josh. xv. 63; Judg. i. 21 (Jebus was the stronghold or fortress " of extraordinary strength," while Jerusalem was the name of the adjacent city. The latter, with its king, was captured early; the former held out till the time of David. So Josephus,[1] and other authorities). Jericho, Josh. vi. 24, 26 and Judg. i. 16; iii. 13; 2 Sam. x. 5 (Bertheau, Knobel, and Le Clerc maintain that two different places are meant. Winer thinks that Joshua's imprecation was not meant to preclude inhabiting the city again, but referred to the *rebuilding of its fortifications*. So that, as an unwalled village, it may have been re-inhabited shortly after its conquest by Joshua). Laish, Josh. xix. 47 and Judg. xviii. 27, 28. Midianites overthrown, Num. xxxi. 10 and Judg. vi. 33; viii. 10–12 (it is not said in Numbers that *all* the Midianites were slain; some doubtless escaped. In some two hundred years this remnant would become sufficiently formidable, aided by their allies, "the Amalekites and the children of the east," to harass northern and eastern Israel). We thus see that the theory of *repeated* conquests of the same place or people meets the exigencies of the case satisfactorily.

Announcement made to Mary.   *At a different time to Joseph.*
Luke i. 26–37.   Matt. i. 20.

Strauss and Bruno Bauer maintain that the two accounts are contradictory. But Mary did not at once tell Joseph of the message she had received, because, *first*, she had nothing to *confess*, and it was not suitable to speak of the matter in a tone of triumph; and, *secondly*, she knew that her own word *alone* would not satisfy Joseph; hence she wisely left it to God to put the mind of her husband at rest in regard to the matter.[2] This "pairing of visions," in order to dispose two persons for

---

[1] Ant. v. 2, 2. Compare Ewald, Hävernick, and Stanley.
[2] See, on this point, Ebrard, pp. 167–171; also, Wordsworth, Replies to Essays and Reviews, p. 469.

co-operation in important and worthy matters, finds a parallel in the cases of Cornelius and Peter, and Saul and Ananias.[1]

Apostles called at one time.	*At a different time.*
John i. 35–43.	Matt. iv. 18–22; Mark i. 16–20; Luke v. 1–11.

John describes the first interview of our Lord with the disciples mentioned. They "abode with him that day," but afterward returned for a while to their ordinary employment. Later, at the time indicated in the other passages, they were called to the apostolic office, and gave up their former mode of life. Ebrard[2] has shown that this is the correct explanation; also, that the commission of the "twelve" in Matt. x., was quite distinct from that of the "seventy," as recorded in Luke x.; the former being of a *permanent*, the latter of a *temporary*, nature.

Ark made at one time.	*Not till a later time.*
Deut. x. 3–5.	Ex. xxv. 10; xxxv. 12; xxxvii. 1.

Possibly the ark mentioned in the first passage was a *temporary* one; or Moses may have ordered its construction before he went upon Sinai, and so made it *per* Bezaleel. But a better explanation is, that Moses here, as in many other cases, "connects transactions closely related to each other and to his purpose, without regard to the order of occurrence." The style of the Hebrew historians, as Le Clerc observes, is not to be "tried by the rules of rhetoricians." It is to their disregard of chronological order, to the arranging of their materials *topically*, rather than *consecutively*, — a method of composition entirely in keeping with their simplicity of thought and diction, — that we must attribute numerous minor discrepancies like the following: Christ conveyed into the mountain at the *third* temptation, Matt. iv. 8; at the *second*, Luke iv. 5 (Luke does not follow the order of time here; nor does he *claim* to do so). His preaching began *before* John's imprisonment, John iii. 2, 22, 24; *from* that epoch, Matt. iv. 12, 17; Mark i. 14 (the meaning may be, from that time began to preach *in*

---

[1] See Acts x. 3, 13, 15, and ix. 6, 10–16.
[2] Gospel History, sections 44, 51, and 70.

Galilee, or to preach the *nearness* of the "kingdom of heaven"). Creation,— one order, Gen. i. 11–27; another order, Gen. ii. 4–7, 9, 19–22 (it is conceded by the best authorities[1] that there is a "general correspondence" between the biblical account of creation and the deductions of geological science. When we compare the statements of Gen. i. with those of the succeeding chapter, we discover several disagreements with respect to the *order* of events. Thus,— to give one of the half-dozen similar instances adduced by rationalistic critics,— in the first chapter, the man and woman seem to be represented as created together, *after* the lower animals; in the second chapter the man appears to be created first, then the beasts, lastly the woman.

Now, these differences arise simply from the *condensation of the narrative* in the first chapter, and from the *disregard of chronological order* in the second. In the first, the sacred historian gives a general, yet concise, account of the six days' work; in the second chapter he recapitulates, and, *without following the order of time*, gives some additional details. As Kalisch has well said, "The writer's end is the history of man's fall. The serpent occasions, the wife shares it; it is therefore necessary to introduce the creation of the animals and of woman."[2]

The narrative in the second chapter is "wholly unchronological," the near and the remote being brought together without regard to the order of time. In other words, everything in this supplementary account, is viewed *in its relation to man;* hence he is here placed foremost according to the spirit of the Aristotelian maxim: The posterior in appearance, the prior in idea).[3] Feast of unleavened bread instituted before the exode, Ex. xii. 15; afterwards at Succoth, Ex. xiii. 3 (the second text

---

[1] Such as Agassiz, Dana, and Guyot. See Dr. J. P. Thompson's Man in Genesis and in Geology, p. 19. Also, Davidson, Introd. to Old Test., i. 161.
[2] Commentary on Genesis, p. 113; see, also, p. 82.
[3] See Lange on Genesis, pp. 200–202.

HISTORICAL DISCREPANCIES. 409

is a mere incidental repetition of the command). Israelites already at Sinai, Ex. xviii. 5; not till later, Ex. xix. 2 (the meeting with Jethro seems related *by anticipation*, in order to clear the way for an uninterrupted account of the meeting with Jehovah at Sinai). John acquainted with Jesus *previous to* the baptism, Matt. iii. 14; not till that epoch, John i. 33 (the recognition by John, at the first glance, may have been due not to any previous acquaintance with Jesus, but to the fact that he had been forewarned that the Messiah was about to appear, and felt an intuitive, irresistible conviction [1] that this was He). Levites set apart during the sojourn at Sinai, Num. iii. 6; viii. 14; apparently not till later, Deut. x. 6–8 (Rashi,[2] Hengstenberg,[3] and others say that vs. 6 and 7 of Deut. x. are *parenthetical;* the words "at that time," in vs. 8, referring back to the events described in the first five verses). Persons sealed at a given time, Neh. x. 1–27; their children supposed to have lived a century earlier, Ezra ii. 1–39; Neh. vii. 7–42 (the eighteen or more "coincident names"[4] in these lists do not absolutely prove the identity of the persons. Rawlinson[5] maintains that the names in the first passage are "not personal, but designate families"). Priests consecrated at Mount Sinai, Ex. xix. 22; not till later, Ex. xxviii. 1 (the Israelites were familiar, from the beginning, with the ideas of *priesthood* and *sacrifice*. There is reason to believe that they had priests and forms of worship and sacrifice previous to the giving of the law and the consecration of the Levites. Jewish writers say that in that early time the first-born or the heads of families performed priestly service. This agrees well with the statement that Moses sent "young men of the children of Israel" to offer sacrifice upon a certain occasion).[6]

---

[1] See Ebrard, pp. 196, 197.
[2] Conciliator, i. 246.
[3] Gen. of Pent., ii. 352.
[4] Davidson, Introd. to Old Test., ii. 138.
[5] Bible Com. on Neh. x. 1–28.
[6] See Ex. xxiv. 5. Compare, however, Kurtz, ii. 334–337; iii. 142, 148.

Beersheba named by Abraham.	Named later by Isaac.
Gen. xxi. 31.	Gen. xxvi. 33.

To the rationalistic objection that "identical names of places are not imposed twice," we may reply, in general, that it is "in full accordance with the genius of the Oriental languages and the literary tastes of the people" to suppose that a name may be *renewed*; in other words, that *a new meaning and significancy may be attached to an old name*.[1] This fact sweeps away a host of objections urged against this and similar cases.

The whole series of events served to recall to Isaac's mind the former name and the circumstances which gave rise to it, hence he renewed it. From xxvi. 15, 18 we learn that all the wells dug by Abraham had been filled with earth by the Philistines, but that Isaac re-opened them, and *called them by the old familiar names*. This would seem a sufficient explanation of the case before us.

In much the same way the following examples of a twofold naming are to be solved. Bethel named at one time, Gen. xxviii. 19; at a later time, Gen. xxxv. 15 (at the first time Jacob made a vow that, if God would bless and keep him till his return, the pillar which he had set up should be "God's house."[2] Upon his return, in view of the abundant blessings which he had received, he performed his vow,[3] changing the ideal to an actual Bethel, and thus emphasizing and confirming the original name). Dan named, Gen. xiv. 14; Deut. xxxiv. 1 and Josh. xix. 47; Judg. xviii. 29 (many commentators — Deyling, Eichhorn, Hävernick, Hengstenberg, Jahn, Kalisch, Keil, Lange, Quarry, Zeller, and others — think that in Genesis another town is intended, that commonly termed "Dan-jaan." Possibly the city may have had two names in ancient times —

---

[1] This is the testimony of a scholar thoroughly acquainted with Oriental manners and customs, Prof. J. L. Porter, in Kitto's Biblical Cyclopaedia, ii. 132 (latest edition).

[2] Gen. xxviii. 20-22.

[3] Gen. xxxv. 14, 15.

Laish (or Leshem) and Dan; one of these being more used at one time, the other at another.[1] Le Clerc suggests that the town was originally called Laish, and the fountain Dan, i.e. *judge*; but that the Danites gave the name of the fountain, which corresponded with that of their own tribe, to the city, as a substitute for its former name). Havoth-jair named, Num. xxxii. 41; Deut. iii. 4, 14 and Judg. x. 3, 4 (the old name may have acquired new significance through the second Jair; or, as Kurtz[2] suggests, the entire district may have been lost by the family during the confusion of the time of the Judges, and a portion, thirty of the sixty cities,[3] regained and re-named by the second Jair). Israel named at one time, Gen. xxxii. 28; at a different and later time, Gen. xxxv. 10 (many critics regard the latter instance simply as a ratification and confirmation of the former meaning. Murphy suggests that in the interval Jacob's spiritual life had been declining, and that its renewal is aptly intimated and expressed by the renewal of his name).

Census made at one time.	*At another time.*
Ex. xxxviii. 26.	Num. i. 46.

We have elsewhere seen that the census of the second text was a military enrolment, but was probably based upon the registration accompanying the collection of offerings mentioned in Exodus.

The hypothesis that similar events occur at different times affords a ready solution of the following cases; Christ anointed at one time, Matt. xxvi. 7; John xii. 3; at another time, Luke vii. 37, 38 (the best critics hold that the anointing in the first two passages was quite distinct from that mentioned by Luke). David anointed at one time, 1 Sam. xvi. 13; at another, 2 Sam. ii. 4; upon a third occasion, 2 Sam. v. 3 (the first was a private, prophetic anointing; by the second he was publicly recognized as king over Judah; by the third, as king over both Judah and

---

[1] Kitto, i. 614.   [2] Vol. iii. 469, 470.
[3] **Comp. Judg. x. 4; 1 Chron. ii. 22, 23.**

Israel). Land assigned, Josh. xiv. 5 and xviii. 6 (chapters xiv.–xix. contain an account of the division of the land; vs. 1–5 of the fourteenth chapter form a preface to the narrative, and state the result by anticipation). Officers appointed, Ex. xviii. 25 and Num. xi. 16 (two entirely distinct transactions). Proverb,— origin, 1 Sam. x. 12 and 1 Sam. xix. 24 (the recurrence of the same circumstance afforded fresh ground for the "proverb"). Saul's anointing, 1 Sam. x. 1 and xi. 14, 15; xii. 3. Solomon's anointing, 1 Kings i. 39 and 1 Chron. xxix. 22 (in both the last cases there was need of a formal and supplementary investiture with authority before all Israel). Spices prepared after the Sabbath, Mark xvi. 1; on the day preceding it, Luke xxiii. 56 (Ebrard[1] gives a rendering of the latter text which obviates the difficulty. Otherwise, one of the two parties of women may have made a purchase before, the other after, the Sabbath. Or, the same persons may have bought a part of the spices at one time, the remainder at the other time). Temple furniture removed, 2 Kings xxiv. 13; xxv. 13–17 and Dan. i. 2 (the temple was pillaged several times). Wives repudiated, Ezra x. 3–17 and Neh. xiii. 23–30 (the evil of intermarriage with heathen women was repressed by Ezra, but some twenty-five years later again required severe measures). Year,— beginning, in spring-time, Ex. xii. 2; in harvest, Ex. xxiii. 16 (the first passage refers to the sacred, the second to the secular year).[2]

Christ crucified at the third hour.   *About the sixth hour.*
Mark xv. 25.   John xix. 14–18.

There are three leading explanations of this case. 1st. That the two evangelists give the extreme limits of time,— Mark referring to the beginning of the preparations, and John pointing to the completion of the dreadful tragedy. The words of the former, "It was the third hour," may denote indefinitely that *the third hour was past;* while the phraseology in John, "about the sixth hour," may mean simply that it was *ap-*

---

[1] Gospel History, pp. 445, 446.   [2] Conciliator, i. 126–129.

HISTORICAL DISCREPANCIES.

proaching the sixth hour, So Ewald,[1] apparently. 2d. John, writing in Asia Minor, may have used the Roman official mode of computation, reckoning from midnight, so that the "sixth hour" would be 6 A.M. From this time to 9 A.M. (the "third hour," according to the Jewish reckoning) was occupied by the preliminaries, and by the passage of the procession forth to Golgotha. This is the view of Ebrard, Mr. Garden,[2] Gardiner, Hug, Olshausen, Tholuck, Townson, Wieseler, Wordsworth, and others. 3d. A copyist's mistake, in John, of $\digamma$, 3, for ς, 6. So Alford hesitatingly, Bengel, Beza, Eusebius, Petavius, Robinson, and Theophylact. Meyer follows John's reckoning, leaving the difficulty unsolved.

Christ's entombment three days and nights.   *A less time.*
Matt. xii. 40.   Buried Friday; rose on Sunday.

We have elsewhere called attention to the fact that the Orientals reckon any part of a day as a whole day. In the case before us, one whole and two parts of a day, together with two nights, are popularly styled "three days and three nights." This Oriental manner of designating intervals of time is found in other portions of scripture,[3] and obtains in modern times. Dr. Robinson[4] found, in his own case, that "five days" of quarantine really meant "only three whole days and small portions of two others."

Christ's infancy, — order of events.   *A different order.*
Matt. ii. 1-23.   Luke ii. 4-39.

It is objected by Strauss[5] and his school that the two accounts are incompatible, since Matthew omits the residence at Nazareth before the nativity, the circumstances which brought Joseph and Mary to Bethlehem, and the presentation in the temple; while Luke does not mention the visit of the Magi, the murder of the innocents, nor the flight to Egypt.

---

[1] Life of Christ, p. 325.   [2] Smith's Bib. Dict., ii. 1102
[3] Compare 1 Sam. xxx. 12, 13.   [4] Later Bib. Res. pp. 625, 626.
[5] New Life of Jesus, ii. 91. See, also, Schleiermacher, Life of Jesus, pp. 46, 48 (Thirlwall's translation).

To this we reply that the argument from the *silence* of an author amounts to very little. That particular aspect of the case which he wished to present, or the knowledge already possessed by those to whom he was writing, might render it inexpedient or superfluous for him to mention all the circumstances, as otherwise he would have done.

In the case before us, the following is the probable order of events: Journey of Joseph and Mary from Nazareth to Bethlehem; birth of the child; presentation in the Temple; visit of the Magi; flight of the family to Egypt; return and settlement at Nazareth.[1]

Eusebius, Epiphanius, and Patritius[2] maintain that, after the presentation in the Temple, Joseph and Mary returned to Nazareth (Luke ii. 39), and, having arranged their affairs there, came back to Bethlehem (which must have possessed very strong attractions for them), with a view to make the latter place their home. Wordsworth thinks they came to Bethlehem the second time on the occasion of one of the great annual feasts. At this time they received the Magi not in a stable, but in a "house" (Matt. ii. 11), and from this city they fled into Egypt. Ebrard[3] satisfactorily explains the omission of some circumstances by one evangelist, and of others by the other.

Daniel continued till first year of Cyrus.   *Till his third year.*
Dan. i. 21.   Dan. x. 1.

In the first text, "continued" means either that he retained his position, or better that he continued in Babylon, till that epoch, at which time the exiles received permission to return. So Bleek, Davidson, and Michaelis. Hengstenberg[4] takes the passage as implying that Daniel lived to see that glorious epoch, but not at all that he *died* at that time.

---

[1] So Robinson, Gardiner, Wieseler, and others.
[2] Kitto, ii. 548, note; Andrews' Life of our Lord, pp. 84–89.
[3] Gospel History, pp. 186–189.
[4] Gen. of Daniel, pp. 54–56.

HISTORICAL DISCREPANCIES.

Deluge, — duration 150 *days.*   *Lasted but* 40 *days.*
     Gen. vii. 24; viii. 3.   Gen. vii. 4, 12, 17.

As Knobel[1] says, the rain continued during the entire one hundred and fifty days, of which the forty form a part; yet we must distinguish its more moderated continuance from the first forty days' storm. Moreover, the subsidence or sinking of a portion of the earth's surface, denoted by the "breaking up of the fountains of the great deep,"[2] doubtless continued also. The one hundred and fifty days bring us down from the seventeenth day of the second month, the beginning of the rain, to the seventeenth day of the seventh month, when the ark rested upon the mountain. On the first day of the tenth month the summits of the mountains were visible. Then forty days (viii. 6) bring us to the tenth day of the eleventh month, when Noah opened the window of the ark, and sent forth the raven. Between this event and the first sending of the dove probably seven days intervened (compare vs. 7 and 8; also, "other seven days," in vs. 10). These, with the two "sevens" mentioned in vs. 10 and 12, make twenty-one days, which bring us to the six hundred and first year, first month, first day, when the "face of the ground was dry,"[3] that is, when the *water* had disappeared. On the twenty-seventh day of the second month the *mud* had dried, so that it was suitable for Noah and his family to go forth.[4] This suggestion removes the supposed contradiction that the earth became dry at two different times.

Drought, — duration three years.   *Apparently three and a half.*
     1 Kings xvii. 1; xviii. 1.   Luke iv. 25; James v. 17.

The "third year" may be reckoned from the time when Elijah began his sojourn with the widow of Zarephath; or, the *drought* begun six months before the *famine* did — the last two texts referring to the drought.

Esau settled in Seir, at one time.   *Not till a later period.*
     Gen. xxxii. 3.   Gen. xxxvi. 6, 8.

The writer, in the first passage, speaks of the "country of

---

[1] Die Genesis, p. 85.   [2] Chap vii. 11.   [3] viii. 13.   [4] viii. 14.

Edom" by anticipation. Probably Esau, at the time alluded to, was sojourning temporarily in Seir; or he may have been there on a warlike expedition. At a later period he took up his abode there.

Exodus occurred in fourth generation. *In the sixth generation.*
Gen. xv. 13, 16. 1 Chron. i. 34; ii. 1, 3-9.

The best critics hold that the term "generation," in the first passage denotes a *century*.[1] The "four hundred years" may be taken here as a round number; otherwise, they may begin with the birth of Isaac, while the "four hundred and thirty" of Gal. iii. 17 may date from the call of Abraham.[2]

Fast observed on the ninth day. *On the tenth day.*
Lev. xxiii. 32. Lev. xvi. 29.

The fast extended from the evening of the ninth to that of the tenth day. Hence it was spoken of as occurring on either day.

Several cases of a kindred nature may be considered here: Feast, — duration, seven days, Ex. xii. 15; six days, Deut. xvi. 8 (in the latter passage the seventh day is specified separately). God's work ended on the seventh day, Gen. ii. 2; on the sixth day, Ex. xx. 11 (Murphy: "To finish a work, in Hebrew conception, is to cease from it, to have done with it"). Interval before passover, Matt. xxvi. 2 and John xii. 1 (the latter passage refers to a somewhat earlier time, to which, also, the *sixth* verse of Matt. xxvi. reverts). Interval before transfiguration, Mark ix. 2 and Luke ix. 28 (Luke's expression, "about an eight days," *includes* the two extreme days). Jordan crossed within three days, Josh. i. 11; iii. 2; on about the eighth day, Josh. ii. 22; iii. 1, 2 (possibly, as Kimchi thinks, Joshua sent the spies two or three days *before* the announce-

---

[1] According to Fuerst and Gesenius, the Hebrew term דּוֹר means not only a *generation*, but also a *century*. So the Latin "seculum" originally meant an *age* or *generation*, but in later times came to denote *a century*.

[2] So Jacobus, Murphy, Wordsworth, and the earlier commentators.

ment, so that, in ii. 1, we should read, "Joshua *had sent*," etc. Or, the "three days" might be "the latest time that could be allowed the people to prepare for crossing."[1] More probably the unexpected detention of the spies slightly disarranged Joshua's plans, so that the crossing was deferred three or four days).

Feast observed under Zerubbabel.   *Not subsequent to Joshua.*
Ezra iii. 4.   Neh. viii. 17.

The second passage means simply that there had been *no such* celebration. The children of Israel "had not *done so*"; the whole congregation had not since Joshua's time dwelt in booths, as in the present instance.

Heaven prepared from eternity.   *Not till after Christ's ascension.*
Matt. xxv. 34; Heb. iv. 3; xi. 16.   John xiv. 2, 3.

The word "prepare," in the first texts, denotes *to create;* in the last case, *to adapt to one's character and needs.* Heaven, *as a place*, was created from eternity; but the process of its adaptation to any given soul, in order to preserve the fitting relation to that soul's character and progress here below, may not be completed till the soul's earthly probation terminates. That is, a *mutual* preparation — *of the soul for heaven* and *of heaven for the soul* — may be now in progress.

Holy Spirit existing before man.   *Not till later.*
Gen. i. 2; Ps. civ. 30.   John vii. 39.

The text at the right does not refer at all to the *beginning* of the Spirit. The ellipsis is to be supplied in some such way as follows: "The Spirit which they that believe on him should receive, for the Holy Spirit was not yet [received by them]; because that Jesus was not yet glorified." The verb which is expressed suggests that which is to be supplied.[2]

Holy Spirit bestowed before Pentecost.   *Not till that time.*
John xx. 22.   Acts i. 5, 8; ii. 1-4.

In the first text, the words "Receive ye," etc., some hold

---

[1] This is Keil's view.
[2] Codex B. followed by Lachmann and Meyer, supplies δεδομένον; Chrysostom, δοθέν; Alford, ἐνεργοῦν.

that the *imperative* is here used for the *future*, "Ye shall receive." So Kuinoel.[1] Alford: "The presence of the Lord now was a partial and temporary fulfilment of his promise to return to them; the imparting of the Spirit now was a symbol and foretaste of what they should receive as Pentecost."

Ishmael about sixteen years of age.   *Apparently very young.*
    Gen. xvii. 24, 25; xxi. 5-8.   Gen. xxi. 14-18.

The English version of verses 14–18 is peculiarly infelicitous, and makes a wrong impression. The "child" was *not* placed upon Hagar's shoulder, nor cast under the shrub, nor held in the hand, as an infant might have been. The Hebrew word here rendered "child," denotes, not only an infant, but also a *boy* or *young man*.[2] Ishmael was at the time some sixteen years of age. The growing boy would be much more easily overcome by the heat, thirst, and fatigue of wandering than his mother, the hardy Egyptian hand-maid. When he yielded to exhaustion she hastily laid him, fainting and half-dead, under the shelter of a shrub. Even after he was refreshed with water, he needed to be "held," that is, supported and led, for a time.[3]

Israelites bondage 400 *years.*   *Apparently a less time.*
    Gen. xv. 13.   Gen. xii. 4; xxi. 5; xxv. 26; xlvii. 9.

Two diverse theories are advocated by critics with regard to the duration of the servitude in Egypt. 1st. Many[4] hold that its actual length was *less than two hundred and fifteen years.* They maintain generally that the "four hundred years" begin with the birth of Isaac, and the "four hundred and thirty,"[5] with the call of Abraham. Isaac was born in the twenty-fifth year of Abraham's sojourn in Canaan; Jacob was born in

---

[1] Compare, on the other hand, Winer's Grammar of N. T. Idiom, p. 312.

[2] So Fuerst and Gesenius. The same word is applied to Joseph when *seventeen* years of age, Gen. xxxvii. 2, 30.

[3] So Keil, Kurtz, Lange, and others in substance.

[4] Bengel, Baumgarten, Mr. Browne (Kitto, i 509, and Ordo Saeclorum, pp. 295-316), and Mr. R. S. Poole (Smith's Bible Dict., i. 442-444), and others.

[5] Ex. xii. 40.

Isaac's sixtieth year, and was one hundred and thirty when he descended to Egypt. This would leave but two hundred and fifteen years for the whole sojourn in Egypt; only a portion even of this latter period being spent in actual servitude. This hypothesis is open to weighty objections, some of which are: that the free, independent, nomad life of Abraham, Isaac, and Jacob, previous to the descent into Egypt, does not properly come under the head of *servitude* and *affliction* predicted in Gen. xv. 13; that a large portion of the period was spent in Canaan,[1] while but *one* land, that of Egypt, is mentioned in the prediction; that the former country could not, in view of the Divine promise to Abraham, be characterized as a "land not theirs"; and that, on this hypothesis, the grandfather of Moses must have had in the lifetime of the latter 8600 male descendants, of whom 2750 were between thirty and fifty years of age![2]

2d. It is maintained by the majority of modern critics[3] that the sojourn *in Egypt* occupied the whole four hundred or four hundred and thirty years. This theory, which allows ample time for the increase of the Israelites, and which meets the demands of the case in other respects, encounters the following objections: that Paul[4] reckons "four hundred and thirty years" between the promise to Abraham and the giving of the law (here, however, since the precise length of time did not affect his argument, we may suppose that he follows the commonly received view of his day, or, as Lange says, he may have regarded *the death of Jacob* as "the closing date of the time of the promise"); that the time was but four generations[5]

---

[1] See Gen. xxvi. 2, 3.
[2] Num. iii. 27, 28; iv. 36. Compare Green's "Pentateuch Vindicated," p. 129; Kurtz, Vol. ii. 144, 145; Smith's Bible Dict., i. 450, 451.
[3] Delitzsch, Ewald, Gesenius, Hävernick, Hengstenberg, Hofmann, Jahn, Kalisch, Keil, Knobel, Kurtz, Lange, Michaelis, Ranke, Reinke, Rosenmüller, Tiele, Tuch, Winer, etc.
[4] Gal. iii. 17.
[5] Gen. xv. 16.

(we have seen that this is equivalent to four hundred years); and that not enough names are given in the genealogy to cover so long a period (it has been conclusively shown by Kurtz and others, that the omission of several names in a genealogy was common; and that the words "bear" and "beget" are used with reference to somewhat remote ancestors.[1] Hence it is inferred that in Ex. vi. 18–20 several generations have been omitted).

Israelites dwelt in Heshbon 300 years.	*A longer period.*
Judg. xi. 26.	Various texts.

If, following Josephus,[2] we allow twenty-five years for Joshua's period of rule, and ten years for Eleazar and the elders[3] who outlived Joshua, adding also the several periods of judgeship, and of servitude previous to Jephthah, as recorded in the Book of Judges, we obtain three hundred and twenty-nine years; sufficiently near to the round number above.

Jacob's age at his flight, forty years.	*Seventy-seven years.*
Gen. xxvi. 34; xxviii. 5.	Gen. xli. 46, 53; xlv. 6.

Joseph was some thirty-nine years old at the time his father, aged one hundred and thirty, went down to Egypt; hence he was born when his father was ninety-one years old. But Joseph's birth occurring in the fourteenth year of the sojourn with Laban, it follows that Jacob, instead of being only forty years old,[4] was actually seventy-seven,[5] at the time of his flight into Mesopotamia. Besides, since Isaac was one hundred years old at the time of Esau's marriage, and lived to the age of one hundred and eighty, we have a period of *eighty years* for Jacob's tarry with his parents, his sojourn in Mesopotamia, and his return to his father at Hebron.[6]

---

[1] See striking examples in Gen. xlvi. 15, 18, 22.
[2] Antiq. v. 1. 29.
[3] Josh. xxiv. 31, 33.
[4] So Von Bohlen and Lützelberger.
[5] So Lange, Murphy, Keil, Kurtz, Hengstenberg, etc.
[6] Gen. xxxv. 27.

HISTORICAL DISCREPANCIES.   421

Jacob's sons, — eleven born in thirteen years.   *Within seven years.*
    Gen. xxix. 20, 21; xxxi. 41.   Gen. xxix. 30, 31; xxx. 25.

Jacob served the "seven years" for Rachel, *after* his marriage with her.[1] In the first four years after the complex marriage, Leah bore four sons and Bilhah two; in the fifth and sixth years Zilpah had also two. In the sixth and seventh Leah bore two more children, and in the latter year Rachel bore Joseph.[2] Thus Jacob might have eleven sons born to him in seven years.

Kennicott, Horsley, and Beer maintain that, according to the Hebrew text of Gen. xxxi. 41, Jacob actually spent *forty* years in the employ of Laban, and that all his children, except Joseph, were born during the first thirty-four years.[3]

Jehovah, — name unknown.   *Well-known.*
And I appeared unto Abraham, unto Isaac, and unto Jacob, by *the name of* God Almighty, but by my name JEHOVAH was I not known to them. Ex. vi. 3.   Name appears in the original of the following passages, Gen iv. 1, 26; v. 29; ix. 26.

Some[4] think that the name was introduced in Genesis by anticipation, that Moses "antedated" a name which had just come into use for the first time; others[5] take the meaning to be, not that the *name* was not known before, but that its *full meaning* was previously unknown; others that those special attributes of God, or that aspect of his character, which the name "Jehovah" indicates, had not been disclosed before.

Judges, — period, about 300 years.   *Four hundred and fifty years.*
  Some twenty texts in Judg. and 1 Sam.   Acts xiii. 20.

Adding together the several periods of rest, judgeship, and oppression specified in the above twenty texts, and allowing twenty years for Joshua's rule, we obtain four hundred and fifty years. But the best critics discard this method of reckoning, and hold that some of the judges were contemporaries, ruling in different portions of the land at the same time. The text from

---

[1] Gen. xxix. 27–30.   [2] So in substance Lange and others.
[3] See Bib. Com., i. 177, 178.   [4] Ebrard and Ewald.
        [5] Aben Ezra, Calvin, Hävernick, Munk, etc.

Acts has really no bearing upon the subject, since, according to the order of the Greek in the four oldest and best manuscripts, the correct rendering is, "He gave them their land as a possession about four hundred and fifty years; and, after that, he gave [to them] judges until Samuel the prophet."[1] It may be added that the chronology of the book of Judges is very uncertain, there being *more than fifty* different methods of reckoning the same.[2]

Levites' service began at thirty.	*At twenty years of age.*
Num. iv. 3; 1 Chron. xxiii. 3.	1 Chron. xxiii. 24; 2 Chron. xxxi 17.

In Moses' time the Levites from the age of twenty-five were employed in the lighter kinds of service;[3] while, for the transportation of the heavier materials of the tabernacle when the Israelites were on the march,[4] men older and stronger were required.[5] After the temple was built, its much less onerous service permitted the standard of age to be lowered to twenty years. After the age of fifty, the Levites were simply to "keep the charge," or guard in the tabernacle, but were exempted from all laborious duties.[6]

Light created in the beginning.	*Sun and moon on the fourth day.*
Gen. i. 3.	Gen. i. 14–19.

The question is often sneeringly asked, "How is it that the Bible represents light as existing *before* the sun and moon were created"?

Humboldt,[7] followed by Wagner and Schubert,[8] calls attention to the fact that light exists independent of the sun, that the earth becomes "self-luminous" in *the northern light;* that the earth, as well as other planets, particularly Venus, is capable in itself of *developing* a light of its own.

Such interpreters of science as Agassiz and Guyot have

---

[1] Smith's Bib. Dict., ii. 1514, note.   [2] Keil, Commentary, p. 276, note.
[3] Num. viii. 24.   [4] Num. iv. 4–15, 24–26, 31–33.
[5] So Abarbanel, Aben Ezra, Lightfoot, Outram, and Reland.
[6] Num. viii. 25, 26.   [7] Cosmos, i. 97, 188, 189 (**Sabine's trans.**).
[8] See in Kurtz' Bible and Astronomy, pp. 427–432.

shown that light results from *molecular action or combination*.[1] Hence, the command, " Light be," was simply another way of saying, " Let molecular action begin," — whereupon light was at once evolved. Professor Dana[2] says, "At last, through modern scientific research, we learn that the appearance of light on the first day, and of the sun on the fourth — an idea foreign to man's unaided conceptions — is as much in the volume of nature as that of sacred writ."

> " ' Let there be light,' said God, and forthwith light
> Ethereal, first of things, quintessence pure,
> Sprung from the deep, and from her native east
> To journey through the aery gloom began,
> Sphered in a radiant cloud, for yet the sun
> Was not; she in a cloudy tabernacle
> Sojourned the while." [3]

Lord's supper instituted at Passover. *Upon the preceding day.*
Matt. xxvi. 17–30; Mark xiv. 12–26;   John xiii. 1, 2; xviii. 28.
Luke xxii. 1, 13–20.

Of the two leading theories the first is, that the Lord's supper was instituted on the evening following the fourteenth day of Nisan, at the legal time of the passover. Robinson[4] maintains that the term " passover " sometimes comprises the *whole paschal festival*, or the feast of unleavened bread which began with the passover proper ; that the expression " to eat the passover " may mean " to keep the paschal festival "; and that the " preparation of the passover," John xix. 14, denotes simply the customary " preparation " *for the Sabbath,* which occurred in that paschal week. In this view, which relieves the difficulty, a host of critics [5] substantially concur.

[1] Thompson's Man in Genesis and in Geology, pp. 15–32.
[2] Bibliotheca Sacra, January, 1856, pp. 114, 118.
[3] Paradise Lost, Book vii., line 243–249.
[4] English Harmony, pp. 200–205.
[5] So Andrews, Bochart, Davidson, Fairbairn, Gardiner, Hengstenberg, Lange, Lewin, Lightfoot, Milligan, Norton, Olshausen, Robinson, Schoettgen, Stier, Tholuck, and Wieseler.

Others[1] hold that the Saviour and his disciples *anticipated* the passover by one day, partaking of a substitute upon the thirteenth day of Nisan. They suggest that there were two distinct days, both legal (one *real*, the other *apparent* time) for keeping the passover; or that the Jews had fallen behind a day in the computation, and our Saviour corrected their error; or that they at this time purposely delayed a day. Both of the above theories find very able and ingenious defenders.

Man's days one hundred and twenty years.   *A different period.*
Gen. vi. 3.   Gen. xi. 11, 13, 32.

Either, there shall be a respite of one hundred and twenty years before the deluge, or human life shall gradually diminish to that length.[2]

Moses feared the king of Egypt.   *Did not fear him.*
Ex. ii. 14, 15; iv. 19; Acts vii. 29.   Heb. xi. 27.

He feared the king at first, but braved his anger at a later period.

Peter's denials at one time.   *At another time.*
Matt. xxvi. 34; Luke xxii. 34; John xiii. 38.   Mark xiv. 30.

The four evangelists agree as to the *number* of the denials; but Matthew, Luke, and John represent them as occurring before the crowing of the cock; Mark as occurring before the cock should crow "twice." Mr. Warington,[3] disregarding this trivial difference, takes the essential substance of Christ's words to be that, "in a few hours' time, ere early dawn, Peter should thrice deny his Master whom he now professed himself so ready to die for."

Alford, Whitby, and many commentators note that cocks are accustomed to crow twice, — at or near midnight, and not far from day-break. Inasmuch as *few persons hear* the *first* crow-

---

[1] Alford, Bleek, Caspari, De Wette, Ebrard, Ellicott, Erasmus, Ewald, Grotius, Ideler, Lücke, Meyer, Neander, Sieffert, Suicer, Tischendorf, Tittmann, Westcott, Winer, Wratislaw, in substance.

[2] See authorities in Bib. Com., on Gen. vi. 3.

[3] On Inspiration, pp. 140, 141.

ing, the term generally denotes the *second*. All the evangelists refer to this latter; but Mark with greater precision designates it as the " second crowing."

It seems probable that no one of the evangelists has mentioned *all* the denials by Peter during that sorrowful night. As the accusation was caught up, reiterated, and flung in his face by one and another of the servants and the guard, the terror-stricken man, in his agitation and in his anxiety to clear himself, *would be likely to repeat the denial a considerable number of times, and in every variety of phrase.* And, meanwhile, he would naturally be shifting about from place to place. This hypothesis accounts for the difficulty as to the *persons* who accosted him, and the *places* where he was when the denials were uttered.[1]

Samuel judged Israel all his days.	Resigned at Saul's accession.
1 Sam. vii. 15.	1 Sam. viii. 5; xii. 1.

Samuel laid down the civil, but retained the ecclesiastical authority; so that, as Ewald[2] says, "he is still, as before the change, the revered prophet." This appears clear from xi. 7, where an edict is issued in the name of Saul and of Samuel.

Samuel's meeting with Saul, in seven days.	Some two years after.
1 Sam. x. 8.	1 Sam. xiii. 8-11.

Some think that the first appointment was kept, xi. 14, 15, and a second made, to which latter the thirteenth chapter refers. But Ewald[3] and Keil take the passage at the left as a mere general direction, that, if at any time Saul went down to Gilgal to offer sacrifice, he was to wait there till Samuel arrived.

Seed time and harvest unfailing.	Interrupted at times.
Gen. viii. 22.	Gen. xli. 54, 56; xlv. 6.

The Hebrew word rendered "cease," in the first text, means

---

[1] See, on these points, Whately's Essay on Dangers to Christian Faith, p. 353 (2d edition); Journal of Sacred Literature, April, 1854, p. 84–92; Ebrard's Gospel History, pp. 425–427; Andrews' Life of our Lord, pp. 473–475, 488–496.

[2] History of Israel, iii. 42.

[3] History of Israel, iii. 29.

to come to an end, to cease to be. A temporary interruption is not precluded. Besides, an unbroken succession of *seasons* is promised, but not necessarily of *crops.*

Sepulchre visited at sunrise.	At the early dawn.
Mark xvi. 2.	John xx. 1.

Ebrard[1] thinks that Mary Magdalene — the only woman specified by John — came *first* and *alone* to the sepulchre. If so, she may have come " early, when it was yet dark "; while the other women did not arrive till " the rising of the sun." Or, of the two parties of women,[2] Mary Magdalene with her friends may have come at the earlier, the others at the later time.

Otherwise in the loose popular sense, the expression "rising of the sun" may denote *the early dawn,* when the rays of the coming sun just begin to redden the east. Thus, in Ps. civ. 22, it is said, respecting young lions, " The sun ariseth, they gather themselves together, and lay them down in their dens "; yet it is well known that wild beasts do not wait for the actual appearance of the sun; at the break of day they retreat to their lairs.[3] Upon any of the above hypotheses, there is no discrepancy in the case.

Temple built 480 years after exodus.	At a different time.
1 Kings vi. 1.	Numerous texts in earlier books.

As to the oft cited text, Acts xiii. 20, we have elsewhere seen that it has no bearing upon the present question. The period of time intervening between the exodus and the building of the temple is variously reckoned by scholars at from 480 to 741 years.[4] The Septuagint gives 440 years; Josephus,[5] 592; Browne,[6] 573; Clinton,[7] 612; Rawlinson, 580 to 600. On the

---

[1] Gospel History, pp. 447, 448.
[2] See infra, p. 328, note.
[3] See Robinson's Harmony, p 212; also, compare Judg. ix. 32, 33.
[4] See some fourteen different estimates, Ordo Saeclorum, pp. 6, 7.
[5] Antiq. viii. 3, 1.
[6] Ordo Saeclorum, p. 703.
[7] Fasti Hellenici, Essay on Scripture Chronology.

other hand, Bähr, Cassel, Ewald,[1] Keil, Rösch,[2] Thenius, Winer,[3] and others accept the number 480 as authentic. If we adopt the latter hypothesis, we may follow Bachmann, Cassel, Keil,[4] and others, in making several of the periods of rest, oppression, etc., in the Book of Judges, *synchronous*, thereby adjusting the whole amount so as to harmonize with 1 Kings vi. 1.

Or, we may regard the 480 as a numerical error; or, with Rawlinson, as " an interpolation" of a comparatively recent date.

Wandering of Israelites forty years.	*Somewhat less time.*
Num. xiv. 33.	Num. xxxiii. 3; Josh. iv. 19.

The deficiency was merely *five days*. In the first text, a round number is employed. Other examples of the use of round numbers are, Ex. xvi. 1, 13, 14, 35 and Josh. v. 10–12; also 1 Kings vi. 1 and 37, 38.

Worship of God, — beginning.	*Not till a later time.*
Gen. iv. 3, 4.	Gen. iv. 26.

The latter passage is of doubtful interpretation. It *may* refer to the first institution of the regular, solemn, public worship of Jehovah, in place of the former private, arbitrary, irregular service as seen in the sacrifices of Cain and Abel.[5]

Murphy thinks that at this time men first began to *address* God in prayer and thanksgiving. Previously their worship had been mute adoration.

V. MISCELLANEOUS.

Altar, — material, earth.	*It was wood.*
Ex. xx. 24.	Ex. xxvii. 1, 8.

The altar in question was a kind of coffer, made of stout acacia planks covered with plates of bronze. When about to be used, its interior was filled with earth or stones, the whole

---

[1] Vol. ii. pp. 368, 369.
[2] In Studien und Kritiken, 1863, pp. 712–742.
[3] Real-Wörterbuch, ii. 327–329.
[4] See their respective Commentaries upon the Book of Judges.
[5] So Kurtz, Vol. i. p. xvi.; also, Lange.

being levelled, so as to form a kind of hearth. It was, therefore, strictly speaking, an *altar case*,[1] "hollow with boards."

Barley, — *field*.	Lentiles, — *field*.
1 Chron. xi. 13.	2 Sam. xxiii. 11.

It is doubtful whether the two passages refer to the same incident. If they do thus refer, עדשים, *lentiles*, has been confounded with שערים, *barley*.

Cattle of Egypt, — all died.	*Some animals survived.*
Ex. ix. 3, 6.	Ex. ix. 19–21; xiv. 7, 9.

The first passage *seems* to imply that all the horses, asses, camels, oxen, and sheep of the Egyptians, died; yet, the latter passages show that their cattle and horses did not all die.

1st. The term "all" is often used in a loose sense to denote *the mass, the great majority*, — such a quantity that what remains is nothing in comparison.[2] This use of the word is due in part to "the want of universal terms in Hebrew."[3]

2d. The plague was limited to animals "*in the field*," ix. 3. Sir Gardner Wilkinson[4] tells us that some animals were *stall-fed* in Egypt. This explains the restrictive clause, "in the field"; as also, the existence of cattle among the Egyptians *after* the plague.

3d. The Hebrew word rendered "cattle," in the text referred to in the ninth chapter, denotes neat cattle, and the smaller animals, but *seldom, if ever, includes horses*.[5] These considerations obviate the difficulty.

Crooked straightened.	*Cannot be straightened.*
Isa. xl. 4.	Eccl. i. 15; vii. 13.

The first text refers to *moral* defects. The design and tendency of the Gospel is to remedy these; to change dis-

---

[1] See Jahn, Bib. Archaeol., § 329; Kurtz, iii. 142; also, Ex. xxvii. 8.
[2] So Aben Ezra, Ben Gershon, and Keil. See examples of this use, 1 Sam. i. 21 and 22; Matt. iii. 5 and Luke vii. 30.
[3] R. S. Poole in Smith's Bible Dict., iii. 2541.
[4] Ancient Egyptians, i. 96 (2d series); similarly Abarbanel and Rashi.
[5] Gesenius says the word is "strictly used only of sheep, goats, and neat cattle, excluding beasts of burden. ... More rarely asses and camels are also comprehended."

honesty and perversity into equity and simplicity, and haughtiness into humility.

The other passages refer to *natural* or *constitutional* defects. As a rule, these are remediless. One born an idiot can never, by any process of education, become a man of talent; a person born without eyes can never have the defect remedied by human skill. Zöckler, with Hengstenberg and Hitzig, observes, " Human action and effort, in spite of all exertion, cannot alter that which has once been arranged and fixed by God." In the Vulgate, Eccl. i. 15 is rendered singularly, thus: "*The number of fools is infinite.*"

Earth founded upon the seas.   *Founded upon nothing.*
    Ps. xxiv. 2.   Job xxvi. 7.

The first passage asserts that the earth is established *above* the waters, so that they will not overflow and destroy it; the second text — the words of an uninspired man — may refer to the scientific truth that the earth hangs free without support in space.

Earth saturated.   *Needed moisture.*
    Gen. i. 9, 10.   Gen. ii. 6.

Some [1] assert that the fact of the earth's being moistened by an ascending mist or exhalation, does not harmonize with its previous submergence in water. As if the earth upon emerging from the briny moisture which could not support vegetation, would not *afterward* become dry, and need dews and rains!

Golden calf, burnt and ground.   *Burnt, stamped, and ground.*
    Ex. xxxii. 20.   Deut. ix. 21.

Goguet [2] and Stahl [3] say that natron, which abounds in the East, has, like tartaric acid, the power of reducing gold to powder, — and this the sooner, if the gold be previously heated. Moses, having pulverized the gold in this way, mixed it with water, and caused the Israelites to partake of the nauseating liquid.

[1] See in Davidson's Introd. to Old Test., i. 86.
[2] Smith's Bible Dict., i. 345.
[3] Hawks, Monuments of Egypt, p. 228.

Davidson[1] explains the case, as follows: In preparing ores of gold and silver for the smelter, *stamps*, or massive beams shod with iron, and weighing as much as eight hundred pounds, are used. These are lifted by machinery, and let fall upon the ore contained in iron troughs. If overstamped, or "stamped dead," as it is termed, the fine particles float away and are lost. Gold, from its great malleability, is peculiarly liable to suffer thus. The gold of which the calf was made was designedly and indignantly overstamped; and, when cast into the stream, would float away. As this author thinks it would impart no special taste to the water.

Wilkinson[2] mentions that, in the towns of Egypt, certain persons were employed to pound various substances in large stone mortars with heavy metal pestles. When well pounded, the substance was taken out, sifted, and the larger particles returned to the mortar. This process was continued, till a sufficient degree of fineness was secured.

Moses may have cast the image into the fire to change its form; or — if it were made of wood and covered with plates of gold — to destroy its combustible part, afterwards employing some one of the processes above described.

Images taken away.	*They were burned.*
2 Sam. v. 21.	1 Chron. xiv. 12.

The Hebrew expression rendered to *take away* may also mean *to destroy*.

Leadership of the cloud satisfactory.	*Not reliable.*
Ex. xiii. 21, 22.	Num. x. 29-31.

Geddes and others[3] object that if the cloud had been a reliable guide, the Israelites would not have needed Hobab to be to them "instead of eyes," as knowing "how they were to encamp in the wilderness." But, *God is not wont to do that for*

---

[1] Introd. to Old Test., i, 254, 255.
[2] Ancient Egyptians, iii. 180, 181; Hengstenberg, Egypt and Books of Moses, p. 217.
[3] See in Graves on Pentateuch, p. 481 (sixth edition).

man which the latter might do for himself. The pillar of cloud determined the *general route* to be taken, the *place* of encampment, and the *length of tarry* in each location; yet *human prudence* was by no means precluded with respect to arranging the encampment so as to combine most advantageously the circumstances of water, pasture, shelter, supply of fuel, medicinal or nutritive plants or substances, and the like, in or near the station. In all these particulars, Hobab's experience, and knowledge of the desert, would be exceedingly useful, as supplementary to the guidance of the cloud.[1]

Manna, — taste, like wafers made with honey.	Like fresh oil.
Ex. xvi. 31.	Num. xi. 8.

The Jewish interpreters and Kurtz say that, in its natural state, it tasted like "cakes with honey," but cooked or ground, like "fresh oil." The Septuagint employs in the first passage a word which is interpreted by Athenaeus and the Greek scholiasts as denoting "a sweet kind of confectionery made with oil."

Molten sea, — appendages, knops.	Otherwise called oxen.
1 Kings vii. 24.	2 Chron. iv. 3.

The "knops" may have been in the form of miniature oxen. Or, as De Wette and Rawlinson think, here may be a copyist's error, פקעים, *knops* or *gourds*, for בקרים, *oxen*.

Mosaic law, — character, cruel.	Conducive to happiness.
Deut. xxxiii. 2.	Deut. xxx. 16.

The words "fiery law," in the first text do not imply *cruelty* in the law, but may refer to the illuminating power of that law, or to the marked exhibitions of divine glory when the decalogue was given.[2]

It may be added that those who stigmatize the Mosaic law as "cruel," are probably not aware that in point of clemency it compares favorably with the laws of other nations in ancient, as well as modern times. In the Mosaic law only some *seventeen*

---

[1] Kurtz, Vol. iii. pp. 214, 215, 258, 281.   [2] Ex. xix. 18.

capital crimes are mentioned.¹ The laws of the Roman kings, and the twelve tables of the *decemviri* were full of cruel punishments.² In the English code, about two hundred years ago, there were *one hundred and forty-eight* capital crimes, "many of them of a trivial nature, as petty thefts and trespasses upon property." In England, in the eighteenth century, it was a capital crime to break down the mound of a fish-pond, to cut down a cherry-tree in an orchard, to steal a handkerchief or other trifle, of above the value of twelve pence, privately from another's person. In Sir Wm. Blackstone's time (A.D. 1723–1780), no less than *one hundred and sixty*³ offences (almost *ten times* as many as in the Mosaic code), were declared by act of parliament to be capital crimes, worthy of instant death.⁴

These facts should silence those who are perpetually inveighing against the " barbarity of the Mosaic code."

Mount inaccessible.	Might be approached.
Ex. xix. 12, 21–24.	Ex. xix. 13, 17.

The Israelites were commanded to " set bounds" about the mount; perhaps, to build a fence or hedge of some kind. At the blast of the trumpet they were to leave their encampment, and go up to the foot of the mountain. But they were forbidden to " break through" the bounds or barrier, that is, to pass a certain limit, under penalty of death.⁵

Nothing new on earth.	Some things are new.
Eccl. i. 9, 10.	Isa. xliii. 19; lxv. 17; Jer. xxxi. 22.

Obviously, in relation to the Creator, nothing is new, for nothing is unforeseen or unexpected to him. And something similar may be said of man, viewed *as a race*, since the phenomena of nature recur in regular order, and history ever tends

---

¹ Wines, Laws of the Ancient Hebrews, p. 263.
² Montesquieu, Spirit of the Laws, Book vi. chapter 15.
³ One writer says, " nearly three hundred"; see "Romilly," in Appleton's New American Cyclopaedia (first edition).
⁴ Blackstone's Commentaries, iv. 4, 15–18 (Christian's edition, New York, 1822).
⁵ **Kurtz**, iii. 115, 116

HISTORICAL DISCREPANCIES.   433

to repeat itself. But, with reference to *any specific man* or *generation* of men, many things are "new."

Paschal offering, a lamb or kid.	Might be from the herd.
Ex. xii. 5.	Deut. xvi. 2.

The Hebrew word "seh" means both *a lamb*, and *a kid*.[1] This fact relieves some apparent incongruities in our version. In the second text, the term "passover" includes not only the proper paschal sacrifice, but also the offerings[2] (some of which were taken from the "herd") of the succeeding six days; as is clear from the next verse: "seven days shalt thou eat unleavened bread therewith." As to Ex. xii. 9 compared with Deut. xvi. 7; the Hebrew term "bäshal" means sometimes *to cook in water;* at other times, *to roast or broil*.[3]

Parable of the talents.	Of the pounds.
Matt. xxv. 14–30.	Luke xix. 11–27.

Strauss asserts that these are discordant versions of the same parable; but Chrysostom, Gerhard, Alford, and Trench,[4] have shown that they are separate parables, addressed to quite distinct groups of hearers, in different states of mind, and needing different admonitions.

Strange gods, real existences.	They are nothing.
Ps. xcvi. 4, 5; Isa. xliv. 9, 10, 17.	1 Cor. viii. 4, 5; x. 19.

Paul, in asserting that "an idol is nothing in the world," does not deny the *existence* of the idol, but simply that it has *any power* to help or harm the worshipper. As Crusius has remarked, not the *existence*, but the *divinity*, of the idol is called in question.

Sun and moon put to shame.	Their glory increased.
Isa. xxiv. 23.	Isa. xxx. 26.

The two passages combined are a poetic prediction that in a coming day, the light of the sun and the moon, though increased

---

[1] See Ex. xii. 5.
[2] Num. xxviii. 16–19.
[3] Compare 2 Sam. xiii. 8; 2 Chron. xxxv. 13; particularly, the latter text.
[4] On Parables, p. 220 (American edition).

sevenfold, will be outdone and thrown into the shade by the revelation of the transcendent glory of Jehovah.

Version of affair, — one form.   *A different form.*
Gen. xlii. 7-20, 30-34; xliii. 3-13.   Gen. xliv. 16-34.

Tuch refers the variation to the inaccuracy of the narrator, Judah. It may be that the agitation and alarm of the speaker modified his narrative to some extent. At all events, his accuracy is not vouched for by the sacred historian.

Vessels made for the temple.   *Not made at the time.*
2 Chron. xxiv. 14.   2 Kings xii. 13, 14.

The statement in Kings simply amounts to this; that none of the money contributed was employed in making vessels, *so long as the repairing of the temple was in progress.* What became of the surplus that remained this author does not tell us. But the chronicler supplements the narrative with the information that this surplus was *afterwards* expended in making vessels for the temple.[1]

Waters of Egypt turned to blood.   *Some not changed.*
Ex. vii. 20, 21.   Ex. vii. 22, 24.

We may take the word "all," in the nineteenth and twentieth verses, in the loose popular sense,[2] as implying *far the greater part;* the exceptions being so few and insignificant that the author overlooks them entirely. Some water remained unchanged, upon which the magicians operated, and which the Egyptians drank during the interval. Kurtz[3] thinks that only *Nile-water*, whether in the river or in vessels, was changed, the water in the wells being unaffected. Mr. R. S. Poole[4] suggests that "only the water that was seen" was smitten, that the nation might not perish. Mr. Alexander[5] thinks that "the

---

[1] So Bähr, Keil, and Rawlinson.
[2] So Keil, and Hengstenberg (Egypt and Books of Moses, pp. 109, 110). The latter points out the use of *universal* terms throughout the narrative, "all the trees" broken by the hail, etc. The idiom is a very common one in all languages.
[3] Vol. ii. p. 271.
[4] Smith's Bible Dict., iii. 2540.
[5] Kitto, i. 749.

water when filtered through the earth on the bank of the river, was restored to its salubrity." This agrees with the statement that "all the Egyptians digged round about the river for water to drink" (vs. 24). Any one of these hypotheses obviates the difficulty.

Water upon Mt. Carmel abundant.   *The drought very severe.*
1 Kings xviii. 32–35.   1 Kings xvii. 7; xviii. 5.

A rationalistic author sarcastically observes that the writer of Kings, in representing Elijah as using so much water[1] at his sacrifice, apparently forgot the long-continued drought, which, having lasted more than two years, must have dried up the mountain streams and the river Kishon supplied by them.

Whence did Elijah obtain water? Blunt[2] thinks that, since Carmel is upon the coast, sea-water was employed. Bähr suggests that the brook Kishon was not dry, and that the water may have been obtained thence. Robinson[3] expresses the opinion that the transaction took place at the foot of the mountain; perhaps, at some Tell (hill) near the permanent fountains of the Kishon.

But Dean Stanley,[4] with Van de Velde, J. L. Porter, Rawlinson, Tristram, and Prof. C. M. Mead,[5] speak of a perennial fountain, a little below the summit of Carmel, from which the water was almost certainly obtained. Stanley, quoting Van de Velde, describes it as "a vaulted and very abundant fountain, built in the form of a tank with a few steps leading down to it, just as one finds elsewhere in the old wells or springs of the Jewish times." Prof. Mead, at a recent visit, found the water in this fountain more than nine feet in depth, and suggests that it may have been considerably deeper in Elijah's time. He says that the "trench" dug by the prophet would contain some

---

[1] Fuerst and Gesenius say that the word rendered "barrels" in our version, means *buckets* or *pails.* Translated "pitcher," Gen. xxiv. 14–20.
[2] Coincidences, p. 199.
[3] Physical Geography of the Holy Land, p. 31, and note.
[4] Sinai and Palestine, p. 347, and note. Comp. Josephus, Ant. viii. 13, 5.
[5] Bibliotheca Sacra, Oct. 1873, pp. 672–696.

twelve to twenty-four quarts only. He found upon the summit of Carmel, and not very far distant from the aforesaid fountain, "a rocky surface, artificially smoothed, about eight feet square, *around the edge of which had been dug a groove an inch or two in depth.*"

This may have been the very spot where Elijah vindicated the patriarchal faith, and where Jehovah "answered by fire" the prayer of his servant the prophet.

We have now reviewed carefully, yet of necessity rapidly, the "discrepancies" of the Bible. We have aimed to include all that are worthy of even a cursory glance; and we trust that the candid reader will feel that, in the great majority of cases, we have stated, or at all events suggested, fair and adequate solutions. When we consider the long interval of time — from eighteen to thirty-three centuries — which has elapsed since the several books of scripture were written; and that during all but four centuries of this time they have been circulated and transmitted *in manuscript;* and the additional fact that our knowledge of antiquity is exceedingly limited and imperfect, — many minute, and sometimes important, circumstances pertaining to every event having passed irrecoverably from the memory of mankind, — when these disadvantages which attend the investigation of the subject are taken into account, it surely can not be too much to believe that, if in any instance the explanation adduced should seem inadequate, a knowledge of *all* the circumstances of the case would supply the missing link, and solve the supposed discrepancy to the complete satisfaction of every reasonable mind.

BIBLIOGRAPHICAL APPENDIX.

NOT to enumerate the various Harmonies of Scripture, which may be regarded as constituting a distinct department, the following would seem to be the principal works occupied wholly or mainly with the consideration of the discrepancies of the Bible.

Among the patristic writers, Eusebius, Chrysostom, Augustine, and Theodoret devote certain treatises, or portions thereof, to the subject. But from the latter part of the fifth to the beginning of the sixteenth century little attention was bestowed upon this branch of sacred literature, and almost nothing is extant pertaining thereto.

With the era of the Reformation a new impulse was given to biblical study, and the discrepancies received a considerable share of attention, as the subjoined list will evince.

The supposed date of *first* publication is indicated by full-faced figures. With reference to the *size* of books there is much difference between ancient and modern designations.

The first two works are of an introductory character.

Staalkopf, Jac. Introductio in historiam Conciliatorum Biblicorum. 4to. Lipsiae, **1724.**

Alardus, Nicolaus. Bibliotheca Harmonico-Biblica, quae praeter historiam harmonicam, tradit notitiam scriptorum harmonicorum. 8vo. Hamburgi, **1725.**

Julianus Pomerius, *Abp. of Toledo,* fl. A.D. 680. Ἀντικειμένων, sive contrariorum in speciem locorum utriusque Testamenti, libri duo. folio, Basileae, 1530; 8vo. Coloniae, 1533, 1540; Parisiis, 1556.

The first edition was published anonymously; some later editions under the name of Julian.

This work has been attributed to several different authors; but with most probability to Bertharius, Abbot of Monte Cassino, who, according to Walch, was killed by the Saracens, A.D. 884. It includes two hundred and twenty-one cases.

Althamer *Brenzius,* Andreas. Diallage; hoc est, Conciliatio locorum Scripturae, qui prima facie inter se pugnare videntur. 8vo. Norimbergae, **1527,** 1528, 1588.

    Some sixteen editions were published. The work is in two parts, and comprises one hundred and sixty discrepancies, which are solved in a neat and perspicuous manner.

Rabe, Ludwig. Conciliationes locorum S. Scripturae in specie pugnantium. 8vo. Argentorati, **1527,** 1550; Noribergae, 1561.

    In two parts, and including one hundred and twenty discrepancies. The materials of the work are extracted from the writings of Augustine.

Cumirano, Serafino. Conciliatio locorum communium Sacrae Scripturae, quae inter se pugnare videntur. 2 vol. 8vo. Parisiis, **1556,** 1559, 1576; 3 vol. Antuerpiae, 1557—1561.

    Revised by Leander de Sancto Martino (originally John Jones), Duaci, 1623.

Baltanas (*or* **Valtanas**) **Mexia,** Domingo de. Concordancias de muchos pasos dificiles de la divina historia. 8vo. Sevilla, **1556.**

Obenhein, Christoph. Novi Testamenti locorum pugnantium ecclesiastica expositio; adjectae sunt etiam quarundam euangelicarum quaestionum solutiones. 8vo. Basileae, **1563.**

    In Acta apostolorum ecclesiastica expositio locorum. 8vo. Basileae, **1563.**

Camara, Marco **de la.** Quaestionarium conciliationis simul et expositionis locorum difficilium Sacrae Scripturae, in quo DC. Scripturae loca exponuntur. 4to Compluti. **1587.**—Also, Venetiis, 1603.

Montoya, Pedro Lopez **de.** De Concordia Sacrarum Scripturarum, 4to. Matriti, **1600.**

Mettinger, Joannes. Harmonia in utroque Testamento; sive conciliationes eorum, quae in sacris biblicis sibi invicem adversa videntur. 8vo. Lavingae, **1601.**

Sharp (*Lat.* **Scharpius),** John. Symphonia Prophetarum et Apostolorum, in qua ordine chronologico loci Sacrae Scripturae, specie tenus contradicentes, conciliantur. 4to. Genevae, **1625,** 1639, 1653, 1670.

    This author solves some seven hundred cases with considerable acuteness.

Walther, Michael. Harmonia Biblica; sive brevis et plana conciliatio locorum Veteris et Novi Testamenti adparenter sibi contradicentium. 8vo. Argentorati, **1626,** 1630; Noribergae, 1649, 1654 (enlarged edition, 1696).

According to Horne, this work is marked by considerable learning and industry.

Menasseh Ben Israel. Conciliador o de la conveniencia de los Lugares de la S. Escriptura, que repugnantes entre si parecen. 4to. Vol. i. Francofurti, **1632;** Vol. ii. Amsterdam, 1650.

——Conciliator, sive de convenientia locorum S. Scripturae, quae pugnare inter se videntur. 4to. Amstelodami, 1633.

——The Conciliator, a Reconcilement of the Apparent Contradictions in Holy Scripture. Translated, with Notes, by E. H. Lindo. 2 vols. 8vo. London, 1842.

This work, restricted to the Old Testament, solves four hundred and seventy-three cases of discrepancies, by the usually ingenious, though sometimes fanciful, methods peculiar to the Jewish rabbies.

Thaddaeus, Joannes. S. S. Scriptura, a se nec diversa, sibi nec adversa, hoc est, Conciliatorium Biblicum, in quo paria mille et supra S. Codicis Locorum specie tenus contradicentium, conciliantur. 12mo. Amstelodami, **1633,** 1648, 1696; Francofurti, 1648, 1687, 1696, 1702; Londini, 1662; Haffniae, 1717.

——The Reconciler of the Bible, wherein above two thousand seeming contradictions are fully and plainly reconciled. By J. T., Minister of the Gospel. London, 1656.

Thaddaeus, Joannes, *and* **Man,** Thomas. The Reconciler of the Bible inlarged, wherein above three thousand seeming contradictions throughout the Old and New Testament are fully and plainly reconciled. By J. T. and T. M. folio, London, 1662.

Singularly enough, in the last two cases the numbers are made up by *counting each discrepancy twice;* so that the first of these editions really contains but one thousand and fifty cases, and the second only some one thousand five hundred. This work comprises a multitude of trivial discrepancies, and omits many of the more important.

Magri, Domenico. Αντιλογίαι, seu contradictiones adparentes et conciliationes Sacrae Scripturae ab ipso collectae. 12mo. Venetiis, **1645,** 1653; Parisiis, 1665, 1675, 1685.

Streat, William H. The Dividing of the Hoóff, or seeming contradictions throughout Sacred Scriptures, distinguish'd, resolv'd and apply'd. 4to. London, **1654.**
This is characterized as a work of little value.

Mayer, Heinrich. Manuale biblicum in quo Sacrae Scripturae certa quaedam testimonia quae sibimet contradicere videntur, omnino concordare docentur. 12mo. Friburgi Brisgoiae, **1654.**

Arnoldus, Nicolaus. Lux in Tenebris; seu brevis et succincta Vindicatio simul et Conciliatio locorum Vet. et Novi Testamenti. 4to. Franeckerae, **1662,** 1665, 1680; Françofurti et Lipsiae, 1698.
A voluminous work, of some twelve hundred pages, directed chiefly against Papists and Socinians, yet discussing incidentally certain discrepancies. It hardly belongs to our department.

Matthiae, Christian. Antilogiae Biblicae, sive Conciliationes dictorum Scripturae Sacrae, in speciem inter se pugnantium, secundum seriem Locorum Theologicorum in ordinem redactae; editae a Joh. Schelhammero, Jun. 4to. Hamburgi, **1662,** 1700, 1726.

Santa Cruz, Emanuel Fernandez de. Antilogiae totius Scripturae. 2 tom. fol. Tom. i., Segoviae, **1671;** Tom. ii., Lugduni, 1677. A 2d ed. of Tom. i., Lugduni, 1681.

Bleiswyck, Jan C. van. Bybel-balance ende Harmonieboeck. 4to. Delfft, **1675.**

Ridder, Franciscus. Schriftuerlyk licht ouer schynstrydende, duystere en misduyde texten der heiligen schrifture. 4to. 5 delen. Rotterdam, **1675.**
Walch speaks of this work as copious and elaborate.

Cuper, Franciscus. Conciliatio locorum utriusque foederis, quae contraria esse videntur. In his "Arcana Atheismi revelata." 4to. Roterdam., **1676.**

Le Fevre (*Lat.* **Faber**)**,** Jacques (*died*, A.D. 1716). Conciliatio locorum Sacrae Scripturae quae contradicere invicem videntur. 12mo. Parisiis, **1683** (?) [Fabricius styles this the *second* edition], 1685.
This work is said to be an enlargement of that of Magri, mentioned above.

Toornburg, K. Concordantiae locorum dissonantium Sacrae Scripturae [Belgice]. 8vo. Alcmariae, **1695.**
The *original* title of this work I have not been able to find.

Pontas, Jean. Scriptura Sacra ubique sibi constans; seu Difficiliores Sacrae Scripturae in speciem secum pugnantes, juxta sanctorum ecclesiasticorum Patrum theologorumque sententiam conciliati. 4to. Parisiis, **1698.**
One volume only, relating to the Pentateuch, was published. Darling says of it; "A learned and able work, containing three hundred and thirty questions with answers."

Heermann, David (*also known as* **Bibliander**). Richtige Harmonia oder Uebereinstimmung hundert solcher Sprüche und Oerter welche in H. Schrifft vorkommen und einander scheinen zuwider zu lauffen. 3 Theile. 8vo. Görlitz, **1705** — 1710; 4 Theile, Görlitz, 1707—1717.

Surenhuys, Willem (*Lat.* **Surenhusius,** Gulielmus). ΒΙΒΛΟΣ ΚΑΤΑΛΛΑΓΗΣ, in quo secundum Theologorum Hebraeorum formulas allegandi, et modos interpretandi conciliantur loca ex V. in N. T. allegata. 4to. Amstelaedami, **1713.**
Discusses some one hundred and sixty-five cases of disagreement between citations in the New Testament and the original passages in the Old. This work properly belongs to a distinct department.

Baruh, Raphael. Critica Sacra examined; or an attempt to show that a new method may be found to reconcile the seemingly glaring variations in parallel passages of Scripture. 8vo. London, **1775.**

Cooper, Oliver St. John. Four Hundred Texts of Holy Scripture with their corresponding passages explained. 12mo. London, **1791.**
Includes fifty-seven instances of disagreement.

Evanson, Edward. The Dissonance of the four generally received Evangelists. 8vo. Gloucester (England), **1792,** 1805.

Falconer, Thomas. Certain principles in Evanson's "Dissonance of the four generally received Evangelists" examined. Bampton Lectures for 1810. 8vo. Oxford, **1811.**

Strauss' "Life of Jesus," with the numerous replies to it, might, equally with the last two works, claim a place in our catalogue.

Fuller, Andrew. The Harmony of Scripture; or an attempt to reconcile various passages apparently contradictory. 8vo. London, **1817.**

A posthumous tract, comprising thirty cases of discrepancy. See, also, Fuller's Works, Vol. i. pp. 667–684 (Philadelphia ed., 3 vols.).

Cox, John Hayter. Lectures on the Harmony of the Scriptures; designed to reconcile apparently contradictory passages. 8vo. London, **1823.**

Treats of nineteen discrepancies.

Longhurst, S. A Common-place Book, or Companion to the New Testament; consisting of Illustrations of difficult passages; apparent Contradictions and Inconsistencies reconciled. Richmond and London, **1833.**

Nork, F. Biblische Mythologie des Alten und Neuen Testaments. Versuch einer neuen Theorie zu Aufhellung der Dunkelheiten und scheinbaren Widersprüche in den canonischen Büchern der Juden und Christen. In two parts. 8vo. Stuttgart, **1842.**

Davidson, Dr. Samuel. Sacred Hermeneutics, Developed and Applied. 8vo. Edinburgh, **1843.**

A portion of this work, pp. 516—611, is devoted to our subject, and resolves some one hundred and fifteen apparent contradictions (Compare reference, p. 25, infra, note).

There are, of course, many other works which bear indirectly upon the subject. Brief disquisitions are extant, by Lightfoot, Knatchbull, Ludlam and Whately. Several pamphlets, on both sides of the question, have been published in this country, and in England.

The above is believed to be, for substance, the literature of the Discrepancies.

INDEX OF SCRIPTURE CITATIONS.

GENESIS.	PAGE	GEN.	PAGE	GEN.	PAGE
		vi. 19, 20,	387	xiv. 24,	319
i. 2,	139, 417	vii. 2, 3,	387	xv. 13,	416, 418, 419
3,	422	4, 11, 12,	415	16,	338, 416, 419
9, 10,	429	17, 24,	415	18,	148, 318, 374
11–27,	408	viii. 1,	57	xvii. 1–3,	60
14–19,	422	3, 6, 7, 8,	415	5,	17
26,	60, 159	10, 12, 13, 14,	415	6,	395
27,	158	21,	68	7,	148
31,	4, 68	22,	425	8,	282
ii. 2,	395, 416	ix. 2,	354	10, 14,	260
3,	395	3,	246	15,	281
4–7,	408	6,	159, 258	16,	281, 395
6,	429	21,	252	17,	281, 317, 318
9,	408	22,	84	24, 25,	418
17,	6, 393	24,	84, 303	xviii. 10, 14,	74
18,	291	25,	84, 302	20, 21,	58
19–22,	408	26,	421	25,	83, 201
iii. 4,	6	x. 29,	395	xix. 14,	355
5,	158	xi. 5,	58	xx. 2,	26
8,	58, 76	11,	424	2–18,	317
16,	308	12,	352	3,	376
22,	60, 158	13,	424	11,	318
iv. 1,	421	26,	392	12,	281
3,	427	29,	281	xxi. 5, 5–8,	418
4,	81, 427	31,	364	10,	304
5,	81	32,	392, 424	14–18,	418
12, 13,	258	xii. 1,	364	23,	244
16,	58	4,	317, 392, 418	24,	242, 244
26,	421, 427	5,	364	31,	410
v. 1,	158	6, 7,	357, 378	xxii. 1,	79
1–32,	14	11–20,	317	2,	237, 380, 396
2,	159	19,	26	5,	270
5,	393	xiii. 15,	318	6, 10,	259
24,	206	18,	395	12,	56, 74
29,	421	xiv. 7,	394	xxiii. 7,	225
vi. 3,	424	12,	281	xxiv. 14–20,	435
6,	4, 66, 68	13,	319	55, 60,	281
7,	68, 207	14,	318, 410	xxv. 1, 2,	318
9,	159	16,	281	5,	305

443

INDEX OF SCRIPTURE CITATIONS.

GEN.	PAGE	GEN.	PAGE	EXOD.	PAGE
xxv. 6,	295, 305, 380	xxxvi. 26,	312	ii 25,	81
22, 23,	163	31,	395	iii. 1,	396, 354
26,	315, 418	xxxvii. 2,	418	2,	396
31–33,	345	25,	339	10,	377
xxvi. 2, 3,	419	28,	339, 348	21, 22,	300
6–11,	318	30,	418	iv. 18,	354
7,	26	35,	193	19,	377, 424
15, 18, 33,	410	36,	339	20,	351
34,	321, 336, 420	xxxix. 2,	172	21,	91
36,	345	4–6,	270	24,	248
xxvii. 1–29,	345	20, 21, 22,	348	31,	344
36,	315	xl. 3, 4,	348	vi. 3,	421
42–45,	345	15,	348, 394	9,	344
xxviii. 2,	345	xli. 12,	270	10–13,	377
5,	351, 420	46, 53,	420	18,	351
9,	336	54,	425	18–20,	420
19, 20–22,	410	56,	367, 425	23,	336
xxix. 2, 4,	363	57,	367	vii. 11, 12,	120
5,	351	xlii. 1–5,	367	20, 21, 22, 24,	434
12,	281	7–20,	434	viii. 1,	301
20, 21,	421	30–34,	434	7,	120
27–30,	421	xliii. 3–13,	434	15,	89, 90
30, 31,	97, 286, 421	11, 15,	367	20,	126
xxx. 16,	314	xliv. 16–34,	434	27,	301
18,	315	xlv. 6,	420, 425	32,	89
20,	316	xlvi. 3, 4,	345	ix. 3, 6,	428
23, 24,	315	7,	384	12,	89
25,	421	8–26,	389	19–21,	428
xxxi. 11, 13,	74	15,	384, 420	34,	89, 90
17,	295	18, 20,	420	x. 1,	89
41,	421	21,	384	7,	205
53,	242	27,	389	25, 26,	301
xxxii. 3,	415	xlvii. 9,	418	xi. 1,	301
28,	411	31,	345	3,	248, 302
30,	73	xlviii. 1,	345	10,	89
xxxiii. 18–20,	357	5,	305	xii. 2,	412
19,	378	8, 10,	363	5,	433
xxxiv. 14, 17,	281	15, 16,	225	7,	377, 378
xxxv. 2, 4,	378	xlix. 9,	127	9,	433
8,	379	10,	149	15,	408, 416
10,	411	33,	345	31–33,	301
11,	395			35, 36,	300
14, 15,	400	**EXODUS.**		38,	342
16–19,	367	i. 17,	292	40,	418
24–26,	367	18–20,	290	43, 48,	260
27,	420	20,	292	49,	305
xxxvi. 2,	321, 336	ii. 10,	315	xiii. 3,	408
3,	336	14, 15,	424	13,	224
6, 8,	415	16, 21,	339	21, 22,	430
12,	352, 394	16–21,	355	xiv. 7, 9,	428
20,	321	18,	354	13, 30,	363
24,	321, 337	22,	338	31,	120

INDEX OF SCRIPTURE CITATIONS.   445

EXOD.	PAGE	EXOD.	PAGE	EXOD.	PAGE
xv. 3,	92	xxii. 18,	307	xl. 17,	396
6,	207	21,	302	20,	390, 396
13–17,	396	25,	306		
20,	309	28,	62	**LEVITICUS.**	
25, 26,	236	29,	224	i. 1–17,	236
xvi. 1,	427	xxiii. 1–33,	221	5, 8, 11,	356
2, 3,	340	3,	296	ii. 1–16,	236
13, 14,	427	10, 11,	297	iii. 1–17,	236
16,	343	14–16,	387	2,	219
23,	395	16,	412	iv. 1–35,	236
31,	431	31,	282	3,	114
34,	396	33,	221	14, 22, 23,	241
35,	342, 427	xxiv. 3–8,	220	26,	236
xvii. 1–7,	374	5,	409	v. 1–19,	236
9,	395	9, 10,	73	15, 18,	245
14,	207	13,	395	vi. 1–30,	236
xviii. 2–6,	351	18,	351	vii. 1–38,	236
5,	354, 409	xxv. 10,	407	xi. 13–19,	391
7,	225	15,	242	21, 23,	246
13–26,	284	18, 20, 34,	226	xii. 3,	12, 13
23, 24,	350	xxvii. 1,	427	6, 7,	230
25,	350, 412	8,	427, 428	xvi. 29,	416
27,	355	xxviii. 1,	409	xvii. 3, 4,	367
xix. 2,	409	xxix. 1–46,	236	11,	236
11,	376	14,	114	13,	220
12, 13, 17,	432	18, 36,	235	xviii. 1–30,	281
18,	376, 431	45,	102	5,	104
19,	76	xxx. 12–14,	345	16,	292
21–24,	432	13,	385	21,	237, 266
22,	409	xxxi. 15,	234	22–24,	266
xx. 1–26,	221	17,	56	25, 28,	266
3, 5,	225	18,	63	26,	305
4, 5,	226	xxxii. 20,	429	xix. 13,	300
5,	78, 84, 86	26, 27,	285	26,	244
8,	233, 395	33,	207	34,	305
11,	56, 234, 416	xxxiii. 3,	63	xx. 1–27,	281
12,	287	7,	396	2,	237
13, 14,	255	11,	73	21,	292
15,	300	14, 15, 17,	63	23,	266, 267
16,	290	20,	73	27,	307
17,	249, 282	23,	73, 75	xxii. 12,	283, 284
24,	427	xxxiv. 5–7,	59	xxiii. 1–44,	387
xxi. 1–36,	221	6, 7,	82	18, 19,	384
2,	303	10–27,	220	27–29,	223
7, 11,	304	18–23,	387	32,	416
14,	255	20,	224	33–39,	223
16,	302	28,	221	42, 43,	343
20, 21,	298	33–35,	355	xxv. 4, 6, 20, 21, 22,	297
23–25,	299	xxxv. 12,	407	32–34,	395
29, 30,	261	xxxvii. 1,	407	39–41,	303
xxii. 1–31,	221	xxxviii. 8,	239	44,	302
8, 9,	62	26,	345, 411	46,	298, 303

446 INDEX OF SCRIPTURE CITATIONS.

LEV.	PAGE	NUM.	PAGE	NUM.	PAGE
xxv. 47–54,	303	xiii. 26,	373	xxvi. 38, 40,	384
xxvi. 9,	81	29,	338	62,	382
30, 44,	68	xiv. 12,	322	64, 65,	357
xxvii. 26,	225	25,	365	xxvii. 12,	373
		30,	63	14,	345
NUMBERS.		33,	427	xxviii. 1–31,	387
i. 2, 3,	345, 358	45,	365, 405	16–19,	433
10,	305	xv. 24,	241	27, 30,	384
23,	385	32, 36,	234, 235	xxix. 1–40,	387
45,	358	39,	250	5,	236
46,	344, 358, 411	xvi. 12–14,	353	xxxi. 8,	366
49,	358	18–24,	353	10,	406
ii. 2, 3,	150, 378	24–27,	353	18,	255
10,	352	31–33,	352	xxxii. 8,	350
17,	366	32,	353	13,	95
32,	345	35,	352	19, 32,	375
iii. 6,	409	40,	333	41,	411
10,	333	xviii. 12, 13,	296	xxxiii. 3,	427
12, 13,	224	15,	224, 296	19–36,	371
27, 28,	419	16, 17,	224	30–33,	372
29,	352	19,	296	38,	363
39,	382	21, 24,	289	44–48,	372
iv. 3, 4–15,	422	xx. 1,	373	44–49,	371
5, 6,	242	10,	279	xxxiv. 10–12,	374
15, 20,	94	12,	248, 345	xxxv. 2, 7,	288
24–26,	422	13,	374	2–8,	395
31–33,	422	18–21,	335	4, 5,	388
36,	419	19, 20,	335	13,	385
v. 11–31,	258	27, 28,	363	14,	375
vi. 5,	246	xxi. 3,	405	19,	256
23,	356	8,	226	31,	261
vii. 12,	150	10–20,	371	xxxvi. 8,	283, 284
viii. 14,	409	11–35,	372		
24, 25, 26,	422	16–20,	372	**DEUTERONOMY.**	
x. 12,	372	20, 21,	373	i. 1,	375
14,	150	xxii. 1	372	6, 9, 14,	357
21,	366	20, 21,	69	9–13, 15	350
29,	354	22,	69, 333	20, 21,	338
29–31,	430	xxiii. 10,	208	22,	350
29–32,	355	19,	63	37,	248
33,	366, 372	xxiv. 2, 7, 16,	394	39,	161
xi. 4–6,	340	20,	208, 394	ii. 4, 8,	335
8,	431	25,	366	7,	340
16,	378, 412	xxv. 1–3,	255, 266	14,	342
24–26,	378	4,	95	19,	365
xii. 1,	339	5, 7, 8,	285	26,	373
3,	248	6–14,	385	28, 29,	335
4,	378	9,	382	30,	89, 91
8,	76	11–13,	68	iii. 4, 14,	411
16,	372	xxvi. 10,	352	27,	373
xiii. 1, 2,	350	11,	353	iv. 10–15,	376
16,	395	14,	385	12,	76

INDEX OF SCRIPTURE CITATIONS.

DEUT.	PAGE	DEUT.	PAGE	DEUT.	PAGE
iv. 15,	73	xv. 19,	225, 296	xxxii. 51,	345, 373
23,	226	20,	296	xxxiii. 2,	60, 431
41,	385	xvi. 1–7,	377	xxxiv. 1,	373, 410
v. 2, 5,	357	1–16,	387	7,	354
15,	234	2, 7,	433	10–12,	355
17,	256, 265	8,	416		
26,	76	xvii. 2, 3, 7,	225	**JOSHUA.**	
vi. 4,	60	9,	284	i. 11,	394, 416
13,	242	14, 15,	229	14,	375
16,	82	xviii. 1, 7,	356	ii. 4, 5,	290
vii. 1, 7,	344	10,	244, 308	22,	416
1–4,	266	10–12,	195	iii. 1, 2,	416
2–4,	389	11,	308	3–6,	366
16,	92	21, 22,	148	iv. 19,	394, 427
22,	403	xix. 15,	117	20,	394
viii. 2,	56	17,	284	v. 5, 7,	260
3, 15,	340	xx. 11, 15,	258	9,	394
ix. 3,	403	16–18,	258, 266	10–12,	427
9, 18,	351	19,	279	13, 14,	225
21,	429	xxi. 2,	284	vi. 24, 26,	406
x. 3–5,	407	11–14,	263	vii. 1,	312
5,	390	15,	295	4,	344
6,	363, 372	17,	304	24, 25,	237
6–8,	409	18–21,	287	24–26,	84, 85
7,	372	xxii. 3,	204	viii. 3–9,	381
8, 9,	356	13–21,	258	12, 13,	381
16,	166	xxiii. 3, 4,	235	28,	403
17,	81	7,	271	34, 35,	347
22,	344	19,	306	x. 15, 21,	374
xi. 2, 7,	357	20,	305	23, 26,	405
24,	374	xxiv. 1, 2,	263, 292	28,	186
25,	344	xxiv. 7,	303	36, 37,	405
30,	394	16,	84, 238	38, 39,	405
xii. 15, 16,	367	xxv. 5,	292	40,	324
17, 18,	296	17, 18,	94	42,	403
19,	288	xxvii. 1–26,	281	43,	374
24,	220	14, 15,	347	xi. 1, 10,	405
27,	219	15,	226	11,	186
xiii. 1–3,	120, 121, 126	xxix. (17) 18,	325	14, 15,	324
3,	56	20,	78	16, 17,	376, 404
6–11,	225	xxx. 1,	134	18,	403
xiv. 7,	246	6,	166	19,	338
12–18,	391	16,	431	20,	89, 90
19,	246	xxxi. 2,	354	21,	322, 405
21,	305	9,	363	22,	322
22–26,	224	16, 17,	148	23,	376, 404
26,	251	25,	363	xii. 7,	375, 404
27,	288	26,	363, 391	8,	376, 404
28, 29,	289	xxxii. 4,	76, 83, 97	10,	348, 406
xv. 3,	305	11,	63	10–23,	404
4, 11,	356	13, 14,	340	12,	348, 403
12,	303, 304	39,	60	14,	405

JOSH.	PAGE	JOSH.	PAGE	JUDG.	PAGE
xii. 16,	348, 403	xxiv. 1,	377	ix. 1–57,	323
21, 23,	348, 405	14,	344, 394	8,	340
xiii. 1,	404	23,	344	13,	251
1–6,	376	26,	377	32, 33,	426
9–12,	374	31,	420	x. 1–18,	323
25,	365	32,	357	3,	411
30,	385	33,	420	4,	385, 411
xiv. 1–15, 5,	412			xi. 1–40,	323
6,	323	**JUDGES.**		17, 18,	335
12, 13,	405	i. 1, 1–36,	403	26,	420
15,	395	1–19,	150	30–40,	237, 238
xv. 1–63,	412	8,	406	37–40,	240
8,	375	9–11,	405	xii. 1–6,	370
13,	150, 395	10,	321	xiii. 22,	73
13–19,	322	11–13,	405	xv. 14, 15,	142
14,	321	11–15,	322	xvii. 9,	336
15–17,	405	16,	355, 406	xviii. 1, 2, 8,	368
21–32,	387	17,	405	27, 28,	406
26–32,	369	19,	55	29,	410
33,	368	20,	321	30,	338
42,	369	21,	406	xix. 29,	257
63,	348, 404, 406	22,	404	xx. 15, 46, 47,	387
xvi. 1–10,	412	22–25,	348, 403		
2,	395	26,	395	**RUTH.**	
10,	348	27,	405	i. 1, 21,	335
xvii. 1–18,	412	28,	324		
11,	348	29,	403, 404	**1 SAMUEL.**	
12,	348, 404	30, 33,	324	i. 1,	335
14,	404	34,	344	9,	396
15–18,	369	35,	324	11,	239
xviii. 1,	377	ii. 1–3,	266	21, 22,	428
1–28,	412	1–6,	403	ii. 10,	207
6,	412	7,	344	22,	239
28,	375	8, 9,	403	23, 24,	335
xix. 1,	369	22,	324	30, 31,	63, 67
1–6,	388	23,	376	iii. 3,	396
1–51,	412	iii. 1–7,	266	13,	335
2–6,	373	2, 4,	324	21,	377
2–7,	369	9,	150	iv. 3,	377
9,	369	13,	406	vi. 6,	89
40, 41, 40–48,	368	20, 21, 26,	255	19,	14, 92
47,	368, 406, 410	iv. 4,	308, 309	vii. 13,	?44
xx. 7, 8,	385	5,	308	15,	425
xxi. 2, 3,	395	11,	354, 355	viii. 2,	352
23, 24,	368	14,	308	5,	229, 425
41,	395	21,	255	7,	229
43,	376	24,	405	19,	359
xxii. 2,	344	v. 31,	204	ix. 1,	351
7,	375	vi. 33,	406	3,	204
11–34,	344	vii. 1–25,	323	16,	344
xxiii. 5,	404	viii. 1–35,	323	17,	359
16,	148	10–12,	406	20,	204

INDEX OF SCRIPTURE CITATIONS. 449

1 SAM.	PAGE	1 SAM.	PAGE	2 SAM.	PAGE
x. 1,	412	xviii. 25, 27,	382	x. 18,	382
1–9,	379	xix. 24,	358, 412	xi. 5–7,	370
5,	344	xx. 1,	114	17,	347
8,	425	42,	244	xii. 9,	347
12,	412	xxi. 1,	320	23,	193
20, 21, 24,	359	9,	370	24,	295
24, 25,	395	12–15,	332	31,	264
xi. 2,	264	xxii. 3, 4,	364	xiii. 5,	359
14, 15,	412, 425	xxiii. 19,	26	8,	433
xii. 1,	425	xxiv. 6,	26	xiv. 27,	380
3,	412	xxv. 25,	315	33,	225
11,	323	xxvi. 1, 9,	26	xv. 7,	393
17,	229	19,	80	xvii. 25,	316, 320
xiii. 1, 2,	402	xxvii. 3–6,	332	xviii. 5,	270
5,	344	xxviii. 6,	359	6,	369
8–11,	425	15, 17, 19,	193	8,	207
12, 13,	345	18,	345	15,	331
14,	222	19,	199	18,	380
17,	344	xxix. 4,	333	xx. 23–26,	332
xiv. 3,	320	6–9,	332	xxi. 1,	241
18, 37,	360	xxx. 1,	403	2,	338
49,	352	12, 13,	413	8,	238, 385
50, 51,	351	17,	403	9, 14,	238
xv. 2, 3,	92, 93	xxxi. 2,	352	18,	373
2–8,	394	3–5,	359	19,	336
6,	355	6,	360	xxiii. 8,	383
7, 8,	403			8–39,	334
10, 11,	63	**2 SAMUEL.**		11,	428
18,	94	i. 6–10,	359	27,	312
22,	236	ii. 4,	411	xxiv. 1,	79, 333, 334
29,	63, 98	8,	360	9,	389
35,	358	10, 11,	400	10,	222
xvi. 2,	99	iii. 2–5,	295	13,	393
6–11,	385	3,	333	14,	96
13,	411	14,	382	24,	390
14,	142	v. 3,	411		
14–23,	360	5,	400	**1 KINGS.**	
18,	362	6, 9,	370	i. 39,	412
21,	331, 361	14–16,	332	ii. 5–9,	256
21–23,	360	21,	430	11,	393
xvii. 12–31,	360	vi. 10,	339	19,	225
15,	331	23,	385	27,	68
25, 34–36,	362	viii. 1,	369	iii. 2, 3,	323
39,	80, 362	2,	264	7,	270
42,	362	3,	25, 374	iv. 26,	383
54,	370	4, 13,	382	31,	351
55–58,	360	16–18,	332	v. 11,	385
56,	362	17,	320, 332	13, 15,	362
xviii. 1–5,	360	18,	333	16,	382, 383
2,	331	ix. 6,	225	vi. 1,	426, 427
9, 10,	360	x. 5,	406	2,	382, 383
10, 11,	142	6,	320	14,	396

INDEX OF SCRIPTURE CITATIONS.

1 KINGS.	PAGE	1 KINGS.	PAGE	2 KINGS.	PAGE
vi. 17,	383	xix. 11, 12,	58	xiv. 3, 7,	271
37, 38,	427	15, 16,	339	17,	399
vii. 14,	339	xxi. 1,	364	23,	399, 401
15, 20,	383	13,	356	29,	191
16, 26,	382	19,	364	xv. 1,	399, 401
24,	431	xxii. 15,	276	2,	399
42,	383	19–23,	98	8,	401
48,	384	37, 38,	364	27,	399, 402
viii. 9,	390	41,	396	30,	399, 401
12,	101	49,	346	32,	399, 402
22, 23,	231	51,	396, 398	33,	401, 402
46,	159			xvi. 2,	399
65, 66,	223	**2 KINGS.**		5, 7, 9,	319
ix. 22,	362	i. 10,	355	10–16, 15,	319
23,	382	17,	400	20,	364
26–28,	378	ii. 11,	216	xvii. 1,	399, 402
28,	383, 395	12,	257	8,	77
x. 1,	80	14,	355	34, 41,	242
19, 20,	226	23, 24,	270	xviii. 2,	399
22,	378	iii. 1,	398	14–16,	340
xi. 1–3,	295	18, 19,	279	25,	205
3,	390	iv. 33,	231	xix. 85,	363
14,	333	34,	355	xx. 1, 4, 5, 6,	63, 64
32, 36,	387	vi. 19,	276	xxi. 17,	351
xii. 4,	362	23, 24,	344	xxii. 3,	401
21,	387	viii. 7–15,	339	14, 15,	309
25,	375	16,	401	xxiii. 4,	401
xiv. 12–17,	375	17,	319	5–12,	348
xv. 2,	317, 323	18,	320	30,	349, 376
3,	222, 317	25,	398	34,	335, 349
5,	222	26,	319, 320, 398	xxiv. 6,	346, 374
8,	323	27,	355	7,	344
10,	396, 398	29,	359	8, 12,	400
10, 13, 14,	323	ix. 1–10,	339	13,	412
16,	398	25,	364	14, 16,	384
20,	373	26,	356, 364	17,	349, 352
32, 33,	398	27,	364, 365	xxv. 1, 6,	377
xvi. 8, 10,	399	28,	365	7,	363
15,	402	29,	398	8,	393
20,	364	x. 13, 14,	319	13–17,	412
21, 22, 23,	402	36,	400	17,	382
29,	396	xi. 3–5,	370	19,	383
xvii. 1,	415	4–19,	350, 351	27,	400
7,	435	5–7,	370		
22,	201, 355	xii. 1,	398, 400	**1 CHRONICLES.**	
xviii. 1,	415	13–14,	434	i. 34,	416
5,	435	xiii. 1,	400	36,	352
26–29,	232	10,	398, 400	41,	312
27,	276	21,	201	51,	352
32–35,	435	23,	81	ii. 1, 3–9,	416
40,	265	xiv. 1,	398	6,	312, 351
xix. 3, 8,	379	2,	399	10,	336

INDEX OF SCRIPTURE CITATIONS. 451

1 CHRON.	PAGE	1 CHRON.	PAGE	2 CHRON.	PAGE
ii. 13,	316	xx. 4,	373	xxii. 1,	319, 346
13–15,	385	5,	336	2,	398
16,	316	xxi. 1,	333	6,	359
17,	320	5,	389, 390	8,	319
18,	323	11, 12,	393	9,	364
19,	324	25,	390	xxiii. 1–20,	350
22, 23,	385, 411	xxiii. 3,	422	4, 5,	370
50,	323	7,	338	xxiv. 14,	434
53,	368	8,	351	xxvi. 10,	352
iii. 1,	333	24,	422	xxviii. 1,	399
5–8,	332	xxiv. 3–6,	68	5, 16, 20,	319
15,	349, 352	xxv. 3,	385	21, 24,	319
16, 19,	352	xxvi. 21, 22,	351	27,	304
22,	385	30,	375	xxx. 2, 3,	340
iv. 28–31,	373	xxviii. 3,	222, 331	9,	97
v. 1, 2,	305	9,	71	17–20, 26,	340
vi. 16–27,	336	xxix. 15,	177	xxxi. 17,	422
20,	338, 351	22,	412	xxxii. 23, 27–29,	340
22,	351			xxxiii. 5, 6,	308
22–28,	353	**2 CHRONICLES.**		11–17,	351
28,	352	ii. 6,	102	15,	348
31,	353	10,	385	xxxiv. 3,	348
33,	353	14,	339	3–7,	401
69,	368	18,	382	xxxv. 13,	433
vii. 6,	384	iii. 1,	396	18,	340
15, 16,	351	4,	382	24,	376
viii. 33,	351, 352	15,	383	xxxvi. 4,	335
38,	32	iv. 3,	431	6,	374
ix. 1–34,	337	5,	382	9,	400
39,	351	13,	383	10,	352
x. 6,	360	19,	384	13,	89
13,	345	vii. 10,	223		
14,	359	12, 16,	102	**EZRA.**	
xi. 10,	334	19, 20,	102	i. 9, 10, 11,	383
11,	383	viii. 10,	382	ii. 1–39,	409
11–47,	334	18,	383	2–60,	352
13,	428	ix. 1,	308	3–35,	385
26,	334	21,	378	5,	380
29,	312	25,	383	6–65,	381
xiii. 3,	360	xiii. 2, 4–12,	317	36–39,	390
xiv. 3–7,	332	xiv. 1,	398	69,	381
12,	430	3, 5,	323	iii. 2,	352
xv. 17, 18, 21,	339	xv. 16,	323	4,	417
xvi. 34,	92	19,	398, 399	v. 1,	352
xvii. 4–6, 12,	331	xvi. 1,	399	vi. 14,	352
xviii. 1,	369	4,	373	ix. 1, 2,	389
3,	25	7–12,	323	x. 3–17,	412
4, 12,	382	xix. 7,	81		
16,	320	xx. 35, 36,	346	**NEHEMIAH.**	
xix. 6, 7,	320	36, 37,	378	vii.7–42,	409
18,	382	xxi. 16, 17,	346	7–62,	352
xx. 3,	264	18, 19,	398	10,	380

452   INDEX OF SCRIPTURE CITATIONS.

NEH.	PAGE	PSALMS.	PAGE	PSALMS.	PAGE
vii. 11–67,	381	i. 3,	173	l. 22,	207
32,	403	ii. 8,	302	li. 2,	166
70–72,	381	9,	116, 207	5,	161
viii. 17,	417	11,	241	9,	207
ix. 17,	82	v. 4,	76	16,	235
x. 1–28,	409	6,	205	17,	207
9–13,	387	vi. 5,	193	liii. 5,	242
14–27, 32,	385	vii. 8,	228	lv. 15,	271
xi. 3–36,	337	11,	82	23,	180
xii. 1,	352	ix. 11,	103	lviii. 3,	161
1–7,	390	17,	214	lix. 4,	114
8, 9,	387	x. 1,	70	lx. Title,	382
xiii. 23–30,	412	xi. 6,	209	lxii. 12,	97
		xiv. 2, 3,	159	lxix. 24, 27,	271
JOB.		xvii. 14,	180	28,	207
i. 1,	159	xviii. 11,	101	lxxi. 17,	73
6, 7,	362	xix. 1,	72	lxxii. 17,	115
19,	347	xxiv. 2,	429	lxxiii. 7, 12,	180
ii. 7,	172	3, 4,	159	11,	58
10,	279	xxvi. 7,	73	16–18,	181
iii. 10,	347	xxx. 5,	95	24,	197
13,	191	xxxii. 1,	221	27,	204
18,	197	xxxiv. Title,	318, 332	28,	70, 73
vii. 9,	200	10,	173	lxxiv. 12,	251
viii. 4,	347	21,	180	lxxvi. 2,	103
ix. 10	73	xxxv. 6, 8,	271	lxxviii. 55,	283
22,	88	xxxvii. 3,	173	58,	78
x. 21,	197	9,	205	69,	215
xi. 7,	72	20,	204	lxxxi. 12,	77
12,	161	21,	300	lxxxiii. 15,	209
xii. 6,	180	25,	177	17,	209, 271
xiii. 23,	114	34,	205	lxxxv. 5,	95
xiv. 4,	161	36,	206	lxxxvi. 2,	159
12,	200	37,	208	lxxxvii. 2, 3,	228
21, 22,	188, 190	38,	205, 208	lxxxviii. 5, 6, 11, 12,	197
xv. 14,	161	xl. 5,	73	xc. 2,	60
xvi. 9, 12–14,	207	6,	152	xci. 4,	16, 63
xix. 10,	205	xli. 1,	296	xcii. 9,	203
17,	347	xlii. 9,	16	15,	83
xxi. 7, 8,	180	xliv. Title,	353	xciv. 5,	207
9, 14,	181	1–3,	283	23,	203
xxii. 23, 24,	174	23,	57	xcvi. 4, 5,	433
xxiv. 5, 6, 12,	182	xlv. Title,	353	xcvii. 2,	101
20, 24,	181	2,	115	7,	60
xxvi. 5,	195	xlvi. Title,	353	c. 2,	241
7,	429	1,	70	cii. 25, 26,	215
xxvii. 13, 14, 22,	182	xlvii.–xlix. Titles,	353	ciii. 8, 9,	95
xxxi. 18,	161	xlix. 10,	178, 204	civ. 5,	215
xxxvi. 14,	180	l. 6	201	15,	251
xxxviii. 1,	76	13, 14,	235	22,	426
xlii. 7–9,	162	21,	58	30,	417
12,	172, 175, 208			35,	206

INDEX OF SCRIPTURE CITATIONS. 453

PSALMS.	PAGE
cvi. 18,	352
33,	345
cix. 6–10,	271
12, 13, 18, 19,	271
cxii. 2, 3,	174
cxv. 17,	195
cxix. 110,	221
147, 148,	19
155,	214
156,	82
176,	221
cxxi. 4,	57
cxxiii. 1,	103
cxxviii. 3,	230
cxxxii. 13,	228
cxxxvii. 8, 9,	272
cxxxviii. 6,	81
cxxxix. 2–4,	56
7–10,	58
21,	306
22,	273, 306
cxliii. 2,	228
cxlv. 3,	72
8,	78
9,	78, 92, 97
18,	70
20,	203, 205
cxlvi. 4,	195
cxlvii. 5,	72

PROVERBS.	
i. 22,	72
26,	96
28,	71
29, 30,	72
iii. 13,	176, 254
15,	254
17,	176
iv. 18,	197
v. 4,	325
18, 19,	295
vi. 34,	78
viii. 11,	176
17,	71
x. 15,	175
27,	180
xi. 31,	182
xii. 21,	172
22,	290
xiii. 21,	180
22,	280
24,	97

PROV.	PAGE
xiv. 21,	296
32,	214
xv. 6,	174
xvi. 7,	178
xvii. 15,	306
22,	250
xviii. 6,	261
22,	291
xix. 9,	204
xx. 1,	251
9,	159
xxi. 28,	204
xxii. 1,	176
15,	161, 278
24,	245
xxiii. 29–32,	251
xxiv. 24,	306
xxv. 27,	248
xxvi. 4, 5,	278
xxvii. 2,	247
4,	78
22,	278
xxviii. 1,	242
13,	221
14,	89, 90
xxx. 8, 9,	175
30,	354
xxxi. 4, 5,	253
6, 7,	251

ECCLESIASTES.	
i. 4,	215
9, 10,	432
15,	428
18,	176, 254
ii. 2,	250
13,	254
15,	176, 254
iii. 1, 4,	250
18–20,	184
20,	199
vi. 8,	254
vii. 1,	176
3, 4,	250
9,	245
13,	428
15,	178, 204
16, 17,	233
20,	159
29,	161
viii. 2,	292
12, 13,	180

ECCL.	PAGE
viii. 14,	172
15,	250
ix. 5, 6,	193
10,	188
xi. 9,	250
xii. 7,	184

CANTICLES.	
v. 10, 16,	127
vi. 8,	390
viii. 6,	78

ISAIAH.	
i. 11–13,	235
13,	233
15,	89
16,	166
20,	207
28,	203, 206
iii. 13,	103
v. 20, 23,	306
vi. 1,	73
10,	264
vii. 15, 16,	161
viii. 9,	207
ix. 1, 2,	151
6, 7,	118
17–21,	399
x. 5,	98
xiii. 9,	205
xiv. 9,	191, 195
10,	195
xxiv. 23,	433
xxvi. 10,	181
14, 19,	200
20,	82
xxvii. 4,	82
xxix. 20,	206
xxx. 10,	177
26,	433
xxxviii. 18,	193
xxxix. 2, 6,	340
xl. 4,	428
5,	181
25,	159
28,	56, 72
xlii. 1,	139
3,	116
xliii. 13,	18
19,	432
xliv. 9, 10, 17,	433
22,	207

454 INDEX OF SCRIPTURE CITATIONS.

ISA.	PAGE	JER.	PAGE	EZEK.	PAGE
xlv. 5,	60	xxiii. 31,	177	xxxiii. 13,	171
7,	76	xxv. 1,	400	19,	88
15,	70	xxix. 11,	76, 77	xxxv. 12,	206
17,	432	xxx. 16,	207	xxxvi. 5,	78
19,	71	xxxi. 22,	432	25, 26,	166
23,	211	xxxii. 27,	55	xliii. 22,	114
xlviii. 16,	60, 62	31,	228	xliv. 29,	114
xlix. 6,	119	xxxiii. 16,	138	xlv. 22,	114
15,	57	xxxiv. 3,	363	xlvii. 13,	305
liii. 2, 3,	127	xxxvi. 9,	393	xlviii. 4, 5,	305
9,	114	30,	346, 374		
lv. 6,	71	xxxvii. 5,	344	**DANIEL.**	
7,	196	xl. 10,	252	i. 1,	393, 400, 402
lvi. 2,	233	xlvi. 2,	400	2,	412
lvii. 1,	88, 204	li. 8,	205	5, 18,	402
2,	88	lii. 12,	393, 402	21,	414
15,	102	23, 25,	383	ii. 1,	402
21,	214	28,	400	48,	331
lviii. 6,	302	28–30,	385	iii. 12,	331
lxi. 1, 2,	150, 151	29,	402	16, 18,	292
lxiii. 17,	90	31,	400	vi. 10, 11,	231
lxv. 1,	71			13,	392
17,	432	**LAMENTATIONS.**		vii. 9,	73, 74
20,	180	iii. 22,	92	13,	131
lxvi. 1,	58, 102	38,	76	14,	131, 137
		44,	70	23,	207
JEREMIAH.		v. 21,	166	ix. 26,	205
i. 5,	270			x. 1,	414
ii. 10, 11,	343	**EZEKIEL.**		xii. 2,	199, 200, 209
22,	227	v. 7,	343		
iv. 8,	82	xi. 12,	343	**HOSEA.**	
14,	166, 227	xii. 13,	363	i. 2,	255
vi. 20,	235	xiii. 10–16,	177	iv. 2,	242
vii. 9,	95	13, 14,	206	6,	205
22, 23,	235	xiv. 9,	99	11,	251
ix. 4,	262	xvi. 47,	343	vi. 6,	235
xii. 1,	180	xviii. 2,	85, 88	viii. 7,	209
xiii. 14,	93, 95	4,	84	xiii. 9,	205
15–17,	95	5,	178, 228		
xv. 6,	64	9,	88, 178, 228	**JOEL.**	
xvii. 5,	262, 287	19,	88	iii. 8,	302
10,	56	20,	84, 203	12,	103
xviii. 7–10,	64, 148	24,	169, 170		
11,	76	25,	83	**AMOS.**	
xx. 7,	99	31,	166	i. 13,	264
xxii. 11,	349	32,	96, 225	iii. 6,	77
19,	374	xx. 3,	70	vi. 1,	394
30,	346	24–26,	104	viii. 14,	200
xxiii. 6,	138	25,	77	ix. 2, 3,	58
19,	209	xxi. 3, 4,	88		
23,	58	xxii. 28,	177	**JONAH.**	
24,	58, 103	xxiv. 14,	63	i. 3,	58

INDEX OF SCRIPTURE CITATIONS. 455

JONAH.	PAGE	HABAKKUK.	PAGE	MALACHI.	PAGE
iii. 4, 5,	148	ii. 4,	228	i. 2, 3,	97
10,	64, 148	iii. 3,	60	14,	99
MICAH.		4,	63	ii. 14, 15,	295
iii. 4,	89	7,	339	15,	263
vi. 16,	77			16,	263
vii. 2,	204	ZECHARIAH.		iii. 1,	151
5,	262	i. 3,	166	6,	63
		ix. 9,	131	15,	82
NAHUM.		xi. 12, 13,	153	iv. 1,	214
i. 2,	78, 82	xii. 11,	376	1–3,	205

MATTHEW.	PAGE	MATT.	PAGE	MATT.	PAGE
i. 2–16,	388	vi. 7, 8,	232	xii. 41, 42,	210, 214
11,	389	13,	79, 253	49, 50,	203
12,	346, 389	19,	174, 280	xv. 5, 6,	191
16,	325	21,	174	22,	239
17,	388	25,	19, 280	24,	119
20,	406	34,	280	xvi. 4,	155
ii. 1–23,	413	vii. 1, 2,	284	13,	108
11,	414	1–29,	331	27,	182
iii. 5,	428	8,	71	28,	155
12,	211	21,	231	xvii. 12, 13,	347
14,	409	viii. 5,	346	xviii. 3, 4,	161, 162
17,	153	12,	210, 213	15,	293
iv. 7,	83	21, 22,	287	20,	114
8,	407	26,	153	xix. 1,	119, 327
10,	293	28,	369, 387	5,	291
12,	407	ix. 2,	153	7,	263
14–16,	151	30,	327	8,	263, 295
17, 18–22,	407	x. 1–42,	407	18,	285
v. 1, 2,	368	2–4,	322	21,	253
1–48,	331	5, 6,	119	26,	55
3,	174	9, 10,	154	28,	202
4,	251	15,	210	xx. 9–12,	210
5,	177	23,	135	16,	172
14,	129	28,	186	17,	327
16,	279	34–36,	118	20,	347
17,	120	37,	97	23,	110
22,	277	xi. 3–5,	120, 121	29,	327
25, 26,	211	14,	348	30,	386
32,	263	22,	210	xxi. 1,	327
33–37,	243	28,	116, 179	1–11,	132
39,	298	30,	179	2, 3,	155
44,	271, 276	xii. 1–5,	234	5, 7,	384
48,	169	32,	139, 211, 241	19,	155
vi. 1,	279	40,	413	31,	217
1–34,	331	41, 42,	202	38,	358
5, 6,	231	xiii. 12,	83	41,	363
		34,	331	xxii. 12,	209

INDEX OF SCRIPTURE CITATIONS.

MATT.	PAGE
xxii. 13,	210
18, 19,	156
30,	155
31,	156
32,	156
xxiii. 2, 3, 8,	293
9,	257, 287
10,	257
16–22,	243
17,	277
33,	116
xxiv. 3,	146
14,	135
15, 16,	156
21,	132
24,	121
29, 30,	132
36,	113
51,	203
xxv. 14–30,	433
30,	203, 210
31, 32,	201
34,	417
41,	210
46,	211
xxvi. 2, 6,	416
7,	411
11,	114
17–30,	423
18,	151
21–29,	156
34,	424
52,	259, 298
63,	242
64,	156
xxvii. 5,	349
6, 7,	347
9, 10,	153
34,	325
37,	154
44,	384
48,	325
xxviii. 1,	391
1–10,	327
2, 5,	386
9,	330
10,	369
16,	367, 369
17,	367
18,	110
19,	257, 370
20,	114

MARK.	PAGE
i. 2,	151
11,	153
14,	407
15,	165
16–20,	407
21, 29,	377
ii. 5,	153
26,	320
iii. 5,	275
16–19,	322
29,	211, 241
iv. 12,	38
40,	153
v. 1,	369
19, 43,	327
vi. 5,	110
8, 9,	154
32, 45, 53,	367
vii. 26,	119, 339
27,	119
viii. 12,	155
38,	209
ix. 1,	155
2,	416
13,	347
44, 46, 48,	209
x. 7–9,	295
13, 14, 16,	270
18,	159
24,	174, 175
25,	175
30,	174
35,	347
46,	386
xi. 2, 3,	155
7,	384
13,	111
14,	155
xii. 9,	363
15,	156
25,	155
26, 27,	156
38, 40,	206, 293
xiii. 10,	135
14,	156
32,	111, 113
xiv. 12–26,	423
13, 14,	151
18–24,	156
30,	424
62,	156

MARK.	PAGE
xv. 23,	325
25,	412
26,	154
xvi. 1,	391, 412
1–14,	327
2,	426
5,	386

LUKE.	
i. 5,	336
26–37,	406
27,	336
33,	137
36,	336
61,	338
ii. 4–39,	413
9,	386
36–38,	309
39,	414
52,	111, 113
iii. 2,	320
22,	153
23,	325, 326
27,	346
35, 36,	352
iv. 5,	407
18, 19,	150, 151
25,	415
v. 1–11,	407
20,	153
vi. 12,	114, 231
13–16,	322
17,	368
20,	174, 368
24,	174
25,	250
26,	176
27–29,	299
30,	280
35,	280, 306
35, 36,	264
37,	284
45,	159
46,	231
vii. 3,	346
15,	201
22,	327
30,	428
37, 38,	411
viii. 25,	153
27,	387
52, 53,	337

INDEX OF SCRIPTURE CITATIONS. 457

LUKE.	PAGE	LUKE.	PAGE	JOHN.	PAGE
ix. 3,	154	xxii. 8, 10, 11,	151	v. 13,	114
10–17,	367	13–20,	423	16,	235
27,	155	14–20,	156	22,	120, 201
28,	416	30,	202	27,	120
30, 31,	195	31,	179	28,	199, 200
52,	119, 358	34,	424	29,	200
53,	358	36,	259, 298	31,	117
56,	116	43,	117	34,	118
59, 60,	287	69, 70,	108	35,	129
x. 1–20,	407	xxiii. 26,	324	36,	121
23,	219	34,	271	37,	73, 76
33–37,	119	38,	154	vi. 15,	136
xi. 8,	232	39–41,	384	32,	134
10,	89	43,	198	51,	128
19,	121, 126	56,	412	53,	38
xii. 4,	185, 277	xxiv. 1–12,	327	66,	39
5,	187	1–53,	386	vii. 1,	277
16–20,	196	4,	386	24,	284
21,	174	10,	391	34,	71
33,	280	15,	114	39,	417
47, 48,	210	25,	277	viii. 14,	117
xiii. 5,	165	27,	331	15,	120, 201
24,	19, 71, 261	33, 36,	367	40,	106
32,	169	39,	63	51,	183
xiv. 26,	97, 286	49,	139, 369	58,	111
xvi. 18,	263	50, 51,	367	ix. 5,	129
20,	177			39,	120, 201
22,	177, 188	JOHN.		x. 9, 11,	128
23,	188, 199	i. 1,	106	15, 17, 18,	130
26,	199	9,	129	28,	169, 172
27, 28, 30,	193	14,	106	30,	106
xvii. 11, 16,	119	18,	73, 109	36,	108
20, 21,	136	21,	347	40,	327
xviii. 1, 7,	232	33,	409	xi. 3, 4,	184
16, 17,	162	35–43,	407	11–14,	191
35, 38,	386	36,	127	14,	184
xix. 10,	108, 116	44,	377	15,	114, 184
11–27,	433	ii. 1–11,	252	17,	327
30, 31,	155	15,	298	26,	178, 183
xx. 16,	363	24, 25,	111	34,	111
23, 24,	156	iii. 2,	121, 407	44,	353
35. 36,	155	6,	162	45,	184
37,	156	13,	216	54,	327
38,	156, 195, 197	17,	120	xii. 1,	327, 416
xxi. 17,	172	22, 24,	407	3,	411
20, 21,	156	34,	139	27,	117
23,	133	35,	110	40,	90, 92
24,	132, 133	36,	211	47,	120, 201
27,	132	iv. 3, 4,	119	xiii. 1, 2,	423
33,	215	24,	63	33,	198
xxii. 1,	423	39, 40,	358	38,	424
3,	140	40, 41,	119	xiv. 2, 3,	417

INDEX OF SCRIPTURE CITATIONS.

JOHN.	PAGE	ACTS.	PAGE	ACTS.	PAGE
xiv. 16,	141	ii. 1–4,	417	xvi. 6,	370
23,	103	4,	140	7,	139
26,	139	17,	139	xvii. 26,	298
27,	118	18,	139, 309	30, 5, 165, 215, 232	
28,	107	23,	130	31,	106, 201
xv. 5,	128	34,	198	xviii. 26,	309
13,	130	iii. 15,	130	xix. 34,	232
15,	31, 330	17,	358	xx. 9, 10,	337
26,	141	21,	214	28,	107, 139
27,	118	iv. 8,	139	xxi. 9,	309
xvi. 3,	358	19,	292	xxii. 9,	359
12,	31, 330	34, 35,	253	xxvi. 14,	359
13, 14,	139	v. 3,	99, 140, 141	23,	201
22,	250	4,	141	xxviii. 25,	139
28,	106	29,	292		
30,	111	31,	165	ROMANS.	
33,	179	vii. 4,	392	i. 13,	18
xvii. 3,	60, 107	5,	318	20,	72
9,	131	14,	389	24, 25,	77
12,	170	15, 16,	357	ii. 5,	85
17,	168	29,	424	6,	85, 210
22,	106	30, 32,	74	7,	187
xviii. 28,	423	48,	102	9, 10,	339
31,	220	52,	130	11,	81
36,	136	59,	198	13,	167
xix. 7,	220	60,	191, 271	14, 15,	164
14,	423	viii. 27,	308	16,	201
14–18,	412	29,	139	29,	213
17,	324	32,	128	iii. 18,	159
19,	154	37,	108	20,	167
29, 30,	325	39,	139	23,	159
xx. 1,	391, 426	ix. 1,	248	28,	167
1–18,	327	6,	407	iv. 2,	167
1–31,	386	7,	359	5,	306
12,	386	10–16,	407	v. 8, 10,	130
17,	330	x. 3,	407	12,	165, 183
19,	367	9,	231	18, 19,	165
22,	417	13,	279, 407	20,	241
29,	219	15,	407	vi. 9,	201
xxi. 1–25,	386	3+,	81	11,	208
16,	279	38, 44,	139	vii. 10,	77, 105
17,	111	xi. 18,	165	18,	230
		xii. 7,	386	viii. 14, 15, 16,	109
ACTS.		xiii. 2,	139	26,	131, 141
i. 3,	331	20,	421, 426	27,	139, 141
5,	139, 417	21,	149	28,	172
8,	417	22,	222	29,	170
9, 12,	367	39,	241	30,	170, 172
13,	322	48,	214	38, 39,	170
18,	347, 349	xv. 10,	83, 104	ix. 1,	243
24,	56	28,	139	11,	162
25.	171, 199	xvi. 1, 3,	260	11–13,	83

INDEX OF SCRIPTURE CITATIONS.   459

ROM.	PAGE	1 COR.	PAGE	GALATIANS.	PAGE
ix. 16,	249	viii. 11,	172		
18,	90, 92	ix. 22,	294	i. 8,	170
x. 5,	104	24,	249	10,	294
xi. 26,	213	x. 8,	382	13,	248
32,	214	19,	249, 433	ii. 3, 4,	260
33,	72	20, 21,	249	6,	81
xii. 14,	276, 306	25,	246	8,	247
20,	25, 275	33,	294	16,	167
xiii. 1, 2,	292	xi. 1–34,	310	20,	230
3, 4,	92	3,	308	iii. 1,	277
5,	292	4,	310	11, 12,	167
14,	280	5,	309	13,	115, 120
xiv. 5,	233	14,	246	17,	416, 419
6,	244	23–26,	156	21,	105
10,	201	xii. 3,	231	29,	149
14,	246	8, 11,	139	iv. 8–11,	245
15,	172	31,	249	10,	244
xv. 2,	294	xiii. 1–3,	171	24,	104
20, 30,	261	1–13,	273	28,	149
33,	92	7, 8,	262	v. 2,	260
xvi. 5,	310	xiv. 1–40,	310	15,	206
12,	309	33,	77, 92	20,	308
27,	186	34,	308, 309	22, 23,	142
		35,	309	vi. 2, 5,	257
1 CORINTHIANS.		39,	249		
i. 14, 17,	257	xv. 5–8,	386	**EPHESIANS.**	
29,	247	6,	368	ii. 1,	208, 393
ii. 8,	358	9, 10,	247	3,	164
10, 11,	139	15,	217	5, 6, 10,	166
15,	202	20,	201	19,	178
iii. 6, 8,	106	21,	200	20,	128, 129
11,	129	22,	214	iii. 8,	247
17,	205	24, 25, 28,	137	iv. 18,	393
iv. 15,	257	31,	208	25,	290
v. 12,	284	36,	277	26,	245
vi. 2, 3,	202	51,	134, 183	30,	139
9.	217	52,	134, 200	v. 14,	166
10,	217, 251	xvi. 19,	310	22, 24,	308
vii. 1,	291	22,	272, 275	25, 33,	286
2,	291, 295			vi. 4,	287
6,	143	**2 CORINTHIANS.**		6,	294
8,	291	iii. 7, 13,	355	9,	81
12,	143	v. 6,	197	17,	129
18,	260	8,	198	24,	187
23,	293	10,	201, 210		
25,	144	21,	114	**PHILIPPIANS.**	
26, 27,	291	vi. 16,	103	i. 21,	197
32, 33, 38,	291	xi. 5,	247	23,	198
40,	144	17,	143, 247	ii. 5, 6,	107
viii. 4, 5,	433	18,	247	7,	112
6,	60	20,	206	8,	112, 117
8, 9–13,	249	xii. 11,	247	10, 11,	211

INDEX OF SCRIPTURE CITATIONS.

PHIL.	PAGE
ii. 12, 13,	167, 251
15,	129
iii. 11, 12, 15,	169
19,	208
iv. 3,	309
4,	251
5,	134

COLOSSIANS.

ii. 3,	111
5,	114
8, 9,	107
14,	207
16,	233
iii. 3,	208
9,	166, 290
10,	166
20, 21,	287
22,	293

1 THESSALONIANS.

ii. 4,	294
iv. 6,	300
14,	199
15,	19, 134
15–17,	183
17,	134
v. 19,	139

2 THESSALONIANS.

i. 8,	202
9,	203, 205
ii. 1, 2, 3,	134
7,	18
9,	121, 126
9–12,	99
11,	40, 77
13,	169

1 TIMOTHY.

i. 17,	73
ii. 3, 4,	214
5,	106, 131
6,	119
8,	231
11, 12,	309
iii. 15, 16,	129
iv. 7,	307
10,	214
16,	262
v. 6,	208
8,	280

1 TIM.	PAGE
v. 19, 20,	293
23,	251
vi. 9, 10,	253
15, 16,	185
16,	70, 73, 101
17,	174, 253
18,	253
20,	307

2 TIMOTHY.

i. 10,	185
ii. 14,	261
24,	19, 261
25,	165, 265, 279
iii. 12,	178
16,	143
iv. 14,	275

TITUS.

ii. 11,	214

HEBREWS.

i. 1,	4
8,	106, 137
ii. 4,	121
17,	111
iii. 8,	90
iv. 3,	417
9,	218
13,	56
15,	114
v. 7,	117
8,	114
vi. 4–6,	170
13,	243
17,	244
18,	55, 98, 244
vii. 14,	150
19,	104
26,	114
viii. 1,	128
ix. 4,	390
26,	128
27,	183, 185
28,	128
x. 4,	236
5, 6,	152
11,	236
26–29,	170
27,	206
31,	96
38,	88

HEB.	PAGE
x. 39,	170
xi. 5,	206, 217
8,	364
12,	318
13,	178, 363
16,	149, 407
17,	380
21,	345
27,	424
32,	239
33,	363
37,	173
39,	149, 363
40,	149
xii. 6,	172, 179
8,	179
11,	172
17,	232
23,	202
29,	93, 95
xiii. 4,	255, 291
14,	177
20,	128

JAMES.

i. 2,	253
5, 6,	89
13,	79, 82
17,	63
19, 20,	245
25,	104
ii. 5,	175
12,	104
14, 17, 21,	167
22, 24,	167
25,	290
26,	167
iii. 15,	254
16,	261
17,	254
iv. 3,	89
8,	70
v. 1–3,	174
11,	92
12,	243
17,	415
19, 20,	262

1 PETER.

i. 2,	168
17,	81
18, 19,	107

INDEX OF SCRIPTURE CITATIONS.

1 PET.	PAGE
ii. 7,	127
8,	40, 128
11,	178
13, 14,	292
18,	293
23,	276
25,	128
iii. 5, 6,	308
9,	276
13,	172
17, 18,	195
18–20,	191
iv. 6,	193, 195
7,	134
v. 8,	362

2 PETER.	
i. 19,	148
20, 21,	146
ii. 4,	362
21, 22,	170
iii. 7,	203, 216
9,	214
10,	216

1 JOHN.	PAGE
i. 8,	159
ii. 1,	131, 159, 241
iii. 2,	109
6, 9,	159
14, 15,	286
iv. 9,	109
16,	92
v. 7,	60, 62
14,	89
16,	241
18,	179
20,	108

JUDE.	
3,	261
6,	362

REVELATION.	
ii. 11,	183, 184
iii. 1,	208
iv. 6–8,	227

REV.	PAGE
iv. 8,	218
v. 5,	127
12,	115
vi. 9,	191
10,	191, 275
16,	116
vii. 14,	128, 173
x. 5,	243
6,	243
xi. 18,	205
xii. 12,	362
xiii. 13, 14,	121
18,	24
xiv. 10, 11,	203, 212
13,	218
xix. 11, 13, 15,	116
xx. 9,	206
10,	212
11,	216
12,	182, 202
13, 15,	210
xxi. 3,	103
8,	214, 290, 308

GENERAL INDEX.

Aaron, death where, 363.
Abel-beth-maachah, names, 373.
Abigail, father of, 316.
Abijah, mother, 317; hypocrisy, 317.
Abraham, equivocation, 26; temptation, 79; sacrifice of Isaac, 238; difficulty with Pharaoh, 317; with Abimelech, 317; inheritance gained, 318; prolonged virility, 318; weakness and timidity, 318; marriage with Keturah, 318, 339; destination, 364; sons, 380; age at migration, 392.
Absalom, sons, 380; tarry at home, 393.
Achan, children slain, 87, 237.
Adam, death when, 393.
Adultery tolerated and forbidden 255.
Agag mentioned prematurely, 394.
Ahab, deceived by Micaiah, 98; death where, 364; death when, 396.
Ahaz, favoring religion, 319; invincible, 319; burial where, 364.
Ahaziah of Israel, reign begun when, 398.
Ahaziah of Judah, brethren's fate, 319; grandfather, 320; death where, 364; age, 398; reign begun, 398.
Ahimelech, high-priesthood, 320.
Ai, destruction, 403.
Altar, material, 427.
Amalek mentioned prematurely, 394.
Amalekites, destruction, 94, 403; location, 365.
Amasa, father of, 320.
Amaziah, reign begun, 398.
Ambuscade, number of men, 381.

Ammonites, torture, 264; allies, 320; land taken, 365.
Anah, nationality, 321.
Anak, sons' fate, 321.
Analogy of Bible and nature, 33.
Anatomists, disagreement, 11.
Angels seen, number, 386.
Anger approved and condemned, 245.
Animal-food, use restricted and unrestricted, 246; kinds prohibited and allowed, 246.
Animals, number employed by Christ, 384; number sacrificed, 384.
Announcement made to Mary and to Joseph, 406.
Apostles, lists of names, 322; called when, 407; distinct from the "seventy disciples," 407.
Arah, sons, number, 380.
Ark, location, 366; contents, 390; construction when, 407.
Arrangement, different methods and principles, 9.
Asa, mother, 323; removal of high places, 323; ten years' tranquility, 398.
Assassination sanctioned and forbidden, 255.
Authorship, differences, 6.
Avenging of blood provided for and discountenanced, 256.
Azariah, reign begun, 399; ended, 399.

Baal, prophets slain, 265.
Baasha, death when, 399.
Bacon, Francis, Christian Paradoxes, 8.

GENERAL INDEX.

Balaam, return whither, 366; permission and prohibition of journey, 69.
Baptism enjoined and neglected, 257.
Barley and lentils, field, 428.
Beasts, slain where, 367; number entering Noah's ark, 387.
Bedan, judge of Israel, 323.
Beersheba named twice, 410.
Benevolence of God, he withholds and bestows blessings, 89; hardens men's hearts, and they do it, 89; is warlike and peaceful, 92.
Benjamin, birth-place, 367; number of sons, 384.
Benjamites, number slain, 387.
Bethel, conquered when, 403; named twice, 410.
Bethsaida, twofold location, 367.
Bethshemites, 50070 slain, 92.
Bible, analogy to nature, 33; compared with other books, 47; moral influence undiminished, 50.
Bleek, definition of miracle, 122.
Blessing gained by those who see and those who see not, 219.
Blind men, number healed, 386.
Blood, poured and sprinkled, 219; covered with dust and poured out, 220.
Boasting tolerated and repudiated, 247; Paul's case, 247; Moses' case, 248.
Brown, Dr. Thos., definition of miracle, 124.
Burdens, our own and others, to be borne by us, 257.

Caleb, father of, 323.
Calling men "father," forbidden and exemplified, 257.
Canaan cursed, 84, 302.
Canaan, land, in state of famine, 367; conquered speedily, 403; extent of subjugation, 404.
Canaanites, extirpated, 265, 324; spared for test of Israel, 324; destroyed suddenly, 403.
Capital punishment inflicted and omitted, 258.
Captives, spared and put to death, 258; number taken by Nebuchadnezzar, 384.

Cattle of Egypt, extent of destruction, 428.
Census of Israelites, made when, 411.
Chapiter, length, 382.
Chastity tested in diverse ways, 258.
Children, of Bethel, slain by bears, 270; treatment, 287.
Christ, divinity, 106; omnipotence, 110; omniscience, 111; omnipresence, 114; holiness, 114; mercy, 116; courage and fortitude, 117; veracity, 117; mission, 118; miracles, 120; modes of representing him, 127; sacrifice, 130; intercession, 131; coming, 131; kingdom, 136; name, 138; execution, 220; bearing of the cross, 324; last drink, 325; genealogy, 325; last tour, 327; concealment of miracles, 327; resurrection, 327; revelation of truth, 330; use of parables, 331; approach by centurion, 367; ascension, 367; first re-appearance, 367; first sermon, 368; number of appearances 386; conveyance upon mountain, 407; beginning of preaching, 407; anointing, 411; crucifixion, 412; entombment, 413; infancy, order of events, 413.
Christ, execution. *See* Execution of Christ.
Christians, bearing of weapons by, permitted and forbidden, 259.
Chronology, Oriental methods, 13.
Circumcision, instituted and discarded, 260; not to be omitted, yet neglected forty years, 260; profitable, yet useless, 260.
Cities, location, 368; pertained to what tribe, 368; Canaanitish, smitten when, 404.
Cities of refuge, number, 385.
Cities and villages, number, 387.
City, Levitical, dimensions, 388.
Collusion of sacred writers disproved, 36.
Coming of Christ, in humility and in grandeur, 131; before and after "times of Gentiles," 132; near and far off, 134; before and after world evangelized, 135.

464　GENERAL INDEX.

Commutation for murder, not allowed, yet permitted, 261.
Computation, different methods, 11; Oriental methods in general, 13; Hebrew methods, 396.
Concubine, wife of inferior rank, 295.
Conduct of David, strayed and did not stray, 221; heart perfect, yet he sinned, 222.
Contention and strife enjoined and forbidden, 261.
Conversion of men, effected by oneself and by another, 262.
Convocations and feasts, number, 387.
Country of two demoniacs, 369.
Courage and fortitude of Christ, shrank, yet shrank not, at death, 117.
Covenant, basis, religious laws and civil laws, 220.
Covering of sin approved and denounced, 221.
Coveting enjoined and prohibited, 249.
Creation, order of events, 408.
Creation of man, made like God; this likeness acquired, 158; made in divine image; with sexual distinctions, 159; made like God; none like him, 159.
Crimes specified, different lists, 221.
Critic's imagination, source of discrepancies, 25, 28.
Crooked made straight, 428.

Dan named twice, 410.
Daniel, exaltation, 331; tarry at Babylon, 414.
Dates, difference, source of discrepancies, 3.
David, perils in wilderness of Ziph, 26; sparing Saul in cave, 26; temptation to number the people, 79; general conduct, 221; perfectness of heart, 222; detention at Saul's court, 331; building of temple forbidden, 331; officers' names, 332; relation to Achish, 332; sons' names, 332; sons' priesthood, 333; tempter, 333; warriors' names, 334; capture of Philistine city, 369; three anointings, 411.

Death of man, all must die, but some die not, 183; Lazarus not to die, yet did die, 184; man's death like a beast's, and different, 184; death ceases, and still exists, 185; men immortal, yet God only so, 185; men kill souls, and cannot kill them, 186; immortality possessed, and to be acquired, 187.
Deaths by plague, number, 382.
Debir conquered several times, 405.
Degrees of future punishment, alike and different, 210.
Deluge, duration, 415.
Demoniacs, number healed, 387.
Descent of Christ into hades, patristic view of, 192.
Design of the Discrepancies, 30.
　To stimulate the intellect, 30.
　Illustrate analogy of Bible and nature, 33.
　Disprove collusion of sacred writers, 36.
　Lead us to value spirit above letter, 37.
　Serve as a test of moral character, 38.
Destruction of the earth, indestructible, yet to be destroyed, 215.
Disciples, outfit, 154; tarry, where, 369.
Discrepancies, number, 1.
　Origin, 3.
　Design, 30.
　Results, 41.
　Ethical, 219.
　Historical, 312.
　Miscellaneous, 427.
Distrust enjoined and precluded, 262.
Divinity of Christ, is God and man, 106; one with, yet distinct from, the Father, 106; equal with, yet inferior to Him, 107; Son is God, and Father only God, 107; is Son of God, and Son of man, 108; only Son of God, yet men are sons, 109.
Divinity of Holy Spirit, is God, yet subordinate, 141.
Divorce allowed and restricted, 263.

GENERAL INDEX. 465

Doctrinal Discrepancies, 55.
  Pertaining to God, 55.
  To Christ, 106.
  To Holy Spirit, 139.
  To Scriptures, 143.
  To Man in relation to the Present, 158.
  To Man in relation to the Future, 183.
Dor conquered twice, 405.
Drought and famine, duration, 415.
Duration of future punishment, unending, yet will terminate, 211.
Duty, revelation of, gradual, 4.

Earth, destruction, 215; dried twice, 415; founded, 429; saturated, 429.
Ebrard, illustration of messenger, 328.
Edomites hated and not hated, 271; hindered Israel's passage, 335; inhospitable, 335; slain, how many, 382.
Edwardses, the two, case, 26.
Effort, human, encouraged and depreciated, 249.
Egyptians visible and not seen, 363.
Ehud, slaughter of Eglon, 255.
Ela, reign, duration, 399.
Elhanan, victim, 336.
Eli, family discipline, 335.
Eliakim, predecessor, 335.
Elijah, mockery of Baal's prophets, 276; journey to Horeb, 379.
Elimelech, indigence, 335.
Elisabeth, tribal descent, 336.
Elisha, deception of Syrians, 276.
Elkanah, nationality, 336.
Employments of heaven, incessant praise, yet rest and quiet, 218.
Enemies, treatment, cruelty employed and prohibited, 264; case of Ammonites, 264; of Moabites, 264; of Baal's prophets, 265; of young Bethelites, 270; of Edomites, 271; enemies cursed and loved, 271; treated kindly, and put to pain, 275; ridiculed, and addressed mildly, 276.
English letters, similarity, 20.
Ephraim, land located, 369.

Epithets, opprobrious, forbidden and employed, 277.
Esau, wives' names, 336; settlement in Seir when, 415.
Eternity of God, his origin from eternity, yet in time, 60.
Ethical Discrepancies, 219.
  Duty of man to God, 219.
  Duty of man to himself, 245.
  Duty of man to fellow-men, 255.
Eutychus, death, 337.
Execution of Christ, lawful and unlawful, 220.
Exode of Israelites, time, 416.
Extent of salvation, all Israel saved, yet only a portion, 213; all men saved, yet some not saved, 214.
Extirpation of Canaanites, grounds, 266.

Faith and works, contrast, 8, 167.
Famine, duration, 393.
Fast, observance enjoined and neglected, 223; of seventh month, on what day, 416.
Fear of persecutors forbidden and exemplified, 277.
Feast, of unleavened bread, instituted when, 408; duration, 416; of tabernacles under Zerubbabel, 417.
Final judgment. *See* Judgment, final.
First-born sons dedicated and redeemed, 224.
Firstling animals redeemed and not redeemed, 224; redeemed with money and not thus, 224; sanctified and not sanctified, 225.
Folly, remediable and irremediable, 278; answered in one way, and in a different, 278.
Forces, Josiah's, stationed, 370.
Foreskins, number, 382.
Fruit-trees spared and destroyed, 279.
Fruits of Holy Spirit, love and vengeance, 142; gentleness and fury, 142.
Future punishment, nature, 203; instruments, 209; degrees, 210; duration, 211.

Genealogical lists, diverse, 325, 337.

Generations, number, 388.
Gershom, relatives' names, 338.
Gezer, names, 373; conquest when, 403.
Gibeonites, nationality, 338.
Gifts of returned captives, amount, 381.
Gilgal mentioned prematurely, 394.
God, omnipotence, 55; omniscience, 56; omnipresence, 58; eternity, 60; unity, 60; immateriality, 63; immutability, 63; inaccessibility, 70; inscrutability, 72; invisibility, 73; holiness, 76; justice, 83; benevolence, 89; mercy, 92; veracity, 98; habitation, 101; position, 103; law, 104; work ended, 416; worship begun, 427.
Golden calf, destruction, 429.
Goliath, armor, placed where, 370; head carried whither, 370.
Good works exhibited and concealed, 279.
Gospel, preached where, 370.
Greek letters, similarity, 20.
Greek terms descriptive of future punishment, 212.

Habitation of God, in light, and in darkness, 101; in chosen temples, and not in them, 102; in eternity, and with men, 102; in heaven, and in Zion, 103.
Hair, long, worn by men, 246.
Halting-places of Israelites, 371.
Havoth-jair, number of cities, 385; named when, 411.
Hazael, anointed by whom, 339.
Hazor conquered twice, 405.
Heads of people, number, 385.
Heaven, occupants, 216; employments, 218; preparation when, 417.
Hebrew letters, similarity, 20.
Hebrew midwives, case, 290.
Hebrew numbers, method of expressing, 13.
Hebrew terms, descriptive of future punishment, 204.
Hebrews' land, premature mention, 394.
Hebron mentioned prematurely, 395; king conquered when, 405.

Heretics treated harshly and gently, 279.
Hezekiah, indigence, 340; passover, 340; age at accession, 399.
Hiram, mother, nationality, 339.
Historical Discrepancies, 312.
  Concerning persons, 312.
  Concerning places, 363.
  Concerning numbers, 380.
  Concerning time, 392.
  Miscellaneous, 427.
Hodge, Prof. C., definition of miracle, 121.
Holiness of Christ, is holy and is sin, 114; blessed and a curse, 115.
Holiness of God, author of evil, yet not its author, 76; jealous and free from jealousy, 78; tempts men and tempts them not, 79; respects and respects not persons, 81; angry and not angry, 82; may be and cannot be tempted, 82.
Holy Spirit, personality, 139; divinity, 141; fruits, 142; beginning, 417; bestowment, 417.
Horeb, relation to Sinai, 376.
Hormah, conquered when, 405.
Horsemen, number, 382.
Horsemen or footmen, 382.
Hosea's wife, unchastity, 255.
Hoshea, reign begun, 399.
House and porch, height, 382.
"Howland will case," 36.
Human effort. *See* Effort, human.
Hypothesis, logical value, 52.

Idolatry forbidden and practised, 225; punished and passed by, 225.
Idol-meats non-essential, yet to be shunned, 249.
Image-making sanctioned and forbidden, 226.
Images disposed of, how, 430.
Imagination of critic, source of discrepancies, 25.
Immateriality of God, a spirit, yet material, 63.
Immutability of God, unchangeable and repenting, 63; satisfied and dissatisfied, 68; destroys and destroys not, 68; abhors and does not abhor, 68; permits and forbids, 69.

GENERAL INDEX.   467

Improvidence enjoined and forbidden, 280.
Inaccessibility of God, approachable and not accessible, 70; all and not all seekers find, 71; early seekers succeed and fail, 71.
Incest, alleged case of Abraham, 281.
Inscrutability of God, attributes revealed and hidden, 72; wonders recounted and numberless, 73.
Inspiration, relation to authorship, 6; not limited to the same phraseology, 7.
Inspiration of Scriptures, all inspired, yet portions uninspired, 143.
Instruments of future punishment, shame and a whirlwind, 209; a worm and a tempest, 209; darkness and fire, 210.
Intellect stimulated by discrepancies, 30.
Intercession of Christ, only Mediator, yet Spirit intercedes, 131; intercedes for world and not for world, 131.
Intermediate state of man, dead unconscious and conscious, 188; dead asleep and awake, 191; devoid of, yet possess knowledge, 193; exercise mental powers, and not so, 195; in darkness and in glory, 197; not with Christ, yet righteous with him, 198; in same place, yet in different places, 199; in the dust, yet saints with God, 199.
Interval before passover, 416; before transfiguration, 416.
Invisibility of God, seen and unseen, 73; similitude visible and not visible, 76.
Isaac, equivocation, 26, 318; sacrifice by father, 237.
Ishbosheth, reign begun, 400.
Ishmael, age at expulsion, 418
Israel, support, 345; sight, 363; reception of new name, 411. See also " Jacob."
Israel, sin ineffaceable and may be removed, 227; boundary, 374.

Israelites, claim to Canaan, 282; condition in desert, 340; dwellings, 343; imitation of heathen 343; hearkening to Moses, 344 practice of idolatry, 344; repulse of Philistines, 344; resistless might, 344; comparative strength, 344; death in wilderness, 357; halting-places, 371; station where, 373; return whither, 374; arrival at Sinai, 409; duration of bondage, 418; tarry in Heshbon, 420; length of wanderings, 427.
Jacob, name derived, 315; brought out of Egypt, 345; errand, 345; mode of securing birthright, 345; support, 345; daughters, 384; family, 389; age at flight, 420; time of sons' birth, 421.
Jael, slaughter of Sisera, 255.
Jair, cities, number, 385.
Jebus, conquest when, 406.
Jeduthun, sons, number, 385.
Jehoahaz, reign begun, 400; duration, 400.
Jehoash, reign begun, 400.
Jehoiachin, son, 346; age at accession, 400; capture, 400; deliverance, 400.
Jehoiakim, successor, 346; death where, 374; fourth year, 400.
Jehoram, sons' fate, 346.
Jehoshaphat, league with Ahaziah, 346.
Jehovah, name unknown, 421.
Jehu, anointed by whom, 339.
Jephthah, sacrifice of daughter, 239.
Jericho captured twice, 406.
Jeroboam, residence, 375.
Jeroboam II. contemporary with Uzziah, 401.
Jerusalem, a delight and a provocation, 228; belonged to what tribe, 375; burned when, 393; captured when, 393; change of name, 395.
Jesse, number of sons, 385.
Jesus approached by centurion and elders, 346. See also under " Christ."
Jethro, identity, 354.
Jewess, marriage restricted to tribe, 283.

468 GENERAL INDEX.

Joab, crimes punished, 256.
Job, flocks and herds, size, 175; survival of his children, 347.
John, identity with Elias, 347; acquaintance with Jesus, 409.
Jonah (Jonas), sign adduced, 155.
Joram, of Israel, reign begun, 400.
Jordan, meaning of phrase "this side," 375; time of crossing, 416.
Joseph, derivation of name, 315; purchasers' nationality, 339; imprisonment, 348; keeper, 348; deportation, 348.
Joshua, conquest of kings, 348; of Canaan, 376; reception of name, 395.
Josiah, extirpation of idolatry, 348; sons, 349; death where, 376; reformation begun, 401.
Jotham, duration of reign, 401.
Judah, duration of reign, 149.
Judas, manner of death, 349.
Judges, appointed by whom, 350; period of rule, 421.
Judging of David, desired and deprecated, 228.
Judging of others forbidden and allowed, 284.
Judgment final, of man, ascribed to God and to man, 201; attributed to and disclaimed by Christ, 201; administered by God, and by men also, 202.
Judicial purpose of discrepancies, 38.
Just man's life by faith and by works, 228.
Justice administered by different judges, 284.
Justice of God, is just and unjust, 83; punishes for others' sins, and not so, 84; slays the good and spares them, 88.
Justification of man, by faith and by works, 167.

Kadesh, situated where, 373.
Keturah, connection with Abraham, 318, 339.
Killing of men forbidden and sanctioned, 285.
Kindred hated, yet loved, 286; parents honored and slighted, 287; children slain, yet cherished, 287.

Kingdom of Christ, not of world, yet within Pharisees, 136; endless and will terminate, 137.
Kings in Israel, premature mention, 395.
Kish, father of, 351.
Kohath, son of, 351.
Korah, manner of death, 352; family's fate, 353.

Laadan, posterity, 351.
Laban, father of, 351.
Laish captured twice, 406.
Land assigned twice, 412.
Laughter praised and condemned, 250.
Law, given where, 376.
Law of God, tends to liberty and to bondage, 104; perfect, yet perfects nothing, 104; tends to life and to death, 104.
Lazarus, death, 184; mode of egress from tomb, 353.
Leadership of cloud, nature, 430.
Letters, similarity of Hebrew, 20; of Greek, 20; Hebrew used as numerals, 21; Greek used as numerals, 24; letters transposed, 313; letters confounded, 392.
Levites portion, were settled, yet sojourners, 288; had stated revenue, yet deemed mendicants, 289; part at inauguration of Joash, 350; number, 382; classes, 387; dimensions of cities, 388; land mentioned, 395; set apart when, 409; beginning of service, 422.
Light, beginning of existence, 422.
Lord's supper, described, 156; time of instituting, 423.
Lot, daughters of, 282.
Luz mentioned prematurely, 395.
Lying countenanced and prohibited, 290.

Machir, wife of, 351.
Mahol, sons of, 351.
Maiden, decease, 337.
Malefactors, reviling, number, 384.
Man, creation, 158; sinfulness, 159; repentance, 165; regeneration,

166; justification, 167; sanctification, 168; perfection, 169; final perseverance, 169; righteous, earthly lot, 172; wicked, earthly lot, 180; death, 183; intermediate state, 188; resurrection, 200; final judgment, 201; duty to God, 219; duty to himself, 245; duty to fellow-men, 255; fear upon beasts, 354; life, duration, 424.
Manasseh, repentance, 351.
Manna, taste, 431.
Man, own way followed and not followed, 250.
Manuscripts, errors, 19; date, 45.
Marriage, approved and disparaged, 291; with a brother's widow enjoined and prohibited, 292.
Mercy of Christ, is merciful and unmerciful, 116; spares reed and wields rod, 116.
Mercy of God, is unmerciful and merciful, 92; his anger fierce and slow, 95; lasting and brief, 95; to fall into hands, fearful and not so, 96; laughs at, yet not pleased with sinner's overthrow, 96; just and merciful, 97; hates some, yet kind to all, 97.
Meribah, location, 374.
Micaiah, ironical words to Ahab, 276.
Michal, sons of, 385.
Midianites overthrown, 406.
Milton, description of hospital, 33.
Miracles of Christ, proof and not a proof of divine mission, 120.
Miscellaneous Discrepancies, 427.
Mission of Christ, peace and war, 118; universal and limited, 119; to Samaritans and to Jews only, 119; to fulfil and to redeem from law, 120; to judge and not to judge world, 120.
Modes of representing Christ, despised and honorable, 127; uncomely and lovely, 127; a lion and a lamb, 127; high-priest and a sacrifice, 128; vine and stone, 128; shepherd and sheep, 128; door and bread, 128; light of world, and men are lights, 129; foundation and men are foundations, 129.

Moabites, punishment, 264.
Molten sea, contents, 382; appendages, 431.
Monarchy sanctioned, yet offensive to Jehovah, 229.
Moral character tested by discrepancies, 38.
Moral purity of Scripture, purity enjoined, yet impure ideas suggested, 144.
Mosaic law, character, 431.
Moses, self-praise, 248; name derived, 315; wife's nationality, 339; family sent back, 351; last, 351; decrepitude, 354; father-in-law, 354; rank among prophets, 355; veil, 355; book received, 363; outlook, 373; commission given where, 377; fear of Pharaoh, 424.
Motherhood, blessed and to be expiated, 230.
Mount of law, accessibility, 432.
Mourning commended and discountenanced, 251.
Murder, punishment commuted, 261; forbidden and sanctioned, 285.

Naboth, sons' fate, 356.
Name of Christ, has divine name, and a city also bears it, 138.
Names, plurality, 17, 314, 373; changes, 17; errors in, 25, 312; different forms, 314; derivation, 314.
Nature, contradictions in, 33.
Nature of future punishment, continued misery and end of consciousness, 203; wicked perish and righteous perish, 204; sinners annihilated, and annihilated objects still exist, 204; wicked cut off, and Messiah cut off, 205; wicked destroyed; destroyed persons yet living, 205; sinners destroyed; destroyed things exist, 205; sinners consumed; consumed things exist, 206; wicked was not, and Enoch was not, 206; wicked devoured, and pious devoured, 206; God's adversaries and widows' houses devoured, 206; sin-

470 GENERAL INDEX.

ners devoured ; persons devoured by forest, 207 ; wicked and righteous torn and broken, 207 ; wicked broken ; things broken remain, 207 ; wicked blotted out ; things blotted out exist, 207 ; wicked and righteous have an end, 208 ; wicked and righteous die, 208.

Nebuchadnezzar, his encampment where, 377; nineteenth year, 402 ; dream explained when, 402.

New, nothing on earth, 432.

Obed-edom, nationality, 339.
Obedience due to rulers, yet withheld, 292 ; due to masters, yet to God only, 293 ; to scribes, yet they must be shunned, 293.
Objects, difference of writers, 7.
Occupants of heaven, Christ only and Elijah also, 216 ; flesh and blood excluded, yet Enoch there, 217 ; publicans and harlots there, but no impure, 217.
Offender rebuked privately and publicly, 293.
Officers, appointed when, 412.
Officers, chief, number, 382.
Omnipotence of Christ, all powerful and not almighty, 110.
Omnipotence of God, power absolute and limited, 55 ; unwearied and weary, 56.
Omnipresence of Christ, everywhere and not in all places, 114.
Omnipresence of God, ubiquitous and not everywhere, 58.
Omniscience of Christ, all-knowing and ignorant,111.
Omniscience of God, all-knowing and ignorant, 56 ; attentive and forgetful, 57 ; sleepless and slumbering, 57.
Omri, reign begun, 402.
Ophir mentioned prematurely, 395.
Oriental idiom, peculiarities, 14, 145.
Oriental methods of notation, 13.
Oriental modes of dress, 145.
Origin of Discrepancies, 3.
    Difference of dates of passages, 3.

Differences of authorship, 6.
Differences of stand-point or of object, 7.
Different methods of arrangement, 9.
Different methods of computation, 11.
Peculiarities of Oriental idiom, 14.
Plurality of names or synonymes, 17.
Different meanings of same word, 18.
Errors in manuscripts, 19.
Imagination of critic, 25.
Other sources of discrepancies, condensation of narrative, 10, 29 ; deficient knowledge of circumstances, 29, 436.
Overseers, number, 382.

Parable of talents, 433.
Paran, wilderness, location, 372.
Park, Prof. E. A., definition of miracle, 122.
Paschal offering, kind, 433.
Passover, slain where, 377.
Patristic view of intermediate state, 192.
Paul, moral state ; nothing good in him, yet Christ in him, 230 ; his boasting elucidated, 247.
Pekah, duration of reign, 402.
Penal object of discrepancies, 40.
People, number, 381, 389.
Perfection of man, saints perfect, and Paul not perfect, 169.
Perseverance, final, of man, apostacy impossible, yet some fall, 169 ; Christians indestructible and destroyed, 172 ; called all saved, yet some perish, 172.
Personality of Holy Spirit, an intelligence and an influence, 139.
Persons, discrepancies concerning, 312 ; slain, number, 383 ; another case, 383 ; sealed when, 409.
Peter, residence, 377 ; denials, 424.
Pharaoh, hardening of heart, 90.
Piety evinced ; profession a proof and not a proof 231.
Pillar of cloud, use, 430.
Pillar of temple, length, 383.

GENERAL INDEX.   471

Pleasing of men practised and condemned, 294.
Polygamy tolerated and discouraged, 295.
Pomegranates, number, 383.
Poor, favored and not favored, 296; present and absent, 356.
Position of God, sitting and standing, 103.
Potter's field, purchasers, 347.
Prayer, public and in private, 231; incessant and brief, 232.
Predictions of Scripture, privately and not privately explained, 146; sure, yet not always fulfilled, 148; divine promise absolute yet conditional, 148; promise to Judah fulfilled and not so, 149.
Priests, dues, first-born and firstlings, and not these, 296; designation, 356; number of classes, 390; time of consecration, 409.
Produce of seventh year, for the poor, and for owner, 297.
Promises, reception, 363.
Property in man recognized and precluded, 298.
Prophecy. *See* Predictions.
Proverb, origin, 412.
Psalms, imprecatory, explanation, 272.
Punishment. *See* Future Punishment.
Purchaser of sepulchre, 357.
Purity, 251. *See also* Moral Purity of Scriptures.

Quotations of Scripture, passages and incorrect quotations, 150; passage and condensation, 151; passages and expansion, 151; passage and inexact version, 152; passage and wrong reference, 153; forms of report, and variations, 153.

Rahab, case, 290.
Ransom, amount, 385.
Regeneration of man, he is active and passive, 166.
Repentance of Esau, unable yet his duty to repent, 232.

Repentance of man, his own act and God's gift, 165.
Resistance exemplified and interdicted, 298.
Results of Discrepancies, 41.
  Text not unsettled by them, 41.
  Moral influence of Bible not impaired, 50.
Resurrection of man; dead raised and not raised, 200; resurrection universal and partial, 200; Jesus raised first; others raised previously 201.
Retaliation, allowed and discouraged, 299.
Retribution, earthly; recompense here and hereafter, 182.
Righteous, earthly lot, no evil, yet some evil, 172; prosperity and misery, 172; prosperity a reward and a curse, 174; poverty a blessing and undesirable, 175; riches a blessing, yet not to be desired, 175; wisdom cause of happiness and sorrow, 176; a good name a blessing and a curse, 176; righteous beg not, yet some beg, 177; possess the earth, yet are sojourners, 177; pilgrims and strangers, yet not so, 178; they surely live, yet some die, 178; are persecuted, yet not persecuted, 178; handled roughly, yet not touched, 179; their yoke easy, yet burdensome, 179.
Righteousness, excess and deficiency perilous, 233.
Robbery of Egyptians forbidden and countenanced, 300.
Rulers' knowledge of Jesus, 358.

Sabbath, sanctioned and repudiated, 233; instituted for diverse reasons, 234; mentioned prematurely, 395.
Sabbath desecration prohibited and countenanced, 234.
Sacrifice of Christ, died for friends, yet for enemies, 130; laid down life and was murdered, 130.
Sacrifices, appointed and disavowed, 235; expiatory, and not expiatory, 236.

472   GENERAL INDEX.

Sacrifices, human, sanctioned and stringently prohibited, 237.
Salah, father of, 352.
Salathiel, father of, 346.
Salvation, extent, all Israel, yet only a portion saved, 213; universal and partial, 214; work of God and of man, 251.
Samaritans, inhospitality, 358.
Samuel, artifice, 99; first-born, 352; visit to Saul, 358; judgeship, 425; meeting with Saul, 425.
Sanctification of man through truth and through spirit, 168.
Sanctuary, location, 377.
Sarah, beauty and charms, 317.
Satan, imprisonment, 362.
Saul, king, sons, 352; election, 359; death, 359; family's fate, 360; ignorance of David, 360; journey, 379; reign, 402; anointings, 412.
Saul of Tarsus, attendants hearing the voice, 359; position, 359.
Schleiermacher, definition of miracle, 122.
Science, discrepancies in, 35.
Scriptures, comparison with classics, 46; inspiration, 143; moral purity, 144; predictions, 146; quotations, 150.
Seedtime and harvest, 425.
Sennacherib, army, survivors, 363.
Sepulchre, time of visit to, 426.
Service of God, with fear and with gladness, 241.
Shakespeare, text, compared with that of Bible, 47.
Shekels paid by David, number, 390.
Shemaiah, sons, number, 385.
Shimei, punishment, 256.
Significations of word, opposite, 18.
Sihon, heart hardened, 91.
Simeon, cities and towns, 369, 373.
Simeonites, number, 385.
Similar events, identity, 26.
Sin, forgiveness, all sin pardonable, yet some not so, 241.
Sinai, relation to Horeb, 376.
Sinfulness of man, none without sin, yet some sinless, 159; made upright and made sinful, 161; born sinful, yet infants sinless,
161; children of wrath and keepers of law, 164; sinners through Adam, and righteous through Christ, 165.
Sinners' feeling, fear yet no fear, 242.
Sin-offering, of one kind and another, 241.
Slavery and oppression, 298, 302; ordained and forbidden, 302; Hebrew slavery allowed and precluded, 303.
Slaves, emancipation, in seventh and in fiftieth year, 303; female, manumitted, and not so, 304.
Solomon, tyranny, 362; destination of fleet, 378; gifts to Hiram, 385; number of wives, 295, 390; anointings, 412.
Sons sharing estate equally and unequally, 304.
Speaker, upon a certain occasion, 363.
Spices, time of preparation, 412.
Spies, sent by whom, 350.
Spirit of Bible above its letter, 37.
Stalls, number, 383.
Stand-point of writers, different, 7.
Staves of ark, fixed and removable, 242.
Stone removed from well, 363.
Strange gods, character, 433.
Stranger, treatment, loved and not loved, 305; impartially treated, yet not so, 305.
Strong drink allowed and forbidden, 251.
Stuart, Prof. M., on future punishment, 212.
Substitute for Bible not to be found, 51.
Sun and moon ashamed, 433.
Swearing and oaths countenanced and prohibited, 242.

Taanach, conquered when, 405.
Tabernacle, location, 378; premature mention, 396.
Tabernacles, feast observed, 417.
Tables of shew-bread, number, 384.
Talents, number, 383; parable, 433.

GENERAL INDEX. 473

Temple, length, 383; number of vessels, 383; premature mention, 396; mount, 396; furniture removed, 412; erection, 426; making of vessels, 434.
Temptation desirable and not so, 253.
Testimony, premature mention, 396.
Text of Scripture, not unsettled, 41; of Old Testament, 42; of New Testament, 44.
Thermometer, illustration, 12.
Things in ark, number, 390.
Thnetopsychism, origin, 185.
Thompson, Dr. J. P., on Oriental chronology, 13.
Time, errors in, causes, 392; methods of computation, 11, 396.
Times, observance, may be, and may not be observed, 244.
Timnah, relationship, 352.
Trench, Abp., definition of miracle. 122.
Trespass, recompense made to the Lord and to the priest, 245.
Tribes, loyal, number, 387.

Unclean birds, number, 391.
Unity of God, one and a plurality, 60.
Usury exacted of no poor man and no Hebrew, 306.

Various readings, value, 36.
Veracity of Christ, witness true and untrue, 117; received and received not testimony, 118.
Veracity of God, cannot lie, and sends lying spirits, 98; denounces and sanctions deception, 99.
Version of affair, 434.
Vessels made for temple, 434.
Visitors at sepulchre, number, 391; time of their visit, 426.

Voltaire, treatment of the Bible, 27.

Wandering of Israelites, duration, 427.
Washington, birth-day, 11.
Water of Egypt, changed, 434.
Water on Mount Carmel, abundant, 435.
Wealth not to be, yet may be retained, 253.
Wicked, earthly lot, long-lived and die early, 180; prosper and do not prosper, 180; see and see not divine glory, 181; sin with impunity, yet punished, 181; punishment affirmed and denied, 182.
Wicked, treatment, hated and loved, 306; justified properly and improperly, 306.
Wisdom, profitless and valuable, 254.
Witchcraft, treatment, punished and contemned, 307.
Wives, foreign, repudiated, 412.
Woman, a certain, nationality, 339.
Woman, condition and rights, should be subject and bear rule, 308; should be silent, and may prophesy, 309.
Worship of God, beginning, 427.

Xenophon, Memorabilia, compared with the gospels, 10.

Year, kinds, 11; beginning, 12, 412; fractions counted for whole, 12.

Zebedee, wife, request, 347.
Zebulon, name derived, 316.
Zechariah, father of, 352.
Zedekiah, relationship, 352; view of Babylon, 363.
Zerubbabel, father of, 352; feast of tabernacles, 417.